2A 2D 7A
3A
4
5D

Eichle

CADOGAN GUIDES

"Intelligently organized and obviously well researched, these books strike a balance between background and sightseeing information and the practicalities that travelers need to make a trip enjoyable.

—Harriet Greenberg, *The Complete Traveller Bookstore, New York City*

Other titles in the Cadogan Guide series:

THE CARIBBEAN
GREEK ISLANDS
INDIA
IRELAND
ITALIAN ISLANDS
THE SOUTH OF FRANCE
SPAIN
TURKEY

Forthcoming:

AUSTRALIA
FLORENCE AND TUSCANY
ITALY
JAPAN

ABOUT THE AUTHOR

Part Scottish, part English, RICHENDA MIERS is a novelist, free-lance journalist and travel writer, who has lived and worked for many years in Scotland. Her husband is in a Highland regiment, her son was born in Inverness and two of her daughters went to Scottish Universities. The family shares a home in the Outer Hebrides.

PLEASE NOTE

Every effort has been made to ensure the accuracy of the information in this book at the time of going to press. However, practical details such as opening hours, travel information, standards in hotels and restaurants and, in particular, prices are liable to change.

All prices are quoted in pounds sterling. The exchange rate is approximately £1 = $1.43.

We intend to keep this book as up-to-date as possible in the coming years. Please write to us if there is anything you feel should be included in future editions.

CADOGAN GUIDES

SCOTLAND

RICHENDA MIERS

Illustrations by Pauline Pears

Series Editors: Rachel Fielding and Janey Morris

The Globe Pequot Press

Old Chester Road
Chester, Connecticut 06412

ACKNOWLEDGEMENTS

This book is for my husband Douglas, with thanks for his patience during its creation.

I would also like to thank: the staff of the Scottish Tourist Board who have given me invaluable help, advice and information; Charles MacLean, Angus Fairrie, Anne White, Sue Brown, Martin Morland, Mary Wood and my mother-in-law Honor Miers, for their useful local knowledge; Francis Pearson for advice on what to read; Doctors Gibbs, Clark and Moffett, for making it possible for me to undertake the research, and finally, Rachel Fielding and Janey Morris for their guidance and good humour.

Manufactured in the United Kingdom

ISBN 0–87106–834–6

CONTENTS

Introduction *Page 1*

Geography *1* – The Cities *2* – Climate *2* – The Scots *2* – Religion *3* – Livelihoods *3* – The Tourist Season *3* – Castles and Historic Houses *3*

Scottish Scrapbook *Page 4*

Clans *4* – Tartan *4* – Gaelic *5* – National Symbols *5* – Ceilidh *5* – Crofting *6* – Celebrations *6* – Midges *6*

Part I

General Information *Page 8*

Travel and Tours *Page 8*
– Getting to Scotland *8* – Tours *8* – Tourist Offices *8* – Getting to Scotland from England *9* – Getting around Scotland *12* – Ferry Services in Scotland *14* – Holidays for the disabled *17* –
What to take with you *Page 18*
– Documents: Passports, Health Certificates, Driving Licences *18* – Health and Travel Insurance *18* – Electric Current *19* – Clothes *19* – Customs *19* –
On arrival in Scotland *Page 20*
– Where to stay *20* – Eating out *25* – National dishes *26* – Drinking in Scotland *27* – Time Zone *27* – Money and Banks *28* – Credit cards *28* – Post offices and stamps *28* – Telephone *29* – Maps *29* – Tipping *29* – Toilets *30* – Public Holidays *30* – Church *30* – Embassies and Consulates *31* – Guides and Help *31* – Shopping in Scotland *31* – Tracing your ancestors *33* – Leisure activities *33* – Historic buildings and sites *38* –

Part II

History *Page 40*

Part III

Edinburgh *Page 52*

Part IV

Glasgow *Page 79*

Part V

Borders *Page 93*

Part VI

Dumfries and Galloway *Page 120*

Part VII

Lothian *Page 151*

Part VIII

Stratchclyde *Page 181*

Part IX

Central *Page 233*

Part X

Fife *Page 250*

Part XI

Tayside *Page 275*

Part XII
Grampian *Page 306*

Part XIII
Highlands *Page 342*

Part XIV
The Islands *Page 405*

Scottish Monarchs *Page 462*

Some Milestones in Scottish History *Page 462*

Biographical Notes *Page 465*

Suggested Reading *Page 469*

Index *Page 471*

LIST OF MAPS

Scotland
Scottish Tourist Boards *Page 21*
Edinburgh *Page 55*
Glasgow *Page 82*
Borders *Page 95*
Dumfries and Galloway *Page 123*
Lothian *Page 153*
Strathclyde (South) *Page 183*
Strathclyde (North) *Page 211*
Central *Page 236*
Fife *Page 252*
Tayside *Page 277*
Aberdeen *Page 308*
Grampian *Page 313*
Highlands (East) *Page 344*
Highlands (West) *Page 358*
Highlands (North) *Page 377*
Skye, Rhum, Eigg, Muck & Canna *Page 407*
Outer Hebrides, Western Isles *Page 422*
Orkneys *Page 442*
Shetlands *Page 453*

INTRODUCTION

Scotland's magic is as elusive as its folklore. To find its true nature you must dig below the myth, romance and whimsical nonsense that has grown over it and touch the bare bones, stripped of tartan and haggis, monsters and porridge, whisky and bagpipes.

About 2,700 million years ago, this tiny land was part of North America, separated from England by an ocean. All the world was still in the melting-pot; land-masses drifted around like flotsam, colliding and splitting, erupting and reforming, until Scotland was born—the most beautiful miniature country of them all. Nowhere else will you find scenery to match it: smoke-grey mountains; wild moorland carpeted with mulberry-red heather; mossy glens shaded by rowans and birches and gnarled oaks; rivers and burns that rush in tumult over slabs of granite and shallow, stony beds, slicing through steep-sided gorges hung with ferns and lichens; deep, mysterious lochs with peat-coloured water overlaid by fragments of early morning mist; sunsets that make you weep.

But there is more to the magic than mere beauty and you must explore the country yourself to find the key to its enchantment. This book is designed to help you on your way.

Geography

It is tempting to think of Scotland as an island: the sea is never more than 60 miles (96 km) away. The country was divided into regions a few years ago, some of which are obvious, others less so. Looking at the map, you have the Borders region in the south-east, with gentle, rolling farmland running north to the Lammermuir Hills, the Moorfoots and the Pentland Hills. In the south-west is Dumfries and Galloway, washed by the Solway Firth to the south and the North Channel to the west. North of Borders is Lothian, on the southern shore of the Firth of Forth, with Edinburgh at its heart. Strathclyde is north of Dumfries and Galloway, running up the west of the country to Loch Linnhe. It embraces Glasgow and several islands to the west including Mull, and includes also half of Loch Lomond to the east. North and west Strathclyde is highland and island scenery, deeply indented and very beautiful. Central region is literally the hub of the country, an area north of the line between Glasgow and Edinburgh, with the lovely Trossachs in the middle. The little "Kingdom of Fife" lies between the Firths of Forth and Tay in the east, surrounded on three sides by water. North of the Tay is Tayside and then Grampian, taking up the great shoulder of land that juts into the North Sea to the east, below the Moray Firth, dominated by the massive Grampian Mountains. All that is left, running west and north, is the Highland region, slit in the east by the Great Glen that runs in a north-east/south-west diagonal from Inverness to Fort William. Highland is the largest of the regions, with great tracts of mountain and moor, almost surrounded by water. Off the west coast lie the islands of Skye and the Hebrides: off the north coast lie the Orkneys and the Shetland Islands.

The Cities

Edinburgh, Glasgow, Aberdeen and Dundee are the four main cities of Scotland and here you will find entertainment and tourist facilities of the highest standard, with a huge variety of activities and places of interest. Inverness is called the capital of the Highlands.

Climate

People tend to joke about the Scottish climate and it is portrayed in a popular post-card showing someone sitting in a deck chair under an umbrella in pouring rain, with the caption "Having plenty of weather here in Scotland". In fact, with a bit of luck, you can go back home from a holiday in Scotland with a deep tan that was not entirely inflicted by the wind, and a packet of photographs showing idyllic blue skies and brilliant sunshine.

Unpredictability is the main drawback for holidaymakers, but when you get a good spell of weather you will look around and wonder why anyone ever goes away from Scotland for a holiday.

It is worth remembering that places in the north of the country have an average of 18 to 20 hours of daylight in the summer, and that resorts on the east coast are noted for their hours of sunshine. In the far north, in the middle of the summer, it is never completely dark.

The average annual mean rainfall in Edinburgh is 26 inches (65 cm) almost exactly the same as that in London and Rome, and palm trees and tropical vegetation on the west coast must say something about the climate there.

Rainfall is highest in the west and particularly on the western mountains. North and south of Fort William on the west coast the mean annual rainfall is over 100 inches (254 cm): with a mean rainfall for August of 6.2 inches (15.7 cm). Due east, in Montrose, the mean annual rainfall is 25–30 inches (63–76 cm), with a mean rainfall for August of 2.8 inches (7.1 cm).

Temperatures are obviously lower as you go north. In July, the mean temperature in the south of Scotland is 59°F (15°C), while in the far north it is 54°F (12.2°C).

Fort William has a mean number of hours of sunshine in August of 110, against 149 in Montrose.

In general, you can expect plenty of rain in the west, but a mild temperature; far less rain in the east but a much more bracing climate with colder winds. Winter, in the Highlands, when the precipitation is mainly snow, can be very beautiful, with clear skies and sun, though temperatures may seldom rise above freezing.

The Scots

If you read the History section, you will see that Scots are descended from many different races. They have never been wholly conquered, nor wholly integrated. There is no typical Scot, any more than there is a typical American. He is most certainly not the music-hall Jock, staggering home on Saturday night in kilt and tam o' shanter, singing 'Glasgie belongs to me'. His canny generosity has been misinterpreted as meanness; his diffidence as dourness. In reality, his kindness can be overwhelming and his shrewd wit as refreshing as the swift-flowing waters of his Highland streams.

Religion

When St Columba brought Christianity to Scotland in the 6th century it was in a Celtic form which was soon replaced by Roman Christianity as practised elsewhere in Britain. From the early 8th century until the Reformation, Scotland was entirely Roman Catholic. The reforming Protestants began to make their mark in the 16th century and having established their Protestant church, they then began to squabble about Episcopacy. This ended with the triumph of Presbyterianism and the formal establishment of the Church of Scotland.

From then on, the majority of Scots have been Presbyterian and the History section in this book summarises the awful struggles that went on before the Presbyterians and Episcopalians were able to come to terms with each other. At the Reformation, however, large parts of the Highlands and the Hebrides clung to Catholicism, strengthened by the immigration of the Irish who came over looking for work, and you will find whole islands and communities that are entirely Catholic.

Livelihoods

Crofting and fishing are the main occupations in the Highlands, though crofting is often subsidised by another job. Scotland's industry is concentrated around the Clyde and the Forth, with the oil-related industries on the North Sea oil fields developing in the north-east. You will find some of the best farmland in Britain in the Lowlands.

The Tourist Season

Tourism is developing rapidly and the main season is from about Easter to the end of September. July and August are peak holiday times and you should book hotels well in advance. You will find that many of the castles, historic houses and smaller museums close for the winter as do some of the hotels in the remoter districts.

Castles and Historic Houses

Having been a country continually at war defending itself from its neighbours and from the invaders who came over the sea, Scotland has more than its share of castles and fortified houses. Many are little more than piles of stones, many have been well restored, as ruins, and a number are still inhabited but are open to the public.

SCOTTISH SCRAPBOOK

Two men in Kilts

Clans

The Scottish clan system was once an integral part of the way of life, particularly in the highlands and islands. Every member of the clan bore the name of the chief, whether related by blood or by allegiance and each was one of the clan family and in no way servile. Mac means son of... The chief was the father, ruler and judge and the strength of the clan lay in his justice, kindness and wisdom, and in the loyalty of the members of the clan, to him and to one another.

Today, clan feelings still run strong, especially in the veins of expatriots, but the clan name is now no more than an umbrella for historical museums, annual gatherings and ceremonial, with the chief as a figurehead, appearing in a tartan costume redolent of moth balls. He has no more authority over the clan family, now, than anyone else bearing his name.

Tartan

You won't find the average Scotsman striding over his native hills swathed in tartan. On the whole, kilts are kept for ceremonial or formal occasions and a great many Scotsmen don't even own one. The mystique that has grown up round clan tartans is put into perspective by the story of the irate chieftain, towering over one of a coach party, seeing round his ancestral castle: "By what right are you wearing my tartan, my man?" "By the right of purchase, at fifteen pounds a yard, my lord."

It is known that Highlanders wore some sort of brightly coloured, striped and checked material as far back as the 13th century, though whether the designs, or "setts" were related to clans or to territories is not known for certain. The wearing of Highland dress was banned in 1746, for 36 years (see History) and during that time many of the old patterns were lost or forgotten. It was not until Hanoverian George IV appeared at Holyrood in 1822 in an astonishing Highland outfit that the fashion for tartan was revived and in a wave of enthusiasm, a large number of "clan" tartans were hastily designed. It is these relatively modern patterns that make up most of the enormous range of tartan that we see today.

Gaelic

Gaelic is still the first language in the Outer Hebrides, but even there, with an influx of non-Gaelic speakers, the children are growing up speaking English among themselves. Elsewhere it is no longer a living language, though it is self-consciously paraded in some places to impress visitors. If you want to hear it, go to church in the Outer Isles on a Sunday when there isn't a visiting priest from the mainland. The locals are far too courteous to speak it among themselves when they know that they have a non-Gaelic speaker in their midst.

National Symbols

The patron saint of Scotland is St Andrew and the national flag is the "saltire", a white St Andrew's cross on a pale blue background. The cross is positioned diagonally because St Andrew refused to be crucified on a vertical cross in case he seemed to be trying to be equal to Jesus. The reason for the adoption of the saltire for Scotland is said to date from a battle in the eighth century, between an invading Northumbrian army and the unusual alliance of a Pict and Scot army under their two kings. These two prayed for victory and saw the saltire in the saxe-blue sky, made of cloud. They agreed that it was an omen and having defeated the Northumbrians they decided to adopt it as the national flag of their united kingdoms. It's a nice story and the fact that they were not united for at least another hundred years is neither here nor there.

The origin of the thistle, as the emblem of Scotland, is said to date from 1263 when Alexander III defeated the Norse King Haakon at Largs. Trying to set up an ambush, or a surprise attack, one of the Norsemen trod on a thistle and made such a din that he alerted the Scots army.

Ceilidh—pronounced Kay-ly

Parts of rural Scotland, as you go north, seem to have been undisturbed by the passage of time and you will find remote crofting communities that still keep to the old ways. The coming of electricity has brought with it the television and this has effectively murdered a community life that once centered round the '*Ceilidh*'—a Gaelic word meaning visit. The crofters gathered in one of the houses after work, sitting round the central peat fire whose smoke escaped out of a hole in the roof. They told stories and sang songs, passing their folklore from one generation to the next. Their music stirred the soul: mouth-music, straight from the heart; Gaelic songs; pipe music. That tradition is dying out now, though you can still find private *ceilidhs* in the islands. Today they tend to be more commercial, organised by hotels and dance halls, but you will hear some good music even if the old atmosphere has gone.

Crofting

A croft is a small-holding, consisting of a few acres, as many sheep as the land will support, sometimes a few cows and poultry. If there is arable land it will be tilled.

The family dwelling is the croft-house (often mistakenly called the croft) and the crofter is the owner or tenant of the croft. Since the Clearances (see History), The Crofting Commission has kept very careful control of crofters' rights.

Celebrations

Scotsmen love to celebrate and many opportunities are found to do so. Perhaps the best known is "Hogmanay", New Year's Eve, when the new year is welcomed with enormous enthusiasm that often results in sore heads and a few broken bones. After midnight, "first-footing" takes place, when people go round calling on their friends, bearing a bottle of whisky. In the Hebrides, the whole population seems to be on the move for the first week of January. Each community moves outwards from its own centre in ever increasing circles with ever decreasing momentum. Many amusing stories are told. Three days into January, Angus was seen trying to get into the driving seat of his car. "Angus; you are in no state to drive that thing". "Away with you, man: I'm far too drunk to make it up the hill on my feet".

St Andrew's Day, on 30 November, is celebrated with dinners and tartan gatherings for the dancing of Reels. Robert Burns' birthday is celebrated on 25 January, with many fervent quotations from the poet's works and a ceremonial "addressing of the haggis" which Burns referred to as "great chieftain o' the puddin' race". Hallowe'en, on 31 October, is greeted with glee by the children, who go round the houses "Trick-or-treat-ing": a gift of a sweet or some other treat, popped into the proffered "poke" or bag, will spare you from having a trick played on you.

Midges

The west side of Scotland and the islands are plagued by a particularly virulent breed of "midge" unequalled in persistence anywhere else in the British Isles. Grown men have been reduced to gibbering wrecks under their vicious attacks. They are at their worst in warm, humid conditions and if you are contemplating camping or picknicking during the midge season you must have lots of the strongest repellent. In truth, they can completely ruin an outing—but it is worth remembering that they won't follow a boat offshore.

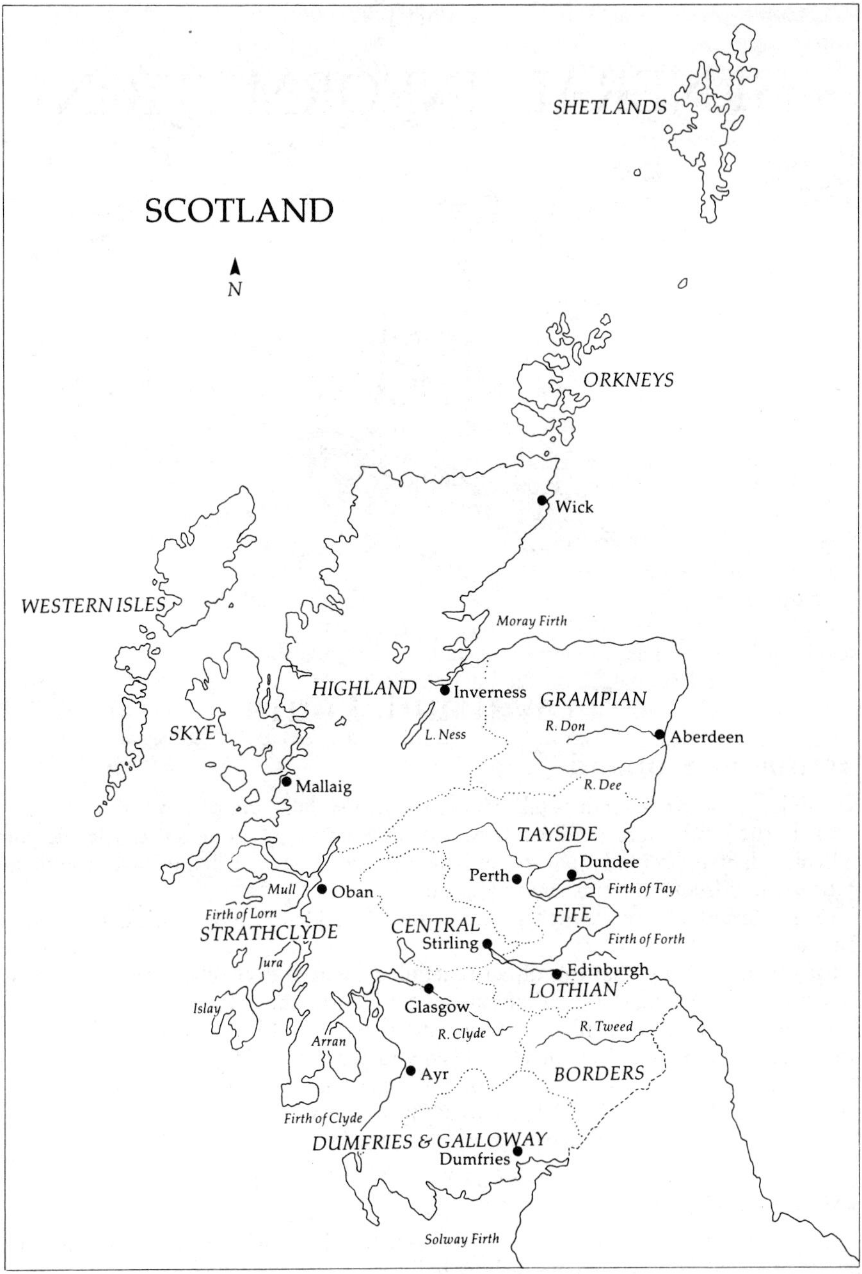
SCOTLAND
N
SHETLANDS
ORKNEYS
Wick
WESTERN ISLES
Moray Firth
HIGHLAND
Inverness
GRAMPIAN
SKYE
L. Ness
R. Don
Aberdeen
Mallaig
R. Dee
TAYSIDE
Dundee
Perth
Mull
Oban
Firth of Tay
Firth of Lorn
FIFE
STRATHCLYDE
CENTRAL
Stirling
Firth of Forth
Jura
Edinburgh
LOTHIAN
Islay
Glasgow
R. Tweed
R. Clyde
Arran
Ayr
BORDERS
Firth of Clyde
DUMFRIES & GALLOWAY
Dumfries
Solway Firth

Part I

GENERAL INFORMATION

Dee Valley Bridge

Travel and Tours

Getting to Scotland

Scheduled air and sea services take you to the British Isles from all over the world.

From the USA, there are direct services with Northwest Orient to Prestwick Airport in Scotland, 30 miles (48 km) or so south of Glasgow. A free coach then takes you to the station where frequent trains run to Glasgow.

From Canada, there are flights from Toronto and Halifax to Prestwick, operated by Air Canada.

European airlines that run direct scheduled services to Scotland include: British Airways, from Milan, Paris, Frankfurt, Dusseldorf, and Munich; Air UK, from Amsterdam, Bergen, Copenhagen, Oslo, Stavanger; KLM Royal Dutch Airline, from Amsterdam; SAS from Copenhagen, Oslo and Stavanger; Lufthansa, from Dusseldorf; Scandinavian Airways from Oslo, Stavanger and Copenhagen; Icelandair, from Copenhagen and Reykjavik; JAT Yugoslav Airlines from Dubrovnik.

Visitors from other countries must travel via England.

Tours

There are a variety of tour operators who offer travel-inclusive packages which suit a variety of tastes: golfing holidays, fishing holidays, historic trails, scenic tours etc. You should consult your travel agent for details. For example, **for Americans,** Abercrombie and Kent, tel 800-323 3602, run tours through lovely Highland scenery in a restored steam train, *The Royal Scotsman*. The tours last from three to six days and you sleep in luxury Victorian and Edwardian coaches and eat gourmet food. A six-day trip in a state compartment (the most expensive) costs US$ 3,330. Caravan Tours, tel 800-621 8338 offer a 15 day holiday for Americans which includes the air fare from New York, escorted motorcoach tours of Scotland and Ireland, free entrance fees, evening entertainment, first class hotels, all breakfasts, one lunch and eleven dinners, all for US$ 2,367.

There are a great many such tours well worth finding out about if you prefer someone else to plan your holiday for you. Other tour operators in the USA equally worth consulting are Galleon World Travel, tel 800-223 1588; Kemwel, tel 800-468 0468; Maupintour, tel 800-255 4266; Scottish Citylink, tel 800-468 0468; Clansman Scottish, tel 800-468 0468; Journeys Thru Scotland, tel 714-499 4410 and Golf Links International, tel 800-541 6898 who specialise in de luxe independent golf tours.

Tourist Offices

Each area in Scotland has its own Tourist Board which will provide lots of helpful local information (see p. 22 for details). In addition there is a network of over 140 information centres throughout the country. The Head Office of the **Scottish Tourist Board** is at 23 Ravelston Terrace, Edinburgh EH4 3EU, tel 031-332 2433. In London contact the Scottish Tourist Board at 19 Cockspur Street, London SW1Y 5BL, tel 01-930 0601. Information and advice on visiting Scotland can be obtained outside the United Kingdom at your nearest British Tourist Authority (BTA) office. The following list gives the addresses of the main BTA offices:

Australia: Associated Midland House, 171 Clarence St, Sydney, N.S.W. 2000, tel 02-29 8627.

Belgium: Rue de la Montagne 52 Bergstraat, B 2, 1000 Brussels, tel 02-511 43 90.

Brazil: Avenida Ipiranga 318-A, 12° Andar, Conj 1201, Edificio Vila Normanda, 01046 Sao Paulo=SP, tel 257-1834.

Canada: 94 Cumberland Street, Suite 600, Toronto, Ontario M5R 3N3, tel 416-925 6326.

Denmark: Møntergade 3, DK-1116 København, tel 01-12 07 93.

France: 63 Rue Pierre-Charron, 75008 Paris, tel 1-42 89 11 11, Voyagel: 36 14 91 66 type VGL.

Germany: Neue Mainzer Str 22, 600 Frankfurt am Main 1, tel 069-238070.

Hong Kong
Suite 903, 1 Hysan Avenue, Causeway Bay, Hong Kong, tel 5-764 371

Ireland: 123 Lr Baggot Street, Dublin 2, tel 01-614188

Italy: Via S. Eufemia 5, 00187 Rome, tel 678-4998 or 678-5548, tlx 622690.

Japan: 246 Tokyo Club Building, 3-2-6 Kasumigaseki, Chiyoda-ku, Tokyo 100, tel 03-581 3603.

Mexico:
Edificio Alber, Paseo de la Reforma 332-5 Piso, 06600 Mexico DF, tel 533-6375/76.

Netherlands: Aurora Gebouw 5e, Stadhouderskade 2, 1054 ES Amsterdam, tel 020-85.50.51, tlx 13395 bta br.
New Zealand: 8th Floor, Norwich Union Building, Cnr Queen & Durham Streets, Auckland, tel 09-31446.
Norway: Fridtjof Nansens plass, 0160 Oslo 1; Postal address: Postboks 1554 Vika, 0117 Oslo 1, tel 02-41 18 49.
Singapore: Singapore Rubber House, 14 Collyer Quay 05-03, Singapore 0104, tel 2242966, 2242967 (Ansaphone), tlx 28493 BTA SIN.
South Africa: 7th Floor, JBS Building, 107 Commissioner Street, Johannesburg 2001, PO Box 6256, Johannesburg 2000, tel 011-296770.
Spain: British Tourist Authority, Torre de Madrid 6/4, Plaza de Espana, 28008 Madrid, tel 91-241 13 96.
Sweden: For visitors: Malmskillnadsg 42 1st Floor. For Mail: Box 7293, S-103 90 Stockholm, tel 08-21 24 44.
Switzerland: Limmatquai 78, 8001 Zurich, tel 01-47 42 77 or 47 42 97, tlx 58632 BTACH.
USA, Chicago: John Hancock Center, Suite 3320, 875 N. Michigan Avenue, Chicago, Illinois 60611, tel 312-787 0490.
USA, Dallas: Cedar Maple Plaza, Suite 210, 2305 Cedar Springs Road, Dallas, Texas 75201, tel 214-720 4040.
USA, Los Angeles: World Trade Centre, 350 South Figueroa Street, Suite 450, Los Angeles, CA 90071, tel 213-623 8196.
USA, New York: 40 West 57th Street, New York, N.Y. 10019, tel 212-581 4700.

Getting to Scotland from England

By air

British Airways and British Midland Airways fly direct to Edinburgh and to Glasgow, Abbotsinch, from London Heathrow Airport. British Caledonian Airways fly to both cities from Gatwick Airport. You can get to Heathrow on the Underground, Piccadilly line, and to Gatwick from Victoria Station, London. Flights take just over an hour and there are buses and plenty of taxis to take you on to Edinburgh or Glasgow. All airlines offer special economy fares with conditions, such as having to book and pay ahead, with no cancellation refund.

A single standby fare, at off-peak times (between 11 am and 3 pm) to either Edinburgh or Glasgow will cost you about £43 by British Airways and British Midland. British Airways apex (book and pay 14 days ahead) costs £72 return. British Midland key fare (book and pay in advance, no cancellation refund) costs £92 return. British Caledonian offer a £48 standby, and a £75 return if you book and pay ten days in advance, with no cancellation refund. The full return fare starts at about £132, British Midland.

British Airways have a "pexfare" (book and pay 14 days in advance) Heathrow, London, to Inverness, return £103. Their saver fare, from Heathrow, London, to Aberdeen starts at £43 single standby. Their return saver from Heathrow, London, to Benbecula is £169 and from Heathrow, London, to Shetland is £180.

There are also many special "package" offers. For example British Airways offer London Heathrow to Orkney, including return flight, self-drive car, insurance and one tank full of petrol (about 300 miles, 488 km) at £190 per head. Ask your travel agent for details.

Useful telephone numbers

British Airways, Terminal One, Heathrow Airport, London, tel 01-759 2525.

British Midland Airways, Terminal One, Heathrow Airport, London, tel 01-745 7321.

British Caledonian Airways, Gatwick Airport, near Crawley, Sussex, tel 01-668 4222.

By train

British Rail run regular train services to Scotland. You leave from Kings Cross Station, London, to Edinburgh, and from Euston Station, London, to Glasgow. The journey takes about five hours and there are at least 15 trains a day to both cities. A full second class return will cost you about £85 to Edinburgh, and £79 to Glasgow. A saver return costs from £45 to £55 between London and Edinburgh, depending on when you travel, and from about £38 to £48 between London and Glasgow. A sleeper costs £15. The inter-city trains are modern and comfortable and you can book seats in advance. In addition, there are direct trains to other big towns in Scotland from London, or convenient connections from Edinburgh and Glasgow. Overnight sleeper connections from London and Bristol operate to Edinburgh, Glasgow, Dundee, Perth, Aberdeen and Inverness. During the holiday season you should book well in advance.

There is also a motor-rail service to the main cities, if you want to take your car but don't want the tedious drive north.

By bus/coach

Several coach companies operate between London and Scotland, usually running at least one day coach and at least one overnight. The journey from London to Edinburgh or Glasgow takes about eight hours, with 40 minute stops at (at least) two service stations. The coaches are reasonably comfortable, with toilets. Most have a snack service and show a film. Prices vary and there are often special offers. Normally it costs about £14 single to Edinburgh and about £12.50 single to Glasgow.

Useful Addresses

Eastern Scottish Coaches, Victoria Coach Station, 164 Buckingham Palace Road, London, SW1, tel 01-730 0202. Arrives at St Andrews Square, Edinburgh, tel 031-556 9464.

Scottish City Link, Victoria Coach Station, 164 Buckingham Palace Road, London, SW1, tel 01-730 0202. Arrives at Buchanan Bus Station, Glasgow, tel 041-332 9191.

US Agent: The Kemwel Group, 105 Calvert Street, Harrison, NY 10528, tel 800-468 0468.

Cotters Coaches, depart from 35 Woburn Place, Russell Square (near Euston),

London, WC1, tel 01-930 5781. Arrives at Lothian Road, Edinburgh, tel 031-228 6045, and 12 Crimea Street, Glasgow, tel 041-221 8042

Stagecoach Express, depart from Kings Cross Coach Station, Kings Cross, London, N1, tel 01-388 2267 (Main office Perth, tel 0738–33481). Arrives at Waverley Bridge, Edinburgh and Parks City Coach Terminal, Sauchiehall Street, Glasgow, tel 041-333 9472.

By car

An excellent network of motorways means that you can drive comfortably from London to Edinburgh in seven hours, sticking to the 70 mph (112 kph) limit. The M1, A68 and the A1 (M) are the quickest routes to Edinburgh, and the M1, M6 and A74 provide the quickest routes to Glasgow.

Getting around Scotland

Once you are in Scotland, a rail system that takes you to the far north and out to the far west, an efficient inter-island ferry service, and a comprehensive island-hopping air service, are all available to help you explore. Alternatively, it is easy to hire a car or join one of the many coach tours.

By air

British Airways and Loganair operate various internal services around the mainland and out to the islands.

Useful telephone numbers

The following numbers apply to **Loganair**

Glasgow Airport, Abbotsinch, Glasgow, tel 041-889 3181.
Inverness Airport, Inverness, tel 0667-62332.
Aberdeen Airport, Dyce, Aberdeen, tel 0224-723306.
Lerwick Airport, Shetland, tel 059-584 246.
Kirkwall Airport, Orkney, tel 0856-3457.
Stornoway Airport, Lewis, tel 0851-3067.

The following numbers apply to **British Airways**.

Glasgow Airport, Abbotsinch, Glasgow, tel 041-887 1111.
Edinburgh Airport, Edinburgh, tel 031–333 1000.
Inverness Airport, Inverness, tel 0463-232471.
Aberdeen Airport, Dyce, Aberdeen, tel 0224-722331.
Wick Airport, Wick, tel 0955-2215.

Travelpass

A Travelpass takes you as far as you like and as often as you like, over virtually the entire Highlands and islands of Scotland, it gives you unlimited travel on most ferry, rail, postbus and bus routes in the Highlands and islands, and includes travel by bus or train to Edinburgh and Glasgow. If you show your Travelpass in any of the tourist information centres, they will book that night's accommodation for you. With your Travelpass, you get a comprehensive transport guide with timetables and maps. You can buy a Travelpass at any of the mainline stations in Britain. The price varies, depending on when you buy it and for how long you want it to last. Americans can get one from Britrail Travel International Inc, 630 Third Avenue, New York, NY, 10017, tel 212-599 5400.

By train

Once you are in Scotland, as well as the main inter-city routes, there are routes that run through the very best of Highland scenery. Aberdeen–Inverness, Glasgow–Stranraer, Glasgow–Oban, Perth–Inverness are all very attractive journeys. The Kyle Line runs from Inverness across Scotland to Kyle of Lochalsh, a lovely stretch of country which links up with the five minute ferry to Skye. The famous West Highland Line from Glasgow up to Fort William and on to Mallaig is a trip that is fun to make just for the beauty of the journey, particularly if you are a railway enthusiast. The journeys are made in preserved locomotives and coaches, authentically decorated in the style of the old trains.

British Rail offer all sorts of excellent bargain tickets and it is well worth checking at any station for full details. For example:

Rail Cards

Young person, aged 16 to under 24, £12. This give you up to half price on all fares.

Senior citizen, men 65, women 60, from £7 to £12 depending on which you buy.

Family Railcard, £15.

Freedom of Scotland

Starting from Berwick-on-Tweed or Carlisle, you get unlimited travel to all stations in Scotland and as passengers on Caledonian Macbrayne and Firth of Clyde Steamers: Silver Fare, 7 days, £38; Gold Fare, 14 days, £55.

All Line Rail Rover

This gives you unlimited travel to all stations in the British Isles, including passenger fares on Caledonian Macbrayne, Firth of Clyde, and Sea Link to the Isle of Wight: Silver Fare, 7 days, first class £200, second class £120. Gold Fare, 14 days, first class £300, second class £190.

Useful telephone numbers

Kings Cross Station, Kings Cross, London, N1, tel 01-837 4200.

Euston Station, Euston Road, London, NW1, tel 01-387 9400.

Waverley Station, Waverley Bridge, Edinburgh, tel 031-556 2451/2477.

Central Station, Argyle Street, Glasgow, tel 041-202 2844.

For information in the **USA** contact Britrail Travel International Inc, at:

630 Third Avenue, New York, NY 10017, tel 212-559 5400.

333, N. Michigan Avenue, Chicago, IL 60601, tel 312-263 1910.

By bus

You will find good bus services throughout most of Scotland. In the very rural areas there is usually a "postbus" service, when you can catch the mini bus that carries the mail, an experience that is often memorable for the social outing as much as for the transportation. There are large numbers of bus companies and you should enquire locally, or ask in the tourist office, for details.

By car

Car hire firms operate from the airports and stations, and there are always local firms which will rent you a car: the more rural you get, the better the bargain usually. For example, in the Outer Isles you get considerable reductions for a rusty old banger whose doors are tied on with rope.

You drive on the left in Scotland as in the rest of the British Isles. Road signs are similar to those in Europe. There is a speed limit of 70 mph (112 kph) on all motorways. Parking in town s is usually restricted to parking meters and car parks. A single yellow line by the kerb means you can't park by day; a double yellow line, and zigzag lines by pedestrian crossings mean no parking at any time.

Main roads are generally good in Scotland, although not always dual carriageways, so you can get trapped behind caravans (trailers) and big lorries. For exploring the country properly, you should get to the area you want on the main roads and then get off onto the minor roads. In rural areas there are a great many single track roads with frequent passing bays. These are never to be used for parking and are also for slow cars to pull into, to allow faster ones to overtake. When touring in the far north, you should remember that petrol stations are not numerous and some close on Sundays. It is law in Britain for all drivers and front seat passengers to wear seat belts.

Hitch-hiking

It is neither more nor less chancey to thumb a lift in Scotland than anywhere else: maniacs and rapists exist all over the world. In populated areas you should be extremely wary. In the islands, however, locals will invariably stop and offer you a lift without being thumbed. It is part of their instinctive hospitality and you will always be safe to accept. It is probably true to say that in all rural areas you are safe to accept lifts from local people but not always from outsiders.

Ferry services in Scotland

Caledonian Macbrayne

Caledonian Macbrayne provide a steamer service to the Western Isles, with roll-on, roll-off car ferries, restaurants, bars, and, in some, sleeping accommodation. For full information write to Caledonian Macbrayne, The Ferry Terminal, Gourock, PA19 1QP, tel 0475-33755.

They offer mini cruises, driveaway, island hopscotch, or car rover tickets. You can

also get day excursions, family tickets and excursion returns. They publish a comprehensive brochure with details. For example the following are available.
Island Hopscotch: between Oban–Craignure, Fishnish–Lochaline, Mallaig–Armadale, Uig–Tarbet, Stornoway–Ullapool, valid for three months £57 to £69, depending on season, for any car. For passengers £11 to £14.
Car rover: 8 to 15 day season tickets for cars and passengers from £62 to £92 for smallest car plus from £22 to £30 for each of the passengers and driver.

Standard price examples
Oban–Barra or South Uist
£26.40 to £31.40 for smallest car on and off season, single.
£35.70 to £45.10 for smallest car, on and off season, excursion return.
£83.30 for smallest car for a six-journey ticket. Season ticket.
Driver and passengers
£8.80 to £10.60 single fare, per head.
Skye: Kyle of Lochalsh–Kyleakin
£2.20 to £2.65 for all cars, on and off season, passengers 23p–35p.
Mull: Oban–Craignure
From £9.60, single, for cars, driver and passengers from £1.60, single, each.
Arran: Ardrossan–Brodick
From £9.20, single, for cars, drivers and passengers from £1.95, single, each.

For Americans, Caledonian Macbrayne are represented by The Kemwel Group, 105 Calvert Street, Harrison, NY 10528, tel 800-468 0468.

P&O ferries
P&O ferries provide a steamer service between Aberdeen and Lerwick in Shetland, and Scrabster and Stromness in Orkney, with roll-on, roll-off ferries.
Aberdeen–Lerwick
From £87.50 to £96, return, for smallest cars, depending on season.
From £24 to £27, single, each for drivers and passengers, depending on season, children half price.
Scrabster–Stromness
From £36.50 to £43.50, return, for smallest cars, depending on season.
From £7.20, single, each for drivers and passengers, depending on season, children half price.

For full details write to P&O Ferries, PO Box 5, P&O Ferries Terminal, Jamieson's Quay, Aberdeen, AB9 8DL, tel 0224-572615. (No US representative.)

Routes to the islands*

From Ullapool
You go from Ullapool to Stornoway in Lewis. There are two boats a day except on Sundays and the journey takes three and a half hours.

*Please note that the frequency of ferry services given here applies to summer. In winter, boats to the islands are less frequent.

From Uig

You go from Uig in Skye to Tarbert in Harris. There are nine boats a week excluding Sundays and the journey takes one and three quarter hours.

You also go from Uig in Skye to Lochmaddy in North Uist. There are nine boats a week excluding Sundays and the journey takes from one and three quarter hours to four hours, depending on the route.

From Oban

You go from Oban to Lochboisdale in South Uist. There is one boat a day except on Sundays and the journey takes from six to eight hours, depending on whether the boat calls in at Barra on the way.

You also go from Oban to Castlebay in Barra. There are four boats a week excluding Sundays and the journey takes five and a half hours.

You go from Oban to Coll, Tiree and Colonsay. There are three to four boats a week and the journey takes between two and five and a half hours.

You go from Oban to Lismore. There are two boats a day except on Sundays and the crossing takes three quarters of an hour.

You go from Oban to Craignure on Mull. There are seven boats a day and four on Sundays. The journey takes three quarters of an hour.

From Lochaline

You go from Lochaline to Fishnish on Mull. There are 15 boats a day except on Sundays and the journey takes quarter of an hour.

On Tuesdays and Thursdays there are also cruises from Oban that go to Mull, Staffa and Iona, and passengers are ferried ashore, if the weather permits, to spend an hour on Iona.

From Fionnphort

You go from Fionnphort on Mull to Iona. There are frequent daily boats, and eight on Sundays and the journey takes five minutes.

From Mallaig

You go from Mallaig to Rhum, Eigg, Canna and Muck. There are from one to three boats a week and the trips take from one and a half to five hours.

You go from Mallaig to Armadale in Skye. There are four boats a day, from Monday to Saturday, and it takes half an hour. There are no boats on Sunday.

From Kyle of Lochalsh

You go from Kyle of Lochalsh to Kyleakin on Skye. The boats run continuously in daylight and the journey takes five minutes.

From Ardrossan

You go from Ardrossan to Brodick on Arran. There are four boats a day and three on Sundays and the journey takes an hour.

From Claonaig
You can also go from Claonaig to Lochranza on Arran. There are seven boats a day, six on Sundays and the journey takes half an hour.

From Wemyss Bay
You go from Wemyss Bay to Rothesay in Bute. There are eight boats a day and seven on Sundays and the journey takes half an hour.

From Colintraive
You can go from Colintraive to Rhubodach in Bute. There is a frequent daily service and the journey takes five minutes.

From Tayinloan
You go from Tayinloan to Gigha. There are four boats every day and the journey takes 20 minutes.

From Kennacraig
You go from Kennacraig to Port Ellen and Port Askaig on Islay. There are three boats a day and two on Sundays and the journey takes two hours.

From Port Askaig
You go from Port Askaig on Islay to Feolin on Jura. There are eight boats a day and one on Sundays and the journey takes five minutes.

From Largs
You go from Largs to Great Cumbrae. A boat goes every half an hour and the journey takes ten minutes.

From Scrabster
You go from Scrabster to Stromness in Orkney. There is one boat a day including Sundays and the journey takes two hours.

From John o' Groats
You can cross from John o' Groats to Burwick in Orkney. There are two boats a day except on Sundays, and four between July and August. The journey takes three quarters of an hour.

From Aberdeen
You can go from Aberdeen to Lerwick in Shetland. There are three boats a week and one on Sundays and the journey takes 14 hours.

Holidays for the disabled

As in the rest of Britain, Scotland is not yet well adapted to make travel for the disabled easy. There are no facilities to enable people in wheel-chairs to get on and off trains and buses unaided. In trains, people in wheel chairs must travel in the guards van. However, there are several associations that are dedicated to making it possible for disabled people to get about and to have holidays that they can enjoy.

The Holiday Care Service, 2 Old Bank Chambers, Station Road, Horley, Surrey, tel 0293-77 4535, will send free information on accommodation, transport and facilities available for holidays for the disabled, with publications and guides.

Holidays on Wheels (Tours) Ltd, 8 Worthington House, Myddelton Passage, London EC1R 1XQ, tel 01-833 3600 will also send details of the holidays they arrange in Scotland for disabled people, their relatives and friends.

What to take with you

Documents

Passports

Anyone coming to Scotland from abroad is required to have a valid national passport. Citizens of the USA, and most Commonwealth, European and South American countries do not need visas.

Health Certificates

Visitors arriving from any area that is currently infected with Yellow Fever will be asked to produce a certificate of vaccination. Infected areas change as epidemics come and go, and you should consult your doctor or health authority before you travel.

No other health certificates are required.

Driving Licences

A full national driving licence is all that is required to drive your own or rented cars. If you are bringing your own car, do check that you are properly insured and bring the vehicle registration certificate or green card with you.

Health and Travel Insurance

The National Health Service (NHS) will cover emergency medical treatment for members of the EEC and for anyone whose country has a reciprocal health arrangement with Britain. Check with your doctor. For immediate emergency treatment, anyone can go to the casualty department of the local hospital where they will be stitched together free.

Anyone coming to Scotland from abroad is strongly advised to take out a comprehensive health insurance. Your travel agent will advise you and often arrange it for you. If you have to go into a NHS hospital you are liable to have to pay £120 a day and if you take private treatment in that same hospital you will also pay the consultant's fees, etc. Insurance is cheap; illness can be very expensive.

For very little extra cost, you can take out a comprehensive holiday insurance, and it is well worth doing so. This will cover health, personal luggage, loss of money, refund of cancellation charges, personal accident, personal liability and departure delay. The rates are usually extremely good and your Travel Agent will arrange it for you.

Electric Current

The electric current is 240 V AC. Plugs generally have three square pins and take 3, 5 or 13 amp fuses. Foreign visitors should bring adapters to use their own appliances.

Clothes

What clothes you take obviously depends on what sort of holiday you intend to have and what time of year you will be in Scotland. Because of the unpredictability of the weather, whatever time of year you choose, plenty of sweaters and waterproof clothing are essential if you are to enjoy the country to the full, and comfortable, sturdy shoes. Rubber boots are useful if you are not pressed for luggage space, but they are not very comfortable for walking long distances in. If you go prepared for rain and cold, the chances are that you will have hot sunshine and drought. Scottish waters are cold but if the sun shines you might regret not bringing bathing things. Very summery clothes are seldom needed.

Customs

In addition to all personal effects you intend to take with you when you leave (with the exception of those goods listed below), duty free allowances for import into the UK are (the figures in brackets are the allowances for goods obtained duty-free and tax paid in EEC countries):

Alcohol	1 (1.5) litres spirits or alcoholic drink over 22% alcohol by volume) or 2 (3 litres) of alcoholic drink under 22% alcohol, fortified or sparkling wine plus 2 (5) litres of still table wine.
Tobacco	200 (300) cigarettes or 100 (150) cigarillos or 50 (75) cigars or 250 (400)g tobacco. If you live outside Europe, 400 cigarettes or 200 cigarillos or 100 cigars or 500g of tobacco.
Perfume	50g/60cc/2 fl oz (75g/90cc/3 fl oz)
Toilet Water	250cc/9 fl oz (375cc/13 fl oz)
Other goods	To the value of £28 (£163)

Prohibited and restricted goods include narcotics, weapons and obscene publications and videos.

You should carry dated receipts for valuable items you bring in with you such as cameras and watches or you may be charged duty.

On arrival in Scotland

Where to stay

The choice of accommodation in Scotland is enormous, ranging from superb, top quality luxury hotels to simple bed and breakfasts. The price is not always a reliable guide. The Scottish Tourist Board have a large number of brochures covering every single area in the country, including the islands. Each region produces its own local publication and in them you will find valuable information about what to do and see; addresses of local facilities; and a comprehensive accommodation guide, listing hotels, guest houses, bed and breakfast places, caravan sites (trailer parks), self-catering houses and camp sites. Each entry gives you full details of the price and facilities, and many of them give photographs. It would be impossible within the scope of this book to include a full list. A selection are given within the text for each district, but you are strongly advised to use the list below and to send off for whichever of the brochures covers your chosen area.

You can pay as little as £5 a night for bed and breakfast and find a clean house, a warm welcome and a thumping good breakfast. You can go to a hotel and pay £110 to sleep in a double, four-poster bed or £130 for a suite with a jacuzzi. You can rent a whole house or cottage for as little as £50 a week, or as much as £500. There is an enormous amount of "packages" on offer, including, fishing, golfing, shooting and stalking. There are boating packages and skiing packages and specialist holidays which include heritage trails, whisky trails, and Taste of Scotland trails. Details of all these are given in the various brochures of the Scottish Tourist Board.

In the hotels mentioned in this book, the prices given are the minimum price for one person. There are seasonal variations and single rooms are usually more expensive, per head, than double. You can get good value in a hotel for £10 a night, if you are lucky. You can rent static caravans (trailers) for anything from £40 a week upwards, and you can park your own caravan (trailer/camper) for as little as £2 a night. Camp site facilities vary and are not, on the whole, as sophisticated as those you will find elsewhere, but very often the scenery makes up for the primitive plumbing!

Many bed and breakfast places will serve you an evening meal and all hotels provide a full service.

The following list gives you the addresses of the various tourist boards. Each number corresponds with an area on the map. If you write to these boards, they will send you their brochures; otherwise, you can call in at the office on arrival.

Each office can give you up to date information on local events, things to see and do in the area and any help you may need in fixing up where to stay and what route to take. They will also advise on such things as fishing permits, the golf courses in the area, and local excursions.

SCOTTISH TOURIST BOARDS

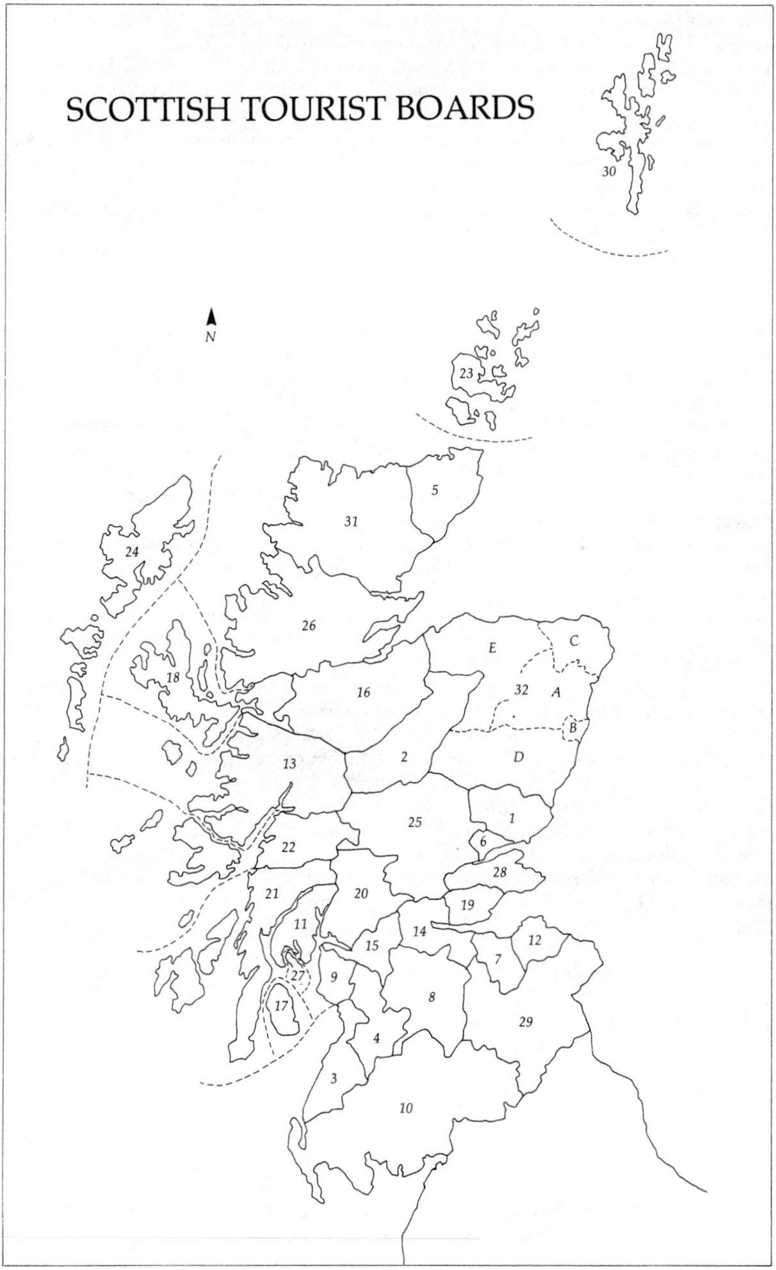

SCOTLAND

1. Angus Tourist Board, Tourist Information Centre, Market Place, Arbroath DD11 1HR, tel Arbroath 0241-72609/76680. Holiday Brochure on request
2. Aviemore and Spey Valley Tourist Organisation, Main Road, Aviemore PH22 1PP, tel Aviemore 0479-810363 (24 hours). Colour Accommodation Brochure: Free. Spey Valley Guide: £1.50 (includes p&p)
3. Ayrshire & Burns Country Tourist Board, Tourist Information Centre, 39 Sandgate, Ayr KA7 1BG, tel Ayr 0292-284196. Brochures: "A Visitor's Guide to Ayrshire and Burns Country", "Ayrshire and Burns Country Accommodation Guide"
4. Ayrshire Valleys Tourist Board, 62 Bank Street, Kilmarnock, Ayrshire KA1 1ER, tel Kilmarnock 0563-39090. Brochure: "Ayrshire Valleys Holidays '87"
5. Caithness Tourist Board, Tourist Office, Whitechapel Road, Wick, Caithness, tel Wick 0955-2596. Brochure: Accommodation Guide
6. City of Dundee Tourist Board, Freepost, The Tourist Information Centre, Nethergate Centre, Dundee DD1 4ER, tel Dundee 0382-27723. Free Brochures on request
7. City of Edinburgh District Council, Department of Public Relations & Tourism, Waverley Market, Princes Street, Edinburgh, tel Edinburgh 031-557 2727. Brochure including Accommodation Register on request
8. Clyde Valley Tourist Board, South Vennel, Lanark ML11 7JT, tel Lanark 0555-2544. Free colour accommodation guide and leaflets. Free Covenanters Trail and A74 Guide. "Historical Tours in Clyde Valley": £1.00. "Welcome Guide": 30p inc p&p
9. Cunninghame District Council, Tourist Information Centre, The Promenade, Largs KA30 8BG, tel Largs 0475-673765. Brochure on request
10. Dumfries & Galloway Tourist Board, Douglas House, Department FJ6, Newton Stewart DG8 6DQ, tel Newton Stewart 0671-2549/3401. Accommodation and Bargain Breaks: Free. "Things to See and Do": £1.00
11. Dunoon & Cowal Tourist Board, Tourist Information Centre, Dunoon, Argyll PA23 7HL, tel Dunoon 0369-3785 (24 hours). Brochure: Inclusive Holidays in Dunoon and the Cowal Peninsula, and "Where to Stay" accommodation
12. East Lothian Tourist Board, Tourist Information Centre, Town House, Dunbar, tel Dunbar 0368-63353. East Lothian Brochure and Accommodation Register
13. Fort William & Lochaber Tourist Board, Cameron Centre, Cameron Square, Fort William PH33 6AJ, tel Fort William 0397-3781 (24 hr service). Brochure: "Fort William and Lochaber"
14. Forth Valley Tourist Board, Burgh Halls, The Cross, Linlithgow, West Lothian EH49 7AH, tel Linlithgow 0506-844600. Free Brochure on request
15. Greater Glasgow Tourist Board, 35–39 St Vincent Place, Glasgow G1, tel Glasgow 041-227 4880. Brochure on request
16. Inverness, Loch Ness & Nairn Tourist Board, 23 Church Street, Inverness IV1 1EZ, tel Inverness 0463-234353 (24 hr service). Accommodation and Information Brochures: Free
17. Isle of Arran Tourist Board, Tourist Information Centre, Brodick Pier, Brodick, Isle of Arran, tel Brodick 0770-2140/2401. Colour Accommodation Register & information available: Free
18. The Isle of Skye & South West Ross Tourist Board, Tourist Information Centre, Portree, Isle of Skye IV51 9BZ, tel Portree 0478-2137. Brochure "Where to Stay in 1987": Free. Colour Souvenir Guide: £1.60 inc p&p. Isle of Skye by Car: £1.30 inc p&p
19. Kirkcaldy District Council, Tourist Information Centre, South Street, Leven KY8 4PF, tel Leven 0333-29464. Information on request
20. Loch Lomond, Stirling & Trossachs Tourist Board, PO Box 30, Stirling, tel Stirling 0786-75019 (24 hr service). Brochure and Accommodation List: Free. Colour Souvenir Guide: £1.40
21. Mid Argyll, Kintyre & Islay Tourist Board, Area Tourist Office, The Pier, Campbeltown, Argyll PA28 6EF, tel Campbeltown 0586-52056. Brochure: "Mid Argyll, Kintyre & Islay—Where to Stay in 1987"
22. Oban, Mull & District Tourist Board, Boswell House, Argyll Square, Oban, Argyll, tel Oban 0631-63122. Brochure: "Oban, Mull & Lorne": Free. Official Guide: £1.30
23. Orkney Tourist Board, Freepost, Kirkwall, Orkney KW15 1BR. Brochure: "Orkney 1987"

24. Outer Hebrides Tourist Board, 4 South Beach Street, Stornoway, Isle of Lewis PA87 2XY, tel Stornoway 0851-3088. Brochure "The Outer Hebrides Where to Stay 1987"
25. Perthshire Tourist Board, Freepost, PO Box 33, Perth PH1 5LH. Colour guide book, accommodation and special rail travel information: Free
26. Ross & Cromarty Tourist Board, Tourist Information Centre, Gairloch, Ross-shire IV21 2DN, tel Gairloch 0445-2130 (24 hr service). Brochure: "Ross and Cromarty"—Where to Stay 1987"
27. Rothesay and Isle of Bute Tourist Board, The Pier, Rothesay, Isle of Bute PA20 9AQ, tel Rothesay 0700-2151 (24 hr service). Brochures: "Where to Stay and Package Holidays 1987"
28. St Andrews & NE Fife Tourist Board, Information Centre, South Street, St Andrews, Fife KY16 9JX, tel St Andrews 0334-72021. Brochure: "Holiday Information Pack"
29. Scottish Borders Tourist Board, Municipal Buildings, High Street, Selkirk TD7 4JX, tel Selkirk 0750-20555. Brochures: "Scottish Borders 1987—Accommodation and Information": Free. "Official Visitors Guide to the Scottish Borders": 85p
30. Shetland Tourist Organisation, Market Cross, Lerwick, Shetland, tel Lerwick 0595-3434. Brochures: "Shetland—The Natural Choice", "Shetland Holidays 87", "Travel Guide to Shetland": All Free
31. Sutherland Tourist Board, Area Tourist Office, The Square, Dornoch IV25 3SD, tel Dornoch 0862-810400. Brochures: "Where to Stay in Sutherland 1987": Free. Sutherland Guide: 65p
32. Scotland's North East, Freepost, Aberdeen AB9 7AR, tel Aberdeen 0224-632727. Free brochure including accommodation, individual free brochures for districts in Scotland's North East from:

32a.-32b. Aberdeen & Gordon Tourist Boards, St Nicholas House, Broad Street Aberdeen AB9 1DE, tel Aberdeen 0224-632727

32c. Banff & Buchan Tourist Board, Collie Lodge, Banff AB4 1AU, tel Banff 02612-2789

32d. Kincardine & Deeside Tourist Board, 45 Station Road, Banchory AB3 3XX, tel Banchory 03302-2066

32e. Moray District Tourist Board, 17A High Street, Elgin, Moray IV30 1EG, tel Elgin 0343-2666 or 3388

Youth Hostels

There are 80 youth hostels in Scotland, marked on most maps by a triangle. They fall into three grades, A, B and C, some having central heating, hot showers, carpets, etc, and all offering dormitory accommodation and self-catering facilities. Anyone over the age of five may use a youth hostel. Membership costs from £1 to £4, depending on age. Overnight accommodation costs from £1.80 to £3.50 depending on age and the grade of the hostel. For full details, write to SYHA, 7 Glebe Crescent, Stirling, FK8 2JA, tel 0786-72821.

Hotel descriptions and categories

If the address of the hotel is not shown in this book it means it is in a place too small to bother with street names, or it is instantly obvious, or the name of the hotel indicates the place it is in. In order to give you some idea of the facilities available in the hotels mentioned in this book, they have, where possible, been divided into a list of six categories. Each category is further subdivided under the three headings: bedrooms, services, meals (in that order). Thus categories 5, 4, 3 means: bedrooms—category 5, service—category 4, meals— category 3.

Categories

Bedrooms

1. Pretty basic, with use of public bathrooms and toilets.

2. Basin in bedroom with hot and cold water, or private bathroom.
3. Central heating and basin or private bathroom.
4. At least 33% of the bedrooms have bathrooms en suite.
5. At least 75% of the bedrooms have private bathrooms en suite as well as TV or radio.
6. All bedrooms with private bathrooms en suite. Colour TV (if reception available), telephone in rooms. Some suites available.

Services
1. Beds made and rooms cleaned. Breakfast room.
2. As above plus public lounge.
3. As above plus early morning call and tea, or tea making facilities in bedroom. Porter on request. Dining room.
4. As above plus separate TV lounge. Central heating throughout. Shoe cleaning facilities.
5. As above plus night porter on duty, shoe cleaning and lounge service until 11 pm.
6. As above plus valet service, 24 hour laundry service except at weekends. All night lounge service. Two or more lounges including a bar lounge. Bookstall. Hairdressing arranged.

Meals
1. Breakfast, sometimes continental.
2. Full Scottish breakfast (usually with cereals or porridge, something cooked, toast, etc and tea or coffee) and evening meal (high tea or dinner).
3. Full breakfast, lunch and dinner. Choice of main courses.
4. Full breakfast, lunch and dinner, choice of all dishes. Table service.
5. All the above plus choice of Scottish or continental breakfast. Continental breakfast available in bedrooms. A la carte menu. Meals can be ordered until at least 9.30 pm. (Sundays or off season 8.30 pm.)
6. All the above plus coffee shops, buttery, grill room, or a second restaurant. Meals can be ordered until at least 11.30 pm. (Sundays or off season, 9.30 pm.) All meals served in bedrooms if wanted.

Scottish Tourist Board gradings

In addition to these general gradings, an impartial team of inspectors, employed by the Scottish Tourist Board, is in the process of visiting over 2,000 hotels, guest houses, bed and breakfast establishments, and self-catering houses to assess their quality. You will see more and more saxe-blue oval signs at the entrance to accommodation, telling you that the establishment has been visited and assessed for quality.

The signs will show the year they were inspected and will include a classification from "Listed" up to one to five crowns. "Listed" means that the place meets minimum Scottish Tourist Board standards. The crowns indicate the range of facilities—the more crowns, the more facilities. They do not tell you how good the facilities are, merely that they exist. On top of this, the sign will usually display a grade, "Approved", "Commended", or "Highly Commended". This indicates the quality of the establishment.

In the more rural areas, and indeed in the towns, don't be put off by the lack of en suite bathrooms in the smaller hotels. What they lack in modern facilities is invariably made up for in the friendly hospitality of the staff. Very often you will find that "public bathroom" means that you have sole use of a bathroom across the passage.

Useful publications
As well as the individual area publications that you can get from local tourist centres, the Scottish Tourist Board publish a number of useful brochures that cover the whole country. For these you should write to **The Scottish Tourist Board, 23 Ravelston Terrace, Edinburgh, EH4 3EU, tel 031-332 2433.**

Scotland: Where to Stay: Hotels and Guest Houses. (free)
Scotland: Where to Stay: Bed and Breakfast. (free)
Scotland: Self-Catering Accommodation. (free)
Scotland: Camping and Caravan Parks. (free)
Scotland 1987. (free)
Adventure and Special Interest Holidays. (free)
Ski Holidays in Scotland. (free)
Holiday Guide Off-peak brochure. (free)
Water Sports in Scotland. (free)
Golf in Scotland Map. (free)
Events in Scotland. (free)
Mary, Queen of Scots. (free)
See Scotland at Work. (free)
Scotland Touring Map. (£2.25)
Scotland: 1,001 Things to See. (£2.50)
Walks and Trails. (£1.50)
Scotland: Hill Walking. (£1.75)
Enjoy Scotland Pack. (£4.50)

Eating out

You can eat as well in Scotland as anywhere and the cities have a range of eating places that are as international as a map of the world. You can choose between "haute cuisine" that will satisfy any gourmet; good plain cooking at a reasonable price; and fast-food and carry-out establishments where you can get anything from hamburgers and pizzas to baked potatoes with delicious fillings and good old fish and chips wrapped up in newspaper.

In the cities you can usually get lunch and dinner at very flexible hours, but in the smaller places you should aim to have lunch between 12.30 pm and 2 pm, and dinner between about 7 pm and 9 pm. If you know that you will be late it is wise to make arrangements in advance. "High tea" is an alternative to dinner, usually served between 4.30 pm and 6.30 pm, and is an extremely sustaining meal that consists of a main course followed by bread, cake, biscuits, etc, washed down by cups of tea—a very British meal.

Some of the country's best restaurants are to be found tucked away in unexpected, out-of-the-way places. These are mentioned in the relevant sections within this book.

Two examples are The Peat Inn, in Fife, and Blair Findey Lodge, in Glenlivet.

Prices vary enormously. You can get a good two course meal for £5 (without drink) or you can pay £50 and come away bloated and disappointed. Ask around, and concentrate on traditional food with local, fresh ingredients, cooked in the simplest ways. Beware of breadcrumbs: they tend to hide mass produced, frozen food that has just emerged from a microwave oven.

National dishes

Scotland has an unmatched reputation for salmon, both fresh and smoked. The development of fish farming has increased the availability but it has to be said that "wild" salmon is unquestionably more delicious than that which has been reared in a farm, which tends to be rather fatty. The Scottish Tourist Board brings out a *Taste of Scotland* booklet every year offering details of over 200 hotels and restaurants that specialise in good Scottish cooking.

Apart from the salmon, national dishes include trout, sea fish, shell fish, game, beef and lamb. Almost without exception you should go for these served in the traditional ways without too much "dolling up". Poached salmon with mayonnaise, new potatoes and cucumber; a freshly caught mackerel, fried so that its skin is crisp and curling, with wedges of lemon and watercress; an Aberdeen Angus fillet steak, medium-rare, an inch thick, with a green salad of just lettuce, chives and a hint of garlic; well-hung roast grouse with game chips, fresh petit pois, fried breadcrumbs, bread sauce, and gravy. These will linger in your memory long after any dish that has been wrapped up in an exotic sauce and given a pretentious name.

You should try haggis, but take it easy. It is made of the heart, liver and lungs of a sheep, mixed with suet, oatmeal and onion, highly seasoned and sewn into the sheep's stomach. It is usually eaten with "bashed neeps" (mashed turnip or swede) and washed down with neat whisky! Try black pudding, too: its unusual flavour is strangely addictive.

Arbroath smokies are fresh haddock, dry salted and smoked in pairs; a delicate, mild flavour makes them particularly delicious and the best way to eat them is cold, with brown wholemeal bread and butter, a generous squeeze of lemon juice and plenty of freshly ground black pepper.

Porridge is no longer a national habit but you can always get it in hotels if you ask. The popular myth that Scotsmen eat their porridge with salt, standing up or walking about, is quickly disproved when you discover how many of them sit down and tuck into it heaped with sugar and cream!

Scottish cheeses are various and worth pursuing. Crowdie is unique to Scotland, a sort of creamed cottage cheese, which you should try on oatcakes, another national speciality.

Shortbread is known all over the world and no one makes it better than the Scots. You will find many local variations of the standard buttery biscuit, Yetholm Bannock, for instance, a very rich shortbread with crystallised ginger, to be found in the Borders.

Cock-a-leekie soup is a delicious broth made from game birds and leeks.

Scotch pies are to be found all over the country; small round pies made of hot water pastry and filled with minced meat. You eat them hot.

Cranachan, if properly made, is memorable; double cream, and sometimes crowdie, is mixed with toasted oatmeal, sweetened and eaten with fresh soft fruit, preferably raspberries which are another of Scotland's specialities.

Drinking in Scotland

Among the myths that need to be taken with a pinch of salt is the whisky myth! The average canny Scot will go for the two bottles of cut-price blended whisky that he can get for the price of one bottle of vintage malt. On the whole, malt whisky is kept for special occasions—or exported. There is a large number of brands and every connoisseur will swear to the unquestionable superiority of his particular fancy. However, experiments involving the transfer of a "favourite" malt into a bottle with a rival label will often prove that it is the eyes rather than the taste buds that dictate which is the best.

Traditionally, malt whisky should be drunk neat, without ice; any additions are believed to spoil the flavour. No other country in the world has the essential ingredients for that unique taste that makes Scotland's whisky so special: that magical blend of snow melt, peaty water, and carefully malted barley. A true Scotsman drinks whisky, or asks for "a dram"; he will never ask for "Scotch" unless he is abroad and in danger of being served with a foreign imposter.

Most of the distilleries are on Speyside, north-east of Aviemore, in the north, or on the islands of Islay and Jura and a large number of them run guided tours so that you can see the process of whisky making and taste the results. You can take the malt whisky trail, on Speyside, a 70 mile (112 km) voyage of discovery, taking in six distilleries. Guided tours last about an hour and you can get details from the tourist information centres.

Scotsmen prefer to do their drinking seriously, in bars, though chic wine bars and English-type pubs are mushrooming in the towns. You may hear, in a true bar, someone ordering "a pint of heavy and a chaser". This will turn out to be a pint of bitter and a dram of whisky—the accepted way to spin out the precious *uisge beatha*, Gaelic for "water of life".

Licensing laws in Scotland permit public houses to stay open for 12 hours a day or longer with special extensions, but not all of them choose to do so. Generally, a bar will be open from 11 am to 2.30 pm, and from 5 pm to about 11 pm, with reduced hours on Sunday. Most city centre bars will stay open till at least midnight. Residents in licensed hotels may buy drinks at any time. Minors (children under 18) may not be served drink in a public house or restaurant, nor may they be sold alcohol in a shop. Some establishments provide special family rooms where children may join their parents, but they must not drink here. Few bars will allow children in, and landlords stand to lose their licenses if they break the law in this respect.

Time Zone

Scotland time is Greenwich Mean Time in winter. From the end of March to late October, British Summer Time (daylight saving time) is one hour ahead of GMT.

Money and Banks

You are allowed to bring into Scotland banknotes, travellers' cheques, letters of credit, etc, in any currency and up to any amount. There is no restriction on the amount of travellers' cheques changed.

The decimal currency in Britain is based on the pound sterling (£) divided into one hundred pence (100p). Notes are issued to the value of £50, £20, £10, and £5. Scottish banks issue their own notes, including a £1 note, which is acceptable at face value throughout the British Isles. English notes are acceptable in Scotland. Coins are issued to the value of £1, 50p, 20p, 10p, 5p, 2p, and 1p. Some of the pre-decimal coins are still in circulation.

If you want money when the banks are shut you can get it at branches of the larger travel agents, such as Thomas Cook, at counter desks in larger hotels, or at one of the many independent *bureaux de change*. It is wise to check in advance the rate of exchange and the commission charged.

Main banks are open during the following times: Monday, Tuesday, Wednesday: 9.30 am–12.30 pm; 1.30 pm–3.30 pm. Thursday: 9.30 am–12.30pm; 1.30 pm–3.30 pm; 4.30 pm–6 pm. Friday: 9.30 am–3.30 pm. Some of the banks in the city centres are open weekdays from 9.30 am to 3.30 pm.

Banks are shut on Saturdays, Sundays and public holidays. Scotland is prone to having public holidays at unexpected times so keep your eyes out for advance warning.

In rural areas, banks list their opening hours (which are sometimes different) and in some places there are travelling banks.

Credit Cards

Most large shops, department stores, banks and high class restaurants, and some garages will accept international credit cards, but it is always wise to check first. Very few of the smaller shops will accept them. The following are the most generally accepted: American Express, Diners Club, Visa, Mastercard, Eurocard, Blue Card.

Post Offices and stamps

Main post offices are open from 9 am to 5.30 pm, Mondays to Fridays and from 9 am to 1 pm on Saturdays. Sub-post offices, often to be found incorporated into village shops, close for a half day during the week. In very rural areas they may only open on weekdays from 9 am to 1 pm.

Letters sent to you "Post Restante" to any main post office, will be kept for three months and then returned to sender.

Post boxes in Scotland are red. Some still have VR on them, dating them to Victorian times. First class letters, for next day delivery in Britain, cost 18p; second class cost 13p, for delivery within five days. If you don't include the postcode letters may take longer to arrive.

Airmail letters to the USA cost 31p, to Europe, 22p, to Asia, India, Australia, New Zealand, 34p. All Aerogrammes cost 26p. Airmail letters take about five days to travel. Please note that these charges are liable to increase.

Telephone

Telephoning is easy and there are a large number of public 'phone boxes. The familiar red kiosks are gradually being replaced by more modern hooded booths and the old disc dials by press-button numbers. You will find public 'phones in pubs, hotels, many garages, and big departments stores, as well as at stations, airports and in the streets. In remote rural districts you will often find a kiosk in the middle of nowhere, serving the scattered community.

The minimum charge for calls is 10p and the dialling codes for all the British exchanges should be displayed in the kiosk.

Useful numbers
Directory Enquiries—192
Operator Services—100
Emergency—999
Telegrams—100

International Direct Dialling is possible to most countries and cheaper than via the operator. Consult the operator for the codes.

Maps

A good map is essential if you are to enjoy your holiday to the full. Bartholomew's half inch maps are good but you need many of them and they are expensive. There is a very adequate *Ordnance Survey Motoring Atlas* (£3.25), 3 miles: 1 inch, (Scottish Highlands and Islands, 7 miles: 1 inch), which you can buy in most garages and bookshops.

A "tourist map" of the whole of Scotland, marking special attractions is a useful addition to your collection. There are several including the *Scotland Touring Map*, published by Geographia Ltd, 63 Fleet Street, London, EC4Y 1PE. This has more than 20 different classifications of tourist information including castles, historic houses, forests, parks, golf courses, skiing, picnic sites, camping/caravan sites and beaches. It is a good map for £1.25. Most map centres will stock it.

If you plan to walk or climb then you must get the appropriate Ordnance Survey sheets, scale 1:50,000.

Tipping

There are no hard and fast rules about tipping and few people will refuse a tip. Waiters, taxi drivers, hotel staff, porters and hairdressers will be disappointed if you don't tip them, even when some restaurants and hotels include a service charge. 10% of the cost of a meal or of a taxi journey is a good guide.

Be careful, however, in rural places, if a highlander comes to your rescue in an emergency. You can offer to contribute to the petrol if given a lift, rather than hand out a tip. A bottle of whisky is often the best way of saying thank you if a highlander has put himself out for you—taken you in his boat as a friend, towed your car to the nearest garage, "fixed" the leak in your petrol tank...

Toilets

The standard of public lavatories in Scotland varies from extremely clean and luxurious to extremely sordid. Service stations on motorways are usually excellent; hotels, restaurants and cafes are usually all right; Public Conveniences in towns can be rather squalid, as can the lavatories provided in some bars. Most big garages have public lavatories, as do department stores.

Public Holidays

New Years Day—January 1—the only statutory public holiday in Scotland. Bank Holidays are mainly for banks only and include: January 2, the Friday before Easter, the first Monday and last Monday in May, the first Monday in August, November 30 (St Andrew's Day), December 25 (Christmas Day), December 26.

Most towns and districts have local public trades' and other holidays which vary from place to place and from year to year. It is worth asking at the local Scottish Tourist Board Information Office for their annual leaflet, Public Holidays in Scotland.

Church

The Church of Scotland

The Presbyterian and United Established Church of Scotland is the church to which the majority of Scottish Presbyterians belong today. When the Free Church and the United Presbyterian Church joined together in 1900, to become the United Free Church, some of the congregations, particularly in the Highlands, remained outside this union. These churches retain the name Free Church, colloquially referred to as the "Wee Frees".

The Episcopal Church of Scotland

The Episcopalian Church in Scotland is in full communion with the Church of England and uses similar forms of worship.

Roman Catholic

At the Reformation, a large part of the population, particularly in the Highlands and some of the Hebrides, remained faithful to the old religion, and still do so today. This has been strengthened by the large influx of Irish people.

Visitors who are not used to the fierce sabbatarianism that exists in some Presbyterian communities should be careful not to offend locals on Sundays. However, tourism has resulted in considerable relaxation of some of the more rigid rules that used to endure.

Embassies and Consulates

All foreign embassies are in London. The following lists some of the Consulates in Edinburgh:

Australia: Hobart House, Hanover Street, tel 031-226 6271.
Austria: 33/4 Charlotte Square, tel 031-225 1516.
Belgium: 89 Constitution Street, tel 031-554 3333.
Denmark: 50 East Fettes Avenue, tel 031-552 7101.
Finland: 50 East Fettes Avenue, tel 031-552 7101.
France: 7 Wemyss Place, tel 031-225 7954.
Germany: 16 Eglinton Crescent, tel 031-337 2323.
Greece: 9 Regent Terrace, tel 031-556 1701.
Iceland: 5 Grange Road, tel 031-667 2166.
Italy: 6 Melville Crescent, tel 031-226 3631.
Monaco: 39 Castle Street, tel 031-225 1200.
Netherlands: 8/12 George Street, tel 031-225 8494.
Norway: 50 East Fettes Avenue, tel 031-552 7101.
Portugal: Gogar Park House, tel 031-339 5345.
Spain: 51 Lauderdale Street, tel 031-447 1113.
Sweden: 6 John's Place, tel 031-554 6631.
Switzerland: 6 Moston Terrace, tel 031-667 2386 (or 061-236 2933).
U.S.A.: 3 Regent Terrace, tel 031-556 8315.
Vietnam: 8 Succoth Place, tel 031-337 1926.

The Scottish Tourist Board administrative office is at 23 Ravelston Terrace, Edinburgh, EH4 3EU, tel 031-332 2433.

Guides and Help

The Scottish Tourist Guides Association operates a network of fully qualified guides, who will accompany you anywhere you wish in Britain. Specialised tours and walks in Edinburgh and other centres can also be arranged. Their address is 9 Jordan Lane, Edinburgh, tel 031-447 7190.

Shopping in Scotland*

Tweed and Wool

No one should leave Scotland without having bought a good selection of the marvellous tweeds, tartans and knitwear that lie waiting to lure you into every mill shop and weaving shop around the country. You can visit little sheds where the weaving is still done on hand looms, mostly in the islands and parts of the Highlands. They are invariably sign-

* Please note that craft centres for each area are given at the end of each part.

posted from the road. Hardwearing Harris tweed is acclaimed all over the world: to be authentic it should be woven in the home of the crofter on a hand loom with Scottish wool (but not necessarily wool from Harris). The textile mills in the borders almost all have their own shops and some have opened up centres further north: Pringles, in Inverness and Edinburgh, for instance. Perhaps the best place of all, and the most tempting, is Campbells of Beauly, Inverness-shire.

Glass

You can buy lovely Scottish glass and there are a number of glass works where you can watch it being blown, moulded and engraved. Edinburgh Crystal have their glassworks at Penicuik. Caithness Glass have centres in Perth, Oban and Wick, with shops where you can buy their lovely range of glassware.

Jewellery and ornaments

You can buy the traditional accessories to Highland dress, set with cairngorms and amethysts, in wrought silver and gold, in the good jewellers, such as Hamilton and Inches, in Edinburgh. For jewellery made from local stones you should look for the many little workshops and craft shops that are dotted over the Highlands.

Horn-work

With such a large deer population, both decorative and functional objects carved from horn are made all over Scotland. Take home a shepherd's crook, called a crommach, with a handle carved from ramshorn or, if your luggage isn't designed to take something of 5 ft (1.5 m) or more in length, go for a horn salt spoon or drinking bowl.

Food and Drink

You should try and squeeze a side of smoked salmon into your suitcase but make sure it is well wrapped. It is expensive and you can get it in most places. If you want to be sure of good quality and the most reasonable price go to Clark Brothers, The Harbour, Musselburgh, tel 031-665 6181.

Buy shortbread and Dundee cake, in tins. They keep forever and are a good reminder of a Scottish holiday.

When you get to the duty free shop at the airport, your choice lies between the malt whisky you have adopted as your "special" (if in doubt, Glenfiddich won't let you down) and Drambuie, Scotland's whisky liqueur.

Shopping hours

The normal shopping hours are from 9 am to 6 pm, though some shops shut at 5.30 pm. Bakeries, dairies, newsagents and some big supermarkets open earlier. Many shops have an early closing day each week (1 pm) which varies from place to place, or from district to district in the cities. Some shops stay open until 7 pm or 8 pm at least one night a week, mostly in the cities.

VAT (Value Added Tax) is at present 15%. It is charged on many of the things you buy and can sometimes be reclaimed by people from abroad who are going to export what they buy. Ask about the retail export schemes: you will have to fill in forms.

Tracing your ancestors

For many reasons, not least the Highland Clearances in the 17th and 18th centuries, a large number of exiled Scots, and descendants of exiled Scots, return to the land of their origins hoping to trace their family history. It is often a fascinating and rewarding journey into the past and brings to light all sorts of hitherto unknown facts, as well as the odd skeleton in the cupboard or black sheep! It can be a daunting task when you have little information to go on and it is essential to start with a good researcher. Probably the best in Britain, who will set your feet on the right path, is Census Searches, The Lady Teviot, 12 Grand Avenue, Hassocks, West Sussex, tel 07918-4471.

Leisure Activities

There is something for everyone to do in Scotland; so much so, in fact, that it is often hard to choose.

Angling
(See Fishing.)

Canoeing
Canoeing is possible all round the coast and on many of the rivers, where the fast flow is often ideal for "white water" canoeing. There are many water sport centres where you can hire canoes. The Scottish Sports Council, 1–3 Colme Street, Edinburgh, tel 031-225 8411, runs outdoor training centres where courses include canoeing. If you have no experience you should not put to sea in a canoe!

Climbing and Hill Walking
Climbing and hill walking are among Scotland's greatest attractions, with possibilities ranging from hair-raising rock climbing in the Cuillin Hills, down to pleasant rambling along signposted routes on the moors and uplands. There are some lovely coastal footpaths, as well as nature trails, woodland trails, city strolls and long distance footpaths.

Long distance footpaths include the West Highland Way, which runs for 95 miles (152 km) from Milngavie on the outskirts of Glasgow to Fort William on the south end of the Great Glen. You get a marvellous range of Lowland and Highland scenery, on the old drove roads, forestry tracks, an old military road and a railway track bed.

The Speyside Way runs for 60 miles (96 km), from Glenmore Lodge, near Aviemore, to Spey Bay on the Moray Firth, with splendid and very varied scenery along the route.

The Southern Upland Way runs from Portpatrick in Dumfries and Galloway, east to Cockburnspath in the Border Region, and is 212 miles (339 km) long. It is signposted and well marked all the way and you can get leaflets that make it more interesting.

Walking and hill climbing in the Highlands offer you an endless choice of new places to explore and conquer. There are more than 270 mountains over 3,000 ft (914 m) high and nicknamed "Munros" after Sir Hugh Munro, who collated these hilltops in his

Glen Orchy

"Munro's Tables". It has become a popular sport to climb as many Munros as possible. From Glasgow and Edinburgh you have several high hills within easy reach by car for a day's outing. The Arrochar Alps, the peaks north-west of Loch Lomond, and particularly the Cobbler 2,891 ft (867 m) are an example. The Trossachs Hills are popular, and also Ben Vorlich, 3,231 ft (969 m), near Lochearnhead.

North of Loch Tay is Ben Lawers, another Munro at 3,984 ft (1,195 m) and looked after by the National Trust for Scotland. It has exceptional alpine flowers. Perthshire has many good hills to climb, including Schiehallion, 3,554 ft (1,066 m) near Loch Rannoch. The hills around Glen Lyon also provide opportunities for hill climbing. Glencoe has a good variety of walks and climbs ranging from easy to very challenging.

Further north is Scotland's highest mountain, Ben Nevis, 4,406 ft (1,322 m), with several routes up including a well marked tourist route. There are also a number of other high hills in Lochaber. To the north west, the highest peaks of the Grampians are truly arctic in the winter, but splendid walking for experienced climbers. The eastern edge of the Grampians, around Glen Clova, and the Lochnagar area, accessible from Deeside, are also popular.

North of the Great Glen you have Torridon, in the west, offering spectacular rock scenery, equalled only by the peaks of the Inverpolly Nature Reserve north of Ullapool and including the distinctive Stac Polly, 2,009 ft (603 m), Canisp, 2,779 ft (834 m) and Guilven, 2,399 ft (720 m). Ben Hope, south-west of Tongue, is Scotland's most northerly Munro, at 3,042 ft (913 m).

Rock climbers should head for the Cuillins in Skye, or Glencoe, Lochnagar, Creag Meaghaidh (near Loch Laggan), Beinn Trilleachan (Glen Etive) and An Teallach (south of Ullapool), all of which will keep you more than occupied.

Ski lifts for walkers are available at Cairngorm, Glencoe and Glenshee. These chairlifts are open for hill walkers in the non-skiing season only and give easy access to some of the higher terrain.

However settled and fine the weather may look when you are starting out on a walk, there are certain precautions that you should always take if you are going any distance off the road. Bear in mind that the weather changes rapidly in the hills and that other lives may be at risk if you get lost and have to be rescued. Always tell someone where you are going, what time you are leaving and what time you expect to return. Display a note in your parked car with this information. Consult someone local about your planned route and keep an eye on the weather. Carry a compass and a good map, 1:50,000. Wear warm, waterproof clothing and suitable footwear. Wellington (rubber) boots are not comfortable for long distance walking and climbing.

Curling

Curling, traditionally Scotland's winter game, is usually played on indoor rinks these days. It has been played in Scotland for over 450 years and is described as "a sort of bowls on ice". For information on where you can go to watch or participate, ask the Scottish Sports Council, 1–3 Colme Street, Edinburgh, tel 031-225 8411.

Diving or sub-aqua

Diving, or sub-aqua, is very popular. The wonderful clarity of the sea around the coast, full of highly coloured sea animals and plants, makes Scottish waters among the best in the world for diving. There is a big choice of good places where you can dive. The four places listed here are outstanding. In the north there is Scapa, in the Orkney Islands. Four of the sunken German fleet, scuttled at the end of the First World War, lie untouched below the clear waters of this huge anchorage and offer marvellous scope for wreck diving. You can charter boats from several places around the coast and get air.

On the east coast, St Abbs Head is well-known among divers for its exceptional sub-aqua quality. This stretch of coast, down to Eyemouth, is good for beginners, being reasonably shallow with lovely marine life. The weather can be bad, so you must be prepared to hang around sometimes.

On the west coast the waters around Oban are excellent for diving, with a good air supply and plenty of boats to charter in Oban. The Sound of Mull is littered with wrecks, and there is good sub-aqua cliff scenery.

The Summer Isles, in the north–west, are also ideal for diving. For more information contact Scottish Sub-Aqua Club, 16 Royal Crescent, Glasgow, tel 041-332 9291.

There are three sorts of fishing in Scotland: game, sea and coarse (fresh water) fishing. Fishing for salmon and sea trout can be expensive and you can pay more than £10 a day for a short section of the Tweed near Peebles. For the same price you might get 30 miles (48 km) of river for a fortnight's trout fishing. Prices vary enormously and you should take local advice. Wild brown trout are found in rivers and lochs all over Scotland, and there are plenty of sea trout if salmon conditions are unfavourable.

The principal and most famous rivers for salmon flow east, but those that flow west can also give excellent sport. Your hotel will usually arrange fishing for you and give advice. Otherwise the local tourist information centre will tell you all you want to know.

Sea fishing is extensive with such a lot of coastline. Porbeagle shark, halibut, cod, bass, hake, ling, skate and turbot are but a few of the fish you can expect to find. There is never a shortage of charter boats, and in most places you will find plenty of experienced locals who will take you out. Ask in your hotel, or in the tourist information centre.

For coarse fishermen there are pike, perch, eel, grayling, roach, chub, bream, dace, gudgeon and tench for a start. Again, your hotel will advise or the local tourist information centre.

The seasons for fishing are as follows: Coarse fishing: no close season. Trout fishing: 15 February to 6 October. Salmon fishing: varies from river to river, starting from January in some places, though as late as March in others, and going through to as late as 31 November.

The following are useful addresses for fishermen:

Scottish Anglers National Association, 307 West George Street, Glasgow, tel 041-221 7206.

Central Scotland Anglers Association, 53 Fernieside Crescent, Edinburgh, tel 031-664 4685.

The Scottish Federation of Sea Anglers, 18 Ainslie Place, Edinburgh, tel 031-225 7611.

Scottish Federation for Coarse Angling, Tigh-na-Fleurs, Hill o' Gryfe Road, Bridge of Weir, Renfrewshire, tel 0505-612580.

Scottish Sports Council, 1–3 St Colme Street, Edinburgh, tel 031-225 8411.

Gliding

Gliding is possible in some areas in Scotland and some clubs offer temporary membership and instruction. Consult the Scottish Sports Council, 1–3 St Colme Street, Edinburgh, tel 031-225 8411.

Golf

Golf is Scotland's national game. There are more than 400 golf courses in Scotland, probably the highest concentration in the world. A few of these are exclusive, some are world famous, most are open to visitors with the minimum of formalities. Charges are reasonable and the courses are almost always well maintained and playable nearly all year round. Good golfing bases include East Lothian, with its Muirfield course, Fife, with St Andrews; Aberdeen; Moray Firth coast; Ayrshire coast, with Turnberry; Dornoch; and Perthshire, with Gleneagles, Callander, Crieff and Rosemount. Smaller centres include the Solway Firth; Borders; Speyside; and, in the islands, Arran with seven courses.

Prices vary. You can play on some municipal courses for as little as £1.50 per round to over £12 a round on St Andrews Old Course or at Muirfield. A few of the exclusive clubs require introductions from their members, others prefer you to be a member of a recognised golf club. With the majority, however, you can just turn up and play, though it is advisable to ring up first. Tourist information centres will have details of local clubs.

The following are some of the most famous courses in Scotland, playing host to international competitions. As such they tend to have more restricted playing times for visitors than the average courses and you should check before you go.

Carnoustie Golf Club, Angus, tel 0241-53249. Unrestricted.

The Honourable Company of Edinburgh Golfers, Muirfield, Gullane, East Lothian. Play only with a member.
Turnberry Golf Club, Turnberry Hotel, Ayrshire, tel 06553-202. Two courses. Unrestricted.
Royal Troon Golf Club, Troon, Ayrshire, tel 0292-311555. No weekend play. Handicap Certificate required.
Royal Dornoch Golf Club, Dornoch, Sutherland, tel 0862-810219. Unrestricted.
The Old Course, St Andrews Golf Club, St Andrews, tel 0334-73038. No Sunday play. Unrestricted.
Gleneagles Hotel Golf Courses, Gleneagles Hotel, Auchterarder, tel 0764-3543. Unrestricted.
Nairn Golf Club, Nairn, tel 0667–52103. Unrestricted.

For further information, including a full list of all golf courses in Scotland, write for *Scotland, Home of Golf* from Pastime Publications, 15 Dublin Street Lane South, Edinburgh. There are a number of tourist organisations that specialise in organising golfing holidays. The Scottish Tourist Board, 23 Ravelston Terrace, Edinburgh, tel 031-332 2433 will send you full details.

Ornithology
Ornithology is a marvellously rewarding pastime in Scotland. There are a large number of nature reserves and bird sanctuaries all over the country. Because of the remoteness of some of the Highland areas you can expect to see birds so rare that many people have never even heard of them. Fair Isle is perhaps the most rewarding place for bird watchers and you can stay there. For details, write to Fair Isle Lodge and Bird Observatory, Fair Isle, tel 03512-258. You can get more ornithological information from RSPB Scottish Office, 17 Regent Terrace, Edinburgh, tel 031-556 5624.

Pony trekking
Pony trekking is a wonderful way of seeing the country and you don't have to be an experienced rider to do it. There are many places from which to start, with a choice of day trekking or trekking and camping. The local tourist information centres will give you addresses: most tourist maps mark them with a horse shoe. The Scottish Tourist Board publishes a leaflet called *Pony Trekking and Riding Centres in Scotland*, but you may find out more by asking around locally.

Skiing
Skiing is becoming increasingly popular and resorts are developing rapidly. Conditions vary enormously. At times it is only for the more experienced skier, when the slopes are icy and pitted with rocks! Consult the Scottish Tourist Board booklet, *Ski Holidays in Scotland*. You can book in London, at 19 Cockspur Street, London, SW1Y 5BL, tel 01-930 8661. The main centres are Cairngorm, Glencoe, Glenshee and The Lecht, and the booklet gives you full details of the many packages on offer.

You can also go dry skiing at any time of the year (except when the slopes are covered in snow). The largest artificial slope in Britain is at Hillend, in the Pentland Hills just outside Edinburgh. There are also slopes at Aviemore, Glasgow, Aberdeen, Bearsden, Cairnwell and Polmont.

Shooting and stalking

Scotland is ideal shooting country, with farmland, mixed woodland and moorland. There is a long tradition of good game management. The estuaries and marshes provide excellent scope for wildfowling, and there are good stocks of deer in the forests and high moors in the Highlands. Game shooting species include pheasants, snipe, grey partridge, woodcock, grouse, capercailzie and ptarmigan. Permitted wild fowl species include many varieties of duck and geese.

Rough shooting is for wood pigeon, rabbit and hare, for which there is no close season. Deer species include red deer, roe, fallow and sika.

No game shooting is allowed on Sundays and a certificate is required by anyone owning or using either a rifle or a shotgun. Before you shoot game you must get a game licence, which is available in all main and branch post offices throughout the country.

All other species of wild life, both bird and mammal are strictly protected in Scotland by the Wildlife and Countryside Act.

A large number of hotels will fix up shooting and stalking for you and the local tourist boards will advise you on contacting estates and on shooting seasons.

Water sports

Water sports are available all over the country, including sailing, wind surfing, water skiing and swimming. Coastal resorts invariably have sailing clubs where you can get tuition and hire boats and equipment. There are a large number of inland water sport centres on the lochs. For full details get the *Scotland Holiday Afloat* booklet from the Scottish Tourist Board or tel 0382-21555 or 0577 62816.

Leisure Centres

Leisure Centres are springing up all over Scotland. Here you can play squash, tennis, badminton, bowls, table tennis, ice hockey, etc. You can also do aerobic dancing, judo, karate, skating and a whole lot more.

Tourist offices will tell you which centre is open in your area.

Historic buildings and sites

National Trust for Scotland

Many of Scotland's historic buildings and conserved land are under the care of the National Trust for Scotland (NTS), a charity that was set up over 50 years ago to promote the preservation of the country's heritage. Nearly 100 properties, including castles, small houses, islands, mountains, coastline and gardens come under the protection of the NTS. These places are visited by more than one and a half million people each year. Most of the properties are open from April to October, and admission charges range from 10p to £1.70 for adults: many are free. You can join the National Trust for Scotland for £12 a year, and this means you can visit all National Trust properties free of charge in England, Wales and Northern Ireland, as well as in Scotland. For further information, write to the National Trust for Scotland Head Office, 5 Charlotte Square, Edinburgh, EH2 4DU, tel 031-226 5922.

Ancient Monuments
The Ancient Monuments division of the Scottish Development Department are responsible for the care and upkeep of many of the country's historic ruins, buildings and sites. In this book, wherever you see "open at standard Ancient Monument times" these times are as follows. April–September: Monday–Saturday, 9.30 am–7 pm, Sunday 2 pm–4 pm. October–March: Monday–Saturday, 9.30 am–4 pm, Sunday 2 pm–4 pm.

Other Public Bodies of Landowners
The Forestry Commission own vast areas of land, much of which is available for public use.
The Nature Conservancy Council.
The Royal Society for the Protection of Birds.
The Scottish Wildlife Trust.
Privately owned castles and houses.

Some of the inhabited castles and historic houses that are open to the public are privately owned and each have their own opening times and admission charges. Wherever possible, this book gives you an idea of times and charges, but these change from year to year and sometimes from season to season and should always be checked if possible.

Good Value for Visitors
There is an "open to view" ticket that you can buy which entitles you to free entrance to 563 places of historic interest: castles, abbeys, stately homes, famous gardens, etc, in Scotland, England, Wales and Northern Ireland. You can buy these from major tourist information centres (£17 adult, £8.50 children). Tickets are valid for a month, starting from the date of your first visit. With your ticket you get a large illustrated map showing all the places together with information about opening times. You also get free or reduced entry to many museums, as well as discount at certain museum shops.

Americans who are flying with British Airways can get a voucher for US$23 (adults) US$11.50 (children) when they buy their air ticket. This can be exchanged at the tourist information centres at Prestwick Airport, Waverley Market in Edinburgh, or Murray's Green in Jedburgh.

This, then, is Scotland. You stand on the threshold: it is up to you to unlock the door.

Part II
HISTORY

Coat of Arms

You don't have to be an historian to enjoy the magic of Scotland. No one could resist its unparalleled scenery, its enormous variety of outdoor activities, its unique culture and folklore and the very special character of its people. But there is no doubt that a superficial knowledge of the main events that made the country what it is will enhance your pleasure as you explore its many attractions. Boring ruins become enchanted castles when you know the background of their destruction. Mysterious symbols carved on stones acquire a fascination when you know that the hand that engraved them belonged to a man who lived 3,000 years ago.

Pre-Historic

Scotland was inhabited as far back as the Stone Age, at least 5,000 years ago. Evidence of anything before that was eradicated by the Ice Age. Those early settlers left clues to their existence in their burial sites and their middens (dung heaps)—enough to tantalise archaeologists, but not enough to leave more than a shadow of their identity. They were nomadic Celts, coming from Asia and Europe, through England and Ireland, arriving, wave after wave of them and settling for long enough to leave traces of their culture and way of life, before vanishing into obscurity. Historians puzzle over their mysterious stone circles and monoliths, and over the true purpose of their brochs (massive stone towers built near the sea in the far north, about 2,000 years ago).

The Romans

The Romans arrived in AD 82 and with them came the first record of Scottish history, written by the historian, Tacitus. Tacitus describes how his father-in-law, Agricola, defeated an army of tall, red-haired men on an unidentified hillside in the north-east, in the Battle of Mons Graupius.

The Romans called their victims "picti" the painted ones, from which the name "Picts" was derived. They failed to subdue them. Highly trained legionaires could not compete with hostile tribes who faded into the mountains and forests and marshes, refusing to fight army-to-army, preferring to lay cunning ambushes for their aggressors. The Romans fell back, having lost the entire Ninth Legion in a savage massacre.

In 121, Hadrian built a wall between the Solway and the Tyne, hoping to contain the barbarians in the north, but the wall was so frequently attacked that another was constructed between the Forth and the Clyde in 141–2, the Antonine Wall. This proved to be no more effective and was soon abandoned.

Exasperated, the Romans withdrew to Hadrian's Wall and an uneasy peace existed between the north and south until the middle of the 4th century. The Picts then resumed their ferocious attacks while Saxons began to invade from the north-east. The Roman empire was in decline: more and more legions were being recalled to fight nearer home. By the end of the 4th century the Romans abandoned Scotland completely, leaving the untamed Picts to defend themselves against new invaders.

The coming of Christianity

Four races now dominated Scotland, which was then called Alba, or Alban. The Celtic Picts were the most powerful, occupying the land from Caithness to the Forth; the Teutonic Angles, or Anglo-Saxons, occupied Bernicia, south of the Forth; the Britons, another Celtic race who had moved in from Wales, occupied the western lands south of the Clyde. Finally there were the Scots; Celts who had come over from Ireland during the 3rd and 4th centuries and settled north of the Clyde, establishing the Kingdom of Dalriada and eventually giving their name to all of Scotland.

St Ninian founded the first Christian centre at Whithorn, near the Solway Firth, in 397, and started on the daunting task of converting the pagans. Then came Columba from Ireland, in 563, a clever man of royal birth who seems to have been exiled in some sort of disgrace. He established himself on the island of Iona, continuing St Ninian's work, and sent missionaries to the mainland and to the other islands. These penetrated further and further into Pictland. Columba's influence was political as well as religious and he did much to consolidate the strength of the Scots. By the end of the 7th century the four kingdoms of Alban were nominally converted to Christianity—a Celtic Christianity, not yet in line with that dictated by the Vatican.

Norse Invasion

Norsemen began to attack from the north at the end of the 8th century, conquering Orkney and Shetland, the Western Isles, Caithness and Sutherland, while the four kingdoms continued to fight amongst themselves, weakening their resistance to outside attack.

The Birth of Scotland

In 843 Kenneth MacAlpine, King of the Scots, achieved some sort of union between Scots and Picts, making himself king over all the territory north of the Forth and Clyde, which then became Scotia. The Picts, who had been dominant for more than 1,000 years, vanished for ever. They were an enigmatic people whose history is unrecorded and unknown; an elusive ghost-race who will perhaps never be fully understood. It was not until 1018, however, that Malcolm II defeated the Angles and brought Bernicia, or Lothian, into the kingdom. He was succeeded, in 1034, by his grandson Duncan I who already ruled the Britons and so the four kingdoms were finally united into one Scotland, except for those parts occupied by the Norsemen.

The Norman Influence

Duncan I was killed in 1040 by Macbeth. Macbeth was then killed by Duncan's son, Malcolm III, Malcolm Canmore, in 1057. *Ceann Mor* is Gaelic for big head, referring to Malcolm's status rather than to any anatomical defect, or conceit.

It was Malcolm Canmore's second wife, Margaret, who made his 36 year reign memorable. She was an English princess, sister of Edgar the Atheling. She and her brother had taken refuge in Scotland after the Norman Conquest of England, in 1066. Margaret, who was extremely pious and later canonised, set about Anglicising the Celtic church. She brought in English clergy and established an English court and it was her influence that civilised Scotland and transformed it into a kingdom more similar to Norman England.

Inspired by the presence in his court of his English brother-in-law, Malcolm coveted the English throne. He made several border raids into Northumberland and Cumbria, forcing William the Conqueror to invade Scotland to subdue him. In order to prevent the subsequent destruction of Scotland, Malcolm was then forced to pay homage to William at Abernethy in 1071. He continued to harass the English until he was treacherously killed while laying siege to Alnwick Castle in 1093. Queen Margaret, already mortally ill, survived him by only three days. She died thanking God for her grief, believing that it purified her soul.

David: the founder of Cathedrals

David I, the ninth son of Malcolm Canmore, inherited the throne in 1124 from a succession of unremarkable monarchs, and he ruled for nearly 30 years.

David had been brought up in England and had many Norman friends. He was married to a Norman heiress: his sister, Maud, was married to King Henry I of England. His reign brought many changes. He gave large Scottish estates to his Anglo-Norman friends. Old Celtic families merged with the French-speaking incomers in south Scotland; the Highlanders retained their traditional clan system and took little notice of their southern neighbours.

David founded many cathedrals, churches and monasteries; he granted royal charters to towns, permitting markets and fairs; he tried to establish a national judiciary; he encouraged foreign trade and selected a body of advisers from his court to help him.

The Auld Alliance

Malcolm IV was only 11 years old when he inherited the throne from his grandfather David, in 1153. Known as Malcolm the Maiden, he ruled for only 12 years before he died, to be succeeded by his brother, William-the-Lion. William established an alliance with France in 1165, "The Auld Alliance" and tried to invade England. He failed, was taken prisoner and sent to Normandy, where he was forced to sign the humiliating "Treaty of Falaise". This placed Scotland under feudal subjection to England. Fifteen years later, when the English king, Richard Coeur de Lion, needed money for a Crusade, he agreed to annul the Treaty of Falaise in return for 10,000 marks.

The end of the Norse occupation

England and Scotland were at peace, then, for more than 100 years. Alexander II succeeded to the throne in 1214, and directed his attention to the Western Isles, whose lords gave their allegiance to Norway. It was his son, Alexander III, however, who managed to expel the Norsemen from the Hebrides. He did this by defeating old King Haakon IV of Norway in the Battle of Largs, in 1263. The Hebrides became part of the kingdom of Scotland again, but the Lords of the Isles paid little heed to any authority but their own.

Alexander continued to foster prosperity in Scotland, along the same lines as his great-great-grandfather, David I. He married the English Princess Margaret, daughter of Henry III. Their daughter, also Margaret, married King Eric of Norway and thus links were forged with both countries. Alexander had a long and successful reign. He outlived his first wife and three children and married again in an attempt to father an heir. He was, however, killed six months later when thrown from his horse and left his grand-daughter Margaret of Norway to succeed him, under the regency of John Balliol. Balliol was a powerful Norman-scot: his wife, Devorguilla, founded Balliol College in Oxford.

Wars of Independence

Edward I of England, determined to unite Scotland to England, immediately proposed a marriage between his son Edward and the eight year old Maid of Norway. This poor little queen died at sea, however, on her way to Britain, and Edward declared himself to be overlord of Scotland. There were several claimants to the Scottish throne, the strongest being those of John Balliol, son of the regent, and Robert Bruce. Both were Anglo-Norman nobles with estates in England and Scotland, given to their ancestors by David I. They were descended from David's youngest son and had both fought in Edward's army.

Edward came north in 1291 and awarded the crown to John Balliol in Berwick Castle, believing him to be more easily manipulated than Robert Bruce. He then ordered Balliol to pay homage to the English throne and accept himself (Edward) as Scotland's overlord. He also insisted that Scotland should contribute to English defence costs and join with them in an invasion of France. Balliol was a weak man, known to his subjects as "Toom Tabard", Empty Coat, but these demands were too much for him and he prepared to invade England. Edward was supported by many of the Scottish nobles who owned estates in England, including Robert Bruce and he defeated Balliol who was forced to renounce his crown.

Edward, "The Hammer of the Scots", progressed through Scotland, compelling nobles and lairds to sign a roll, "The Ragman's Roll". This acknowledged him to be their king. He then returned to England, taking with him the Stone of Destiny, brought from Ireland seven centuries earlier and believed to embody special powers. It was used in the coronation of Scottish kings. Edward thought that he had finally conquered Scotland. He had not.

William Wallace

William Wallace was a young Scot from the south-west, outlawed in 1297 for killing the sheriff of Lanark in revenge for the murder of his wife. In exile Wallace became the leader of a fast-expanding resistance movement against English repression. In September 1297 he led a resounding defeat of the English at the Battle of Stirling Bridge, kindling new hope in Scottish hearts, and paving the way to freedom from English tyranny. The following year he was defeated by Edward and had to go into hiding. He evaded capture for seven unhappy years before he was betrayed. He was paraded through the streets of London, tried on a series of trumped-up charges and condemned to death. It was a particularly vicious execution. He was hanged, drawn and emasculated, his entrails being burnt before his eyes as he died. Quarters of his body and his head were displayed throughout Britain. During those final years of Wallace's life, Edward ravaged Scotland in his attempt to crush further resistance.

Robert Bruce

Robert Bruce, son of John Balliol's rival, had served Edward in his youth. Like his father, he had a claim to the throne, as did Balliol's nephew, Red John Comyn. These two men met at Greyfriars Kirk, in Dumfries, presumably to discuss plans for ridding their country of English domination. A quarrel arose between them and Bruce killed Comyn, in the kirk, thus committing sacrilege as well as murder. Excommunicated by Rome and hounded by the Comyns, he went to Scone and had himself crowned king of Scotland, in May 1306.

Edward hurried north and defeated Bruce, a month later, at Methven.

Outlawed, his friends and allies dead, Bruce went into hiding. During this time of exile, probably on the island of Rathlin, off the Irish coast, he encountered the legendary spider, whose determination and persistence finally enabled it to swing from one rafter to another on its frail home-spun web. If the spider could succeed, then so could he. Bruce returned to Scotland in 1307 on the death of Edward I, overcame all other claimants to the throne and defeated Edward II at Bannockburn in 1314. He reigned for a further 15 years and died of leprosy, at Cardross Castle on the Clyde in 1329.

Struggles for Power

Bruce was succeeded by his five year old son, David II, with Thomas Randolph, Earl of Moray, as regent. The 42 years of David's reign were troubled times for Scotland. Encouraged by Edward III of England, the Scottish nobles, who had been disinherited earlier by Bruce for backing the English, tried to put Toom Tabard's son, Edward Balliol, on the throne. Moray was killed, as was his cousin the Earl of Mar, who succeeded him as regent. Balliol was crowned king of Scotland, at Scone, but not for long. Irate Scottish nobles rose up in fury and chased Balliol from the country.

David, who had been sent to France for safety at the age of ten with his child-wife Joan, was brought back to Scotland in 1341. He was captured by the English, at the Battle of Neville's Cross, however, and spent the next 12 years in England. He was very content with the easy life of Edward III's court, while his regent, Robert Stewart, grandson of Robert Bruce, continued to harass the English. Beguiled by his love for England, David consented to name Edward III's son as his heir. However, Scotland was not in favour of such a betrayal and when David died in 1371, they put Robert Stewart on the throne, the former regent and the first Stewart king.

The Stewarts

Robert had been a good regent—better than he now was as king. Anarchy, rebellion and internal squabbles disturbed the peace he strove for. Border raiding was rife, causing continual devastation in the south, and the whole country seethed in a turmoil of lawlessness. Robert II died in 1390 and was succeeded by his son, Robert III

Crippled by a kick from a horse, Robert was in poor health. He allowed his brother, the Duke of Albany, to assume power and he abdicated in 1399 because of his disabilities. For the next 25 years Scotland was ruled by regents, including Robert's son, David, Duke of Rothesay. Rothesay disappeared in mysterious circumstances, allegedly starved to death by his uncle, the Duke of Albany, who once again took office—this time as regent.

The ailing Robert III sent his grandson and heir, James, to France, in 1406, fearing that Albany had plans to remove him from succession. The young prince was, however, captured by pirates and handed over to the English. Too shocked to go on living, Robert died a month later, leaving Albany in full power for 18 years while James was held hostage. Powerful nobles in Scotland seized the opportunity to consolidate their strength. They expanded their estates and built up private armies, many of them becoming as powerful as kings. Most notable among them was the Douglas family, whose lands and subjects rivalled those of the king. Meanwhile, in the north-west, the Lords of the Isles allied themselves with the English and continued to live their own lives with little regard for central government.

Anarchy

James I returned to his throne in 1424, at the age of 29, with an English bride, Joan Beaufort, cousin of Henry VI. Reared and educated in England, he had had a good grounding in statesmanship and in military strategy. He found his country in turmoil. His nobles were far too powerful and anarchy, poverty and lawlessness were rampant. His first step was the wholesale execution of the Albany family, in 1425, and the seizure of their considerable estates. In 1427 he summoned the Highland chiefs and arrested 40 of them: Alexander of the Isles retaliated by burning Inverness. Further rebellion from the west was subdued and James managed to redress the balance of power in the Lowlands by annexing many of the earldoms that had threatened his supremacy.

James achieved a great deal for Scotland, restoring law and order and introducing a number of much-needed reforms. Inevitably, his decisive methods won him enemies and in 1437 three of them stabbed him to death, leaving his six year old son James II as his heir.

The Powerful Douglases

Scotland was once again ruled by regency, and once again the nobles, in particular the

Douglas family, became too powerful. In 1440, the regent, Sir William Crichton, invited the 14 year old Earl of Douglas and his younger brother to dine with the boy-king at Edinburgh Castle. This came to be known as the "Black Dinner": a black bull's head, symbol of death, was brought into the Great Hall, and the two Douglas youths were murdered, in front of the eight year old king. For a while, the Douglas family were subdued.

James II came to his throne in 1449 at the age of 19. He continued to establish the reforms so dear to his father, but was threatened by an alliance between the Douglases, Crawfords and John of the Isles.

Perhaps remembering the "Black Dinner" of his youth, he summoned the Earl of Douglas to Stirling Castle and stabbed him to death. With English help the Douglases attempted revenge and James defeated them completely at the Battle of Arkinholm, killing three of the murdered earl's four brothers. The power of the Douglas family, known as the Black Douglases, was squashed. James was killed in 1460 when a canon exploded during the siege of Roxburghe.

His son, James III, was nine years old and so Scotland was once more ruled by regents, until his accession at the age of 19. He married the King of Norway's daughter who brought with her the islands of Orkney and Shetland as part of her dowry.

James was an intellectual, better fitted for an academic life than for a crown. He antagonised his nobles who rose against him. They hung his favourites and proclaimed his son, James IV, to be king in his place. James III tried to regain power, fighting the rebels at Sauchieburn, near Stirling, in 1488. His horse bolted and threw him. Badly injured he begged for a priest and the man who stepped forward to administer the last rites, stabbed him to death.

Renaissance in Scotland

James IV, the most popular of the Stewart kings, was 15 when he came to the throne. He was clever and charming, a good leader, pious and energetic, generous, flamboyant and sensual. His mistresses bore him a number of bastards. During his reign, the Renaissance came to Scotland: art and education blossomed and James led the way. He authorised the building of beautiful palaces and churches. His court was elegant and cultured and the country was at peace, growing in prosperity. But the peace was not absolute: on the doorstep the Lords of the Isles continued to live as they always had, fiercely patriarchal, their loyalties all directed to their own clans and chieftains. James, who had taken the trouble to learn Gaelic, decided to visit the western Highlands and islands, hoping to win the friendship of the clans. His attempts were viewed with suspicion, thus he desisted and appointed overlords to rule them. This resulted in an uprising of the Macdonalds and the Macleans, in 1503: they stormed Inverness and burned it.

Flodden

In 1503, James married 12 year old Margaret Tudor and signed a treaty of perpetual peace with England. But in 1511, his brother-in-law, Henry VIII of England, joined the Pope, the King of Spain and the Doge of Venice in a Holy League against France. James passionately desired a united Europe. Determined to maintain a balance of power, therefore, he renewed the Auld Alliance with France and tried, in vain, to mediate.

In 1513, threatened from all direction, France appealed to Scotland for help. James in turn appealed to Henry, who replied with insults. Against all advice, in August 1513, James led a Scottish army across the Tweed, to Flodden Field, where the army was massacred by the superior forces of the English. The king, his nobles and most of Scotland's best men were killed in a battle that was as pointless as it was valiant: it was perhaps Scotland's greatest tragedy. The country was left leaderless, its army slain, its new king James V, a toddler and its regent, Margaret Tudor, with divided loyalties.

There followed a period of more turmoil and intrigue until the king was old enough to take office and try to restore order to his country. Ignoring several offer of brides, he chose French Madeleine, who only lived for two months after their marriage. The following year he took a second French wife, Marie de Guise-Lorraine, who bore him two sons both of whom died.

James was an ingenuous man. He liked to disguise himself as a commoner and mingle with his subjects, posing as the Guidman Ballangeich, fooling no one but himself, and getting into several unfortunate escapades.

He squabbled with the English, aggravated his nobles, and tried to invade England. His pathetic, mutinous army, quarrelling amongst itself, was defeated by Henry VIII's army, at Solway Moss, in 1542. Sick and despairing, James returned to Falkland Palace where he heard that his wife had just given birth to a daughter. The news was too much for him and he died, leaving as his heir Mary, Queen of Scots only a few days old.

Mary, Queen of Scots: The Rough Wooing

Henry VIII, determined to take Scotland into his realm, proposed a marriage between Mary and his delicate son, Edward. A marriage treaty was arranged with the regent, Arran, but the Queen Mother, Marie de Guise, had other plans. Mary was crowned queen of Scotland, at Scone, with the approval of the Three Estates (the church, the nobles and the burghers). Furious to be thus snubbed, Henry set about what became known as the Rough Wooing. He devastated the south of Scotland and earned the bitter hatred of the Scots. Mary was sent off to France at the age of five, where she stayed for 15 years, marrying the French Dauphin. While she was away, learning French ways, Protestants were gaining power in Scotland, resenting the Catholic French influence. The regent, now Marie de Guise, backed by the French, denounced all Protestants as heretics. This so enraged John Knox, a powerful and energetic reformer, that he incited his followers to destroy the Catholic churches and religious houses. The regent queen was deposed in 1559 and Catholicism was abolished. At this point, Mary's French husband died and she returned to her country as queen; no longer Mary Stewart, but Mary Stuart because the French have no "w" in their alphabet.

The seven unhappy years that followed were so fraught with violence, treachery and intrigue, and so overlaid with romance that they seem to dominate Scottish history.

Mary in Scotland

Mary was not yet 20 when she landed in Scotland in 1561. French in education and attitude, a devout Catholic, high-spirited, passionate, sensual and beautiful, she had the best intentions. She had no desire to tangle with the Protestants. She was not a bigot; she merely wished to be allowed to practise her own religion in peace. This horrified John Knox and his followers, who found her light-hearted ways obnoxious.

In 1565, she married her cousin, Henry Stewart, Lord Darnley, a dissipated Catholic youth, four years her junior, and distrusted by all. Within a year, when Mary was six months pregnant, Darnley became jealous of her Italian secretary, Rizzio, and murdered him with the help of his friends, in the presence of his wife. She never forgave him. When he himself was murdered, the following year, some hinted that Mary may have known of the plot. Eight weeks later, she married James Hepburn, Earl of Bothwell, a buccaneering Protestant of great charm and little honour. He had abducted and raped Mary in order to marry her, having hastily divorced his wife.

Bothwell had been heavily implicated in the murder of Darnley and this ill-advised action sparked off an inferno of protest from both Catholics and Protestants. Mary, publicly humiliated, was forced to abdicate in favour of her baby son, James VI. Her half-brother, James Stewart, Earl of Moray, bastard son of James V, was proclaimed regent. Mary fled to England and threw herself on the mercy of her cousin, Elizabeth I. But Elizabeth, without an heir, could not forget Mary's claims to the English throne. Mary was imprisoned for 20 years, and then beheaded.

Conflict within the Reformed Church

After another spell of regency, James proclaimed himself king in 1583 and found himself to be the head of a country divided between Catholics and Protestants. He aspired to be an impartial king and incurred the animosity of both factions. A Protestant himself in name, if not belief, James had no wish to antagonise his Protestant cousin Elizabeth of England and spoil his chances of inheriting her throne. He concluded an alliance with England and made no more than a formal protest when Elizabeth agreed to the execution of his mother in 1587.

The new, Protestant religion in Scotland now presented problems. It was divided between the extreme Presbyterians, who wanted a religion of the purest simplicity with equality of ministers and no bishops or elaborate ritual, and James' English form of Protestantism, with bishops appointed by the crown and a formal liturgy. He tried to impose his will on the Kirk, but failed. Presbyterians grew more and more averse to Episcopacy and their religion became less and less formal, with extempore prayers replacing those in the prayer book.

Union of Crowns

In 1603, Queen Elizabeth I died, appointing James as her heir. Thus, he became James VI of Scotland and I of England. He hurried to London and only returned to Scotland once, preferring the pomp and magnificence of the English court, and the ritual of the Church of England. But he still tried to foist Episcopacy on his northern subjects and to reinstate formal worship. He died in 1625 and his son, Charles I, succeeded him.

The Covenanters

Charles, reared in England and a devout Anglican and Episcopalian, had no love for the Kirk. When he went north for his coronation in 1633, his subjects were scandalised by the Popish practices he brought with him. He authorised the revision of the English prayer book in an attempt to produce one for Scotland that might replace extempore prayer. This act produced violent opposition, riots and protest. Important men and nobles rebelled against the enforcement of the use of the new prayer book. Thousands flocked to Greyfriars Kirk, in Edinburgh, in February 1638 to sign the National Covenant, a document that condemned all Catholic doctrines and upheld the "True Religion". Copies of the Covenant were carried all over the Lowlands and signed, amidst strong national feeling. The Covenant, however, was somewhat ambivalent: its signatories swore, not only to uphold the True Religion, but also to be loyal to a king who demanded the Episcopacy that they shunned. Thus, loyal subjects of the crown found themselves torn betwen obedience to the king and obedience to their new religion.

When civil war broke out in England, the Covenanting Scots agreed to go to the aid of the English Parliamentarians, on condition that Presbyterianism was adopted throughout England and Ireland, as well as Scotland.

In 1649, Charles I was defeated by Cromwell and executed. The Scots grasped this opportunity to advance their quest for stability and invited his exiled son, Charles II, to Scotland where he was crowned king, on the condition that he supported the Covenant. Furious, Cromwell invaded Scotland. Charles went back into exile and Cromwell ruled both countries until the Restoration of the Monarchy, in 1660.

The Killing Times

Charles II now ignored all the promises he had made, and sought to reintroduce Episcopacy. This rekindled the fervour of the Covenanters, who fled into the hills and worshipped in secret "Conventicles". In 1670, these conventicles were declared to be treasonable, and there then followed the "Killing Times", when thousands of fanatic Covenanters were slaughtered, retaliating with brutal reprisals.

The Jacobites

Charles II died of apoplexy in 1685 and was succeeded by his brother, James VII/II, Scotland's first Catholic sovereign for 120 years. During his brief reign, James tried unsuccessfully to introduce tolerance for all religions. He was deposed in 1688 by his daughter Mary and her Dutch husband, William of Orange. He fled to France and William and Mary were crowned King and Queen. Some Scots, mostly Highlanders, remained true to James, however. The Jacobites, as they were called, rose, under Graham of Claverhouse and almost annihilated William's army in a savage battle at Killiecrankie, in 1689. But Claverhouse was killed, leaving them leaderless, and they lost heart and returned to their Highlands.

The Massacre of Glencoe

The government, uneasy about the rebellious Highlanders, issued a proclamation, ordering all the clans to take an oath of allegiance to the Crown by the first day of 1692. Circumstances prevented MacIan MacDonald of Glencoe from taking the oath until after the deadline. This provided the government with a chance to rid itself of any likely threat from one of the most powerful clans. A company of Campbell soldiers, commanded by a relation of MacIan's, Captain Campbell of Glenlyon, billeted themselves on the MacDonalds in Glencoe. Under orders from higher authority, they rose up at dawn and slaughtered their hosts. The barbarity of the Massacre of Glencoe produced public outcry. The king denied all fore-knowledge: as a gesture, he sacked his Secretary of State, the Master of Stair, who had instigated the deed.

The Union of Parliaments

In 1695 Scotland's economy was shattered, by an unsuccessful attempt to colonise the Darien Peninsula, between North and South America. The failure of this Darien Scheme, mostly due to fever and inhospitable Spaniards, brought about the Treaty of Union, in 1707, uniting the parliaments of England and Scotland. This carefully worded document brought advantage to both countries: it gave Scotland a badly needed boost to her economy and the right to Presbyterianism, and removed the threat of further war between the two countries.

But the signing of the Treaty of Union forced the Scots to accept a Hanoverian succession to the throne, and Jacobite loyalties still prevailed in the Highlands. James Edward Stuart, son of the deposed James VII/II, was regarded by many as Scotland's king. The Old Pretender, as he was called by Hanoverians, made three unsuccessful attempts to regain his throne. In 1708 he only got as far as the Firth of Forth. In 1715 he persuaded the Earl of Mar to rally an army of Highlanders. Mar raised the Scottish standard and proclaimed James king. The rising looked promising; a battle was fought at Sherrifmuir in which the result was inconclusive. The Old Pretender escaped to France, leaving the Highlanders to fend for themselves. In 1719, a final attempt was made, backed by the Spanish; but the supporting fleet was lost in a storm and the Highlanders dispersed.

Stringent measures were put into effect to quell the clans. General Wade built a series of military roads and forts, opening up the Highlands and linking the strategic strong points, at Fort William, Fort Augustus and Fort George. He raised a regiment of clansmen, loyal to the Whig government, the Black Watch, whose duty it was to keep order among the resentful clans.

George I came to the throne in 1714, an unattractive German who disliked the British as much as they disliked him. When he died, his son, George II was equally Germanic and unsuitable to rule over those Highlanders who still clung to their Jacobite dreams. This was excuse enough.

The end of the Jacobite dream

Exiled in Rome, the Old Pretender's son, Prince Charles Edward Stuart, was a brave young man with a great deal of charm and magnetism. He pawned his mother's rubies and set sail for Scotland, landing in Eriskay on 2 August 1745, with the intention of winning the crown for his father.

At first his reception was daunting: Macdonald of Boisdale told him to go home. "I am come home," he retorted. MacLeod, and Macdonald of Sleat refused to help, but Macdonald of Clanranald stood by him. Cameron of Lochiel was reluctant to encourage what he believed to be romantic folly, but he was won over and on 19 August the standard was raised in Glenfinnan and the Old Pretender proclaimed King James VIII/III, with Prince Charles as his regent.

Subsequent events are well known. Clansmen flocked to the prince as he marched on Edinburgh, capturing Perth on the way. He held glorious court, at Holyrood, defeated General Cope's soldiers at Prestonpans, and gathered more and more support. He led his motley army south, hoping to attract more Jacobites on the way, with the intention of taking London. Meeting little resistance, they got as far as Derby, only 120 odd miles

(192 km) from their target, but at this point the prince's prudent advisers insisted that to go any further was madness. Furious, the prince had to give in and on 6 December 1745, the weary Highlanders turned round to march back to Scotland. Pursued by Hanoverian troops, they struggled north until, in April 1746, they were slaughtered in battle, on Culloden Moor near Inverness. They were starving, exhausted, untrained and ill equipped. The prince escaped, with a price of £30,000 on his head, and spent the next five months in hiding in the western Highlands and islands. Aided by brave Flora Macdonald, he escaped eventually to Europe, where he lived in pathetic and rather squalid exile for the rest of his life, dying in Rome in 1788.

The Suppression of the Highlands

The English and the Lowland Scots were determined to squash the rebellious Highlanders forever. They enforced the Act of Proscription in 1747, banning Highland dress, the bearing of arms and even the playing of the pipes. Jacobites who had not died at Culloden were either executed or transported. The old way of life was dead. The act was repealed in 1782, but by this time it was no longer relevant. Many of the clan chiefs, seduced by the lure of London, had leased their northern lands to English sheep farmers.

The Highland Clearances

Between 1780 and 1860, thousands of crofters were evicted from their homes to make way for the sheep, in what became known as the Highland Clearances. By the end of the 19th century, the rural Highlands were almost deserted. Many of those who were turned from their homes emigrated to Canada, America, New Zealand and Australia.

Scotland at Peace

In the Lowlands, it was a different story. No longer inhibited by the constant threat of war, Edinburgh flourished; an elegant cultural centre where art, music and literature blossomed. Sir Walter Scott, 1771–1832, was a leading influence. George IV, who ruled until 1830, paid a state visit to Edinburgh, flamboyantly dressed in Royal Stewart tartan. Holyrood was opened up and Scotland paid willing homage to their king. Queen Victoria fell in love with Scotland and bought the estate of Balmoral in 1852, bringing more and more enthusiastic followers to adopt a Scotland-mania.

Scottish physicians, engineers and inventors led the world. A flourishing cotton industry collapsed in the 1860s when the American Civil War cut off supplies of raw cotton: heavy industry developed instead. Glasgow, once the biggest tobacco importer in Britain, led the world in shipbuilding. Expanding industries meant expanding labour forces: there were concentrations of population in industrial areas. Starving Highlanders, dispossessed of their crofts, flocked to the towns, joined by immigrant Irish escaping the potato famine.

Modern Scotland

Two world wars in the 20th century proved that Scotsmen are still the bravest of all men. Today, although an integral part of Great Britain in spite of periodic cries for devolution, Scotland retains that fierce pride and independence that has endured throughout so many centuries of its bloodstained history.

Part III
EDINBURGH

Castle

All things to all men, Edinburgh is one of the most beautiful and fascinating cities in the world. Its history is violent and romantic; its culture enormously versatile, as exemplified by its International Festival. It is the capital city and yet no more typical of Scotland than London is of England or Washington DC of America. Outsiders are often jealous; you may hear them say that Edinburgh is "stuffy, stuck-up, pompous". It may be all of those things; it is also a lively city, bursting with enterprise at all levels and all ages.

The large university attracts as many English students as Scottish. The Festival brings visitors from all over the world. Murrayfield is a powerful magnet for rugger enthusiasts: the Murrayfield Roar can be heard from miles away and on big match days, the streets reflect the fortunes of the opposing teams. Twice-host to the Commonwealth Games, Edinburgh's sporting facilities are second to none.

The stones of the city are honed by a pervasive east wind: they say you always spot a native of Edinburgh—when he rounds a corner anywhere in the world, his hand will fly instinctively to clutch at his hat. Listen to the shrewd cynicism of the Edinburgh taxi-driver; talk to the little walnut-faced lollipop man who has shepherded children across the road in all weathers with the same rough humour for years; sit down on the bench in Princes Street Gardens beside the neat, ordinary-looking old woman who is about to go into hospital and is worried about who will look after her cat. These are the real people of Edinburgh, just as much as the professionals for whom the city is renowned: the doctors, the lawyers, the businessmen and accountants.

The unwritten history of Edinburgh goes back to the Picts, who existed in a cluster of wooden huts on the rocky slopes of the castle crag, choosing the windy heights for greater security. The Romans built a fort at Cramond, west of the town, and a naval harbour from which the Emperor Severus embarked on his northern campaigns. When the Angles of Northumbria invaded Lothian in the Dark Ages, their King Edwin built up a ruined fortress on the rock, *Dun Eadain*, meaning literally Fortress-on-a-hill. This became Edwin's Burgh.

Small communities settled around the castle walls, tradesmen supplying the needs of those in the garrison, but it was not until the 11th century, in the reign of Malcolm Canmore, that Edinburgh began to develop as a town. Queen Margaret persuaded her husband to move from Dunfermline into Edinburgh Castle and from then on, buildings flew up.

Robert Bruce granted the town a Royal Charter in 1329. James II transferred the status of 'capital' to Edinburgh from Perth, when he held his parliament there in 1450. During the 16th century the city suffered a dreadful battering from Henry VIII's 'Rough Wooing' after his marriage proposal for the infant Queen Mary and his sickly son Edward had been turned down. Mary spent most of her short, tragic reign based in Edinburgh, riding out from its walls on frequent excursions. When her son James VI inherited the English throne, he moved down to London, only returning once to his native land. For a while, then, Edinburgh retreated into the shadows, with brief leaps into the sunlight, as when Prince Charlie marched into the town in 1745 and took over Holyrood Palace and the hearts of the townspeople, for five crazy, unreal weeks of feasting and triumph, before his march south and his sad, ignominious retreat to the bloodbath of Culloden.

From the death-throes of the Jacobite rebellion, peace finally emerged and with it, in the 18th and 19th centuries, a sudden glorious explosion of culture and the arts. Literature, painting, music, architecture: all began to flourish in this richly productive new age, giving birth to such men as Walter Scott, Allan Ramsay, Henry Raeburn, William MacTaggart, Robert Louis Stevenson and many others. It was Walter Scott who was largely responsible for the success of the triumphal visit of the Hanoverian King George IV, in 1822, resplendent in gaudy tartan. This was the first royal visit for more than 100 years, discounting that of Prince Charlie. When Queen Victoria's passion for her "dear, beloved Scotland" made the country socially acceptable to other southerners, Edinburgh began to attract more and more eager Scotia-philes, and tartan, porridge and bagpipes became all the rage.

Modern Edinburgh has everything you could want: excellent shops, haute cuisine, first-class entertainment at all levels and so many things to see that it would be impossible to run out of new things to explore. On the whole, the places of interest are in a very compact area and far the best way to enjoy them to the full is to put on a pair of comfortable shoes and abandon your car: parking is not Edinburgh's strongest point, especially during the tourist season.

As you wander through the streets of Edinburgh you will find plenty of places where you can relax for a while over a cup of coffee and a sticky cake, or a glass of wine and a slice of pizza, or whatever else you need to revive your flagging spirits. There are masses of cafes and wine bars, tucked away down steps, or in the wynds (alley ways), or on the main streets. When the sun shines you can even sit at tables in the street, though the licensing laws are such that it is not always possible to drink alcohol at pavement tables.

If your stay in Edinburgh is limited, don't try and see it all: you won't manage to and you won't enjoy what you do see. If you only have one day, for instance, your best bet is to confine your sightseeing to The Royal Mile. If you start at the Castle, which will take you a good two hours, and then wander down towards Holyrood, taking in lunch at one of the many places on the way, and looking in at all the interesting features you pass, and finish up at Holyrood, another two hours, you and your feet will be more than ready to go back to your hotel to freshen up before hitting the night-spots.

If you have two days, you should explore the New Town on the second day, including a couple of the art galleries or museums, with perhaps an hour or so browsing among the shops in the Princes Street area. If you have three days you should certainly devote most of a morning or afternoon to the National Gallery, or to the Modern Art Gallery if you prefer modern paintings: half a day at the National Gallery is excellently counterbalanced by spending the other half in the Botanic Gardens.

WHAT TO SEE
A very good way to start your visit to this lovely city is to go to the award-winning Visitor Centre, **The Scottish Experience**, at the west end of Princes Street, beyond the Caledonian Hotel. This is open daily except Sundays, adults £1.60, children 80p. There are two major shows: an audio-visual history of Edinburgh and an intriguing three-dimensional map of Scotland, with six audio-visual tours introduced by Magnus Magnusson. You get an excellent introduction to the city and you come dashing out, determined not to miss anything.

The Old Town

Edinburgh Castle

(Open daily throughout the year, with good guided tours: adults £2.00, children £1.00)

The castle is a "must": its history is the history of the city and its position makes it the focus of attention. Allow plenty of time—at least two hours, more if possible—and try to go on a reasonably clear day so that you get full advantage of the lovely views. The castle guides, in dark green uniform, many of them ex-servicemen, are a limitless fund of knowledge and they will take you way back into the history of every corner and stone, as you toil upwards on the rough, cobbled pathways. If you prefer to be independent (and you will miss a lot of good anecdotes, if you dispense with a guide) then this itinerary gives you the castle's main attractions

Along the Esplanade
The Esplanade, below the castle gate, slopes surprisingly steeply upwards: it is here, during the Edinburgh Festival, that the Edinburgh Military Tattoo is staged, drawing vast crowds night after night, year after year, always combining displays of British military skills with those of other countries, and always ending with that most moving of all Scotland's hat-tricks, the floodlit Lone Piper on the Battlements, his haunting music reaching out across the darkened arena to echo in your heart for evermore. Most

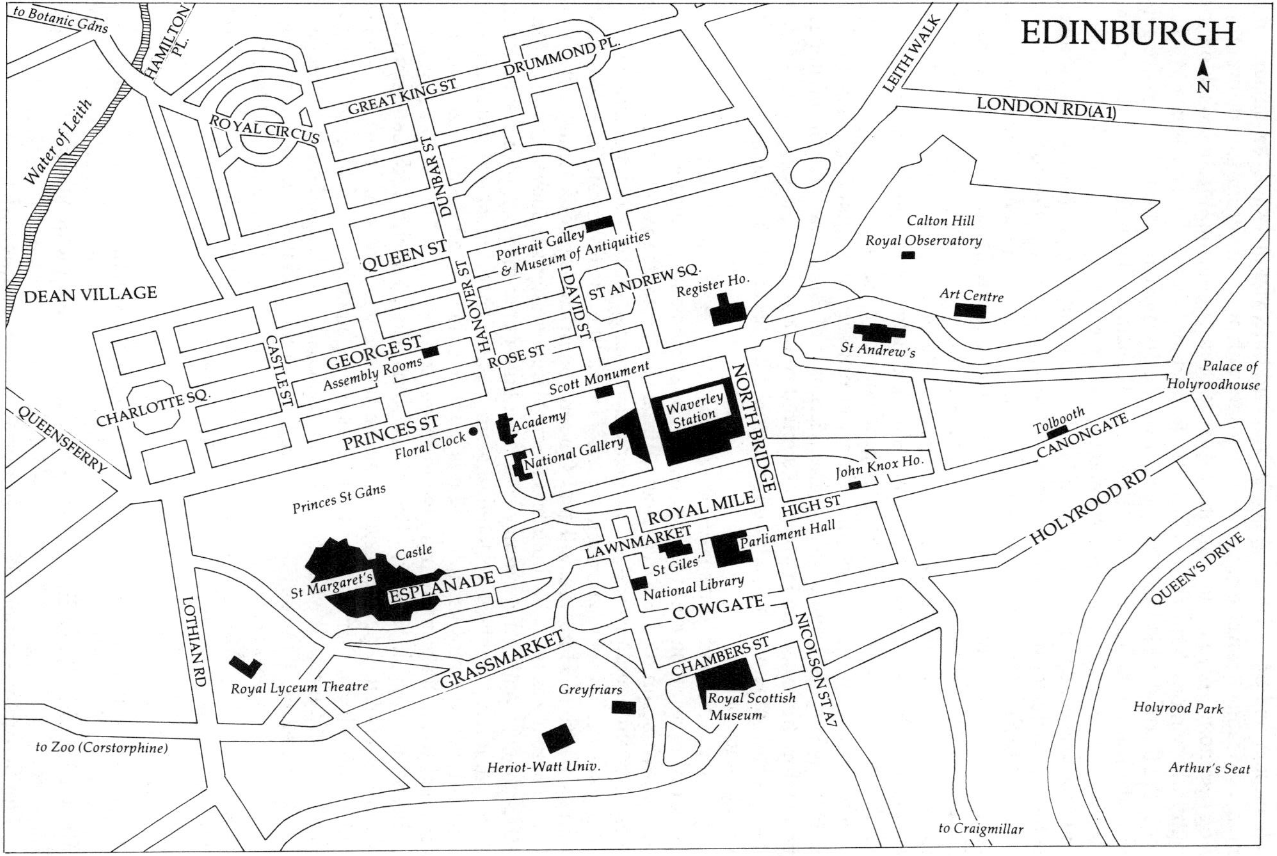
EDINBURGH
N
LONDON RD(A1)
LEITH WALK
Calton Hill
Royal Observatory
Art Centre
St Andrew's
Palace of
Holyroodhouse
Tolbooth
CANONGATE
HOLYROOD RD
QUEEN'S DRIVE
Holyrood Park
Arthur's Seat
to Craigmillar
John Knox Ho.
HIGH ST
NICOLSON ST A7
Parliament Hall
NORTH BRIDGE
Waverley
Station
Register Ho.
ST ANDREW SQ.
Portrait Galley
& Museum of Antiquities
ROYAL MILE
LAWNMARKET
St Giles'
National Library
COWGATE
CHAMBERS ST
Royal Scottish
Museum
Greyfriars
Heriot-Watt Univ.
GRASSMARKET
ESPLANADE
Castle
St Margaret's
Princes St Gdns
Royal Lyceum Theatre
LOTHIAN RD
to Zoo (Corstorphine)
QUEENSFERRY
CHARLOTTE SQ.
CASTLE ST
GEORGE ST
Assembly Rooms
PRINCES ST
Floral Clock
Academy
National Gallery
Scott Monument
ROSE ST
ST DAVID ST
HANOVER ST
DUNBAR ST
QUEEN ST
GREAT KING ST
DRUMMOND PL.
ROYAL CIRCUS
HAMILTON PL.
to Botanic Gdns
Water of Leith
DEAN VILLAGE

Wednesday and Saturday evenings, in May and June, you can watch the ancient ceremony of Beating the Retreat, on the Esplanade, with pipes and drums and plenty of stirring ceremony. As you come into the Esplanade you can see the **Witches Well**, on your right, where more than 300 witches were burned, between 1479, and as late as 1722.

At the top of the Esplanade you go across the dry moat and through a massive gateway, flanked by statues of Robert Bruce and William Wallace. Ahead of you the path slopes up to the right, towards the **Portcullis Gate** which dates from 1574. Just before this you can see, up on the left, a memorial stone to Sir William Kirkaldy of Grange, a colourful character of the 16th century who helped to murder the notorious Cardinal Beaton (see St Andrews) and was a leader of the Lords of the Congregation in the Reformation. He was an accessory to the murder of Mary, Queen of Scots' secretary, Rizzio, and he later received her surrender at Carberry Hill and was mainly responsible for her final defeat at the Battle of Langside. After her imprisonment in England, he changed his loyalties, went over to her side and held Edinburgh Castle in her cause until he was forced to surrender, after which he was hanged.

Above the impressive Portcullis Gate you can see the **Constable's Tower**, later known as **Argyll's Tower** because the Marquess of Argyll was held in the dungeon here before his execution in 1661. The mixed construction of the steep path, being of cobbles and smooth stones, allowed grip for the horses and free-running tracks for the vehicles they pulled.

Keeping to the path as it snakes upwards past the Argyll Battery, you will come to the tourist administration area with a postcard and souvenir shop. Beyond this is the **Regimental Museum of the Royal Scots**, Britain's oldest infantry regiment, full of regimental trophies, uniforms, flags, weapons, documents, pictures and memorabilia.

Beyond the museum, through Foog's Gate is the highest platform in the castle, **King's Bastion**. Here you will find **Queen (or St) Margaret's Chapel**. This tiny Norman gem was probably built by Queen Margaret after she moved to the castle, in 1076, though some believe it may have been built in her memory, by her son David I. Although it has often been restored, this simple little chapel must look much the same now as it did when it was built, and it is possible to hold weddings and baptisms here, provided you don't want to invite too many guests.

Beside the chapel, on King's Bastion, is **Mons Meg**, a mighty 15th-century cannon about whose history people disagree. Some say she was forged in Mons, in Belgium, others will tell you that she was hastily cobbled together by a local blacksmith and his family, to help James II when he took Threave Castle in 1455 and finally subdued the Black Douglases. This story has some credence as the land that was given to the blacksmith as a reward was called Mollance, or Mons, and his wife's name was Meg! Whatever the true story, Mons Meg was taken to the tower of London in 1754, but returned to its present home at the insistence of Sir Walter Scott

Crown Square

Signposted to the right, off the path up to King's Bastion, is Crown Square, round which stand the Scottish National War Memorial, the Crown Room, Queen Mary's Apartments, the Old Parliament or Banqueting Hall and the Scottish United Services Museum.

The Scottish National War Memorial, on the right, is perhaps one of the most dignified and poignant in the world. It combines a record of the gallantry of the many Scots who died for their country, with a tranquil chapel built up out of the rock, that seems to embody the sense of freedom that they bought with their lives.

Further round Crown Square, on the east side, you come to the **Crown Room** in the **Old Palace** that dates from the 15th century. The regalia that you see here has its origins in medieval times, and is thus older than the English crown jewels in London, which are almost all post-Restoration (Cromwell having destroyed the earlier ones). The crown, made of Scottish gold, decorated with 94 pearls, 10 diamonds and many other precious stones, is said to have been used by Robert Bruce in 1306; set on his head by a brave woman, Isobel of Fife, Countess of Buchan, acting for her brother whose hereditary right it was to crown the king, but who was too frightened to do so. (This lion-hearted woman was captured by the English and hung up in a cage from a wall in Berwick, as a punishment.) The crown was last used when Charles II was crowned at Scone in 1651. Looking at it, behind its glass case, you cannot fail to be stirred by the thought of the part it played in Scotland's history. The glittering sword of state, was given to James IV by Pope Julius II. During the troubled times of the Civil War, the Scottish regalia was hidden for safety (see Dunnottar Castle, Grampian) and then, after the Act of Union in 1707, packed away in a chest and forgotten for about 100 years. Then along came that tireless patriot, Walter Scott, who organised a search, and the regalia was discovered, in the same room in which you can now see it displayed.

Still in the Old Palace, signs direct you through to **Queen Mary's Apartments**. Here you will see the tiny cupboard of a room in which Mary gave birth to James VI, in 1566. An intriguing mystery hangs over that accouchement and it doesn't take a lot of imagination to picture what may have happened in this airless little room, so long ago, where the young queen endured the pains of labour, surrounded by her anxious, loyal women. A tiny oak coffin was discovered behind panelling in a recess in the room, in 1830, during restoration work. The coffin contained the remains of an infant, wrapped in silk, with a 'J' worked into the shroud. No one will ever know the story behind this pathetic little relic: it was re-interred, carrying its secret with it and leaving our minds seething with speculation. But it is worth remembering that it was thought to be crucial, for Scotland's security, that the queen gave birth to a live son. Mary had suffered some nasty shocks during her pregnancy, including the murder of her secretary, Rizzio, before her eyes. It has been remarked that portraits of James VI show a definite similarity to portraits of John, second Earl of Mar, whose mother looked after the infant king after his birth.

Further round, along the south side of Crown Square you come to the **Banqueting Hall**, once the Old Parliament Hall, dating from the 15th century and extensively rebuilt by James IV. It is a vast chamber with a high open-timber roof and contains displays of weapons on the walls. It is sometimes used for social gatherings on ceremonial occasions such as the queen's birthday. Go up to the gallery at the end and look down on the chattering crowd of sightseers and think back to 1440 and the day of the 'Black Dinner'. The Black Douglases were getting altogether too powerful for the liking of those who ruled Scotland for the eight year old King, James II. They summoned fourteen year old William, Earl of Douglas, and his younger brother, to attend a banquet in the presence of the boy-king. A black bull's head was brought in, signifying a death sentence, and the two young Douglases were murdered, in front of King James.

In one of the dungeons that you can see below the Banqueting Hall, the ninth Earl of Argyll was held before his execution in 1685. He was a staunch Protestant who supported Monmouth's rebellion against James VII/II; but he was defeated and executed. French prisoners were also imprisoned here during the Napoleonic wars.

On the west and east side of Crown Square, you can see **The Scottish United Services Museum**, which covers the history, dress, weapons and equipment of all three services.

The views from the castle are wonderful. Stop on your way out and look over the northern and southern walls of the Esplanade: to the north you look over Princes Street, the New Town, the suburbs, the Firth of Forth and away to the grey-blue hills of Fife. To the south you see the Pentlands, with the Moorfoots and Lammermuirs to the east and the distant shape of Ben Lomond and the mountains of Argyll to the west

The Royal Mile

A walk down the Royal Mile from the castle to Holyrood could take you days if you stop to explore every historic or interesting feature on the way. There is not space to mention more than just a few features here and you are well advised to get hold of Bartholomew's excellent "Visitor's map of central Edinburgh and the Royal Mile", from any bookshop and many of the tourist souvenir shops. This gives you a numbered map of the Royal Mile with each feature described. As you go down, you pass plenty of coffee shops, restaurants and wine bars, to refresh you along the way.

The Royal Mile offers little cameo glimpses into the past. From the 11th century onwards this area became a warren of close-packed houses, struggling upwards, shouldering each other for light and air, a maze of wynds and yards and twisting stairways: a steaming, stinking, screaming cauldron of humanity. During the 18th and 19th centuries, the richer inhabitants of the Old Town emerged from their overcrowded houses, crossed the stretch of putrid water that was called the Nor' Loch, below the northern face of the castle rock, and began to build the New Town, with its gracious spread of Georgian houses and squares. In 1816, town planners decided to drain the stinking Nor' Loch. In the meanwhile, the buildings in the Old Town became tenements for the poor, who moved in, many families to a building, and huddled together in overcrowded squalor. Today, many of these houses are being restored and re-inhabited by the descendants of the original occupiers: a social reversal that repeats itself in cities all over the world

Castle Hill

As you leave the Esplanade and enter Castle Hill, you pass Castle Wynd Steps on the right, leading down to the Grassmarket. At the top is **Cannonball House**, so called from the ball embedded in its western gable, which is said to have been fired from the castle in 1745, towards Holyrood during its occupation by Prince Charlie.

Opposite, on the left, is the **Outlook Tower** (open daily from 9.30 am to 6 pm: adults £1.25, children 60p). You can climb this and can look at the city through the **Camera Obscura**, a cunning contraption of mirrors that gives you an intriguing, reflected bird's-eye view. There are also view-finders and telescopes, round the roof, and special exhibitions.

Next to the Outlook Tower, past **Semple's Close**, is the Assembly Hall of the General Assembly of the Church of Scotland (not always open to the public). It is on the site of a palace where Mary of Guise, mother of Mary, Queen of Scots, lived in the 16th century. Plays are staged in this magnificent hall during the Edinburgh Festival

Lawnmarket

A little further down on the left you come to **Gladstone's Land**, 1617, with its original arcaded front, the only true example left in the Royal Mile. Below this is **Lady Stair's House** (open every day except Sundays: admission free). It dates from the early 17th century and is now a museum, with a lot of relics of those three literary giants: Burns, Scott and Stevenson. Lady Stair was a leading hostess of Edinburgh society in the 18th century.

Across from Lady Stair's House is **Brodie's Close**. Dean Brodie was the model for Robert Louis Stevenson's character Jekyll and Hyde. Brodie was a respectable citizen by day and a notorious thief by night who was hanged in 1788. On the corner of Lawnmarket and George IV Bridge you can see three brass studs in the road: these mark the site of the last public execution, in 1864, and a little further down, in front of **Parliament Square**, the heart-shaped stones in the road mark the site of the old city jail, law courts and tolbooth, demolished in 1817. It is a city tradition to spit on the spot. It was here, in 1650, that the head of gallant Montrose, was displayed on a pike

Parliament Square

St Giles Cathedral lies within Parliament Square, which covers the old churchyard. John Knox is buried somewhere here, near his statue behind the cathedral. Everyone must form their own impression of St Giles: for some, its unadorned Presbyterian gloom seems to have banished all traces of the God whose house it claims to be. It seems strange that a church that was once the centre of anti-episcopal rioting, where the clergy were physically assaulted for trying to retain episcopalian ritual, should still be called a cathedral—a word that means the seat of the bishop! A church is thought to have stood here as early as the 9th century, but the present Gothic building dates from the 15th century. It has been much restored, not always to advantage, and it contains many interesting relics and monuments. Near the entrance to the side chapel, south of the nave, you can see a tablet marking the traditional spot from which Jenny Geddes flung her stool at the clergyman, striking the first blow for the Covenanters in the 17th century.

The flags of the Scottish regiments, known as The Regimental Colours, hang above the nave—glorious banners embroidered with the battle honours of the regiments. These Colours are treated with enormous respect and honour; when brought out on parade people stand up when they pass, and men salute them.

You must pay a fee to see the **Chapel of the Thistle**, in the east corner of the cathedral, designed by Robert Lorimer in 1911. It is tiny and ornate, in honour of The Most Ancient and Most Noble Order of the Thistle—deliciously out of place among these dark, forbidding walls.

Parliament House (open all year, Tuesday to Friday, 10 am to 4 pm: admission free) stands just behind St Giles. Now the home of the Scottish Law Courts, it was the home of the Scottish Parliament until after the Union in 1707. The Great Hall has a splendid hammerbeam roof and lovely stained glass. A Greek façade, added in 1808, hides the original front, but you can see how it once looked from George IV Bridge, round the corner

High Street

The 17th-century **Tron Church**, a little way down past St Giles, was so called because of the tron, or weighing beam that stood nearby. This tron served to check the weights used by the merchants: those found using under-weight measures were nailed to the tron by their ears! Locals who, in their student days, celebrated Hogmanay, or the birth of the New Year, will have hazy recollections of storming up the Mound, just before midnight, then staggering down the High Street, as this part of the Royal Mile is called, to gather and touch the tron, in salute to the New Year.

John Knox's House (open daily except on Sundays: adults £1, children 60p) is on the left-hand corner where the High Street narrows before Netherbow Port. It dates from 1490 and is a delightful old house with an outside stair, recently restored to reveal its original walls, fireplaces and painted ceilings. John Knox is believed to have lived here from 1561 to 1572 and it is thought that he died in one of the upstairs rooms. Inside you can see many relics of his life, with pictures of Edinburgh as it was in the past. Whether he lived here or not, he has managed to stamp his dynamic personality into the soul of the building. It is easy to dismiss him as a dark, melancholy fanatic, brandishing fire and brimstone and everlasting damnation, but there was much more to him than that. He had a sharp wit and a shrewd worldliness, and presumably had "charisma" for, at the age of 51, he took as his second wife, a girl of 16 who gave him three daughters.

The Museum of Childhood lies opposite John Knox's House (open daily except Sundays: adults 40p, children 20p). It holds a fascinating collection of objects related to childhood in the past; not just toys and games, but books children used to read and medicines they were given. It is of as much, if not more, interest for adults as for children

Canongate

The High Street now becomes Canongate—the road up which the canons, or clerics, walked, from Holyrood Abbey into the walled town. Canongate was once the smart residential quarter of the aristocracy. **The Canongate Tolbooth**, 1591 (open daily except Sundays: admission free), is another museum, showing Highland dress and tartans. On the ground floor there is a brass rubbing centre.

Beside the Tolbooth is **Canongate Church**, 1688, built for the congregation that James VII ousted from Holyrood Abbey. Opposite is **Huntly House** (open daily except on Sundays: admission free). Dating from the 16th century, it is now a museum showing Edinburgh life through the centuries.

Next door, on the same side of the road, is **Acheson House**, 1633, now the Scottish Craft Centre (open every day from 10 am to 5 pm except Sundays: admission free).

Queensberry House, a 17th-century building, is further down, also on the right. It is a private hospital. As you pass it, spare a thought for the poor little kitchen boy who used to turn the spit there. While the second Duke of Queensberry was busy accepting a bribe to help push through the Act of Union in 1707, his oldest son and heir, a homicidal lunatic, was equally busy roasting the kitchen boy on his spit. He was caught, but not before he had begun to eat his victim.

Holyrood

Holyrood Abbey

Holyrood Abbey, at the foot of the Royal Mile, has a history that has marched in tandem with that of the Castle, since it was founded in 1128 by David I, on the spot where tradition has it that he was saved by a miracle from being gored to death by a wild stag. The name Holy Rood (or Cross) is derived from the following story. It is believed that a fragment of the True Cross was brought to Scotland by saintly Queen Margaret in the 11th century and incorporated into the new abbey as a shrine by her son David. If this was so, the holy relic did not survive: perhaps it was carried off by Edward I, at the beginning of the 14th century, when he took away the Stone of Destiny from Scone. Only a shell now, with a glorious, soaring Norman arch, the abbey makes a beautiful silhouette against the evening sky, its ghosts reaching out from the ancient stones. It was a favourite royal residence: James II was born and crowned here in the 15th century; he and his two successors were married in the church, as was Mary (to Darnley in 1565). Several monarchs were buried at Holyrood and Charles I was crowned here.

Holyrood Palace

Holyrood Palace, or the Palace of Holyroodhouse, now the Queen's official residence in Edinburgh, is open to the public when she isn't there (open daily except Sundays in the winter: adults £1.40, children 70p). It was built during the reign of James IV, around 1500. With the abbey, it took a severe bashing during the "Rough Wooing" (see History) in 1544. It is the ghost of Queen Mary that bewitches you in every corner as you pass from room to room, for it was here that so many of the well-known events took place that were to pass down through history and become engraved forever on the minds of every history student.

Here she came, the bright-eyed, high-spirited, sensual young widow of 19, fresh from the French court, accustomed to French ways. Here she received Knox, and was berated by him for attending mass in her chapel. Here, in 1565, she married dissolute, Catholic Darnley, four years her junior, a vicious youth who suspected her of infidelity with her Italian secretary, Rizzio, and who helped to murder Rizzio, in front of Mary when she was six months pregnant. As you stand in the tiny supper room, it is easy to imagine Mary, starting up from the table, cumbersome with her unborn child, staring down at Rizzio who clawed at her skirt, abject and cowering, begging her to save him: listening to his screams as they dragged him away and then to the awful silence. And finally, it was here that Mary married Bothwell, a squalid, hole-in-the-corner business that brought a swift end to her tragic reign.

Of happier memory, although only lasting for a short time, were those five weeks, in 1745, when Prince Charles Edward Stuart held court at Holyrood: riding out in the morning to review his troops, spreading his magnetic charm at the magnificent Court levees in the evening, the darling of Edinburgh society, the dazzling focus of all female eyes.

In the 150 ft (45.7 m) long picture gallery, you must not miss one of Scotland's best practical jokes. The gallery holds 111 portraits of Scottish monarchs, commissioned by the government in 1684 and completed in two years by a Dutchman called James de Witt. Many of the portraits are of fictitious characters and many of them, as Walter Scott commented when he saw them, "lived several centuries before the invention of oil paints". De Witt was paid £120 per annum for this daunting commission of monarchs "in large, royall postures" and had to provide his own materials. One can only guess at the emotion of the official who received and hung these travesties of art.

The quaint, turreted lodge on the edge of the palace grounds, to your left as you approach from Canongate, is called **Queen Mary's Bathroom**. Some say that the queen bathed here in white wine. If this were true then she was liable to catch pneumonia, walking back to her apartments through the cold Edinburgh wind

Holyrood Park and Surrounds

If outdoor Edinburgh takes your fancy, you should explore **Holyrood Park**, that great open space that stretches away south and east of the palace (though you may not have the energy to do so at the end of your tour of the Royal Mile). The steep hill that rises abruptly to the south of the palace car park is **Arthur's Seat** and you certainly need your energy to climb to the top, though it is less of a slog than it looks and the easiest way up is from **Dunsappie Loch** to the east. The name has no connection, alas, with the legendary King Arthur: it might relate to Prince Arthur of Strathclyde, but it is more likely to be a corruption of *Ard Thor*—the Gaelic for "height of Thor". Glorious views from the top will make the effort of climbing there well worth while. (Should you happen to be in the area of Arthur's Seat on the eve of May Day, you will notice crowds of people heading up the slopes through the darkness, like colonies of ants. On May Day, it is traditional to greet the dawn from the top although, to judge from the empty bottles and beer cans that litter the place the next day, it is likely that quite a few people don't manage to keep their eyes open throughout the pre-dawn revelry!)

Salisbury Crags are also part of the park—the rocky peaks to the west of Arthur's Seat. There are three lochs in the park, **Duddingston Loch** in the south-east being a bird sanctuary preserving a surprising variety of bird life so close to the city. The village of Duddingston, to the east of the Loch, was the encampment for Prince Charlie's army for six weeks in 1745, during which time he reigned supreme in Holyrood Palace.

Meadowbank (open daily) north-east of Holyrood Park, is a huge leisure centre, internationally known as the venue for the Commonwealth Games. It has every sort of facility and you can hire whatever equipment you need.

Restalrig Church, just east of Meadowbank, was destroyed in 1560 when John Knox and his fanatic followers were busy with their reforms. They branded it "a monument of idolatry" and pulled it apart. Later it was restored. The small hexagonal chapel beside it, with a lovely groined roof resting on a central pillar, was the chapel of a college founded by James III in 1478. When it was restored in the 20th century, the new floor was split open by a spring of water below it, believed to be a spring once used to cure eye diseases. The original chapel that stood over the spring was called St Triduana: there was in fact no saint of that name and the name comes instead from a three-day fast practised by the old Celtic church

The Grassmarket

If you have any energy left when you have "done" the Royal Mile, and perhaps revived yourself with a glass of cold lager in one of the taverns on the way back up the hill, you should dip down into the Grassmarket. You can either go down the Castle Wynd Steps, by Cannonball House at the top of Castle Hill, or down Victoria Street that leads off George IV Bridge just before the Central Library. Both ways are picturesque: **Victoria Street** has some nice shops in it including an excellent print shop where you can get prints of many Scottish scenes and buildings; a good memento to take home from a holiday and very reasonably priced. There are also some tempting antique and bric à brac shops. The Grassmarket opens out at the bottom, a long, wide oblong, now a peaceful backwater, once the scene of several ignoble events. Among parked cars and trees, you will see an innocent-looking cross in a railed enclosure at the foot of Victoria Street. This marks the site of the gallows where more than a hundred Covenanters were hanged in the 17th century for refusing to give up their right to worship God in their own way.

Another of the Grassmarket's victims was a certain Captain Porteous, who died in circumstances that could easily be dressed in 20th-century clothes. In 1736, a crowd was getting restless after an unpopular execution, just up the hill in the Lawnmarket: Porteous ordered the Guard to fire: some people were killed and Porteous was tried for murder but was acquitted. The angry mob dragged him from the Tolbooth Jail and administered their own rough justice, hanging him from a dyer's pole in the Grassmarket.

The attractive 17th-century **White Hart Inn** is also in the Grassmarket. Both Burns and Wordsworth stayed there, and, looking at the building, you get the impression that its appearance hasn't changed at all.

A part of the **Flodden Wall** can still be seen if you climb the steps in the **Vennel** (vennel meaning alley) from the south-west corner of the Grassmarket up to Heriot Place. This wall was hastily built to protect the city after the awful defeat at Flodden in 1513, when the victorious English army seemed too close for comfort. A quick strengthener in The White Hart might encourage you to finish off your tour of the Old Town, all within a few minutes walk of the Grassmarket

The Rest of the Old Town

The National Library of Scotland, on George IV Bridge, opposite the Central Library, was founded in 1682 and is one of the four largest libraries in Britain. As well as enjoying the right to claim a copy of every book published in the British Isles, the library owns a wonderful collection of illuminated manuscripts and documents relating to Scottish history, including the original copy of the last letter Mary, Queen of Scots wrote to her cousin Elizabeth on the eve of her execution. You can also see the written order that set in motion the Massacre of Glencoe in 1692.

Greyfriars Bobby is further on down George IV Bridge, opposite the entrance to Chambers Street. This is the statue of an endearing Edinburgh character—a Skye terrier that watched over his master's grave for 14 years, from 1858, being fed by local people and being granted Edinburgh citizenship in order to save him from being destroyed as a stray dog.

Set back beyond Greyfriars Bobby, across Candlemaker Row, you can see **Greyfriars Kirk**, another of the Old Town antiquities. It was here that the adoption and signing of the National Covenant took place in 1638—that "great marriage day of this nation with God", as Lord Warriston called it, and leading to even greater bitterness, hatred and bloodshed than before. Ironically, 1,400 Covenanters were imprisoned in the Kirkyard, in 1679.

Greyfriars Bobby

The National Museum of Scotland (open daily: admission free) is less than five minutes walk round the corner into Chambers Street, a splendid Victorian building with a great soaring glass interior and a range of exhibits that are so diverse you could wander happily for days and not feel bored. Its collections include art, archaeology, ethnology, natural history, technology and social history, covering the whole world.

The University Old College is in South Bridge, beyond the museum. It is of both aesthetic and morbid interest. It is Robert Adam's largest work in the city and, built in 1789, it contains good examples of Adam's distinctive interiors. The upper library was designed in 1830 by William Playfair. The building stands partly on ground that belonged to Kirk o' Field, where Darnley met his nasty end (see History).

The **Talbot Rice Art Centre** is also here (open daily except Sundays, 10 am to 5 pm: admission free). The centre contains an old master gallery and an exhibition gallery where the collections change about every five weeks. The Torrie Collection, with important paintings and bronzes came to the Talbot Rice from Sir James Erskine of Torrie; some pieces of this collection date from the 16th century. The exhibitions are mainly of contemporary art.

The New Town

When, in the 18th and 19th centuries, the wealthy inhabitants of the Old Town moved off the castle ridge and built themselves gracious houses to the north, they created what is now called the New Town, an elegant spread of crescents and squares, gardens and lovely town houses, the whole area a delight to walk through on a fine day.

Princes Street is unique: where else in the world can you find a main shopping street on one side of the road and lovely gardens backed by a cliff-top castle on the other? When the town planners decided to drain the stinking Nor' Loch, in the 19th century, they cleverly agreed to leave the south side of Princes Street open, with no buildings—the effect is breath-taking. As you come down any of the side streets into Princes Street from the north, up on the ridge you see the silhouette of the roofs and spires of the Royal Mile, a marvellous frieze of architecture leading dramatically up to the Castle. If you should manage to catch this view at dawn you will remember it for the rest of your life.

The shops on the north side of the street cater for all tastes and purses, from up-market stores to trendy boutiques, and the wide pavement is usually jammed with shoppers.

When you are exhausted, or have no money left, you merely cross the road and go into **Princes Street Gardens**, in the basin that was the Nor' Loch. Here you can sit on one of the seats and recover your strength—in the summer, anyway. Terraced lawns and flowerbeds, shaded by old trees, make a perfect haven from the exhausting jostle of the shops. You can feed the very tame grey squirrels that live here, or the pigeons that strut fearlessly at your feet. On the first day of spring, which can come any time from April till June in Edinburgh, you can witness a miraculous "rebirth" at lunchtime in the gardens. The city's workers erupt into the sunshine with their lunch packets, throw off their winter coats and lie around on the grass like holidaymakers on a Mediterranean beach. In the gardens, there is an open-air cafe in the piazza, where you can have a snack, listening to music from the bandstand nearby, where lunchtime music is played in the summer. Also in the gardens is the amazing **Floral Clock**, a horticultural showpiece that is well worth seeing.

The Scott Monument, at the eastern end of the gardens, will be familiar from photographs. You can climb its 287 steps for 45p on weekdays, for a splendid view of the city. Somehow, this very Victorian monument, erected in 1840, seems entirely suitable and just the sort of thing that Sir Walter might have designed for himself. He and his dog look out from under a great canopy, set with niches containing many of Scott's characters. The stone is blackened with city grime: it is not beautiful but it is undeniably impressive.

Waverley Market is beyond the Scott Monument, above Waverley Station. Only recently opened, it is a most attractive and imaginatively designed indoor shopping precinct, on several levels, light and airy with a fountain and pool in the middle and bistro-style cafes around. Apart from the shops and waggon-stalls, this is a colourful, cheerful place for a rest and a snack and you will usually find live entertainment going on near the fountain in the summer.

Calton Hill rises beyond the east end of Princes Street; a well-known part of the Edinburgh skyline, with its semi-Parthenon at the top, built as a war memorial for the

Napoleonic wars and left unfinished when funds ran out. If you climb the hill, and you should, you can go up the 102 ft (31.1m) high **Nelson Monument**, erected 1815, for an even better view (open daily: admission 40p). The buildings of the old Royal Observatory are open, too, but you must apply to the custodian for entry. (The present observatory is on Blackford Hill, due south, where there is a visitor centre (open daily all the year: adults 65p, children 35p). Here you can learn about the work of astronomers all over the world.)

Moving north from Princes Street you come to **George Street**, running along the ridge, with wonderful vistas down the intersections towards the Firth of Forth and across to Fife.

St Andrew's Square lies at the east end of George Street, a mixture of old and new buildings, dignified but somehow lacking the character of other squares in the New Town. The coach station is in the north-east corner, with a taxi rank just outside.

Charlotte Square is at the west end of George Street and here you have all the elegant charm of the New Town distilled. Robert Adam designed it but died before it was finished: it is accepted as one of his masterpieces and renowned throughout Europe. Even when it is full of cars you can still feel some of that old graciousness that must have rubbed off onto the beautiful façades of the houses.

The Georgian House (open daily from April to December: adults £1.20, children 60p) lies within Charlotte Square. It has been restored and furnished as it would have been by its late 18th-century owners, and it gives you a wonderful picture of the domestic and social conditions that surrounded a wealthy family in those days.

If you have time to spare and the weather is fine, wander north from Charlotte Square and explore the other crescents and squares that lie beyond: **Moray Place, Ainslie Place, Randolph Crescent**, round attractive gardens, linked by well-proportioned streets.

Art Galleries

Edinburgh's art galleries are magnificent and you could spend many days exploring them and still have some in reserve. If you have time you should try to fit in at least one a day during your visit. If you have to choose only one, you should not miss The National Gallery.

The National Gallery of Scotland (open daily from 10 am to 5 pm and from 2 pm to 5 pm on Sundays, with extended hours during the Edinburgh Festival: admission free) stands at the foot of the Mound, back from Princes Street across an attractive piazza that is a favourite haunt of buskers. The gallery was built in the middle of the 19th century with a new wing added in 1978, and it is a treasure trove that lures you back whenever you have moments to spare.

The new wing, downstairs, has a permanent collection of Scottish paintings which are changed from year to year and sometimes removed to make way for special exhibitions. Here you can see works by that great painter of Scottish scenes, William McTaggart; portraits by Allan Ramsay, whose masterly portrayal of women is so lifelike that you feel you know them personally; marvellous works by David Wilkie, whose "social history" pictures seem to sum up the life of ordinary people in Scotland in the 18th and 19th centuries, including the heart-rending picture "Distraining for rent", bucolic "Pitlessie Fair", and "The letter of introduction" with one of Wilkie's famous dogs seeing off the young man. There are splendid portraits by Raeburn, including a self-portrait, and work by a great many more Scottish artists. Downstairs, too, there is a library, a print room and a prints and drawings gallery. Every January, you can see 38 watercolours by Turner on display, a lovely collection whose colours are so delicate that they are only allowed into the light for one month each year.

In the main part of the gallery, on two floors, there is a large collection of European and British paintings, many of which will be familiar from art books and magazines. For instance, to name but a few: "Madonna and child", attributed to Verrocchio and brought to Britain by John Ruskin; Raphael's "Holy family with a palm tree"; Titian's "Diana and Actaeon"; Tintoretto's "Descent from the Cross"; Rubens' "Feast of Herod"; Rembrandt's voluptuous "Woman in bed" and many, many more. You will see paintings by El Greco, Velazquez, Vermeer, Claude, Watteau, Courbet, Delacroix, Pissaro, Degas, Daumier, Sisley, Gauguin, Monet, Cézanne, Renoir, Van Gogh, Goya, Gainsborough, Hogarth, and Constable. Upstairs, in a room of their own and easy to miss, are "The Seven Sacraments", by Poussin, with colours so rich and deep that you almost get indigestion looking at them.

The Royal Scottish Academy, of painting, sculpture and architecture (open daily during exhibitions: adults £1.20) is just beside the National Gallery, facing onto the Mound. It was founded in 1826 to promote Fine Arts in Scotland and it holds two main exhibitions a year: The Annual Exhibition, in the summer, and the Festival Exhibition. These very enormously and cover all aspects of Fine Art.

The Portrait Gallery (open all the year: admission free, except for special exhibitions) is at the east end of Queen Street. Here are memories of Scotland's heroes and villains, kings and regents, tyrants and philanthropists. The gallery holds good exhibitions, often displaying photographic portraits which are as exciting as the old master paintings.

The National Museum of Antiquities (open all year, admission free except for special exhibitions) is opposite the portrait gallery. Here you will see relics from Scotland's history that go right back to the first settlers: excavated artefacts from Stone Age man; early Christian carved stones and crosses; pagan carvings; implements; pottery, and many other artifacts. Perhaps the most fascinating exhibit in the museum is the treasure that was dug up from Traprain Law in 1919: 4th-century Christian and pagan silver-gilt bowls, goblets, jewellery, clasps, etc, possibly buried there by pirates.

The Fine Art Society (open on weekdays from 9.30 am to 5.30 pm and 10 am to 1 pm on Saturdays: admission free) is at 12 Great King Street, ten minutes walk north from the Museum of Antiquities and easy to miss. A flag hangs over the doorway and you ring the bell, as if going to a private house: indeed, once you are inside it is as if you are in someone's very beautiful home. On three floors, you can see an often-changing display of the Society's many paintings, with the downstairs rooms furnished in a style that adds to the feeling that you are on a social visit.

The City Art Gallery (open daily: admission free, except for special exhibitions) is tucked away behind Waverley Station. This gallery houses the city's art collection, including many Scottish works, and holds a number of first class exhibitions from all over the world.

The Modern Art Gallery (open daily: admission free) in Belford Road, north-west of Princes Street, was opened in 1984 in what was formerly a school. It has made the best possible use of a fine building, set back behind a grass sward dotted with trees and sculpture, including some by Henry Moore. The gallery houses an excellent collection of 20th-century paintings, sculpture and graphic art, by such masters as Picasso, Braque, Matisse, Hockney, Caulfield and many more. There is a nice little licensed restaurant downstairs, with a friendly staff comprised mainly of impoverished students

Cathedrals

Among Edinburgh's many churches of all denominations, there are two cathedrals, not counting St Giles.

St Mary's Episcopal Cathedral, 1879, is in Palmerston Place, west of Princes Street. You will see its central spire from all over the city. In the grounds is the charming, little, late 17th-century house, **Easter Coats House**, which is now the cathedral's music school. As well as services, the cathedral holds public concerts throughout the year, with the programme posted up outside.

St Mary's Metropolitan Catholic Cathedral, is at the east end of Queen Street, round the corner from York Place. Its all-male choir has been acclaimed as being among the best in the land, "... because they sing not as trained professionals, but with their hearts...". At the start of a high mass, the choir, starting with the trebles, moves in procession into the church through a door from the vestry and the sound of their voices, swelling and deepening as they move forward, and filling the entire building with glorious sound, is an experience not quickly forgotten

The Environs of Edinburgh

The Botanic Gardens

The Botanic Gardens (open all year round: admission free) north of the city between Inverleith Row and Inverleith Terrace, deserve almost daily visits from early spring till late autumn, to appreciate their ever-changing beauty. The herbacious border is spectacular, backed by a gigantic beech hedge. There are glasshouses and pavilions full of exotic vegetation, steamy-hot and lush, where you almost believe you have been transported to some tropical jungle. The rock garden is huge, full of rare alpine plants, rising in miniature mountains from the water garden and sweeping lawns. You don't get that prim "keep-off-the-grass-don't-feed-the-birds" feeling in these gardens: they are beautifully kept but somehow informal, making you want to lie on the grass on hot summer days

Warriston Cemetery

Not many people would think to seek an hour or two of delightful peace among the dead, but you can do this in Warriston Cemetery! Just to the east of the Botanic Gardens, you will find it by following the Water of Leith northwards, across Inverleith Row and along Warriston Road. The cemetery was bought by a property speculator who then found that some of the graves were too recent to allow excavation: it is now a public, secret garden, half-tended, just enough so that you can walk in it but not so much as to spoil its lovely wild, undiscovered aspect, with forgotten graves overhung with trailing creepers, shaded by fine trees. You find yourself wandering here in the dappled sunlight, pausing to read the inscriptions, brushing aside a swathe of Old Man's Beard to examine a draped urn or a marble angel. There is no feeling of bereavement here: it is all tranquillity and the ghosts are happy. Don't, however, go through the tunnel that leads under the road into an older part of the cemetery: there is an evil presence here, so tangible that you almost feel a physical shock

Leith

Leith, to the north-east, is the historic port of Edinburgh and contains more and more wine bars, bars and restaurants which open up along the waterfront to give delicious refreshment. You can sit either outside (in summer) or inside and enjoy good views of maritime activity within the port. The English used to batter Leith during their many campaigns against Edinburgh. Mary, Queen of Scots landed here when she came back from France to take up her loaded crown in 1561: one can't help wondering what a mixture of feelings—of hope, excitement and anxiety—raced through her mind as she received her first Scottish hospitality. Two years before, her mother, Mary of Guise, used Leith as headquarters during her struggles with the Lords of the Congregation, probably in Water Street.

Charles I played golf on Leith Links and it was while he was playing here in 1641 that he was stopped, mid-putt, and told the news of the Irish rebellion. Cromwell built a fort in Leith which the Jacobites captured in 1715. George IV landed in the port in 1822 making his celebrated visit to Edinburgh, organised by Sir Walter Scott. It was at that time that he showed himself to his northern subjects in an astonishing tartan outfit, complete, some say, with tights.

Andrew Lamb's House, in Burgess Street, is owned by the National Trust. This four-storey building, with a projecting staircase tower, was built as a house and warehouse combined and is now an old people's day centre. It was here that Mary was entertained on arrival in 1561, by Andrew Lamb, one of the rich merchants of Leith.

Trinity House, in Kirkgate, Leith, was founded as an almhouse in 1555, rebuilt in Victorian times, and contains four portraits by Raeburn which you can see on request. The much-restored **Church of St Mary**, nearly opposite, was built in the 15th century.

The Dean Village

North-west of the city centre, as you take the main road north, you cross the **Dean Bridge**, often unaware of the attractive Dean Village that lies in the valley below. There was a grain-milling community here for 800 years, straggling along the Water of Leith, the old buildings now being restored and converted into comfortable flats and houses. You can walk for miles along this waterway and forget that you are close to the heart of a busy city.

Dean Village

Lauriston Castle

Lauriston Castle (open daily in the summer except on Fridays and at weekends in the winter: adults 80p, children 40p) is further to the north-west, off Cramond Road South, overlooking the river in the suburb of Davidson's Mains. The original 16th-century tower has been extended into the present beautiful house where you can see some good paintings, furniture, tapestry and 'Blue John Ware'.

The Zoo

The zoo (open daily all the year: adults £2.40 children £1.20) is at Corstorphine as you go west out of Edinburgh on the A8. It is one of the biggest zoos in Britain, with a large collection of mammals, birds and reptiles. An eerie experience for insomniacs or early risers, is to climb **Corstorphine Hill** at dawn, and watch the sun rise over the city: you stand there, entranced, as the whole Lothian plain comes alive, and suddenly, very close to you, you hear the harsh, unfamiliar roar of some African beast, greeting the dawn from its cage. For a petrified moment your heart literally stands still—and then you remember that you are on the perimeter fence of the zoo!

Craigmillar Castle

Craigmillar Castle (open daily except Fridays: adults 50p, children 25p) is three and a half miles (5.6 km) south-west of the city centre on the A68. (The journey out was through open countryside in the days when Mary, Queen of Scots used to ride out with her court.) The massive ruins of the castle stand high and proud above a straggle of modern buildings that threatens to encroach from all sides and yet fails to diminish its aloof splendour. These mellow, well-preserved walls, dating from the 14th century, have witnessed some of the darker moments of Scotland's history. In 1475, James III imprisoned his brother, John, Earl of Mar, in the keep, accusing him of "conspiracy". Later, Mar died from "... overzealous bloodletting".

Craigmillar was Mary's favourite country retreat: the village nearby became known as Little France, when the overflow from her court used to take lodgings there. It was here, in 1566, at the Craigmillar Conference, that Mary was urged by her lords (including Bothwell) to divorce Darnley.

The great banqueting hall on the first floor is served by four stairways and it is easy for the mind to furnish it with hanging tapestries, straw on the flagged floor, blazing logs in the vast open hearth and a minstrel in the gallery below the barrel-vaulted ceiling. You can get right up to the roof, with lovely views across to Arthur's Seat, the Firth of Forth with the hills of Fife beyond, and the soft contours of the smoke-grey Pentlands on the south-western horizon. The two ancient yew trees that still flourish in the courtyard are relics from the days when they were believed to ward off evil spirits (a more prosaic explanation for their presence being that their wood was needed for making bows).

The Edinburgh Butterfly Farm

The Edinburgh Butterfly Farm (open daily: adults £1.75, children £1) is six miles (9.7 km) south of the city, well signposted, on the A7. This is a must for butterfly collectors: there are over 1,000 of them, flying around in a tropical rainforest, complete with waterfall and bubbling pools. You really feel you are in another country as you wander through the enormous glasshouse, with all those exotic beauties flitting and hovering around you, and you quite expect to have a touch of malaria when you emerge.

The Edinburgh International Festival

In 1947, after the Second World War, when people were trying to pick up the pieces of the past and get back to normal life, the Edinburgh Festival was born. It is now one of the world's leading festivals of drama, music and art, and takes place in August. International companies perform concerts, ballet, opera, drama; and all are of the highest standard. The Festival takes a theme, each year (The Auld Alliance, for instance) and many of the performances and exhibitions relate to that. For three weeks the city is transformed; packed out with Festival crowds, accommodation booked for months ahead; taken over by an air of frenzy as people try to cram as much as possible into the time.

Perhaps almost as well-known is the **Edinburgh Fringe** that has grown up round the main Festival. Every spare inch that can be used as a theatre is grabbed: old kirks, halls, back rooms, basements, attics, schools. Students and drama companies from all over Britain and abroad, perform every possible sort of entertainment, from monologues and poetry readings, street shows and acrobatics, to full-scale drama and opera. The list of productions runs into many hundreds (nearly 900 in 1985!) and although they go on most of the day and well into the small hours, it is not possible to see them all. Until the reviews begin to come out, no one has any idea what is good, and once something gets a rave review you must run at top speed to the Fringe Office in the High Street, if you want a ticket. Everyone goes just a little mad, during the Festival, and it is a recurring madness that is packed away after it is all over, so that you think it is gone forever, until the following year when it reappears as virulent as before. The **1987 Edinburgh International Festival** will be held from 9 to 31 August and the **1988** Festival from 14 August to 3 September.

The Military Tattoo takes place every night of the Festival on the castle esplanade. For one and a half hours you watch a wonderful pageant of military skills, with massed bands, pipes and drums, dancers, displays, precision drills, and piping. Each year the organisers manage to find something different, as well as the set favourites, and you can never be sure whether the climax is going to be a Bulgarian belly dancer or a parade of Indian elephants. With the flood-lit castle as a dramatic backdrop and the brilliant staging of each event, culminating in the Lone Piper on the battlements, the Tattoo is one of the most popular attractions of the Festival, year after year.

The Edinburgh International Film Festival runs at the same time as the main Festival and has a reputation for discovering new talent. You can see a tremendous range of international films, over 70 new feature films, documentaries, shorts, etc, with discussions and conferences and a chance to see and meet some of the leading film makers in the world. You can get preliminary programme details from June onwards, from: Department F, Edinburgh International Film Festival, 88 Lothian Road, Edinburgh, tel 031-228 2699.

TOURIST INFORMATION

Edinburgh Tourist Centre, Waverley Market, 3 Princes Street, tel 031-557 2727.

Festival Offices, 21 Market Street, tel 031-226 4001.

Fringe Office and Society, 170 High Street, tel 031-226 5257.

Tattoo Office, 1 Cockburn Street, tel 031-225 1188.

Guides and Help, 9 Jordan Lane, tel 031–447 7190 (for specialised tours and walks in Edinburgh).

Leisureline, tel 031-246 8041 (for a selection of the main events of the day between 1 May and 30 September).

WHERE TO STAY

The choice is enormous and you should consult the Tourist Centre. Book well ahead during the summer and especially during the Festival. The following is a small, random selection of hotels in the city centre—an easy walk or short taxi ride from the station.

Expensive

Caledonian Hotel, west end of Princes Street, tel 031-225 2433. B&B from £46.50: categories 5,6,6: 254 bedrooms en suite. The Caledonian has a long established reputation for comfort and impeccable standards of service; there is a number of bars and restaurants, including the elegant Pompadour Restaurant, inspired by Louis XV's mistress, Madame de Pompadour.

Edinburgh Sheraton, bottom of Lothian Road, tel 031-229 9131. B&B from £50:

categories 6,6,6: 263 bedrooms en suite. This brand new hotel stands back behind fountains and a paved garden and is well up to the standard of all Sheraton hotels.

Roxburghe Hotel, Charlotte Square, tel 031-225 3921. B&B from £47.50: categories 6,5,6: 73 bedrooms en suite. A comfortable, old-established hotel with excellent service and food, overlooking Edinburgh's loveliest square.

The George Hotel, east end of George Street, tel 031-225 1251. B&B from £59: categories 6,6,6: 195 bedrooms en suite. The hotel has all possible comforts and amenities.

Moderate

North British Hotel, east end of Princes Street, tel 031-556 2414. B&B from £29: categories 5,5,6: 201 bedrooms, 172 en suite. This is the Victorian dowager of Edinburgh's hotels. It is situated over the station and has several bars and a good service and the Cleikum Restaurant.

Cheap

Osbourne Hotel, 53/9 York Place, tel 031-556 5746. B&B from £14: categories 5,5,4: 25 bedrooms, 19 en suite. A comfortable townhouse hotel within a few minutes walk of Princes Street.

Thistle Hotel, 59 Manor Place, tel 031–225 6144. B&B from £14: categories 4,3,3: 10 bedrooms en suite. A friendly hotel in the west end, a few minutes walk from Princes Street.

Maitland Hotel, 33 Shandwick Place, tel 031-229 1467. B&B from £12: categories 4,3,4: 27 bedrooms, 11 en suite. A Georgian house near the centre in the west end, once owned by the Earl of Maitland. It offers a variety of package holidays which include dinner, B&B, and visits to many parts of the city.

Arden Hotel, 17/20 Royal Terrace, tel 031-556 8688. B&B from £15: categories 4,4,2: 45 bedrooms, 33 en suite. A family-run hotel in magnificent listed Georgian Terrace, with wooded gardens front and back, in the east end below Calton Hill.

Kildonan Lodge Hotel, 27 Craigmillar Park, tel 031-667 2793. B&B from £12: categories 3,3,5: 9 bedrooms. A friendly atmosphere, ten minutes walk from the city centre with special bargain offers in the spring.

EATING OUT

Again, the choice is endless and today's "in" place may be old-hat tomorrow. You need to ask around: the following are just a few suggestions—and it is always wise to book.

Expensive

Pompadour Restaurant, Caledonian Hotel, tel 031-225 2433. Remembering Scotland's Auld Alliance with France, this elegant restaurant is decorated in the style of Louis XV's famous mistress Madame de Pompadour, its bar overlooking the castle. So long as you don't mind having to put on a jacket and tie, and don't mind music while you eat, you can't hope for a better meal anywhere. For £15 you can get two courses without wine, but you should be prepared to spend more.

Prestonfield House, Priestfield Road, tel 031-667 8000. A 17th-century house in attractive grounds where peacocks strut and highland cattle graze. Excellent food in a country house atmosphere: dinner from £18, lunch from £8.50—both excluding wine.

Moderate

Martin's Restaurant, 72 Rose Street North Lane, tel 031-225 3106. A personally run, intimate restaurant; aptly described as "a country restaurant in the city". First class food. A two course dinner without wine from about £10 and lunch, plat du jour from £5. Highly recommended.

Howard Hotel, 36 Great King Street, tel 031-557 3500. Classical Scottish dishes: try the kipper and whisky mousse, poacher's broth, and Flummery Drambuie. Original Georgian dining room, good two course dinner without wine from about £11.50.

Restaurant Alphorn, 167 Rose Street, tel 031-225 4787. Genuine Swiss atmosphere, good service, moderately priced. You can get a two course dinner from about £10.

Creperie Francaise, 8a Grindlay Street, (by Lyceum Theatre), tel 031-229 5405. Excellent French food, in friendly, casual atmosphere. Two course dinner from about £10.

Cafe Royal Oyster Bar, Register Place, tel 031-556 4124. If you saw the film *Chariots of Fire*, you will recognise this 1830's restaurant with its dark gleaming wood and reflecting glass. Marvellous "traditional" atmosphere. Two course dinner from £8.

On the Waterfront at Leith there are several good seafood restaurants with a marvellous "waterfront" atmosphere, tables outside and excellent fish dishes. Try **The Shore Bar**, Shore St, tel 031-553 5080; **Skippers**, 1a Dock Place, tel 031-554 1018; **The Waterfront Wine Bar**, 1c Dock Place, tel 031-554 7427.

Cheap

Le Caveau Club des Vins, 13b Dundas Street, tel 031-556 5707. Checked tablecloths, candles in bottles, friendly "bistro" atmosphere, reasonable two course meal from £6.

Bannermans, 212 Cowgate, tel 031-556 3254. Built in the 1770s as a shell-fish warehouse, then a dwelling, and later, a tavern called "The Bucket of Blood", Bannermans has managed to retain its original tavern atmosphere, with plenty of bare wooden surfaces: you almost expect to see rushes on the floor. Traditional Scottish folk music, live, on Sundays, Tuesdays and Wednesdays. Excellent soup and a main course for £2. Highly recommended for atmosphere.

The Bungalow, 23 Brougham Place, tel 031-229 2537. Very good curries of all sorts and strengths. Far Eastern rattan decor. Not too expensive. Meal from £5, and one course is all you'll manage.

Ferri's Pizzeria, 1 Antigua Street, tel 031-556 5592. Happy Italian atmosphere (genuine). Good for children and extremely reasonable. You can eat well for from £5.

La Fayette, 22 Brougham Place, tel 031-229 0869. Small, intimate, French atmosphere. Two course meal from £7.

Madogs, 38 George Street, tel 031-225 3408. This American-inspired cocktail bar, specialising in exotic cocktails that make your mouth water just looking at them, has seating for 50. It is known for its hamburgers but there is a wide alternative choice. You can get good food from £5.

Merchants Brasserie, Merchant Street, tel 031-225 4009. Small, friendly atmosphere in converted tartan warehouse. Two course dinner from £10. Plat du jour lunch from £6.50.

ENTERTAINMENT

A new information centre and ticket service has been opened at 31/2 Waverley Bridge, just beside the station, where you can go for advice on theatre and concert ticket availability. You can get information here about events in Edinburgh and you can also find out about the many coach tours around the area, and get tickets for them.

You will find top class opera, concerts, drama, ballet, variety shows, etc in Edinburgh's theatres, and the latest films in the cinemas.

Theatres

The Playhouse, at the top of Leith Walk, tel 031-557 2590.

The Usher Hall, Lothian Road, tel 031-228 1155.

The Kings Theatre, Leven Street. Recently done up and restored to its original Georgian splendour, tel 031-229 1201.

Royal Lyceum Theatre, Grindlay Street, near the Usher Hall, Scotland's largest repertory company, tel 031-229 9697.

The Netherbow, High Street, a multi-arts centre with a large variety of shows and exhibitions, tel 031-556 9579.

Theatre Workshop, 34 Hamilton Place, tel 031-226 5425.

Traverse Theatre, West Bow, off the Grassmarket. A leading experimental theatre, tel 031-226 2633.

Caley-Palace, Lothian Road, is a "rock venue" as well as a cinema, tel 031–229 7670.

Cinemas

Edinburgh Filmhouse, Lothian Road. All the good films you ever missed, or longed to see again, tel 031-228 6382.

ABC Film Centre, Lothian Road. Several screens showing both recent films and oldies, tel 031-229 3030.

Odeon Film Centre, Clerk Street. Same as above, tel 031-667 3805.

Dominion, Newbattle Terrace. Same as above, tel 031-447 2660.

Caley-Palace, see above, in Theatre section.

SHOPPING IN EDINBURGH

Princes Street and George Street, together with their transversal streets and the whole area between them are the main shopping area in the city centre. Jenners, in Princes Street, is the "Harrods" of Edinburgh: if you can't get what you want anywhere else, they usually have it. There is any number of tweed, tartan and wool shops. The Tartan Gift Shop, in 96 Princes Street will probably have what you want, with its "seconds" shop at 10 North Bridge, by the North British Hotel, and another at 108a Rose Street, where you can often pick up a bargain.

Rose Street and its lanes, running parallel between Princes Street and George Street, is a lively street, humming with bars and restaurants, hot-food take aways and boutiques. Many of the shops here are "fun" places, with gimmicky knick-knacks and craft work. Les Cadeaux, 121 Rose Street, sell a good range of china, crystal and gifts, and they run a shipping service to the USA.

The St James Centre, at the east end of Princes Street, is an indoor shopping complex, with a John Lewis ("never knowingly undersold") and many smaller shops.

Waverley Market, already mentioned, is most attractive to wander about in, with lots of specialist shops and representatives of larger stores elsewhere.

Hamilton & Inches, at 87 George Street, sell antique and modern silver and jewellery, Highland accessories, watches, clocks, crystal and china: an old-established shop of the class that high-born grandparents remember.

You will find plenty of gift shops in and just off the Royal Mile, as well as antique shops and bars and restaurants.

Cockburn Street, that winds down from the High Street to Waverley Station, is very much a young people's shopping street, crammed with boutiques and wonderfully way-out fashions, colourful and full of atmosphere.

The Grassmarket and the area around it is good shopping territory. There is a well-stocked print shop, already mentioned, in Victoria Street, where you can buy framed and unframed prints of almost anywhere in Scotland for reasonable prices. There are second-hand bookshops here and several antique shops worth browsing in.

Among the shops and boutiques in the Grassmarket is Droopy and Brown, 70–72, who have built up a reputation for their own design of clothes: "...classic fashion but not neat little navy blue suits..." It is well worth a visit for all ages from 18 to 80.

Campus, at 42 Grassmarket, pride themselves on stocking top design clothes as well as more ordinary fashions, so that they usually have something for all ages and tastes.

Stockbridge, down by the Water of Leith, in the New Town, has a village community atmosphere of its own and here you will find some good shops. St Stephen Street, at the bottom of north-west Circus Place, is lined with antique and junk shops. Some are high class and expensive, some are a delightful clutter of other people's cast-offs where you can re-stock your wardrobe, buy a box of old 78 rpm records, or a glass jar full of buttons. Many of Edinburgh's students are dressed from head to foot with bargains from St Stephen Street.

On the corner of St Stephen Street, Galloways is an antique shop that also does very high class interior decoration, with lots of tempting things if you are doing up your house.

In Raeburn Place, further down, there are two "Herbys": a licensed delicatessen, and a take-away. Between the two of them you will find everything you could possibly want for an impromptu picnic: mouth watering cheeses, pâtes, cold-cuts, bread, etc.

The James Pringle Woollen Mill, in Bangor Road, has a splendid range of tartans, tweeds and knitwear. They also have a "trace your clan" computer. They are open every day from 9 am to 5.30 pm (10 am on Sundays).

CRAFT CENTRES IN EDINBURGH

Acheson House, Canongate, is the Scottish Craft Centre, with a wide variety of displays, things to buy and information.

The Adam Pottery, 76 Henderson Row, tel 031-557 3978. This is a one-man studio producing hand-thrown stoneware. Visitors can watch whatever process is underway at the time.

Crucible Pottery, 38 Merchiston Avenue, is another studio where you can watch hand-thrown and decorated pottery being created.

Jennifer Jackson Designs, 45 Bernard Street, Leith, tel 031-554 1720. Here you can watch dress design, cutting and manufacture, by appointment, and free of charge.

Maggie Belle Designs, 4 Forth View, Newcraighall Road. You can watch souvenir dolls being hand made, painted and dressed.

Cosy Knits, 166 Canongate. You can watch the intricate designing and knitting of garments. Also at Ace Knitwear, 250 Canongate, you can see the linking, washing, steaming and labelling of garments; and also at Helga Wade Knitwear, 12 Upper Grove Place.

Roxclox of Edinburgh, 4 New Broom Park, Granton Park Avenue Industrial Estate. Go there if you want to see wall tiles, clocks, barometers, lamps, candleholders, etc, being made out of Isle of Skye marble using diamond machinery.

The Celtic Craft Centre, 93/101 High Street. Here you can see kilts, dirks, *skean-dhu's* and bagpipes being made.

You can watch tapestry and rug-weaving on Highland Law Looms, at Milly Donaldson, 23 Torphichen Street, and hand weaving by Carol Anderson, 11 Blackford Road.

SPECIAL EVENTS IN EDINBURGH: 1987

The year 1987 is the 400th anniversary of the execution of Mary, Queen of Scots. There are special events all over Scotland to mark this historic tragedy. The following are to take place in Edinburgh.

At Holyrood, all year except May and July: a display of Mary, Queen of Scots' artifacts, including a guided tour of her apartments and a display of some of her belongings.

At the Wax Museum, 142 High Street, all year: Mary, Queen of Scots theatrical tableaux.

Edinburgh University is holding a Mary, Queen of Scots quatercentenary concert on 6–7 February.

Huntly House Museum, in Canongate, throughout the summer: an exhibition of Mary's stay in Edinburgh.

The Portrait Gallery, from July to September: Mary, Queen of Scots quatercentenary exhibition.

The Scottish Record Office, in Register House, at the east end of Princes Street, from July to September: "The Queen and the Scots", an exhibition of manuscripts.

There is to be an opera, "Maria Stuart", by Malay Theatre of Leningrad, in August, the theatre to be decided.

OTHER EVENTS IN 1987

25 April: Edinburgh's Twentieth Annual Concert of the Kevock Choir.
21–24 June: Royal Highland Show.

7–29 August: Military Tattoo (1988, 12 August–3 September).
8–24 August: Film Festival.
9–31 August: International Festival (1988, 14 August–3 September).
28–30 August: Antiques Fair.
August (date to be decided)—Dunedin Dancers International Folk Dance Festival.
20–22 November: Winter Antiques Fair.

Part IV

GLASGOW

Gourock

People have become so used to thinking of Glasgow as the ugly, sprawling warm-hearted, boisterous, earthy, working-class hub of industrial Scotland that few have noticed what has been happening over recent years. The "Gorbals Image" (so brilliantly encapsulated in a book called *No mean city*, by A. McArthur, written in the 1950s and still in print) has gone. Glasgow is still no mean city, but it is a city with a punchy, 20th-century image, no longer struggling among the tatty ruins of its slum tenements. It is a rapidly developing, modern city with a motorway system that enables you to drive right through its heart at 50 mph—which is more than can be said for London or Edinburgh.

Edinburgh, with its international Festival and its gracious Georgian buildings and its historic past, has won itself the title of Cultural Centre of Scotland: it is now true to say that Glasgow is close on its heels and threatening to overtake it, if it has not already done so! Quietly, almost stealthily, it has moved up into the front rank, and that dirty old slum-infested tramp that was "Glasgie" is now offering as much top-class entertainment as anywhere in the country. Indeed, Glasgow has recently been nominated as Britain's European City of Culture for 1990—much to the chagrin of Edinburgh and other British cities.

Home of the Scottish Opera, one of Scotland's most prestigious possessions, as well as the Scottish National Orchestra, Glasgow now owns the Burrell Collection, to which people fly in from all over the world especially to visit. The Mayfest, only a few years old, is rapidly gaining international acclaim, as is the Folk Festival in July. The Third Eye Arts Centre is the best in Scotland, stimulating great interest from people all over Britain and abroad.

the blossoming culture in every field of Fine Art are mere facets in a glittering diamond. You will find, in the preceding chapter on Edinburgh, long lists of things to do and see; a great parade of attractions and amusements as glossy as mink: compared with that, this chapter may seem disappointingly bare and lacking in specific descriptions. Glasgow is not easily revealed on paper: its magic lies not in its tangible, visible, material assets, but in its soul. It is an elusive magic: a will o' the wisp vitality; a vibrant atmosphere; a bewitching character that you can only discover for yourself.

Go out into the streets of the city to find it; go into the bars and cafes; go down to the waterfront and into the markets; go shopping. Keep your ears and your eyes open; get into conversation with the man on the news-stand; the ticket-collector; the out-of-work dosser; the sharp-faced, sharp-tongued housewife with henna-ed hair in rollers under a pink chiffon scarf. Talk to the students and the barmen; the taxi-drivers and the old-age pensioners. That is how you will uncover Glasgow's charms.

If comparisons must be made, and perhaps this is inevitable with two major cities so close to each other, you could say that Glasgow is to Edinburgh what New York is to Washington. The Glaswegian is to the Scottish music hall what the Cockney is to the English, and as in all parodies, there is some truth in the image but only in self-mocking overstatement. The Glaswegian is a blend of the Irish who came over in their starving hundreds during the potato famine, and the deposed Highlanders, driven from their crofts by sheep farmers. He has the lyrical, romantic charm of the former and the gentle courtesy of the latter, combined with the Celtic wit and sensitivity of both. He adds to this endearing mixture a shrewd, worldly cockiness that stems from his independent spirit and courage. There is no one else quite like him, anywhere in the world.

It is amusing to reflect that when supercilious Edinburgh consisted of just a cluster of Pictish huts round a wooden fort, St Mungo was busy in Glasgow, establishing a church from which the present cathedral grew, on a site that had already been consecrated by St Ninian, two centuries before in the 4th century. So, although it cannot boast an impressive saga of glamorous royal dramas, its recorded history goes right back to the dawn of Christianity and relates to the fortunes of the church from that time.

Assuming that legend is born from fragments of fact, a Pictish princess was banished from Traprain Law (see Lothian) in the 6th century and cast adrift on the Firth of Forth in a coracle. She landed at Culross (see Fife) and was taken in by St Serf (or Servanus) and cherished while she gave birth to a son, Kentigern. St Serf baptised mother and child and brought the child up, giving him the affectionate nickname of Mungo (or Munchu) the Latin-Welsh endearment for "dearest friend". Mungo went out as a missionary: in fulfilment of a prophesy, he took the bones of a holy man, Fergus, and carried them until God told him to stop. Glasgow Cathedral now stands on that spot, with the bones of Fergus lying interred there. The town that grew up around the church was called Glas Cau—the green place, and in the mild, dampish climate that prevails the land would indeed have been very green and fertile.

Glasgow's coat of arms incorporates a salmon, a ring, a tree, a bird and a bell, all of which are related to the patron saint. Mungo saved the honour, and the life, of a queen by arranging for a ring that she had given her lover to be found in a salmon in the river, and returned to her to be shown to her suspicious husband. The tree is a branch that burned miraculously, enabling Mungo to rekindle the monastery fire that he had been entrusted to keep alight. The bird was a robin, a favourite of St Serf's, killed by accident and brought back to life by Mungo. The bell was one given to Mungo on his ordination and taken everywhere with him.

Glasgow's wonderfully self-confident motto "let Glasgow flourish" stems from the rather more cautious invocation that was inscribed on the 16th-century bell on the Tron Church: "Let Glasgow Flourish Through the Preaching of the Word and Praising Thy Name".

The city saw some moments of secular history: William Wallace defeated the English in a battle in 1300, over what is now the upper end of the High Street. The university was founded in 1451 by Bishop Turnbull, only 40 years after St Andrews. Mary, Queen of Scots' final bid for power after her escape from Leven Castle, in 1568, took place at Langside, near Queen's Park. She watched the battle from her horse, at Castle Knowe, riding forward into the mêlée to encourage her loyal troops, who were, even so, soon defeated. Cromwell came to Glasgow in 1650, and heard himself denounced as a "sectary and blasphemer" by the Rector of the university, Zachary Boyd, in a two-hour sermon. Cromwell appears to have taken this public humiliation with rare humour, inviting Boyd to dinner and making him sit through three hours of prayer! Bonny Prince Charlie lodged in the town on his way to Culloden, in 1745.

Separated from America by only the Atlantic, Glasgow merchants grew rich on the import of tobacco and sugar, after the Union of Parliaments in 1707. The Clyde, once a shallow salmon river, was deepened by dredgers and the city flourished as a major port, developing into the world's leading shipbuilding centre. Times of recession always hit hardest at areas of heavy industry, however, and Glasgow's docks are no longer the hives of activity that they used to be: Clydeside no longer reverberates to the ceaseless clang and clatter and fizzle of thriving shipyards. The Clyde is no longer the busy waterway it once was. But Glasgow has shaken itself free of dependence on heavy industry and diversified its economy so successfully that it is now a centre of modern technology that covers almost every form of manufacture.

Glasgow is like any strong personality: on first acquaintance one feels daunted and nervous and perhaps a little shy. But perseverance will uncover the warm character under the awe-inspiring façade and it soon becomes a "dear, familiar place". Walk down to the river and stand on one of the bridges at night: the lights and reflections transform the work-a-day city into a fairy-story kingdom of ethereal beauty.

A slogan has recently made its way on to car stickers, tee-shirts, billboards, and knick-knacks: a beaming yellow "Mr Happy" is displayed with the words: "Glasgow's miles better". This double-edged caption somehow sums up the ebullient spirit of Scotland's most warm-hearted of cities.

WHAT TO SEE

Glasgow Cathedral

Glasgow Cathedral (open standard Ancient Monument times: admission free) is a good place to start, as it is on the site of the church built by St Mungo, and it is around this church that the city of Glasgow grew. It is the city's parish church and is less than a mile (1.6 km) east of the city centre. You can still see traces of the original buildings, dating from 1197, in the lower church, which is the chief glory of the cathedral. The crypt,

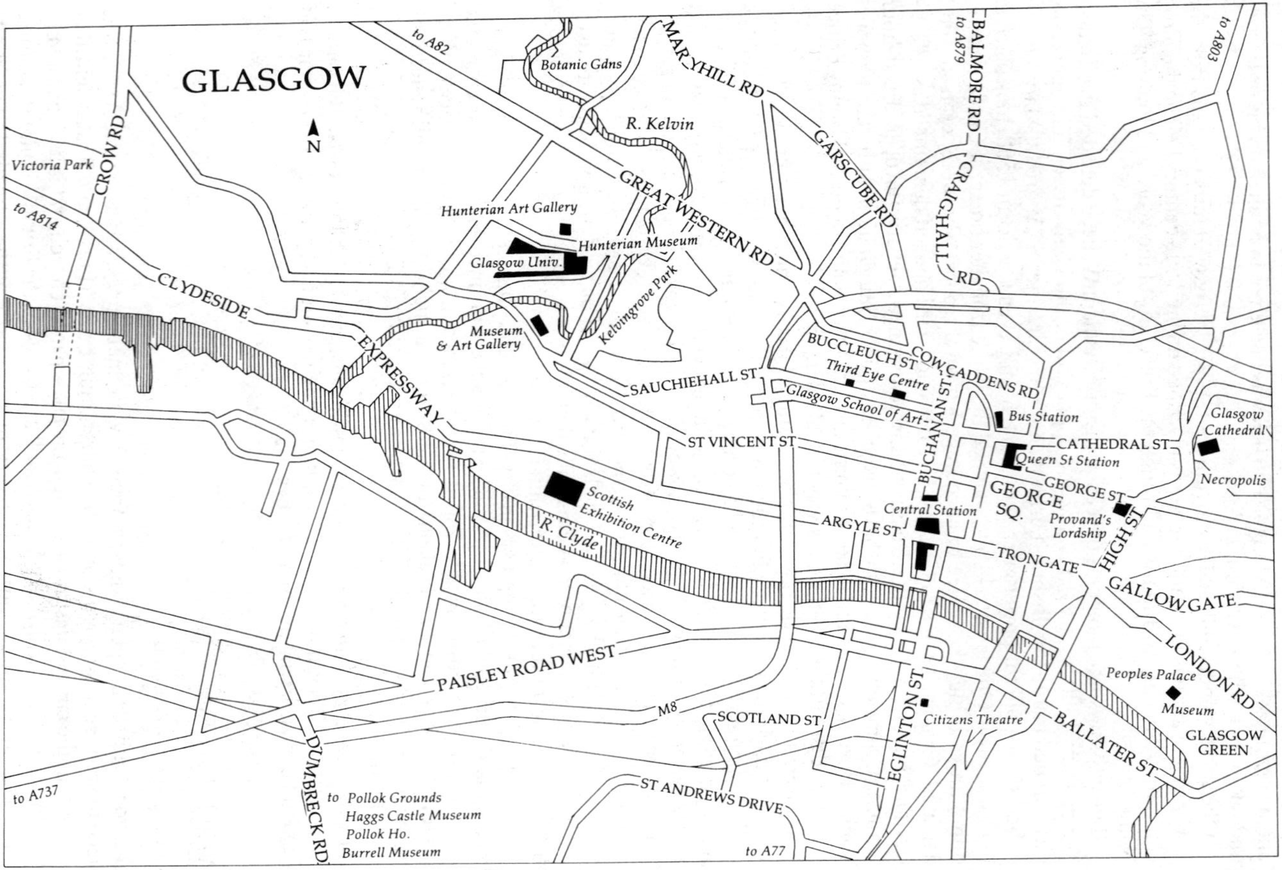
GLASGOW
N
to A82
Botanic Gdns
MARYHILL RD
to A879
BALMORE RD
to A803
R. Kelvin
Victoria Park
CROW RD
GARSCUBE RD
CRAIGHALL RD
GREAT WESTERN RD
Hunterian Art Gallery
to A814
Hunterian Museum
Glasgow Univ.
CLYDESIDE
Kelvingrove Park
Museum & Art Gallery
EXPRESSWAY
BUCCLEUCH ST
Third Eye Centre
COWCADDENS RD
SAUCHIEHALL ST
Glasgow School of Art
BUCHANAN ST
Bus Station
Glasgow Cathedral
ST VINCENT ST
CATHEDRAL ST
Queen St Station
Necropolis
GEORGE SQ.
GEORGE ST
Scottish Exhibition Centre
Central Station
Provand's Lordship
ARGYLE ST
R. Clyde
TRONGATE
HIGH ST
GALLOWGATE
LONDON RD
PAISLEY ROAD WEST
Peoples Palace
Museum
M8
SCOTLAND ST
EGLINTON ST
Citizens Theatre
BALLATER ST
GLASGOW GREEN
ST ANDREWS DRIVE
to A737
DUMBRECK RD
to Pollok Grounds
Haggs Castle Museum
Pollok Ho.
Burrell Museum
to A77

choir and tower were built in 1233, the rest being added at various stages in the succeeding years. During the appalling destruction of church embellishment, in the Reformation, the last Catholic archbishop, James Beaton, stripped Glasgow Cathedral of its finery and carried the treasures off to France, together with the archives, for safekeeping. Unfortunately, in the later turmoil of the French Revolution, these were lost and have never been found. In 1578, when the iconoclasts of the Reformation threatened to destroy the cathedral entirely, the city's trade guilds intervened, and, miraculously, managed to prevent them: thus, today you can see the finest example of pre-Reformation Gothic architecture in Scotland. Austere, as all Presbyterian churches seem to be, it is even so very fine inside, with St Mungo's tomb in the crypt, under magnificent fan-vaulting, and a rood-screen with carvings of the seven deadly sins on its corbels.

The cathedral stands on a slope embedded with horizontal grave stones, and backed by the **Necropolis**, on a hill behind, giving a splendid sky-line of elaborate monuments, overshadowed by a Doric column from which John Knox keeps a stern eye on the city.

Provand's Lordship

Provand's Lordship (open daily: admission free) is in Castle Street, opposite the cathedral. It dates from 1471 and is the only other pre-Reformation building of interest. Built as a priest's house, it is very well preserved and has been turned into a museum where you can see 17th- and 18th-century furniture, tapestry and pictures, as well as the key of Leven Castle, where Mary was imprisoned (see Tayside). She may have stayed in this house when she came to Glasgow in 1567 to visit her husband Darnley, who was sick with some disfiguring disease that has been diagnosed as anything from smallpox to syphilis, before taking him back to Edinburgh—and murder. It is the oldest house in the city, and was visited by both James II and James IV during their reigns in the 15th and 16th centuries.

George Square

George Square is at the heart of the city, 20 minutes stroll west of the cathedral, a splendid hub surrounded by fine buildings. There is something pleasantly continental about the square on a sunny day, like the main piazza of any Mediterranean town, where crowds gather to pass the time: visitors in shirt sleeves, slung about with cameras, linger among the trees and statues. Parades are sometimes held here and if you are lucky, you can watch and listen to the bands of pipes and drums of various Scottish regiments, beating retreat on summer evenings. The square is dominated by a statue of Sir Walter Scott on an 80 ft (24.4 m) high column (a column that was first intended for a statue of George III). This mighty monument was the first to be set up in honour of Sir Walter, in 1837, although he was barely ten years old when the square was laid out, in 1781. He towers over Queen Victoria, Prince Albert, Robert Burns, James Watt, and many others, wearing his plaid across the wrong shoulder for convention, as was his custom. In the middle of the square you will find the **Municipal Information Centre**, where you can find out anything you want about the town.

The imposing building along the entire eastern side of George Square is the **City Chambers**, and you can have a free conducted tour of its sumptuous interior any weekday, except Thursdays (tel 041-221 9600). It is a splendid show of Italian Renaissance architecture, with a loggia, a great staircase, marble columns, soaring vaulted ceilings and a banqueting hall. As you go round you half expect to see some gilded potentate, attended by bowing courtiers, step out from behind one of the columns to hold an audience in the Council Chamber.

The Scottish Design Centre (open daily, except Sundays) is in St Vincent Street, leading off the south-west corner of George Square, and you should certainly go there if you are interested in contemporary design. You can see an average of 500 items that have been selected from the Design Index of 10,000 British manufactured goods. It is a place where you can keep pace with Britain's progress in the field of design, and where you can make up your own mind whether the country is going up or down hill. There is a shop where you can buy some of the goods on display and a cafe.

Museums and Galleries

Glasgow's **Art Gallery and Museum** (open daily, from 10 am to 5 pm; 2 pm to 5 pm on Sundays, admission free) occupy a vast red-sandstone building on the western side of **Kelvingrove Park,** about one and a half miles west of the city centre. Ranking among Britain's best, this place deserves many hours of your time, if you are to see everything that is displayed. It was built as recently as 1901 and has a splendidly solid, Victorian feeling about it. An enormous central hall soars to the full height of the building, used sometimes for organ recitals and special exhibitions.

The museum has fascinating archaeological collections, including a reconstruction of the Antonine Wall, and some Bronze Age cists with their contents. You can also see displays of armour, ethnological exhibits, natural history and social history. The engineering collection is so big that it is not possible to display everything, so if you have a special interest you should ask at the enquiry desk.

The art gallery claims to have one of the finest collections owned by any city, beautifully displayed in upper galleries leading off the balcony that encircles the central hall. On the balcony there are sculptures (including works by Rodin and Epstein), ceramics, silver, jewellery, and furniture displays (including work by Charles Rennie Mackintosh, the Glasgow-born architect who had a considerable influence on European design in the late 19th, early 20th centuries).

Among the art gallery's many treasures you can see Giorgione's "The Adultress brought before Christ", Rubens' "Nature adorned by the Graces", Rembrandt's familiar "Man in armour" and Ribera's "St Peter". Other artists include Delacroix, Corot, Millet, Manet, Degas, Raeburn, Allan Ramsay, Reynolds, Hogarth, Whistler and Turner. There are lots of Impressionists and Post-Impressonists; a Glasgow gallery, and a gallery for recent and contemporary paintings. Perhaps the best known painting in the gallery is Salvador Dali's "Christ of St John of the cross". It is dramatically hung at the end of a corridor and you walk towards it as if walking down a long avenue, your eyes gradually taking in the rich colour and the almost three-dimensional perspective. Familiar as the painting must be to most people, sold all over the world on holy cards, postcards and in life-sized reproductions, you will, even so, get a queer jolt of emotion when you see it for the first time. Around it there is a comprehensive description of its conception, with illustrations. Dali was inspired by a 16th-century drawing of the crucifixion by a Spanish Carmelite friar who became known as St John of the Cross. He painted the picture in 1951, saying that he wanted to create a Christ who would be "... as beautiful as the God that He is". He succeeded.

Kelvingrove Park is an ideal setting for the art gallery and museum. It has a peaceful, academic feeling, with the River Kelvin flowing through its 85 acres (34.4 ha), and was twice used for international exhibitions at the turn of the century as well as for the Scottish National Exhibition in 1911. You can hear concerts several times a week in the summer, in the amphitheatre on the river bank. Strolling among the trees, lying on the grass, listening to the music—it is hard to believe that you are close to the pulsating heart of this vibrant city. In winter, when the frost sharpens the skeleton trees and your breath hits the cold air like smoke, you can walk in Kelvingrove Park in the early morning and feel you are the only person awake in the city. And then the sun comes up over the roof tops to the east, painting the walls of the university on its hill to the north-west a glorious fiery pink and you want to fling out your arms and shout with joy. Usually, you don't, because by that time the early joggers have begun to emerge, as well as the man with his road-sweeping equipment.

Glasgow University was founded in 1451, as just a few classes in the cathedral crypt. It then moved to the High Street, south of the Cathedral Square, and was finally moved to Kelvingrove in 1870 where it expands continually to cater for more than 10,000 students.

The Hunterian Art Gallery (open daily except on Sundays: admission free) is in Hillhead Street, running north from the university and being part of it. In it you will find a comprehensive collection of work by Charles Rennie Mackintosh as well as a large number of Whistler's paintings. There are also works by Rembrandt, Chardin, Stubbs, Pissarro, Reynolds, Sisley and many more. You can see sculpture, including work by Rodin, in the courtyard.

The Hunterian Museum (open daily except on Sundays: admission free) is also part of the university and is Glasgow's oldest museum, with geological, archaeological and ethnographical collections among its many exhibits. Glasgow is proud of Charles Rennie Mackintosh and you will find memorials to him all over the city:

The Glasgow School of Art, for instance (open on weekdays when the school is open and by arrangement, tel 041-332 9797), is in Renfrew Street, ten minutes west of George Square, and is said to be one of Mackintosh's most outstanding designs. He designed it in 1896 and each façade of the building reflects a different facet of his imaginative style. You can ask for a conducted tour whenever one of the staff is free.

The Willow Tea Room, 217 Sauchiehall Street, fifteen minutes north-west of George Square, is another memorial to Charles Rennie Mackintosh. Restored to his original design, it is furnished with chairs and tables of his design and you can get light lunches and tea, between 9.30 am and 5 pm.

The Headquarters of the Charles Rennie Mackintosh Society (open Tuesday, Thursday, Friday and Saturday: free) is in the former Queen's Cross Church, at 870 Garscube Road, north of the Willow Tea Room. Built in 1897 Art Nouveau Gothic style, the church has an information centre, reference library and book stall.

The Third Eye Centre (open daily except on Mondays: admission free) is at 350 Sauchiehall Street, in a Grecian building that caused a stir when it was designed by Alexander Thomson in 1865. This is Scotland's largest, liveliest contemporary arts centre; a dynamic example of how the city has exploded into the forefront of the arts scene. Founded in 1975, it contains galleries, a studio theatre, a bookshop, cafe and bar. It holds an average of 30 exhibitions a year, usually accompanied by a descriptive publication, and these exhibitions tour internationally as well as nationally. Programmes include drama, dance, music, readings, talks, films and festivals. A visit to the Third Eye Centre jerks you out of complacency and makes you very aware of just how much Glasgow has reinterpreted its sobriquet of "no mean city".

The Regimental Museum of the Royal Highland Fusiliers (open weekdays: admission free) is also in Sauchiehall Street, at number 518. Here you can see uniforms, pictures, medals, documents, photographs, trophies, and memorabilia, going back over the 300 years of the regiment's history.

The Tenement House (open daily in the summer, weekends only in winter: admission, adults 90p, children 45p) at 145 Buccleuch Street, a few blocks north of Sauchiehall Street, is a must for anyone who is interested in the social history of Glasgow. It is a first-floor apartment in a red-sandstone tenement built in 1892, restored to give you a realistic insight into the living conditions of the working-class family who lived here for half a century. There are two rooms, as well as kitchen and bathroom, with the original kitchen range, period furniture and fittings. You can almost see the overworked mother, standing over her "jaw-box" sink, admonishing her brood of children, anxiously awaiting the tipsy return of her man, on payday.

The People's Palace (open daily: admission free) is on the eastern side of Glasgow Green, half an hour's easy walk south-east of George Square, and so called because it was built in 1898 as a cultural centre for the people in the east end of Glasgow. It is a splendid museum, devoted to the story of the city from 1175 to the present, including the growth of trades and industry, trade unions, labour movements, women's suffrage entertainment and sport. Among its many exhibits are the purse and a ring belonging to Mary, Queen of Scots; a bible that belonged to the notorious Archbishop Beaton (see St Andrews, Fife) and an organ built by James Watt. You can see portraits of many famous Glaswegians and there is a cafe and shop. There is also an exotic Winter Garden, with tropical plants and birds.

Glasgow has a number of museums of specialist interest. From the People's Palace, you should cross the river and go south-west to Albert Drive.

The Museum of Transport (open daily: admission free) is at 25 Albert Drive, and is one of the most renowned of its kind, opened in 1964 in huge premises that were adapted from part of the municipal transport works. Most forms of transport are represented, from bicycles and motor cycles and a delightful painted and carved caravan, to six railway engines, some of which are 100 years old. There are trams, horse-drawn vehicles, commercial vehicles and cars. The Clyde room is a shipping gallery with splendid models. Old photographs show you many of the exhibits in use.

Haggs Castle (open daily: admission free) is at 100 St Andrew's Drive, a mile to the west of the Museum of Transport. Built in 1585, and much restored, Haggs Castle was opened in 1976 as a museum for children, although only the snootiest of adults could fail to be fascinated by some of the very imaginative exhibits. You can see a reconstructed Victorian nursery; an 18th-century cottage interior, and period gardens. Children are encouraged to use the workshops for museum-based activities such as spinning, weaving, candle-making and other crafts.

The Museum of Education (open weekdays, with free conducted tours) is in Scotland Street, a short walk north of Haggs Castle. Housed in a Charles Rennie Mackintosh building, the museum has a display of school furniture and equipment over a span of 80 years. Recent complaints that cuts in the education budget will hamper the chances of modern schoolchildren are reduced to laughable proportions when you see the facilities and equipment that were responsible for the education of some of Scotland's leading industrialists, economists, doctors, historians, artists, writers, and academics!

The Burrell Collection

The Burrell Collection (open daily: admission free) is Glasgow's newest treasure attracting many thousands of visitors from all over the world. Only recently opened, it is three miles south-west of the city, well signposted off the main roads and motorways and with a good bus service from all over the city. To appreciate it fully, you should plan to spend a whole day in **Pollok Country Park**, visiting the Burrell in the morning, with a pause for a leisurely lunch in the restaurant there, before going on to Pollok House in the afternoon. You won't enjoy it properly if you try to fit it into a day of general sightseeing.

A specially designed complex in the park houses the fabulous collection of works of art, given to Glasgow by the wealthy industrialist, Sir William Burrell (1861–1958) in 1944. Sir William joined his father's shipbuilding firm at the age of 15 and even then he had begun to collect paintings, against the wishes of his father who would have preferred him to spend his money on more "manly" pursuits! By the time he was 96, he had some 8,000 objects, an average of two acquisitions a week! He was a careful collector, canny in his haggling, sometimes missing an important piece because he refused to pay inflated prices. Ideally, you should take several bites at the Burrell Collection, to avoid aesthetic indigestion.

From outside, as you emerge from your car in the big car park, you see a building that seems to be all sharp angles, glass, red-sandstone and wood, designed to give the best possible light and perspective to the treasures inside. It is beautifully laid out and you feel you are walking out of doors, in opulent courtyards and arcades, as you wander through the building. The building has recently won a prestigious architectural award for its design. You will see oriental art works, stained-glass, porcelain, silver, paintings, sculpture, carpets, crystal, and tapestries. There are rooms that have been taken from Sir William Burrell's house, Hutton Castle. The beauty and sheer diversity of the collection plays on your senses and you move from display to display in a daze, marvelling that one man can have collected so much in a lifetime. This is a place you will find yourself being drawn back to time and again, whenever you re-visit Glasgow.

Pollok House (open daily: admission free) is in the same grounds as the Burrell Collection, and is a much older-established show-piece that is now sometimes neglected in favour of its dazzling neighbour. This is a pity. It was built in 1750 and given to Glasgow in 1966 by the Maxwell Macdonald family, including the 361 acres (146.1 ha) of garden and parkland, and it contains one of the finest collections of Spanish paintings to be found anywhere in Britain. There are also many works by other European masters, 18th- and 19th-century furniture, silver, ceramics and crystal. It is a lovely house in a fine setting and should certainly not be missed out.

Outdoor attractions

The Zoo (open daily from 9 am to 7 pm, or till dusk: adults £1.70, children from three years old upwards, £1) is in Calderpark, six miles (9.7 km) south-east of Glasgow on the A74. Here you can see lions, polar bears, leopards, monkeys, camels, deer, elephants, wallabies, porcupines and a lot more besides, making a good outing when the children have grown tired of sightseeing.

The Fossil Grove (open daily: admission free) in Victoria Park west of Kelvingrove, is a place you should not miss. In 1887, when this park was being laid out, workmen, cutting a path across an old quarry, revealed this fragment of a 230 million year old forest. The weird stumps and roots were formed by the setting of mud, within the bark of the trees: trees which, compressed for millions of years, became the coal that fired the Clydeside furnaces in the 20th century. As you stand and look at this remarkable relic, you feel strangely humbled: the worries and stresses of yesterday and tomorrow suddenly seem rather trivial.

The Botanic Gardens (open daily till dusk: admission free) are in Great Western Road, north of Kelvingrove. The gardens cover 42 acres (17 ha), with flowers, trees and shrubs and a famous collection of orchids. The Kibble Palace, a splendid Victorian glass pavilion, houses a luscious collection of tree ferns, and plants from the temperate zones of the world.

"**The Barras**", Barrows (open every weekend from 9 am to 5 pm), at Gallowgate, north of Glasgow Green, is Glasgow's flea-market—internationally renowned. With over 800 traders, selling anything you want from the mass of stalls, barrows and shops all along Gallowgate, the market is a shopper's delight. But you don't have to be intent on shopping: it is wonderfully light-hearted, festive place to idle away a sunny day. You drift along among a noisy crowd, fingering beaten copper pots, leatherwork, straw mats, wicker baskets, silks and batiks, cottons and man-made fibres, polished wood and plastic urns. Stalls, like still-life paintings, piled with fruit and vegetables, jostle with tables of health-foods, cheese booths and fish slabs. You are quite likely to be serenaded by a street performer; touched for a fiver by a conscience-stabbing down-and-out, or have your wallet slid dexterously from your pocket or bag as you haggle over the price of a strip of foam-rubber. For more information, go to 244 Gallowgate, or tel 041 552 7258.

Festivals

While Glasgow does not aspire to anything on the scale of the Edinburgh Festival, it has more than its share of festivals throughout the year and it would not be surprising to find that some of these might move into the front line over the next few years, given the enthusiasm and enterprise mushrooming in the city's cultural pastures.

The Mayfest has only been going for a few years and is already attracting international companies with first class reputations. Drama, music, ballet, opera and art; all flood the theatres and halls and galleries for the month of May, incorporating various side-shoots of a "fringe" character.

In February there is an annual **Festival of Music, Speech and Dance**, at Pollok, providing a launching-pad for plenty of new talent.

The Flower Festival in Glasgow Cathedral takes place at the beginning of June and is a glorious celebration of nature in an ideal setting.

The Glasgow Folk Festival lasts for a week every July, during which time the city hums and vibrates with folk music by groups that arrive from all over the world, especially Scandinavia and northern Europe. Indoors and out, you can hear a reverberating crescendo of folk music of all kinds, with ceilidhs and musical gatherings going on in the evenings.

The Easterhouse Festival is another enterprising parade of drama, music, ballet and opera, at Easterhouse every August.

TOURIST INFORMATION

Greater Glasgow Tourist Board, 35/39 St Vincent Place, tel 041-227 4880. A large and extremely helpful staff will tell you more or less anything you want to know about Glasgow and the surrounding area, in the way of tourist attractions, facilities and accommodation. You can get a free copy of their accommodation brochure and they will help and advise on booking, both for accommodation and for activities and trips.

Municipal Information Bureau, George Square, tel 041-221 7371. You can get any information you want about the city from this useful office right in the centre of the square.

Scottish Tourist Guides Association, 16 Colebrook Street, tel 041-339 5254. For information on guided tours throughout the country.

British Telecom: Dial-a-what's-on-service, tel 041-248 4000. An excellent resume of what's on in Greater Glasgow each week, from theatre to festival, baby show to marathon, carnival to pop concert.

Treasures of Scotland Tours, 3 Silk Street, Paisley, tel 041-887 1143. Good specialised tours of Scotland.

Mayfest Central Office, Mayfest Office, 7 Burgh Hall Street, Glasgow, tel 041-334 3450 or 041-357 3450. For up-to-date information on Glasgow's Mayfest.

WHERE TO STAY

There is a large choice of hotels, guest houses and bed and breakfast places in Glasgow, ranging from luxurious to simple, expensive to cheap, and you should look at the Tourist Board brochure for a full list with descriptions and details. (You can get this from the Information Office in St Vincent Place.) The following is a small selection.

Expensive

Albany Hotel, Bothwell Street, tel 041-248 2656. B&B from £35: categories 6,5,6: 248 rooms en suite. A large, modern friendly 4-Star hotel that won the 1986 Hotel of the Year award. Good food.

Copthorne Hotel, George Square (until recently, The Diplomat), tel 041-332 6711. B&B from £30: categories 5,5,5: 152 rooms en suite. This elegant, listed 18th-century hotel incorporates the house in which Sir William Burrell grew up. It has recently been done up with all the latest facilities. International cuisine with a reasonable table d'hôte dinner or à la carte. You can eat in the conservatory or in the window on the Square Restaurant.

Crest Hotel, 377–383 Argyle Street, tel 041-248 2355. B&B from £30: categories 5,5,5: 123 rooms en suite. A 4-Star city centre hotel with all modern comforts and a friendly staff.

e
Hotel, 7 Park Terrace, tel 041 332 9438. B&B from £22: categories 6,5,6: [illegible] bedrooms en suite. Dating from 1865, Beacons has a friendly relaxed atmosphere and overlooks Kelvingrove Park. Good reasonably priced food.

Buchanan Hotel, 185 Buchanan Street, tel 041-332 7284. B&B from £18: categories 5,3,5: 50 bedrooms, 45 en suite. An old-fashioned Victorian hotel with friendly personal service. The Buonasera is their Italian restaurant, serving Italian and continental food.

Kelvin Park Lorne Hotel, 923 Sauchiehall Street, tel 041-334 4891. B&B from £19: categories 5,5,6: 80 bedrooms en suite. A modern hotel, recently renovated, with a friendly relaxed atmosphere. The restaurant has been designed in the Charles Rennie Mackintosh style, you get good food at a reasonable price. There is also a bar-diner, where you can listen to live folk music and enjoy a decor of "island scenery", complete with boat and fishing nets.

Cheap

Burbank Hotel, 67–85 West Princes Street, tel 041-332 4400. B&B from £15: 36 bedrooms, 26 en suite. All modern conveniences in a splendidly Victorian decor. The staff are friendly, the food very reasonable and you get a full Scottish breakfast.

Central Hotel, Gordon Street, tel 041-221 9680. B&B from £15: 214 bedrooms, mostly en suite. In Victorian surroundings with a warm friendly welcome. Food very reasonable; there is a carvery buffet and you can "eat Scottish".

EATING OUT

As in Edinburgh and any other big city, eating places tend to come and go in popular estimation. The larger hotels mostly have good restaurants where you can eat a set meal or à la carte, and bar meals are usually sold. Ask around for the smaller "in" places. Here are a few suggestions (and remember, it is always wise to book ahead).

Expensive

The Buttery, 652 Argyle Street, tel 041-221 8188. In the style and decor of a Victorian gentleman's club, you can eat well in the relaxed atmosphere of the buttery from about £15.00.

Poachers Restaurant, Ruthven Lane, Byres Road, tel 041-339 0932. Small, privately-owned restaurant in 1870 farmhouse, where you get fresh Scottish produce cooked when ordered: prime meat, fish, shellfish and game. Dinner from £14.50.

Rogano, 11 Exchange Place, tel 041-248 4050. Dating from 1876, the Rogano was remodelled in 1935 when the *Queen Mary* was being built on the Clyde, in classic Art Deco style and is now renowned for its atmosphere. Specialises in seafood. Dinner from £15.

Moderate

The Colonial Restaurant, 25 High Street, tel 041-552 1923. In the merchant part of old Glasgow, the Colonial uses only fresh ingredients: fillet of beef Mod Nan Eilean; fresh shellfish from Seilving Island; fresh chanterelles from Fort William. Dinner from £10.50.

Hospitality Inn, 36 Cambridge Street, tel 041-332 3311. Garden cafe restaurant in American style, or elegant Prince of Wales cocktail bar and restaurant. Dinner from £10.50.

Kensington's Restaurant, 164 Darnley Street, tel 041-424 3662. Small intimate restaurant tucked away in a quiet backwater on the south side of the city. West coast sea-food, venison, game, Scottish beef and lamb. Speciality: Scottish puddings. Dinner from £10.50.

Albany Hotel, see above. Members of Taste of Scotland, the Albany serves good Scottish food in the Four Seasons Restaurant and you will get a good dinner for under £10.00, without wine. There is also a self service carvery with a chef on duty on the end of the carving knife.

Scotts Corner, Kelvin Park Lorne Hotel, see above. A "village in the city", Scotts Corner is popular for its homely atmosphere and live folk music in "island" scenery. Avocado with crab, Loch Alsh scallops. Delicious dinner from £9.

Ubiquitous Chip, 12 Ashton Lane, tel 041-334 5007. Plants, a waterfall, batiks and murals, in a lively cobbled courtyard restaurant. Original and traditional recipes using best Scottish ingredients. Good dinner from £10.50.

Cheap

Baby Grand, 3 Elm Bank Gardens, Charing Cross, tel 041-248 4942. Likened to a New York cafe, Baby Grand specialises in fish and you can get dinner from £5, while you listen to the Baby Grand, whose mood varies depending on the pianist: jazz, soul, blues, requests.

Entresol Restaurant, Central Hotel, see above. In an olde worlde setting you can eat haggis and trimmings, fillet of sole Bressay, whisky cream crowdie. A good Scottish meal without wine for £6.50.

Ewington Hotel, 132 Queens Drive, tel 041-423 1152. West-coast fresh seafood, home made soups such as Cullen Skink, Aberdeen Angus beef. Dinner from under £8.

ENTERTAINMENT

Among the many places of entertainment in Glasgow you will find top class drama, music, ballet, variety shows, etc.

Theatres

Theatre Royal, Hope Street, tel 041-331 1234. Home of Scottish Opera and frequently host to the Scottish Ballet, Scottish Theatre Company, National Theatre, Ballet Rambert and other international companies.

Kings Theatre, Bath Street, tel 041-552 5961. Drama, family entertainment, shows, musical and amateur shows.

Citizens Theatre, Gorbals Street, tel 041-429 0022/8177. Glasgow's Repertory Theatre, opened in 1878 as a Music Hall.

Mitchell Theatre, Granville Street, tel 041-221 3198. Meetings, lectures and amateur dramatics.

Glasgow Theatre Club, in Tron Theatre, 38 Parnie Street, tel 041–552 5961. Actors and musicians meet in a club atmosphere.

City Hall, Candleriggs, tel 041-552 5961. A versatile stage where you can see anything from the Scottish National Orchestra to pop and folk concerts.

Henry Wood Hall, Claremont Street, tel 041-221 4952. In what was Trinity Church, this classical concert hall is the home of the Scottish National Orchestra.

Pavilion Theatre, Renfield Street, tel 041-332 1846. Family entertainment variety, pop, rock, and pantomimes.

Cinemas

Odeon Film Centre, Renfield Street, tel 041-332 8701. Three screens.

ABC Cinema, Sauchiehall Street, tel 041-332 9513. Five screens.

Glasgow Film Centre, Rose Street, tel 041-332 6535. One screen.

SHOPPING IN GLASGOW

You can get anything you want in Glasgow. The main shopping area radiates out from George Square and you will find branches of most of the leading chain stores in the city. Don't miss a visit to the Barras, the market, in Gallowgate, every weekend.

For tweeds, tartans and woollen things, try The Edinburgh Woollen Mill, 72 St George's Place, or Loch Lomond Mill, 61 King Street, or Pitlochry Knitwear Company, 130 Buchanan Street, or The Scotch House, 87 Buchanan Street.

For stylish new collections of fashionable clothes, people are talking about The Warehouse, 61–65 Glassford Street. For trendy clothes, try Graffiti, 63 Queen Street. If you want hand knitted originals, go to Cruise Clothes, in Renfield Street. For shoes and handbags try Sarti, in the Mews Arcade. Bambolini, 165 Hyndland Road, is the shop for fashion-conscious babies. Flip, in Queen Street, specialise in American style clothes. For leather and suede fashions, go to Vous, 425 Great Western Road.

CRAFT CENTRES IN GLASGOW

Laura Grant, 10 Edzell Drive, Newton Mearns, Glasgow. Here you can watch toy designing and manufacture. Tel 041-639 4838 for appointments.

Leading Studio, Clyde Workshops, Fullarton Road, Tollcross, is a stained glass workshop, where you can watch the design, manufacture and restoration of all sorts of stained glass.

Maskot Puppet Theatre, 39b Otago Street. A puppet centre with craft workshop for professional, amateur, community and youth training. You can watch the re-stringing, of marionettes, the carving of wooden puppets, mask-making in leather, latex, celastic and sculpture.

SPECIAL EVENTS IN GLASGOW: 1987

February:	Annual Festival of Music, Speech and Drama, Pollok.
May:	Mayfest.
	European Karate Championships.
June:	Flower Festival, Cathedral.
	Horse Show and Country Fair.
July:	Folk Festival.
August:	Easterhouse Festival.
	World Netball Championships.
	Sports Festival for the Disabled.
	World Pipe Band Championships, Bellahouston Park.
September:	The Glasgow Marathon.
	Coaches Marathon.
5 November:	Bonfire Night Spectacular.

Part V

BORDERS

Dryburgh Abbey

Sweeping views across an undulating checkerboard of fertile farmland characterise the Borders on the Scottish side of the Tweed. Further north, under the brooding shoulders of the Lammermuirs, Moorfoots and Pentlands, you can find traces of Iron Age settlements. In dramatic contrast is the savage coast-line with cliff-hung fishing towns and villages, some of which are little changed since the days when smugglers teemed in the warrens of twisting wynds and closes, evading the excisemen in underground hideaways.

Every inch of this borderland was fought over, bitterly and often, from pre-historic times until the middle of the 17th century: many ruins bear witness to those violent times. Buildings and whole towns were sacked and hastily rebuilt: most settlements were fortified. The four magnificent abbeys, Melrose, Jedburgh, Kelso and Dryburgh, built in the 12th century by David I, and within only a few miles of each other, were destroyed and repaired many times before the Reformation led to their final decay.

It was not just the invading English who caused havoc: the Border Reivers were the powerful border families who warred amongst themselves, raiding each other's territory and stealing the cattle. Ballads and folk tales have romanticised them: in reality they were savage and barbaric.

Textiles, farming and horse-breeding play an important part in Borders economy: the rivers are internationally famous for their salmon and trout.

Much has been written in prose, poetry and song, trying to capture the elusive spirit of the Borders; perhaps Sir Walter Scott, that son of Edinburgh who spent the last years of his life at Abbotsford and made the Borders his domain, wrote most.

The Borderer will be polite to you and hospitable, but you may notice a reticence in him, inherited from his ancestors who were forced to regard all strangers with suspicion and caution.

SPECIAL ATTRACTIONS

The turbulent days of the Border Reivers are remembered today with annual Common Riding Festivals, in several of the towns, each with its own local variation, remembering the days when the men rode out from the town to check the boundaries. These celebrations provide lighthearted entertainment and pageantry during the summer months; they last from a few days up to a week and usually incorporate some special event in local history, as well as a 'ride' when a great cavalcade of riders streams out of the town to 'inspect the marches'. Some of the Border Ridings that you should look out for include: The Peebles Beltane Festival, The Earlston Civic Week, Galashiels Braw Lads Gathering, Hawick Common Riding, Melrose Summer Festival, and Selkirk Common Riding. All are in June. In July are the following: Duns Summer Festival, Jedburgh Border Games, Kelso Civic Week, Innerleithen St Ronans Border Games, Kelso Games, and Lauder Common Riding. The Coldstream Civic Week usually takes place in August.

Game fishing is famous in the Borders. You can get permits and advice from tackle shops, some post offices, sport shops, hotels and the tourist information centres—for river and loch fishing. The Tweed is most famous as a salmon river, but there is an endless variety of both game and coarse fishing, not only on the tributaries, like the Ettrick, Teviot, Whiteadder and Till, but in many smaller streams and lochs. The Scottish Tourist Board publishes a book *Angling in the Scottish Borders*, which you can get for 75p from any of its information offices. It also has a useful leaflet, *Discover Scotland, Fishing,* available free from any of its offices. For further information about fishing see p. 35.

Riding is good in the Borders, the country being well suited to it and Borderers being knowledgeable horse breeders. Ask in your hotel or go to the local tourist information office for details. Most tourist maps show riding centres, marked with a horse shoe. See also p. 37.

Walking is rewarding in the Borders, with an endless choice of lovely routes, both lowland-riverside, and upland, but not too challenging.

Golfers will find plenty of good courses throughout the region. Sub-aqua divers should go to St Abbs Head, one of Scotland's most famous stretches of coast line for diving. Going south to Eyemouth you will find wonderful marine life in clear water. In places it is shallow—40 ft (12.2 m) or so—and therefore ideal for beginners. The weather can be variable here and it is sometimes necessary to wait around for calm.

TOURIST INFORMATION

The tourist offices in the Borders region are generally only open in the tourist season. If you want any information during the closed season, or wish to get hold of any of the brochures, write to the Edinburgh Tourist Information and Accommodation Service, Waverley Market, Princes Street, Edinburgh, tel 031-557 2727.

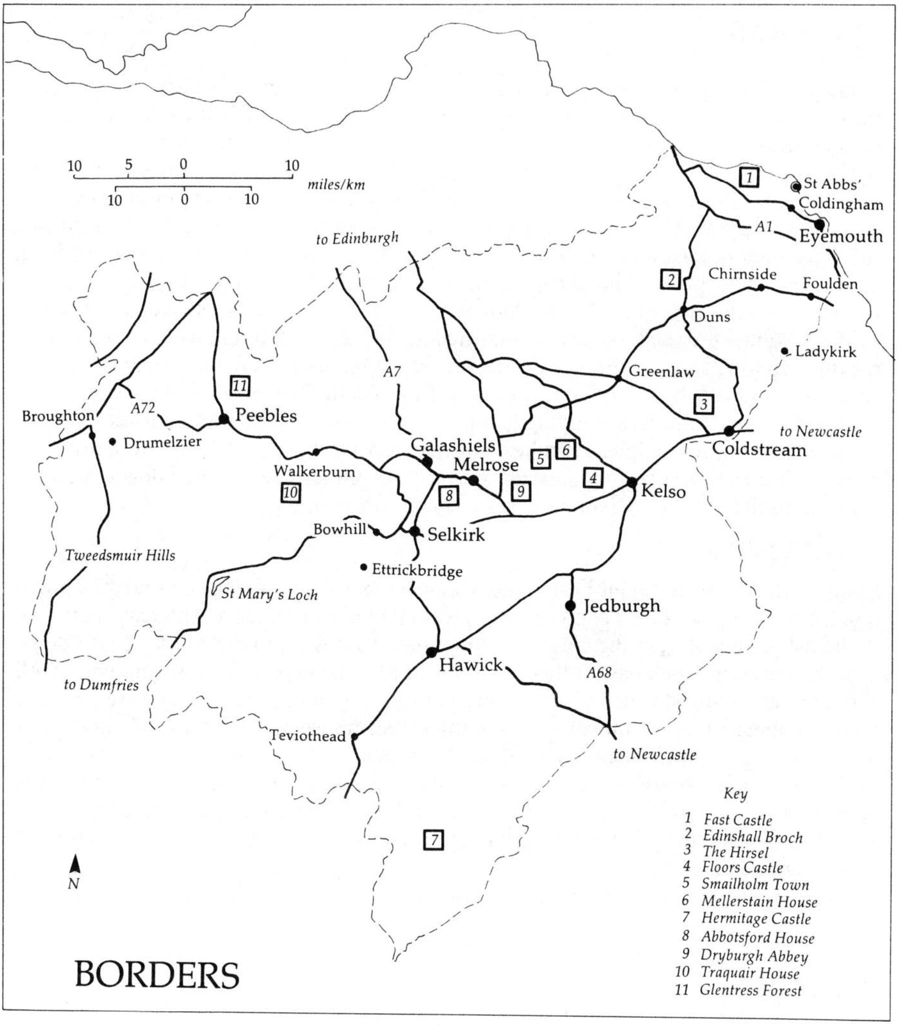
10 5 0 10
10 0 10
miles/km
to Edinburgh
St Abbs'
Coldingham
A1
Eyemouth
Chirnside
Foulden
Duns
Ladykirk
Greenlaw
A7
Broughton
A72
Peebles
Drumelzier
to Newcastle
Coldstream
Galashiels
Melrose
Walkerburn
Kelso
Bowhill
Selkirk
Ettrickbridge
Tweedsmuir Hills
St Mary's Loch
Jedburgh
Hawick
A68
to Dumfries
Teviothead
to Newcastle
N
BORDERS
Key
1 Fast Castle
2 Edinshall Broch
3 The Hirsel
4 Floors Castle
5 Smailholm Town
6 Mellerstain House
7 Hermitage Castle
8 Abbotsford House
9 Dryburgh Abbey
10 Traquair House
11 Glentress Forest

The coast and north-east corner

Eyemouth

Fishing and smuggling played an important part in forming the characters of those whose descendants live along the coastal fringe of the Borders. Not far into Scotland, Eyemouth is a small seaside town with a busy commercial fishing industry that includes the export of shell-fish. When James VI/I (see History) granted it a Free Port Charter, in 1597, it became a thriving centre for smugglers. The intricate design of the older part of the town provided a maze of hiding places and escape routes and many of the houses still have hidden chambers and secret passages: it is said that more than half of Eyemouth is underground. The cliffs around are honeycombed with caves. Even today as you stand on the harbour wall and look out to sea, you find yourself thinking back to Friday 14 October, 1881—a day that dawned too bright and too still, with the barometer reading too low. The fishing fleet sailed out to sea: at noon there was a terrifying dark stillness, followed by a sudden storm—a tornado that devastated the fleet. Many drowned at once; others, struggling home, were smashed on the rocks outside the harbour in sight of their helpless families. Only six boats got back safely; 23 were lost; 129 Eyemouth men were drowned, leaving 107 widows. Other fleets up and down the coast suffered in the same way. Not an event you can easily forget.

WHAT TO SEE

Eyemouth Museum (open Easter and May–October, 10 am to 6 pm, Sundays 2 pm to 6 pm: adults 70p, children and OAP 35p) was opened in 1981 as a centenary memorial to the fishing disaster, in the converted Georgian Auld Kirk, in the Market Place down near the harbour. Look out for the tapestry, a most striking piece of contemporary work with pictures of the storm, sea scenes and the names of all the boats that were lost with the men aboard them. You can also see the wheel-house of a modern fishing boat as well as the fishing and farming history of this region.

Eyemouth Harbour, recently improved and enlarged, is long and narrow and teeming with maritime life. Fish boxes are stacked in open-sided sheds surrounded by all the clutter of the sea: nets and derricks and craft of all sizes and great, ribbed skeletons of hulls propped in cradles.

Gunsgreen House, opposite the harbour, is alleged to have secret passages leading to the water.

Coldingham

Coldingham just up the coast on the A1107, is an attractive, twisting village with the remains of a 13th-century priory, the choir of which is now the parish church. A magnificent arch rises with splendid dignity from the ruined foundations, ancient gravestones and fragments of carved masonry scattered at its feet. Making an impressive foreground to a distant seascape, the priory was mostly demolished by Cromwell in

1648. It bore the right of sanctuary for lawbreakers, the boundary within which they were safe being marked by crosses. If you go down to the beach you can collect pretty coloured pebbles which make unusual ornaments, polished and displayed in glass jars.

St Abbs

St Abbs, a mile (1.6 km) north-east on the B6438, is another pretty village clinging tenaciously to the cliffs, with narrow zig-zag streets running steeply down to the harbour, lined by brightly painted terraced fisher cottages, some of which still have their quaint 'doll's house' sheds in front. St Abbs is a holiday village now, with just a few lobster boats replacing the trawlers that used to go out for haddock, cod and turbot. Boats still come in during bad weather for shelter. Down in the harbour you will see upturned boats, piles of nets, tottering piles of creels and boxes backed by the old stone tackle-sheds. St Abbs has one of the few sandy beaches on this bit of coast.

St Abbs Head is a rugged promontory just north of the village—a towering headland of black volcanic rock, pounded by the sea, with a lighthouse at the tip. Parking is limited at the lighthouse but it is an invigorating walk, across cropped turf dotted with sheep and wind-stunted trees, the restless sea in the background. You can go over the lighthouse at the keeper's discretion. This desolate headland is a wildlife reserve and you can see many different species of sea-bird: guillemots, like a host of chattering waiters; razorbills, with their cut-throat razor beaks and their endearing courting ritual; shags, stretching out their black wings to dry their feathers, and many more. The air is vibrant with their noise.

Fast Castle

Fast Castle, about three miles (4.8 km) to the west, out on Wheat Stack below Telegraph Hill, is a lovely walk along the cliffs, but take care where you put your feet—the path can be hazardous. All you can see now are the tattered remains of what was once a notorious fortress, used by wreckers and robbers, perched half-way up the cliff. You can get down to it from the cliff above if you are careful. Its origins are not known: it was a stronghold of the Home family (pronounced 'Hume') by the end of the 14th century. Margaret Tudor, Henry VIII's sister, stayed there on her way to marry James IV, leaving her entourage of 1,500 attendants at Coldingham Priory. She was fourteen years old at the time. What can have been her thoughts as she stood in her bedchamber, fresh from the magnificent English court, and looked out across that bleak sea with her heavy-lidded eyes. The year was 1503: in ten years time she was to weep for her faithless husband, in an upstairs room in Linlithgow, one of the many flowers of the forest that were 'a' wede awae' on Flodden Field. Fast Castle was the model for Scott's 'Wolf's Crag' in *The Bride of Lammermoor.*

Ayton

Ayton is a cross-road village, south-west of Eyemouth. Here you can't help noticing **Ayton Castle** (open 2 pm to 5 pm on Sundays—or by appointment, tel 03902-212), a vast red Victorian pile, clearly seen from the road. This architectural extravaganza is so ostentatious that it is easy to believe the local legend that it developed from its foundations without plans or architect, its creator crossing the river each day to order the erection of yet another tower or turret or crow-stepped gable according to his mood. This splendid example of Scottish Baronial at its most fanciful, was in fact designed by Gillespie Graham in 1846, on the site of an ancient fortalice that was destroyed by the English in the 15th century.

Beyond the church, near the imposing entrance to the castle, in a graveyard that is a carpet of snowdrops in early spring, are the ruins of a pre-Reformation church. Among these ivy-covered stones, perched above a chattering river, emissaries of Scots and English kings often met to arrange short-lived truces during the years of the border wars. Many ancient bones lie buried far below the present layer of graves in this tranquil resting-place and the huge castle, standing high on the sky-line, seems to intrude like a brash newcomer on the ancient ruin.

Foulden

Foulden, to the south, is little more than a brightly painted row of cottages on a cobbled terrace on one side of the road, facing a green beyond which the land falls gently away to the Cheviot Hills on the southern horizon. The Flemish-style cottages seem to be gazing out over the magnificent view, their gabled eyebrows forever raised in surprise. To the left of the row, in the old school house, the door to the post office is set back behind four delightfully incongruous fluted columns.

By the church you can see a restored two-storeyed tithe barn, with an outside stair and crow-stepped gables, where the minister stored the grain given him by his parishioners as a stipend.

Chirnside

Chirnside, due west of Foulden, is where the racing driver Jim Clark was born and is buried. The church has a beautiful 12th-century Norman doorway on the south wall. Inside you will see a charming plaque, dated 1572, telling you to 'Helpe the Pur'. In 1674, the Chirnside minister's wife was buried in this churchyard, wearing a valuable ring. The wicked sexton, returning at night to rob the grave, tried to hack off the ring with a knife. The corpse sat up, screamed and rushed to the manse, yelling: "Open the door, open the door, for I'm fair clemmed wi' the cauld". (She later mothered two sons who founded the Original Secession Church!)

TOURIST INFORMATION
Aulk Kirk, Market Place, Eyemouth, tel 0390-50678. This is open from April to October.

WHERE TO STAY
(See pp. 23–25 for description of categories.)
Home Arms, Church Street, Eyemouth, tel 0390-50201/50505. B&B from £9.75: categories 1,1,4. A small, family hotel by the sea with ten bedrooms and living-in owners. Shooting parties can be arranged.

Dolphin Hotel, North Street, Eyemouth, tel 0390-50280. B&B from £9.50: categories 2,3,3. A small, family-run hotel by the beach, with six bedrooms. You can get bar meals and there is live music and a beer garden.

Glenerne Hotel, Albert Road, Eyemouth, tel 0390-50401. B&B from £9.50: categories 3,3,2. Small privately-owned comfortable hotel with eight bedrooms, overlooking the port. Home cooking a speciality.

EATING OUT

Contented Sole, Harbour Road, Eyemouth, tel 0380-50268. An inexpensive, cheerful harbourside tavern with a friendly atmosphere.

LOCAL SPECIALITIES

'Eyemouth Pale' is a lighter, more delicate version of smoked haddock, which you can get in all the fish shops. Eyemouth Tart is a delicious confection made with walnuts, currants and coconut.

LOCAL EVENTS

July: The Children's Picnic and Herring Festival, an annual event in Eyemouth.

Duns

Heading inland towards the heart of the Borders you come to the small county town of Duns, straggling uphill from a solid looking church on a green mound with narrow streets behind, where buildings seem to jostle each other, all set at odd angles in no apparent order. In the square among this charming clutter of random buildings stands the Victorian-Gothic town hall, like a matronly dowager frowning reprovingly on the frivolous antics of the proletariat.

SPECIAL ATTRACTIONS

Duns has a horse-show, in May, a Summer Festival in July, which is their Common Riding Celebration and the Berwickshire Agricultural Association Show, in August.

WHAT TO SEE

Duns Nature Reserve is reached by a footpath from the top of Castle Street. It has pleasant walks and a short, steep climb up **Duns Law.** The town used to cling to the south-west slope of this hill until the English completely destroyed it in 1545 as part of Henry VIII's revenge for being refused Mary, Queen of Scots as a daughter-in-law: it was rebuilt in its present position within fifty years. On top of the Law you can see a stone with a hole in it: a Covenanting army flew its standard here, in 1639, awaiting a battle that never took place. Their general, Leslie, is thought to have had his headquarters in the elegant **Duns Castle.** The stone at the castle gate was erected by Franciscans, claiming Duns to be the birthplace of Johannes Duns Scotus, a great medieval scholar who questioned the teachings of Thomas Aquinas.

The Jim Clark Memorial (open in the summer: adults 50p, children 25p) is clearly signposted on the west side of the town. Its trophy room displays the trophies of the world champion racing driver who was killed in 1968.

Manderston

Manderston (open in the summer, Thursdays and Sundays, 2 pm to 5.30 pm: £2.00, grounds only £1) is two miles east of Duns, and is one of the finest Edwardian stately homes in Scotland, with 56 acres of gardens where the rhododendrons are well worth seeing. In the house you can see the only silver staircase in the world: spare a thought for whoever has to keep it clean!

Edinshall Broch

Edinshall Broch is four miles (6.4 km) north of Duns on the north-east shoulder of Cockburn Law and has the sturdy remains of one of the Iron Age towers, unique to Scotland and rare so far south. The twenty to thirty minute climb from a pine wood by the road is clearly marked. You cross a suspension bridge over **Whiteadder Water**, which cascades down over gleaming slabs of granite below you, the sound of its turmoil carrying far across the bleak moorland. Scattered piles of stones on the grassy slopes are relics of those settlers who roamed the desolate hillside with their beasts, huddling for refuge within the tall, double-walled tower, honeycombed with chambers and galleries. The massive walls that you can see were the base of a tapering tower about 40 ft (12.2 m) high, its one passage-entrance easily defended.

Greenlaw

Greenlaw, on the **Blackadder**, is a little town south-west of Duns and has a remarkable church whose tower was built to resemble a church spire but which contained the prison. Known locally as Hell's Hole, it has a sinister grid-iron gate, or yett, and barred windows. Originally the courthouse was also joined to the house as if to emphasise the connection between the Wrath of God, and Justice.

TOURIST INFORMATION
Coldstream, Henderson Park, tel 0890-2607, from April to October.

WHERE TO STAY
Barniken House Hotel, 18 Murray Street, Duns, tel 0361-82466. B&B from £11.50: categories 3,4,4: 4 bedrooms. A Georgian house in the town, family-run, specialising in good food and personal service.

Purves Hall Hotel, Greenlaw, tel 089084-558. B&B from £18: categories 5,3,4: 8 bedrooms en suite. Fully licensed, beautiful hotel set in ten acres of peaceful countryside. Ideal for family holiday, with swimming and tennis in the grounds.

Castle Hotel, Greenlaw, tel 03616-217. B&B from £12: categories 4,5,5. Built as a coaching inn in 1835, Georgian style in the heart of the village. Friendly, family-run hotel with good food.

EATING OUT
Purves Hall Hotel (see above) specialises in local fish, meat and game, with excellent smoked-fish creams. Dinner from £10.

Whitchester Christian Guest House, near Duns, tel 03617-271. Has no licence, but the home-made soups and local-produce dishes are good. Dinner from about £5.

Coldstream

Literally a border town Coldstream clings to the banks of the Tweed, seeming to ignore the rumble and grind of the traffic that thunders continually up its narrow main street. The Tweed, winding through its broad valley, casts a spell over this area, each bend and pool and cascade having its own special character and beauty. The fast, dark currents slide and whirl seawards carrying memories of the past when the mingled blood of Scots and English so often stained the water. Coldstream was the first place where it was easy to cross the river: many armies passed this way and camped on the banks.

SPECIAL ATTRACTIONS
The Common Riding Celebrations take place at the beginning of August, during Coldstream Civic Week. There is also the Borders Country Fair at The Hirsel, every June.

WHAT TO SEE
If you walk out across the bridge to the middle you can see a plaque marking the spot where Robert Burns, Scotland's best loved romantic poet, first put a foot across the border into England in 1787.

On the north side of the bridge is a tiny "marriage house", much used by fugitive lovers from England in the 18th century. The figure in a frock-coat, just beyond, who stands Nelson-like on a fluted column, dispatch papers in hand, lightening-conductor pointing heavenwards from the back of his head, was a popular Victorian MP—Charles Marjoriebanks.

Henderson Park is a formal garden overlooking the river off the Main Street. Look for the engraved stone, erected by the Coldstream Guards, recording how, in 1660, their predecessors crossed the Tweed nearby, following their beloved General Monk, to crush Cromwell and establish Charles II on the throne. Although they were not raised here, they later adopted their title of Coldstream Guards in honour of this historic event.

General Monk's Headquarters (open in the summer every afternoon except on Mondays: adults 35p, children 15p) is a small museum in the town's asymmetrical "square". It is a simple building, with iron gates across a large door, and it houses regimental and local history exhibits.

Abbey Road leads down from the Main Street to where a Cistercian priory stood for four centuries until it was destroyed by the English in 1545. No trace remains today but human bones were excavated in 1834, some of which may have been the sad remains of bodies that arrived here, piled on waggons, Flodden's dead, brought to the Lady Abbess for burial.

The Hirsel, seat of the Douglas-Home family, is signposted by a white board pinned to a tree on the western edge of the town. The house is not open to the public but you can walk in the park at any time of the year, leaving a donation in the honesty box in the car park. A picturesque stable-yard has been converted into a **Folk Museum**, each stall containing domestic displays under such headings as: wash house; joiner's shop; forestry; archaeology. You can get maps and guides in the information room and there are toilets and a coffee shop.

Ladykirk

Ladykirk, a few miles north of Coldstream, is just a handful of houses surrounding a cruciform church—a pale rose-coloured church that is worth travelling a long way to see. Built in 1500, its solid buttresses, topped by carved finials, support the tremendous weight of an overlapping slabbed-stone roof, and a curiously oriental tower that was added in 1743 by William Adam. The delicate blush of the exterior seems to glow in daylight as if lit from within translucent walls.

James IV was almost drowned crossing the Tweed here and he vowed to build a shrine, dedicated to Our Lady, in gratitude for his survival. Ladykirk was the fulfilment of his promise: a magnificent rarity in a land where the house of God, since the Reformation, is so often grimly austere.

Inside this well-restored gem, a spiral stair leads up to the original living-quarters of the priest, with a small window from which he could watch the altar. James often visited Ladykirk, and he knelt at prayer here before the Battle of Flodden in 1513. Sit in one of the pews for a moment, and you can almost catch an echo of that poignant lament, composed by a woman over two hundred years after Flodden, that enshrines the whole tragedy of the battle.

We'll hear nae mair lilting, at the ewe-milking;
Women and bairns are heartless and wae:
Sighing and moaning on ilka green loaning—
The flowers of the forest are a' wede awae.

TOURIST INFORMATION
Coldstream, Henderson Park, tel 0890-2607 from April to October.

WHERE TO STAY
Crown Hotel, Market Square, Coldstream, tel 0890-2558. B&B from £9: categories 1,3,3: 4 bedrooms. A small hotel with a friendly, relaxed atmosphere.

Lynnside Guest House, 1 Abbey Road, Coldstream, tel 0890-2682. B&B from £7.50: categories 1,2,2. A family-run house in the Market Square close to the museum and only a few yards from the River Tweed.

Hotel Majicado, 71 High Street, Coldstream, tel 0890-2112. B&B from £10: categories 3,3,4. Small, intimate family hotel, personally supervised by owners. First hotel in Scotland on banks of Tweed.

Newcastle Arms Hotel, 50 High Street, Coldstream, tel 0890-2376. B&B from £10: categories 3,3,2: 7 bedrooms. Small family-run hotel with TV lounge, dining room, bar and lounge. Pets welcome. Coach parties catered for.

EATING OUT
Most hotels in this area will give you a good meal, and you can dine well for around £10. Go for the local specialities where they are offered: game, fish, meat and vegetables.

Kelso

Two famous border rivers, the Teviot and Tweed, meet under the walls of Kelso, a compact market town facing south across lush green plains towards the Cheviots. Originally called Calkou (Chalk-hill) Kelso was never strongly fortified, relying on its status as an Abbey town for immunity from attack. However, being on the threshold of Scotland, it was in fact frequently sacked by the English: it was also the last staging post for Scottish armies on their way south. The Old Pretender was proclaimed king in the market place in 1715 and his son, retreating north after his march on London in 1745, stayed here.

In spite of shocking architectural vandalism in the 19th century, when the town hall's piazza was filled in and a monstrous bank was built on a corner, the elegant Georgian square is still very fine, almost Flemish in style, its spaciousness a marked contrast to the narrow streets of most border towns, crammed behind defensive walls.

SPECIAL ATTRACTIONS
The Kelso Races take place in the winter months, from October to April. The Berwickshire Hunt has its point-to-point in Kelso in February, and the Buccleuch and Jed Forest point-to-point takes place in April. April is also the month for the Kelso Horse Show. The Great Tweed Raft Race, takes place in May, followed by the Kelso Dog Show and Kelso Games, in June. Kelso Civic Week, in July, celebrates the Common Riding Festival, and this is followed by the Border Union Agricultural Show, also in Kelso. The Scottish Horse Driving Trials take place at Floors Castle in August, and in September there are the Kelso Ram Sales.

WHAT TO SEE
Kelso Abbey (open at standard Ancient Monument times: admission free) was founded by David I in 1128, the monks having been moved there, inexplicably, from Selkirk. All that can be seen today is the façade of the north-west transept, the tower and a small part of the nave. This was once the most powerful ecclesiastical establishment in the land and one of the most wealthy, collecting revenue from dozens of parishes, manors, granges, mills and fisheries. The infant James III was crowned here in 1460. In 1523 the English began their attacks on the abbey, tearing off the roofs and firing the monastic buildings. In 1545 they completed the work, slaughtering a hundred brave defendants, including twelve monks.

By 29 Roxburgh Street you can see a horseshoe set into the road marking the spot where Prince Charlie's horse cast a shoe in 1745.

The graceful five-arched bridge over the Tweed was built by Rennie in 1801 as a model for the now demolished Waterloo Bridge, two of whose lamps now adorn it.

Floors Castle

Floors Castle (open most days in the summer: adults £1.80, children £1.20), home of the Duke of Roxburghe, two miles (3.2 km) north-west of Kelso, was built by William Adam between 1721 and 1725, and added to by William Playfair in 1849. It is an immense mansion, flanked by vast pavilions, its minarets and cupolas giving it an almost Eastern look and is best appreciated from a distance. A tree in the grounds marks the spot where James II was killed by an exploding cannon in 1460. Inside, you can see a magnificent collection of tapestries, porcelain and paintings.

Floors Castle advertises itself as being the "ancestral home of Tarzan," having been the location of the film "Greystoke". Its more romantic claim to fame is that it was the setting for the formal proposal of marriage by Prince Andrew to Miss Sarah Ferguson, now the Duke and Duchess of York, in the spring of 1986.

Mellerstain House

Mellerstain House (open daily except Saturdays in the summer: adults £1.50, children 50p) in stately parkland eight miles (12.9 km) north-west of Kelso, was partly built by William Adam in 1725 and finished by his son Robert in 1778. It is one of Scotland's finest Georgian mansions, with formal Italian terraced gardens sloping gently down to a lake. In front is a mile-long avenue of giant beeches, oaks and firs. Inside, you can see the original Robert Adam ceilings and plaster work, especially in one of the two libraries. The elegant furniture includes pieces by Chippendale, Sheraton and Hepplewhite. Among the paintings you can see works by Gainsborough, Allan Ramsay, Constable and Veronese.

Smailholm Tower

Smailholm Tower (open daily in the summer except on Tuesdays and Fridays: adults 50p, children 25p) is seven miles (11.3 km) west of Kelso and is a typical 16th-century border peel tower. It stands by a loch on a rocky crag, gaunt and forbidding, 57 ft (17.4 m) and five storeys high, with store rooms below and living quarters above. Walter Scott, who spent some of his youth nearby, was so impressed by Smailholm that he described it in *Marmion*. It seems incongruous that such a stern-faced fortress should contain a museum of dolls and tapestries, until you discover that the theme of the display is Scott's "Minstrelsy of the Scottish Border".

Roxburghe

Roxburghe was once a mighty walled Royal burgh, about 2 miles south of Kelso, so large that in the 12th century, some of its inhabitants had to be re-housed outside the town. This great metropolis was so bitterly fought over and so frequently annexed by the English, that the Scots decided, in 1460, that the only way to keep it permanently from their enemies was to remove it from the map. All you can see today are the earthworks of the castle.

TOURIST INFORMATION
Turret House, Kelso, tel 0573-23464. It is open from April to October.

WHERE TO STAY
Sunlaws House Hotel, Heiton, Kelso, tel 0573-5331. B&B from £28: categories 6,5,5: 14 bedrooms en suite. Owned by the Duke and Duchess of Roxburghe, Sunlaws is in quiet woodland and offers good service, good food and a relaxing atmosphere.

Cross Keys Hotel, The Square, Kelso, tel 0573-23303. B&B from £15: categories 4,5,5: 25 bedrooms, 18 en suite. One of Scotland's oldest coaching inns, completely modernised, overlooking the attractive Flemish-style square.

Ednam House Hotel, Bridge Street, Kelso, tel 0573-24168. Prices on application: categories 5,4,4: 33 bedrooms, 27 en suite. A fine Georgian mansion dating from 1761, in three acres (1.2 ha) of garden, overlooking the River Tweed, yet close to the town centre.

Queens Head Hotel, 24 Bridge Street, Kelso, tel 0573-24636. B&B from £9.50: categories 3,4,3: 10 bedrooms, 1 en suite. An 18th-century, listed coaching inn near the abbey and cobbled square, and the River Tweed.

EATING OUT
Floors Castle, Kelso, tel 0573-23333. In the old stable courtyard and, on fine days, on the verandah, you can get an excellent lunch in a splendid setting. Try Floors game pâte, or the fresh or smoked local salmon. Good home baking from the castle kitchen. Lunches only, for under £5.

Sunlaws House Hotel, see above. Very good food: dill-cured salmon; Eyemouth lobsters; West coast oysters; local game and fish. Dinner from £10.

LOCAL SPECIALITIES
Yetholm Bannock is a very rich shortbread with crystallised ginger.

Jedburgh

Jedburgh lies in the valley of the Jed water surrounded by green pasture land and woods whose vivid autumnal colours are a delight. Its proximity to the border made it the target of many raids and its position on one of the main routes north brought a succession of armies through its streets. Built round its abbey, this beautiful little town is packed tight with history. The men of Jedburgh were renowned for their brave resistance to invasion, defending their town with gruesome tenacity. "Jeddart Handba" a local game played with a hay-stuffed leather ball is said to originate from when Jedburgh (or Jeddart) men returned from a successful routing of the English and played ball with the heads of their victims!

SPECIAL ATTRACTIONS
The Jedburgh Festival is held annually in July, a week of pageantry dominated by the Jeddart Callants—the young men of Jedburgh—who re-enact the Common Ridings of the past. The Jedburgh Border Games are also held in July. In 1987, to mark the 400th

anniversary of the execution of Mary, Queen of Scots, Jedburgh is to hold a Mary, Queen of Scots Festival, from Easter onwards, with a special Banquet at Ferniehirst Castle in June.

WHAT TO SEE

Jedburgh Abbey (open standard Ancient Monument times, except October–March, closed Thursday afternoons and Fridays: adults 50p, children 25p), has a history spanning several centuries. Fragments of Celtic carved stonework, found during the careful and effective restoration of the abbey, suggest that it was built on the site of a 9th-century church that appears in the records of Lindisfarne.

Founded as a priory in 1138, by David I, and raised to Abbey status in 1147, it was frequently sacked by the English, the most devasting attack being by Hertford in 1544 during his ruthless execution of the orders of Henry VIII. It stands now on a green sward, its mellow stone still supporting graceful arches and windows, including the lovely rose window, called St Catherine's Wheel. You can dream of the past in this ruin, on a fine day when the sun picks up the colours of the intricately carved masonry and you can hear echoes of plain-chant in the walls.

Jedburgh Castle (open daily in the summer: adults 10p, children 5p) was built at the top of Castlegate in 1823 as the county prison, stands on the site of one that was built around the same time as the abbey. It was a popular royal residence; Alexander III chose it as the place for his wedding feast when, desperate for an heir, he married his second wife Jolande in the abbey in 1285. It was at this feast that the spectre of Death appeared, prophesying the death of the king: an event that happened six months later when he fell from his horse. Frequently occupied by the English and in fact ceded to them under the Treaty of Falaise in 1174, it was destroyed by order of the Scottish Parliament to keep it from the enemy. It is now the **Castle Jail Museum** with reconstructed rooms showing the "reformed" system of imprisonment in the early 19th century and giving an insight into the social history of those days.

Queen Mary's House (open daily in the summer: adults 50p, children 35p) in Queen Street, is haunted with memories of Scotland's tragic queen. Mary came here in 1556, still married to Darnley, to preside over the Court of Justice at the Assizes. She stayed in this house, reputedly because it was the only one with indoor sanitation. During her stay she heard that James Bothwell had been wounded and was seriously ill at Hermitage Castle, 20 miles (32.3 km) away. Perhaps already in love with the attractive earl, she rode over to Hermitage and back again, all in the same day, to visit him. As a result she became critically ill of a fever from which she nearly died: her attendants opened the window at the crises of her fever, to let her soul fly free. Years later she was to say: "Would that I had died, that time in Jedburgh." Darnley came to visit her while she was ill and when she was better she rode back to Edinburgh with Bothwell, now also recovered, in her entourage. The charming, ochre-coloured house has high crow-stepped gables and a turret stair: the steep roof was once thatched. It has been beautifully restored and is much as it was when Mary was there: you can see the great hall, withdrawing-room and fireplace and the stuffy little room where she lay so ill for a month, near to the chamber occupied by her famous four Marys: Mary Beaton, Mary Seton, Mary Carmichael and Mary Hamilton. Among the fascinating exhibits in the museum you can see one of the rare portraits of Bothwell, done in 1565; a facsimile of

Queen Mary's House, Jedburgh

Mary's death-warrant, signed by her cousin Elizabeth, and her watch, apparently found in the marshy land near Hermitage Castle 200 years after she lost it on her impulsive visit to Bothwell.

TOURIST INFORMATION
Murray's Green, tel 0835-63435/63688, open March to November.

WHERE TO STAY
Ferniehirst Mill Lodge, Jedburgh, tel 0835-63279. B&B from £15: categories 3,4,2: 11 bedrooms, 8 en suite. A quiet, private hotel overlooking the river, with good food, personally supervised by the owners.

Glenbank Hotel, Castlegate, Jedburgh, tel 0835-62258. B&B from £13.50: categories 4,3,5: 9 bedrooms, 6 en suite. A Georgian house in lovely gardens, in a quiet residential area only five minutes walk from the town centre.

Spread Eagle Hotel, Jedburgh, tel 0835-62870. B&B from £8: categories 3,3,2: 10 bedrooms. A small, family-run hotel in the town centre, reputed to be the oldest in Scotland, and claiming that Mary, Queen of Scots slept there.

EATING OUT
Carters Rest, Abbey Place, Jedburgh, tel 0835-63414. Restaurant and bar meals with many traditional Scottish and European specialities. Reasonable dinner from £7.50.

See also under Kelso, p. 105.

Hawick

Substantially built in a fold of the hills on the banks of the Teviot, Hawick owes its prosperity to the thriving textile mills along the river, many with their own shops, and to the well-stocked timber yards in the area. The proud hub of this bustling town is a bronze statue in the High Street, an armoured youth on a charger, holding a standard above his head. In 1514 a band of English troops, looting their way through the Borders, were carelessly camped at nearby Hornshole, knowing that the death-toll from the Battle of Flodden the previous year had reduced the fighting strength of the border towns to nothing but old men and boys. The Callants—teenaged youths—of Hawick rode out in a brave, ragged band, routed the English and returned with the enemy standard.

SPECIAL ATTRACTIONS
The Callants' routing of the English in 1514 is an event incorporated into the week-long festival which takes place every August.

Rugby is the town's ruling passion; Hawick has contributed players to the Scottish International team over many years. The Hawick Rugby Sevens take place in April. In June Hawick holds its Common Riding Festival, and in August the town also holds a Summer Festival.

WHAT TO SEE
Wilton Lodge Museum (open in the summer except on Tuesdays and Fridays: adults 20p, children 10p) in Wilton Lodge Park on the western outskirts of the town shows exhibits related to the textile industry as well as displays of Borders history and archaeology, and local natural history. It also houses an art gallery with monthly exhibitions. William Wallace visited here in 1297 and you can still see the tree where he is supposed to have tethered his horse. The park has walks, gardens and sports facilities.

Teviothead

There is a poignant memorial, nine miles (14.5 km) south-west in the village of Teviothead, on the A7. The memorial is a stone, set into the wall of the graveyard opposite the kirk and it is dedicated to the 16th-century freebooter, Johnnie Armstrong and his band of followers. Armstrong rode up to this bleak and lonely place from Langholm, further south, hoping to win the favour of his teenaged sovereign, James V. He offered the service and allegiance of his men and himself, but the young king, intent on cleaning up the lawless Borders, was not won over. Armstrong and his band were hanged from a make-shift gallows at Caerlanrig to the south-west.

Hermitage Castle

Hermitage Castle (open at standard Ancient Monument times: adults 50p, children 25p) is less than ten miles (16.1 km) south of Hawick and is well signposted. Stark and indestructable, it stands on a grassy platform surrounded by extensive earthworks, an angular fortress with fierce, frowning arches. On all sides, bleak moorland rises in peaks from where watch could be kept in all directions, including across the border into England. Even in sunshine, with the swift, sparkling Hermitage Water at its feet, it has a grim aura about it. A 14th-century tower, built round a small courtyard can still be seen with the later additions of massive square towers and walls set with holes and corbels that once supported a continuous walkway, high on the exterior walls, reached through rectangular doorways. Close by are the ruins of St Mary's Chapel and traces of the medieval village that grew up round the castle.

Legends of such horror and cruelty surround this melancholy lump of history that it is no wonder locals believed the weight of its iniquities would eventually cause it to sink into Hades, though it shows no sign of doing so yet.

The first man to build on the site, was Nicholas de Soulis, in the 13th century. He was so cruel and evil that his neighbours and servants carted him off to **Ninestone Rig**, a mile to the north-east, wrapped him in a sheet of lead, and boiled him to death.

The 11 ft-long grave that you can see outside the walls of the little kirkyard which lies beyond the castle, is believed to contain the mortal remains of the Cout of Keilder, a giant baron who came to Hermitage to slay de Soulis. He was drowned by his intended victim, in a deep pool in the river that is still known as Cout of Keilder Pool. A "gallant Scottish patriot", Alexander Ramsay of Dalhousie, was lowered into the pit-prison that you can still see in the castle. He existed for many days on a trickle of grain that fell from the granary above, but eventually he starved to death.

Mary, Queen of Scots came to Hermitage Castle to visit Bothwell when he lay wounded in a room above the bakehouse, after a battle. One can see her, galloping across the moors, flinging herself from her horse, running up the spiral stair and bursting impetuously into her lover's room. She could only stay to comfort him for a short time before hurrying back to Jedburgh, perhaps already aching from the fever that nearly killed her.

WHERE TO STAY

Teviotdale Lodge Country Hotel, Commonside, Hawick, tel 045085-232. B&B from £15: categories 4,4,4: 8 bedrooms, 4 en suite. A family-run hotel with traditional Scottish food and comfort.

Mansfield House Hotel, Weensland Road, Hawick, tel 0450-73988/73207. B&B from £18: categories 5,4,5: 10 bedrooms, 8 en suite. A country house hotel in ten acres (4 ha) of ground, a mile (1.6 km) from the town centre.

Elm House Hotel, 17 North Bridge Street, Hawick, tel 0450-72866. B&B from £12: categories 5,4,5: 15 bedrooms, 11 en suite. A comfortable, friendly, family-run hotel near the town centre.

The Buccleuch Hotel, 1 Trinity Street, Hawick, tel 0450-72368. B&B from £13: categories 4,4,4. 17 bedrooms, 5 en suite. A comfortable family-run hotel, with colour TV. Tea and coffee making facilities in the bedrooms and good home cooking.

Borthaugh House Hotel, Hawick, tel 0450-75379. B&B from £17.50: categories 3,3,5: 5 bedrooms, 2 en suite. A Victorian mansion built for the Duke of Buccleuch, in extensive grounds.

EATING OUT

The Old Forge, Newmill on Teviot, tel 0450-85298. A converted blacksmith's forge where the atmosphere is unhurried and friendly. You will get a very reasonable meal here from a fixed-price menu.

LOCAL SPECIALITY

Teviotdale, or Benalty Pie is a delicious savoury batter pudding.

Selkirk

Selkirk means "kirk-of-the shieling", a peaceful, rural connotation that no longer applies to this sturdy little town on the hillside above the valleys of the Ettrick and Yarrow, its spires and gables visible for miles, its textile mills tucked away along the river banks. These valleys were once extensive forests, hunting ground for kings and refuge for fugitives. Selkirk men are still called "Souters" (shoemakers) from the days when cobbling was the main occupation: Prince Charlie ordered 4,000 shoes from Selkirk for his barefooted army.

Of the 80 Selkirk men who rode out to fight at Flodden in 1513, one returned, throwing down a captured English standard at the feet of the waiting families in silent tribute to his fallen friends. The standard is preserved in the public library.

SPECIAL ATTRACTIONS

The capturing of the English standard during the Battle of Flodden is an event commemorated during the annual Common Riding Festival every June, one of the most spectacular of these Borders celebrations. **Earlston**, near Selkirk, also have a Common Riding Festival in June, during Earlston Civic Week. In September, Selkirk is the venue for the Yarrow and Ettrick Pastoral Society Annual Show.

WHAT TO SEE

The Market Place, which is triangular, has a statue of Sir Walter Scott on a 20 ft (6.1 m) pedestal in front of the Town Hall. Scott was county sheriff here for 33 years. In the **Town Hall** (open weekday afternoons in summer or by arrangement) where Court Sessions were heard in the days of Sir Walter's jurisdiction, you can see mementoes of him, and of many other famous "Souters".

The Museum of Old Ironmongery (open on weekdays, with a donation box) is off the Market Place, with displays of Victorian and Edwardian domestic articles and the 1910 town ambulance, which can't have been a comfortable ride for someone in the grip of acute peritonitis.

A statue of **Mungo Park**, the 18th-century explorer, stands at the east end of the High Street. He was born four miles (6.4 km) away at Foulshiels and gave up medical practice to devote himself to exploring the Niger, in which he was finally drowned while escaping in a canoe from hostile natives.

The Flodden Monument is just beyond Mungo Park's statue. It is a statue of a standard bearer, with the poignant inscription "O Flodden Field".

At Linglie Mill (open all year: admission free) in Riverside Road, you can watch glass paperweights being made with all their range of patterns and colours.

In the street called **West Port**, look for the plaque over a shop doorway, marking where Montrose lodged in 1645 before his defeat at the battle of Philiphaugh. After the battle, General Leslie and his bloodthirsty Covenanter army butchered the remains of Montrose's army, including hundreds of women and children, without mercy, in the name of their God.

Newark Castle

Newark Castle, four miles (6.4 km) west of Selkirk (which you can see on application to the Buccleuch Estates) is where a hundred of these luckless victims were shot. Even without its grim history—and you find yourself looking for bloodstains and shot-scars on the walls, and listening for the echo of the screams—it is an impressive ruin. It stands five storeys tall, a tower house within a curtain wall on a green mound above the fast flowing river, was once a royal hunting seat for the Forest of Ettrick, with the 15th-century arms of James I on the west gable. This castle was the setting for Walter Scott's *Lay of the Last Minstrel.*

Bowhill

Bowhill (open daily in the summer, except Fridays: adults £2, children 75p) is on the way to Newark. It is the home of the Scotts of Buccleuch, built about 1785, a sumptuous Georgian mansion surrounded by lovely wooded hills that dazzle the eye in autumn. Here you can see, in a truly gracious setting, works of art that include paintings by Leonardo da Vinci, Gainsborough, Reynolds, Claude, Canaletto, Guardi and Raeburn; proof copies of books by Walter Scott; relics of the Duke of Monmouth, and a good deal more. There is an adventure playground in the park and nature trails, as well as a gift shop and a tea-room. There is also pony-trekking.

St Mary's Loch

St Mary's Loch, 14 miles (22.5 km) south-west of Selkirk, is a delightful three mile stretch of reed-fringed water among gentle hills, a popular spot for sailors and for fishermen. You can stop for refreshment at **Tibbie Shiel's Inn**, on the southern shore of the loch, called after the innkeeper who used to serve Walter Scott, Thomas Carlyle, Robert Louis Stevenson and James Hogg (the poet who was Scott's protégé, known as the Ettrick Shepherd). These literary giants used to come here for convivial gatherings. Hogg lived nearby and you can see his statue on the wooded hillside overlooking the inn.

TOURIST INFORMATION
Halliwell's House, Selkirk, tel 0750-20054, open April to October.

WHERE TO STAY
Ettrickshaws Hotel, Ettrickbridge, tel 0750-52229. B&B from £17: categories 4,5,4: 6 bedrooms en suite. This hotel is *very* highly recommended for an unforgettable break. It is a family-owned and managed Victorian mansion in ten acres (4 ha) of peaceful grounds, with fishing if you want it. The food is renowned. If you are lucky, you may persuade the proprietor, Peter Slaney, to play his grand piano for you.

Philipburn House Hotel, a mile (1.6 km) out of Selkirk on the A708 to Peebles, tel 0750–20747/21690. B&B from £22: categories 5,4,5. An attractive 18th-century house in five acres (2 ha) of grounds, with its own swimming pool and a friendly hospitable welcome. You can dine in poolside and garden restaurants, and you will find the hotel mentioned in most major international travel and good food guides.

Woodburn House Hotel, Heatherlie Park, Selkirk, tel 0750-20816. B&B from £13: categories 3,4,5. A country house hotel in four acres (1.6 ha), overlooking Selkirk and the surrounding Borders countryside. It has its own fishing and riding and a miniature farmyard.

EATING OUT

Ettrickshaws Hotel, see above. The food is out of this world, served with great imagination. Dinner from £10.50.

Philipburn House Hotel, see above. Renowned for its food. Try saddle of roe deer in port wine and bilberry sauce, or gratin of langoustine, or Loch Fyne gravlax with dill cream. Dinner from £15.

WHAT TO BUY

Most of the mills in and around Selkirk have their own mill shops, where you can buy lovely tweeds and woollen goods.

Galashiels

Galashiels (Shieling-on-the Gala) is a busy town that concentrates on the manufacture of textiles. Plain and unpretentious, it lies snugly among green hills and fast flowing rivers. Milling since 1622, Galashiels built the first Scottish carding machine in 1790 and is particularly famous for its tweed and woollen hosiery. (The name "tweed", incidentally, comes not from the river but from a printing error by an English clerk employed by James Locke of London in 1829, who misread a blotted work—tweels—on a consignment note, "tweels" being the Scots word for cloth. The internationally renowned Scottish College for Textiles is in the town, launching pad for many aspiring designers.

SPECIAL ATTRACTIONS

Galashiels holds its Common Riding celebrations in June, with the Braw Lads Gathering. The Melrose Summer Festival, also in June, and Lauder Common Riding in July are two other similar celebrations in the area.

WHAT TO SEE

The Galashiels War Memorial is a splendid reconstruction of a peel tower with a death-roll engraved on a bronze tablet set into the wall, serving as a backdrop to a magnificent statue of one of the Border Reivers, sitting on his horse, proud and vigilant. The town crest is interesting and you can see it on the wall of the **Municipal Buildings**. It consists of a fox, reaching up for some plums, with the motto "Sour Plums", and commemorates the incident in 1337 when men of Galashiels disposed of a band of English soldiers who were looking for wild plums in the woods.

Abbotsford House

Abbotsford House (open daily from the third Monday in March to 31 October, 10 am to 5 pm: Sundays 2 pm to 5 pm, adults £1.20, children 60p), lies two miles (3.2 km) to the south-east of Galashiels and was Sir Walter Scott's home for the last 20 years of his life. He bought a farm here in 1811 but was not happy with its name—Clarty Hole—"clarty" being a Scots word meaning dirty, smelly, with certain farmyard connotations; he decided on Abbotsford in memory of the monks from Melrose who used to cross the river nearby. He demolished the farmhouse and, bit by bit, as the money came in from his books, built the house you see today. When financial disaster overcame him his creditors made him a present of the house. Mock Scots Baronial, it is Sir Walter's monument to himself with ideas of design borrowed from many sources: a cloister from Melrose; a porch from Linlithgow; a ceiling from Roslin. Now a museum, it is a compulsory pilgrimage for any true Scott enthusiast. You can see his personal possessions, the rooms just as they were, and the extraordinary range of things he collected; a lock of Bonny Prince Charlie's hair, for instance, and one of Robert Burns drinking tumblers. All the most romantic names in history seem to be represented here, and when you've had enough of nostalgia you can go and inspect the library with 9,000 volumes in it. There is also a teashop serving light refreshments.

Melrose Abbey

Melrose Abbey (open standard Ancient Monument hours: adults £1, children 50p) is three miles south-east of Galashiels, was perhaps the most beautiful of the four abbeys founded by David I in the Borders in the 12th century. Established in 1136 to replace a Celtic monastery at Old Melrose nearby, it was, like its sisters, sacked frequently by the English and as frequently rebuilt by its monks. Much of its mellow stone still remains, soaring upwards, a triumphant harmony of arches, towers and windows, all most splendidly decorated. Don't miss the enigmatic carving of a pig playing the bagpipes. Robert Bruce's heart is buried here in its casket, having failed to make it to the Holy Land. In fulfilment of a vow that he had made to the king before he died, his friend Sir James Douglas cut out his heart and set off to the Holy Land, where it was to be buried. But Douglas was killed on the way, fighting against Moors, in Spain, and the heart was returned to Scotland and buried in the abbey. The Abbey has its own museum with local history and a room devoted to excavations from the Roman fort at Trimontium.

The Melrose Motor Museum (open daily in summer, weekends in winter: adults 75p, children 25p) is near the abbey, and is a private collection of about 20 vintage cars as well as motor cycles and cycles, old signs, posters and memorabilia.

Priorwood Gardens (open daily: admission by donation), belonging to the National Trust for Scotland, are also close to the abbey, and all the flowers you see here are suitable for drying. There is an orchard walk, picnic area, tourist information centre and a shop where you can buy dried flowers.

Dryburgh Abbey

Dryburgh Abbey (open at standard Ancient Monument times: adults £1, children

50p), only five miles (8 km) from Melrose to the south-east, completes the quartet of 12th-century Border abbeys. It is a beautiful ruin, in a loop of the Tweed, its cloister buildings more complete than those of other Scottish monasteries, though little remains of the church itself, which is all in the clean, warm-coloured local stone. In common with the other abbeys, Dryburgh was continually ravaged by the English until 1545 when Hertford, acting for Henry VIII, left it a smoking ruin. It was robbed of its usefulness, but not of its tranquil beauty, or its atmosphere of sanctity. Look out for Walter Scott's tomb, behind a railing, and for that of Earl Haig, the First World War leader. The lovely cedars of Lebanon that throw their shade across the grass were brought back from the Holy Land during one of the Crusades.

Scottish Museum of Woollen Textiles

The Scottish Museum of Woollen Textiles (open weekdays all the year, and daily in the summer: adults 25p, children 15p) is at Walkerburn, half way to Peebles on the A72 from Galashiels. The museum's somewhat uninspiring name houses an extremely interesting collection, showing the history of the wool industry, its development from a humble cottage industry, with the original wool and cloth patterns, through to the thriving activity it is today. There is a mill shop where you can treat yourself to some of the local products.

TOURIST INFORMATION
Bank Street, Galashiels, tel 0896-55551. It is open April to October.

WHERE TO STAY
Kingsknowes Hotel, Selkirk Road, Galashiels, tel 0896-3478. B&B from £22: categories 5,4,5: 10 bedrooms, 7 en suite. A 19th-century mansion house full of character and overlooking the River Tweed, Abbotsford and lovely Borders countryside.

Woodlands House Hotel, Windyknowe Road, Galashiels, tel 0896-4722. B&B from £18: categories 6,4,5: 9 bedrooms en suite. The house was built in 1860 for a mill owner and the hotel is graded as 3-Star by the AA and the RAC.

Abbotsford Arms Hotel, Stirling Street, Galashiels, tel 0896-2517. B&B from £10: categories 3,4,5: 10 bedrooms, 5 en suite. A small family-run hotel, recently renovated. First class home-made food in both bar and restaurant, reasonably priced. Graded 2-Star by the AA and the RAC.

Tweed Valley Hotel, Walkerburn, tel 089687-220. B&B from £14: categories 5,5,5: 16 bedrooms en suite. An Edwardian country house overlooking the River Tweed. Sauna and solarium; fishing and riding.

EATING OUT
Redgauntlet Restaurant, 36 Market Street, Galashiels, tel 0896-2098. Small, intimate restaurant in the centre of the town. Excellent local beef, lamb and fish; home-made soups and pâtes; Scottish puddings and cheeses. Dinner from £7.50.

Tweed Valley Hotel, Walkerburn, see above. Try the Tweed valley game casserole as well as local salmon and trout. Dinner from £6.

Peebles

Flanked by wide greens, the River Tweed hurries on its way through Peebles, a peaceful old town with narrow streets leading to quaint yards and charming buildings with carved lintels. You can still see traces of the wall that was built to protect the town from the ever-destructive English. Cromwell garrisoned his troops here and, as early as the sixth century, St Mungo came to Peebles, baptising his converts from the well that bears his name.

SPECIAL ATTRACTIONS

The Beltane Festival is held every June, stemming from pagan roots, and incorporating Peebles Common Riding of the Marches. The Peebles sheepdog trials are also held in June, a splendid demonstration of the skills of these highly intelligent animals. In August you can attend the Peebles Agricultural Show, and in September there are the Peebles Highland Games, and the Peebles Art Festival.

WHAT TO SEE

The Tweed Bridge, with five elegant stone arches, decorated with ornate lamp standards, dates from the 15th century.

The Chambers Institution (open on week days: admission free) was once the townhouse of the Queensberry family, and was given to the town by William Chambers, the publisher. With the help of a grant from Andrew Carnegie, the institute was enlarged to house reading rooms, libraries, two museums and an art gallery.

Cross Kirk is the 13th-century ruined nave and west tower of a Trinitarian friary, with the foundations of the cloister buildings. When the English burnt down the collegiate church of St Andrew, Cross Kirk was used as the parish church.

Neidpath Castle (open daily in summer: adults 75p, children 20p), a 13th-century castle just west of the town, stands high on a green mound by the Tweed. Its mellow ochre walls, nearly 12 ft (3.6 m) thick in places, withstood the bombardment of Cromwell's troops in the mid 17th century for longer than any other castle south of the Forth. You can still see the pit prison and some of the original vaults and you can climb right up to the roof and look out over miles of wooded hills and valleys. As you walk along the grassy path to this regal castle you may notice a few yew trees. These are all that remain of a once famous avenue (the Neidpath Yews) from which bows were made for crusaders. The majority of the yews were cut down to pay the gambling debts of that debauched old reprobate, "Old Q"—William Douglas, Duke of Queensberry, in 1795. Wordsworth was so shocked by this vandalism that, during his tour of Scotland in 1803, he wrote the sonnet "Composed at Neidpath Castle" starting: "Degenerate Douglas, oh, the unworthy lord ... who sent forth word... To level with the dust a noble horde, A brotherhood of venerable trees."

Kailzie Gardens (open daily: adults 90p, children 40p) are just east of Peebles with a rose garden, fine herbacious border, shrubs, greenhouses, art gallery, shops and a licensed tea room. Here you can walk in lovely woods along a sparkling burn, where the ground is golden with daffodils in spring.

Glentress Forest

Glentress Forest is three miles (4.8 km) east of Peebles with several signposted walks one of which leads to **Cardie Hill Fort**, with its grass-covered ramparts, and another to **Shielgreen Tower**, of which little now remains. At the entrance to the park look out for a trio of tall wooden figures, unornamented and wonderfully graceful in their simplicity, carved from local wood.

Traquair House

Traquair House (open daily in the summer: admission charge), eight miles (12.9 km) south-east of Peebles, dates from the 10th century and is said to be the oldest inhabited mansion in Scotland. The house seems to give off an air of bustling domesticity as you walk round it, that is a pleasant contrast to the museum-like atmosphere of most stately homes. The grey harled walls rise to four storeys with corbelled turrets and a steeply pitched roof, not unlike a French château. Twenty seven monarchs have visited Traquair, notably Mary, Queen of Scots, with Darnley and their infant son, whose cradle you can see.

The "Bear Gates" that bar the entrance to the avenue were clanged shut in 1796 by the staunch Jacobite laird, and will never be re-opened until a Stuart rules Scotland again. At one time the Tweed ran so close to the house that its owner could fish for salmon from his windows: finding, however, that he could also swim in his cellars, James Stuart, the 17th-century laird, diverted the course of the river so that it now flows a quarter of a mile away. The grounds offer woodland walks, a maze, craft workshops and exhibitions. Ale is still produced in the 18th-century brewhouse and there is an annual Traquair Fair, in August.

Dawyck House Gardens

Dawyck House Gardens (open daily in the summer: admission 50p a car), eight miles (12.9 km) south-west of Peebles, were created by Sir James Nasmyth in 1720, under the influence of his mentor Linnaeus, a great Swedish botanist. Here you can walk among rare trees and shrubs from all over the world, twisting and climbing until you come to a pretty Dutch bridge over a waterfall.

Drumelzier

Drumelzier, nine miles (14.4 km) south-west of Peebles, is one of the legendary sites of Merlin's grave, Britain's most elusive magician. Thomas the Rhymer, the 13th-century seer, said: "When Tweed and Powsail meet at Merlin's grave, England and Scotland shall one monarch have." The day Elizabeth I died, when James VI of Scotland inherited the English throne also, the River Tweed burst its banks and flooded across Drumelzier into the neighbouring Powsail. This seems conclusive proof!

Broughton

Broughton, ten miles (16.1 km) south-west of Peebles, is a village in the valley of Biggar

Water, below layers of gentle rounded hills. **Broughton Place** is a treasure which you might miss if you aren't looking out for the signs, up a steep drive. It is a 20th-century castle, designed by Sir Patrick Spence in the 1930s, in the style of the Border fortresses. It looks startlingly authentic against its background of blue-grey hills and inside is a first class **Art Gallery** which you can visit in the summer. Many contemporary artists and craftsmen show their work here and if you are lucky you may see some of the outstanding watercolours painted by its father-and-son proprietors, Ian and Graham Buchanan-Dunlop.

TOURIST INFORMATION

Chambers Institute, Peebles, tel 0721-20138. It is open April to October.

WHERE TO STAY

Cringletie House Hotel, Eddleston, Peebles, tel 0721-3233. B&B from £21: categories 4,4,4: 18 bedrooms, 11 en suite. A privately owned, personally run hotel two miles out of Peebles with wonderful views from all the rooms. BTA commended and recommended by all main tourist guides.

Drumore Guest House, Venlaw High Road, Peebles, tel 0721-20336. B&B from £8: categories 2,2,2: 3 bedrooms. A hillside house with panoramic views.

Peebles Hotel Hydro, Innerleithan Road, Peebles, tel 0721-20602. B&B from £20: categories 5,5,4: 139 bedrooms en suite. The hotel stands in 30 acres and has a swimming pool, jacuzzi, saunas, solaria, gym, games room for badminton, tennis and squash, golf, riding, pitch-and-putt.

EATING OUT

Cringletie House Hotel, see above. Scottish meat and fish with fresh vegetables and fruit. Lunch from £7.50, dinner from £10.

Drumore Guest House, see above. Fresh local meat and fish: Scottish dishes. Dinner from £7.50.

Peebles Hotel Hydro, see above. Good Scottish meat and fish. Smoked salmon. Lunch from £7.50, dinner from £10.

Beechwood Tea Room and Country Shop, West Linton, tel 0968-82285. Scottish breakfasts a speciality. Local meat and game; Scottish cheese and local vegetables. Lunch and dinner from £5.

The Old Bakehouse Tearoom, Main Street, West Linton. (Unlicensed) open 10 am to 5.30 pm. Everything is home-made: soups, steak pie, tarts, scones, doughnuts, shortbread, macaroons. From £5.

CRAFTWORK IN THE BORDERS

Many of the old crafts are being revived in Scotland and some new ones are developing. In a number of the workshops and studios the public are welcome to go and see the work in progress, often giving a fascinating insight into how things are created.

The people listed below are all happy to see you and you can often buy the finished products. It is best to ring first if there is a telephone number.

Ceramics

Cushat Ceramics, The Smithy House, Stichill, Kelso, tel 0573-7204. Slipcast and pressmoulded animals, in stoneware.

George Nitsche, Duns Pottery, 57 Castle Street, Duns. Stoneware, earthenware, domestic and decorative.

Thom McCarthy, Ettrickbridge Pottery, Main Street, Ettrickbridge, tel 0750-5247. Handthrown porcelain and stoneware pottery.

The Kelso Pottery, The Knowes, Kelso, tel 0573-24027. Domestic stoneware pottery: throwing, glazing, decorating in rich colours.

Oxnan Pottery, Oxnan, Jedburgh, tel 0835-4217. Hand thrown domestic and garden pots.

Pentland Ceramics, 2 Roxburgh Mill, Kelso, tel 0573-5294/5211. Stoneware pottery, tableware and individual pots.

Glass making

Lindean Mill, Galashiels, tel 0750-20173. Hand-blown glass.

Liz Rowley, Dod Mill House, by Lauder, tel 05782-335. All stages of glass cutting, leading, soldering, puttying for stained glass work, mirrors, boxes, windows, also copper foil work.

Knitwear and Crotchet

Denholm Knitwear, Denholm Village, Hawick, tel 0450-87332. Fully fashioned knitting on frames and machines, including some Fair Isle.

Glenavan of Tweeddale, 4 Traquair Road, Innerleithen, tel 0896-830894. Hand manufacture of knitted garments, design, assembly and finishing.

Nether Mills, Huddersfield Street, Galashiels, tel 0896-2091. Pure wool tweeds, tartans and knitwear.

Macramé and Embroidery

Mary Johnstone, Palace, Crailing, near Jedburgh, tel 0835-5225. Embroidery in metal threads, silk and wool. Vestments.

Weaving

Lesley's Weaving Workshop, 8 Newby Court, School Brae, Peebles Handwoven cushions, scarves, rugs, jackets, handspun sweaters—mohair and Shetland.

Woodwork

Monteviot Woodcraft, Tower Workshop, Harestane Mill, near Jedburgh, tel 0450-87446. Woodturned articles made from locally grown hardwood.

Mossburnford Woodcraft, The Smiddy Workshop, Jedburgh, tel 0835-4296. Wide range of woodworking, making furniture and ornaments.

Pinecraft, Unit 2 Burnfoot Annex, Hawick, tel 0450-8335. Household furniture handmade in pine, mahogany or oak.

Whim Looms, Whim Square, Lamancha, West Linton. Hand-weaving looms, woven rugs.

Basketmaking
Sheaf House Craft Studio, Sheaf House, Allanton, Duns, tel 0361-981 550. Basket making in cane and willow.

Part VI

DUMFRIES AND GALLOWAY

Henry Moore's King and Queen

You will find every sort of land- and seascape in this south-western corner of Scotland: machair, around the Solway Firth and the estuaries; dramatic cliffs and rocks on the Rinns of Galloway; lochs and rivers cutting deep valleys through forest and farmland; bleak, high moorland inhabited only by sheep. Bluebells and gorse, saxifrage and broom, paint a blue and yellow landscape, giving way to checkered greens and browns in the uplands. This lovely region enjoys some of the mildest weather in the whole of Britain; parts of the coast rival the Mediterranean and gardens with palms and sub-tropical plants are not uncommon. But if you go and stand on the Mull of Galloway in a south-westerly gale, or climb into the hills round Wanlockhead in winter, you will feel a long way from the tropics.

Galloway is derived from the Gaelic *gallgaidhel*—land of the stranger. It was here, early in the 6th century, that the Celtic Christian Scots from Ireland landed, driving out the aboriginal Picts, before moving northwards and establishing the kingdom of Dalriada. Earlier than that, St Ninian brought the first message of Christianity to Whithorn, in AD 397. Many churches and abbeys were built in the area, becoming places of pilgrimage for monarchs of Scotland and for people travelling from distant lands. Frequent wars, the Reformation and Henry VIII's "Rough Wooing" in the 16th century, reduced most of these to ruins, but you can still see the shells of their former splendour today.

Towns near the border suffered their share of hammering from the English and settlements on the coast had to be fortified against invasion from the sea. The hills and remote places saw bloody battles between government armies and Covenanters in the 17th century, with dreadful atrocities being committed by both sides.

Apart from the extreme east, this is an isolated corner, off the main route to anywhere else, closer to Ireland than to much of the rest of Scotland, attracting little industry, cut off by hills to the north and east, and by the sea to the west and north. Fishing and farming are important to the economy. In early days smuggling was rife, providing employment for Robert Burns, among others, who spent his last years in Dumfries as an exciseman.

The people reflect their history: they have the gentle courtesy of the Celt, the self-reliance of country people, the blarney of Ireland and the pride of all Scots.

SPECIAL ATTRACTIONS

As in the Borders, some of the town and villages that lie close to the border with England have annual Common Riding celebrations, in memory of the days when the men used to go out and check the marches, to make sure that no Border Reiver had been at work, stealing the cattle. These festivals last for up to a week and incorporate events in local history, as well as plenty of pageantry and entertainment. In June there is Dumfries' Gude Nychburris Festival, and Lockerbie's Common Riding Festival. In July there is Annan's Riding of the Marches and Moffat's Gala Week, and Langholm's Common Riding Festival. Sanquhar has a similar festival in August.

Apart from sightseeing, Dumfries and Galloway is an ideal place for sailing and all kinds of water sports, including water-skiing and wind-surfing; fishing; golf; riding and birdwatching. There are also many marvellous walks, both coastal and inland, forest and hill-walking. Your hotel will advise you on where to go for any of these activities, or the local tourist information office.

TOURIST INFORMATION

If the tourist information office is closed in the off season, you can get information, advice and brochures from the Scottish Tourist Board, 23 Ravelston Terrace, Edinburgh EH4 3EU, tel 031-332-2433.

From East to West

Gretna Green

Coming from England, on the A74, you cross the Scottish border into Dumfries and Galloway at Gretna Green. From the romance that has grown up around this famous village it is difficult to untangle the squalid reality of an era when a great many innocent females were duped by men whose ambitions could not stand the test of a formal betrothal with parental consent. Runaway lovers, cheated of "irregular marriages" in England by the 1754 Hardwicke Marriage Act, were able to cross the border until 1856 and be married by declaration, before a witness. Even in the 20th century couples came north because until the Age of Consent was altered in 1969, Scotland was the only place where parental consent was not required after the age of 16. The border villages of

Gretna and Springfield, now by-passed by the A74, vied with each other for the considerable profit that could be made from these often disastrous unions. Today they continue to exploit them by displaying the marriage houses where the ceremonies took place. Springfield lost its trade to Gretna in 1830, when the building of the Sark Bridge caused it to be by-passed by the main north–south route.

WHAT TO SEE

The Old Blacksmith Shop, or Smithy, at Gretna (open all the year: admission 20p) has a museum where you can see the marriage room, anvil, and many photographs and documents relating to those days.

Prince Charlie's Cottage is a little house by Gretna Green Kirk thought to be where the prince spent a night in 1745 after his march south.

Solway Moss is just north of Gretna, on the border. It is an inhospitable wasteland of bog. In 1542, James V lost his army in battle here, against the English, many of them perishing in the treacherous marsh as they tried to retreat. James died soon afterwards, it is said, of despair.

The Clochmaben Stone is on the shore of the Solway Firth not far south of Gretna. It weighs at least ten tons (10.2t) and is thought to be the remains of a stone circle, possibly connected with a shrine to Maponos, god of youth and music: a very appropriate trysting place for runaway lovers! Fairs were held here in the Middle Ages and it was the site where border disputes were discussed and settled, under daylight truce.

Kirkpatrick Fleming

Kirkpatrick Fleming lies three miles (4.8 km) north-west of Gretna, and here you can see a cave where Robert Bruce hid for three months. Accessible now by path, it was then reached by swinging down the cliff on a rope. The cave was originally cut out of the rock by Stone Age man. Locals will tell you that it was here, and not on Rathlin Island, or anywhere else making similar claims, that Bruce took courage from the persistent spider.

Kirtlebridge

At Kirtlebridge, off the A74 three miles (4.8 km) further on, you can see the 15th-century **Merkland Cross**, nine ft (2.7 m) high, with intricate carvings, erected in memory of a Maxwell who was killed in battle.

TOURIST INFORMATION

Annan Road, Gretna Green, tel 0461-37834. It is open Easter to October.

WHERE TO STAY

The Crossways Inn, in the middle of Gretna, tel 0461-38284. B&B from £13: categories 6,6,5: 6 bedrooms. A small, friendly pub.

Gretna Chase Hotel, also in Gretna. B&B from £15: categories 4,4,5: 9 bedrooms. It is slightly larger than the Crossways Inn.

Gretna Hall Hotel, in Gretna, tel 0461-38257. B&B from £11: categories 3,3,4: 116 bedrooms, 62 en suite.

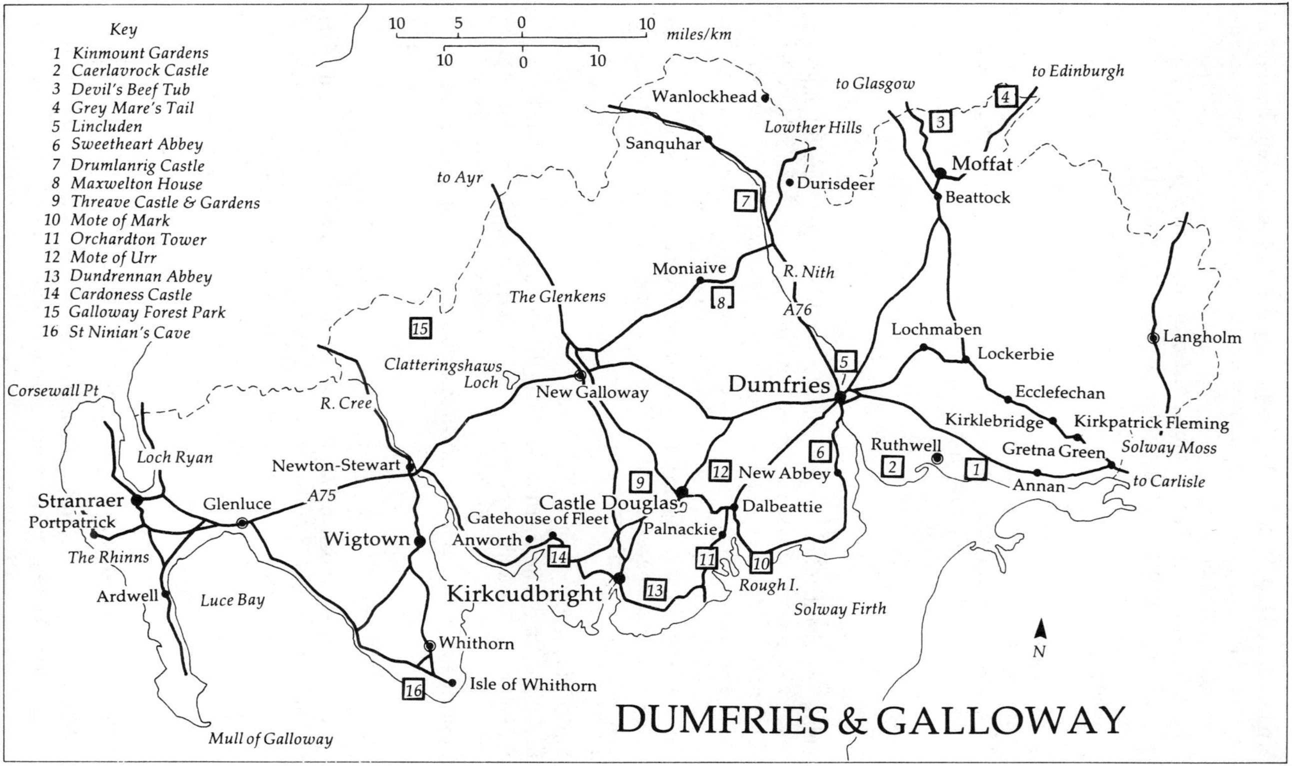

DUMFRIES & GALLOWAY
Key
1 Kinmount Gardens
2 Caerlavrock Castle
3 Devil's Beef Tub
4 Grey Mare's Tail
5 Lincluden
6 Sweetheart Abbey
7 Drumlanrig Castle
8 Maxwelton House
9 Threave Castle & Gardens
10 Mote of Mark
11 Orchardton Tower
12 Mote of Urr
13 Dundrennan Abbey
14 Cardoness Castle
15 Galloway Forest Park
16 St Ninian's Cave
10 5 0 10 miles/km
10 0 10
to Ayr
to Glasgow
to Edinburgh
Wanlockhead
Lowther Hills
Sanquhar
Durisdeer
Moffat
Beattock
Moniaive
The Glenkens
R. Nith
A76
Lochmaben
Lockerbie
Langholm
Ecclefechan
Kirklebridge
Kirkpatrick Fleming
Solway Moss
Gretna Green
to Carlisle
Annan
Ruthwell
Dumfries
New Abbey
Dalbeattie
Palnackie
Rough I.
Solway Firth
Castle Douglas
Gatehouse of Fleet
Anworth
Kirkcudbright
Clatteringshaws Loch
New Galloway
R. Cree
Newton-Stewart
A75
Wigtown
Whithorn
Isle of Whithorn
Glenluce
Luce Bay
Mull of Galloway
Corsewall Pt
Loch Ryan
Stranraer
Portpatrick
The Rhinns
Ardwell
N

Kirkconnel Hall Hotel, a bit further up the A74 at Ecclefechan, tel 05763-277. B&B from £11: categories 5,3,4: 30 bedrooms, 22 en suite. This hospitable hotel is set in a Georgian mansion.

The Riverside Inn, in Canonbie, just over the border on the A7, tel 05415-295/512. B&B from £19: categories 5,3,4: 6 bedrooms en suite. On the River Esk, this great little place won the AA Inn of the Year award, with a rosette for the high standard of its cooking.

EATING OUT

Kirkconnel Hall Hotel, see above. You will get a good meal, reasonably priced.

The Riverside Inn, see above, provides the best value in the area. Its cooking won a rosette, and you can get a very good dinner from £10.

Langholm

Coming into Scotland on the A7 from the south, you go through Langholm, about ten miles (16 km) north of Gretna, a pleasant little mill town where the waters of the Esk, Wauchope and Ewes meet. You will notice two contrasting styles in this town: a narrow, twisting old-town, with its market place and town house, and a more spacious, stately-looking quarter, across the river, developed in the 18th century when Langholm became a flourishing textile centre. The town has its Common Riding celebrations in July, with a great charge of riders through a narrow bend and up the hill from the square—a very dramatic stampede.

WHAT TO SEE

Langholm Castle, now a ruin, was once the stronghold of the Armstrongs, kinsmen of the freebooter Johnnie Armstrong of Gilnockie, around whom several ballads have been woven, and who was finally hanged by James V in 1529 (see Teviothead, Borders). A descendant of this family was Neil Armstrong, first man on the moon in 1969.

Gilnockie Tower

Gilnockrie Tower (open by appointment, tel 0541 80976), once called Hollows, or Holehouse, five miles (8 km) south of Langholm, dates from the 16th century and was one of Johnnie Armstrong's strongholds. Ruffian he may have been, but it is hard not to feel a twinge of admiration for him, as you look up at this romantic tower, with crow-stepped gables and a carved parapet-walkway round the top, standing high above the Esk valley. It has recently been restored.

Craigcleuch Scottish Explorers Museum

This museum (open daily in the summer: or by arrangement with the enterprising founder, Mr David Young, tel Langholm 80137: adults £1, children 50p) is two miles (3.2 km) north-west of Langholm, in sheltered parkland surrounded by trees and shrubs, overlooking the Esk valley. This 19th-century Scottish Baronial mansion contains an amazingly diverse collection of rare objects from all over the world gathered up by early Scottish explorers. Here you can see exquisite carved coral and ivory, African wood-carvings, pre-historic ornaments and implements, Chinese silk paintings, wall hangings, tribal art, hunting trophies and skins. There is something here for everyone and you can even buy some of the pictures. Outside, you can walk and picnic by the river with lovely views through two hills known as the "Gates of Eden" to the north.

Westerkirk

In 1757, Thomas Telford was born at Westerkirk, which is north-west of Craigcleuch on the Esk and here you can see a memorial to this giant of the Industrial Revolution, who built roads and bridges all over the country, serving his apprenticeship on his own local bridges.

TOURIST INFORMATION
High Street, Langholm, tel 0541-80976.

WHERE TO STAY
Riverside Inn, Canonbie (see Gretna Green) a real treat.

Eskdale Hotel, in Langholm, tel 0541-80357. B&B from £11.50: categories 4,4,5: 14 bedrooms, 3 en suite.

EATING OUT
Riverside Inn, Canonbie (see Gretna Green).

Annan

Going west from Gretna Green you come to Annan on the northern shore of the Solway Firth. Although its history goes back a long way, the town was too frequently torn apart in border disputes to show much sign of antiquity today. In 1317 it was recorded that "the Vale of Annan lay so wasted and burned that neither man nor beast was left". If you are lucky, you may see haaf-net fishermen, standing up to their chests in the water, holding out their awkward nets, framed like football goal-posts. Shrimp-canning is one of the towns valuable industries and in the 19th century the beautiful tea-clippers used to be made here. The blind poet, Dr Thomas Blacklock, lived here; a man who did an enormous amount to promote the genius of Robert Burns and who prevented him from emigrating when times were hard. Annan celebrates the Riding of the Marches in July.

WHAT TO SEE
The Brus Stone, which has been built into the wall of the **Town Hall**, is a carved tablet from a castle built by the Brus lords. It is inscribed with the name Robert de Brus, thought to be King Robert the Bruce. This poignant relic was stolen in the 19th century and lost for 100 years before someone found it in North Devon in 1916.

Kinmount Gardens

Kinmount Gardens (open daily from Easter to November: adults 25p, children 15p), four miles (6.4 km) west of Annan, has lovely walks in woods beside a lake, and is especially attractive in the azalea and rhododendron season.

Ruthwell

Ruthwell (pronounced Rivvel) is two miles (3.2 km) further west. Stop off at the church and in an apse built specially for it, you will find the 7th-century **Ruthwell Cross**, one of Scotland's greatest treasures, with incredibly clear sculpted figures and vine scrolls and birds and animals. The Runic inscriptions, the longest and perhaps oldest known in Britain, have been deciphered by scholars and are extracts from a devotional poem, "The Dream of the Rood", the oldest poem in the English language, written by 7th-century Northumbrian poets. The arms of the 18 ft high cross are modern, but this in no way detracts from the awe-inspiring grace and charm of this ancient relic. The reason why it is so well preserved is that it was buried some time in the 17th century by the minister, to protect it from the rabid iconoclasm of the Presbyterian reformers. The man who discovered the hidden cross and re-erected it was Rev Henry Duncan, who also established Scotland's first savings bank, in Ruthwell in 1810. The cottage where this first bank was founded is now a **Museum** (open all the year round: admission free) at which you can learn all about the early days of the savings bank movement.

The National Nature Reserve, lies beyond Ruthwell, between the mouth of the Nith, and Lochar Water. It is 13,594 acres (5,501 ha) of wild salt-marsh and mud-flats, a marvellous sanctuary if you are a nature-lover. It is the most northerly breeding ground of the Natterjack toad, an endearing little fellow whose hindlegs are too short to let it hop, so it has to run. You can visit the reserve all year round.

Caerlavrock Castle (open at standard Ancient Monument times: adults 50p, children 25p) is a massive triangular-shaped ruin on the western edge of the nature reserve, its shape governed by *that* of the rock on which it was built just a few feet above the high-tide level at the mouth of the Nith. Aptly described by a medieval monk as 'shield-shaped' the castle managed to hold off 3,000 English troops under Edward I for two days, in 1300, defended by only 60 men. Adding considerably to its impregnability, it is surrounded by treacherous sinking-mud and swampland. Built in 1290, the castle was a Maxwell stronghold and it has an elegant Renaissance interior designed by the first Earl of Nithsdale in the 17th century. There is something very French about its three-storey façade, surrounding the triangular courtyard, decorated with sculpted doors and windows. Sadly, the Covenanters destroyed it not long after the first Earl's improvements. You can still see the Maxwell crest and motto, above the door.

TOURIST INFORMATION
Whitesands, Dumfries, tel 0387-53862. It is open from Easter to October.

WHERE TO STAY
Queensberry Arms Hotel, 47 High Street, Annan, tel 04612-2024. B&B from £20:

categories 5,4,5. A cheerful hotel full of atmosphere in the town centre, offering packages for golf and fishing holidays.

Warmanbie Hotel, Annan, tel 04612-4015. B&B from £17.50: categories 5,3,6: 6 bedrooms en suite, stands in secluded woodland grounds overlooking the River Annan. The bedrooms have private bathrooms and colour TV. Good food and wine and special rates for three nights or more.

EATING OUT

Both hotels above will give you a good meal, at a reasonable price.

LOCAL SPECIALITY

Pinneys, at Brydhill, Annan are high class fish smokers where you can get very good smoked fish pâtes as well as smoked salmon, trout, mackerel, etc.

Lockerbie

Less than ten miles (16 km) north of Annan and now, mercifully, by-passed by the A74, Lockerbie has been an important centre for lamb and cattle sales for a long time. Once a small hamlet, it grew up around the 16th-century whinstone tower, behind the police station, which was the home of the Johnstones, bloodthirsty rivals to the Maxwells. These two families fought each other bitterly and often, the Johnstones habit of slashing their captives' faces being known as "the Lockerbie lick". One Johnstone lady brained a Maxwell lord with the front-door key of her castle!

By the end of the 18th century, Lockerbie was a substantial town, with lamb sales held annually on **Lamb Hill**. These sales were great occasions for the whole of Annandale; boisterous, colourful fairs, with sideshows and booths and noisy, jostling crowds.

WHAT TO SEE

Birrenswark, or **Burnswark** as it is sometimes called, has a distinctive outline which can't be missed. It is a steep, flat-topped hill south-east of Lockerbie visible for miles round. This commanding position was the site of a large fort, many centuries BC, with circular huts inside sturdy ramparts. Along came the Romans, besieged the inhabitants and moved in, leaving the foundations you can see today. It is well worth the 940 ft (286.5 m) climb, not just for the tremendous view you get from the top but for the great feeling of ancient history that you experience, standing among those ancient ramparts and ditches. In 937 a ferocious battle took place here, the Battle of Brunanburh between the Saxon-English and the united Scots and Norse armies, with victory for the English.

Lochmaben

Lochmaben, four miles (6.4 km) west of Lockerbie, is a small town with a history that goes back to the 12th century when Robert Bruce's forebears were powerful, and in fact it is one of the places claimed as the birth-place of King Robert himself. The scant remains of the 13th-century castle, on a promontory at the south end of Castle Loch, is a pathetic travesty of what used to be a 16-acre concourse, with four moats. It was one of James IV's favourite places in the 16th century though his preferences were often influenced by whatever female charms were available in the area. Mary, Queen of Scots came here with Darnley and it is said that she introduced the "vendace" to the lochs. These are small rare fish that are considered a great delicacy and have to be netted because they won't take bait. A lot of the buildings in Lochmaben were built with stone from the ruined castle.

Spedlins Tower

Spedlins Tower, now a ruin, is three miles (4.8 km) north of Lochmaben. It was once haunted by a rather gruesome ghost. In the 17th century the local miller, Porteous, was locked in the dungeon by the laird who then rode off to Edinburgh, forgetting about his prisoner. Porteous starved to death, eating his own flesh in an attempt to survive, and his ghost haunted the tower until they managed to confine it to the dungeon by laying a black-letter Cranmer bible on the cellar steps!

Rammerscales

Rammerscales (open selected afternoons in May, late August and September or by arrangement in the season, tel 038781 361: adults £1, children 50p) is a Georgian manor house a couple of miles (3.2 km) south of Lochmaben on the B7020. It was built for Dr James Mounsey who was the personal doctor to the Tsarina Elizabeth of Russia in the 18th century. Inside, you can see an elegant pillared hall with a circular staircase, an excellent library and a modern art collection. You can also walk in the lovely grounds.

Ecclefechan

Ecclefechan six miles (9.7 km) south-east of Lockerbie, was the village in which Thomas Carlyle was born in 1795. The **Arched House** (open daily except Sundays, in the summer, or by arrangement, tel 05763 666: adult 60p, children 30p), so called because of its arched gateway, was his birthplace; a pretty, while house that is now a museum. The house was built by his father and uncle and inside you can see a fascinating collection of Carlyle memorabilia, including some of his correspondence with Goethe. This great literary genius who refused burial in Westminster Abbey, is buried below a simple granite slab in the churchyard, an unfussy monument to a brilliant man who loathed ostentation. Among the many things Carlyle wrote was *Sator Resartus* (Tailor Repatched) in which he describes a village, "Entepfuhl" which you will recognise as Ecclefechan. Carlyle's mother learnt to read so that she could decipher the letters he wrote to her.

Moffat

Moffat is an attractive, quiet town 16 miles (25.7 km) north of Lockerbie and bypassed by the A74. The very wide High Street is dissected by a splendid double avenue of lime trees and the **Colvin Fountain**, a cairn of boulders with a huge bronze ram on top, that underlines the town's importance as a sheep-farming centre.

In 1633, Rachel Whitford, a bishop's daughter, tasted the water from a spring to the east and recognised the strong tang as that of sulphur. Within 100 years, peaceful little Moffat, deep in its valley among the hills, became one of the most fashionable spas in Europe, attracting the ailing rich from far afield.

It was here in 1759, that James Macpherson produced his first "Ossianic" fragments, poems that he swore he had "... translated from the Gaelic of Ossian, the son of Fingal". The authenticity of these poems was hotly debated by Dr Samuel Johnson, among others, and although many scholars were convinced that they were genuinely collected from oral tradition, others believed that Macpherson composed them straight from his own head when he was a student.

WHAT TO SEE

The Devils Beef Tub

The Devils Beef Tub is six miles (9.7 km) north of Moffat on the A701. It lies just off the road and the signs will direct you. This is an incredible natural corral, deep among the hills, where Border Reivers used to drive their stolen cattle, hiding them in the black abyss with swirling mist rising eerily from a tiny stream in the bottom.

Grey Mare's Tail

Grey Mare's Tail, one of the highest waterfalls in the country is ten miles (16.1 km) north-east of Moffat. Here Loch Skene pours in a single cascade, 200 ft down into Moffat Water. From the car it seems to hang motionless in the air, but if you approach it, its spray fills the air like mist and the sound of its water becomes a roar. The National Trust for Scotland own the land around the falls, which is beautiful country rich in wildflowers and supporting a rare herd of wild goats. You should be very cautious, walking here, there are some precipitous edges to fall over.

TOURIST INFORMATION
Churchgate, Moffat, tel 0683-20620.

WHERE TO STAY
(See also Gretna.)

The Dryfesdale Hotel, just north of the town on the A74, on a hill, tel 05762-2427. B&B from £20: categories 5,4,5: 10 bedrooms, 8 en suite. It is privately owned and managed, in seven acres (2.8 ha) of grounds, with riding, shooting, fishing and golf available. Egon Ronay and Ashley Courtenay recommended, its rooms all have TV and a telephone. There is an à la carte restaurant and you can get bar meals.

The Beechwood Country House Hotel, off Harthope Place in Moffat, tel 0683-20210. B&B from £19: categories 5,4,5: BTA commended. It has a 2-star rating by AA and was awarded a rosette for cooking. Self-catering also available.

Moffat House Hotel, in the High Street, tel 0683-407. B&B from £15: categories 4,4,4: 15 bedrooms, 11 en suite. It is an imposing Adam mansion in one and a half acres (0.6 ha).

Auchen Castle Hotel, Beattock is a mile north of Beattock on the A74, tel 06833-407. B&B from £15: categories 5,4,4: 28 bedrooms en suite.

EATING OUT

The Beechwood, see above, with an AA rosette for cooking, specialises in local salmon, trout, venison and game, in season. Dinner from about £14.

Auchen Castle Hotel, see above, where you can get dinner from about £10. Uses local ingredients: beef, lamb, salmon, grilse and sea-trout, oysters and mussels, Ayrshire ham and bacon.

LOCAL SPECIALITY

Moffat Toffee Shop, Moffat. This is a first class "sweetie shop", renowned for its delicious Moffat toffee.

Dumfries

Dumfries stands serenely on the banks of the Nith, 16 miles (25.7 km) west of Annan, and surrounded by lush farmland, woods and beautiful gardens. Its history is as blood-stained as that of any border town, its inhabitants known for their brave opposition to invasion. William-the-Lion made it a Royal Burgh in 1186 and it was granted a charter in 1395 by Robert III. Bronze and Iron Age relics have been excavated nearby and it is almost certain that there was a Roman settlement with a Roman road up Nithsdale. Edward I captured the now vanished castle; Robert Bruce murdered Red Comyn here in 1306; Bonny Prince Charlie passed through in 1745. Robert Burns lived and died in Dumfries and described the town as "Maggie by the banks of Nith, a dame wi' pride eneuch".

The name Dumfries comes from Dun, or Drum, Phreas—the fort, or ridge, in the brushwood. The town was home to Norwegian exiles during the Second World War.

SPECIAL ATTRACTIONS

There is an annual Gude Nychburris Festival (Good Neighbours) in June, incorporating many historic events from the past including the granting of the charter and the Border Marches, another of the Common Riding celebrations, incorporating goodwill among neighbours and the crowning of the Queen of the South.

WHAT TO SEE

Dumfries Museum (open daily in the summer and closed on Sundays and Mondays in the winter: admission free) is in an attractive watermill built about 1730 and recently restored in lovely grounds. Inside, in "period" rooms, you can see a wide range of local exhibits: archaeological, natural history; Roman altars, early Christian monuments and costumes and, of course Burns memorabilia. There is a "camera obscura" dating from 1836, giving you an ingeniously reflected bird's eye view of the town and surrounding countryside.

The Auld Brig, a six-arched footbridge above a caul (weir) that was created in the 18th century to provide power for the grain mills, is a successor to a wooden bridge put up by Devorguilla Balliol in the 14th century. (See Sweetheart Abbey, below.) The present bridge dates from 1432 but was considerably restored since the 17th century when floodwater reduced it from nine, or even thirteen, arches, to the present six.

Old Bridge House (open daily in the summer: admission free) at the end of the bridge, dating from 1662, is a folk museum where you can get a splendid insight into life in Dumfries over the centuries.

You might catch the echo of an ironic chuckle from that most earthy of romantic poets, Robert Burns, as you stand in the High Street, in front of Greyfriars Church and look up at the splendidly sentimental statue of him, a white marble Adonis, lounging against a tree-stump, hand on heart, clutching a posy of flowers, his dog resting its faithful head on his rustic boot. Burns stares out over the town wearing a rather vapid expression that does not quite match his colourful life.

The Globe Tavern and the **Hole in the Wa'**, two of the poet's favourite inns are in the High Street. Both are crammed with Burns memorabilia and and it is hard to believe that he died nearly 200 years ago, so living is his memory in these stones. It is said that his tragically early death at the age of 36 was brought about by collapsing in the snow after a "night wi' the boys" in The Globe, and lying there long enough to catch a chill. The barmaid at The Globe bore one of his many children. Burns lived in Dumfries for the last four and a half years of his life, working as an excise man and writing nearly 100 of his best known works including "Auld Lang Syne".

Burns House (open all the year round, daily except Tuesdays from September to June, daily in July and August: adults 30p, children 15p) is a must for Burns enthusiasts. You will find it in what is now Burns Street but which was called Mill Vennel, when he lived and died there. He called it "Stinking Vennel" on account of the open drain that ran down the alley carrying effluent from the meat market to the river. Here you can see more mementoes of his short life; the house has recently been restored.

An elaborate **Mausoleum** in the grounds of **St Michael's Church** contains the body of Burns, and those of his wife Jean Armour and five of their children. Like the statue in the High Street, this splendid Grecian temple with the muse of poetry, sculpted by Turnerelli, coming on Burns at the plough, is somehow too mawkish for the man. This monument was erected in 1815, when it cost £1,450.

Robert Burns seems to dominate Dumfries and it would be easy to miss the plaque in Castle Street, all that remains of the **Monastery of Greyfriars**. It commemorates the event which was one of the turning points in Scottish history, when Robert Bruce stabbed to death Red Comyn, his rival claimant to the crown, in a quarrel. Having thus disposed of opposition with the double crime of murder and sacrilege, Bruce was then able to seize the throne.

Midsteeple, 1707, is in the middle of the town. It is the former tolbooth with a plan on the wall of how Dumfries was in Burns' day. This imposing building was also the prison and ammunition store.

In **The County Hotel**, there is a panelled room, upstairs, known as Prince Charlie's room, where the prince held a council of war in 1745.

Lincluden Abbey (open standard Ancient Monument times, except closed on Thursday afternoons and Fridays: adults 50p, children 25p) stands on the northern outskirts of the town on a grassy plateau within a bend of Cluden Water. It has managed to retain its tranquil charm in spite of the modern houses that surround it. The abbey was founded for Benedictine nuns in the 12th century: in 1339 the nuns were thrown out by Archibald the Grim and the abbey became collegiate. Archibald's son, the fourth Earl of Douglas, son-in-law of Robert III was killed fighting for France against England. His wife, Princess Margaret, endowed a chapel in the south transept of Lincluden in memory of her husband and was herself buried in the canopied tomb that you can still see in the ruins today, richly decorated and inscribed. You can also see plenty of Douglas signatures on the walls in the form of coats of arms, shields, etc, as well as some carvings on the rood screen showing scenes from the life of Christ.

Drumcoltran Tower

Drumcoltran Tower (open at standard Ancient Monument times: admission free) is eight miles (12.9 km) south-west of Dumfries and is a 16th century, simple oblong tower-house among farm buildings. It stands three storeys high with a wheel-stair in a projecting turret. A hoard of Bronze Age rapiers was found in a ditch nearby.

Sweetheart Abbey

Sweetheart Abbey, (open standard Ancient Monument times: adults 50p, children 15p) is at **New Abbey**, seven and a half miles (12.1 km) south of Dumfries. It is one of Scotland's most poignant monastic ruins and was founded in 1273 by Devorgilla Balliol—mother of King John Balliol, the luckless "Toom Tabard"—who also founded Balliol College in Oxford. Devorgilla was buried here with her husband's embalmed heart, which she had carried around with her in an ivory and silver casket, since his death: her "sweet, silent companion". The abbey became known as Dulce Cor, or Sweet Heart, and you can see Devorgilla's tomb, marked by a raised platform of turf with a cross cut in it, in front of the high altar.

The warm red sandstone shell of the abbey dominates the pretty little village of New Abbey with its main street lined by single-storey whitewashed cottages, curving up to the gates of what used to be the precincts. You can still see part of the enormous boulder wall that used to encircle the grounds.

Arbigland

The grounds of Arbigland (open on Tuesdays, Thursdays and Sundays in the summer: adults £1, children 50p) are 12 miles (19.3 km) south of Dumfries. On a sandy bay overlooking the estuary of the Nith, you can wander in beautiful woodland, water-gardens and formal gardens. In a humble cottage south of the estate road, John Paul Jones was born in 1747, and grew up. This flamboyant character, whose father, John Paul, was gardener at Arbigland, served a prison sentence for murder and then made his home in America. A brave, dashing sailor, he fought for the Americans in the War of Independence, helping to establish their navy, and led several daring raids on English and Scottish territory in command of an American brig. A true mercenary at heart, he fought for France and for Russia and died in Paris. There are many glamourised stories of his exploits, including one in which he returned some treasure, plundered by his crew, to its owner—a lady who lived on the Solway Firth.

TOURIST INFORMATION
Whitesands, Dumfries, tel 0387-53862.

WHERE TO STAY
The Cairndale, English Street, Dumfries, tel 0387-54111. B&B from £16: categories 4,5,5: 45 bedrooms, 20 en suite. Close to the town centre, this imposing Victorian sandstone hotel is privately owned, with a warm atmosphere, good food and wine.

The Station Hotel, in Lovers Walk, Dumfries, tel 0387-54316. B&B from £17: categories 6,5,5: 30 bedrooms en suite.

The Criffel Inn Hotel, in The Square, New Abbey, tel 0387-85305. B&B from £14: categories 3,3,3: 5 bedrooms. It is Egon Ronay recommended and stands between Sweetheart Abbey and the restored Corn Mill. A friendly atmosphere and good home cooking.

EATING OUT
The Station Hotel, in Dumfries, see above, will give you an excellent Scottish meal for about £8. Try the Galloway Sirloin Independence; local beef stuffed with Arbroath smokie and cooked the way you specify.

Sanquhar

If you follow the River Nith 27 miles (43.4 km) northwards on the A76, you come to the small, main road town of Sanquhar, whose chief interest is historic rather than scenic. Two Covenanters' declarations were pinned to Sanquhar's mercat cross: the first, by Richard Cameron in 1680, the second, by James Renwick in 1685, both protesting against the Episcopalian leanings of James VII/II during the "Killing Times" (see History). An obelisk marks the site of the cross, and it is hard to conjure up now just what hysterical bitterness must have pervaded the atmosphere then, when crowds of angry Covenanters stood around, pledging their lives for The Cause. Richard Cameron was killed but his followers were granted an amnesty by William III, and it was from them that the regiment of the Cameronians was founded—now disbanded.

WHAT TO SEE
In the **Tolbooth** is a small museum designed by William Adam, in 1735, with an attractive clock tower and double external steps. You must hunt out the curator, Mr Johnston (either by asking around or by ringing Sanquhar 303) and he will show you over and tell you anything you want to find out about the district. Ask him about **The Admirable Crichton**, the 16th-century genius and child prodigy, who was born at **Elicock Castle**, two miles (3.2 km) to the south, and killed in an unfortunate brawl in Mantua when he was only 22.

Wanlockhead

Wanlockhead is one of the highest villages in Scotland, almost on the Strathclyde border north-east of Sanquhar, and over 1,300 ft (396.2 m) up in the moors. It is reached through a narrow valley that climbs beside the Mennock Water, through curiously unreal-looking, mottled green and brown hills. The village is a wedge-shaped cluster of houses built on turf mounds, nestling in a bowl in the austere landscape.

The **Scottish Lead Mining Museum** (open July and August, 1 pm to 8 pm or by appointment, small fee) is in a rebuilt miner's cottage, with mining artifacts and a beam-pumping engine outside. You can also see a disused walk-in lead mine if you don't suffer from claustrophobia. Gold was once panned from the streams in the hills here; a piece weighing four to five oz (approx 130 g) is now in the British Museum. The lonely, heather-covered moorland was a haunt of Covenanters, who used to hold their illegal conventicles up here, with look-outs on guard on surrounding peaks to warn of approaching soldiers, during the Killing Times in the 17th century.

The Southern Upland Way is for the energetic. It passes through Wanlockhead and is clearly sign-posted.

Durisdeer

At Durisdeer, to the south, on the A702, don't miss the delightfully "Baroque-Arcadian" **Queensberry Aisle** in the 17th-century church there. Durisdeer itself is a pretty hamlet, tucked away at the entrance to the **Dalveen Pass**. A key to the Aisle can be got from the cottage nearby.This mausoleum contains a white marble monument, designed by Van Nost, in memory of the second Duke and Duchess of Queensberry who died in 1711 and 1709, respectively. The duchess lies supine, with her husband propped on an elbow beside her, like lovers on a pastoral tryst, surrounded by twisted columns, garlands and cherubs. Above the romantic-looking couple there is a scroll, extolling their virtues: it doesn't mention that their heir, Lord Drumlanrig, had, in 1707, murdered and tried to eat a spit-boy, in Queensberry House, Edinburgh!

Drumlanrig Castle

Drumlanrig Castle (open most days in the summer: adults £2, children £1) is three miles (4.8 km) to the south-west, off the A76, and is a gorgeous pink-sandstone Renaissance palace, on a low hill beside the Nith. This impressive pile, with its mass of turrets and windows, was built in 1689 for the first Duke of Queensberry. The Duke moved in, spent one night, didn't like it and moved out again, having virtually ruined himself paying for his folly. When the castle was inherited by the fourth Duke, the notorious "Old Q" in 1778, he sold the beautiful avenue of lime trees to help pay his gambling debts. On his death the Duke of Buccleuch inherited the estate and it is now open to the public and well worth a visit.

You will see state rooms panelled with carved oak, beautiful French furniture, many treasures, and among the paintings, works by Rembrandt, Holbein, Murillo, Ruysdael and Rowlandson, and portraits by Kneller, Reynolds and Ramsay. There are nature trails and an adventure play area in the lovely grounds.

Maxwelton House

Maxwelton House (house—open by arrangement, tel 08482-385; garden—Monday to Thursday afternoons in the summer; Annie Laurie's Boudoir—same times in July and August only: admission charge) is near **Moniaive**, about nine miles (14.5 km) south-west of Drumlanrig on the A702. It was the birthplace of Annie Laurie, for love of whom the ardent young Jacobite, William Douglas of Fingland, wrote the well-known poem, set to music and reshaped in 1835, in which he declared he would "... lay me doon and dee ... for Bonnie Annie Laurie". In this 14th-century house you can see an early kitchen as well as dairy and farming implements.

WHERE TO STAY

Blackaddie House Hotel, Blackaddie Road, Sanquhar, tel 06592-270. B&B from £12: categories 3,4,4: 7 bedrooms, 3 en suite. This family run hotel lies in pleasant grounds on the banks of the Nith. You get colour TV in each room, tea/coffee making facilities, and very reasonably priced food. There is a children's playground in the garden, a golf course 500 yards away and trout and salmon fishing available.

Mennockfoot Lodge Hotel, is two miles (3.2 km) out of Sanquhar on the A76 to Dumfries, tel 06592-270. B&B from £12: categories 3,3,4: 9 bedrooms, 3 en suite.

Castle Douglas

Eighteen miles south-west of Dumfries, Castle Douglas' history goes way back to when Iron Age builders created two crannogs on **Carlingwark Loch** below the town. These islets, built on wooden platforms and submerged in shallow water, provided extra protection for the inhabitants of the huts on top. Horse-shoes, excavated from the shore of the loch which the **Civic Park** now covers, are thought to date from a shoeing-forge that served the horses of Edward I's army when he was hammering the Scots. The town was once the village of Carlingwark, changing its name in honour of a pedlar called William Douglas who made his fortune in Virginia and returned to his homeland in 1789, buying up the village and developing it into a prosperous cattle market.

WHAT TO SEE

Threave Castle

Threave Castle (open at standard Ancient Monument times: admission free; ferry fee: adults 50p, children 25p) one and a half miles (2.4 km) west of Castle Douglas stands on an island in the river Dee, a grim and yet magnificent Black Douglas stronghold dating from 14th century, and is the last of their fortresses to surrender to James II, in 1455, during his struggle to throw off their powerful grip on his kingdom. James won his victory with the help of Mons Meg, that mighty cannon that you can now see in Edinburgh. Contrary to general belief, local tradition claims that Mons Meg was forged especially for the battle by a Galloway blacksmith called McKim: Mons being a contraction of Mollance—the land he was given as a reward—and Meg being his wife. Square and stark, the 70 ft (21.3 m) tower had five storeys, each containing a single room linked by a spiral stair, surrounded by a curtain wall and four drum towers. You will see a stone projecting above the doorway; this was "The Gallows Knob" and Archibald the Grim, the aptly named, 14th-century Earl of Douglas used to boast that it "never lacked a tassel". Covenanters stormed the castle in 1640 and demolished the interior.

Threave Gardens (open daily, all the year round: adults £1.20, children 60p) are a mile (1.6 km) south of the Castle. You have to go there to appreciate the importance of this National Trust for Scotland creation. Here is a school of practical gardening, whose fortunate students receive a two-year training in gardening skills that might once have been learnt at the knee of that almost extinct breed, the head gardener. Students live in the Victorian house in the grounds and between them and their instructors, they maintain a garden that it is a joy to walk in. You can also explore the National Trust for Scotland **Visitor Centre** and the **Threave Wildfowl Refuge** where you can see many species of wild geese and ducks. (Access to the nature reserve is limited, in the breeding season: adults £1.05, children 50p.)

Palnackie

In Palnackie, four miles (6.4 km) south–east of Castle Douglas on the mouth of the Urr, you can watch glass-blowing, welding and sculpting at the **North Glen Gallery** (open daily).

Dalbeattie

Dalbeattie, six miles (9.7 km) to the east of Castle Douglas, is renowned for the beauty and durability of its granite which was used to strengthen buildings all over the world. The Eddystone Lighthouse, the Thames Embankment, lighthouses in Ceylon, paving stones in Russia and South America, are just a few instances in which this Galloway granite was used. Dalbeattie Civic Week, at the end of July, is a week full of entertainment and fun of all kinds.

Woodside Studio Gallery, in William Street (open daily: admission free) has exhibitions of paintings of local interest where, if you are lucky, you may pick up a good Galloway landscape or seascape.

The Mote of Mark

The Mote of Mark, lies south of Dalbeattie on the Urr Water. Here you can see the remains of a prehistoric hillfort, looking over the National Trust for Scotland bird sanctuary of **Rough Island**. Across the water to the west there is the only circular tower house in Scotland, **Orchardton** (open at standard Ancient Monument times and you can get the key from the custodian who lives in a cottage nearby: admission free). It is a delightful sturdy 15th-century tower in an attractive wooded dip.

The Mote of Urr

The Mote of Urr, three miles (4.8 km) north of Dalbeattie, is another fortified hill. It is an almost circular mound, rising in three tiers, on a platform surrounded by a deep trench; a splendid relic of Saxon–Norman occupation.

TOURIST INFORMATION
Markethill, Castle Douglas, tel 0556-2611. It is open Easter to October.
Car Park, Dalbeattie, tel 0556-610117. It also is open Easter to October.

WHERE TO STAY
The Merrick Hotel, King Street, Castle Douglas, tel 0556-2173. B&B from £8: categories 3,3,5: 6 bedrooms. Rated 1-Star by the AA and RAC, Relais Routiers approved. A private hotel offering comfortable accommodation, good home cooking and bargain breaks.

Kings Arms Hotel, St Andrews Street, Castle Douglas, tel 0556-2097. B&B from £14: categories 3,3,4. Rated 2-Star by the AA. Egon Ronay recommended. A friendly atmosphere with bargain breaks offered.

Maxwell Arms Hotel, Maxwell Street, Dalbeattie, tel 0556-610431. B&B from £9: categories 3,3,4. A friendly, family-run hotel, the oldest in the town. Good food from local produce. Golf, fishing and riding available.

Clonyard House Hotel, Colvend, by Dalbeattie, tel 0556-63372. B&B from £11: categories 5,3,4. A country house hotel in four acres (1.6 ha) of lawns and woodland, near the sea. Family-run, known for its good food and wine, at reasonable prices.

Baron's Craig Hotel, Rockcliffe, by Dalbeattie, tel 0556-63225. B&B from £26: categories 5,4,4. rated 3-Star by the AA and RAC. Egon Ronay and Ashley Courtenay recommended; BTA commended. A country-house hotel in 11 acres (4.5 ha) of lovely grounds, overlooking the Solway Firth. Sailing, swimming, fishing, golf, riding all available locally.

EATING OUT
Clonyard House Hotel, see above. Good local dishes: Solway scallops, venison, game, local salmon and beef, Border tart. Try their Atholl Brose—a deliciously warming drink made of whisky, honey, cream and oatmeal. Dinner from £8.

Baron's Craig Hotel, see above. You will get a good dinner here from about £12.

OF LOCAL INTEREST
You can visit The Creamery, in Dalbeattie and watch the local cheese being made. Book through the tourist information office.

Kirkcudbright

Beware! If you first meet Kirkcudbright (pronounced Kir-coo-bry), on a sunny spring day when the blossom is out and the early flowers in bloom, you may find it impossible to move on and explore anywhere else in Scotland. Sturdy, gaily painted houses and old streets beside the water at the mouth of the Dee make this one of Scotland's most enchanting towns. It was a medieval port and a royal burgh, named after the Kirk of St Cuthbert, when the saint's bones rested there on the way to interrment in Durham. With its mild, almost Mediterranean climate and glorious sea views, the town is popular with painters and has a thriving art colony. This whole area is known as "The Stewartry", dating from the time when Balliol lands were confiscated and placed under a royal "steward"—hence also the origins of the Stewart/Stuart dynasty.

SPECIAL ATTRACTIONS
The six-week Kirkcudbright Summer Festivities in July and August provide Scottish Nights, a Raft race, a puppet festival, sports, walks and a Floodlit Tattoo in front of MacLellan's Castle.

WHAT TO SEE
MacLellan's Castle (open standard Ancient Monument times: adults 50p, children 25p) is an impressive ruin off the High Street, dating from 1582, and built by Thomas MacLellan with stones from a ruined friary which once stood here. The jagged fangs of this castellated mansion draw you to it from across the town. In the huge great hall, look for the remarkable single stone lintel that spans the ten and a half ft (3.2 m) aperture and also for the small closet behind the fireplace with a peephole, hinting at all sorts of intrigue and concealment in the past.

Broughton House (open daily in the summer except Sundays and on Tuesday and Thursday afternoons in the winter: adults 50p, children 30p) in the High Street, was built in the 18th century. It was the home of E. A. Hornel, one of the first settlers of the Kircudbright artists' colony and a renowned artist himself. Hornel died in 1933 and left this lovely Georgian house to the town, with a marvellous collection of books and manuscripts on Galloway, a treasure-trove for the researcher. The colourful gardens slope gracefully down to the river.

The Tolbooth, also in the High Street, dates from the 16th century, with an outside stone stair. Several witches were imprisoned here, as was John Paul Jones (see Arbigland), convicted for causing the death of a seaman, but later freed.

The Stewartry Museum (open daily in the summer, except on Sundays: adults 50p, children 25p) is the place to go if you want to know more about the buccaneering life of John Paul Jones. The museum is in St Mary Street, where there is a special exhibition devoted to him. You can also see displays relating to everyday life in the Stewartrys, both historic and domestic, going back to prehistoric times. There are also works by local artists, especially Jessie M. King who was a contemporary of E. A. Hornel.

Just north of the town you will see a power station, in itself no great beauty but built on the site of **Tongland Abbey** which had a colourful history. One of its abbots was murdered as he stood at the altar, in 1235, and its most famous abbot was John Damian, an alchemist. Damian enjoyed the patronage of James IV, the king who would undoubtedly have been a leading entrepreneur today and whose enquiring mind encouraged many experiments. In an attempt to show the king that it was possible for man to fly, Damian leapt off the walls of Stirling Castle in his presence: he broke his thigh. The Tongland Power Station has conducted tours for those more interested in modern engineering than in anecdotal history.

Dundrennan Abbey

Dundrennan Abbey (open at standard Ancient Monument times: adults 50p, children 25p), seven miles (11.3 km) to the south-east, has little of its former splendour but its roofless aisles and transepts, its pointed arches and blind arcading reverberate with the echo of yet another act in the tragedy of the life of Mary, Queen of Scots. Founded for Cistercians in 1142, and falling into ruin after the Reformation, the abbey provided the queen with her final resting place before she embarked for England from Port Mary: it is not known whether she slept here or merely rested. She arrived in tattered, shabby clothes, her head shorn for disguise, and sat somewhere in these ruins to write a final letter to her cousin Elizabeth of England, begging for sanctuary. It is heartbreaking to picture her tall, slender, elegant figure, passing through the exquisite 13th-century pointed doorway that you can still see, between two lovely windows, into the chapter house, to receive the care of the abbot and his monks.

Gatehouse of Fleet

The Murray Forest Centre, north-west at Gatehouse of Fleet, has a **Log Cabin Centre**, an information office, picnic sites and signed forest walks.

In the ruin of the old church in tiny, peaceful **Anworth**, to the west, there is a fascinating gem for anyone who enjoys the study of old grave-stones. You will see an elaborate Gordon tomb, inscribed with an epitaph to a Lady of Cardoness who died in 1628, beginning:

> Ze gaizers on this trophee of a tombe
> Send out ane grone for want of hir whois lyfe
> Twyse borne on earth and now is in earthis wombe
> Lived long a virgine now a spotless wife...

If you manage to get to Glasgow Cathedral, you will find the tomb of the Hamiltons of Holmhead, inscribed in 1616:

> Yee gazers on this trophie of a tomb
> Send out ane grone for want of her whose life
> Once born of earth, and now lies in earth's womb,
> Liv'd long a virgin, then a spotless wyfe.

There is an ancient Pictish stone near the church, carved with a cross, indicating that this was an early Christian settlement.

Cardoness Castle

Cardoness Castle (open standard Ancient Monument times: adults 50p, children 25p), a mile (1.6 km) south-west of Gatehouse of Fleet, is a 15th-century tower house, four storeys high and very fine, with a vaulted basement. Although it lacks a roof it gives you a good idea of what it must have been like, with the original stairway, stone benches and elaborate fireplaces. In the Dark Ages, the owners, called de Cardine, got so carried away celebrating the birth of an heir that, it is said, they all went skating on the loch before the ice was strong enough to hold them and that was the end of them.

Dirk Hatteraick's cave, is near Kirkdale Burn on the shore beside the coast road going west. It is the largest of several caves in this area. Hatteraick was a notorious smuggler and so caves were important in his life.

Barholm Castle can be found by going down to the mouth of the burn, through a lovely, wooded glen. The 16th-century ruin was the refuge of John Knox in the days when he was a fugitive. If you walk about half a mile (0.8 km) up the track you come to two great Neolithic burial tombs, **Cairn Holy**. The first is a stone cist with standing stones; the second has a double burial chamber. The imagination is stirred, as you stand in this lonely spot among these ancient stones and think of those distant mourners performing their mysterious rites.

TOURIST INFORMATION

Harbour Square, Kirkcudbright, tel 0557-30494. It is open May to September.

Car Park, Gatehouse of Fleet, 055-74 212. It is open Easter to October.

WHERE TO STAY

Arden House Hotel, Tongland Road, Kirkcudbright, tel 0557-30544. B&B from £13: categories 4,4,5: 10 bedrooms, 4 en suite. This is an old mansion a mile from the harbour on the way to Castle Douglas. It has good home cooking, good company and dancing every weekend. There is a private putting green, tennis court and beer garden, and barbecues in the summer.

The Selkirk Arms Hotel, High Street, Kirkcudbright, tel 0557-30402. B&B from £14: categories 3,3,5: 26 bedrooms, 9 en suite. This hotel is in the heart of the town with a large, secluded garden. You can get bar meals or go to the à la carte restaurant, and there are barbecues in the summer.

The Cally Palace, clearly signposted in Gatehouse of Fleet, tel 05574-341. B&B from £30: categories 6,6,5: 49 bedrooms en suite. It stands in 100 acres (40.5 ha) of magnificent wooded parkland, with lochs. The hotel offers a wide range of indoor and outdoor activities and you can get special winter and spring weekend breaks.

EATING OUT

The Selkirk Arms Hotel, see above, has good Scottish dishes using local fresh ingredients. Dinner from about £10.

The Cally Palace, see above, has an excellent, varied menu with local ingredients. Dinner from about £12.

New Galloway

Although it was only a village, 18 miles (28.9 km) north of Kirkcudbright, New Galloway was created a royal burgh in 1633 so that the Gordon laird of nearby **Kenmure Castle** (a private residence) could have easy access to a market. Surrounded by wild moorland and forest, the landscape was transformed in 1929 by Scotland's first hydroelectric development, with reservoirs where rivers and burns once ran, looking remarkably natural in spite of dams.

WHAT TO SEE

Lochinvar Castle

Lochinvar Castle is on an islet three miles (4.8 km) north-east of New Galloway, off the

A702 and along a track to the left of the road. If you had to recite "Young Lochinvar" as punishment for crimes in your youth you might feel some sort of compensatory delight in finding traces of Lochinvar's birthplace—bringing reality to what may once have seemed legend. When, in Scott's "Marmion", brave Lochinvar came out of the west, to rescue fair Ellen from having to marry a "laggard in love and a dastard in war", it must have been from here he set out.

Clatteringshaws Loch

Clatteringshaws Loch is about five miles (8 km) west of New Galloway. Here you will come to the **Galloway Deer Museum**, a converted farmsteading (open daily in the summer: admission free). You can see and learn all about not only deer but all other aspects of wild life in this area, with geology and history, wild goats and a live trout exhibition.

Bruce's Stone is reached by following the National Trust for Scotland signs up into the moor north-west from Clatteringshaws Loch. This marks the site of the Battle of Rapploch Moss in 1307, when Robert Bruce defeated the English by rolling massive boulders down onto them.

The Galloway Forest Park, formerly Glen Trool Forest, covering 150,000 acres, or 240 sq. miles (ha), has been opened up by the Forestry Commission so you can walk through the many trails, surrounded by exceptionally lovely scenery as well as a wealth of wild-life, including roe deer, red deer and wild goats. Lonely moorland, peat-bog, hills, lochs and fast-flowing rivers and burns, all dominated by the great bulk of Merrick, 2,770 ft (610 m), make a visit here unforgettable. It is a good idea to get one of the guide-books, sold locally, with information and details of the many walks as well as of the camp-sites, picnic areas and special viewpoints.

TOURIST INFORMATION

Newton Stewart, Dashwood Square, tel 0671-2431. It is open Easter to October.

Gatehouse of Fleet, Car Park, tel 055-74 212. It is open Easter to October.

Kirkcudbright, Harbour Square, tel 0557-30494. It is open May to September.

Castle Douglas, Markethill, tel 0556-2611. It is open Easter to October.

WHERE TO STAY

Ken Bridge Hotel, a mile (1.6 km) out of New Galloway on the A213 to Castle Douglas, tel 06442-211. B&B from £10.50: categories 3,4,3: 10 bedrooms, 1 en suite. This friendly hotel in an old farmhouse has been in business for 200 years. It has its own fishing.

Leamington Private Hotel, High Street, New Galloway, tel 06442-327. B&B from £10: categories 3,3,4: 9 bedrooms, 1 en suite. This hotel gives you a good welcome.

EATING OUT

See Kirkcudbright and Newton Stewart.

Newton Stewart

Nineteen miles (30.5 km) south-west of New Galloway, on the banks of the River Cree,

Newton Stewart grew around the first easy place to ford the river. It is an attractive holiday centre and market town, surrounded by wooded moors and fertile farmland on the reclaimed mud-flats of the estuary. From here you can enjoy a marvellously varied holiday; walking, fishing, boating, bird-watching, sight-seeing or just relaxing in the mild, often hot, sunshine. It is a good base from which to explore the enormous Galloway Forest Park, to the north (see p. 141).

Wigtown

Seven miles (11.3 km) south of Newton Stewart on the western shore of Wigtown Bay, Wigtown is another pleasant little holiday resort. Here you will see two mercat crosses, the second, rather ostentatious one having been erected to celebrate the victory at Waterloo in 1816. The railed enclosure in the large town square was for penning up cattle at night, a practice that was necessary not only to stop them straying, but also to keep them safe from reivers.

Wigtown will always be remembered for its two martyrs, Margaret Lachlan, aged 62, and Margaret Wilson, aged 18. In 1685, these two women were convicted of having attended twenty conventicles—the illegal Covenanter prayermeetings. They were tied to stakes in the estuary and drowned by the rising tide watched by a large, avid crowd. Margaret Wilson was deliberately placed so that she could witness the final throes of her older companion: she was then half-rescued and given the chance to "repent". She refused and was re-secured to her stake.

WHAT TO SEE

The graves of the two women, **The Wigtown Martyrs**, together with those of six other Covenanter martyrs, are in the churchyard where you can see the ruins of two former churches beside the present parish church. These sad memorials are food enough for thought, as is the monument on the hill above the town, but it is not until you see the simple pillar, on the shore where the drownings took place, and watch the tide rising over the estuary mudflats, that the full horror of that appalling event really hits you.

Torhouse Stone Circle

The Torhouse Stone Circle, is about five miles (8 km) west of Wigtown. There are 19 standing stones forming a complete circle 60 ft (18.3 m) in diameter with three more across the centre. As with all other standing-stone circles, historians can only guess at their original purpose.

TOURIST INFORMATION

Dashwood Square, Newton Stewart, tel 0671-2431.

WHERE TO STAY

Bruce Hotel, Queen Street, central Newton Stewart, tel 0671-2294. B&B from £18: categories 5,4,5: 17 bedrooms, en suite. The AA and RAC rate it as 3-Star and it is

Egon Ronay and Ashley Courtenay recommended. This quiet, family run hotel has lovely views of the Galloway hills. The food is good.

Creebridge House Hotel, a couple of minutes walk from the bridge, tel 0671-2121. B&B from £16: categories 5,4,5: 17 bedrooms, 15 en suite. In pleasant grounds, this hotel is Egon Ronay recommended and a member of Taste of Scotland. Fishing is available.

Galloway Arms Hotel, Victoria Street, in the middle of Newton Stewart, tel 0671-2282. B&B from £17: categories 5,4,5: 25 bedrooms, 16 en suite. A friendly atmosphere and good Scottish cooking. Egon Ronay and Les Routiers recommended. The AA and RAC rate it as 2-Star.

Kirroughtree Hotel, a mile (1.6 km) from the middle of Newton Stewart, just off A712 to New Galloway, tel 0671-2141. B&B from £28: categories 6,5,5: 24 bedrooms en suite. The AA rates it as 3-Star and rosette, Merit Award Egon Ronay grade 1, awarded the 1985 international trophy as the most outstanding hotel and recognised as one of Britain's most luxurious country house hotels. Exceptional food prepared by a master chef.

Rowallan House Hotel, Corsbie Road, five minutes walk from the centre of Newton Stewart, tel 0671-2520. B&B from £14.75: categories 5,3,5: 5 bedrooms, en suite. A comfortable friendly hotel in its own grounds. All rooms have TV and tea/coffee making facilities.

Fordbank Country House Hotel, less than a half mile (0.8 km) out of Wigtown on the road to Bladnoch, tel 09884-2346. B&B from £12: categories 4,3,5: 4 bedrooms, 3 en suite. A friendly family-run hotel, with good food, attractive garden and bird garden; river, loch and sea fishing available. Golf nearby and good walking country all round.

EATING OUT

Creebridge House Hotel, see above. You get a good dinner with local fresh ingredients, including lobster and game. Dinner from £10.

Kirroughtree Hotel, see above. Award-winning cuisine. Dinner from about £12.

OF LOCAL INTEREST

The Creetown Gem Rock Museum, opposite Creetown Clock Tower, open daily, has displays of gems and minerals from all over the world. There is a polishing workshop, three display halls, a giftshop and tearoom.

Cree Mills in Newton Stewart are renowned for their mohair products.

Whithorn

About ten miles (16.1 km) south of Wigtown you come to Whithorn (from the Anglo-Saxon "huit aern" for "white house"). Whithorn is thought to be the birth-place of St Ninian. Born some time in the middle of the 4th century and of royal descent, Ninian went to Rome on a pilgrimage and returned here in 397 as a consecrated bishop. He built a white-plastered stone church which became known as Candida Casa, and from here he set about converting the Britons and southern Picts to Christianity.

WHAT TO SEE

The Pend, is a lovely, deep 17th-century arch flanked by 15th-century pillars which support a stone panel carved with the Scottish coat of arms as it was before the Union, in 1707.

A **Museum** (open at standard Ancient Monument times: adults 50p, children 25p) found within The Pend, is well worth visiting before doing anything else because it gives an excellent and very clear description of the significance of Whithorn and the vital part it played in the birth of Christianity in Britain. There are some fascinating early Christian crosses and stones with explanations that make you long to go and read up all the books about this most crucial time in our history.

Your ticket includes entry to **the Priory** which was built on the site of Candida Casa: you can still see the 13th-century nave and a doorway in the south wall that was built by Fergus of Galloway who founded the priory in 1126. It was a place of pilgrimage for more than 400 years, until "idolatry" was made illegal in 1581 by the reformers. Many of Scotland's monarchs paid regular visits to the shrine: James IV walked from Edinburgh on one occasion. Mary, Queen of Scots was the last monarch to go, in 1563, during her tour of the west.

Isle of Whithorn

Isle of Whithorn, three miles (4.8 km) south-east of Whithorn village, on the south-east tip of the peninsula, is a little port built on what was once an island. You can see here the ruin of a 12th-century chapel dedicated to St Ninian, built on the site of one that was probably for the use of the pilgrims who came from abroad, for whom special safe-conducts were granted.

St Ninian's Cave

St Ninian's Cave lies three miles (4.8 km) to south-west of Whithorn. This is believed to have been the saint's private oratory and there are early Christian crosses, carved on the rocks. There is something very moving about this tiny corner of Galloway: whether you are a Christian or not, you cannot fail to wonder at the strength of the faith of those first missionaries, working among barbaric pagans, sowing the seeds that grew into the Christian church as we know it today.

Archaeological Sites

If archaeology interests you, the coast road north-west along **Luce Bay** from the Isle of Whithorn to **Glenluce** links up several pre-historic sites on or near the shore.

The Wren's Egg Stone Circle, is on the left after **Craiglemine**, and **Barsalloch Fort**, an Iron Age fort, surrounded by a horseshoe ditch, on a cliff 60 ft (18.3 m) above the sea, is by **Barsalloch Point**. Archaeologists found the remains of Mesolithic fishermen here, over 6,000 years old. If you come in summer, the foreshore is a glorious blue carpet of saxifrage.

Drumtrodden Stones, less than three miles (4.8 km) inland from Barsalloch, have Bronze Age cup-and-ring markings carved in the rock.

Druchtag Motehill, to the north beyond Mochrum village, is a typical early medieval earthwork mound, with traces of the stone buildings.

Chapel Finian, little more than a few stones now, beside the A747, and five miles (8 km) north-west of Port William, was a 10th-century chapel dedicated to St Finbarr. The chapel was built here in this little inlet for pilgrims landing from the sea on their way to either Whithorn or Glenluce.

Glenluce Abbey (open at standard Ancient Monument times, weekends only in the winter: adults 50p, children 25p) at the head of Luce Bay was restored during this century and is now a ruin so interesting that you will want to go back to it many times. Founded in 1190 by Roland, Lord of Galloway, its 15th-century vaulted chapter house is almost intact, entered by a round, curiously carved doorway. Inside, a single octagonal pillar stands in the middle, supporting the stone vaulting-ribs on carved corbels, each arch being decorated with twined foliage, grotesques and emblems. All this is aesthetically satisfying, but of even greater interest to some, will be the baked-clay water pipes and drains that have been excavated, laid by those monks so long ago and yet still sound today. These traces of early plumbing are fascinating, most expertly put together and possibly a great deal more durable than the unfortunate development of modern plastic drains!

A 13th-century wizard, Michael Scot, is said to have lived here and to have saved the community from extinction by luring the plague, that had attacked them, into the abbey and shutting it up in a vault and starving it to death! He is also said to have occupied the witches who helped him at his work by commissioning them to spin the ropes of sand that you will see, south of the abbey at **Ringdoo Point**, revealed as broken strands of sand when the tide goes out.

TOURIST INFORMATION

Dashwood Square, Newton Stewart, tel 0671-2431. It is open Easter to October.

Port Rodie Car Park, Stranraer, tel 0776-2595. It is open Easter to October.

WHERE TO STAY

Castlewigg Hotel, clearly signposted from Whithorn, just outside the village, tel 09885-213. B&B from £10: categories 3,3,5: 6 bedrooms. A country house hotel in its own grounds, 150 yards (137 m) off the main road, privately owned and family run. There is a friendly atmosphere and you can go river and sea fishing, clay pigeon shooting, and boating from the harbour nearby.

Monreith Arms Hotel, in Port William, tel 09887-232. B&B from £11.30: categories 3,3,4: 13 bedrooms, 1 en suite. This is a friendly hotel.

Corsemalzie House Hotel, in Port William, clearly signposted, tel 098-886 254, B&B from £18: categories 5,5,5: 15 bedrooms en suite. The AA and RAC rate it as 3-Star and it is Ashley Courtenay recommended. A country house hotel in 40 acres (16.2 ha) of garden and woodland, it is peaceful and secluded. It is privately owned and family run. Taste of Scotland food served in the bar and restaurant. Fishing and shooting available.

EATING OUT

Corsemalzie House Hotel, see above. Bladnoch salmon and trout, local meat, beef a speciality, game in season. Dinner from £10.

Stranraer: The Rhinns of Galloway

Stranraer is a busy port and the market centre for the area, as well as being a popular holiday resort. Very sheltered, at the head of **Loch Ryan**, ten miles west of Glenluce, it is the gateway to the Rhinns of Galloway, the name given to the hammer-head peninsula that juts from the south-west tip of Scotland. Although it isn't a beautiful town it can give you all the amenities you could ask for on holiday, with numerous hotels and guest houses, golf courses, good beaches, excellent trout and sea fishing, boating and exploring. Frequent car-ferries make the two-hour crossing to Larne in Northern Ireland.

It is odd to think, as you walk about the bustling, modern town, that below your feet lie the oystershells that were thrown out by Mesolithic settlers, 6,000 years ago. Looking out across Loch Ryan you can picture it in Roman times when they used the sheltered anchorage for their galleys, in their expeditions against the Gallovidians, calling it "Rericonius Sinus".

WHAT TO SEE

Old Castle of St John was a 16th-century, L-shaped edifice. What is left of it is tucked away in a back street, surrounded by ugly buildings. Claverhouse occupied the castle during his relentless persecution of the Covenanters in 1682: his victims were imprisoned in the dungeons where many of them perished. You can get a wonderful view from the parapet walk.

North West Castle Hotel, opposite the pier, was the home of Sir John Ross, the 18th-century Arctic explorer who sailed in search of the north-west passage and discovered the true position of the north magnetic pole. A passionate seaman, Ross built his house as much like a ship as possible, a flamboyant, castellated mansion with the dining room modelled like a ship's cabin with rounded stern.

The Wigtown District Museum, London Road, Stranraer (open daily except Sunday: admission free) will give you more information about Sir John Ross. It is a local history museum with emphasis on dairy farming.

The Castle Kennedy Gardens (open daily in the summer: adults £1, children 50p) are well worth an unhurried visit. These gardens were laid out by the second Earl of Stair, who died in 1747, having been ambassador in France and inspired by the gardens of Versailles. Not slow off the mark, the Earl used soldiers of the Royal Scots Greys and the Inniskilling Fusiliers (who were in the area to quell Covenanters) to build his garden for him around his home, **Castle Kennedy**, which you can now see as a ruin, softened by swathes of ivy, on an isthmus between two lochs. After the castle was burned down in 1715, the gardens were sadly neglected for years, until 1847, when they were rescued and restored to their original 17th-century design. The shrubs are spectacular and the pinetum was the first one to be grown in Scotland. The present Scots–French mansion, Lochinch Castle, a private residence, was built in 1867 to replace Castle Kennedy.

Exploring the Rhinns of Galloway you will be pulled up in delight at the many lovely views that open up seawards.

Castle Kennedy, Stranraer

Lochnaw Castle

Lochnaw Castle, to the north-west, was the seat of the Agnews, hereditary sheriffs of Galloway from 1451 to 1747. Although the present building is mainly 17th-century, it dates from an earlier one of which the 15th-century tower remains.

Corsewall Point

Corsewall Point is reached by a rough track and the **Lighthouse** is on the northern tip of the Rhinns, with the dominating cone of **Ailsa Craig** rising from the sea to the north. Robert Louis Stevenson's grandfather built the lighthouse. You are a lot closer to Belfast, on this tip, than you are to Edinburgh!

Portpatrick

Portpatrick is on the west of the peninsula and is a thriving holiday resort and fishing village. Only 22 miles north-east of Donaghadee, in Ireland, this was once the port for the main route west, but south-westerly gales frequently made docking hazardous, so the port was moved to sheltered Stranraer. Portpatrick is an idyllic holiday centre with lovely coastal scenery, sandy bays, a golf course, a picturesque little harbour and some good walks. In summer you could easily be in some Mediterranean resort: the landscape is bright with flowers, the air deliciously scented with their perfume. It is said that St Patrick landed here on a visit from Ireland.

Dunskey Castle

Dunskey Castle, a gaunt, jagged ruin dating to the 16th-century, stands on a headland a mile to the south and you need to take great care walking on the cliff paths which are not suitable for young children.

Kirkmadrine Stones are another place of interest to the archaeologist, and lie eight miles (12.9 km) south of Stranraer on the southern arm of the Rhinns. The 5th/6th-century stones are to be found against the church wall, with a description that explains their significance. Some bear Latin inscriptions and the "Chi-Rho" symbol, formed by a combination of the first two letters of Christ's name in Greek. These ancient stones prove that St Ninian managed to establish Christianity in this area.

Ardwell House Gardens

Ardwell House Gardens (open daily in the summer: admission by donation) are nine miles (14.5 km) south of Portpatrick. Go there to have a look at the lovely, almost tropical gardens as well as the good views across the water.

At **Ardwell Bay**, on the precipitous west coast, there is a narrow rock spit, cut off by a wall, where you can see one of the few brochs in the south-west, unusual in that it had two entrances, one to seaward and one to landward. Those early settlers would certainly have had the advantage of anyone trying to invade them by sea.

Logan Botanic Gardens

The Logan Botanic Gardens (open daily in the summer: admission 50p per car) are on the west coast of the peninsula, 14 miles (22.5 km) south of Stranraer. They are a compulsory stop for garden-lovers and a glorious riot of sub-tropical plants, tree-ferns, cabbage palms and the Brazilian *Gunnera manicata*, the largest-leafed outdoor plant in Britain. Plants from all over the world flourish in the mild climate and you feel you are walking in some exotic foreign land.

When you have had enough of the gardens, walk through to the **Logan Fish Pond**, a tidal pool in the rocks, 30 ft (9.1 m) deep and 53 ft (16.1 m) round, created in 1800 to make a fresh-fish larder for Logan House. It was damaged by a mine during the last war and re-opened in 1955. There are usually about 30 fish in it, mainly cod, which are so tame that they can be fed by hand.

The Mull of Galloway

The Mull of Galloway is a dramatic headland with cliffs 200 ft (61 m) high on the southern tip of the Rhinns. You can stand here, buffeted by the wind and salt spray, and watch a boiling cauldron, far below, at certain times and conditions when seven tides meet and do battle together. You can see over the lighthouse at the keeper's discretion.

Double Dykes is the name of the trench across the western end of the point and is said to be the last defence of the Picts, retreating from the Scots who had driven them down the peninsula early in the 6th century.

TOURIST INFORMATION

Port Rodie Car Park, Stranraer, tel 0776-2595.

WHERE TO STAY

North West Castle Hotel, opposite the castle in Stranraer, tel 0776-4413. B&B from £19.75: categories 6,6,5: 78 bedrooms en suite. Truly Scottish hospitality here, with excellent food and modern accommodation. Winner of Scottish Tourist Board award for "food, welcome and hospitality" and well earned. You can get weekend bargain breaks in winter and spring.

George Hotel, in the middle of Stranraer, tel 0776–4413. B&B from £15: categories 4,5,5: 31 bedrooms, 15 en suite. The RAC rate it as 3-Star and it has a high standard of comfort and very good food. There are mid-week and weekend bargain breaks.

Fernhill Hotel, overlooking the sea in Portpatrick, tel 077681-220. B&B from £18: categories 4,4,5: 15 bedrooms, 9 en suite. The AA and RAC rate it as 3-Star and it is Ashley Courtenay recommended. Excellent food, polite, friendly service. You can get golf packages very reasonably.

Portpatrick Hotel, in Portpatrick, tel 077681-333. B&B from £16: categories 3,5,3: 58 bedrooms, 28 en suite. A friendly hotel which will arrange fishing, golf, etc for you.

EATING OUT

All the above hotels will give you a good meal. The hotel prices are reasonable; for instance you will get bar lunches and suppers from about £5 and dinner from £10 in the Fernhill.

Bay House Restaurant, Cairnryan Road, Stranraer, tel 0776-3786. Try the Bladnoch whisky pâte; local fish and game; Bladnoch fillet steak; salmon and lobster in season. Dinner from about £10.

CRAFTWORK IN DUMFRIES AND GALLOWAY

The people listed below are happy to have visitors in their workshops, to watch them in the various stages of their craftwork. It is always a good thing to ring first, if there is a telephone number.

Ceramics

Laurieston House Pottery, Wallaceton, Dunscore, Dumfries, tel 472–038 782. Handthrown, decorated domestic earthenware.

Milestone Pottery, Jocksthorn Cottage, Wamphray, Moffat, tel 05764-291. Handthrown pottery, including domestic stoneware.

Dolls and Toys

Windows and Wood, Close Cottage, Boreland, Lockerbie, tel 057-66 272. Toys, wooden handmade dolls, puppets, marionettes, furniture, stained glass windows.

Glass

David Gulland, Skairkilndale, Barrhill Road, Kirkcudbright, tel 0557-31072. Glass engraving.

North Glen Gallery, Palnackie, Castle Douglas, tel 055-660 200. Many forms of glassblowing and some metalworking.

Jewellery and Silverwork
Creetown Gold and Silversmithing Workshop, 93 St John Street, Creetown, Newton Stewart, tel 067-182 396. Jewellery making and silverware.

Printed and Dyed Textiles
Tuar Fabrics, Blacknest House, Thornhill, Dumfries, tel 0848-30745. Handprinted kitchen aprons, tea cosies, handkerchiefs, tea towels.

Woven Textiles
Glen Cree Ltd, Newton Stewart, tel 0671-2990. Woven brushed mohair; rugs, stoles scarves, knitting yarn.

Part VII

LOTHIAN:

Excluding Edinburgh

Tantallon Castle

On a clear day you can stand on certain summits and see almost all Lothian in one sweep, 50 miles (80 km) from east to west, 15 miles (24 km) from north to south. It is a shallow dish of fertile plain falling away from the southern peaks, northwards to the sea and the Firth of Forth, with the blue hills of Fife beyond. It is a land- and seascape like none other in Scotland: a patchwork of farmland that is some of the richest in Britain and with hills that can be bleak and snowbound in winter and a joy to walk in at other times. It also has 70 odd miles of coastline made up of sheer rock cliffs, wide sandy beaches, quaint fishing ports, windswept dunes and isolated nature reserves. Dotted over the plain and out in the Firth you can see massive humps and wedges of volcanic rock that provided splendid vantage points in the days when every acre was fought for; among them are Traprain Law, the Bass Rock and Arthur's Seat.

Although Lothian has Edinburgh at its centre, it is by no means merely the city's dormitory. Lothian has always retained its own staunch independence, an independence that kept it aloof from the rest of Scotland until the 11th century when Malcolm II drew the kingdoms together. The Romans called it Votadini in the days when it was the Southern Pictish nation, with Traprain Law as its capital, and it may have been from the Pictish King Loth that it got its name. After the Picts faded into obscurity, Lothian formed the northern part of Bernicia, inhabited by the Angles.

The land was mined for coal as far back as the 12th century; farming has always been important and large fishing fleets once crowded the sheltered harbours along the coast.

East Lothian has one of the highest averages of sunshine in Britain. Its people are hard working men of the soil and intrepid seamen, clear-eyed and proud, straightforward and reliable, their roots going deep into their land since long before history was recorded.

There is no shortage of things to do in Lothian. Apart from sightseeing, golf perhaps heads the list of outstanding attractions. Muirfield, at Gullane, is internationally renowned, and there are a large number of good courses throughout the region. If golf is not for you, there are all types of water sports along the coast, with sailing centres at Dunbar, North Berwick, Musselburgh and several of the smaller coastal villages. There are also lovely walks to the hills and along the many miles of coast, with a large variety of birds to look out for.

You can go riding or pony trekking, fishing (both sea and river) or skiing on the dry-ski runs at Hillend. With Edinburgh on your doorstep, you can always take off for the city, for a day of culture, shopping or sightseeing. Your hotel, or the nearest tourist information office will give you full details of what is available locally, and will usually fix up permits, etc for you.

TOURIST INFORMATION

If the local tourist information office is closed for the winter, you can always get advice, information and brochures from The Scottish Tourist Board, 23 Ravelston Terrace, Edinburgh, EH4 3EU, tel 031-332 2433.

The Lothian coast from east to west

Dunbar

Dunbar was an important fishing port 300 years ago giving jobs to 20,000 workers. The harbour is quiet now, though it still has a small fishing fleet. Smuggling once flourished: in 1765, 8,000 lbs of contraband tobacco passed through the port. Today it is a rapidly developing holiday resort with a record of the lowest rainfall and highest sunshine in Scotland. Edward I defeated the Scots here in 1295 and his son Edward II escaped from the harbour by sea, 19 years later, after his defeat at Bannockburn. In 1650, Cromwell fought and defeated the supporters of Charles II in Dunbar, killing 3,000 and taking 10,000 prisoners.

The town sprawls round a wide High Street, squared off at the north end by **Lauderdale House**, built by Robert Adam and once used as a barracks. The 17th-century steepled **Town House**, in the middle of the High Street is the oldest civic building in constant use. The town holds a veteran and vintage Vehicle Rally in August—with everything from motorcycles and buses, to Rolls Royces.

WHAT TO SEE

Dunbar Castle is best seen from the edge of Lauderdale House barrack square, whence you can look down on it and read the detailed description of its history which is

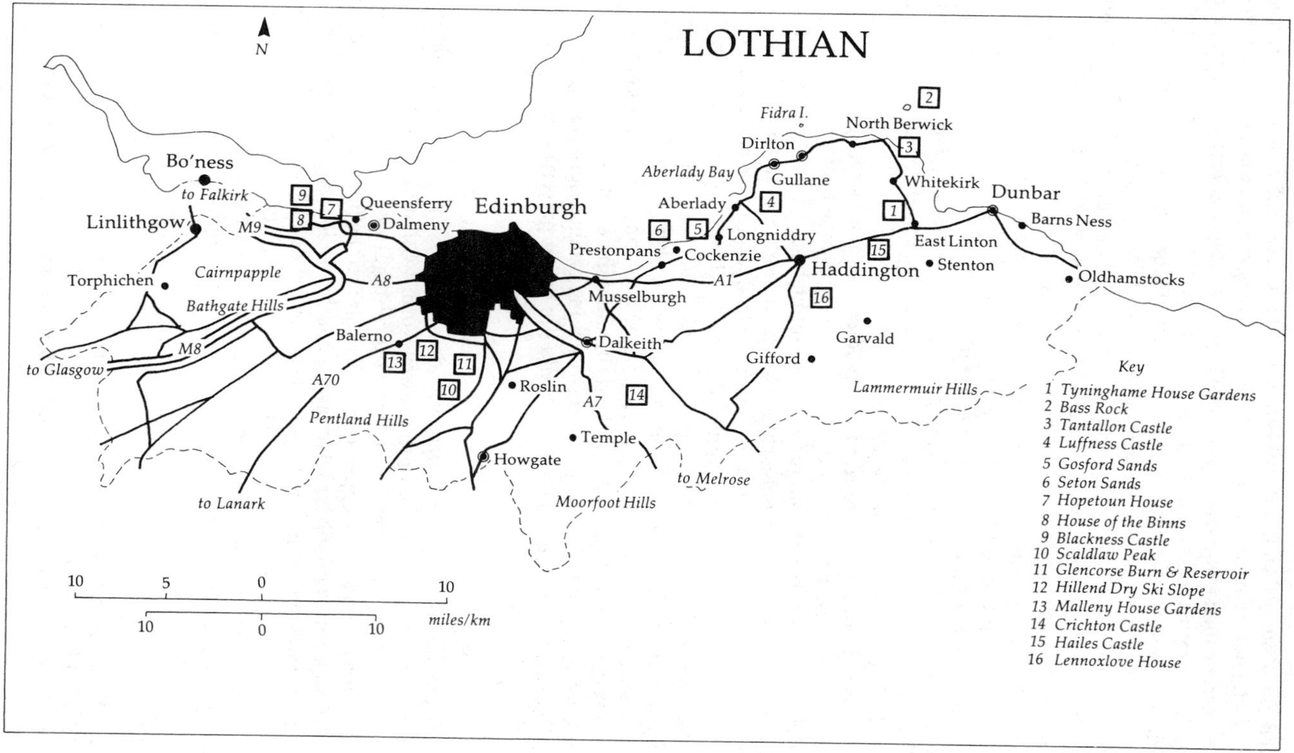
LOTHIAN
N
Bo'ness
to Falkirk
Linlithgow
M9
Queensferry
Dalmeny
Edinburgh
Torphichen
Cairnpapple
Bathgate Hills
A8
M8
to Glasgow
Balerno
A70
Pentland Hills
to Lanark
Roslin
Howgate
A7
Temple
Moorfoot Hills
to Melrose
Dalkeith
Musselburgh
Prestonpans
Cockenzie
Longniddry
Aberlady
Aberlady Bay
Gullane
Dirlton
Fidra I.
North Berwick
Whitekirk
A1
Haddington
East Linton
Stenton
Dunbar
Barns Ness
Oldhamstocks
Garvald
Gifford
Lammermuir Hills
1
2
3
4
5
6
7
8
9
10
11
12
13
14
15
16
10
5
0
10
10
0
10
miles/km
Key
1 Tyninghame House Gardens
2 Bass Rock
3 Tantallon Castle
4 Luffness Castle
5 Gosford Sands
6 Seton Sands
7 Hopetoun House
8 House of the Binns
9 Blackness Castle
10 Scaldlaw Peak
11 Glencorse Burn & Reservoir
12 Hillend Dry Ski Slope
13 Malleny House Gardens
14 Crichton Castle
15 Hailes Castle
16 Lennoxlove House

displayed on a board. Only one jagged fang-like tower and a few scattered stones remain of what was once an extensive fortress guarding the gateway to the eastern plain, sprawled across menacing sea-lashed rocks, overhanging the narrow entrance to the harbour. The original castle was built in the 11th century for Cospatrick, Earl of Northumbria, deposed by William the Conqueror and made Earl of Dunbar by his cousin Malcolm Canmore. The focus of many battles it is particularly noted for a siege in 1339, when Black Agnes, Countess of Dunbar, and her ladies, held it for six weeks against the English. This brave woman mocked the great siege engine, called a "sow", which was used against the castle. She and her ladies leant over the battlements and wiped the walls with their dainty handkerchiefs where the sow's missiles had hit. When Bothwell abducted Mary, Queen of Scots, in 1567, he brought her to Dunbar Castle and it was here that he raped her, though many believe it was not rape. It was to Dunbar that they fled, less than six weeks later, playing out the final act in Mary's tragedy. The castle was demolished by her half-brother, Regent Moray, after her final defeat, and later, Cromwell used its stones to improve the harbour.

Picturesque **Dunbar Harbour** has cobbled quays round an outer and inner basin, restored warehouses, a coast-guard station, working fishing boats, piles of netting and lobster creels, pleasure craft and the ever vigilant lifeboat. Kittiwakes throng the rocks, wheeling and screaming above the ruined castle. In northerly and easterly gales, waves pour over the harbour walls. Picture it in the old days, the boats packed tight in the basins, men busy on deck, sorting and landing the catches, the quays alive with the chatter of the women, gutting the great heaps of slithering silver herring.

The John Muir Country Park, on the western outskirts of the town, is called after a 19th-century conservationist, born in Dunbar, who founded America's national parks. Many acres of wild and beautiful coastland surround the mouth of the Tyne, where you can walk along the cliffs, go fishing, sand-yachting, sailing, surf-riding or swimming, play golf, or just enjoy the large range of wild life that is preserved here.

Tyninghame House Gardens

Tyninghame House Gardens (open weekdays in the summer: adults 70p, children 25p), four miles (6.4 km) to the west, are well worth a visit in the summer. The house is not open at present but it makes a perfect focal point in the grounds, with its rose-coloured turrets and crow-stepped gables, surrounded by fine old trees. You can stroll among shrubs and statuary, parterre lawns, and herbacious borders; or sit in arbours enjoying the mingled scents and blends of colour; or you can slip into the secret garden and stand entranced, serenaded by a choir of birds. Don't miss the ruin of 12th-century St Baldred's chapel, a romantic gem tucked away among smooth banks of grass, with two richly ornamented Norman arches, soaring in triumph beneath the trees.

Barns Ness

Barns Ness is about three miles (4.8 km) east of Dunbar where the road runs straight out to the lighthouse on a rock promontory beyond a campsite. Here there is a wild life preserve, a geology trail with an old lime kiln, and splendid bracing bathing from the clean white sands.

TOURIST INFORMATION
Town House, Dunbar, tel 0368-63353. It is open all year.

WHERE TO STAY
Bayswell Hotel, Bayswell Park, Dunbar, tel 0368-62225. B&B from £18: categories 6,5,5: 12 bedrooms en suite. The hotel on the cliff, with lovely views across to May Island and the Bass Rock, is rated as 2-star by the AA and RAC. All have colour TV, telephone and tea/coffee making facilities. The kitchen is Taste of Scotland and the hospitality won an award. You can get bargain breaks and golf is on the doorstep.

Battleblent Hotel, West Brans, Dunbar, tel 0368-62234. B&B from £19.50: categories 5,4,5: 7 bedrooms en suite. This hotel has a friendly atmosphere.

Bayview Hotel, Bayswell Road, Dunbar, tel 0368-62778. B&B from £11: categories 3,4,5: 6 bedrooms, 1 en suite. On the sea front, overlooking May Island and the Bass Rock, it is only a few minutes from the harbour and High Street. It serves British and Italian food, personally supervised by proprietors.

St Beys Guest House, 2 Bayswell Road, Dunbar, tel 0368-23571. Prices on application. Categories 3,4,5: 6 bedrooms, 1 en suite. Colour TV and tea/coffee making facilities. The hotel offers special golf packages, i.e. four nights dinner, B&B, plus special golf ticket for £79.

EATING OUT
All hotels serve meals

The **Bayswell Hotel**, see above, with its lovely views from the dining room, will give you a Taste of Scotland dinner from about £8. (Dunbar trout, haggis, Fenton Barns turkey, local beef, lamb, port, Home baked Eyemouth Tart, shortbread.)

North Berwick

North Berwick is about ten miles (16 km) north-west along the coast from Dunbar and was created a royal burgh by Robert III around the end of the 14th century. The town developed into a seaside holiday and golfing resort during the 19th century. It has lots of sunshine thus making it still popular today. A compact town flanked by two bays with a rocky headland between them, it is the main shopping centre for the area. Narrow, one-way streets, teeming with bustling holiday crowds in summer, lead down to the tiny, sheltered harbour, full of boats, surrounded by warehouses converted into flats. Lobster creels, nets and fish-boxes mingle on the quay with the spars of pleasure boats and hulls of sail-boards and, just beyond, an open-air swimming pool has been built into the rock, high above the sea. Among the many sailing events during the year, are the European Mirror Dinghy Championships, in August.

WHAT TO SEE
North Berwick Museum (open daily in the summer, and from Fridays to Mondays from Easter to the end of May: admission free) is in School Road. It is a cosy little museum on the upper floor of the old school where you can pick up a good idea of the local social history, archaeology, and wild life, with special exhibitions.

The Auld Kirk stands on a rocky spit near the harbour. All you can see of this notorious 12th-century ruin today is the whitewashed nave, south aisle and foundations. When James VI/I was nearly drowned in a freak storm off the Bass Rock, he blamed a well established coven of witches in North Berwick, alleging that some of them had had the temerity to row round his foundering ship in a sieve! The witches were arrested one dark night as they performed some rather nasty rituals in and around the Auld Kirk, presided over by their "Devil", Francis, Earl of Bothwell, nephew of Mary's Bothwell, who lived at Hailes Castle nearby. The subsequent trial of 94 witches and 6 wizards was based on confessions extracted by gruesome torture and attended by the king who was inspired to write a book on the subject.

North Berwick Law, is the volcanic rock that towers 613 ft (184 m) above the town. If you have the energy you should climb the path up its steep flank for a wonderful view out to sea, over to the hills of Fife and across the Lothian plain to the Lammermuirs, Moorfoots and Pentlands, with a view indicator to help you get your bearings. This was once one of a chain of warning beacons and in the Dark Ages it was crowned by a Pictish fort. Now it is occupied by a watchtower that was used to look for invaders during the Napoleonic wars, and some other, more modern, buildings used in the First World War. There is also an arch made from the jawbones of a whale, a relic from the days of whale fishing in the North sea.

The Bass Rock

The Bass Rock, another volcanic plug, is an island one and a half miles (2.4 km) offshore, 350 ft (105 m) high and a mile round and is a familiar wedge-shaped landmark for sailors. You can take boat trips from North Berwick to cruise round it but special permission is needed to land, a feat not always possible in rough weather. St Baldred, the hermit, died on the rock in the 7th or 8th century and you can just make out where his cell was, half way up, on a terrace on the south side. Near the lighthouse you can also see the ruins of a castle owned by the Lauder family. In 1406, James I, the twelve year old heir to the throne, sheltered on the Bass on his way to sanctuary in France, before being captured at sea and held hostage in London for eighteen years. Many Covenanters, a number of whom subsequently died, were imprisoned on the rock during the "killing times" in the 17th century. Later, four Jacobites held out against all attempts to capture them, provisioned by the French for four years. The Bass Rock is now a famous gannetry as well as a haven for other sea birds and seals. If you sail too close to its guano-whitened cliffs on a hot day you will get a rich smell!

Tantallon Castle

Tantallon Castle (open standard Ancient Monument times, except on Tuesdays and alternative Wednesdays in winter: adults £1, children 50p) is three miles (4.8 km) east of North Berwick, and however limited your time is in Lothian, you should make sure you include a visit to it. Dramatic and proud, this impressive ruin stands on the edge of a sheer cliff overhanging the booming sea, between two bays. Dating from the 14th century, it was a stronghold of the powerful Douglas family who leased it (when it was a much smaller fortalice in the 14th century) from the Earls of Fife. This was an unusual practice in those days. These were the Red Douglases, Earls of Angus, who "rose upon the ruins of the Black" Douglases when they were finally subdued by James II. These Red Douglases became a menace to the crown, ruling their domains with a total disregard for authority. They flaunted their personal armies and lived just as they pleased, especially when the devious Tudor widow of James IV, Margaret, married their leader, the Earl of Angus in 1514, and they became arch manipulators in the power struggle over the boy king James V. They built on to, and strengthened, Tantallon and it provided a perfect stronghold for this arrogantly audacious, power-loving family. The castle's massive curtain walls cut it off on its headland, whence it could be supplied by sea, impregnable against the impotent battering of frustrated rivals. It took Cromwell's artillery twelve days of devastating bombardment before Tantallon was eventually "dinged doun". The three ditches that you can see to landward were to repel siege engines and potential invaders. The walls are 14 ft (4.2 m) thick and the well 100 ft (30 m) deep, bored through the rock. Seen silhouetted against the sea, especially as the sun comes up out of the east, Tantallon is one of the most heart-stopping ruins in Scotland. It is always accessible on the outside.

Whitekirk

Whitekirk, two miles (3.2 km) south of Tantallon on the A198, was once the site of a holy well, now lost in the field opposite the church. Among the many pilgrims who visited it in the 15th century, was a papal delegate who later became Pope Pius II. He walked there from Dunbar, barefooted in the snow, to give thanks for rescue from a shipwreck. This pilgrimage earned him rheumatism in his feet for the rest of his life. The imposing red sandstone church dates from the 12th century, well restored after it was burnt by zealous suffragettes in 1914. The name Whitekirk, for such a dominantly red building is explained by the use, in earlier times, of whitewash or harling to cover the sandstone.

Dirlton

Dirlton is three miles (4.8 km) westwards along the coast from North Berwick. It is one of the prettiest villages in the area, built in the style of a medieval feudal township and is a peaceful backwater with pantiled cottages, 17th-century church, session house, old school and inns round two wide, tree-lined greens.

Dirlton Castle (open standard Ancient Momument times: adults £1, children 50p) overlooks the upper green from a rocky mound. It is an impressive 13th-century ruin. Situated in the middle of the village, it was the last castle in the south of Scotland to resist Edward I and was finally demolished by General Monk, for Cromwell in 1650. Surrounded by lawns, a garden and a 17th-century bowling green, it has a 17th-century dovecote with 1,100 nests, in the east corner. This is a relic from the days when pigeon meat was a valuable supplement to the diet in the lean winter months. As you wander among the mellow stones of this castle it is eerie to think of a coven of witches, possibly those of North Berwick, who were imprisoned here before being half strangled and publicly burnt at the stake on Dirlton Green.

Yellow Craig, a popular sandy beach backed by woodland, is reached by a lane leading a mile (1.6 km) seawards from the eastern edge of the village. It has a caravan park, picnic sites and a nature trail along the coast. If you climb the small hillock that rises from the trees you are ascending into fiction; this was the model for Spyglass Hill in Robert Louis Stevenson's *Treasure Island.* The sandy bay, fringed with buckthorn and marram grasses overlooks **Fidra Island**, a menacing lump of black basalt rock, eroded by wind and sea, for which you need your own boat to visit. There was a Celtic monastery on Fidra: Romanised in 1165, it was a popular place for pilgrimages and its ruins can still be seen.

Gullane

Gullane is a seaside golfing mecca about five miles (8 km) west of North Berwick. It is an overgrown village with numerous hotels, guest houses and holiday flats, centering around attractive Goose Green. Church land until the Reformation, it developed more recently into a holiday centre for the wealthy, with Muirfield among its golf courses and a magnificent sandy beach. The Open Golf Championship is a great event at Muirfield, in July. Pronunciations vary, from Gillan and Gullan, to Goolan: Gillan was once considered "posh" but Gullan and Goolan date from further back.

St Andrew's Collegiate Church is said to have fallen into ruin when James VI/I objected to the minister smoking tobacco, and in the 16th century, transferred the parish two miles (3.2 km) east to Dirlton.

Gullane Hill, on the west flank of the village, was formed by wind-blown sand, a process that still continues. Sand has silted up **Aberlady Bay** on the west side of the hill and created a well-known bird sanctuary and nature reserve, with over two hundred recorded species of birds including all five members of the tern family. A wooden footbridge leads from the roadside car park into the reserve.

Luffness Castle (open to the public by appointment only: 08757 218, admission free) overlooks Aberlady Bay. It dates from the 16th century, with a 13th-century keep built on the site of a Norse camp. You can still see the moat, curtain walls and towers. The castle was built by the Scottish-Norman family, de Lindsay, one of whom was regent for Scotland when Alexander III was a boy. He died on a Crusade and offered land to the monk who carried his embalmed body home. The ruins of the monastery that was built on the promised gift of land are near the castle, with the tomb and effigy of the crusading laird.

Aberlady

Aberlady is now no more than a straggling village on the south-west shore of the bay. It was once a thriving trading port, until the Peffer Burn silted up. Attractive pantiled cottages border the main street, with the Quill Gallery, pretty inns and a mercat cross that lost its top during the Reformation. In the church, with its 15th-century tower and vaulted stone basement vault, you can see part of an 8th-century Celtic cross with interwoven bird carvings. The original "louping-on stane" at the gate was the mounting block.

Myreton Motor Museum (open daily: adults 75p, children 25p) is a mile (1.6 km) to the east. Here, surrounded by farmland, is a varied collection of vintage cars, old road signs, advertisements, petrol-pumps, cycles, motor-cycles, military vehicles and memorabilia from early motoring days.

Gosford Sands are less than a mile (1.6 km) beyond Aberlady to the south-west. They overlook the Firth of Forth and have a network of tracks and picnic sites, backed by quaintly wind-sculpted trees behind the wall of Gosford Estate. This long, rock-strewn beach is ideal if you want to stretch your legs or enjoy a good blow before getting into the suburbs of Edinburgh.

TOURIST INFORMATION
Quality Street, North Berwick, tel 0620-2197. It is open all year.

WHERE TO STAY
Point Garry Hotel, West Bay Road, North Berwick, tel 0620-2380. B&B from £7.50: categories 4,3,5: 15 bedrooms, 8 en suite. The hotel overlooks the West Links golf course and the Firth of Forth and offers a golf package of four nights, dinner, B&B, and five days golf for £120.

The Marine Hotel, Cromwell Road, North Berwick, tel 0620-2406. B&B from £30: categories 5,5,5: 86 bedrooms en suite. A luxury golf hotel with special golf packages from £45. It overlooks West Links golf course and the Firth of Forth and is an imposing stone-turreted building with a warm welcome. Guests have free use of snooker rooms, squash courts, tennis courts, sauna cabin, solarium, putting green, open-air heated swimming pool, darts, table tennis and children's play room.

Castle Inn, Dirlton, tel 062085-221. Price on application. 9 bedrooms. A small friendly inn with an olde worlde atmosphere, looking across the green to the castle.

Open Arms Hotel, Dirlton, tel 062085-241. B&B from £20: categories 5,4,5: 7 bedrooms en suite. Renowned for its food. Overlooks green to castle.

The Golf Inn Hotel, Main Street, Gullane, tel 0620-843259. B&B from £8.50: categories 3,3,5: 13 bedrooms, 2 en suite. A friendly, family run hotel. Restaurant, pool tables, darts and skittle alley, in the middle of Gullane and handy for the golf courses.

Greywalls Hotel, Muirfield, Gullane, tel 0620-842144. B&B from £43: categories 6,6,6: 24 bedrooms en suite. A well known luxury hotel built by Lutyens at the turn of the century. It lies on the eastern edge of Gullane in well-kept grounds, with a comfortable country house atmosphere. It is recommended by all the leading good food and hotel guides.

Kilspindie House Hotel, Aberlady, tel 08757-319. B&B from £12.50: categories 4,3,5: 12 bedrooms en suite. A friendly hotel in the middle of this attractive village,offering winter and weekend bargains.

Greencraig Hotel, Aberlady, tel 08757-301. B&B from £30: categories 5,4,5: 6 bedrooms en suite. A friendly hotel on the bay as you drive in from Dunbar.

EATING OUT
Open Arms Hotel, see above. Classic Scottish dishes with several unique recipes. You can get a good dinner from £10.

Greywalls Hotel, see above. Highly recommended food from fresh Scottish produce. Try turbot mousse with purée-ed scallops and watercress salad, or chicken, veal and asparagus terrine. Delicious puddings. Not cheap but worth it. Dinner from £18.

Kilspindie House Hotel, see above. Good Scottish food. Try Rob Roy steak Balmoral, or Jacobean pancakes. Dinner from £8.

Musselburgh

Musselburgh, nine miles (14.4 km) beyond Aberlady, is the next sizeable town south-west along the coast. It lies at the mouth of the River Esk whose tidal flats were once carpeted with mussel beds. A stream of A1 traffic pounds through the heart of the town, diminishing its peace but not robbing it of its history. The Romans had a fort here, to supply their camp at Inveresk and 5,000-year-old Bronze Age relics have been excavated locally.

Being on the direct route to Edinburgh, Musselburgh was often sacked by invading English armies. In 1332, Robert Bruce's nephew, Thomas Randolph, Earl of Moray and Regent of Scotland, fell ill and was given sanctuary from the English by the citizens of Musselburgh, until he died. The town was called The Honest Toun thereafter and Honesty remains its motto.

The Battle of Pinkie was fought just south-east of the town in 1547, one of Henry VIII's victories during his "Rough Wooing". A mile (1.6 km) south of Inveresk is Carberry Hill, scene of the so-called battle that resulted in Mary, Queen of Scots' surrender and capture. Picture Mary, aged only twenty five, proud to the last, preparing to watch the series of chivalric encounters that were to decide the issue. No one of suitable rank among the rebel nobles stepped forward to take up Bothwell's challenge. There was no fight and Mary decided that her surrender and the promise of a safe conduct for Bothwell were the best solution. There, at Queen's Mount, on Carberry Hill watched by those of her army who had not melted away, she embraced her new husband whose child she was carrying, and watched him ride off. She never saw him again. What can have been in her heart . . . ?

SPECIAL ATTRACTIONS

Honest Toun celebrations are held every July. There is a festival with plenty of pageantry and entertainment, both inside and out. There is also a flourishing Flower Show in August.

From its earliest beginnings, golf was played on Musselburgh Links, now more familiar as a race course, the Royal Musselburgh Golf Club having moved along the river to Prestongrange. (James VI/I was an enthusiastic player and James IV is believed to have played here also. Cromwell stationed his troops on the Links in 1650 after his victory at Dunbar while he "sorted out" the district.) Now they are also the site for an annual shooting contest by the Queen's Bodyguard for Scotland, the Royal Company of Archers.

WHAT TO SEE

The Tolbooth, recently restored, and at the east end of Musselburgh High Street near the mercat cross, was once the town prison. Its unusual 16th-century spire was built from material taken from the chapel of Our Lady of Loretto, nearby, when the Reformation decreed its demolition. The chapel, founded by a hermit, Thomas Douchtie, in 1533, became a great healing centre for the sick on the same scale as Lourdes. When its stones were recycled for secular use the pope was so outraged that he excommunicated the Honest Toun for 200 years! Today a boy's public school occupies the lands of Loretto.

Pinkie House (open to the public Tuesday afternoons during the summer and Christmas terms: admission free) is opposite Loretto and now part of the school. It is an early 17th-century building with later additions and it is well worth a visit. Go and see the magnificent painted gallery on the first floor. It is long and wide, its arched timber ceiling painted in tempera by Italian artists.

Fisherrow is Musselburgh's old harbour with terraces of fisher cottages round the harbour-basin on the waterfront.

Prestonpans

Prestonpans straggles along the coast a couple of miles (3.2 km) to the east forming an almost continuous waterside township with **Port Seton, Cockenzie** and **Longniddry**. This strung out village was the site of the Battle of Prestonpans, when Bonny Prince Charlie defeated General Johnnie Cope in a ten-minute dawn skirmish in 1745. You can see a cairn beside the A1 commemorating the battle. Monks mined coal here as far back as the 12th century and established great open-air pans, heated by coal, for the evaporation of sea water from the Firth, to extract valuable salt.

The Prestongrange Mining Museum (open daily all year: admission free) is on the western outskirts of Prestonpans. Developed on a former colliery site, the museum covers 800 years of mining history. Outside, you can see an 1874 Cornish Beam Pumping Engine with its five-storey engine house. The former power house is an exhibition hall full of mining artifacts and documents. There are steam locomotives and various vintage exhibits. Special "steam days" are held on the first Sunday of each month from April to September. A group of interesting 15th to 17th-century buildings stand in the old part of Prestonpans above the coast road.

There is a ruined 15th-century tower with an attached lectern dovecote, the 16th-century Northfield (a private residence) with elegant corner turrets, and 17th-century, Hamilton House, National Trust for Scotland (open by appointment only).

The 17th-century **Mercat Cross** is the most charming member of this group. It is the only complete and unaltered cross of its kind in Scotland. It has a unicorn-crowned shaft rising from a circular base with pilasters and niches, and a turnpike stair to a platform from which public proclamations were read. It is nice to think that perhaps the town crier in 1745 hurried to this platform to inform the townspeople of the victory of the Stuart prince just down the road.

Seton Collegiate Church (open to the public standard Ancient Monument times except on Tuesdays: adults 50p, children 25p) is a mile (1.6 km) east of Cockenzie and Port Seton. Built on the site of an earlier church, it was established as collegiate in 1492 and you can still see the ruins of the domestic buildings. Among the many ancient and interesting things in the church you can see effigies of the fifth Lord Seton and his wife: he was killed at Flodden in 1513; she built the transept and spire.

Seton Castle (private), an 18th-century building adjacent to the church, stands on the site of Seton Palace. This was frequently visited by Mary, Queen of Scots, the Setons having been loyal supporters of her cause. She came here with Darnley after Rizzio's murder and also the next year, with Bothwell, after Darnley's murder, when she took part in an archery contest, adding another nail to the coffin that was being built for her by her critics. The daughter of the house, Mary Seton, was one of the queen's four Marys.

Seton Sands, nearby, are an extensive holiday park with permanent caravans (on site trailers) and all possible facilities for those who prefer a holiday crammed with entertainment and bustle, rather than one designed to "get-away-from-it-all".

Inveresk Lodge Gardens (open all year except Tuesdays, weekdays 10 am–4.30 pm, weekends 2 pm–5 pm: adults 40p, children 20p) are a mile (1.6 km) south of Musselburgh. This garden of a 17th-century house (a private residence) is run by the National Trust for Scotland and specialises in plants that are suitable for small gardens. It offers a host of tempting ideas for those of us who do not live in stately homes.

TOURIST INFORMATION

Brunton Hall, Musselburgh, tel 031-665 3711. It is open June to mid-September.

WHERE TO STAY

Sweethope House Hotel, Carberry Road, Inveresk, tel 031-665 3005/2336. B&B from £17.50: categories 3,4,5: 11 bedrooms, 9 en suite. A nice old fashioned looking hotel with a friendly staff.

Carberry Hotel and Motor Inn, North Berwick Road, Musselburgh, tel 031-665 2302. B&B from £18: 47 bedrooms en suite. Comfortable modern hotel.

Woodside Hotel, Linkfield Road, Musselburgh, tel 031-665 2155. B&B from £13.50: categories 2,3,5: 8 bedrooms, 7 en suite. A friendly atmosphere.

The Olde Ship Inn, Port Seton, tel 0875-811725. B&B from £12: categories 2,4,4: 6 bedrooms. Nice, old fashioned inn near the sea.

EATING OUT

If you don't want to eat in your hotel, you are so close to Edinburgh that it is worth the few miles to go and try one of the many good food places in the city. (See "Eating Out" in Edinburgh section.)

LOCAL SPECIALITY

There is a little wooden cabin, painted bright red, on the harbour-front in Fisherrow, behind Musselburgh. You can't miss it. Inside you will find Mr Clark, whose smoked salmon, done by him in a little cupboard just inside the door, is the most succulent in Scotland and among the cheapest.

The Lothian Coast: West from Edinburgh

Queensferry

South Queensferry is nine miles (14.4 km) west of Edinburgh, where the Firth of Forth narrows to little more than a mile. In the 11th century, Queen Margaret of Scotland established a free ferry here, to carry not only herself but also the many pilgrims she encouraged to visit the holy shrines at Dunfermline and St Andrews. She built two hospices for the weary pilgrims, one on each bank and the ferry service continued (though latterly not free) until the opening of the road bridge in 1964, linking what became known as North Queensferry and South Queensferry.

You can often see naval ships as far up as the dockyard at Rosyth, and great oil tankers lying at anchor, waiting to take on oil from the man-made island just east of the rail bridge. This is the terminal of the pipeline from the North Sea oil fields. South Queensferry juts into the river between the feet of the two bridges, its main street no longer choked with traffic waiting to catch the ferry. Stretching away on either side are private estates with houses open to the public, farmland and woods with lovely views across the water to the hills of Fife.

SPECIAL ATTRACTIONS

The Burry Man Festival, in August, is the village's annual carnival, with plenty of parades and entertainment bringing colour and life to its picturesque streets.

WHAT TO SEE

The Hawes Inn, facing the old ferry ramp, stands on the site of the southern hospice. It appears in Walter Scott's *The Antiquary* and in Robert Louis Stevenson's *Kidnapped*.

The Queensferry Museum (open weekdays on application to the Burgh Chambers: admission free) lies between the two bridges. Its exhibits give you a good idea of the local history including the building of the rail bridge.

At **Port Edgar**, west of the road bridge, a thriving yacht marina has been developed in the former naval station of *HMS Lochinvar*. Here, you can launch your own boat from the ramp, take part in races and regattas, water ski, or take lessons in sailing and wind surfing. *The Maid of the Forth*, goes from Priory Bank, South Queensferry, to Inchcolm (see Fife), tel 031-331 1454.

Dalmeny House (open every afternoon in the summer from 2 pm–5.30 pm except Fridays and Saturdays: adults £1.70, children £1.10). It lies just east of South Queensferry and is a Tudor, Gothic style house built in 1815 for the Earl of Rosebery whose family has lived here for more than 300 years. Although it isn't old in terms of history, it is a splendid baronial mansion with a Gothic hammerbeamed hall, vaulted corridors and classical main rooms. You can see the fabulous collection of 18th-century French furniture, tapestries and porcelain. Some of the paintings are very fine, especially those of Scottish scenes. Queen Victoria stayed here with Prince Albert in 1842 and commented on the beauty of the setting—you can see why—and the 'excellent modern comforts' of the house.

Dalmeny Village

Dalmeny Village, tucked away below the A90 and some distance from Dalmeny House, has attractive cottages clustered round a green. You won't regret making a detour to see the 12th-century church, dedicated to St Cuthbert. Lovingly restored in this century it must be one of the finest gems of Norman architecture in all Scotland. Its receding arches draw your eye magnetically towards a simple altar and east window. In the pulpit is a carved misericord, possibly unique, on which the weary preacher could surreptitiously perch his bottom between exhortations.

Cramond

Cramond, a couple of miles (3.2 km) to the east, is a pretty 18th-century village at the mouth of the River Almond. If you feel energetic, you can walk to it, along the shore from Dalmeny House. Cramond means literally fort-on-the-river. The fort was Roman, built in about AD 142 to guard the harbour. If you look by the church you can still see the foundations of the fort, with an excellent illustrated plan of how it was. (In the summer, free conducted walks round the village start from the Kirk at 3 pm every Sunday.) To the south, beside an older Cramond Brig than the present 17th-century bridge, James V was violently attacked. The king was given to wandering about the country dressed as a humble farmer, calling himself the Goodman of Ballengiech, and some say that he was thus disguised when he was attacked by the family of a peasant girl to whom he was making love. He was rescued by a local man called Howieson, who gave him water. The king rewarded him with a gift of land on condition that Howieson and his descendants should always have water ready whenever a monarch should pass. George IV, Queen Victoria, George V and the present Queen have all been offered water by Howieson's descendants.

Hopetoun House

Hopetoun House (open daily in the summer: adults £2, children £1) is two miles (3.2 km) west from Queensferry, another lovely walk along the shore if you have time. It is one of Scotland's most beautiful mansions. Originally built at the beginning of the 18th century for the first Earl of Hopetoun, it was rebuilt and enlarged by William Adam and his sons Robert and John, between 1721 and 1754. To get the best picture of its simple, classical beauty, you should go to the end of the avenue and look back at the house, a perfectly proportioned sweep of inspired architecture. Among its sumptuous furnishings and treasures are paintings by Van Dyck, Titian, Rubens, Rembrandt and Canaletto, hung on walls lined with silk and damask.

The gardens were modelled on those at Versailles and landscaped to give views across the Forth to the peaks of Ben Lomond. There is a deer park in the grounds, some rare St Kilda sheep and a nature trail, as well as walks along the river. In the stable block you can see an exhibition called "Horse and Man in Lowland Scotland". When you are exhausted with sightseeing, you can go to the licensed restaurant in the lovely tapestry room and indulge yourself with some smoked salmon, Aberdeen Angus beef, or the new "Houptoun Delight" dessert. All is delicious home cooking. The Antique Dealers Fair is held at Hopetoun, in September, and is a marvellous chance to pick up a bargain if you are a collector.

House of the Binns

The House of the Binns (open daily in the summer except Fridays, from 2 pm – 5.30 pm: adults £1.20, children 60p) is the next stately home, a couple of miles (3.2 km) west along the river from Hopetoun. The curious name stems from *ben*, the Scottish word for hill. The house, dating from 1630 with 19th-century Gothic embellishments stands above parkland with lovely views across the Forth. The moulded ceilings are very fine, and the rooms are beautifully furnished. By far the most intriguing aspect of a visit to The Binns is the memorabilia of the notorious Tam Dalyell (pronounced Dee-el) who raised the Royal Scots Greys here in 1681 and whose father built the house. Stories about General Tam, whose mortal remains were popularly believed to have been removed from the family vault at **Abercorn**, nearby, and carried to a far warmer resting place by the Devil himself, are as spine-chilling as they are apocryphal. Known to his troops as the "Bluidy Muscovite", he was alleged to hold flagellation parties, to munch wine glasses and to have conversations with the Devil—stories that were richly embroidered by his Covenanting enemies. In the house you will see a heavy carved table that was recovered from a muddy pond where it had lain for 200 years, having, it is said, been hurled there by the Devil, a bad loser in a game of cards with Tam. Among the relics of this legendary man are his sword and his bible and the comb with which he groomed his beard, having sworn never to cut a hair of his head after the execution of Charles I until the Restoration of the Monarchy.

Blackness Castle

Blackness Castle (open at standard Ancient Monument times, except Monday afternoons and Tuesdays from October to March: adults 50p, children 25p) is a mile or so (1.6 km) north of the House of the Binns. The castle juts into the River Forth, its northern walls pointed like the prow of a massive battleship, lapped on three sides by the river. The original date of this grim fortress is unknown. The present tower was built in the 15th century when it was one of Scotland's most important fortresses. Besieged by Cromwell, it has in its time been a royal castle, a prison for Covenanters, a powder magazine and a youth hostel. When Scotland and England were joined by the Acts of Union in 1707, Blackness was one of the four fortresses to be maintained at full military strength. If you stand looking out across the water through the gun-slits in the sturdy curtain wall, you can almost hear the roar of cannon fire and smell the acrid tang of spent gunpowder.

The quiet riverside village of **Blackness**, just along from the castle, was a bustling medieval seaport, with warves and warehouses and teeming with all the noise and smell and colour of a busy port which supplied the royal burgh of Linlithgow.

Bo'ness

Bo'ness or **Borrowstownness**, a couple of miles (3.2 km) further west, is of historic rather than scenic interest. The **Antonine Wall** started a mile (1.6 km) to the east, at Bridgeness. This wall was built by the Romans in 1423 between the Forth and the Clyde in an abortive attempt to protect the south from the barbarians in the north (see History).

Bo'ness is also the home of the **Scottish Railway Preservation Society**, and steam enthusiasts should certainly visit the **Bo'ness and Kinneil Railway** where you can take steam train rides at weekends and on certain weekdays in the summer.

Kinneil House

Kinneil House (open standard Ancient Monument times except for Tuesday afternoons and Fridays: adults 50p, children 25p) is a mile (1.6 km) west of Bo'ness, up a steep zigzag drive above the Forth. It was built in the 16th and 17th centuries and saved from demolition in 1936 when workmen uncovered original wall paintings and decorated ceilings that are among the finest in Scotland. This building, miraculously saved from destruction, is now preserved as a museum in an attractive walled garden. Don't miss the bothy (hut) at the back where James Watt built the first steam engine while trying to help solve the problem of flooding in a nearby mine in 1765.

Kinneil Museum (open in the summer only: free) is in the grounds. It gives you a picture of local history from Roman times. There is also an excavated fortlet from the Antonine Wall.

TOURIST INFORMATION
Burgh Halls, The Cross, Linlithgow, tel 0506-844600. It is open Easter to end of September.

WHERE TO STAY
Blackness Inn, The Square, Blackness, tel 0506-834252. B&B from £10: categories 1,2,4. A cheerful, friendly inn where you can be sure of a warm welcome.

Forth Bridges Moat House, South Queensferry, tel 031-331 1199. B&B from £21: categories 6,5,5: 108 bedrooms en suite. A large, modern hotel, very handy for breaking your journey on the way north.

EATING OUT
Hawes Inn, South Queensferry, tel 031-331 1990. Good food in a warm friendly atmosphere. This inn is on the site of Queen Margaret's hospice for pilgrims and overlooks the Forth. Not too expensive. Dinner from £7.

Hopetoun House, tel 031-331 2451/4305. You can eat a self-service or served lunch in the Tapestry Room of this lovely Adam mansion, with good home baking and Scottish food: Scotch smoked salmon, Lorraine soup, Aberdeen Angus beef and special "Hopetoun Delight" pudding. Not expensive. Lunch from £5.

Otherwise, you are close enough to Edinburgh to go and try one of the many good food places in the city. (See "Eating Out" in Edinburgh section.)

The hinterland of Lothian: from west to east

Linlithgow

Linlithgow, three miles (4.8 km) south of Bo'ness, is not far inland. It is in an oasis of rural tranquillity, surrounded by smoothly rounded hills and remote farming communities, where it is easy to forget the ugly sprawl of industrial and mining development that lies just out of sight beyond the horizon.

There was a Pictish settlement here before the Romans came and the first royal palace was recorded in the 12th century. Edward I had his headquarters in the town in 1301 and David II built a royal manor which was destroyed by fire, along with all the town, in 1424. The following year work began on the present palace. Since then this thriving, compact little town has watched over much of Scotland's history.

SPECIAL ATTRACTIONS

In June, the town celebrates the Riding of the Marches, in memory of the days when the men had to check the boundaries against cattle reivers. The celebration consists of a parade, with bands, decorated floats, flutes and drums, and plenty of fun. The Linlithgow Festival takes place in August, with medieval entertainment and pageantry. There is also the Scottish National Canal Rally, on the Union Canal in August.

WHAT TO SEE

The Palace of Linlithgow (open standard Ancient Monument times: adults £1, children 50p), must be one of the country's most poignant ruins. Only pigeons now inhabit the empty shell that stands on a gentle slope of grass overlooking its own loch. Mellow pinkish-ochre walls rise to five storeys, supported on the lower edge by flying buttresses: a roofless square with many of its rooms so well preserved that you only need a little imagination to see how they must have been. Through its gateway in 1513, James IV rode out, against the advice of his lords, to lead his gallant army to tragic defeat at Flodden. His widow, Margaret Tudor, peered in vain from one of the turret window slits. The elaborate fountain in the quadrangle is said to have run with wine when James V gave it to Mary of Guise as a wedding present in 1538 and it was not many years afterwards, in 1542, that their daughter was born in one of the upper chambers. She was the ill-fated Mary who was proclaimed Queen of Scots within a week of her birth. Over-enthusiastic fuelling of domestic fires, possibly with bedding straw, by Cumberland's troops who were garrisoned there, caused the loss of the roof in 1746. The swans on the loch add a royal touch: it is said that they flew away when the Roundheads arrived and returned the day Charles II was crowned at Scone in 1649. Perhaps the best view you can get of the palace is at night, as you drive past on the M9, when you catch a glimpse of it, floodlit against the dark sky.

St Michael's Church is so close to the palace that from a distance it seems to be part of it. As well as providing a place of worship for many of Scotland's monarchs, this large pre-Reformation church has had to endure much harsh treatment since its consecration in 1242. It was rebuilt after the fire of 1424; John Knox's followers despoiled it; Cromwell's soldiers stabled their horses in the aisle and left shot-holes in the walls. While praying for guidance and victory before Flodden, James IV saw a ghost which stood by the altar and warned him of his coming defeat. An open stone crown on the tower was replaced, after the Second World War, by the present astonishing laminated wood-and-aluminium "crown of thorns".

Cockleroy Hill

Cockleroy Hill is on your right, along a little country lane signposted to Preston, due south of Linlithgow. It is not a great feat of mountaineering to climb but it is a pleasant 15 minute stroll through dense pines and up a gentle slope of turf and vivid green moss. Some say the name is derived from "cuckold le roi", and hint at an indiscretion by Mary of Guise, getting her own back for the philanderings of her husband James V. Others, more prosaic, will tell you that the name stems from the Gaelic "cochull ruadh", meaning red-capped hill. The keenness of your eyes is the only limit to the horizon from here. A view indicator points out 36 landmarks including Goat Fell, 66 miles (105 km) away on Arran. You can see the ramparts of a Pictish hill fort beyond the indictor: their look-outs would have been able to give plenty of warning of attack.

Torphichen Preceptory

Torphichen Preceptory (open standard Ancient Monument times, closed Fridays and alternate Wednesdays: adults 50p, children 25p) lies two miles (3.2 km) further south. It was founded as the community of the Scottish Order of the Knights of St John of Jerusalem, in 1153. The 15th-century tower and vaulted transepts are all that remain, together with the nave which was rebuilt in the 17th century and it is now the parish kirk. It stands on the outskirts of the pretty little village, among lawns backed by bracken-covered hills and is a good example of fortified church architecture. There is a folding green-baize table in one of the box pews in the kirk, hinting at a less than spiritual attitude among past parishioners. One of the tombstones in the churchyard is thought to be pre-Christian and there are several with ancient primitive carvings.

Cairnpapple

Cairnpapple is less than a mile (1.6 km) south again, in the **Bathgate Hills**. It is a bleak summit aptly known as "windy ways", with a wonderful panoramic view. Follow the Ancient Monument signs which will point you to a parking bay and a short, easy climb over turf to a lofty site that was used for ritual and burial from possibly 2500 BC until the first century. An underground cist, or tomb (open standard Ancient Monument times, closed Monday mornings and Fridays in the winter: adults 50p, children 25p) has been cleverly reconstructed so that you can go down into it and see exactly how it was. A taped commentary is available to explain all that you will see. It is a strange feeling, standing on that windswept plateau, trying to picture those ancient ceremonies and those 4,500 year old tragedies and tears. (When the cist is shut you can get the key from the curator of the preceptory in Torphichen.)

Beecraigs Country Park

Beecraigs Country Park (open all year: admission free) is also in the Bathgate Hills, between Linlithgow and Bathgate. The park is 700 acres (280 ha) of lovely grounds, where you can indulge in pretty well every sort of outdoor activity as well as look at exhibitions in the Park Centre. There are woodland walks, a deer farm, a trout farm, water sports on the lake, fly fishing, archery, a keep-trim course, orienteering and even rock climbing. (For further information tel 0506-844516.)

TOURIST INFORMATION
Burgh Halls, The Cross, Linlithgow, tel 0506-844600. It is open Easter to end of September.

WHERE TO STAY
St Michael's Hotel, 19–21 High Street, Linlithgow, tel 0506-842217. B&B from £12: categories 3,3,4: 6 bedrooms. Nice, old-fashioned, friendly atmosphere in the middle of the town.

Bonsyde House Hotel, Bonsyde, near Linlithgow, tel 0506-842229. B&B from £11.50: categories 3,3,5: 9 bedrooms. An attractive old hotel on the outskirts of the town. Provides a warm welcome.

Star and Garter Hotel, 1 High Street, Linlithgow, tel 0506-845485. Prices on application. Categories 3,3,5: 6 bedrooms. Conveniently situated in the middle of the town.

EATING OUT
If you don't want to eat in your hotel, there are several small restaurants in Linlithgow where you will get a reasonable meal from about £5. **Alexanders, The Four Marys** and **The Tryst**, are all in the High Street. Or try **Bridge Inn** at Linlithgow Bridge, tel 0506-842777.

North Pentlands

The Pentland Hills run south-west from Edinburgh, sprawling across a width of four to five miles (7 km approximately); high, wild moorland carpeted with heather, bracken and deer-hair grass and laced with reservoirs and tumbling streams. There are dozens of lovely walks, some taking you along the old cattle-drover routes south. The highest peak is **Scaldlaw**, 1,898 ft (569 m).

WHAT TO SEE
Castlelaw Iron Age Fort (open at all times) is clearly signposted off the west side of the A702. It is reached by a short climb through gorse scrub from the road. Here you will find an excellently restored souterrain, or earth-house, with a stone passage and chamber, surrounded by three ramparts. A visit to Castlelaw at dawn, with the sun rising over the Moorfoot Hills to the south-east, bathing the land in a pinkish light, with the mist still clinging to the valley, is well worth the early rise: for a breathtaking moment time seems to collapse, fusing prehistoric with present.

The Flotterstone Inn is just south of Castlelaw on the A702. Here you can sit in the garden in summer beside the swift-flowing **Glencorse Burn**. (At the inn there is a good selection of dishes on the menu at reasonable prices.) From the inn you can walk up beside the burn for about a mile (1.6 km) to the **Glencorse Reservoir**, an attractive pine-fringed stretch of water reflecting the surrounding hills. The naked mud shore and receding water-line too often indicate a shortage of rainfall.

You would never guess, as you gaze across the water, that it covers the remains of the **Chapel of St Katherine in the Hopes**. In the 13th century Sir William St Clair of Roslin had a bet with Robert Bruce. He wagered his head against this Glencorse valley, that his hounds would kill a certain deer that had eluded all huntsmen, before it reached the Glencorse Burn. The deer was brought down at the burn, St Clair won his land and built the chapel on the site in thanskgiving. (He was later killed, with James Douglas, on the way to the Holy Land with Bruce's heart in 1330 (see Dunfermline).)

Roslin

Roslin, or **Rosslyn**, is three miles (4.8 km) east of Castlelaw, in the lee of the Pentlands. It has a fairy-story castle, towering near the treetops and near an historic chapel. Part of the castle has been restored and you can rent it, for an unforgettable holiday. To see it from the outside, park by the chapel and walk round the graveyard and over a narrow foot bridge (once a drawbridge) that spans the **River North Esk**, dizzyingly far below. The castle rises above the trees, suspended high over **Roslin Glen**, with dripping dungeons, an ancient yew tree and legends of buried treasure. Dating from 1304, when the Lamp tower was built, it was the home of the St Clair family. William St Clair, who lived here in the 15th century in sumptuous state (eating off gold plate, waited on by dozens of lords and ladies) decided towards the end of his life to make a fitting memorial to his Creator, in the form of a church.

Roslin Chapel (open April to end October, Monday to Saturday, 10 am–5 pm and on Sundays for worship (Episcopalian): adults 75p, children 30p) was the result. Dedicated to St Matthew and founded in 1446, the chapel was designed to be an enormous cruciform collegiate church. It was never finished. When William died in 1484 enthusiasm for the project dwindled and all that was completed was the present chapel, a chancel and part of the transept, with a vault below. The interior is so richly carved that you get visual indigestion, looking at it. Nearly every inch has been decorated with men and animals, birds and foliage, flowers and insects. You will find the Seven Cardinal Virtues, the Seven Deadly Sins, the Dance of Death and a lot more besides, all created by the finest craftsmen of the day.

Your eye will be drawn inevitably to the famous Prentice Pillar on the south side of the Lady Chapel. The pillar's carving is so delicate that it makes the rest seem almost crude. Legend has it that the pillar was intended to enshrine the spiritual concept, rather than the material form, of the Holy Grail and that for such an important monument St Clair sent his master mason to Italy to find an appropriate design. When the mason returned to Roslin he found that one of his apprentices, inspired by a dream, had carved the pillar that you see today. Incensed with jealous rage, he killed the boy.

Roslin Inn, now the curator's house, beside the chapel, gift shop and cafe, dates from 1662 and has had many illustrious visitors including Boswell, Johnson, Burns, Scott, the Wordsworths and Edward VII, who engraved a memorial to his visit on a window in 1859 when he was Prince of Wales.

The Howgate Inn, a couple of miles (3.2 km) south of Roslin is another inn with literary associations: Walter Scott, Allan Ramsay, Dr John Brown, Henry Mackenzie and Robert Louis Stevenson were among its better known customers. Dr John Brown immortalised the area when he wrote his lovely book *Rab and His Friends* about the dog who goes to Edinburgh every day with the Howgate carriers. (You can see the grave of the carrier and his wife, in the churchyard of St Mungo's in Penicuik.) The Howgate

Inn's food is acclaimed locally and when the weather is fine you can eat outside in the attractive terraced gardens.

Malleny House Gardens

The Malleny House Gardens (open daily in the summer: adults 60p, children 30p) are in **Balerno**, about seven miles (12 km) south-west of Edinburgh, lapped by the Water of Leith. Although the 17th-century house is not open to the public, it is a perfect focal point for the formal gardens, where you can see rare shrub roses and clipped yews, rhododendrons and a variety of other shrubs and plants. The saddle-backed dovecote behind the house has not been inhabited since 1961 when its residents perished from a surfeit of treated grain.

Hillend Dry Ski Slope

Hillend Dry Ski Slope (open all the year) on the northern slope of the Pentlands, is the largest of its kind in Europe. If you are keen on ski-ing, whatever the season, it has a beginners' slope as well as the main run and you can hire equipment and instruction.

TOURIST INFORMATION
Burgh Halls, The Cross, Linlithgow, tel 0506-844600. It is open Easter to end of September.

WHERE TO STAY
See Edinburgh section.

EATING OUT
The Bridge Inn, Ratho, tel 031-333 1320/1251. Canal-side inn with cruising boat restaurant and dancing. Lunch from £5, dinner from £7.50.

The Howgate Inn, 7 West Howgate, tel Penicuik 74244. Excellent food, served indoors and out. Reasonable prices. Dinner from about £8.

A SPECIAL TREAT
The restored apartment in Roslin Castle sleeps eight people and can be taken for as long as you like for an unforgettable holiday in wonderful surroundings. If interested, contact The Landmark Trust, Shottesbrooke, Maidenhead, Berkshire, tel 0628-82 5925.

LOCAL SPECIALITY
In Penicuik you can go on a conducted tour of the Edinburgh Crystal Glass Factory, tel 0968-75128. Here you can see the whole process of glassmaking; blowing, cutting, engraving, etc. There is a small charge for tours and no children under ten are allowed. It is open Monday to Friday, with a shop where you can buy the finished glassware, and a cafeteria.

Dalkeith

Dalkeith, six miles (9.6 km) south-east of Edinburgh on the A68, is a compact, busy town, with a wide, cobbled main street, embraced by two arms of the **River Esk**. In spite of being the junction of several main roads, it has a stately feeling about it, enhanced perhaps by its palace and the historic castles that surround it.

WHAT TO SEE

Dalkeith Park (open every day in the summer and at weekends in November: 65p) where you can roam along the river among the trees, has a "tunnel walk", and adventure woodland play area, nature trails, an 18th-century bridge and an orangery. Although the palace is not open to the public it makes a splendid background to the park. Seat of the Scotts of Buccleuch since the 12th century, it is a large, reddish, neo-classic mansion. It was designed in the 18th century by Sir John Vanburgh around an older castle, with a recessed centre and two projecting wings, modelled on the Dutch Loo Palace. It was here, in 1572, when the palace was known as the Lion's Den, that the notorious James Douglas, Earl of Morton, lay in his sick-bed and held the council which plotted to bring Mary, Queen of Scots to trial. Queen Victoria stayed in the present palace in 1842 and remarked in her diary that she had "... tasted oatmeal porridge, which I think very good ...".

The Collegiate Church of St Nicholas, much restored, is on the north side of Dalkeith High Street. It was first built in the 12th century. In the roofless ruin of the 14th-century choir and apse you can see a double tomb which is believed to contain the remains of the first Earl Morton and his wife Johan, daughter of James I.

Dalkeith Arts Centre (open daily, except Tuesdays and Sundays: admission free) has an outdoor sculpture exhibition.

Newbattle Abbey (conducted tours on written application to the Warden) lies a mile (1.6 km) south-east of Dalkeith and easily seen from the road. It was a 12th-century Cistercian foundation: after the Reformation it was the family seat of the Kerrs, later Marquesses of Lothian, who gave it to the nation as an adult education centre. It was frequently visited by royalty: a murdered mistress of David II was buried here; James IV met his 14 year old bride, Margaret Tudor here; James V stayed here and George IV came, on his famous Scottish bonanza. The monks of Newbattle were among the first to work the local coal mines.

Melville Castle, now an hotel, stands in lovely wooded grounds on the banks of the River North Esk just outside Dalkeith. Designed by James Playfair in the 18th century, on the site of an ancient baronial castle, it looks rather like a toy fort with its Gothic windows, turrets and wings. In the entrance hall you can stand at the foot of the graceful spiral staircase and look up three storeys to a vaulted ceiling with delicate polychrome paintings in moulded framework.

Borthwick Castle

Borthwick Castle stands 5 miles (8 km) south of Dalkeith in a tiny hamlet in the **Moorfoot Hills**, just off the A7. Five hundred years old and the largest complete peel tower in Scotland, it is now a private hotel. Bothwell and Mary came here a month after their marriage, looking for peace, but not for long. The insurgents surrounded them and Bothwell escaped through the postern gate, followed later by Mary, disguised as a man. If you go to the information centre beside the lodge at the gate, you will find details of the history of this area.

Crichton Castle

Crichton Castle (open standard Ancient Monument times but weekends only in the winter: adults 50p, children 25p) stands within sight and signalling distance of Borthwick, two miles (3.2 km) to the north–east on a grassy plateau, high and magnificent above a steep valley. Now a ruin, this was Bothwell's seat and it is said that he kept his divorced wife here after his marriage to Mary. This, however, does not tie in with the belief that Mary came here for refuge after she escaped from Borthwick, on her way to meet up with Bothwell and run to Dunbar. The castle dates from the 14th century and in the courtyard you can see a delightful memento of Bothwell's nephew, Francis Stewart, the half-mad demonist (see North Berwick). He travelled widely in Italy in the 16th century and brought back the idea for this astonishing Italianate piazza. Its walls are of a classical diamond design over pillars, making a remarkable contrast to the more sturdy structure of the rest of the castle. Certainly Mary came here as a guest of Bothwell when she was newly arrived in Scotland, to dance at the wedding of his sister to her half-brother. The chapel-like ruin beyond is a fortified stable.

Crichton Collegiate Church, half a mile (0.8 km) north, has been in continuous use since it was built in 1449 and has some impressive barrel vaulting.

Temple

Temple is a tiny hamlet two miles (3.2 km) west of Borthwick. There, in a tranquil churchyard on a hillside beside a cascading burn, you will find the roofless ruin of a 14th-century church. It is on the site of one built by the Knights Templar, the soldier-monks of the Crusades who had headquarters here until the Pope decided they were becoming too powerful and suppressed them in 1312.

TOURIST INFORMATION
1 Eskdaill Court, Dalkeith, tel 031-663 2881.

WHERE TO STAY
The Dalhousie Castle Hotel, just south of Dalkeith in Bonnyrigg, tel 0875-20153. B&B from £53: 24 bedrooms en suite. This is a friendly, high class hotel and its 4-Star rating is well deserved.

The Buccleuch Hotel, in Dalkeith, tel 031-663 4725. B&B from £12: 10 rooms en suite.

The County Hotel, in Dalkeith, tel 031-663 3495. B&B from £18: 20 rooms en suite.

Eskbank Motel, Dalhousie Road (A7), Dalkeith, tel 031-663 3234/3647. Prices on application. All rooms en suite. It has a reasonable restaurant.

The Melville Castle Hotel, at Lasswade just outside Dalkeith (on A7), tel 031-663

6633. Prices on application. A real castle and a very friendly hotel in lovely grounds. You can even have a marriage ceremony arranged in the private chapel.

EATING OUT

The Cavaliere Restaurant, 124/6 High Street, Dalkeith. A nice, olde worlde restaurant with Italian and French style dinner, as well as a large carry-out menu. Fresh baked pizzas, delicious duck in orange sauce, salmon, mussels, trout, king prawns, etc. Dinner from about £10.

The Dalhousie Castle Hotel, see above. You can't do better than to eat here, but it is expensive, so enjoy every mouthful.

The other hotels above will all feed you well, with dinner from about £10.

Haddington

Haddington is 12 miles (19.2 km) north-east of Dalkeith, mercifully by-passed by the A1, and peacefully spread along the banks of the **River Tyne**. This compact and very beautiful little town was extensively restored by an enterprising town council a few years ago, with a lot of help from local inhabitants: the results are outstanding. The wedge-shaped market square is divided at one end by the fine William Adam **Townhouse** whose church-like steeple was added by Gillespie Graham in 1831, and has a clock that still strikes the curfew at 10 pm and 7 am. Bright colour-washed houses front the main streets with quaint wynds and courtyards leading off giving you charming little vistas through into another, older way of life. Flood water from the river has been known to reach the steps of the mercat cross.

WHAT TO SEE

There are over 130 buildings listed of special architectural or historic interest in Haddington and you should get the excellent illustrated booklet, *A Walk round Haddington*, which is sold locally. There is also an architectural trail map, on the wall of the Townhouse.

The Church of St Mary, a medieval church, is one of Haddington's greatest treasures. Built by the river in the 14th century on the site of at least two previous churches, its chancel and transepts were roofless for 400 years after the Reformation until it was restored to its full glory in 1973. Concerts are often performed here now, honoured by such musicians as Yehudi Menuhin and Louis Kentner. The size of the church gives you an idea of the early prosperity of this area. John Knox, who was born nearby, in 1505, worshipped in St Mary's. Look out for a plain slab on the floor with a very moving inscription on it by Thomas Carlyle, to his wife Jane Welsh, daughter of a Haddington doctor. They were married for 40 years and she is buried in the churchyard.

Haddington House, 1680, in Sidegate, is now the headquarters and library of the Lamp of Lothian Trust, which is responsible for much of the restoration of the church and cultural life of the town. You can reach its restored 17th-century garden (with lovely roses, herbs and a charming paved sunken garden) from Pleached Alley.

The Poldrate Corn Mill, a three-storey, 18th-century mill, is situated beside the Tyne at Victoria Bridge. Its undershot water-wheel and cottages were also restored by the Lamp of Lothian Trust and it is now a community and arts centre. East of the river is called the **Nungate**: malefactors used to be hanged from the hump-backed bridge, a gruesome thought as you look at the attractive river scene where a swan breasts the current and an artist dabs peacefully at a canvas. The bridge led to the now vanished Abbey of Haddington, once known as the Lucerna Laudoniae (the Lamp of Lothian) for its reputation as a lamp of spirituality and learning, until the Reformation.

Traprain Law

Traprain Law dominates the plain east of Haddington, a massive whale-backed hump, part of a volcanic seam that includes North Berwick Law and the Bass Rock. Traprain, 734 ft (220 m) high, was the capital of the Vortadini, or Southern Pictish nation, overlooking the "Scottish Sea" whence invasion frequently threatened. The Picts lived on the rich, fertile lands below, retiring to the summit in times of danger, where you can still see the remains of a fort. Traces of their occupation on the lower slopes include standing stones and souterrains. In 1919 a fabulous hoard of 4th-century Christian and pagan treasure was excavated from the top of Traprain, possibly buried by pirates. You can see it now (a fascinating collection) in the Edinburgh Museum of Antiquities. It includes 160 silver-gilt bowls, goblets and clasps. Conservationists have managed to arrest the stone-quarrying operations at the east end of the Law and it is hoped that the huge, ugly gouged-out wedge will eventually be restored.

Hailes Castle (open at standard Ancient Monument times: adults 50p, children 25p) is below Traprain on the northern side. The extensive ruin dates from the 13th century and was once a feudal stronghold. Built by the Hepburns, later Earls of Bothwell and demolished by Cromwell, it was strategically sited on what was then the main north–south highway and used to charge extortionate tolls from passing travellers. The ruin stands beside a fast-flowing burn on a grassy bank carpeted with bulbs in spring. You can still see the water gate, bakehouse and vaulted pit prison in which prisoners were lowered and left to perish. The 29 year-old lover of the wife of one of the lairds was incarcerated here and it is said that his spirit lingers on, begging for a Christian burial.

Lennoxlove House

Lennoxlove House (open on Wednesday, Saturday and Sunday afternoons from 2 pm–5 pm in the summer, or by arrangement, tel Haddington 3720: adults £1.50, children £1) is a mile (1.6 km) south of Haddington on the B6369. It is the home of the Duke of Hamilton, and stands in pretty woodland, overlooking the Lammermuirs. The 15th-century keep has parapet gargoyles, bartizans and a watch tower penthouse. In the keep and 17th and 18th-century house you can see many good paintings including some by Raeburn, Van Dyck, Janssens, Lely, Augustus John and de Lazlo, as well as exquisite porcelain and furniture. Look out for the death mask of Mary, Queen of Scots and her silver casket in which were found the letters (possibly forged) incriminating her in the murder of Darnley. The house got its present name from the beautiful 17th-century Duchess of Lennox, Frances Teresa Stuart. She was a favourite of Charles II and possibly the model for the original Britannia on the pre-decimal coinage.

Preston Mill, East Linton

Preston Mill

Preston Mill (open daily in the summer and at weekends in winter: adults 85p, children 40p) lies about five miles (8 km) north-east of Haddington on the outskirts of attractive **East Linton**. This really delightful mill, which has been restored by the National Trust for Scotland, stands in a picture-postcard setting, on a green beside the Tyne, where muscovy ducks and mallards bask in the shade of apple trees. It is probably the only mill of its kind in working order. Built of warm red sandstone and mellow pantiles, it has a quaint polygonal kiln with a ventilator, a working water-wheel and wooden machinery. Next door there is a small museum in an out-building.

Athelstaneford

Athelstaneford is a tiny hamlet on a whinstone ridge a few miles north of Haddington. The thing you notice immediately is the St Andrews Cross flying proudly from a flag pole high above a brass mural in the kirkyard. The mural is engraved with a scene from a battle between an invading Northumbrian army and the combined forces of the Picts and Scots, in the Dark Ages. Legend states that the temporarily allied kings, normally at loggerheads, prayed for victory and were answered by seeing a saltire—the diagonal cross of St Andrew—etched in cloud against a blue sky. When they then won their battle, the two kings agreed to make the saltire the national flag of their united kingdoms, with St Andrew as their patron saint; a resolution that was to be broken many times before it became reality.

Stenton

Stenton, six miles (9.6 km) east of Haddington, is just off the A1. It is a delightful and very well preserved small village. You can see a restored tron (a tall, timber weighing scales, used for measuring out wool at the wool fairs) on one of the two tiny greens. Charming red sandstone cottages with pantiled roofs surround the greens, one with its original outside stairway. The old joiner's house lies below, with a picturesque court yard, and beside it stands a farm with a wheel house. Near the school is the Smiddy and the **Oak Inn** which incorporates a picture gallery with frequently changing exhibitions by contemporary artists. Here, you can sit at cosy tables enjoying an excellent light lunch (home-made soups, vol-au-vents with creamy fillings, pâtes, fish creams and cheese washed down with wine) surrounded by the paintings you came to see.

Rood Well is easy to miss. It is on the right as you enter the village from the A1. This 16th-century well, once a popular place for pilgrims, is in a hollow carpeted with St John's Wort. Nearby, the ruins of the old kirk, with crowstepped tower and dovecote, lie in the shadow of the tall pinnacles of the present church.

Pressmennan Glen

Pressmennan Glen, is a mile (1.6 km) south of Stenton, and is reached by forking left at Stenton school. It is a long, wooded hanging valley. Bennet's Burn was dammed in 1819 to form this artificial loch, a lovely deep, dark snake of water and haunt of wild fowl and trout. There is a forest trail that takes about two hours, depending on how often you pause to enjoy the peaceful beauty of the glen.

TOURIST INFORMATION

Brunton Hall, Musselburgh, tel 031-665 6597. It is open June to mid-September.

WHERE TO STAY

George Hotel, 91 High Street, Haddington, tel 062082-3372. B&B from £13: categories 4,3,4: 11 bedrooms, 7 en suite. It is right in the middle of this lovely old town.

Brown's Hotel, West Road, Haddington, tel 062082-2254. B&B from £18: categories 5,4,2: 6 bedrooms, 4 en suite. Nice, old fashioned hotel set back from the road near the centre and with a warm friendly atmosphere.

Maitland Field House Hotel, Sidegate, Haddington, tel 062082-2287. B&B from £15: categories 3,3,3: 13 bedrooms, 2 en suite. A family run hotel in its own grounds overlooking the historic St Mary's Church and Abbey, in Sidegate. Golf concession tickets arranged.

Harvesters Hotel, East Linton, tel 0620–860395/860429. B&B from £20: categories 4,4,4: 10 bedrooms, 7 en suite. Nice secluded hotel.

EATING OUT

Thirty-Nine Restaurant, 39 High Street, East Linton, tel 0620-860716. A small, informal restaurant where you will get nicely cooked traditional Scottish food, with fresh local ingredients and traditional home baking. Dinner from £8 (but you must ring first).

North Lammermuirs

South and east of Haddington, deep valleys cut into the smoothly rounded summits of the high, wild moorland of the Lammermuir Hills. In summer, sheep graze among wine-red heather, whins and cascading burns; skylarks sing and wild thyme scents the air as you walk. In winter the roads are often blocked with snow; all is white, even the hares; tractors go out from remote farmsteads to feed the sheep.

WHAT TO SEE

Garvald

Garvald, three miles (4.8 km) south of Traprain Law, is a small redstone village nestling in a fold of the hills beside the fast flowing **Papana Water**. Behind a grille on the church wall and below a sundial dated 1633, you can see a metal neck-collar (the "jougs") the height of a small man, where they used to tether petty criminals for a spell of punishment.

Nunraw is set back in a fringe of trees above the village to the south-east. It is a 15th-century tower house with later additions. This massive red pile, founded as a nunnery in the 12th century and abandoned during the Reformation, was bought by Irish Cistercians in 1946. It was their monastery while they built their new abbey. Now, the gentle monks in their white and black habits welcome all visitors who come here seeking God.

The new abbey, **Sancta Maria**, is further on up the hill on the right, a starkly simple, mellow brick building, high on the hillside. In the long plain church, the many clear-glass windows look out over desolate moorland. When the wind moans outside and the clouds race across the sky, it is perhaps easy to feel closer to the God people come here to seek.

Gifford

Gifford is four and a half miles (7.2 km) due south of Haddington and is a lovely 17th-century village straggling round a wide main street. You can see the entrance to **Yester House** (a private residence) at the end of an avenue, a graceful wrought-iron and gilded arch between redstone gatehouses with columned pillars topped by urns. It is a pity that you can't go in for on the estate there is the **Goblin Ha'**, a mighty underground hall with a high vaulted roof. This was built in the 13th century by (as tradition has it) Sir Hugo Gifford who was known to be a wizard. Sir Walter Scott could not resist putting such a romantic place into *Marmion*. ("Of lofty roof and ample size, beneath the castle deep it lies.")

In **Gifford Kirk** you can see the "laird's loft" or withdrawing room, with a fireplace for the pampered laird and his family. There is an interesting illustrated history of local buildings on a wall in the main street.

Whiteadder Reservoir lies, dark and mysterious, in a bowl of the Lammermuirs just inside the Lothian border eight miles (12.8 km) to the south-east. There is a sheltered picnic site below the dam surrounded by clumps of trees and you can choose from a number of good walks up into the hills.

Oldhamstocks

Oldhamstocks, still on the border, is eight miles (12.8 km) north-east of the reservoir. This very attractive village, on a plateau above a valley, has its cottages clustered round a wide green with a pump and cross. The curious name comes from the Saxon for "old settlement". As in Gifford, there is an illustrated board in the middle of the village giving the history of local buildings. **The Watch Tower**, 1824, in the kirkyard was used to watch over the graves in order to protect them from the lucrative practice of body-snatching. The 15th-century chancel of the kirk has a stone-slabbed roof. Don't miss the proclamation hanging in the porch, granting the village "... two frie fares yeirlie ... & a ... werklie mercat for buying and selling of horse nolt, sheip meil, malt and all sort of grane, cloath, linnings etc...". What an easy life our ancestors had, before spelling was standardised!

TOURIST INFORMATION

Town House, Dunbar, tel 0368-63353. It is open all year.

WHERE TO STAY

Tweedale Arms Hotel, Gifford, tel 062081-240. B&B from £18: categories 5,4,5: 11 bedrooms, 6 en suite. An attractive 18th-century inn in the middle of Gifford with a very friendly atmosphere.

Goblin Ha' Hotel, Gifford, tel 062081-244. Prices on application. Categories 3,3,4: 7 bedrooms. There is a beer garden and a Boule Court in this hotel in the middle of Gifford, and packages offered if you stay for a minimum of two nights. Good country-style cooking.

EATING OUT

Both hotels above will do you well, with a good dinner from about £10.

CRAFTWORK IN LOTHIAN

The places listed below all welcome visitors to watch them at work. Where telephone numbers are given you should check on times first.

Calligraphy

The Quill Gallery, Aberlady, tel 405-087 57. Illuminated documents, heraldic designs, writing, painting, use of quills as in medieval manuscripts.

Ceramics

The Pottery, Newton Port, Haddington, tel 062-082 3584. Slipcasting, throwing, fettling, glazing, pottery and tiles, sculpture.

Shape Scape Ceramics, The Pottery, Station Hill, North Berwick. Making and decorating semi-porcelain ceramics.

Jewellery and Silversmithing

Carrick Jewellery, 1 Brewster Square, Livingstone, tel 0506-412927. All aspects of jewellery making.

Knitting and Crochet

Ewe Nique Knitwear, Primrose Gallery, 3 Lodge Street, Haddington, tel 062-082 2199. Specialist hand and machine knitwear and design.

Weaving

Lammermoor Woollens, Michell's Close, Market Street, Haddington, tel 062-082 2207. Handwoven tweed clothes, colourful, intricate patterns on hand loom.

Glass

Vitrics Glass, 6 Tyne Close, off Church Street, Haddington, tel 062-082 2520. Designing and sandblasting glass, some kiln work.

Edinburgh Crystal, Eastfield, Penicuik, tel 0968-75128. All aspects of crystal glass-making.

Clothing and Textile

Enigma Bridals, 51–53 Forth Street, North Berwick, tel 0620-4220. Design and manufacture of fabrics in pure new wool and other natural fibres.

Dolls

Penston, near Tranent, tel 0875-610132. Making of reproduction antique porcelain dolls and restoration of antique dolls.

Part VIII

STRATHCLYDE:

Excluding Glasgow

Culzean Castle

The name Strathclyde is deceptive because although "strath" means "broad valley" Strathclyde in fact encompasses much more than that. It includes not only the broad valley of the Clyde, but also what should be the northern part of Dumfries and Galloway, several islands and a large, deeply cleft chunk of the south-western Highlands. You will notice great differences in the scenery of the region, as well as in the people and way of life.

Real Strathclyde is densely populated; a busy industrial sprawl, not beautiful but teeming with life and character. To the south you find farmland and the bright lights of the holiday resorts along the coasts north and south of the Clyde—the playgrounds of Glasgow. Here also, in Ayrshire, is Burns country—a land for dreamers. Then to the north and west, lie miles of lonely moor, mountains and forests, long, narrow sea lochs, enchanted islands and enough water to satisfy the keenest of sailors.

The Clydeside people are like the Glaswegians: the Cockney of the north; an endearing mixture of Celtic charm and shrewd, worldly wit, ready to take on the world single-handed. The farming people to the south are slower, steadier and more cautious; quiet men who will sit by their hearths and recite Burns to you as fluently as if they were making conversation. And in the north and west of Strathclyde you will find the descendants of the Dalriadan Scots, those gentle, slow, courteous Celts whose roots go back to the old clan system, where every man was a member of the clan family, and where justice and kindness were of supreme importance.

Strathclyde has plenty of prehistoric remains. It was mainly in Argyll that the ancient Dalriada Scots from Ireland settled, forming their powerful kingdom. It was here that Columba landed to spread the Christianity that St Ninian had introduced at Whithorn, more than one and a half centuries earlier. As well as the dozens of pre-historic burial mounds, stones and cairns, Strathclyde is dotted with the remains of a number of fortresses, built to defend the land from invaders, and the ruins of many once-beautiful churches and abbeys, destroyed during the Reformation.

The climate is as varied as the landscape: mild and damp like most west coast places, it can also be hot, dry and brilliantly sunny, or brittle-cold with vistas of snow-capped mountains.

There is a large choice of things to do in Strathclyde. You can visit the more populated tourist centres along the coast or travel to the remote areas in the north and west. There are excellent golf courses, riding and pony trekking, every sort of sea sport, fishing, birdwatching, walking and climbing. Your hotel will usually fix you up with fishing or golf, or boat hire: if not, try the local tourist office.

Most of the towns have a summer festival or Civic Week, with gaily decorated streets and an excuse for plenty of light-hearted entertainment and music. In the remoter places, the scenery is so beautiful that you can spend an entire holiday just exploring and discovering more and more lovely places. You will find a large number of castles and historic homes and buildings to visit, and Burns lovers should go on the nostalgic Burns Heritage Trail, taking in all the landmarks in the poet's short life. (For full details, write to Land o' Burns Centre, Alloway, Ayr.)

TOURIST INFORMATION

The local tourist information office is only open in the summer. At other times you can get advice, information and brochures from the Tourist Information Centre, 35–39 St Vincent Place, Glasgow, tel 041-227 4880. You can also try 39 Sandgate, Ayr, tel 0292-284196. This has a 24 hour answering service.

Strathclyde from the south—mainland

Girvan

Girvan is a typical Ayrshire seaside holiday resort, with good sandy beaches, golf courses, a harbour where pleasure-boats mingle with fishing trawlers, and easy access to the lovely Galloway Forest Park to the east and south (see Dumfries and Galloway).

SPECIAL ATTRACTIONS

Girvan has a Folk Festival in May, a Civic Week in June, and an Easter Cycle Race.

WHAT TO SEE

Knockcushion is an attractive public garden with an aviary, above the harbour. There

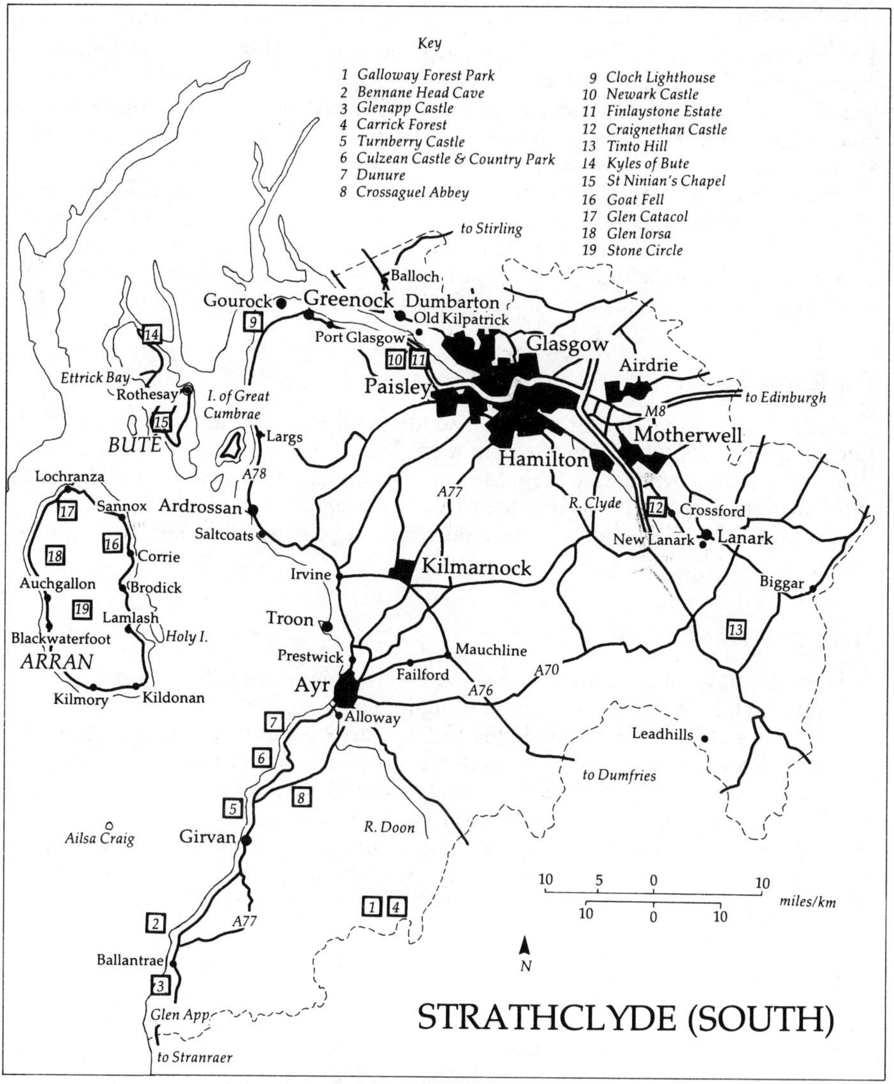

Key
1 Galloway Forest Park
2 Bennane Head Cave
3 Glenapp Castle
4 Carrick Forest
5 Turnberry Castle
6 Culzean Castle & Country Park
7 Dunure
8 Crossaguel Abbey
9 Cloch Lighthouse
10 Newark Castle
11 Finlaystone Estate
12 Craignethan Castle
13 Tinto Hill
14 Kyles of Bute
15 St Ninian's Chapel
16 Goat Fell
17 Glen Catacol
18 Glen Iorsa
19 Stone Circle
to Stirling
Balloch
Gourock
Greenock
Dumbarton
Old Kilpatrick
Port Glasgow
Glasgow
Airdrie
Paisley
to Edinburgh
M8
Motherwell
Hamilton
Ettrick Bay
Rothesay
I. of Great Cumbrae
Largs
BUTE
A78
Lochranza
Sannox
Ardrossan
Saltcoats
Corrie
Auchgallon
Brodick
Lamlash
Holy I.
Blackwaterfoot
ARRAN
Kilmory
Kildonan
Irvine
Troon
Prestwick
Ayr
Alloway
Kilmarnock
A77
R. Clyde
Crossford
New Lanark
Lanark
Biggar
Mauchline
Failford
A76
A70
Leadhills
to Dumfries
R. Doon
Ailsa Craig
Girvan
A77
Ballantrae
Glen App
to Stranraer
10 5 0 10
10 0 10
miles/km
N
STRATHCLYDE (SOUTH)

used to be a hill fort here, and you will see a stone which commemorates the granting of a charter by Robert Bruce, and the fact that he administered justice from this hill.

Ailsa Craig

You can take boats from Girvan to Ailsa Craig, the 1,114 ft (334 m) high volcanic lump that rises from the sea, ten miles (16 km) due west. It is known as Paddy's Milestone because it lies half-way between Glasgow and Belfast. At low tide you can walk the two mile (3.2 km) circumference of the rock, or, if you feel energetic, climb to the top for lovely, if rather windy, views over to Arran and Kintyre, and back to the mainland. Ailsa Craig comes from the Gaelic for fairy rock, a delightfully romantic name for the place where miscreant monks were once sent to cool off, and where persecuted Catholics took refuge during the Reformation. It is now a bird sanctuary, with gannets and puffins among its avian population. The guano can smell quite powerful on a warm day. The special granite used for making curling stones is quarried from Ailsa Craig.

Carleton Castle

Carleton Castle (accessible at all times: admission free) is five miles (8 km) south of Girvan. It was one of the chain of watchtowers, built by the powerful Kennedy family to defend this part of the coast. It is amusing to stand on the cliff here and recall the ballad that tells of the baron who lived in the castle and pushed seven wives, in turn, to their deaths over this cliff. He himself was similarly disposed of by wife number eight, Mary Cullean.

Bennane Head Cave

Bennane Head Cave lies a little further south, on a point three miles (4.8 km) north of Ballantrae. Only the very sure-footed should attempt to visit this macabre spot, the alleged hide-out of Sawney Bean. In the 17th century it is said that a number of wealthy travellers, known to have passed through this area, vanished without trace. Suspicion and local gossip led the authorities to this cave where they discovered Sawney Bean and his large, incestuously-bred family, with an enormous quantity of human bones. Sawney and his ghoulish tribe had been living off the flesh, and the gold, of their unfortunate victims for years! Some accounts of the discovery of the cave describe a gruesome array of "joints" hanging from the roof like hams in a farmhouse kitchen.

Ballantrae

Ballantrae, immortalised by Robert Louis Stevenson, has been twice tricked by literature. Burns wrote a lovely song about the Stinchar valley, which carried the River Stinchar into the sea at Ballantrae, but primly fastidious editors changed it to: "Beyond yon hill where Lugar flows", depriving Ballantrae of its rightful acclaim. Then Stevenson was attracted to the name of the place, and used it for his novel *Master of Ballantrae*, but set the story further south in the Stewartry of Kirkcudbright.

Glenapp Castle (open daily except Saturdays in the summer: admission free) is just outside Ballantrae, at the northern end of **Glen App**. The castle was designed by David Bryce in 1870 and stands in pleasant grounds with an aviary and woodland walks.

Carrick Forest

Carrick Forest starts eight miles (12.8 km) due east of Girvan. It is a vast expanse of wild country away from the holiday crowds and fruit machines. Its mountainous terrain, studded with lochs, makes it very attractive. You can walk here for hours and feel yourself in another world.

Loch Doon Castle (accessible at all times: admission free) can be seen on the shore of its loch, near the border with Dumfries and Galloway. This 19th-century castle once stood on an island in the loch. When the hydroelectricity board raised the level of the water, the ruined castle was dismantled and re-built on its present site. It used to be called Balliol Castle and was owned by King John Balliol, the ineffectual "Toom Tabard".

Turnberry Castle

Turnberry Castle (accessible at all times), is five miles (8 km) north of Girvan up the coast. The castle is a scrap of a ruin on a cliff-top by the lighthouse, which stands on what was the castle's court yard. There are some who claim that Turnberry, rather than Lochmaben, was the birth place of King Robert Bruce, and if this is so, the infant prince grew up with glorious views to inspire him. The castle was brought into the Bruce family by his mother, Margaret, and certainly Robert's supporters used to meet here, to plot his accession to the throne.

More recently, Turnberry is internationally known as a golf centre, with two excellent courses and a huge hotel. It is incredible, looking at the velvet sward today, to think that these golf courses were tarmac-ed and used as an airfield during the war, while the hotel was requisitioned as a hospital. The Open Championships are held in July.

Culzean Castle and Country Park

Culzean Castle (open daily from 1 April to 31 October: adults £1.70, children 85p) and Country Park (open all year round: admission free if on foot, £2.50 for cars) overlooks Culzean Bay about eight miles (12.8 km) north of Girvan. Pronounced Cullain, the castle was built on top of the cliff in 1777 by Robert Adam, incorporating an ancient tower that was one of the many Kennedy strongholds guarding the coast. Built with an eye to grandeur rather than defence, it is a sumptuous mansion full of architectural marvels that dazzle the eye rather than soothe! There is the round drawing room with its specially woven carpet, an oval staircase under a great glass dome, and a profusion of Adam mouldings that make you feel you are encased in Wedgwood china, or icing sugar! When Culzean was given over to the National Trust for Scotland in 1945, it was with the condition that an apartment be set aside for anyone whom Scotland might wish to honour. The first tenant for life was General Eisenhower.

The Culzean Country Park was created in 1970, the first in Scotland, with a Park Centre in the Adam farm buildings. You can see an excellent audio visual show here, giving you plenty of interesting information about Culzean and there are exhibitions, a shop and restaurant. Guided walks take you all over the 565 acres (226 ha) of lovely grounds, including the castle gardens, terraced, with castellated walls, a sunken fountain, rare shrubs from all over the world as well as palm trees, glorious cascades of colour, a camelia house, orangery and seats where you can sit back and admire it all. The grounds include a swan pond, aviary and deer park. Culzean is a day out in itself.

Dunure

Dunure (accessible at all times: admission free), four miles (6.4 km) north of Culzean, is a gaunt ruin on the edge of the cliff. It has a conical dovecote, some walls, overgrown, and its precinct is now used as a car park. Mary, Queen of Scots came here in 1563 during one of the lighter moments of her tragic reign, when she toured her kingdom accompanied by a splendid train of courtiers. It is said that in 1570 the Earl of Cassillis roasted a lay-abbot who came from nearby Crossaguel. The earl did this in an attempt to persuade him to hand over the abbey lands.

Crossraguel Abbey

Crossraguel Abbey (closed Thursday afternoons and Fridays: adults 50p, children 25p) lies a couple of miles (3.2 km) inland from Culzean. Founded in 1244, it resisted the dissolution of the monasteries until in 1592, the Reformation took its toll. It is a scattered ruin, parts of it more intact than most of its fellows, giving you a good idea of what monastic life must have been like in those days. The 16th-century, turreted gatehouse is particularly well-preserved. It must have been peaceful here for the monks, before the purges did away with the old monastic life, surrounded by sweeping green fields and the smell of the sea not far away.

TOURIST INFORMATION

Bridge Street, Girvan, tel 0465-4950. It is open from April to October.

Culzean Country Park, Maybole, tel 06556-293. It is open from April to October.

WHERE TO STAY

Hotel Westcliffe, Louisa Drive, Girvan, tel 0465-2128. B&B from £11: categories 4,4,4: 24 bedrooms, 13 en suite. All rooms with colour TV and tea/coffee making facilities. The hotel stands on the sea front, and has a solarium.

Kings Arms Hotel, Dalrymple Street, in the middle of Girvan, tel 0465-3322. B&B from £14: categories 4,4,5: 26 bedrooms, 11 en suite. A family run, 2-star hotel with telephone, colour TV, video films and tea/coffee making facilities. There is a good restaurant, a cocktail bar and dancing most weekends. (It was in the Kings Arms that John Keats wrote *A Tribute to Ailsa Craig*, in the summer of 1818, three years before his death.)

Southfield Hotel, The Avenue, Girvan, tel 0465-4222. B&B from £11: categories

3,3,4: 6 bedrooms, 5 en suite. A small, friendly hotel with colour TV in the bedrooms and tea/coffee making facilities, and a cocktail bar, serving bar lunches, as well as a dining room. You can get tickets for eight local golf courses when booking for the hotel.

Sands Hotel, 20 Louisa Drive, Girvan, tel 0465-2178. B&B from £8: categories 3,3,2: 9 bedrooms. A friendly hotel on the sea front.

The Royal Hotel, 71 Main Street, Ballantrae, tel 046583-204. B&B from £9.50: categories 4,3,5: 5 bedrooms. A comfortable little hotel in the middle of Ballantrae.

Turnberry Hotel and Golf Courses, Turnberry, tel 06553-202. B&B from £45: categories 6,6,6: 137 bedrooms en suite. This hotel overlooks the sea and the championship golf courses and gives you good value, in comfort, service and food, for every penny you pay.

EATING OUT

Splinters Restaurant, 56 Montgomerie Street, Girvan, tel 0465-3481. Good meals served in red pine "booths" with 1930s music. Fresh shellfish and fish, Scottish beef and lamb. Local vegetables and salads, good puddings. Dinner from £8.

Culzean Country Park Restaurant, Maybole, tel 06556-240. Good Scottish food. A nice way to round off a visit to Culzean. Lunch from £5.

Malin Court, Turnberry, tel 06553-457/9. The restaurant in the hotel overlooks Arran and the Firth of Clyde, and serves good Scottish food with local ingredients. Dinner from £8.

Turnberry Hotel, see above. Excellent food but not cheap. Dinner from £18.

Ayr

Ayr is 22 miles (35.2 km) north of Girvan, and is the main holiday centre on this coast. A large, bustling town, it has every sort of entertainment: good shops, splendid sandy beaches, three golf courses, fishing, and a famous racecourse. It is a town that seems to sparkle with friendliness and fun. There was a settlement here as far back as the 8th century. Early in his struggles for Scotland, Robert Bruce burnt down "The Barns of Ayr" (a temporary barracks) as well as the inhabitants, 500 of the troops of Edward I. For many, Ayr is of supreme importance as the capital of Burns country. Robert Burns was born on 25 January, 1759, at Alloway, just outside the town. Although he only lived there for seven years, much of his youth was spent nearby and he used many local people and scenes for his poems.

SPECIAL ATTRACTIONS

The Ayr Golf week is held in June. In August there is the Flower Show.

WHAT TO SEE

The Burns Heritage Trail, organised by the Scottish Tourist Board, takes you to all the places of importance relating to the poet's life and work. You can get details from The Land o' Burns Centre, Alloway, or from any of the Scottish Tourist Board offices, or from 23 Ravelston Terrace, Edinburgh, EH4 3EU, tel 031-332 2433. This is a must for lovers of Burns!

Burns Statue Square has one of the more impressive of the many monuments that have been erected in memory of the poet, which stands on a pedestal surrounded by flower beds.

The Tam o' Shanter Inn (open daily except Sundays but including Sundays, June to August: adults 35p, children 20p) is in the High Street. This is where Burns often met up with his friend Douglas Graham, his model for the character of Tam o' Shanter. The inn is a typical brewhouse of its time and now a fascinating museum of Burns memorabilia.

The Auld Kirk, down a wynd off the High Street on the banks of the wide river, is where Burns was baptised. As you go through **Kirk Port**, look for the rather morbid "mort-safes" dating from 1655, which were put over freshly filled graves to discourage the body-snatchers! Cromwell supplied the funds to build this church, having used the old one as part of a great fort he built in Ayr, of which little now remains.

The Auld Brig will ring a bell for Burns lovers. Dating from the 13th century it was Ayr's only bridge until a new bridge was built in 1788 and replaced in 1877. Burns wrote a poem, in which he watched the pretentious construction of the new bridge being built, through the contemptuous eyes of the old bridge, prophesying, with uncanny prescience, that the new bridge would not stand the test of time.

In the High Street a plaque marks the site of the old fish market, where all would have been bustle and noise, everyone jostling and calling out and the air heavy with the smell of the fish.

Loudoun Hall (open in the summer or by arrangement, tel 0292-282109: admission free) is in Boat Vennel. It is one of the oldest surviving examples of townhouse architecture in the country. Built for a rich merchant, in the late 15th century, it has been beautifully restored, having previously been condemned as a slum and threatened with a demolition order! It is now a Culture Centre.

Alloway, within the southern suburbs of Ayr, was the village where Burns was born in 1759 and lived for seven years.

The Burns Cottage and Museum (open daily, except Sundays in the winter: adults £1, children 50p, which includes the Burns Monument, next door) incorporates the thatched cottage that was built by Burns' father. Here you can see, among other things, the box-bed in which the poet was born. Family and animals shared the same roof—a practice that helped to warm the living quarters in winter, if also to make them rather smelly. The museum, adjoining the cottage, contains a wealth of Burns memorabilia including the family bible and many of the original manuscripts, such as that of *Auld Lang Syne*.

Burns Monument close to the museum in Alloway, was built in fanciful Grecian style, in 1823, on the **River Doon**. A circular temple, held up by fluted columns stands over a chamber that contains such treasures as Jean Armour's wedding ring, and Highland Mary's bible. (Jean was his wife; Mary was to have been, but she died.) In the gardens around the monument you can see statues of Tam o' Shanter and Souter Johnnie.

Brig o' Doon, the 13th-century, single arched bridge that spans the river here is the one over which Tam o' Shanter escaped on his Maggie, leaving the witches to their "...hornpipes, jigs, strathspeys and reels..." in Kirk-Alloway, after Tam had been on a monumental bender with his "...trusty, drouthy crony—Souter Johnnie...".

Alloway Kirk, scene of the witches orgy, was built in 1510. A tiny shell now, it overlooks the grave of Burns' father.

The Land o' Burns Centre (open all the year: admission free, except for the audio visual show: adults 20p, children 10p) is opposite the kirk. Here you can wallow in Burns' memory. There is an exhibition area and an audio visual show that gives a first-class resume of the poet's life and work.

Burns House (open daily during the summer: adults 50p, children 20p) is in **Mauchline,** 11 miles (17.6 km) east of Ayr. It is the house where Burns lived with his wife, Jean Armour, before and after their marriage in 1788. It has been kept as it was, furnished in the style of that period, and contains many relics of the poet and his times. It was on land here that Burns and his brother farmed without much success from 1784–8, and it was in the kirk here that poor Burns was forced to sit on the "cutty stool" or stool of repentance, a humiliating punishment inflicted by the Elders of the kirk because of his "irregular marriage" with Jean Armour!

At **Failford**, just outside Mauchline, on the River Ayr you can see **Highland Mary's Monument**, where Burns is said to have parted from his beloved Highland Mary Campbell, for the last time before she died.

Prestwick

Prestwick is almost continuous with Ayr, to the north. It was here that legend tells of Robert Bruce, in the early stages of the leprosy that killed him, striking the ground with his lance. He was parched with thirst and exhausted: water gushed from where his lance struck and he was miraculously revived. You can see **Bruce's Well**, in a housing estate south of the town, signposted from the Ayr Road.

Troon

Troon, three miles (4.8 km) north of Prestwick, is another popular seaside resort, with sandy beaches and good golf courses. The name comes from Troone (nose) because of the hook of land that thrusts out to sea.

Kilmarnock

Kilmarnock is 12 miles (19.2 km) north-east of Ayr and 8 miles (13 km) inland. It is the centre of industry in this area, whisky being one of its most important products. The **Johnnie Walker Distillery** must be world famous—its bottles certainly are, and you can have tours of the premises on weekdays. The company was founded in 1820 when an Ayrshire man, John Walker, gave up farming and bought a grocery, wine and spirit business in Kilmarnock.

SPECIAL ATTRACTIONS
Kilmarnock holds a lively carnival for the last week in May. There is also a "Festival of Leisure", in September.

WHAT TO SEE
Kay Park Monument and Burns Museum (closed till further notice, admission by arrangement, tel 0563-26401) is a tall red sandstone tower, with good views from the top. Burns was closely associated with the town and his first collection of poems, the "Kilmarnock Edition" was produced here by John Wilson in 1786. In the museum you can see this rare treasure, a slim, 35 page volume with 44 poems. There are lots of other interesting Burns manuscripts as well.

The Dick Institute (open daily except Sundays: admission free) in Elmbank Avenue, has geological and archaeological exhibits for anyone interested in the local history, as well as an art gallery with frequent exhibitions.

Dean Castle (open daily in the summer: adults 50p) stands in lovely grounds in a wooded hollow in Dean Road. This 14th-century fortified keep with a 15th-century palace, was once the ancestral home of the Boyds. Inside, you can see collections of armour, weapons, old musical instruments and tapestries, with a splendid banqueting hall, a minstrel's gallery and a gloomy dungeon. **The Dean Castle Country Park** (always open: admission free) consists of 200 acres (80 ha) of wood and farm land over which you can wander.

Irvine

Irvine, eight miles (12.8 km) west of Kilmarnock and on the coast, is one of Scotland's new towns, developing from its own industrial estate founded in 1960. But its history goes back a long way, for it was here that William Wallace was deserted by his followers in 1297, when they decided to sign a treaty with the English. Mary, Queen of Scots came to Irvine in 1563 and was entertained in the now ruined 13th-century Seagate Castle. This visit is now commemorated with **Marymass**, a week-long festival every August, which culminates with a procession past the castle and the crowning of a queen. The town also holds a Harbour Festival in July.

The Magnum Leisure Centre is 150 acres (60 ha) of seaside park, with swimming pools, an ice rink, squash courts, theatre, cinema, bars and cafes.

Eglinton Castle

Eglinton Castle (always open: admission free), is two miles (3.2 km) north of Irvine. Here, below the 100 ft (30 m) high tower, built in 1796, a romantic attempt was made to re-establish ancient chivalric ceremonies, in 1839, with the holding of the Eglinton Tournament: a somewhat whimsical Victorian longing for "the good old days".

Saltcoats

Saltcoats, is an industrial town four miles (6.4 km) along the coast north-west of Irvine, with all the associated sprawl of development. It was an important producer of salt in the days of James V. Its **Maritime Museum** (open daily: admission free) has many exhibits of interest for those who enjoy the sea.

Ardrossan, another holiday resort, merging with the northern suburb of Saltcoats, is the terminus for steamers crossing to Arran. The Ardrossan Highland Games are held in June.

Largs

Largs is ten miles (16 km) up the coast from Ardrossan, and is perhaps the most attractive of the resorts on this coast. It is built on a shelf between the hills and the sea, looking across to Great Cumbrae Island and beyond, to Bute. It is a town of hotels and guest houses and every sort of holiday facility, and is the terminal for ferries out to Great Cumbrae.

The Battle of Largs, in 1263, ended Norway's claims to the Western Isles. Alexander III's army waited, while the Norwegian fleet lay helpless in the teeth of October gales, polishing off those who escaped ashore as the galleys foundered. King Haakon of Norway fled with the tattered remnants of his navy, to die in the Orkneys, too dispirited to return home. This historic event is celebrated during the September Largs Viking Festival.

Great Cumbrae

From Largs you can make the ten minute ferry crossing to the island of Great Cumbrae, a quiet place of low hills and sea views. One road, of 12 miles (19.2 km), encircles the island. Great Cumbrae is an ideal place for a family holiday. You can hire bicycles and go out to the beaches with little effort. **Millport**, the only town, curves round a bay. Its beach is a mixture of sand and rocks, and here you can visit the **Museum of the Cumbraes**, in Garrison House (open Tuesday to Saturday in the summer: admission free) with an exhibition of Victorian and Edwardian social history.

The Pencil Monument commemorates the Battle of Largs, a slender obelisk south of Largs, from where it would have been possible to survey the battle.

The Largs Museum (open in the summer with a donation box) will tell you all about the battle, as well as about local history in general.

Muirshiel Country Park

Muirshiel Country Park, nine miles (14.4 km) north-east of Largs in high wooded moorland, gives you a good day out with signposted nature trails, picnic sites and an information centre. Adjoining it is the **Castle Semple Loch Water Park**, at **Lochwinnoch**, where you can sail, row, fish and canoe on the loch.

Gourock

Gourock is 12 miles (19.2 km) north of Largs on the shoulder where the Clyde swings round from the east to flow out to sea. The **Cloch Lighthouse** is an imposing white landmark, essential for guiding shipping. It was built in 1797. You reach the lighthouse before the town.

Half resort, half port, Gourock has a character of its own. It is the home of Caledonian MacBrayne who run many of the west coast ferries, several of which depart from here and it is an important centre for yachtsmen. You get lovely views out over the Firth from the **Kempock Stone**, just east of the town. This 6 ft (1.8 m) high block of grey stone, known as the Granny Kempock, dates from pre-historic times and may have been part of a Druid temple. Superstitious fishermen in the past believed that Granny Kempock commanded the sea. They used to bring her offerings which would be laid before her while they walked round her seven times, begging for fair weather and good fishing. Newly married couples used to pay homage to her also, asking a blessing on their marriage. Gourock Highland Games are held in May.

You will find a great contrast in the landscape round these parts: inland, are remote farms and lonely moorland, while along the river you feel the increasing bustle and splurge of industry as you approach Glasgow.

Greenock

Greenock is an industrial town, the sixth largest in Scotland. It is situated immediately east of Gourock and the suburbs of the two towns merge as the Clyde narrows to a river. At present, with dying shipyards, men out of work, and Port Glasgow (further along), it is rather depressing. But it will recover with that tenacious spirit that is part of the Clydeside character. You need go only a stone's throw inland to find yourself back in the moors again.

SPECIAL ATTRACTIONS
The Greenock Inverclyde Marathon is held here at the end of August.

WHAT TO SEE
The Maclean Museum (open daily except Sunday: admission free) will give you a good picture of the local history. It includes an art gallery.

Port Glasgow, merging with the eastern suburbs of Greenock, was built in the 17th century and was the last deep water port of the Clyde.

Newark Castle (open standard Ancient Monument times: adults 35p, children 15p) is east of the town and dates from the 16th century, with a 15th-century tower. It is a large, turreted mansion house, overlooking the river. It is still almost intact with court-yard, hall and a large number of chambers, an elegant contrast to the industrial sprawl that surrounds it.

Finlaystone Estate

Finlaystone Estate (open all year: adults 60p, children 40p), two miles (3.2 km) west, is an excellent garden centre with lovely woodland walks. People return continually to this very special place: you will find that it has a unique atmosphere that you cannot resist. The beautiful grounds have been lovingly developed by the family who own it, and you almost feel at home, as you lean over a stone balustraded bridge, looking down at an enchanted water garden or wander in the formal gardens, high above the Clyde. When you go into the extremely good garden shop in the old stable block you find yourself welcomed as if you were one of the family. You could easily be asked to help pick a dozen bunches of daffodils, or to carry a bag of compost out to someone's car! The house (open on Sunday afternoons in the summer or by arrangement, tel 047-554285: small fee) has some Victorian relics, flower prints, and an international collection of dolls.

TOURIST INFORMATION

35/39 St Vincent Place, Glasgow, tel 041-227 4880. It is open all year.
The Promenade, Largs, tel 0475-673765. It is open all year.
62 Bank Street, Kilmarnock, tel 0563-39090. It is open all year.
39 Sandgate, Ayr 0292-284196. It is open all year.

WHERE TO STAY

You have an enormous choice of hotels and guest houses and should consult the tourist brochures that you can get through the local information offices. The following are just a small, random selection.

Sundrum Castle, Coylton, near Ayr, tel 0292-570221. Prices on application. In 82 acres (33 ha), a mile (1.6 km) out of Coylton on the Ayr road, this luxury hotel dates from 1373. It has been newly modernised inside, to give every possible comfort in the 25 or so bedrooms. Riding, fishing and shooting in the grounds.

Carlton Hotel Ayr Road, Prestwick, tel 0292-76811. B&B from £24: categories 5,5,6: 39 bedrooms en suite. Rooms have colour TV, telephone, tea/coffee making facilities. A modern hotel in its own grounds only ten minutes from the middle of Prestwick and Ayr. Good restaurant, with live entertainment and dancing most evenings and every weekend

The Pickwick Hotel, 19 Racecourse Road, Ayr, tel 0292–60111. B&B from £22.50: categories 6,5,5: 15 bedrooms en suite. A 3-Star AA and RAC hotel in attractive grounds. Recommended by Michelin, Egon Ronay and Ashley Courtenay. Good food and bar lunches.

The Chestnuts Hotel, 52 Racecourse Road, Ayr, tel 0292-264393. B&B from £14: categories 4,4,5: 14 bedrooms, 8 en suite. A comfortable, 2-Star RAC hotel. Relias Routiers recommended, with Wedgwood "Top 500" award. Rooms with colour TV, baby listening intercom and tea/coffee making facilities. Good food and a warm welcome.

Irvine Hospitality Inn, Irvine, tel 0294-74272. B&B from £27.50: categories 6,5,6: 128 bedrooms en suite. A modern hotel with comfortable rooms.

Elderslie Hotel, Largs, tel 0475-686460. B&B from £17.50: categories 4,4,4: 25 bedrooms, 12 en suite. On the sea front with lovely views over the Firth of Clyde. Good food and a warm welcome.

Gleddoch House Hotel, Langbank, tel 047-554 711. B&B from £32: categories 6,5,5: 20 bedrooms en suite. Special weekend bargains. The hotel stands in 250 acres (100 ha) overlooking the Clyde and the Loch Lomond Hills. It was once a family home, and its rooms are all elegant and comfortable with every possible facility. The country house atmosphere is warm and hospitable and guests have free use of an 18 hole golf course, squash courts, snooker, sauna, and riding. You'd have to look a long way to find a better place to stay.

EATING OUT

There are plenty of places in all the resort towns, and the hotels will all do you well. For a real treat, go to Gleddoch, see above, whose good food won the Taste of Britain Award for Scotland, where you can get a first class dinner from £15.

Paisley

Paisley, ten miles (16 km) south-east of Port Glasgow, has given its name to a design of shawl that must be known internationally. Soldiers, returning from India at the end of the 18th century, brought with them the shawls they had bought in Kashmir. The people of the town adapted these and created the distinctive Paisley design, based on segments of pine cones, which were Kashmiri in origin. The town has its annual Festival in May.

Paisley Abbey was founded in 1171 for Cluniac monks and was almost completely destroyed by Edward I. Rebuilt after Bannockburn, its tower collapsed in 1553, wrecking the nave, and it remained in this state for many years. The present restoration, including work by Robert Lorimer, is the parish church, a lovely, dignified building, austere but full of a deep peace. You can see the Barochan Cross in the abbey, a weathered 10th-century Celtic cross that used to stand on a hillock overlooking Port Glasgow. The tombs of several of the Bruces are in the choir, under a stone-vaulted ceiling, and there is a charming little chapel dedicated to St Mirin, a 6th-century saint who was adopted as Paisley's patron saint.

Paisley Museum and Art Gallery (open daily except Sundays: admission free) has among its many interesting exhibits a fascinating display of Paisley shawls, and plaids, at least 500 of them with their looms and design patterns.

Lanark

There isn't all that much to detain you, south of Glasgow but you should not miss a visit to Lanark on the A73, 23 miles (36.8 km) south-east of Glasgow. The town stands on a plateau high above the upper reaches of the Clyde and is the agricultural market centre for the area. At first glance you might write it off as just another main-road town, with the busy A73 carrying heavy traffic right through its centre, but a closer look will reveal a strong individual character that will invite you to explore further.

The main street is so broad that a long central flower bed, studded with chain-linked pillars, divides it into a dual carriageway. It slopes down between cheerfully painted houses and shop fronts, apparently oblivious of the ceaseless flow of traffic, to the 18th-century parish church that stands like a bulwark at the bottom. Don't let the man in the car behind you prevent you from stopping here to inspect the **Statue of William Wallace** that is in a canopied niche in the face of the tall, colour-washed church tower. It must be one of the most endearing statues ever to have been set up in memory of a hero: a huge, genial, Father Christmas-like figure who seems to be embarrassed by his bare, fat knees. You look up at him and marvel that such an unlikely fellow can have roused the Scots to rebellion and helped them to struggle free from the despair they had fallen into, in 1297. The statue was presented to the town in 1822 by its sculptor, Robert Forrest, who, it is said, taught himself his art. This is easy to believe and you can't help sympathising with the elders of the town who, when presented with the statue, wondered desperately where they should display it. William Wallace lived in Lanark and, when the

English murdered his wife (or mistress) Marion Bradfute, it was here that he struck the first blow for Scottish independence. Every June Lanark celebrates Lanimer Day, which coincides with the Riding of the Marches.

New Lanark

You could easily dash through Lanark and miss New Lanark, for no fuss is made of this delightful backwater, a mile (1.6 km) to the south and only modestly signposted. Stop at the top, as the narrow road takes a final hairpin bend before descending into New Lanark. The view down over the village to the distant **Falls of Clyde** belongs to a painting by Turner. A mist of spray rises from the trees above a glint of foaming water and if the sun is shining and it happens to be autumn, you could not find a more breath-catching view in this part of Scotland. New Lanark was built in 1784 as a model cotton manufacturing village by a rich industrialist, David Dale. His son-in-law, Robert Owen became manager of the estate in 1800 and instituted some very radical innovations, including the founding of the first infant school in Britain. Owen's reforms for better working conditions and "villages of unity" were the forerunners of todays co-operative societies.

New Lanark is a monument to those days of reform. It is in the process of restoration, with the old buildings coming back to life, austere but not ugly, uncluttered by architectural adornment, rising tall and plain from the street, some with outside stairways, overlooking the river. The old bell that summoned the people to work or to pray still hangs high in its belfry. There are exhibitions in the village illustrating clearly its social and industrial history.

Bonnington Nature Reserve

Park at the far end of New Lanark and go down the steps to Bonnington Nature Reserve where a fenced path follows the Clyde a couple of miles (3.2 km) upstream past the falls of **Corra Linn** to those of **Bonnington Linn**. The river tumbles over treacherous black slabs of granite, overhung by pines, oaks and birches, spray rising like smoke. This stretch of the river, known as **The Falls of Clyde** and beloved of many romantic artists, runs through **Corehouse Nature Reserve**.

On the walk you will see **Wallace's Tower**, or **Corra Castle**, far too dangerous to enter but stirring to the imagination. It clings to a rock pinnacle high above Corra Linn, its walls rising directly from the edge of the sheer cliff. Although this reach of the Clyde is harnessed to serve the hydroelectricity power stations and is thus robbed of much of its full splendour, enough water remains to provide salmon with access to their spawning grounds up-river and to give dramatic effects as it pours over gigantic layered slabs of granite. Corra Linn drops 86 ft (25.8 m) in a series of steps, to a dark still lagoon below, set in an amphitheatre of rock, and hung with ever-damp vegetation and precariously rooted trees. Bonnington Linn is about a mile (1.6 km) further on, with two branches of the river descending round a rock island.

Craignethan Castle

Craignethan Castle (open during standard Ancient Monument times: adults 50p, children 25p) is five miles (8 km) north-west of Lanark and about two miles (3.2 km) west of the A72 at **Crossford**. You reach it across an unfenced, green plateau where shaggy cattle roam free among grotesquely gnarled old thorn trees and come abruptly on the castle that stands on a spur between the deeply eroded beds of the Water of Nethan and the Craignethan Burn. This 16th-century stronghold was destroyed after Mary, Queen of Scots was hounded from her throne, because the Hamilton family who owned it had been loyal supporters of her cause. The ruin is well preserved with a keep, passages, basement and well, round an open courtyard. In 1962, excavations unearthed a rare 'caponier'. Buried for nearly 400 years, this dank, stone-roofed vault was built across the floor of a dry moat to protect and conceal handgunners defending the castle. It still contained bones of cattle, sheep, rabbits and chickens from the hasty meals of those 16th-century gunners!

Although he himself denied it, Craignethan is believed to have been the inspiration for Walter Scott's Tillietudlem Castle, in *Old Mortality* and a nearby halt on the long-disused branch railway was called Tillietudlem, in its honour.

Leadhills

South of Lanark, on the border before Dumfries and Galloway, a pink road straggles over humpbacked bridges between dry-stone walls with views across farmland and smooth-turfed hills. Forest and pasture create a patchwork on the hillsides, all shades of green and brown and sepia, dotted with rural cottages, rising to desolate moor and peat bogs where the farms are linked by single telephone wires.

Leadhills, high on this lonely moorland 18 miles (28.8 km) south of Lanark, is second only to Wanlockhead as Scotland's highest village. In the small, windswept cemetery above the tiny village, lie the remains of John Taylor who died at the age of 137, having worked for more than 100 years in the lead mills. It doesn't say much for the toxic effects of lead that we are always being warned about!

Allan Ramsay, the 17th-century poet, was born here, surrounded by the hills that are alive with the ghosts of Covenanters who used their protection for holding conventicles.

Biggar

Biggar lies ten miles (16 km) east of Lanark near the Borders. It is a typical lowland market town, the main road running through its centre, widening to form a market place. The town has Open Golf Championships in May.

WHAT TO SEE

The Gladstone Court Museum (open in the summer: adults 80p, children 40p) is an indoor street museum with shops and shop windows, an intriguing lay-out of all you would have seen walking through the town in the old days: a grocer, photographer, dressmaker, bank, school, library, ironmonger, chemist, china merchant, etc. It is a well designed display that will enchant anyone who used to enjoy "playing shop".

Cadgers Brig at the bottom of the town is the bridge where William Wallace is said to have crossed the burn dressed as a cadger (pedlar) on a spying mission. The bridge is more likely to have been named after the cadgers who came into town over it on market days.

Tinto Hill

Tinto Hill, six miles (9.6 km) south-west of Biggar, dominates the landscape for miles. At 2,220 ft (666 m) high, it begs to be climbed, when the weather is right. It is a long but not too arduous haul through scree and heather and the views from the top are terrific. Keen eyes on a clear day will see 18 counties including peaks in Cumberland, the tip of Ireland, The Bass Rock, Ailsa Craig, Arran and Jura. Tinto is wrapped in legend: William Wallace camped on the hill with his army in the 13th century, and there is a depression in a boulder at the top called, somewhat doubtfully, "Wallace's Thumbmark". Tinto is derived from the Gaelic *teinteach* (place of fire) hinting that it may have been one of the sites for the ancient fire rites of Beltane, sometimes connected with human sacrifice.

TOURIST INFORMATION

Town Hall, Abbey Close, Paisley, tel 041-889 0711. It is open all year.

South Vennel, Lanark, tel 0555-2544. It is open all year.

WHERE TO STAY

Cartland Bridge Hotel, well signposted on the outskirts of Lanark, tel 0555-3084. B&B from £25: categories 3,4,5: 16 bedrooms. A warm friendly atmosphere.

Hopetoun Arms, in the Main Street of Leadhills, tel 06594-234. B&B from £7.50: categories 3,3,2: 3 bedrooms. A friendly family hotel.

Elphinstone Hotel, High Street, Biggar, tel 0899-20044. B&B from £13: categories 4,3,4: 7 bedrooms, 6 en suite. A nice old fashioned inn in the middle of the town.

Hartree Country House Hotel, on the outskirts of Biggar going south, tel 0899-20215/20066. B&B from £18.50: categories 4,3,5: 33 bedrooms, 9 en suite. A large, castellated hotel in nice grounds. A friendly welcome.

EATING OUT

The hotels will all give you a good meal, reasonably priced.

Toftcombs, in Biggar, tel 0899-20142. This has a "Lairds Table" with traditional Scottish food with fresh local ingredients: haugh and kidney soup, Cromarty casserole, Tweed salmon. Diner from £8.

The Islands of South Strathclyde

ARRAN

There is a holiday atmosphere on the ferry from Ardrossan to Brodick on Arran: for an hour, crowds jostle for tables round the bar or in the seating lounges; knapsacks are piled everywhere and the uniform is jeans and fluorescent kagools. If it is raining when you arrive at Brodick don't worry; Arran usually manages to show a smiling face for at least some of the day.

Slightly larger than the Isle of Wight, about 20 miles (32.8 km) from north to south, 9 miles (14.4 km) across and 56 miles (89.6 km) in circumference, Arran has a special charm that few can resist. It is a distillation of the whole country of Scotland, and although its beauty and mild climate attract thousands of holidaymakers it has managed to keep its unique character more or less intact. In no time you can get away from the hotels and guest houses and chalet settlements that ring the island; heading inland you can roam for hours and feel totally remote.

Arran was populated way back before the dawn of recorded history and has ancient stones and burial cairns to prove it. When the Irish Scots came over and settled, in the early 6th century, Arran was part of the kingdom of Dalriada. The Vikings held the island for a time until they were ousted by Somerled, Lord of the Isles, possibly of Norse descent himself. Arran lost much of its crofting population in the 18th century when deer were established, for sport, overrunning the crofts of the tenant farmers.

SPECIAL ATTRACTIONS

There is so much to do on this small island that it would be easier to list what is not available. There is every kind of sea sport including swimming, sailing, windsurfing, water skiing, sub-aqua diving and fishing. Also golf, riding, pony trekking—a lovely way to explore—tennis, squash, bowling, etc. And of course, walking and climbing with such a choice of places to go that you could walk for your entire holiday and never cover the same ground twice once you leave your car.

The birds, wild life and wild flowers are wonderful. There is plenty for geologists and archaeologists to look at, and if none of that is what you want, you can just lie back and look at the glorious views.

GETTING THERE

Car ferry from Ardrossan with train link from Glasgow takes about an hour. In the summer only: ferry between Lochranza and Claonaig, Kintyre, takes half an hour. Further information is available from Caledonian MacBrayne Ltd, Ferry Terminal, Gourock, Renfrewshire, tel 0475-33755.

Brodick

Brodick, the port of Arran, is a large resort-village with plenty of hotels, guest houses and bed and breakfast places, straggling round Brodick Bay, with Brodick Castle overlooking the northern shore.

WHAT TO SEE

Brodick Castle (open daily in the summer, from 1 pm to 5 pm: adults £1.40, children 70p. Gardens and grounds open all year, 10 am to 5 pm: adults 80p, children 40p) was built on the site of a Viking fortress and dates from the 13th century. Given to the National Trust for Scotland in 1958, it was previously the home of the dukes of Hamilton. The magnificent collection of treasures that you will see in the castle are partly the inheritance of Susan Euphemia Beckford, daughter of that enigmatic author of *Vathek*, William Beckford. She married the tenth Duke of Hamilton in 1810 and part of what was left of her father's fabulous collection of art works from all over the world came to her. There is a good guide book which will tell you about the lovely silver, porcelain, paintings and furnishings. The castle gardens are almost exotic enough to have been part of the rich oriental settings in *Vathek*, with great translucent blooms that seem to be made of wax and silk, with leaves of lacquer, scented with essences from Grasse. All this, with the tall, stately red sandstone castle, backed by the sea and surrounded by hills, dominated by Goat Fell, make Brodick a castle you will never forget

The Isle of Arran Heritage Museum (open in the summer: adults 60p, children 30p) shows you what life was like on the island up until 1920.

You can drive right round the island, only losing the sea in a couple of places, or you can cut through the middle on the String Road from Brodick to Blackwaterfoot, or down Glen Scorrodale from Lamlash to Lagg Inn.

Goat Fell, 2,866 ft (860 m) high, north of Brodick, dominates Arran, and you should wait for a clear day before climbing it. There are several ways up, including an easy two hour haul from Brodick. The views from the top make it all worth while. You won't see goats these days but you might, if you are lucky, see golden eagles gliding on the air currents in a corrie below you.

Corrie

Corrie is about five miles (8 km) north of Brodick, a charming village, that is a favourite with artists, with its picturesque white cottages and trim colourful gardens, its harbour and quay and beach, backed by the wooded hills.

You should take time to walk up into some of the glens that cut into the hinterland like the spokes of a wheel. There are two at **Sannox**. These are delightful secret places away from the road, and on the high ground where you find heather, lichens, mosses and alpine willow, and many rare wild flowers such as purple and starry saxifrage. **The Fallen Rocks**, beyond Sannox, are thought to be a landslip from the Palaezoic Age, which sent these massive boulders, some as big as houses, tumbling to the beach. This is a popular place for rock climbers. At Sannox is a 9 hole golf course.

Lochranza

Lochranza (Water of the Rowan Tree) lies two miles (3.2 km) south-west from the northern headland **Cock of Arran**. Here you will see **Lochranza Castle**, a romantic ruin on the tidal flats, backed by rugged mountains. It was built as a hunting seat for Stewart kings, and is an L-plan castle, three storeys high with a pit prison in the vaulted basement. This roofless shell, seen against the flaming skies of a good sunset, is a lovely sight. Also at Lochranza there is a 9 hole golf course.

Going south from Lochranza down the west side of the island the road clings to the sea, with the mountains tumbling down almost onto the beach. Steep-sided **Glen Catacol** takes you inland again up into the hills, through beeches and larch, chestnut and firs, the ground lush with vivid green ferns.

Thundergay and Pirnmill

Thundergay, five miles (8 km) south of Lochranza, gets its strange name from Tor-na-Gaoith (Windy Hill) and two miles (3.2 km) further south, Pirnmill is derived from the bobbin mill that was here in the days when linen was an important industry in the island. The mill has now been converted into holiday flats.

Glen Iorsa runs north-east through marshy bog land, hemmed in by barren hills. It is a great tract of lonely, waterlogged moor, towering below frowning crags, cut by steep ravines and lochans.

Pre-historic Remains of Arran

The south-west quarter of Arran is rich in prehistoric remains. There is the **Auchagallon Stone Circle**, 15 red sandstone blocks which once encircled a cairn; the **Farm Road Stone Circle**, close by (within range of the 9 hole Machrie golf course) and the **Standing Stones at Machrie**, which are slim, primeval monoliths whose mysterious purpose baffles man today.

In addition, don't miss the **King's Caves** at **Drumadoon, Blackwaterfoot**. King Robert Bruce is said to have sheltered here when returning to fulfil his destiny and free Scotland from the stranglehold of English domination. Here, too, legend brings Fionn MacCumhail, the 3rd-century warrior-poet and leader of the Feinn, those elusive Celts who feature in the old sagas. You can just see rock carvings in the King's Caves: typical Pictish hunting scenes and animals.

There are more cairns at **Kilmory** on the south coast, and lovely walks along the shore or up into **Glen Scorrodale**.

Kildonan

Following the road east from Kilmory you reach Kildonan, a scattered farming village with two hotels and a fine sandy beach. There are wonderful views of Pladda Island lighthouse and Ailsa Craig, which rises dramatically from the sea like an iceberg, some 13 miles away on the horizon. On a summer's evening, walk along the shore west towards **Bennan Head**. Look out for a large colony of grey Atlantic seals. Unafraid and curious, they will come quite close to the shore to inspect any passers-by. Here, the mysterious carcase of a large sea-creature was once discovered which baffled the world of science and remains unidentified to this day. Before you reach the headland, there is a winding path hugging the cliffside once used by smugglers in the 18th century. It leads to the road above. From there you can head back down to Kildonan.

Whiting Bay

Whiting Bay lies five miles (8 km) north of Kildonan, and is a popular village with holiday-makers. Straggling along a wide bay, there is a number of shops and hotels, including two or three excellent craft shops, specialising in leather, pottery and wood carving. Visit the Jewellery Workshop, signposted at the north end of the village, where you can buy locally crafted silver and gold jewellery. For evening entertainment, **Naggs**, adjoining the Whiting Bay Hotel, has live music and a disco in the summer. There is a 18 hole golf course with fine views across the Firth of Clyde to the Ayrshire hills beyond.

Follow the signpost to **Glen Ashdale Falls** (at the south end of the village) for a charming walk up a steep, wooded glen to the falls. Here you can picnic and watch the crystal clear waters cascade down to the rocks below. You can also see the **Giant's Graves** (signposted), a stone circle traditionally associated with Finn MacCumhail, the legendary leader of the Feinn.

Lamlash

Completing the circle, you come to Lamlash, three miles (4.8 km) south of Brodick on **Lamlash Bay** which is almost blocked at the mouth by **Holy Island**. This wonderfully safe anchorage, now a yachtsman's haven, provided shelter for King Haakon and his fleet after they had been defeated in the Battle of Largs in 1263, and, in 1548, the ship carrying five year old Mary, Queen of Scots to France from Dumbarton, sheltered here. Lamlash holds sea angling competitions every year and these are renowned throughout Scotland.

You can go out to **Holy Island** by boat and see **St Molio's Cave**, about half way down the west shore, with a stone bed shelf and runic inscriptions on the roof. You can see a fireplace, a gutter on the floor to carry off the water that dripped down from the walls, **St Molio's Well**, with healing qualities, and the **Judgement Stone**, a 7 ft (2.1. m) sandstone table, with seats carved out, where presumably the saint dealt out justice.

TOURIST INFORMATION

The Pier, Brodick, tel 0770-2140/2401. It is open all year.

WHERE TO STAY

There are hotels and guest houses all over the island, as well as a large number of self-catering places, static caravans (trailers) and camp sites. You should get the tourist brochure, which has pictures and details of them all. The following is just a small, selection.

Auchrannie Hotel, in Brodick, tel 0770-2234. B&B from £10: categories 4,3,4: 16 bedrooms, 4 en suite. A nice friendly hotel in secluded wooded grounds, with a log fire in the hall and good Scottish food.

Douglas Hotel, on the sea front in Brodick, near the ferry, tel 0770-2155. B&B from £15: cagetories 3,4,4: 26 bedrooms, 12 en suite. Lovely views and a warm welcome. Live entertainment, dancing, sauna, beauty salon, etc.

Ennismor Hotel, also on the sea front in Brodick, tel 0770-2265. B&B from £9.25: categories 3,3,4: 14 bedrooms, 10 en suite. A comfortable hotel with a nice garden that welcomes children, at reduced prices.

Whiting Bay Hotel, at Whiting Bay, tel 07707-247. B&B from £15: categories 4,4,5: 20 bedrooms, 12 en suite. A friendly staff. High standard of Scottish food, ceilidhs, cabarets, dances and films.

Kinloch Hotel, overlooking the sea at Blackwaterfoot, tel 0770-86 44. B&B from £14.50: categories 5,4,5: 47 bedrooms en suite. Very comfortable with good food, indoor swimming pool, solarium, sauna and squash court.

Lagg Hotel, Lagg, tel 0770-87255. B&B from £20: 18 bedrooms, 9 en suite. 3 crowns. Commended.

EATING OUT

Lagg Hotel, see above. Set-price meal on Fridays and Saturdays only. Incudes starter, fishcourse and choice of roast meat, pudding and coffee. Excellent value, generous helpings. Dinner from £11.50.

Wishing Well Restaurant, Lagg, tel 0770-87255. Recently opened in a converted stables. À la carte menu—seafood a speciality: lobster, when available. Dinner from £8 to £12.

LOCAL SPECIALITIES

Visit the Arran Mustard Factory, The Old Mill, Lamlash, tel 07706-370 and sample some of the unique blends that go into the huge range of mustards.

BUTE

The island of Bute is a popular holiday resort, attracting a great many people in the summer. It is a place for those who like the bright lights and who enjoy the stimulus of other people: don't go to Bute expecting to "get away from it all". But, if you put on your stout walking shoes and head away from the roads, you will be pleasantly surprised at how many hidden corners you will find. Even some of the beaches and coves are relatively empty, so long as you are prepared to walk. Sailors can hire boats which open up a number of secret, inaccessible little bays where it will be just you, the seals and the sea gulls!

SPECIAL ATTRACTIONS

In August, the island has a Highland Festival, culminating in a Highland Games, where you will see plenty of tartan and all the traditional events such as tossing the caber and putting the weight, as well as piping and dancing.

There is something for everyone, on this holiday island: golf, fishing, every sort of water sport in wonderfully clear water, walking, tennis, bird-watching, riding and plenty of entertainment to while away the evenings, in the way of dancing, cabarets, shows and night clubs.

GETTING THERE

Roll-on, roll-off car ferry from Wemyss Bay—an hour's drive or train journey from Glasgow—frequent sailings daily, duration—half an hour. There is a bus service to Wemyss Bay from Anderson Cross Bus Terminal, Glasgow. There is also a scheduled helicopter service from Glasgow Airport. The flights take approximately 15 minutes.

For further information on ferries, contact Caledonian MacBrayne Ltd, The Ferry Terminal, Gourock, Renfrewshire, tel 0475-33755; and on flights, Burnthills Highland Helicopter Service Ltd, Glasgow Airport, tel 041-887 7733

Rothesay

This is the thriving hub of Bute where you will find lots to do.

WHAT TO SEE
Rothesay Castle (open at standard Ancient Monument times except Thursday and Friday mornings in winter: adults 50p children 25p) has enough history and interest to attract any visitor. It was built in 1098, in the days when the Norsemen dominated the islands. It reverted to Scottish hands after the Battle of Largs, in 1263. Added to over the centuries, it is an impressive fortress with high curtain walls and drum towers enclosing a circular courtyard. King Robert Bruce captured it in 1313 and it was his great, great grandson who was first created Duke of Rothesay, a title still held by the heir to the throne of Britain. The castle was used as a headquarters when both James IV and James V tried, with little success, to subdue the arrogant rule of the Lords of the Isles. Cromwell battered it badly during the Civil War and it was burned by Argyll in 1685 during the Monmouth Rebellion; it then lay in ruins until restoration in the 19th century.

The Museum (open daily except Sundays in winter: admission free) lies behind the castle. It will give you plenty of information on local history as well as details of the nature trails around the island.

Kyles of Bute

Going up the north-east side of the island you overlook the lovely Kyles of Bute, the narrow strait that separates the mainland from Bute, with views that make you gasp with delight.

The north-west corner of the island is only accessible on foot, making it wonderfully remote. It has more glorious views.

Ardencraig Gardens (open daily in the summer: admission free) lie south of Rothesay. Here the fuchsias make an incredible mass of exotic colour.

Canada Hill, above **Loch Fad** in the lower middle of the island, gives you panoramic views of the Firth of Clyde, Argyll and Arran. It is an easy climb on a fine day.

St Blane's Chapel is in the southern toe of Bute. It is a 12th-century ruin with a Norman arch, built on the site of a monastery founded by St Blane in the 6th century. It was during that time that the early missionaries were struggling to establish Christianity among a wild, heathen race.

St Ninian's Chapel is half way up the west coast. Here are the foundations of another early settlement where you can still see the surrounding garth wall, on a point by a glorious sandy bay.

Ettrick Bay lies further north. Here you will find another good sandy beach.

You have three golf courses to choose from, as well as yachting marinas, an underwater diving club and a variety of pleasure cruises during the summer which offer you one of the best ways of seeing the lovely coast. You can also charter self-drive boasts from The Pier, in Rothesay.

TOURIST INFORMATION
The Pier, Rothesay, tel 0700-2151. It is open all year.

WHERE TO STAY
The choice is enormous and you should get the brochures from the tourist office, see above. The following is just a very small selection.

Guildford Court, Watergate, Rothesay, tel 0700-3770. Prices on application. A listed building overlooking the harbour where you can get self catering suites, and lounge-bedroom suites, with low weekly, overnight and weekend bargains.

Kingarth Hotel, Kingarth, at the south end of the island, tel 0700-83 662. B&B from £7.50: categories 4,3,3: 7 bedrooms, 3 en suite. A comfortable, friendly hotel with both serviced bedrooms and self-contained chalets. Dining room. Bowling green, near the golf club.

Bayview Hotel, 22 Mountstuart Road, Rothesay, tel 0700-2339. B&B from £10.50: categories 3,3,2: 20 bedrooms. A nice Victorian house on Craigmore Shore, ten minutes from the pier with lovely views of Rothesay Bay. Good food.

Royal Hotel, Rothesay, tel 0700-3044. B&B from £9: categories 4,4,5: 20 bedrooms, 4 en suite. Overlooking the yacht marina, a short distance from the ferry terminus. Cabaret every night during the season. Private loch fishing arranged and special terms for golfers. Good food.

Glenburn Hotel, Glenburn Road, Rothesay, tel 0700-2500. B&B from £14: categories 4,6,5: 100 bedrooms, 47 en suite. Overlooking the water. A friendly, comfortable hotel next door to a heated swimming pool and a golf course, with good food in the dining room and bar meals.

EATING OUT
All of the hotels above provide good food.

North of the Clyde

The pull from the north is getting stronger. Take the **Erskine Toll Bridge** over the Clyde, ignoring the industrial sprawl north of Glasgow. This magnificent sweep of modern engineering replaces a cable-ferry, holding only a few cars, that used to be the only way across here.

The Heatherbank Museum of Social Work (open all year by appointment, tel 041-956 2687: admission free) is about four miles (6.4 km) north-east of the bridge on the A809. It is the only museum of its kind in the world, with over 2,500 slides of life in the 19th and early 20th century,and a 5,000 volume reference library.

Heading west from the Erskine Bridge you pass **Old Kilpatrick** which was the western end of the Antonine Wall. There is nothing to see of it here but a rampart base which is still visible at **Duntocher**, two miles (3.2 km) to the east.

Dumbarton

Dumbarton is a large industrial town, 15 miles (24 km) from Glasgow. Whisky has taken over in importance from the shipbuilding that once flourished on the water-front. Still close enough to Glasgow for its people to have that sharp Glaswegian wit, they combine this with the slower, softer charm that characterises the people of the west. The famous clipper, *Cutty Sark*, was built in Dumbarton in 1869. It was named after the "short shirts" as seen by Tam o' Shanter when he watched the witches orgy in the poem by Burns.

WHAT TO SEE

Dumbarton Castle (open at standard Ancient Monument times: adults 50p, children 25p) stands high in a cleft of Dumbarton Rock, a lump of volcanic basalt, shaped like Gibraltar, and the site of a fortress since pre-historic times. The name is derived from Dun-Bretane (Hill of the Britons). From about the 5th century, this fortress rock was the centre of the kingdom of Strathclyde; it was a royal castle in the Middle Ages; later it was a barracks and now a museum. Mary, Queen of Scots sailed to France from here in 1548, aged five, going to what was possibly the only happy period in her tragic life.

As you toil up the steps you pass Wallace's Gatehouse, where William Wallace was imprisoned before being taken to his trial and barbaric execution in London in 1305. It was Sir John Monteith, governor of Dumbarton Castle at the time, who finally betrayed Wallace, that brave rebel who struck such a memorable blow for Scottish independence. Perhaps Wallace stood at the window of his cell, drawing strength from the magnificent view across the Clyde. Some say that St Patrick was born nearby—a claim made by many other places on this coast and down as far as Cumbria. Certainly he was captured near here in the 4th century and deported to Ireland as a slave.

The town of Dumbarton is modern, but you will still find a few old buildings in it, particularly Glencairn "Greit House", built in 1623, once the home of the Duke of Argyll.

West Loch Lomondside

You have a choice of two routes north from Dumbarton, one being West Loch Lomondside: the boundary with the Central region goes up the middle of the Loch. This road, the A82, which gives you marvellous views, ranging from the loch, with its islands and anchorages, to the hills on the far side, is tortuous to drive along during busy times. It is narrow and twisting, with blind corners, half-way round which you are likely to meet enormous coaches. Take the road in the early morning before the traffic gets going, then you can pause on every bend and enjoy scalp-prickling views, with the mist still clinging to the glassy water and the sun rising over Ben Lomond. The loch is 24 miles (38.4 km) from north to south, its southern end as much as five miles (8 km) wide, narrowing to a long, thin neck in the north.

Balloch

Balloch, at the south end of the loch, is a very popular holiday resort. There you will find the **Maid of the Loch**, the last paddle steamer to have been built in Britain. It sails from Balloch in the summer on a variety of cruises taking you round the islands that are scattered over the loch, and up to the narrow head. The islands, so small and serene-looking, are steeped in history. Before exploring these, visit Cameron Loch Lomond.

Cameron Loch Lomond, immediately north-west of the town beside the loch, is a wildlife reserve (open daily in the summer, admission charge). It has bears, bison, yak, deer and Highland cattle. There is also a children's zoo, a wildfowl sanctuary, attractive gardens, an adventure playground and boating.

Cameron House (open daily in the summer: admission charge) contains various interesting items including rare weapons, a collection of Staffordshire pottery animals, and a replica of a Victorian nursery.

The Islands

Inch Cailleoch (island of the old women) was the burial place of the fierce MacGregor clan. The ruined **Lennox Castle**, on **Inchmurrin** (isle of spears) was where the Duchess of Albany retired, after James I had slaughtered her husband, sons and father in 1425 (not without cause, see History). Many of the islands are part of a nature reserve.

Rossdhu (open in the summer: admission charge) is a house a little way up the western shore, has been the home of the Colquhouns (pronounced Ker-hoon) since the 12th century. The Colquhouns were deadly rivals of the MacGregors, both clans forever fighting for supremacy in this area. The present Rossdhu, built in 1773 possibly by Robert Adam, has period furniture, paintings and a collection of stuffed birds and animals.

Like most places that are popular because of their great beauty, Loch Lomondside can get very crowded. A good way to explore it is by boat: either your own, launched on one of the ramps, or in a hired one, of which there are many.

Helensburgh

The other route north from Dumbarton is the A814 via Helensburgh and Loch Long. This route is as narrow and twisting as the A82, and just as beautiful in places, clinging to the water most of the way and keeping company with the railway.

Helensburgh, at the mouth of the **Gare Loch**, eight miles (12.8 km) north-west of Dumbarton, is a residential resort. The town slopes up from the Clyde with an air of dignified respectability. This is sailing territory and the water is usually speckled with craft of all sizes. There are good shops and plenty of places to stay, with lovely views across the Clyde.

Glen Fruin is within easy walking distance from Helensburgh and if you choose a good day you can roam up here surrounded by grand beauty and solitude and seranaded by the clatter of many streams flowing down from the hills into the valley.

Climb **Ben Chaorach** and look back down into the glen. You may hear the echo of war cries here and sad cries for mercy. In 1603 there was a horrific battle between the Colquhouns and the MacGregors, arising from boundary disputes and accusations of cattle pilfering. The MacGregors slew not only the Colquhoun men, but also their families, who had been shut away in a barn for safety, as well as a party of schoolboys who had been taken along to watch the fun.

Rhu

The less bloodthirsty visitor might prefer to go a little further on to Rhu, a mile (1.6 km) west of Helensburgh, and enjoy the woodland and lovely shrubs at **Glenarn Gardens** (open in the summer: small fee). You can also go to **The Hill House** (open most days: small fee) designed by Charles Rennie Mackintosh in 1902 with a good display of his furniture.

The two routes meet at **Tarbet** where you must go west, if you want to explore the rest of Strathclyde.

TOURIST INFORMATION
Car Park, Balloch, tel 0389-53533. It is open April to September.

Pier Head, Helensburgh, tel 0436-2642. It is open April to September.

WHERE TO STAY
Balloch Hotel, in Balloch, on the southern end of Loch Lomond, tel 0389-52579. B&B from £14.50: categories 3,2,4: 13 bedrooms, 6 en suite. A friendly hotel.

River Lodge Hotel, Balloch Road, Balloch, tel 0389-52052. B&B from £13.75: categories 4,3,6: 11 bedrooms, 6 en suite. A very picturesque hotel, newly renovated. Rooms have colour TV and tea/coffee making facilities. The hotel has a day nursery and a playground, and the food is good.

Commodore Hotel, West Clyde Street, Helensburgh, tel 0436-6924. B&B from £29: categories 5,6,5: 45 bedrooms en suite. A modern hotel, on the sea front.

County Hotel, Old Luss Road, Helensburgh, tel 0436-2033/4. B&B from £12: categories 3,3,3: 7 bedrooms, 2 en suite. A nice family hotel, half a mile (0.8 km) from the town centre.

Ardencaple Hotel, Shore Road, Rhu, tel 0436-820200. B&B from £15.50: categories 4,3,4: 12 bedrooms, 6 en suite. A traditional coaching inn on the shore of Gareloch with excellent food.

Rosslea Hall Hotel, Rhu, tel 0436-820684. B&B from £24.50: categories 6,4,5: 16 bedrooms en suite. In landscaped grounds with lovely views across the Clyde, and good Scottish food.

Tarbet Hotel, Tarbet, tel 03012-228. B&B from £18: categories 5,5,5: 101 bedrooms, 76 en suite. Scottish baronial mansion overlooking Loch Lomond with a comfortable modern interior, friendly staff and nice food.

EATING OUT
The above hotels all serve good food at reasonable prices. You can get a nice dinner from about £8.

The Cowal Peninsula

5 miles west from Tarbet through Glen Coe, you climb the Rest and Be Thankful—

which speaks for itself, even if you are in your car! Here you can see some wonderful views. There is a car park and a stone commemorating the completion of this military road in 1750, part of the network that was constructed to try to keep order in the Highlands after the Jacobite risings.

This is climbers territory, known as the Arrochar Alps. Ben Arthur, known as The Cobbler, 2,891 ft (867 m), towers over Glen Coe to the north and there are four "Munros" to be added to your list of peaks over 3,000 ft (900 m) high: Beinn Ime, Ben Vane and Ben Vorlich marching away to the north-east, and the fourth just beyond the Cobbler.

The Cowal Peninsula stretches to the south like a misshapen lobster claw, washed on either side by Loch Long and Loch Fyne. This is Argyll territory with many an echo of history among its ruins.

WHAT TO SEE

Castle Garrick (open at all times: admission free) is a 14th-century ruin. It can be reached from a minor road south from the Rest and be Thankful and then the track-road down the west side of **Loch Goil**. It is here that the Argylls kept their documents and their prisoners. A remote enough place in those days, the great shell of the keep is impressive even now. The road ends here but you can just see where the loch joins up with Loch Long, to the south.

Creachan Mor, 2,156 ft (647 m) high to the south, is worth climbing. From the top, on a clear day, you can look down on a glorious jigsaw of moor and hill, each irregular piece linked by a gleaming slither of water. Time is the only barrier to exploring the peninsula properly—on foot!

Ardentinny is a track which runs down from Creachan Mor. From here it is not far to the **Younger Botanic Garden**, (open daily in the summer, adults 20p, children 10p), three miles (4.8 km) cross-country, and six miles (9.6 km) by road. This is an extensive woodland with shrubs and a splendid avenue of *sequoias* (Giant Californian Wellingtonias).

Kilmun Arboretum

Kilmun Arboretum, on the northern shore of **Holy Loch**, has some of the tallest trees in Scotland. Holy Loch, now home of a naval base, was so named when a ship, which was carrying earth from the Holy Land, intended as suitably sacred foundations of Glasgow Cathedral, foundered in a storm as it tried to get round the corner into the sheltered Clyde and finished up in this appendix of the mighty river.

Dunoon

Dunoon, the chief resort on the Cowal Peninsula, lies on the coast-road. It was just a village until early in the 19th century, when rich merchants built villas and it developed into a resort. The long, low sprawl of the town is backed by blue-grey hills in a crescent to the north and east.

Steamers run from Dunoon and there is a number of cruises you can take, on the Clyde and around the Cowal Peninsula. Dunoon is an ideal family holiday centre with any amount of places to stay, to suit all pockets, with a huge choice of things to do, on the threshold of some of the finest walking and climbing country that anyone could hope for.

SPECIAL ATTRACTIONS

The Cowal Highland Gathering is one of the town's highlights of the year, on the last Friday and Saturday in August. More than 150 Pipe Bands compete, drawing huge, appreciative crowds.

WHAT TO SEE

Dunoon Castle, of which you can now see only a trace, dates from the 13th century. It was built on the site of an earlier fort, with a colourful history that kept it bouncing back and forth between English and Scottish hands like so many of the strongholds of Scotland. Edward I took it; Robert Bruce re-took it; then Edward Balliol, who was ousted by Robert II. In 1471 the earls of Argyll were made honorary keepers, by James III, on condition that they paid the crown a fee of a red rose, whenever demanded! When Queen Elizabeth II visited Dunoon in 1958 she was presented with a red rose without having to demand it!

Lazaretto Point was the quarantine station for servicemen fighting in the Napoleonic wars. It is hard to feel sorry for these men if you look out at the views they had as they waited for the development of some rare foreign disease.

The Royal Clyde Yacht Club is at **Hunter's Quay**, just north of Dunoon, a hive of activity during the sailing season, with regattas and races among the dozens of boats of all classes.

TOURIST INFORMATION

Dunoon, tel 0369-3785. It is open all year.

WHERE TO STAY

The choice is enormous. The following is a small selection.

Ardentinny Hotel, Ardentinny, Loch Long, near Dunoon, tel 0369-81 209/275. B&B from £16: categories 5,4,5: 11 bedrooms en suite. Packages offered such as three days bed and breakfast and dinner, £85–95. Excellent taste of Scotland food, buttery and patio-garden meals. A really nice hotel overlooking the water, offering boat hire, and free ferry tickets, and free entry into Younger Botanic Garden and Inveraray Castle. The AA and RAC rate it as 2-Star. Egon Ronay, Ashley Courtenay and Michelin recommended. Attractive gardens.

Abbeyhill Hotel, Dhailling Road, Dunoon, a short distance from the sea front, tel 0369-2204. B&B from £17.50: categories 5,4,5: 14 bedrooms en suite. Rated as 2-Star by AA and RAC. Rooms with colour TV. Good food. In attractive grounds.

Ardfillayne Hotel, West Bay, Dunoon, tel 0369-2267. B&B from £18.50: categories 5,4,5: 8 bedrooms en suite. A country house hotel in six acres (2.5 ha) of wooded grounds with lovely views over the Clyde and to the hills of Argyll. Built in

1835, the hotel still has a friendly olde worlde atmosphere, and excellent food in its attractive dining room.

Esplanade Hotel, West Bay, Promenade, Dunoon, tel 0369-4070. B&B from £11.50: categories 3,4,4: 50 bedrooms, 41 en suite. A family run hotel on the Promenade only a few minutes walk from the pier and near the town centre. Special rates for children.

Glenmorag Hotel, West Bay, Dunoon, tel 0369-2227. B&B from £10: categories 3,5,3: 90 bedrooms, 28 en suite. A friendly welcome and good views.

Kilfinan Hotel, Kilfinan, near Tighnabruaich, tel 0700-82 201. B&B from £18.50: categories 6,4,5: 11 bedrooms en suite. A charming, old fashioned hotel on the eastern shore of Loch Fyne. Once an old coaching inn, it still has cosy log fires. The food is excellent, made with local ingredients.

Carrick Castle Hotel, Lochgoil, tel 03013-251. B&B from £15: categories 6,4,4: 21 bedrooms en suite. Lovely views on to the water and a friendly welcome.

EATING OUT

Beverley's Restaurant, 53 Bullwood Road, Dunoon, tel 0369-2267. Good local ingredients in a Charles Rennie MacKintosh-style dining room. Try the whisky syllabub. Candle-lit dinner from about £10.

Enmore Hotel, Marine Parade, Dunoon, tel 0369-2230. Traditional Scottish food. Nice dinner from about £10.

Ardentinny Hotel, see above. Traditional Scottish food in a hotel which has connections with Harry Lauder, and a display of memorabilia related to that much loved Scots singer and comedian. Dinner from £10.

Bouquet Garni Restaurant, Lochgoilhead, tel 03013-206. Fresh local fish and shell fish a speciality. Nice atmosphere. Dinner from about £8.

Kames Hotel, Tighnabruaich, tel 0700-811489. Good local fish and shell fish. Dinner from £7.50.

Kilfinan Hotel, see above. Sea trout and salmon from the hotel's own river, local shell fish and game in season. Dinner from £10.

North Strathclyde: Loch Fyne down to Kintyre

The whole of this north-western area of Strathclyde is beautiful and it would be impossible to mention all the spectacular views. You will find them at every turn of the road and along every path and mountain track you take. Many of the walks are signposted but you should certainly always carry a good map. The more you can explore on foot, the better the rewards will be, for the best places are invariably off the road.

Loch Fyne washes the western shore of the Cowal Peninsula, a long, narrow arm of sea, eating its way into highland scenery that is a mixture of hill and forest, in some parts rising steeply from the water, in others rolling back in great sweeps of farmland. As you drive round it, look out for a caravan in a lay-by at the head of the loch, and a sign saying

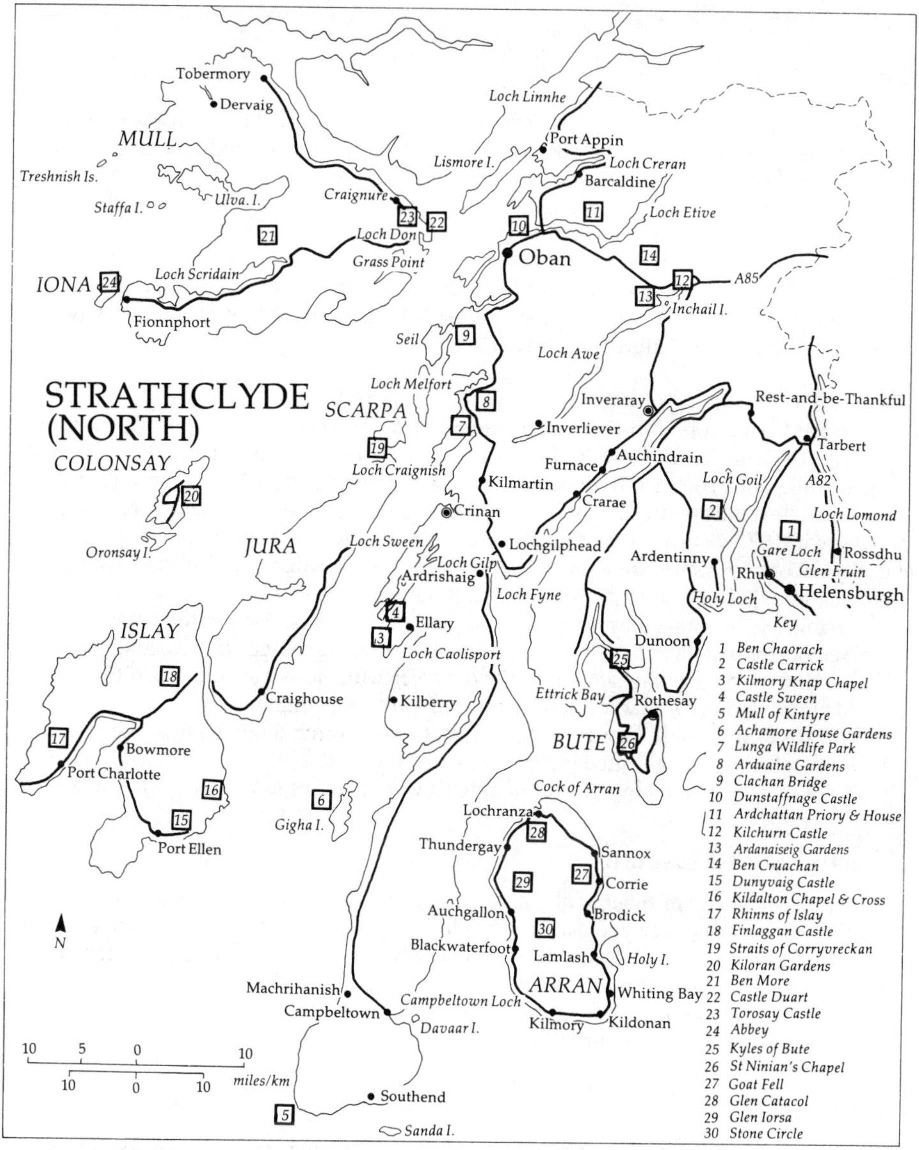
STRATHCLYDE (NORTH)
Tobermory
Dervaig
MULL
Treshnish Is.
Staffa I.
Ulva I.
Craignure
Loch Don
Grass Point
Loch Scridain
IONA
Fionnphort
Loch Linnhe
Port Appin
Lismore I.
Loch Creran
Barcaldine
Loch Etive
Oban
A85
Inchail I.
Seil
Loch Awe
Loch Melfort
SCARPA
Inveraray
Rest-and-be-Thankful
Inverliever
Tarbert
COLONSAY
Loch Craignish
Furnace
Auchindrain
Loch Goil
A82
Kilmartin
Crarae
Loch Lomond
Crinan
Oronsay I.
JURA
Loch Sween
Lochgilphead
Ardentinny
Gare Loch
Rossdhu
Loch Gilp
Rhu
Glen Fruin
Ardrishaig
Loch Fyne
Holy Loch
Helensburgh
ISLAY
Ellary
Key
Loch Caolisport
Dunoon
1 Ben Chaorach
2 Castle Carrick
3 Kilmory Knap Chapel
4 Castle Sween
5 Mull of Kintyre
6 Achamore House Gardens
7 Lunga Wildlife Park
8 Arduaine Gardens
9 Clachan Bridge
10 Dunstaffnage Castle
11 Ardchattan Priory & House
12 Kilchurn Castle
13 Ardanaiseig Gardens
14 Ben Cruachan
15 Dunyvaig Castle
16 Kildalton Chapel & Cross
17 Rhinns of Islay
18 Finlaggan Castle
19 Straits of Corryvreckan
20 Kiloran Gardens
21 Ben More
22 Castle Duart
23 Torosay Castle
24 Abbey
25 Kyles of Bute
26 St Ninian's Chapel
27 Goat Fell
28 Glen Catacol
29 Glen Iorsa
30 Stone Circle
Craighouse
Kilberry
Ettrick Bay
Rothesay
Bowmore
Port Charlotte
BUTE
Cock of Arran
Gigha I.
Port Ellen
Lochranza
Thundergay
Sannox
Corrie
Auchgallon
Brodick
Blackwaterfoot
Lamlash
Holy I.
N
ARRAN
Machrihanish
Whiting Bay
Campbeltown
Campbeltown Loch
Kilmory
Kildonan
Davaar I.
10 5 0 10
10 0 10
miles/km
Southend
Sanda I.

"Loch Fyne Fisheries". Here you can buy a mouth-watering selection of fresh sea food including oysters from the local oyster beds, smoked salmon and delicious scampi.

Inveraray

Inveraray stands on the north-west shore of the loch, a small, 18th-century town with an aura of slightly privileged graciousness. It is a pretty place, curiously un-Scottish, and built in a T-shape with the road north passing through an archway and the parish church dividing the Main Street, on a small mound. Inveraray was once a small fishing village, always a Campbell of Argyll domain. It was sacked by Montrose in 1644. The present town was the creation of the third Duke of Argyll, in 1743, employing Roger Morris and William Adam. Both of these men died before the work was finished by John Adam, son of William, took over the job with the help of Robert Mylne. Between the lot of them they achieved an extremely attractive town.

WHAT TO SEE

Inveraray Castle (open during the summer, daily except Fridays: adults £2, children £1.00) was built in 1770 while the town itself was being built. The castle is a great square pile with round towers topped by cone-shaped turrets, imposing rather than beautiful. It stands on the site of the original village, demolished to make room for it. A bad fire in 1975 destroyed the roof and top floor but these have been rebuilt. The beautifully decorated rooms are a joint achievement by John Adam and Robert Mylne, and provide the perfect settings for the paintings, tapestries, Oriental and European porcelain, 18th-century furniture and many other treasures. Among the paintings you can see portraits by Kneller, Raeburn, Hoppner, Gainsborough, Batoni, and Ramsay. Wandering in the grounds among lovely old trees with views out over Loch Fyne, you could almost believe you were part of an 18th-century painting!

The Inveraray Bell Tower, in the Episcopalian church (open daily in the summer for a small fee) was established in this century by the tenth Duke of Argyll, its peal of ten bells being rung in memory of the Campbells who died in the First World War.

Auchindrain Museum

Auchindrain Museum (open daily in the summer for a small fee) is six miles (9.6 km) south of Inveraray. Here you can see the old "strip-farming" that was prevalent in the Highlands until the end of the 18th century, when villages had communal tenancy of farmland, paying their rent jointly, in this case to the Argylls. The museum has a visitor centre, telling you about the farming methods, and the 18th and 19th-century buildings are all equipped as they would have been then.

Furnace

Furnace is two miles (3.2 km) further on. It holds unhappy memories of the troubled times that reigned during the 18th century. It is so called from the charcoal-burning smelting furnace that was established here to utilise the trees that were felled by order of the Hanoverian government, so that rebel Highlanders still clinging to the Jacobite cause, would have less cover to hide.

Crarae Woodland Garden

The Crarae Woodland Garden (open daily in the summer: adults £1, children free), three miles (4.8 km) to the south, has lovely azaleas and rhododendrons in season, as well as a variety of conifers and rare shrubs.

Lochgilphead

Lochgilphead, 24 miles (38.4 km) south-west of Inveraray, at the head of Loch Gilp, and an appendix off Loch Fyne, is a jolly, bustling holiday resort as well as the shopping centre for the area: the jovial country cousin of the prim, elegant Inveraray. There is an excellent choice of good shops around the wide main street that was the market place. The Mid Argyll Show takes place in Lochgilphead in August.

The Crinan Canal cuts through from Ardrishaig in Loch Gilp to Crinan on the west coast. It was built at the end of the 18th century, with 15 locks in its 9 miles (14.4 km) of waterway, through the top of the Kintyre Peninsula, saving the sailor 130 miles (208 km) of often rough passage. Going down the canal in a small boat is a delightfully peaceful way of passing a fine day, though you have to work the lock gates yourself, straining at the handles that wind up the sluices in the massive wooden gates, and leaning on the great timber arms that swing them open when the water either side is level.

Crinan is a small place round a sheltered harbour and the tidal gate between the canal and the open sea. The Crinan Hotel is one of the best in Scotland if you want a memorable break in lovely surroundings.

South of Lochgilphead

Knapdale

Knapdale, running south from Lochgilphead like a clenched fist, just manages to hang on to the long arm of Kintyre, so nearly an island. It is difficult to say which is the best time to explore this part. Autumn is glorious; the wonderful range of colours shading the hills against the endless views across the water to the islands. So is spring, when the rhododendrons and azaleas are in full glory against the soft new green and the sparkle of water. Perhaps the best time of all is November, just after a light dusting of snow has left its magic touch on what was left of the autumn leaves, muted but still beautiful; the water steel-grey, the hills etched in white.

WHAT TO SEE

Kilberry

Kilberry, on the south-west corner of Knapdale on the B8024, has a collection of 9th and 10th-century stones and some from the Middle Ages, that have been gathered up from the surrounding area and are housed under cover just north of the hamlet, signposted Kilberry Stones, from the road.

St Columba's Cave

St Columba's Cave is 12 miles (19.2 km) north-west of Kilberry on the western shore of **Loch Caolisport** (pronounced Killisport) near **Ellary**. In it is an altar stone and two crosses carved above. Tradition associates this cave with the saint's mission in Scotland and it is not difficult to go along with tradition when you are surrounded by scenery such as is found here. Excavations in the 19th century unearthed evidence that there was a settlement here as far back as 8000 BC, making St Columba comparatively modern! You can see traces of dwellings outside the cave and the ruin of a chapel, as well as a smaller cave, reached by steps. It is nice to think of that charismatic saint spreading his net from here.

Kilmory Knap Chapel

Kilmory Knap Chapel, a 13th-century building, on the southern tip of the peninsular, north of Loch Caolisport contains a collection of sculpted stones and MacMillan's Cross. This cross was elaborately carved in the 15th century, possibly by monks from the monastery at Kilberry.

Castle Sween

Castle Sween, five miles (8 km) north of Kilmory, in a splendid position guarding the entrance to **Loch Sween**, could be the oldest stone castle on the Scottish mainland. It dates from the 11th century and is a great sprawl of a ruin, Norman in style, with buttresses. You can still see the ovens and recesses in the kitchen and the original drain and rubbish-chute in the wall of the round tower. The smell around the outer walls of these castles must have been horrific in summer in the old days!

The castle was a stronghold of MacSweens in the 12th and 13th centuries but they lost their lands when they sided with the English in the 14th century. Robert Bruce besieged it and installed McNeills of Argyll to maintain it, one of whom married a MacMillan. Thus, Knapdale became MacMillan territory. The castle was destroyed in 1647 by Royalists, fighting the cause of Charles I.

This coast is an enchanted land, each mile opening up a fresh view to the islands of Jura and Islay in the west, or down through layers of hills to distant lochs and the sea.

Kintyre: south of Knapdale

Campbeltown

You can drive right round the Kintyre Peninsula, passing through little villages and hamlets, most of which cater for summer visitors. The landscape is similar to that of Knapdale, cut by wooded valleys rising to hilly moorland. The east and west routes meet at **Campbeltown** at the head of **Campbeltown Loch**, a perfect haven for boats in a westerly gale, and subject of that hopeful song: "... O Campbeltown Loch, I wish you were whisky ..." It is a sturdy holiday town and boating centre, and was once an important herring port, with two distilleries.

Flora Macdonald sailed to Carolina from Campbeltown in 1774, emigrating with her family nearly 30 years after her brave actions helped to save the life of Bonny Prince Charlie.

William McTaggart, that great painter of Scottish life and scenery, was born in the town in 1835. He was no doubt inspired by the local land and seascapes.

WHAT TO SEE

The Museum (open daily except Wednesday and Sundays: admission free) in Hall Street has a fascinating demonstration of how vitrified forts were formed.

Davaar Island

Davaar Island is at the mouth of the loch and accessible at low tide along a shingle spit; a tiny lump of rock with a cave in it. Here, in 1887, a man called Archibald Mackinnon, inspired by a dream, painted a picture of the crucifixion on to the rock. It is a moving picture, after the style of el Greco, lit by a shaft of light that streams into the large cave through an aperture.

Machrihanish

Machrihanish, 6 miles (9.7 km) west of Campbeltown, and fully exposed to the fury of Atlantic gales, is a popular holiday village, with several hotels, a golf course, camp site and glorious sandy beaches, as well as the airport.

Mull of Kintyre

The Mull of Kintyre, the southern tip of the peninsula, is a splendid dramatic rocky extremity, with a lighthouse and sheer cliffs. It lies only 13 miles (21 km) from Ireland and is an impressive place in a westerly gale. This was the subject of a song by Paul McCartney sending a number of fans off to the island of Mull, looking for it!

Southend

Southend is tucked round the corner to the east of the Mull. 8 miles (12.9 km) south of Campbeltown. This is another holiday village with a golf course and wonderful sandy beaches with dunes, covered in marram grass, offering shelter from the wind. Here you will also see what little is left of **Dunverty Castle**, which is a jagged tooth of masonry standing above vicious rocks, shrouded in uncomfortable memories. Three hundred of trose's men, fighting the cause of Charles I, were besieged here by the merciless Covenanting General David Leslie. Forced by thirst to surrender, the Royalists, mostly Irish mercenaries, were shamelessly massacred.

Keil, just west of Southend, has a flat rock which is traditionally regarded as the place where St Columba first landed in Scotland. If you look carefully you can see two footprints burnt into the rock where he stood, turning his back on the land that had outlawed him!

Sanda Island

From Southend you can hire a boat and go out to Sanda Island, about 2 miles (3.2 km) to the south where Robert Bruce hid in 1306, while making his way back from Rathlin Island.

Gigha Island

You can get a ferry across to Gigha from **Tayinloan**, half way up the west side of Kintyre. Gigha is Norse for God and indeed this could almost be called a Garden of Eden. On the island you can see the **Achamore House Gardens** (open all year round: adults £1, children 50p). These are a riot of sub-tropical plants and shrubs, all thriving in this mild westerly climate. On a warm, sunny day you can enjoy the scents and vivid colours of exotic blooms and think yourself on some south sea island.

TOURIST INFORMATION
Campbeltown, tel 0586-52056. It is open all year.
Inveraray, tel 0499-2063. It is open April to September.
Lochgilphead, tel 0546-2344. It is open April to September.
Tarbert, tel 08802-429. It is open April to September.

WHERE TO STAY
You have a very big choice of hotels, guest houses, bed and breakfasts, and self-catering places in this area and you should look at the tourist brochure, which gives full details and photographs. The following is just a small, random selection.

Stonefield Castle Hotel, Tarbert, on Loch Fyne, tel 08802-207. B&B from £27: categories 5,5,5: 34 bedrooms, 33 en suite. A large, comfortable white castellated hotel with a friendly staff and good food.

Tarbert Hotel, Tarbert, on Loch Fyne, tel 08802-264. B&B from £13.50: categories 4,4,5: 21 bedrooms, 10 en suite. A comfortable hotel right on the waterfront.

Argyll Arms Hotel, Inveraray, tel 0499-2466, B&B from £13.50: categories 4,4,4: 30 bedrooms, 11 en suite. A friendly hotel in the middle of the town with comfortable rooms and good food.

George Hotel, Inveraray, tel 0499-2111 B&B from £9.50: categories 3,4,4: 14 bedrooms, 2 en suite. Good Scottish hospitality in the middle of the town.

Stag Hotel, Lochgilphead, tel 0546-2496. B&B from £15.50: categories 4,3,4: 24 bedrooms, 17 en suite. Friendly staff and good old fashioned atmosphere.

Argyll Hotel, Lochgilphead, tel 0546-2221. B&B from £12.50: categories 4,3,4: 12 bedrooms, 5 en suite. In the middle of the town with a warm welcome.

Crinan Hotel, Crinan, tel 054683-235/243. B&B from £28.50: categories 6,4,4: 23 bedrooms, 22 en suite. A comfortable hotel in a lovely position overlooking the water. The food is excellent but it is not cheap.

Gigha Hotel, Isle of Gigha, tel 05835-254. B&B with dinner, £27: categories 4,4,4: 9 bedrooms, 3 en suite. A friendly, comfortable hotel on paradise island.

Post Office House, Isle of Gigha, tel 05835-251. B&B with dinner from £11: categories 1,1,2: 3 bedrooms. Hospitable, informal welcome.

Keil Hotel, Southend, near Campbeltown, tel 0586-83253. B&B from £12: categories 3,4,5: 18 bedrooms, 5 en suite. A comfortable, modern hotel by the sea with lovely views.

Royal Hotel, Main Street, Campbeltown, tel 0586-52017. B&B from £15.25: categories 5,5,5: 16 bedrooms, 12 en suite. Very comfortable and friendly in the middle of the town.

White Hart Hotel, Main Street, Campbeltown, tel 0586-52440/53356. B&B from £12.50: categories 3,3,5: 31 bedrooms, 1 en suite. Right in the middle of the town.

EATING OUT

You will get very adequate meals in the hotels at reasonable prices. For an expensive treat, go to the **Crinan Hotel**, see above, and try the seafood, in the **Rooftop** restaurant. It is supplied daily by fishing boats that unload a short distance from the kitchen. Dinner from £15, but it is worth splashing out and forgetting the price.

North from Lochgilphead

The drive from Lochgilphead to Oban, up the west coast, is lovely. The road flirts with the sea, dipping and twisting and pulling away with magnificent views.

WHAT TO SEE

This part of Argyll is drenched in ancient history. Four miles (6.4 km) north-west of Lochgilphead you can see all that is left of **Dunadd Fort**, once the capital of the kingdom of Dalriada, from the 6th to the 9th century. This was a great and powerful political centre, all those years ago, headquarters of the early missionaries, including St Columba, until Kenneth MacAlpine decided it would be sensible to move the capital to Pictland. A hillock and a rock are all that remain, the rock now protected by a glass cover with carvings of a boar, a footprint and some Ogham inscriptions. Historians believe that this was the place where kings were crowned; that St Columba crowned Aidan here in 574, using the disputed Stone of Destiny as the throne. The stone was stolen away to Westminster Abbey by Edward I, and it has been there ever since, apart from a brief holiday in 1951, when it was temporarily "restored" to Scotland.

From Dunadd to **Kilmartin**, a distance of only about three miles (4.8 km), there are a great number of pre-historic standing stones and burial cairns dating from the Stone Age and Bronze Age. They have been well labelled and you find your imagination reeling as you stand here trying to see how it was, all those years ago. If you choose a time when there aren't too many people about, and try to picture those ancient people performing their mysterious rites in this very place, you find yourself strangely moved. Some of the cists have been reconstructed so that you can go inside and see the carvings on the walls.

Carnasserie Castle

Carnasserie Castle is nine miles (14.4 km) north of Lochgilphead. It is the ruined home of John Carswell, the first Protestant Bishop of the Isles, who translated Knox's liturgy into Gaelic in 1567, the first Gaelic book to be published.

Lunga Wildlife Park

The Lunga Wildlife Park, on the **Ardfern Peninsula**, north of Loch Craignish, has indigenous animals in beautiful surroundings, and there is experimental white fish farming in the loch.

Just to the north on **Loch Melfort**, you should visit the **Arduaine Gardens** (open in the summer: adults £1, children free) with their wonderful display of sub-tropical plants: magnolias, rhododendrons and azaleas; water garden and rock garden and many rare trees and shrubs.

Seil

Seil is a hook of land west of Loch Melfort—an island, joined to the mainland by a much-photographed, hump-backed bridge, **Clachan Bridge**, "The only bridge over the Atlantic". From this bridge a narrow road twists down to **Easdale**, where you can see the old slate-quarry workings. Part of the original film of *Whisky Galore* was made here, many years ago, transforming the little township into a stage set.

Sheltered **An Cala** in Easdale, is another beautiful garden with a blaze of blossom and water and rock gardens with lovely views. Boats run from Seil, in the summer, to Mull, Jura and the Corrievreckan whirlpool.

Oban

Oban is 31 miles (50 km) north of Lochgilphead, and is unmistakably a seaside resort; a hive of activity in the summer, quiet and withdrawn in winter. The town is a crescent, rising steeply from the bay round which it is built, its main street fronting on to the harbour. High above stands **McCaig's Folly**, a large circular temple with pillars, built in 1897 by the banker, McCaig, partly to give work to the unemployed and partly as a memorial to his family.

In summer the streets are crowded with holidaymakers, the shops hung with buckets and spades and souvenirs, the harbour full of boats. MacBraynes steamers come and go, to Mull and the Outer Hebrides; the quays are thronged with cars and people and freight. Neat, respectable villas and hotels fringe the town and the cafes and restaurants are packed.

SPECIAL ATTRACTIONS

The Argyllshire Gathering is a great Highland occasion in Oban in August with lots of piping and dancing and traditional games. In September The Oban Gala Day and Street Fair is a colourful carnival, especially when the sun shines.

Oban is an excellent base for sub-aqua divers, with good air supplies in the town and marvellous underwater terrain. The sound of Mull is littered with wrecks and the waters all round offer a wealth of marine life and cliff scenery.

WHAT TO SEE

Dunstaffnage Castle (open standard Ancient Monument times, except in winter closed Thursday afternoons and Fridays: adults 50p, children 25p) is four miles (6.4 km) north of Oban on a rocky promontory guarding the entrance to Loch Etive. It is a splendid, ragged ruin that seems to grow out of the rock. Parts of it stand over 60 ft (18 m) high, its massive walls more than 10 ft (3 m) thick. It was here that Flora Macdonald was held prisoner for a few days after helping Prince Charlie in 1746. Tradition holds that the Stone of Destiny came here from Dunadd, staying until Kenneth MacAlpine moved it to Scone in an attempt to draw together his kingdom of Picts and Scots.

The northern tip of Strathclyde is rugged, mountainous hinterland laced with rivers and cascading burns and cut by Loch Etive, encircled by a road that gives you many lovely views.

White Corries Chairlift

About 60 miles (96 km) from Oban via Tyndrum, in the north-east corner of the region, off the A82, you come to the White Corries Chairlift (open weekends from January to April, and daily in the summer: adults £1.50, children £1). This takes you 2,100 ft (630m) up into the hills with glorious views over Rannoch Moor and into Glencoe.

The coast road north from Oban loops round **Loch Creran**, clinging to the coast in places with more good views. A minor road south from **Barcaldine** takes you to the northern shore of Loch Etive and **Ardchattan Priory** (open at all times: admission free) founded in 1230. It was the meeting place of one of Robert Bruce's parliaments, in 1308, one of the last to be held in Gaelic. You can see the remains of the priory, and curse Cromwell, whose soldiers burned it down. The gardens of **Ardchattan House** (open in the summer: admission free) are next door.

The ideal way to explore this part of the coast is by boat, but you need a competent skipper to navigate the hazardous rocks and currents of these water.

Lismore Island

From Oban, a car ferry (taking an hour) runs six miles (9.6 km) north to Lismore Island in **Loch Linnhe**, or you can catch the passenger ferry from **Port Appin**. This long slither of rock, overlaid with loam and heather, was the seat of the diocese of Argyll from 1200 to 1507, in the days before Luther stirred up the beginnings of the Reformation. There are traces of the miniature cathedral that was here in those early times, incorporated into the parish church, built in 1749.

Bachuil House (open by arrangement, tel Lismore 256: free) is on the island. Here you can see the **Bachuil Mor**, or pastoral staff of St Moluag, the man who converted the island to Christianity in the 6th century. Moluag and Columba are said to have been rivals, the one being a Pict, the other a Celt.

Keep a sharp eye out for seals all round this coast: they bask on the rocks in large numbers, flopping down into the water if disturbed, to pop up and stare at you with their great velvety eyes.

Castle Stalker

Castle Stalker (open by appointment, tel Upper Warlingham 2768, in summer: adults £2.50, children £1, including the boat trip), dating from 1500 and recently restored, was the home of the Stewarts of Appin. It is situated on a tiny islet off Port Appin.

Loch Awe

If you go north from Inveraray, you reach the head of Loch Awe and the east–west route to Oban. The road twists and climbs through a wild glen, with glorious views, till it reaches the loch, a 23 mile (37 km) long serpent of water with thickly wooded shores, islands, and more than its share of midges clinging to the dense vegetation.

Kilchurn Castle can be looked at from the outside. It lies on a commanding site at the north end of the loch. Dating from 1440, it belonged to the Campbells of Breadalbane who occupied it until it was taken over by Hanoverian troops in 1746, with the consent of the Campbells who were anti-Jacobite. The gale that destroyed the Tay Rail Bridge also demolished one of Kilchurn's turrets.

When the level of the loch is low you can see traces of several "crannogs", man-made islands where early settlers built dwellings for greater protection against attack. Some of the islands were used as clan burial grounds, especially **Inchail**, where there is a ruined chapel dating from the 13th century and several graves of the Macarthur clan.

There are good walks either side of the loch. On the west side there is an information centre at **Inverliever**, where you can pick up useful advice and directions for the best trails to take.

Ardanaiseig Gardens (open in the summer: adults £1, children free) are at the north end of the loch. They contain lovely shrubs and flowers and some of the best views of the area.

If you have time to spare and are feeling energetic, climb **Ben Cruachan**, north of the A85, 3,695 ft (1,108 m), from whose lofty summit you will get some of the best views in Scotland. On a clear day you can stand up there with the wind holding you upright, and feel that the whole country lies at your feet.

TOURIST INFORMATION

Oban, Argyll Square, tel 0631-63122. It is open all year.

WHERE TO STAY

Once again, you have such a big choice of accommodation that you must look at the tourist brochure, which fills you in on the range, with all details and photographs. The following is just a small selection.

Crinan Hotel, see previous "Where to stay" section.

Alexandra Hotel, Corran Esplanade, Oban, tel 0631-62381. B&B from £27: categories 5,5,5: 56 bedrooms, 49 en suite. An imposing hotel on the waterfront, with a friendly staff and good food.

Argyll Hotel, Esplanade, Oban, tel 0631–62353. B&B from £12: categories 4,5,5: 29 bedrooms, 6 en suite. Right in the middle of the town, not far from ferries and station. Recently modernised, with friendly hospitality and lovely views out across the bay.

Caledonian Hotel, Station Square, Oban, tel 0631-63133. B&B from £19: categories 5,5,4: 67 bedrooms en suite. In the middle of the town next to the station and the ferries. A comfortable, old fashioned hotel with good food and a warm welcome.

Great Western Hotel, Esplanade, Oban, tel 0631-63101. B&B from £24: categories 3,3,5: 78 bedrooms, 68 en suite. A comfortable hotel overlooking Oban Bay.

Park Hotel, Esplanade, Oban, tel 0631-63621. B&B from £18: categories 3,5,4: 80 bedrooms, 51 en suite. All comforts and a friendly staff. Views across Oban Bay.

Ardsheal House, Kentallen of Appin, Appin, tel 0631-74 227. B&B from £21: categories 4,3,3. 13 bedrooms, 9 en suite. A nice relaxed atmosphere, high on a peninsula with lovely views over Loch Linnhe, in 900 acres. 18th century, with oak panelling, open fires and antiques. Excellent food.

Airds Hotel, Port Appin, tel 0631-73 236. Dinner, B&B from £45: inclusive, categories 5,4,4: 15 bedrooms, 11 en suite. Overlooking Loch Linnhe, Lismore and Shuna islands, and the mountains of Morvern, this hotel has won awards for its accommodation, food and service.

Loch Melfort Hotel, Arduaine, near Oban, tel 08522-233. B&B from £20: categories 4,3,4: 26 bedrooms, 23 en suite. One of the original commended hotels in Scotland, with views out to sea and the islands, including Jura and Sacba. The high standard and warm atmosphere of the hotel bring guests back, and it is a favourite stopping place for west coast yachtsmen.

Loch Awe House Hotel, overlooking Loch Awe, tel 08382 261. B&B from £8: categories 2,3,4: 61 bedrooms. Old fashioned, relaxed, friendly hotel in a lovely setting.

Falls of Lora Hotel, Connel Ferry, near Oban, tel 0631-71 483. B&B from £9.50: categories 4,5,5: 30 bedrooms, 23 en suite. Overlooking Loch Etive, this owner-run hotel gives you a warm welcome and good service and is very comfortable. You can choose between luxury four-poster bedrooms or inexpensive family rooms. The food is good.

Knipoch Hotel, Kilninver, near Oban (six miles (9.6 km) south of Oban on A816), tel 085-26 251. B&B from £20: categories 6,5,6: 22 bedrooms en suite. On the shore of Loch Feochan, with a history dating from 1592. Family-run luxury hotel with good food that has won several awards. Watch the sun setting below the hills of Lorn, across the loch.

EATING OUT

All the hotels above will give you a good meal. For a special treat try the Crinan Hotel, see previous "Eating out" section.

Knipoch Hotel, see above. Excellent dinner from £15.

Airds Hotel, see above. Excellent dinner from £15.

Loch Melfort Hotel, see above. Excellent dinner from £15.

Falls of Lora Hotel, see above. Good Scottish food. Dinner from £7.50.

Balmoral Hotel, Craigard Road, Oban, tel 0631-62731. Traditional Scottish food in candle-lit restaurant. Dinner from £7.50.

Cuilfail Hotel, Kilmelford, tel 085-22 274. Bistro-style, good home cooking. Dinner from £7.

If you are hurrying to catch a ferry in Oban, at night, with no time for a sit-down meal, there is a fish and chip shop on your left as your drive into the main street of the town from Connel Ferry, where you can get a delicious variety of carry-out meals.

The Hebrides: Strathclyde

ISLAY

Islay, the most southerly of the Hebrides, is a favourite holiday island which people fall in love with and return to, time and time again.

Islay (pronounced I-lah) is a land of contrasts, with farmland rising to wild moorland, cut by streams and rivers, and a rugged coastline giving way to great sweeps of sandy beaches and machair. The island is perhaps best known for its whisky. Its eight distilleries scent the air with the pungent smell of smouldering peat. Islay was in the news recently when conservationists managed to prevent Scottish Malt Distillers Co from digging Duich Moss peat, essential for the flavour of Islay whisky. Rare Greenland white-fronted geese fed on the peat moss and it was thought that to cut it might disturb them. The islanders were understandably furious at this interference, pleading that whisky was more vital to their survival than "any bloody goose".

GETTING THERE

There are several ferries a day, from West Loch Tarbert, taking just over two hours. There is a daily Loganair flight from Glasgow airport as well, taking half an hour, and one from Campbeltown, also taking half an hour.

Port Ellen

Port Ellen, in the south, is the chief holiday centre. Here there is plenty of accommodation. The airport is on **Laggan Bay** above the dramatic **Oa Peninsula**, whose sheer cliffs are honeycombed with caves.

WHAT TO SEE

Dunyvaig Castle lies 3½ miles (5.6 km) east of Port Ellen. It is a ruined 14th-century fortress, once the stronghold of the MacDonalds of Islay in the days when the Lords of the Isles considered themselves to be separate from the authority of the Crown.

Kildalton Chapel and Cross is another 3½ miles (5.6 km) further north along this road. It is currently in the process of restoration. The Celtic cross carved from a single block of blue stone and inscribed with early Christian symbols, is perhaps the finest Celtic cross in Scotland. It dates from the 9th century.

The Oa Peninsula runs 5 miles (8 km) south-west of Port Ellen and was once a haunt of smugglers and illicit whisky distillers.

Machrie lies north of Oa. Here there is an 18 hole golf course which is a glorious place to play as it stands beside the sandy crescent of Laggan Bay.

Bowmore is 7 miles (11.3 km) north of Port Ellen. Here you can see the intriguing, round church of **Kilarrow**. Built in 1769, of Italian design, its shape was thus in order to deprive the devil of any corners in which to lurk!

The Rhinns of Islay thrust out from the west side of the island like a great hammer-head.

Port Charlotte, on the south-east shore, has the **Museum of Islay** (all year except weekends in winter: adults 50p, children 25p). The museum is in a converted church and contains an interesting collection of exhibits that cover the history of the island from pre-historic times to the present.

Finlaggan Castle is in the north of the island, on Loch Finlaggan. Here the Macdonalds, Lords of the Isles, had their main stronghold. Near the castle there is an islet where they used to hold their councils, when the 14 chiefs of the Lordship were summoned to a kind of parliament, to advise their overlord. You can picture them, coming in from all over the kingdom of the Isles, in coracles, accompanied by members of their clans, proud men, independent of the Scottish parliament, settling their disputes and problems, often with great wisdom and justice.

TOURIST INFORMATION

Bowmore, tel 049-681 254. It is open April to September.

WHERE TO STAY

There is quite a choice, so you should look in the tourist information brochure, or ask the local office.

Machrie Hotel, Machrie, Port Ellen, tel 0496 2310. B&B from £16.67: categories 4,4,5: 20 bedrooms, 10 en suite. A friendly atmosphere.

White Hart Hotel, Port Ellen, tel 0496-2311. B&B from £12.50: categories 3,3,4: 19 bedrooms, 5 en suite. A relaxed, friendly hotel overlooking the sea.

Port Charlotte Hotel, Port Charlotte, tel 049685-321. B&B from £10.50: categories 3,3,4: 11 bedrooms, 4 en suite. A waterside hotel in Port Charlotte.

Lochside Hotel, Shore Street, Bowmore, tel 049681-265/244. B&B from £18: categories 4,4,4: 9 bedrooms, 7 en suite. An old fashioned, friendly hotel.

EATING OUT

All the hotels above serve reasonable meals. Dinner from about £8. Go for the seafood whenever possible.

JURA

Just off the north-east coast of Islay, Jura has little accommodation for tourists and so is far less frequented. It is wild and rugged; a beautiful, remote haven where you can really relax and get away from it all.

GETTING THERE
The ferry from West Loch Tarbert takes 2¾ hours and from Port Askaig in Islay it takes ten minutes.

Craighouse

This is the only village on the island and here you will find the Jura Hotel, the only hotel on Jura. The island supports herds of deer and stalking can be arranged through the hotel. Here you can also arrange riding, fishing, sea-angling, boating, shooting and waterskiing.

WHAT TO SEE
The **Corryvreckan Whirlpool** is one of the features of the island. It is found off the island's northern tip, in the strait between Jura and Scarba. Known about by all west-coast sailors, the Corryvreckan is both lion and lamb. In the right conditions of tide and weather its mighty maw has been known to suck down whole boats, roaring like an express train. But you can come upon it, by sea, and find only satin-smooth water, ruffled by tiny eddies, that pull gently at your boat, no more.

TOURIST INFORMATION
The Pier, Campbeltown, tel 0586-52056. It is open all year.

WHERE TO STAY
Jura Hotel, Craighouse, tel 049682-243. B&B from £16.50: categories 3,4,4: 18 bedrooms, 4 en suite. A really relaxed, friendly atmosphere in a lovely setting, and good food.

COLONSAY AND ORONSAY

These two tiny islands, joined at low tide, lie ten miles (16 km) west of Jura. They possess delightful havens of craggy hills, woods and a rocky coastline broken by wonderful silver sands. Both islands are ideal for botanists, archaeologists and ornithologists, as well as for people looking for peace and quiet. The wild flowers are glorious, with purple orchids among the many varieties that carpet the machair.

GETTING THERE
The ferry from Oban (passengers only) takes 2½ hours.

WHAT TO SEE

Kiloran Gardens, on Colonsay (open daily: admission free), have a wealth of sub-tropical plants, palm trees, and lovely shrubs.

St Oran's Chapel, on Oronsay, is a ruined 14th-century priory, named after St Oran who was a companion to St Columba. Although the cloisters have fallen this is a splendid ruin with gravestones carved with boats and warriors and hunting scenes. Excavations, of which there are no trace now, revealed that Oronsay was inhabited in the Middle Stone Age. Certainly Norsemen lived here, and some Columban monks, long before the present ruin was built.

From Colonsay you can reach Oronsay on foot. For about three hours, at low tide, and that is about as long as you need to explore.

TOURIST INFORMATION

Oban, tel 0631-63122. It is open all year.

WHERE TO STAY

Isle of Colonsay Hotel, tel 095-12 316. B&B from £10: categories 5,4,4: 11 bedrooms, 8 with private bath or shower. Comfortable and informal, with friendly service.

MULL

Mull, like all Scottish islands, is a kingdom of its own, giving you a lifetime's worth of exploring, walking, climbing and boating. The island, called "isle-with-a-mass-of-hills", is the largest of the inner Hebrides and deserves a whole book to itself. Shaped like a caricature of the British Isles, its south-western peninsula kicking frivolously upwards, it is encircled by roads and deeply cut by lochs. The western seaboard is sprinkled with islands and it is possible to get boat-trips out to these. Some of the hotels charter their own boats. In addition, there are always local men who will take you out fishing or sightseeing. The whole coast is a sailor's paradise. The hinterland is indeed a mass of hills, dominated by **Ben More**, 3,169 ft (950 m), in the west.

You will never forget a holiday on Mull. The island holds a Music Festival, in April, and a Car Rally, in October.

GETTING THERE

Car ferries run quite frequently from Oban to Craignure, taking just under an hour, from Oban to Tobermory, taking about two hours, from Lochaline to Tobermory, taking about an hour, and from Lochaline to Fishnish, taking quarter of an hour. There is also a passenger ferry from Mingary (Kilchoan) to Tobermory, taking half an hour.

Tobermory

The boat from Oban takes you all the way up the Sound of Mull, past **Castle Duart**, a great fortress guarding the south-eastern corner. This is almost the first thing you see as you look at the island. Then you go on to Tobermory where you land. Tobermory meaning The Well of St Mary, is the "capital" of Mull. It has one of the most sheltered harbours in Scotland and tucked round behind a headland is the town which is clustered attractively round the anchorage, its houses rising steeply from the water. It is a cheerful place, full of boats during the season, where you hear yachtsmen hailing each other across the water, having last met up in some other west coast anchorage, maybe years before. "Ceilidhs" erupt spontaneously in the bars and hotels that line the waterfront; dinghies come and go between the boats during long summer evenings.

WHAT TO SEE

Mull and Iona Folk Museum (open week days in summer: adults 30p, children 10p) is in a converted church. Here you can see displays of the island's history.

In the bay beyond the harbour lies the wreck of a Spanish galleon, the *Florida*, part of the Armada, still a focus of attention for treasure seekers today. The ship was driven to seek shelter here in a storm in 1588. Always hospitable, the islanders treated the Spaniards with courtesy, restocking their stores and entertaining them in grand style. But Scotsmen are thrifty, as well as hospitable, and when rumour came that the *Florida* was about to depart, without having paid its dues, a local man, Donald Maclean, went aboard to remonstrate. Although instantly locked up in the ship's cell, he managed to escape, and in retaliation he blew up the ship, together with the vast hoard of gold and treasure it was alleged to have been carrying.

Tobermory has a 9-hole golf course, on the northern tip of the island.

Dervaig

Going west to Dervaig, six miles (9.6 km) from Tobermory, you come to the **Mull Little Theatre**, the smallest professional theatre in Britain whose really first class productions should be booked for well in advance (tel 06884-267).

The west coast road gives you some glorious views out to the scattering of islands that create such wonderful seascapes in these parts, especially if you see them against a setting sun.

Islands

You can go out to the **Treshnish Isles** and to **Staffa**, by boat when the weather is fair, though it is not always possible to land. The organ pipe rock formation on Staffa inspired Mendelssohn in 1829, to write *The Hebridean Overture*. The island of **Ulva** will be familiar to anyone who had to learn the poem *Lord Ullin's Daughter*, in their youth. It concerns the sad tale of "The Chief of Ulva's Isle" and his lover, fleeing her father's wrath and drowning in the ferry, crossing to the island.

Every one of these islands off the main island has its legends and its place in history or literature. Johnson and Boswell came to these islands on their tour of the Hebrides, both writing of the various trips they made.

Staffa 'Fingals Cave'

Port na Croise

More and more beautiful vistas open up as you drive down the west coast or walk up into the hills. A splendid walk is the six miles (9.6 km) track out to Port na Croise on the southern tip of the **Ardmeanach Peninsula**, north of **Loch Scridain**. Here you can see a fossilised pine tree, 40 ft (12 m) high and some 50 million years old!

Castle Duart

Going east from the head of Loch Scridain, 15 miles (24 km), across great stretches of moor and hill, you come to Castle Duart (open daily in the summer: adults £1.50, children 70p). The castle dates from the 13th century, and was always the home of the chiefs of Maclean, although temporarily confiscated after the Jacobite rising in 1745. It was bought back and restored in this century by the then chief, a gallant Hussar colonel who rode with the Light Brigade in the Crimea and died at the age of 100.

As well as the keep, you can see the cell where prisoners were held from the Spanish galleon sunk in Tobermory in 1588. There are relics of the Maclean family and an exhibition of Scouting throughout the Commonwealth.

Grass Point

Just south of Duart, a road takes you out to Grass Point, on **Lochdon**, the old drovers' road once used to get cattle and sheep to the mainland from the little jetty. The seals that you will see on the rocks round the bay are not related to those that you see in the waters round Mull. Grass Point seals are the work of the eminent sculptor, poet and writer, Lionel Leslie. He and his wife bought the Drover's Inn here, after the last war, and built it up with their own hands to what you see today. There is a tea room with home made teas and you can see over the studio and buy local crafts. If you are lucky you can sit and listen to the sculptor himself, a man in his mid-eighties with a wit as sharp as the stone he can no longer see to carve. Grass Point was the landing point for pilgrims going to Iona.

Torosay Castle

You should not miss a visit to Torosay Castle (open daily in the summer: adults £1.50, children 90p), a mile south of Craignure near Duart. This is a splendid 19th-century Scottish Baronial building, with all the embellishments so beloved by the Victorians, designed by David Bryce. The 11 acres (4.5 ha) of terraced Italian style gardens with a statue walk and water garden, were laid out by Robert Lorimer. Among the things to see in the house are some magnificent paintings of wild life by Thorburn, Landseer, Poynter, de Lazlo and Sargent. There are also hunting trophies, a library and an archive room with photographs and scrapbooks going back over 100 years. In the high season you can get boats from Oban direct to Torosay.

Going back to the head of Loch Scridain, the road west through the **Ross of Mull**, with its rugged scenery, takes you out to Iona.

IONA

No one can visit Mull without making a pilgrimage to the "cradle of Christianity", though, in fact, St Ninian was spreading the word for nearly 150 years before St Columba founded his church on Iona in 563. The island is beautiful; a gentle landscape of white cockle shell sand and vivid green slopes, scarred with rust red granite and painted with wild flowers.

The powerful Irish saint, of royal descent, outlawed from his own land, came here with a few followers and set about converting the heathen Picts of Scotland to the Celtic Christianity of his homeland. Many Scots, Irish and Norse kings were buried on Iona and you can see their graves today.

GETTING THERE

The passenger ferry from Fionnphort, on Mull, to Iona, takes five minutes. There is also a Sacred Isles Cruise, on certain days in the summer, leaving Oban at 9.15 am, and sailing via Staffa, to Iona, arriving at 1.30 pm. You get two and a half hours on Iona and arrive back in Oban at 6.45 pm.

WHAT TO SEE

The Abbey

In 1938, George Macleod, a remarkable Presbyterian socialist, settled a new community on the island, to restore the ancient stones and create the present abbey and its domestic buildings. For some, it is not a warm place where you instinctively go down on your knees to say a prayer. For some it is not even a house of God at all, with its post-cards and booklets and stark, unadorned interior thronged with sightseers, slung about with cameras and macintoshes. But for everyone it must be an experience, to come, knowing that St Columba was here, all those years ago.

If you feel a slight tug of disappointment at the "museum feeling" of this very sacred spot, climb the small hill, **Dun I**, to the north of the abbey. From here you can look down on the buildings, and the boats around the pier, and the trails of people in their bright anoraks (parkas), munching their sandwiches and scattering their litter. If you stay very quiet you may catch a faint echo of ironic laughter, and feel a gentle Celtic presence beside you...

TOURIST INFORMATION

Oban, tel 0631-63122. It is open all year.

Tobermory, tel 0688-2182. It is open all year (two hours a day in winter).

WHERE TO STAY

You will find true Highland hospitality in all the island hotels, with friendly service. There are quite a few to choose from. The following is just a small, random selection.

Western Isles Hotel, Tobermory, tel 0688-2012. B&B from £13: categories 5,5,4: 29 bedrooms, 15 en suite. Lovely views.

Suidhe Hotel, Tobermory, tel 0688-2209. B&B from £12: categories 3,3,4: 9 bedrooms, 1 en suite. Hotel on the waterfront.

Ardfenaig House, Bunessan, tel 068-17 210. Dinner & B&B from £40: categories 4,4,3: 5 bedrooms.

Craignure Inn, Craignure, tel 06802-305. B&B from £11.50: categories 1,3,3: 4 bedrooms. A friendly, relaxed atmosphere.

EATING OUT

Back Brae Restaurant, Tobermory, tel 0688-2422. Fresh sea food, and also a carry-out service. Dinner from £6.

The Captain's Table, Tobermory, tel 0688-2313. Local sea food, overlooking the harbour. Dinner from £6.

Martyrs Bay, Isle of Iona, tel 06817-382. Restaurant and spar shop. Snacks, tea and coffee, light meals, bar.

The Keel Row, Fionnphort, Mull, tel 06817-458. Dinner from £6.

The Puffer Aground, Salen, tel Aros, 389. The food here is recommended and you should book for dinner. Dinner from about £8.

COLL AND TIREE

You can get to both islands by boat from Oban, and to Tiree by Loganair. Coll is known for its trout-filled lochs. Tiree's name comes from Tir Eth (the land of corn) and dates from the days when it supplied corn to Iona. The two islands, guarding the north-west coast of Mull, tend to be forgotten. They are flat, crofting islands, with several ruins and a reputation for sunshine, and wind. Gaelic is still a living language here.

WHAT TO SEE

Breacachadh Castle

This castle, on Coll, is a restored 15th-century tower house. It was stronghold of the Macleans of Coll and now the headquarters of the Project Trust. The tourist centre in Oban will arrange for you to have a tour of the castle and croft.

At Totronald you can also see the **Standing Stones**, called Na Sgeulachan (The Tellers of Tales), thought to be the site of an ancient temple.

Broch of Dun Mor

On Tiree you can see the Broch of Dun Mor. It lies on the north coast and is the ruin of one of the tall, hollow towers built for refuge against Norse and other invaders.

There is a 9 hole golf course on Tiree.

TOURIST INFORMATION
Oban, tel 0631-63122. It is open all year.

WHERE TO STAY
You will find true Highland hospitality at all the hotels on these islands.

Isle of Coll Hotel, tel 087-93 334. B&B from £12 (with dinner, £23): categories 3,4,5: 8 bedrooms, 1 en suite.

Tigh-na-Mara, Coll, tel 087-93 354. Dinner, B&B from £16: categories 3,3,5: 6 bedrooms.

Scarinish Hotel, Tiree, tel 087-92 308. B&B from £11: categories 3,3,4: 11 bedrooms.

Tiree Lodge Hotel, tel 087-92 353/368/317. Prices on application. Categories 3,3,3: 10 bedrooms, 1 en suite.

CRAFT CENTRES AND WORKSHOPS IN STRATHCLYDE

All the places mentioned below welcome visitors to their workshops to see them at work creating the various crafts. Where a telephone number is given you should always telephone first to check times.

Ceramics

Rosann Cherubini Ceramic Design, Law Farm, Galston Road, near Tarbolton, tel 0292541-253. Pottery making.

Loanfoot, Skirling, Biggar. Stoneware and porcelain.

Drymen Pottery, The Pottery, The Square, Drymen, tel 0360-60458. Stoneware and pottery: kiln, wheel and glazing.

Mynde Ceramics, 38A Rotchie Street, West Kilbride, tel 0294-822084. Decorated ceramic tiles, screen printed, hand glazed.

Jewellery and Silversmithing

Anne Clare Graham, 31 High Barholm, Kilbarchan, tel 05057-4814. Design and manufacture of jewellery and small boxes.

Woodwork

Clements Midwood, The Cottage, Station Road, Fairlie, tel 047556-751. Hand made original and reproduction furniture, turnery and carving.

Weaving, knitting and toymaking

Rowallan Crafts, Whiting Bay Brodick, Isle of Arran, tel 07707-282. Handwoven tablemats, wallhangings, soft toys. Mohair sweaters.

Part IX

CENTRAL

Stirling Castle

The eastern part of the Central region is a densely-packed industrial area, forming, with Clydeside, a great pulsing core of energy for Scotland, and offering few attractions for the tourist. As if to compensate, however, the surrounding countryside, which can be reached very quickly, is lovely: the Ochils in the north, the Campsie Fells in the south and Loch Lomond to the west, all create natural boundaries, with the beautiful Trossachs at their heart, giving birth to the young River Forth in a landscape that is the Highlands in miniature.

With no sea coast, the climate is gentle and can be hot. Without the lulling sight and sound of the sea, the people are hard-working, brisk and shrewd, tempered by iron-foundaries, and coal mines, tough and resilient, with a sharp penetrating wit and impetuous generosity. This was Pictland, home to those mysterious aboriginal settlers in the land, indigenous long before the Irish Scots, the Angles and the Welsh began to push north, followed by the Romans.

In the Central region you can trace the Antonine Wall, built in c. AD 140, during the reign of Emperor Antoninus Pius, by Roman Legions II, VI and XX, under Quintus Lollius Urbicus, who was then governor of Britain. Hadrian's Wall, built ten years before, was not proving to be strong enough to deter the ferocious barbarians in the north and the Antonine Wall was a somewhat futile attempt to push them back and cut them off. It stretched 37 miles (59 km), from Old Kilpatrick in the west to Bridgeness in the east. Exploring the Central region you will find bits of it well-preserved, and it is a good idea to go first to the National Museum of Antiquities in Edinburgh, or the Hunterian Museum in Glasgow where there are excellent descriptions of how the wall was constructed as well as many relics.

SPECIAL ATTRACTIONS

Among the events that take place in the Central region during the year, Falkirk, in the south, holds the Scottish Brass Band Championships in March. It also has a Canal Festival and a Spring Fling, in May, and a Family Show, in August.

Dollar has a Gala Day and a Hill Race, in June, and a Flower Show in September.

In July, Alva, Luss and Airth all hold their Highland Games, with piping and dancing, plenty of tartan and all the traditional Scottish sports like putting the weight, tossing the caber and high jump.

Stirling is a great place for ceilidhs, and they have a Tartan Week, in July.

Doune and Dunblane share an Agricultural Show, in July and there are more Highland Games in Dunblane in September.

Balquhidder, to the north, has a Beltane Bonfire, in May, recalling pagan ceremonies of the past, and in July there are the Balquhidder, Lochearnhead and Strathyre Highland Games. This provides another chance to see Highland dancing, piping and all the traditional games and sports that are played on these occasions. There is a pro-golf tournament in Callander in August.

Once you get out of the industrial belt, there is no end of things to see and do: lovely walks and climbs, plenty of golf courses, and lots of historic castles and buildings to explore. There is some good fishing, and riding and pony trekking.

As this is a popular tourist area, many of the hotels to the north, lay on a splendid programme of ceilidhs, Scottish dancing and entertainment.

TOURIST INFORMATION

Where the local tourist information office is closed, off season, you can always get advice, information and brochures from the Tourist Information Centre, Dumbarton Road, Stirling, tel 0786-75019.

From the south-east corner

Falkirk

Falkirk, deep in the heart of industrial Scotland, does not, on first acquaintance, tempt you to linger; but there is a mass of history packed in behind its modern face and you should not pass by too quickly. Falkirk was once one of the cattle drovers' main trysting places—hard to picture the scene now in the busy streets: those tough nomads, wrapped against the cold, surrounded by their herds and flocks, pausing to exchange news with others of their kind, seen always in transit. Two battles were fought here; one in 1298, when William Wallace was defeated by Edward I, and one in 1746, when Prince Charles Edward Stuart, retreating north, turned to defeat the government forces who pursued him.

WHAT TO SEE

The Museum is small but extremely interesting (open daily, except on Sundays: admission free). It is in Orchard Street, behind the main car park. Here you will find the history of the area, including a good section on the Antonine Wall, and details of the two battles. Prince Charlie is said to have slept in a cupboard bed in the room above the door of Watson's shoe shop in the High Street opposite the steeple.

He also lodged in **Callendar House**, which you can see in **Callendar Park** surrounded by attractive woodland. The house is not at present open to the public, though publicly owned, but it makes a good centre piece for the park, where you can walk and play golf.

The Antonine Wall

It is near Falkirk that you will see the best sections of the Antonine Wall. There is a part of it in Callendar Park Housing Estate, to the east, and at Watling Lodge, on the western outskirts, by the canal. Here, just by the road, you can see clearly how the wall must have been and there is a description board.

Rough Castle is the best preserved remnant of the wall. It is well signposted, one and a half miles (2.4 km) from **Bonnybridge**, west of Falkirk and is accessible at all times. Even the slag heaps that overshadow the plateau fail to detract from the queer feeling that you get, standing there thinking of those unfortunate legionaries, accustomed to gentler places, condemned to this bleak place, menaced by a wild race of men who appeared from nowhere with blood-curdling war cries and primitive but lethal weapons, and equally easily vanished again. There are information boards, to help your imagination, telling you where there was a fort, barracks, commander's house, granary, headquarters and a bathhouse.

North of Falkirk and now closed are the famous Carron Ironworks, a massive place founded in 1759, where Britain's cannons were once made.

The north-east corner

Kincardine

After all this industrial sprawl you will pine for a day in the country. From Falkirk, head for Kincardine, four miles (6.4 km) north-east across the Forth. Before crossing the bridge, go a couple of miles (3.2 km) up the A905, south of the river towards Stirling. When you pass Airth Castle Hotel turn off left on B9124.

WHAT TO SEE

Not far along the road, a clear sign directs you to **The Pineapple** (always accessible on the outside: admission free) an amazing garden folly, built on the Dunmore estate in 1761 and now owned by the National Trust for Scotland. This is a splendid relic of the

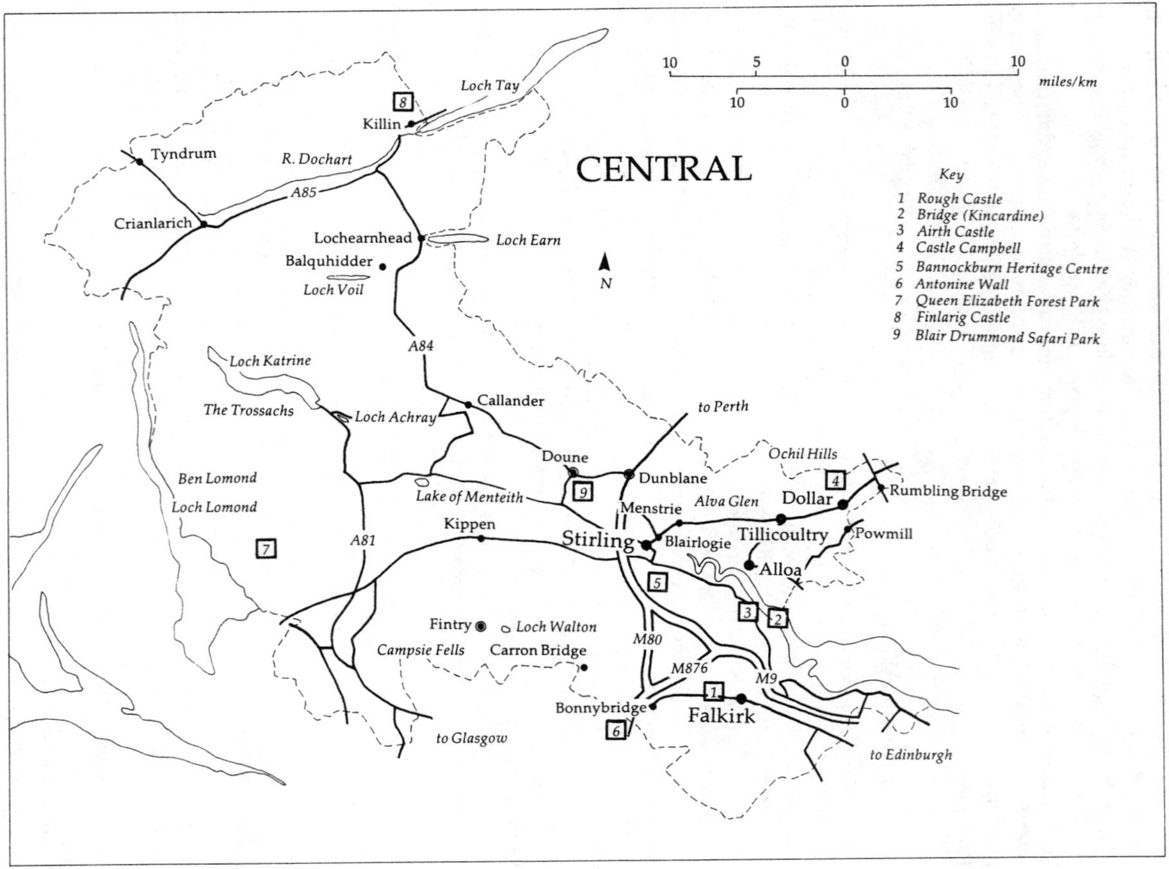

CENTRAL
10 5 0 10 miles/km
10 0 10
N
Key
1 Rough Castle
2 Bridge (Kincardine)
3 Airth Castle
4 Castle Campbell
5 Bannockburn Heritage Centre
6 Antonine Wall
7 Queen Elizabeth Forest Park
8 Finlarig Castle
9 Blair Drummond Safari Park
Loch Tay
Killin
Tyndrum
R. Dochart
A85
Crianlarich
Lochearnhead
Loch Earn
Balquhidder
Loch Voil
A84
Loch Katrine
The Trossachs
Loch Achray
Callander
to Perth
Doune
Dunblane
Ochil Hills
Rumbling Bridge
Dollar
Alva Glen
Menstrie
Ben Lomond
Loch Lomond
Lake of Menteith
Kippen
A81
Stirling
Blairlogie
Tillicoultry
Powmill
Alloa
Fintry
Loch Walton
Campsie Fells
Carron Bridge
M80
M876
M9
Bonnybridge
Falkirk
to Glasgow
to Edinburgh

days when the privileged classes could indulge their fancies with the help of a large labour force. A double wall surrounds a 14 acre (5.6 ha) garden, the space between the walls being for the circulation of hot air from furnaces. On top of the north wall you will see a vast stone pineapple, whose interior forms the domed roof of a circular chamber below. Pineapples were grown here in 1761, under hot-house conditions in the buildings flanking this centre piece, with an army of stokers beavering away to feed the fires that provided the necessary heat. The buildings are now converted to holiday flats which you can rent through the Landmark Trust

Rumbling Bridge

Go back past Airth Castle Hotel south a mile (1.6 km) to the roundabout and cross **Kincardine Bridge**, taking the A977 north for nine miles (14.4 km). Turn off left after **Powmill** to Rumbling Bridge. It would be all too easy to cross the River Devon in Rumbling Bridge and completely miss the significance of its name, so narrow and steep is the gorge as you cross the bridge by car. Park just beyond it where there is a gate through to a path. From here you can see this breathtaking chasm, 120 ft (36 m) deep and so narrow in places that you could shake hands with someone on the far side, if you were both acrobats! From an observation point, well fenced, you can see how the present bridge, built in 1816, spans the older one, built in 1713, with a queer, leap-frog effect. If it strikes you that the lower bridge is alarmingly narrow and lacks any sort of parapet, remember that this was once the main highway!

A path, recently built by Sappers in the British Army, winds upriver from the bridge; securely fenced, much to the relief of those who suffer from vertigo. You get spectacular views of the gorge, with trees clinging tenaciously to the steep limestone rock face, and vivid green ferns and trailing vines, with the river rumbling over the rocks far below. You can walk up to **Devil's Mill**, where the thumping of the water on the boulders sounds like a mill grinding. Downstream from the bridge you get to **Cauldron Linn**, a double waterfall that is impressive after rain.

Castle Campbell

Castle Campbell (open standard Ancient Monument times, except closed on Thursday afternoons and Fridays in winter: adults 50p, children 25p) is three miles (4.8 km) west of Rumbling Bridge, and a mile north of Dollar. You must use your map and look out for the Ancient Monument signs, for the castle is not well advertised. Everyone has a favourite place, to be re-visited and revealed to favourite people: Castle Campbell must be such a place for some. If possible go there on a fine autumn day. If you have time and are reasonably agile, don't drive up the rough track to the car park. Instead, park at the bottom and take the footpath up the burn, through steep, mossy, wooded banks; a secret place overhung with ferns where you must watch where you walk. You will cross narrow foot bridges, getting sudden glimpses of cascading water through rocky ravines. Suddenly, ahead of you, high up and apparently inaccessible, you see the castle and you catch your breath with delight. It soars in lofty isolation on a narrow spur above the rocky, wooded ravines of the Burn of Care and the Burn of Sorrow, backed by a dramatic crescent of bracken-covered hills, copper-coloured in autumn.

Enigmatically, the castle was once called The Gloume (Gloom), yet even with the dismal names of the two burns, it is the least gloomy of any place in the world. Seen in sunlight, with the trees at their fullest autumnal best, it is much more a castle of enchantment.

The present castle dates from the 15th century, built on the site of an earlier fortress and acquired in marriage by the Campbells of Argyll, who changed its forbidding name by Act of Parliament in 1489.

John Knox preached here in 1556, on the grassy slope now called Knox's Pulpit. Montrose's army tried (and failed) to take the castle in 1645. (Some of his troops, of the MacLean clan, having a private feud with the Campbells, wanted an excuse to burn it.) General Monk was also here, nine years later, and his troops made a better job of destruction.

You walk through a vaulted "pend" into the courtyard and there is a substantial amount of the ruin intact. In the tower there is the great hall where you can see the entrance to the pit prison, on the right of the fireplace. You can climb right to the roof for glorious views down across **Dollar Glen** and up into the hills

Dollar

3 miles (4.8 km) west of Rumbling Bridge. The town is famous for its Academy. It has a Gala Day and a spirited Hill Race in June as well as a Flower Show in September.

The Ochils brood over a wide wooded valley running west from Dollar and you can walk for miles, among the ghosts of the Covenanters who took refuge here. **Alva Glen** is five miles (8 km) west of Dollar, beyond the old mill town of **Tillicoultry**, and you reach it through an imposing archway beside the Traquair Knitting Factory in Alva. A zigzag path leads down to the burn and then up the glen into the hills, past **Craighall Waterfall**, a steaming cascade bewitched by "kelpies", those elusive water sprites and river horses

Menstrie Castle

A couple of miles (2.2 km) west of Alva, on the A91, you come to Menstrie Castle (open on Monday, Wednesday and Thursday in the summer, or by appointment: adults 20p, children 10p). This restored 16th-century tower house rises from the middle of a housing development like a toy fort on the nursery floor among a clutter of toys that should have been tidied away. It contains a Nova Scotia exhibition room, run by the National Trust for Scotland in honour of Sir William Alexander, whose birth place is the castle. He was sent off to found a Scots colony in Canada, in 1621, as a reward for his services to the crown. He was an indifferent poet and an unpopular Secretary of State for Scotland, and one thing that is certain is that he would never have permitted the building of a modern housing estate on his doorstep

Blairlogie

Still going west towards Stirling on A91, about one and a half miles (2.4 km) west of

Menstrie, look out for a concealed entrance signed "The Square". This leads to the tiny village of Blairlogie, a delightful huddle of pretty old houses and a white-washed church, built along narrow, winding streets on a ledge below the Ochils among orchards and colourful gardens. Blairlogie is one of the first of the "Hillfoot" communities. It grew up around the castle, a sturdy little fortress on a shelf above the village, not open to the public.

TOURIST INFORMATION
Pine 'n Oak, Kincardine Bridge Road, Airth, near Falkirk, tel 032-483 422. It is open Whitsun to end September, 10 am to 6 pm daily.

WHERE TO STAY
Stakis Park Hotel, Camelon Road, Arnothill, Falkirk, tel 0342-28331. B&B from £34: categories 3,3,5: 55 bedrooms en suite. All the facilities of a very modern, purpose built hotel.

Airth Castle Hotel, Airth, 032483-411. B&B from £23: categories 5,5,5: 22 bedrooms en suite. A real castle, restored from its 14th-century origins, with a good dining room and every comfort.

Rumbling Bridge Hotel, beside the bridge, tel 05774-325. B&B from about £10: 27 bedrooms. Dining room and bar meals. Said to be one of the old drovers' inns, this hotel stands on the edge of the gorge, within sound of the river.

Castle Campbell Hotel, Bridge Street, Dollar, tel 02594-2519. B&B from £10: categories 2,4,4: 7 bedrooms. A small country hotel. Relaxed, friendly atmosphere in lovely scenery, with fishing and golf available.

Gartwhinzean Hotel, Powmill, on A977, tel 05774-595. B&B from £12: 6 bedrooms. A small friendly hotel incorporating an old farm house.

EATING OUT
All the hotels will give you a good meal from about £10. The Airth Castle Hotel makes a special occasion, with its antiquity behind the modern façade.

Carron Valley

Before you head for the proper Highlands, visit the Carron Valley. It is surprisingly rural, even though it lies so close to the industrial belt.

WHAT TO SEE
Five miles (8 km) West of Falkirk, at **Dunipace**, the B818 takes you westwards along the River Carron for six miles (9.6 km) to the reservoir. Just before this, a bridge takes you over to an island picnic spot, surrounded by the white tumult of the river.

Less than a mile (1.6 km) further on beyond the reservoir, just past **Loch Walton**, you should abandon your car and walk across the bracken to the left to the **Loup of Fintry**. Where the **Endrick Water** tumbles in long creaming falls to the valley below, filling the air with its noise and spray.

Campsie Fells

The Campsie Fells to the south west of the Carron Valley give you some satisfying walking territory with plenty of fine views.

WHAT TO SEE

Culcreuch Castle, at Fintry, three miles (4.8 km) west of the falls, was built by the Galbraith clan in 1296. The Galbraiths lived here until their chief, Robert, had to flee to Ireland after a scandal in 1630. The castle has had various owners since then and is now a remarkably well-preserved mansion run as a hotel, with the old keep incorporated. There is lovely parkland, a walled garden and pinetum and loch.

WHERE TO STAY

Culcreuch Castle, Fintry, tel 036086 228—see above. Details on application. B&B from £15. 6 Bedrooms.

Stirling

Stirling will have been beckoning to you from the west as you approached from Dollar, 11 miles (17.6 km) away, and indeed from whichever way you come to it. It rises abruptly from the flat plains: a fortress-crowned rock with a grey town clinging to its steep sides—a colourful but blood-stained history book. Because of its strategic position, Stirling was a fortress town since earliest times; bitterly fought over, bravely defended. Stirling Tartan week is in July, with every sort of Scottish entertainment.

WHAT TO SEE

Stirling Castle

Stirling Castle (open at standard Ancient Monument times: adults £1.20, children 60p) is a must. There is a Landmark Visitors' Centre in the car park where you buy tickets for the castle and you should watch the excellent ten minute film of introduction before starting your tour. Legend credits King Arthur with having taken the castle from the Saxons, adding a touch of romance to a stronghold that seems otherwise too solid for the chivalric wisps of Arthurian tales. What is certain, is that Alexander I died there; Henry II took it as part payment for the release of William the Lion after the Battle of Alnwick; and that same William died there in 1214. In those days it would have been built of timber, superseded by masonry in the 13th century. Continual alteration and restoration have resulted in the castle that you see today, most of it 15th and 16th century with some splendid Renaissance architecture.

Every inch seems drenched in history and interest. Perhaps the most intriguing is the **Douglas Room** where, in 1452, James II summoned the eighth Earl of Douglas, whom he suspected of disloyalty, stabbed him to death and threw his body out of the window at the end of the passage. Tradition held that a skeleton, found in the garden below, in 1797, was that of Douglas. You can't help feeling sorry for the poor, frantic king, trying to heave the gory remains through the window: particularly if you remember that when he was only eight years old, he had been forced to witness the murder of a previous Earl of Douglas, at the notorious Black Dinner in Edinburgh Castle in 1440.

The **Chapel Royal** was the place where the nine month old Mary was crowned Queen of Scots surrounded by scheming nobles and a miasma of conflicting loyalties and ambitions. The chapel was rebuilt by her son, James VI/I, and is now the Memorial Hall for the Argyll and Sutherland Highlanders, whose headquarters and Museum are in the castle.

In the **Lions' Den**, outside the palace, James III and James IV both kept lions. Catching and shipping them must have presented a terrible problem for whoever had the job of supplying them.

You get marvellous views from the castle on a fine day and you should allow several hours if you want to take in all the things there are to see up here. Floodlit at night, it is transformed into a fairytale castle, visible from miles away.

The Old Town

The old part of Stirling town is clustered up the hill to the castle: **Spittal Street** and **Broad Street** contain plenty of interesting old buildings. This includes **Mar's Wark** at the top of Broad Street, which is the remains of a palace that was started in 1570, by the regent, Earl of Mar, but never finished and mostly destroyed during the Jacobite rising in 1746.

The Wallace Monument

A visit to Stirling is not complete without going to see the Wallace Monument (open daily from February to October: adults 80p, children 40p) which is almost as much of a landmark as the castle. It lies one and a half miles (2.4 km) north-east of Stirling and was erected in 1869 on top of Abbey Craig, a Victorian monster of a tower, 220 ft (66 m) high with a mighty statue of Wallace on its wall above the door. Inside you can see the **Hall of Heroes** where you will find yourself the focus of attention from a somewhat mawkish group of marble sons of Scotland (some of whom you could be forgiven for never having heard of). You can also see a two-handed sword, 5 ft 4 ins (1.5 m) long, claimed to be that of Wallace. Don't miss the audio visual history of the Battle of Stirling Bridge. This was fought, and won, by William Wallace in 1297. You can climb 246 steps up to a parapet with dizzying views across the Carse of Forth to the castle on its rocky eminence above Stirling town.

To reach the monument you must climb the final ascent from the car park on foot.

Bannockburn Heritage Centre

From Stirling follow the signs for Bannockburn Heritage Centre (open daily in the summer: adults 60p, children 30p) *not* for Bannockburn. The Battle of Bannockburn actually took place over an area that is now mostly mining country, less than two miles (3.2 km) from Stirling, and dominated by slagheaps and pit head constructions, which are the modern developments of the liberated Scotland that Robert Bruce fought for, and won, in 1314.

The Heritage Centre is on higher ground, to the south-west, at Borestone Brae where Bruce is said to have set up his standard on the evening before the battle. You can see fragments of the "bored-stone" with its socket hole, in the visitor centre where an audio visual theatre gives an excellent history of the battle.

If you walk through the hedge from the car park you come to the imposing **Robert Bruce Memorial Statue**. Bruce was that great general who won his battle mounted on a pony, having instructed his men to dig man traps all over the plain, disguised with branches, and to scatter iron spikes, or calthrops, over the field. You will find that a visit to Bannockburn is more of a historical pilgrimage than a search for scenic beauty!

TOURIST INFORMATION
41 Dumbarton Road, Stirling, tel 0786-75019. It is open all year.

WHERE TO STAY
The choice is very large and you should look at the tourist brochure which gives you full descriptions of what is available, from high class hotels to one-room bed and breakfasts. The following is just a small selection.

Golden Lion Hotel, 8–10 King Street, Stirling, tel 0786–75351. B&B from £15: categories 4,6,5: 78 bedrooms, 37 en suite. This 3-Star AA and RAC hotel is renowned for its Scottish hospitality and good service, as well as its food.

Heritage Hotel, 16 Allan Park, Stirling, tel 0786-73660. B&B from £17: categories 5,5,5: 4 bedrooms en suite. A Georgian town house, elegantly furnished with antiques and original paintings, making a very gracious background to excellent food.

Park Lodge Hotel, 32 Park Terrace, Stirling, tel 0786-74862. B&B from £24: categories 6,6,5: 9 bedrooms en suite. Part Victorian, part Georgian mansion, overlooking the park and the castle, with antique furniture and paintings, a four-poster bed and excellent food.

Cross Keys Inn, Kippen, tel 078687-293. B&B from £11: categories 1,2,4: 3 bedrooms. An 18th-century village inn with a beer garden, and a friendly, relaxed atmosphere. Egon Ronay recommended.

WHERE TO EAT
Good food is available in all the hotels, from between £8 and £15.

Littlejohns Restaurant, 52 Port Street, Stirling, tel 0786-63222. A traditional Scottish atmosphere and Scottish food. Dinner from about £8.

The Settle Inn, 91 St Mary's Wynd, Stirling, tel 0786-75859. Public house built in 1733 with original barrel-vaulted ceiling, full of atmosphere. Dinner from about £7.

The Arches, 35/7 Upper Craigs, Stirling, tel 0786-70972. Family run restaurant with Scottish cooking. Dinner from about £6.50.

Stakis Steakhouse, 52 Upper Craigs, Stirling, tel 0786-75469. Good steaks and special children's menus. Dinner from about £6.

Dunblane

Dunblane is four miles (6.4 km) north of Stirling and by-passed by the A9. It is a small town built around its ancient cathedral in the valley of the **Allen Water**. A narrow main street leads up to the cathedral close, with some fine old buildings around it.

SPECIAL ATTRACTIONS
The Doune and Dunblane Agricultural Show is in July. The Dunblane Highland Games are in September.

WHAT TO SEE

The Cathedral
The Cathedral (open daily, admission free) was founded in 600 by St Blane of Bute, grandson of King Aidan of Dalriada and it still has parts of the old Celtic church in its red sandstone walls. Most of the present building was commissioned by Bishop Clement in the mid-13th century. The roof was stripped after the Reformation but the building was restored in 1892 and is the parish church. This lovely Gothic building has an oval window that you can only see from outside. It is decorated with carved leaves and flowers and is called the **Ruskin Window** because John Ruskin praised it. After a visit to the cathedral, Ruskin said: "... I know not anything so perfect in its simplicity, and so beautiful, as far as it reaches, in all the Gothic with which I am acquainted ...'. You can see his point!

Stand for a moment by the three poignant stone slabs in the cathedral that are in memory of Margaret Drummond and her two sisters, all poisoned in 1502 by scheming nobles. James IV was in love with Margaret. (Some go further and say he was secretly married to her.) Politicians desired a union with England and Margaret Drummond was a threat to this plan. Why her luckless sisters had to be eliminated as well remains a mystery—perhaps they all ate from the same dish. Within a year of this awful crime, James married 14 year old Margaret Tudor and found himself the brother-in-law of bellicose Henry VIII.

The **Cathedral Museum and Library** (open daily in the summer except Sundays, with a donation box) is in the cathedral close. The museum was the Dean's House, built 1624. Here you can discover the local history.

Blair Drummond Safari Park

Blair Drummond Safari Park (open daily in the summer: adults £3, children £2, cars free) is on the River Keith seven miles to the south-west. Here you will see lions, giraffes, tigers, hippopotami, etc. Or take a boat-trip on the lake and see a chimp island. This is definitely a day out for children, with aquatic mammal shows, a pets' corner, adventure playground, a 3D cinema, an "Astraglide", picnic areas, shops, amusement arcades, restaurants and a bar for the exhausted parents. The house, which is a school for handicapped children, is not open to the public.

Doune

Doune, three miles (4.8 km) west of Dunblane, is a small town with wooded hills rising in folds to the north. Stand in the attractive, triangular market square and try to picture the scene when it was a 17th-century sheep and cattle market, to which people flocked from miles away. There would have been ramshackle stalls selling broth and ale; a press of wild-looking men from the hills, herding their beasts; smoke from fires and the smell of animals and unwashed humanity. It was a living, seething scene, full of bawdy jokes and raucous laughter, with an underlying tension and sharp eyes on the watch for trouble between Covenanters and soldiers.

WHAT TO SEE

Doune Castle

Doune Castle (open standard Ancient Monument times: adults £1, children 50p) is one of Scotland's best preserved ruins of a medieval castle. It was built in the 14th century by Robert, Duke of Albany and his son Murdoch, and was annexed by the crown after the wholesale execution of the Albany family by James I. James IV gave it to his queen, Tudor Margaret, who in turn passed it to her second husband, Henry Stuart, Lord Methven. Later it passed to the Earls of Moray who still own it. It is a splendid ruin, easy to restore, in the imagination. The gatehouse is a self-contained complex complete with its own water supply in case of siege. It is built round a large courtyard, protected by two rivers and a deep moat. A long, vaulted passage leads into the court yard with its vaulted chamber on the right where Prince Charlie put the prisoners he took at the Battle of Falkirk.

You can climb up to the **Lords Hall**, on the first floor of the main tower, and picture it when it was filled with smoke from the blazing fire, rushes on the floor, dogs squabbling over bones, a great throng of people jostling for attention from the nobles at the high table. The castle contains a host of domestic details that are fascinating to the modern eye, making it easier to see those distant people living their daily lives, eating and sleeping and loving like anyone today. The gardens were created in the early 19th century by the tenth Earl of Moray. They have a walled garden, a pinetum, lovely shrubs and plants and woodland walks through the attractive glen.

Bridge in Doune

The Bridge in Doune was apparently built by Robert Spittal, in 1535. Spittal was tailor to the wife of James IV. (He also founded Spittal's Hospital in Stirling, so the queen must have paid him well!) Spittal is said to have come to the ferry that preceded the bridge and been refused passage because he had no money on him. He built the bridge to spite the unfortunate ferry man.

Doune Motor Museum

The Doune Motor Museum (open daily in the summer: adults £1.50, children 75p) is in the gardens. It contains Lord Moray's collection of vintage cars and is a must for vintage car enthusiasts. Most of the cars are in working order and the collection includes such makes as Hispano, Suiza, Bentley, Jaguar, Aston Martin, Lagonda, and the second oldest Rolls Royce in the world.

TOURIST INFORMATION

Stirling Road, Dunblane, tel 0786-824428. It is open April to September.

WHERE TO STAY

Cromlix House, Dunblane, tel 0786-822125. B&B from £48.50; categories 5,4,5: 14 bedrooms en suite. This hotel is rated as one of the best in Scotland: a Victorian mansion with warm Scottish hospitality and excellent food. Recommended by Egon Ronay, La Ina Cherry, Andrew Harper Hideaway Report, Wedgwood Plate award.

Pierre's, Doune Road, Dunblane, tel 0786-823141. B&B from £12.50: categories 3,2,4: 4 bedrooms, 2 en suite. A small, comfortable, very friendly hotel with delicious French cooking.

Red Comyn Inn, Perth Road, Dunblane, tel 0786-824343. B&B from £11: categories 3,3,6: 7 bedrooms. A nice old country house in two acres (0.8 ha) of lovely garden, on the A9, in the middle of the town. You can sit in the sun and share your real ale with the squirrels in the beer garden.

Stakis Dunblane Hydro Hotel, Dunblane, tel 0786-822551. B&B from £26: categories 3,3,5: 188 bedrooms en suite. Large, modern, comfortable and convenient.

Stirling Arms Hotel, Stirling Road, Dunblane, tel 0786-822551. B&B from £10: categories 4,3,4: 10 bedrooms, 3 en suite. An old coaching inn on the banks of Allan Water in the middle of the town. Scottish home cooking.

EATING OUT

All the hotels above will do you well, with dinner from about £10; except for the Cromlix, where you will get food you will remember for a long time, and where you should forget the bill and be prepared to spend upwards of £15. Every penny will be worth it.

The Trossachs

Once you get north-west of Doune on the A84 you begin to feel the lure of the Highlands. There is no one particular thing to see in the Trossachs and the surrounding country; it is more an area of unfolding beauty and delight, best explored outside the tourist season and made a thousand times more memorable if explored on foot. You will find that, even in the high season, most sightseers tend to stay within sight of their cars, and you have only to take off away from the roads to shake off the feeling of claustrophobia that can attack when there are too many people around. Autumn and early spring are truly glorious in this land of forested ravines and gullies, spectacular views and stirring legends.

Although people tend to refer to the whole of the area between Callander and Lochearnhead, on the east, and Loch Lomond on the west, as the Trossachs, (meaning "bristly country") in fact the Trossachs proper is only the gorge that runs from Loch Achray to Loch Katrine, a rugged pass barely a mile long (1.6 km). It is thickly wooded and carpeted with bracken and foxgloves, bog myrtle and heather and is scented with wild thyme and honeysuckle. This is a magic place, overlaid by light mists, haunted by birdsong; a fairytale place in which you half expect to break through a tangle of thorns and discover a sleeping beauty—provided you have managed to get off the beaten track.

WHAT TO SEE

Callander

Callander, eight miles from Doune (12.8 km), is a good holiday centre for this area. It is a friendly little town to the east of the popular Trossachs and from here you are within easy reach of lots of invigorating walks up through dense woods into the moors, with streams and rivers rushing down to fill Loch Lubnaig and the River Teith.

Loch Katrine

Loch Katrine, nine miles (14.4 km) west of Callander, is the setting for Walter Scott's *Lady of the lake*. Ellen's Isle is named after the heroine of the poem. In the summer you can take a trip in the Victorian steamer, and cruise along the nine mile (14.4 km) length of the loch, and picture fair Ellen being wooed by the mysterious James Fitz-James, who bore a remarkable resemblance to King James V, that monarch who enjoyed roaming the countryside disguised as the Goodman of Ballengiech.

Balquhidder

Another popular literary association in this area is at Balquhidder, on **Loch Voil**, north of the Trossachs, ten miles (16 km) north of Callander, and just west of the A84. This is where Rob Roy lived, died and is buried. This colourful character, much romanticised by Scott, lived between 1671 and 1734, son of Macgregor of Glengyle. Rob Roy (Gaelic for Red Robert) started life peacefully enough as a herdsman. But the Macgregors had been outlawed for their bloodthirsty habits and life was hard. He took to cattle rustling and smuggling, robbing the rich to pay the poor in Robin Hood style and legends of his daring escapades and narrow escapes around Loch Katrine make good reading, even if, in reality, he was no doubt a rogue and a menace to his neighbours. He died, uncharacteristically, in his bed and you can pay homage to him in Balquhidder churchyard.

Queen Elizabeth Forest Park

If you are feeling energetic, you can walk right through the Queen Elizabeth Forest Park, three miles or so (5 km) south and west of the Trossachs. The park is on the eastern side of **Loch Lomond**. If your energy still holds, climb **Ben Lomond**, 3,192 ft (958 m), for a glorious, bird's-eye view.

Inchmahome Priory

Before you go on north from Callander, take the A81 six miles (9.6 km) south-west to **Lake of Menteith** and catch the ferry to Inchmahome Priory, a beautiful ruin on the largest island of three on the lake. (The weather dictates the running of the ferry: adults £1, children 50p, and the priory is open standard Ancient Monument times, tel Stirling 62421: admission free.)

Founded for Augustinians in 1238, the priory was a refuge for Mary, Queen of Scots for a short while before she was sent off to France to grow up out of range of Henry VIII's "Rough Wooing." It is nice to think of the little girl, in the garden now called **Queen Mary's Bower**, happily playing hide-and-seek, perhaps with the indulgent monks.

Lochearnhead and the north-west corner

Fourteen miles (22.5 km) north of Callander on the A84, you come to Lochearnhead, an attractive little village on the western corner of **Loch Earn**. It has several good hotels and a boating and water skiing centre. The loch runs seven miles (11 km) east to **St Fillans** (see Tayside) a beautiful ribbon of water sheltered by hills and an ideal place for a holiday.

Killin

Killin is five miles (8 km) north of Lochearnhead, on the A85. It sits on the western tip of **Loch Tay**, that long, deep serpent of water that broods mysteriously below two mountain ranges (see Tayside). From Killin, the **Falls of Dochart** carry the **Dochart River** in a magnificent cascade of falls and rapids, swirling and tumbling down to the loch.

WHAT TO SEE
On the lower of two islets below the old bridge in Killin you can see the burial ground of the clan MacNab, the most powerful clan in the district until they emigrated to Canada in the 19th century, an aggressive clan, forever at loggerheads with the neighbouring clans of Neish and Gregor, who were never backward in aggression themselves.

Finlarig Castle

Finlarig Castle (open at all times: admission free) lies half a mile north (0.8 km) of Killin. It was the seat of the sinister sounding Black Duncan of the Cowl, a fierce Campbell chief. The castle is hidden among trees on a mound and you can get to it across an iron bridge opposite the Queen's Court Hotel. Near it you can still make out the gruesome "beheading-pit" It is said that it was the privilege of the gentry to be beheaded, while the common people were hanged from a tree!

This northern corner of the Central region is made up of wild, lonely moorland, densely wooded in places, with sudden glimpses of enchanted river valleys.

Crianlarich

From Killin the A85 takes you 10 miles (16 km) west to Crianlarich, a tiny, isolated village, tucked in among the moors, with the somewhat incongruously energetic-sounding title of "railway-junction". This is where the railway lines from Oban and Fort William join up on their progress south. If you wish to be spared changing trains and stations in Glasgow at crack of dawn, and are in no hurry to catch your steamer from Oban to the Outer Isles, you can get out of the night train from the south, on to the tiny platform at

Crianlarich, and while away two delightful hours before your connection comes along. Eating hot bacon baps (rolls) in the early morning in the station buffet, after a night sitting up in the train, is an experience you don't forget, especially if the weather is kind and you wander off into the hills, leaving your luggage perfectly safely on the platform, and keeping an ear for the approach of your train.

The roads also meet in Crianlarich. You can go back south to west Loch Lomond, or proceed northwards.

Tyndrum

Five miles (8 km) north, on the A82, brings you to Tyndrum, gateway from the Central, into the Highland and the Tayside regions. Here, again, you must choose beneath north and west. Tyndrum has several hotels and gives the feeling of being a holiday stepping-off place, where you are well placed for marvellous walks in all directions, with several hills rising to heights above 3,000 ft (900 m).

TOURIST INFORMATION

Leny Road, Callander, tel 0877-30342. It is open April to September.

Main Street, Killin, tel 05672 254. It is open April to September.

Car Park, Tyndrum, tel 08384 246. It is open April to September.

WHERE TO SAY

Bridgend House Hotel, Bridge Street, Callander, tel 0877–30130. B&B from £20: categories 5,4,5: 7 bedrooms, 5 en suite. An old world atmosphere. Four-poster beds. Scottish food and lovely views.

Gart House, Callander, tel 0877-31055. B&B from £7.50: categories 3,4,1: 6 bedrooms. A secluded 19th century mansion in 12½ acres by the River Teith.

Hotel Marie Stuart, Lochearnhead, tel 05673-273. B&B from £12: categories 3,3,4: 27 bedrooms. The hotel is on the shores of the loch, with a friendly atmosphere, open log fires and good food. Live entertainment at least three times a week.

Lochearnhead Hotel, Lochearnhead, tel 05673-299. B&B from £13.15; categories 4,4,5: 14 bedrooms, 4 en suite. Also on the shores of the loch, a comfortable family-run hotel with a chalet complex, nice food, and friendly service. Moorings and watersports are available.

Ardeonaig Hotel, Ardeonaig, Killin, tel 05672-400. B&B from £18: categories 3,3,3: 14 bedrooms en suite. An old drover's inn, dating from 1680, on the south side of Loch Tay.

Bridge of Lochay Hotel, Killin, tel 05672-272. B&B from £12.25: categories 3,3,5: 17 bedrooms, 7 en suite. The hotel is on the banks of the River Lochay, opposite the golf course, with salmon and trout fishing available.

Alt-Chaorain House Hotel, Crianlarich, tel 08383-283. B&B from £11: categories 4,4,3: 9 bedrooms, 3 en suite. A family house atmosphere, with log fires and friendly service, in a beautiful setting.

Invervey Hotel, Tyndrum, tel 08384-219. B&B from £10: categories 3,3,4: 17 bedrooms. A friendly, family-run hotel near the junction of the A82 and A85, in lovely Highland scenery.

Royal Hotel, Tyndrum, tel 08384-272. B&B from £10: categories 3,3,2: 84 bedrooms, 20 en suite. A large, country hotel, with friendly, relaxed atmosphere.

EATING OUT

Dalgair House Hotel, Callander, tel 0877-30283. Good home cooking with local ingredients in season. Dinner from £6.

Highland House Hotel, Callander, tel 0877-30269. All dishes prepared by the proprietor, with fresh local ingredients. Dinner from £7.

Ledcreich Hotel, Balquhidder, tel 08774-230. Good Scottish cooking. Dinner from £15.

Dall Lodge Hotel, Killin, tel 05672-217. Good Scottish food—try the "cloutie dumplings". Dinner from £7.50.

Alt-Chaorain House Hotel, see above. Tay trout, game pie. Fresh local ingredients. Dinner from £5.

CRAFT CENTRES IN THE CENTRAL REGION

The workshops and studios listed below welcome visitors. Where there is a telephone number given you should telephone first to check times.

Ceramics

Barbara Davidson Pottery, Muirhall Farm, Larbert, tel 03245-554430. Hand thrown pottery.

Glass Making

MacIntosh Glass, Unit 4, Dalderse Avenue, Falkirk, tel 0324-37986. All aspects of glass making.

Village Glasshouse, Queen's Lane (off Henderson Street), Bridge of Allan, tel 0786-832137. All aspects of glassmaking.

Jewellery and Silversmithing

Cornerstone, Cathedral Square, Dunblane, tel 0786-823 696. Gold and silver jewellery making and silversmithing.

Graham Stewart, 91–5 High Street, Dunblane, tel 0786-823696. Jewellery in 18 ct gold and precious stones. Silver spoons and containers.

Part X

FIFE

The Study, Culross

When the new regional divisions were planned in 1975, the tiny kingdom of Fife was to be split horizontally, one half to become part of Tayside and the other, part of Lothian. But the planners reckoned without the people of Fife, who had no intention of being annihilated and who protested so violently that Fife was allowed to remain intact.

The peninsula is bordered on three sides by water and on the west by the Ochil Hills. It used to be a place people went *to*, but not *through*, until the Tay Road Bridge was opened in 1966. Now, a tour of the attractive Fife fishing villages and visit to St Andrews can be included in a journey to the north-east.

A surprising amount of history has soaked into this tiny corner of Scotland with its long coast line, gently rolling low hills, ancient towns and medieval remains. Abernethy, just over the border, in Tayside, was once a Pictish capital, whose overspill left many pre-historic sites to be excavated in the whole area.

Filmgoers may recognise the miles of golden beaches around St Andrews as those used for the running scenes in *Chariots of Fire*.

The Fifer is a stoic: he has had to fight for his independence since time began, as well as to till the fertile soil, fish the abundant sea, and create industry to bring him wealth. He never had much time left over for fancy frills or affectation. You will find him straightforward and down-to-earth: he will look you in the eye when you shake his hand and kick hard if you threaten his independence.

Apart from sightseeing, of which there is more than enough to occupy you in Fife, golf is one of the region's greatest attractions. St Andrews is universally known, and there is a large number of other excellent courses, including those along the coast around Carnoustie. With so much coastline, there are all the water sports, and marvellous stretches of golden sands for family seaside holidays. For the archaeologist, there are a wealth of prehistoric sites to explore and plenty of historic castles and houses for the historian.

SPECIAL ATTRACTIONS

Among the many local events that take place in Fife throughout the year, there is the St Andrews Festival, in February, the St Andrews Festival of Food and Wine, in March, and the Kate Kennedy Procession in St Andrews in April. This is a great occasion for the students of the university. There is a Country Fair at Craigtoun near St Andrews in May, and a half marathon at Glenrothes the same month.

In June you can go to the Strathmiglo Games, the Ceres Highland Games, the Cupar Gala Week, and the East Neuk Seafood Festival. Both Cupar and St Andrews have Highland Games in July, and during this month there is also the Elie Fair, Crail Festival Week, Anstruther Holiday Fair Week, and in 1987, Mary, Queen of Scots' celebrations at both Falkland Palace and St Andrews. Falkland continues to honour Mary, in August, when there is also the Crail Fair, the St Andrews Lammas Fair, the Pittenweem Arts Festival and Aberdour Festival. In September, RAF Leuchars have an open day and in November St Andrews have great celebrations on St Andrews Day (30 November).

TOURIST INFORMATION

Where the local tourist information offices are closed in the winter, you can always get advice, information and accommodation brochures from 78 South Street, St Andrews, tel 0334-72021. It is open all year.

From south-west to north-east

Culross

If you explore Fife from the west, your first stop should be at Culross (pronounced Cure-oss). This miniature town on the shore of the Firth of Forth has been restored by the National Trust for Scotland over the past 50 years. A "showpiece" burgh of the 16th and 17th centuries, it looks almost exactly as it must have done in those days though, like most museums, it can never restore the smell and teeming, boisterous splurge of real life as it was. But, like museums, it gives your imagination an accurate framework on which to build.

Culross was once one of the largest ports in Scotland, comparable in importance to Liverpool. It traded in coal, iron, fish, hand-loom weaving, and salt, extracted from the sea water in salt pans heated by local coal. The combination of the Industrial Revolution and a bad storm that silted up the port, severely damaged the economy and the little town became a backwater until the National Trust moved in, in 1932.

Historically, Culross was the site of a 5th- or 6th-century religious foundation pre-

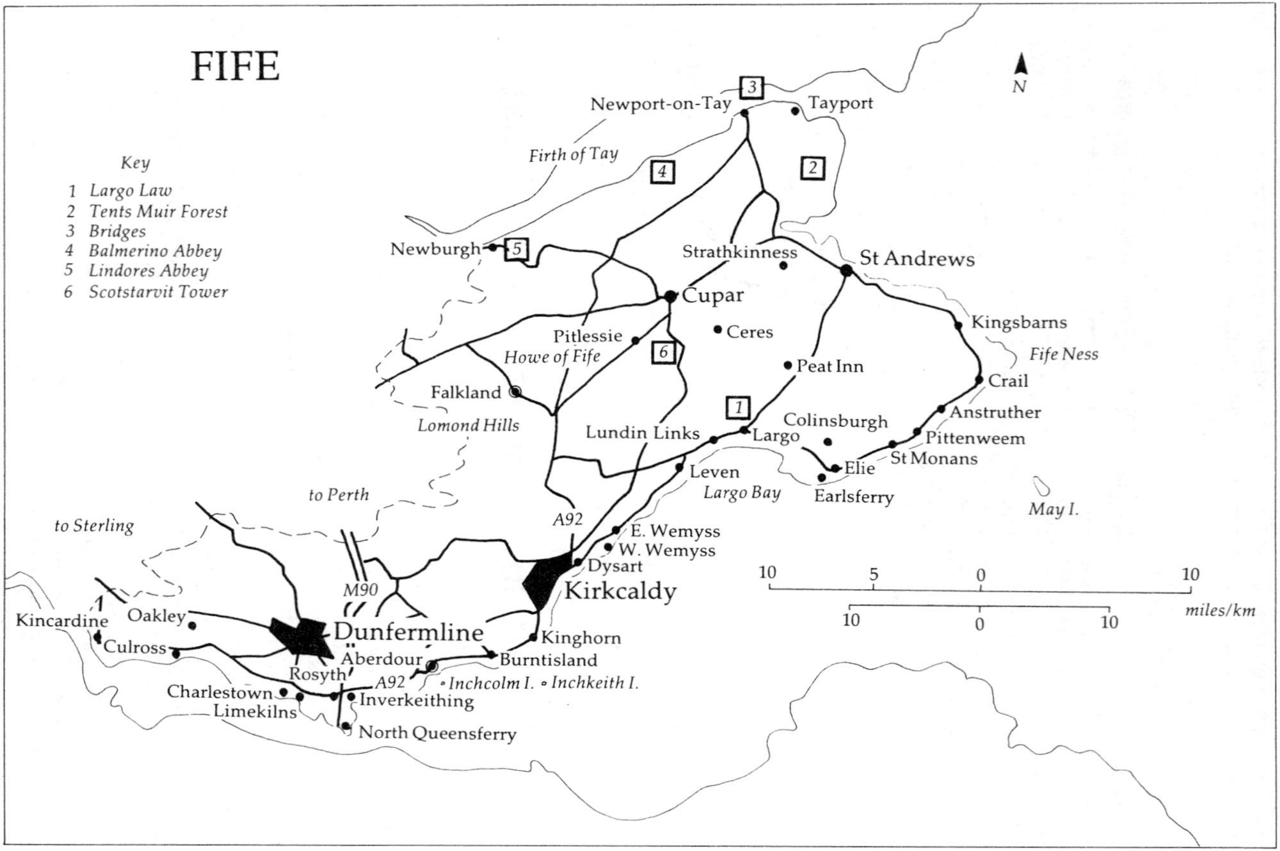
FIFE
Key
1 Largo Law
2 Tents Muir Forest
3 Bridges
4 Balmerino Abbey
5 Lindores Abbey
6 Scotstarvit Tower
N
Newport-on-Tay
Tayport
Firth of Tay
Newburgh
Strathkinness
St Andrews
Cupar
Ceres
Kingsbarns
Fife Ness
Pitlessie
Howe of Fife
Peat Inn
Crail
Falkland
Lomond Hills
Colinsburgh
Anstruther
Lundin Links
Largo
Pittenweem
St Monans
Elie
Leven
Largo Bay
Earlsferry
May I.
to Perth
to Sterling
A92
E. Wemyss
W. Wemyss
Dysart
Kirkcaldy
M90
Kincardine
Oakley
Dunfermline
Culross
Aberdour
Burntisland
Kinghorn
Rosyth
A92
Inchcolm I.
Inchkeith I.
Charlestown
Limekilns
Inverkeithing
North Queensferry
10 5 0 10
10 0 10
miles/km

sided over by St Serf (or Servanus) and St Kentigern was born here (see Glasgow). Leave your car on the outskirts of the old part and explore the steep, narrow, cobbled streets on foot.

WHAT TO SEE

The Palace (open at standard Ancient Monument times: adults £1, children 50p) was built in 1597 by a prosperous merchant, Sir George Bruce, overlooking the river which in those days came much closer to the town. Bruce, trading local salt for valuable glass, cheated James VI of window tax by incorporating half shutters of wood into the windows! You won't find a better example of a Scottish laird's house anywhere else, with Bruce's private counting house, through an iron door. It is stone-vaulted, fireproof and has safes sunk into the walls. The painted ceiling, with allegorical figures, Latin texts and "improving" admonishments is on the second floor and is one of the best in Scotland. The curator has a fund of fascinating stories and manages to bring the place to life for you by pointing out a mass of small domestic details that you might easily miss.

The Palace stands within a walled court, with crowstepped gables, decorated dormer windows, and pantiled roofs. The walled garden rises steeply behind with terraced walks, the whole complex being most attractive.

The Town House, or **Tolbooth** (open daily in the summer, or by arrangement, tel Newmills 880359: adults 40p, children 20p) built in 1626, is on the right of the palace. It has a double outside stair and was restored, with the tower being added in 1783. The National Trust for Scotland have their headquarters here and you can see an excellent audio visual show in the visitor centre, telling you the history of the town and showing how it was rescued from decay. You can see the iron house, or prison, on the ground floor, the council room with a painted ceiling and the debtors' room. The "high tolbooth" or turret, was apparently used for witch-spotting! The tron, or public weighing scales, stood outside the tolbooth, where traders' measures could be checked against the standard weights in case of cheating.

The Study (open all year by arrangement and weekends in April and October, tel Newmills 880359:) is an L-plan, late 16th-century house with a turnpike stair and a small room at the top of its tower, which gave it its name. It is reached by climbing steep, narrow streets, cobbled and paved, behind the Town House until you get to a tiny asymmetrical market place with a reconstructed mercat cross. Inside the house is a small museum with furniture, pottery, pewter of the period and maps illustrating the early town.

The Little Houses of Culross which are privately occupied, can all be enjoyed from the outside. They represent wonderful examples of the domestic architecture of the houses built by the relatively humble working class people of those days, in apparently random positions against each other, straggling up the narrow streets.

Culross Abbey (open daily: admission free) was founded in 1215 for Cistercian monks on the site of St Serf's church. The present parish church, dating from 1300, was rebuilt in 1633 from the original choir and central tower. If you go in you will see a spectacular alabaster monument in memory of Sir George Bruce who built the Palace.

St Mungo's Chapel

Going east from Culross just along the shore you will find the ruin of St Mungo's

Chapel (always accessible, free). Built in 1513, it commemorated the spot where a Pictish princess, after escaping the wrath of her family, landed and gave birth to St Kentigern, affectionately known as Mungo (see Glasgow). You get lovely views across the Forth from here. The flaming stacks of the Grangemouth Refinery on the far shore are eerie and strangely beautiful when seen through the haze they create, or in the half-light, against a darkening sky, reflected in the water.

Charleston

Inland you will find undulating farmland with narrow lanes and sudden splendid views. Along the shore you pass through picturesque little harbours and villages such as Charleston, six miles (9.6 km) east of Culross. This 18th-century village is set round a green on a wooded plateau above the Forth. Charleston harbour, now a tiny haven that dries out at low tide, was built by the 18th-century laird the fifth Earl of Elgin, for sailing ships bringing iron ore and carrying away locally quarried lime. This is Bruce country, for the earls of Elgin trace their descent from King Robert. It was the seventh earl who "acquired" the ancient Greek marble sculptures, mostly a frieze from the Parthenon (now called the Elgin marbles) and sold them to the British Museum for £35,000 (The Parthenon was being used by the Turks, who were then occupying Athens, for target practice!).

Limekilns

Limekilns, a mile (1.6 km) east of Charleston, is an old world village whose pretty cottages were lived in by the seamen whose ships plied from Charleston.

Oakley

Oakley, four miles (6.4 km) inland, north-west of Limekilns, is a mining village built to house miners in the Comrie colliery. Many of the miners came from declining areas in the west, thus creating a strongly Catholic community. The church, endowed by the Catholic laird, Captain Smith-Sligo, in 1958 has some beautiful "vitraille" stained glass and woodwork carved by a local craftsman.

Dunfermline

Dunfermline is two miles (3.2 km) inland, and about seven miles (13 km) east of Culross and was once the capital of Scotland. It is the hub of the south-west corner of Fife, dominated by its abbey and palace that stand above the town like sentinels. The town falls away from this crowning glory, an endearing mixture of Scottish Baronial, modern industrial and ancient ruins. Dunfermline means "fort-by-the-crooked-pool" after a fort that stood in what is now Pittencrief Park, sloping down from the abbey to the south-west.

King Malcolm Canmore lived in Dunfermline in the middle of the 11th century. He was an unremarkable, blood-thirsty, perhaps rather boorish man, until along came saintly Margaret, an English princess, fleeing with her brother from the Norman Conquest. She married Malcolm in 1067 and set about Normanising Scotland, both culturally and ecclesiastically. Edward I held court here during his campaigns against the Scots; Charles II agreed to accept the Covenant while staying in Dunfermline in 1651. The town is probably best known today as the birth place of Andrew Carnegie, 1835–1919, the son of a humble linen weaver, who went to America and made a fortune in steel. One of the best known philanthropists of the modern world, he used his millions for the benefit of mankind in numerous ways, including giving his home town Pittencrief Park, public baths, a library and an annual Festival of Music and Art. Dunfermline has a Civic Week in June, an excuse for all sorts of festivities, parades and entertainment.

Dunfermline must be firmly lodged in many minds as the subject for the ballad about Sir Patrick Spens. Sir Patrick was dispatched on a mission by his king who "...sat in Dumfermling toune, drinking the blude-reid wine...". Poor Sir Patrick put out in a storm, against his better judgement, and perished! "...have owre, have owre to Aberdour ... wi' the Scots lords at his feit...". According to Sir Walter Scott, Spens' voyage was to collect the Maid of Norway in 1290 (see History). But that cannot have been so because there was no king in "Dunfermling toune" at that time which was why they were so anxious to get hold of the Maid.

WHAT TO SEE

The Abbey (open daily: admission free) is reached by steps from a terraced car park. The abbey church, much restored, stands adjacent to the ruined monastery buildings and palace, which are linked to each other by a pend. There was a Culdee chapel on the site where Malcolm Canmore, a widower, married Margaret. Two years later, the queen, horrified by the lax ways of the Celtic church, began to build a new church to be administered in the Norman manner, to which she was accustomed.

The present church stands on the foundations of Margaret's church, some of which you can see through iron grilles in the floor. Frequently sacked and burned over the centuries, today's building is a jigsaw of different tastes and styles, the nave dating from 1128 and the massive buttresses from the 16th century.

In 1818, workmen unearthed a vault with a stone coffin in it, containing a skeleton wrapped in thin sheets of lead. Shreds of cloth of gold clung to the bones and the breast bone had been sawn through, almost conclusively proving that this was the coffin of King Robert Bruce. Bruce died of leprosy in 1329 having begged Sir James Douglas to carry his heart to Palestine and bury it in Jerusalem. (He had always intended to make a pilgrimage to the Holy Land in atonement for murdering his rival for the throne, Red Comyn.) Douglas set off with the heart but was killed in Spain in battle with the Moors. The heart was retrieved from the battle-field, returned to Scotland and buried in Melrose Abbey where it is today.

Bruce's remains were re-interred and you will see a brass plate, set in Italian porphyry, below the pulpit, marking the spot. To celebrate this historic find, an over-enthusiastic architect designed the vast inscription that you cannot fail to notice, written in stone-fretwork round the top of the square tower: "King Robert the Bruce".

Malcolm Canmore and Queen Margaret died within a few days of each other in 1093 and you will see their shrine against the outside wall of the present abbey, where the Lady Chapel once stood. The abbey succeeded Iona as the burial place for Scottish kings.

The Palace (open daily: admission free) is now a ruin. Magnificent against an evening sky, it was built when Margaret and Malcolm got married. You can imagine the queen, walking up each day from Malcolm's Tower, the ruin which you can still see below, in Pittencrief Park, to inspect the progress of her new home. Although she would have chosen to have been a nun rather than a queen, Margaret loved fine clothes, and exotic furnishings and no doubt her palace was very splendid. It provided an admirable setting for her task of 'refining' the rough, Celtic ways of her husband's court.

When Margaret endowed the Benedictine priory, she set up a shrine, with a relic of the True Cross, and encouraged pilgrims to come from miles away to venerate it.

It is hard to believe, when you look at the ruin of the palace and monastery buildings that in the 13th century they were said to be "...big enough to hold two sovereigns with their retinues, at the same time, without inconvenience to one another...'.

Pittencrieff Glen is reached by a gate which is opposite the west door of the abbey. When Andrew Carnegie was a boy, before he emigrated to Pennsylvania to make his fortune, he was forbidden entrance to the privately-owned park. He never forgot this and when he returned with his millions, he bought it and gave it to the people of Dunfermline so that "...no wee child should ever feel locked oot of it, as I was...". So now you can roam at will among lovely shrubs and flowers and trees, along the steep-sided, wooded glen, where birds sing and a burn tumbles down over its rocky bed and no child is ever "locked oot". It is a beautiful place and Queen Margaret, known for her generosity to the poor, would have heartily approved.

Pittencrieff House (open in the summer, daily except Tuesdays: admission free) was built in 1610. It, too, was bought by Carnegie and makes a good focal point in the park. Inside you will see displays of local history, costumes and an art gallery.

The Carnegie Museum (open daily: admission free) is in Moodie Street. Carnegie was born in this small cottage which is now a museum. The rooms are furnished as they were in his life time and the millionaire himself, remarkably life-like in waxen effigy, sits at his desk in his study, looking rather stern, perhaps planning where to bestow his next gift.

Dunfermline Museum (open daily except Sundays: admission free) is at Viewfield. This Victorian villa has displays concentrating on the local history. There is plenty which deals with weaving and the linen industry, both of which enriched the town in the past.

TOURIST INFORMATION

Dunfermline, tel 0383-720999. It is open Whitsun to end of September.

WHERE TO STAY

Red Lion Inn, Lower Causeway, Culross, tel 0383-880225. B&B from £10: categories 3,3,4: 6 bedrooms. A delightful, picturesque inn. A cosy, friendly atmosphere.

The City Hotel, 18 Bridge Street, Dunfermline, tel 0383-722538. B&B from £14: categories 4,5,4: 17 bedrooms. A attractive old building in the middle of the town. Friendly service.

King Malcolm Thistle Hotel, Wester Pitcorthie, Dunfermline, tel 0383-722611. B&B from £26: categories 6,5,5: 48 bedrooms en suite. A modern, purpose-built hotel with good service.

The Auld Toll Tavern, St Leonards Street, Dunfermline, tel 0383-721489. B&B from £10: categories 5,6,4: 4 bedrooms. A cheerful little hotel with a relaxed atmosphere.

Keavil House Hotel, Crossford, tel 0383-736258. B&B from £16: categories 5,5,5: 32 bedrooms. A comfortable hotel with friendly staff.

EATING OUT

The hotels above all serve reasonable food. Dinner from about £7.

Keavil House Hotel, see above, belongs to the Taste of Scotland, and specialises in Scottish dishes such as venison, game, salmon, lamb and beef. It uses fresh local produce. Good dinner from £10.

Rosyth

Rosyth is three miles (4.8 km) south of Dunfermline, on the shore of the Forth. Its dockyard, now in the process of being privatised, has played an important part in British naval history over the years. At one time it was the only naval dockyard where the entire fleet could anchor at any state of the tide. More recently, it was the only place that specialised in the refitting of nuclear and polaris submarines.

St Margaret's Hope is east of the dockyard, near the foot of the Forth Road Bridge. Tradition has it that it was at this rocky promontory that Queen Margaret landed for the first time in Scotland. Perched on a terrace on the point is the house of the admiral who is in command of the navy in Scotland. In the recent past, another admiral, of lesser rank, lived on Castland Hill, across the marsh opposite and these two old salts communicated by hoisting witty signal flags on their respective flagpoles—an essential part of any naval establishment!

North Queensferry

North Queensferry, a mile south-east of Rosyth, was originally the northern terminal of the ferry established by Queen Margaret to carry pilgrims to Dunfermline. (See South Queensferry, Lothian.) It remained a ferry terminal until the road bridge was opened in 1964.

Inverkeithing

It is worth stopping off in Inverkeithing, a stone's throw north of Queensferry. It is an older place than you might think at first glance, for it was granted a royal charter in 1165.

Behind the busy central square in the High Street you will find the 14th-century **Greyfriars Hospice**, restored as a community centre with a small **Museum** (open all the year round from Wednesday to Sunday: admission free). Not only is the museum crammed with items of local interest—religious, military, industrial and domestic history—but it is presided over by a curator who will tell you everything you want to know about the area.

Dalgety Bay

Keeping to the shore road, a couple of miles (3.2 km) east of Inverkeithing, you come to Dalgety Bay, now fringed by a sprawling residential development, but haunted by ghosts.

Donibristle House, stands on the site of the house where, in 1592, "the bonny Earl of Moray" was murdered by an avenging Huntly on the order of the king. There are many versions of the murder story, one being that there was a tunnel from the house down which the unfortunate earl tried to flee, but because his hair had been set alight by his enemies he acted as a living torch for his pursuers. Whatever the story, it is a gloomy enough place now, its once lovely terraces overgrown with weeds.

St Bridget's Church is further along the shore of Dalgety Bay. This charming ruin is an unexpected little place right beside the water. It was dedicated in 1244. The eastern part of the church is the oldest. It was a two storey kirk with a burial vault and laird's loft.

Aberdour

Aberdour, only five miles (8 km) east of the Forth Road Bridge, is a popular holiday resort, known for its silver sands. There is plenty here for a family holiday: golf, water sports, a sailing centre and a little harbour. This picturesque town has a delightful cluster of medieval buildings above it, overlooking the sea. These include St Fillan's Church, the castle and dovecote.

St Fillan's Church is part Norman, like a tiny cathedral, with a leper-squint in the west wall, and an atmosphere of peace and timelessness.

The Castle (open daily except Thursday mornings and Fridays: adults 50p, children 25p) close by, stands on 14th-century foundations with the original tower, added to in succeeding centuries.

The Dovecote, circular in shape, is part of the castle.

Inchcolm

You can get a boat from **Hawkcraig Point**, in Aberdour, tel 0383-860335, to the tiny island of Inchcolm, across Mortimers Deep, the watery grave of poor Sir Patrick Spens (see Dunfermline). Inchcolm is a perfect place to visit on a fine day, the boat trip making it more special. There are usually a few private boats at anchor in the tiny harbour, with much good-natured 'giving-way' to the official cruise boats. On calm days the water is often ruffled by the wakes of powerboats and waterskiers.

The Abbey of St Columba (open, weather permitting, standard Ancient Monument times, except Wednesday afternoons and Thursdays: adults £1, children 50p) is just next door to the landing jetty, overlooking a small rocky bay. It was founded in 1123 for Augustinian monks by Alexander I. A Columban monk hermit, who lived on the island, saved the king when his boat foundered on the rocky shore and building the abbey was the king's act of gratitude. There is a very rough cell at the north-west corner which could have been the hermit's. Although it was often sacked by the English and desecrated during the Reformation, the abbey has been well restored and the monastic buildings are the best you will find in Scotland. You can see the 13th-century octagonal chapter house with stone roof, and a 14th-century cloister with chambers above.

Burntisland

Burntisland, is three miles (4.8 km) along the coast, east of Aberdour. A sturdy town, once famous for its shipbuilding, is now more popular as a holiday resort. Its boatyards have closed down. The town climbs up from the water and on a fine day in the summer you could lie on the beach and think yourself anywhere in the Mediterranean.

WHAT TO SEE

The Church of St Columba, an octagonal building, was the first to be built in Scotland after the Reformation. It was copied from a church in Amsterdam and has a central pulpit and galleries reached by outside stairs. The tower, added in 1749, is joined to the corners of the church by great flying arches. The General Assembly of the Kirk of Scotland was held here in 1601, when, in the presence of James VI, it was proposed that there should be a new translation of the bible, the Authorised Version, published in 1611.

Agricola is said to have used the natural harbour for his fleet in about AD 83, and it is strange to think of those Roman galleys at anchor where pleasure boats are now moored.

Rossend Castle is a splendid 15th-century tower house that was saved from demolition and recently restored. Now it is one of Burntisland's treasures. It is used as offices but you can see it from the outside. It was here that an ardent French poet, Chastelard, hid himself in Mary, Queen of Scots' bedroom in 1563, a crazy escapade that cost him his life. He was executed in St Andrews and died reciting poetry and crying "... adieu, thou most beautiful and most cruel Princess in the world ...". It is tempting to speculate whether the lively, 21 year old widow had led him on, lonely for the French manners she had grown up with.

Kinghorn

Kinghorn is a couple of miles (3.2 km) further along the coast. There you will see a Victorian monument beside the road in the shape of a Celtic cross. This is where Alexander III was thrown from his horse and killed, an event which completely altered the course of Scottish history. The king had been sitting in council with his lords in Edinburgh. They had eaten well and washed down their meal with plenty of wine. He set off to return to his new wife, Jolande, married only six months earlier, in a desperate attempt to get himself an heir (see Jedburgh Castle, Borders). There was a violent storm but he insisted on being taken across the Forth, at Queensferry. On the far side, he refused to shelter till daybreak but set off, galloping eastwards towards Pettycur where his still barren queen awaited him. His horse stumbled on the edge of the cliff at Kinghorn, plunging the country into many years of bitter conflict and power struggles. Kinghorn is now a thriving holiday resort, with a sandy beach, good hotels, a golf course and campsites.

Inchkeith

You need to hire a boat if you want to go out to the island of Inchkeith, south-east of Burntisland. Its strategic position in the Firth of Forth has made it an important defensive stronghold over many centuries, ever since Mary of Lorraine (Queen Regent for the infant Mary, Queen of Scots in the 16th century) invited her French compatriots to fortify and occupy the island to defend Scotland's shores from English invasion. The island was used in the last two world wars, to defend the dockyard at Rosyth and the rail bridge. It is now occupied only by the lighthouse keepers and by thousands of seagulls whose colony has been infected by virulent botualism from one of their scavenging grounds.

The story is told of an experiment that was tried by James IV. He wanted to see what language a child would speak if it had no example to follow. He sent two infants to the island with a totally dumb woman as a nurse. Some say that the children grew up speaking excellent Hebrew, others, that they emerged from the experiment speaking fluent Gaelic!

Kirkcaldy

Once known as "the Lang Toun" Kirkcaldy (pronounced Kirkoddy) stretches along the coast 3 miles (4.8 km) north of Kinghorn. It is a busy seaport, thriving industrial centre, holiday resort, and Fife's main shopping town, with four miles (6.4 km) of seafront and an Esplanade that was built in the early 1920s in an effort to relieve unemployment.

Linen, weaving and textiles were the town's first occupations, until a weaver of sail cloth, Michael Nairn, turned his talents to the invention of linoleum, which quickly erupted into a major industry. It is said that, at the height of the linoleum boom, you could smell Kirkcaldy from many miles away. With the development of man-made fibres and more sophisticated floor coverings, the town's industry has diversified tremendously. Furniture manufacture is now an important part of the economy.

Among Kirkcaldy's famous sons are Thomas Carlyle, the literary genius, Robert and James Adam the architects, and Adam Smith, who wrote *Wealth of Nations*.

SPECIAL ATTRACTIONS

Every April, the Esplanade is closed for five days for The Links Market, the largest and oldest fair in Britain. A great gala of events is presented with plenty of music, colour, pomp and ceremony.

WHAT TO SEE

Kirkcaldy Museum and Art Gallery (open daily: admission free) is in the War Memorial Gardens, next to the station. You can see a good archaeological collection with 300 million year old fossils. You can also learn about local social history, natural history and industry. The art gallery, though small, has a splendid collection including work by many Scottish artists. A whole room has been devoted to William McTaggart, that great master who captured simple every day life and familiar scenes so well. Other artists include Peploe, Lowry, Sickert and Raeburn.

The Industrial Museum (open daily from 2 pm–5 pm in the summer except on Sundays: admission free) is next door. For anyone interested in the growth of Kirkcaldy's linoleum industry, coal mining, and textiles this museum is worth a visit. There is a wheelwright's shop, a forge, a printing press and a lot more.

The McDouall Stuart Museum (open every afternoon in the summer: admission free) is an award winning museum in Dysart, which is an attractive suburb of Kirkcaldy. The museum is in Fitzroy Street, in a building restored by the National Trust for Scotland, with a lintel dated 1575. The house was the birthplace of John McDouall Stuart, the first man to cross Australia from south to north through the central desert, in 1866. The museum tells you all about Stuart and his fascinating, and often hair-raising, expeditions including his encounters with Aborigines and Australian wildlife.

If you explore the heart of Kirkcaldy you will find that it is not just a modern town full of good shops and busy streets: you can wander into the older parts and come upon delightful little wynds and courtyards, and old houses with pantiled roofs and crow-stepped gables, as for example in Kirk Wynd.

Parks

The town has several parks: **Beveridge Park** with flower gardens and a swimming lake; **Dunniker Park**, to the north-west, with a nature trail and golf course, shaded by cedar trees; and **Ravenscraig Park**, along the shore beyond Dysart.

Ravenscraig Castle (open standard Ancient Monument times: adults 50p, children 25p) is dramatically situated beside Ravenscraig Park, on a rocky promontory overlooking the river. It is at present almost cut off by extensive building developments but it is still open to the public. It is worth picking your way through the builders' rubble to visit this substantial ruin, dating from 1460 when James II intended it as a dower house for his wife. He lost interest in it when she died.

James III gave it to the Earl of Orkney in exchange for Kirkwall Castle which he had long coveted, and it was finally demolished for Cromwell in 1651 by General Monk. It was the first castle in Britain to be designed for defence by and against cannon shot and you can still see the wide gun loops in the walls and the massive thickness of the walls. The views out over the Forth are lovely and in the days when such things were important, it was a splendid vantage point against invasion.

West Wemyss and East Wemyss

West Wemyss is one and a half miles (2.4 km) east of Dysart and East Wemyss three miles (4.8 km). They are so called from the many "weems", or caves, that honeycomb this bit of the coast. People have sheltered in these caves for many thousands of years and the graffiti they have left behind them is fascinating, dating back possibly to the Bronze Age (2500 BC). Four of the main caves are accessible and you are allowed to explore them any time, at your own risk. Take a torch. The ruin just east of East Wemyss is called Macduff's Castle, once the stronghold of the Thanes of Fife.

Leven

Leven, three miles (4.8 km) up the coast from the castle, on Largo Bay, is another holiday centre with a good beach and plenty of holiday facilities , including golf and fishing. The harbour was once a busy port, used to ship in provisions to the Royal Palace of Falkland but it is now silted up and used only by pleasure craft.

Lundin Links, also on Largo Bay, is another good family holiday resort. It has a sandy beach, sea fishing and golf. The standing stones that you can see just to the west are thought to have been part of a Druid temple.

Largo

Largo, at the head of the bay, three miles (4.8 km) north-east of Leven, was once an important fishing centre. It is now mainly residential and very popular in summer with its golden crescent of sand. Look out for the **Statue of Alexander Selkirk**, which stands in a niche outside the cottage in which he was born in Lower Largo in 1676. Selkirk was a wild young man who ran away to sea, quarrelled with his captain and was dumped on an uninhabited island, Juan Fernandez, at his own request, where he existed for five years until he was rescued. He and his story were immortalised by Daniel Defoe, in his novel *Robinson Crusoe.*

While you are here you should climb the volcanic cone of **Largo Law**, where an ancient chief is said to have been buried, dressed in silver armour! You will get a good view of Fife from the top.

Colinsburgh

Colinsburgh, inland, four miles (6.4 km) east of Largo, was built by Colin, third Earl of Balcarres, in the early 18th century. He was an ardent Jacobite and he built the village for his soldiers when he realised that the Stuart cause was hopeless.

TOURIST INFORMATION
Forth Road Bridge, Inverkeithing, tel 0383-417759. It is open Easter to end of September.

4 Kirkgate, Burntisland, tel 0592-872667. It is open all year.
Esplanade, Kirkcaldy, tel 0592-267775. It is open all year.
South Street, Leven, tel 0333-29464. It is open all year.

WHERE TO STAY

Forth View Hotel, Hawkcraig Point, Aberdour, tel 0383 860402. B&B from £11: categories 3,3,2: 6 bedrooms. Overlooks the Forth. Friendly, hospitable welcome.

Albert Hotel, Main Street, North Queensferry, tel 0383-413562. B&B from £11: categories 4,3,3: 8 bedrooms. An attractive hotel in the middle of picturesque North Queensferry with a warm, relaxed atmosphere.

Inchview Hotel, 69 Kinghorn Road, Burntisland, tel 0592-872239. B&B from £21: 12 bedrooms en suite. A Georgian, listed, terraced hotel, looking out across the Forth.

Bayview Hotel, St James Place, Kinghorn, tel 0592-890228. B&B from £10.50: 11 bedrooms. Friendly service, with a dinner-dance every Saturday.

Dean Park Hotel, Chapel Level, Kirkcaldy, tel 0592-261635. B&B from £30: 22 bedrooms en suite. In addition, 12 chalets in the grounds with hotel facilities and meals served in main hotel.

Dunnikier House Hotel, Dunnikier Way, Kirkcaldy, tel 0592-266630/268393. B&B from £18.50: 17 bedrooms en suite. Weekend golf packages offered.

Belvedere Hotel, West Wemyss, tel 0592-54167. B&B from £25: 11 bedrooms en suite. A friendly, relaxed atmosphere.

EATING OUT

All the hotels above have reasonable food. Dinner from about £6.

Hawkcraig House, Aberdour, tel 0383-860335. Private house at mouth of the harbour, overlooking Inchcolm Island. Accent on home cooking using prime Scottish produce. Good dinner from £8. Take your own wine, as there is no licence.

The East Neuk of Fife

The nose that juts east from Largo round to St Andrews is called East Neuk, "neuk" meaning corner, and the road that takes you round the coast links up a chain of delightful little towns and villages, each with its own individual charm and character. Picturesque harbours, quaint old houses rising in steep terraces, twisting cobbled streets and a number of good inns where you will get a reasonable meal, all combine to make an exploration of the East Neuk a memorable experience. From Elie, north-east to Crail, and then north-west back to St Andrews, you will find many delights that will tempt you to stop.

WHAT TO SEE

Elie and Earlsferry

Elie and Earlsferry at the eastern end of Largo Bay, six miles (9.6 km) from Largo, are more or less one place. Both are popular resorts with lovely sandy beaches where, if you look carefully, you may find garnets in the sand. Earlsferry is the place where Macduff, Earl of Fife, is believed to have hidden from Macbeth in the 11th-century in a cave at Kincraig Point, before being ferried to Dunbar. The Elie Fair is in July.

St Monance

St Monance, or Monans, three miles (4.8 km) north-east, has a charming cluster of old houses reaching down to the sea. When the wind is in the south-east the spray rises over the churchyard wall to wash the gravestones in the cemetery of a dear little fishermen's church that stands on the edge of the water. The foundations of this church date from 1362 when David II dedicated it to St Monans, or Mirren, an Irish missionary, in gratitude for a miraculous recovery from an arrow wound. The unusual T-shape of the church is thus because the nave was never built.

The town rises steeply from a double harbour, an attractive network of narrow, twisting streets and restored old houses. Miller's Yard, close to the harbour, is one of the oldest surviving boatbuilders in Scotland, established in 1747 and still building traditional fishing boats.

Pittenweem

Pittenweem, meaning place-of-the-cave, a mile (1.6 km) up the coast, is the home port of the fishing-fleets of the East Neuk, with a thriving fish market and an Arts Festival in August. It is an attractive, cheerful town, its old harbour often crammed with fishing boats, its quays stacked with fish boxes and gear. The National Trust for Scotland has done tremendous work on several of the buildings in the town. These include **Kellie Lodging**, a tower, that juts into the High Street, and **The Gyles**, an attractive group of 16th and 17th-century houses by the harbour. You can see the remains of a priory in the grounds of the Episcopal Church, founded in 1114, whose Augustinian monks established a shrine in **St Fillans Cave**, where services are still occasionally held.

Kellie Castle

Kellie Castle (open daily in the summer and weekends in spring and autumn, from 2 pm–6 pm: adults £1.40, children 70p; gardens open all the year round: adults 60p, children 30p) is three miles (4.8 km) inland to the north-west. Kellie dates back to the 14th century, an impressive great pile of mainly 16th and 17th-century domestic architecture, in an attractive setting of landscaped gardens. It was rescued from decay by Professor James Lorimer, in 1875 and his grandson, the sculptor Hew Lorimer, is the resident custodian. It has some splendid plaster work and painted panelling.

Anstruther

Anstruther, a mile (1.6 km) up the coast from Pittenweem and contracted to "Anster" by locals, was once an important fishing centre but is now better known as a holiday resort. It has, however, hung onto its link with its fishing past.

The Scottish Fisheries Museum and Aquarium (open daily except Tuesdays: adults 75p, children 25p) at the head of the harbour, gives you a unique insight into the life and work of a fishing community. You come away filled with admiration for the men who put the haddock on your plate, determined that you will never take a fish supper for granted again.

Kellie Castle

You can also see over the **North Carr Lightship**, in the harbour, which did 43 years service off Fife Ness. Try to picture what life must have been like for the seven man crew in those cramped quarters, particularly in bad weather.

Anstruther has a Holiday Fair week in July.

Crail

Crail is three miles (4.8 km) beyond Anstruther, just before **Fife Ness** which is the tip of the East Neuk, and is another well-restored little fishing town with one of the prettiest harbours in Fife, Crail was a royal burgh in 1310 with rights for trading on the Sabbath (which can't have pleased John Knox when he came preaching here some 200 years later). Picturesque, colour-washed houses and cobbled streets lead down to the harbour and its crow-stepped customs house: a lovely place to sit on the harbour wall, a glass of beer in your hand, the sun on your face, and listen to the sounds of the water slapping at the stones. Crail Festival week is in July.

The Church of St Mary is a 12th century church. The large blue stone at the gate of the church is said to have been hurled there by the Devil, from May Island, five miles (8 km) out to sea! You can see an 8th-century Pictish cross slab in the church and in **Victoria Gardens** the early Christian **Sauchope Stone**. The restored **Tolbooth** dates from the early 16th century and at 62 Marketgate, you can explore the **Crail Museum and Heritage Centre** (open daily in the summer: adults 50p, children 20p) and learn much of the history of this ancient town.

May Island

You can hire boats from Crail or Anstruther, to visit May Island, the largest of the four that command the entrance to the Firth of Forth and once of vital strategic importance. The island is now a bird sanctuary, and among the many birds you will see there are the enchanting puffins with their unreal-looking striped beaks, living in burrows in the turf. Look out for the remains of the **Beacon** which was the first Scottish lighthouse, built in 1636. The present lighthouse was built by Robert Louis Stevenson's grandfather, Robert, in 1816.

Kingsbarns

From Crail, the coast road turns north-west towards St Andrews and you lose the sea for a while. You come first to Kingsbarns, three miles (4.8 km) from Crail, whose name will tell you that this is good farmland. There is a nice story attached to the original owners of **Pitmillie**, just north of the village. In the 11th century before Malcolm Canmore was king he asked a stranger for the loan of "a few pennies". "Not a few: mony pennies", (sic) came the munificent reply. King Malcolm did not forget. When he came into power he granted his benefactor the lands at Kingsbarns and the family became known as "Moneypenny".

St Andrews

As you come down into St Andrews, ten miles (16 km) from Crail, and see the town laid out below you, you get a funny feeling of time collapsing as you try to see the many ghosts of this historic and fascinating town. Many of the stones used to build the older houses came from the ruined cathedral on the eastern edge of the town, towards which the three main streets lead. Scotland's oldest university, founded in 1411, is now the living heart of the town whose medieval spirit is kept young in many ways. For instance, you might be lucky and see the Sunday parade of students processing from the chapel in the scarlet medieval gowns that were introduced so that they could be easily spotted entering brothels. (Divinity students wear black gowns: presumably they were above suspicion!)

According to legend, St Rule, during the 8th century, was shipwrecked on the rocks just to the west of today's harbour. He had with him some of the bones of St Andrew, no one is quite sure why, and he enshrined them on the headland where you can now see the 12th-century ruins of the cathedral.

SPECIAL ATTRACTIONS

In spring, the Kate Kennedy Pageant takes over, with sixty to seventy students parading the streets in costume. In August you can go to the Lammas Fair, Scotland's oldest surviving medieval market, with showmen from all over Britain setting up stalls and booths in the streets—a bright, colourful carnival that lasts for two days. There are also the St Andrews Festival in February, the Festival of Food and Wine, in March, St Andrews Highland Games, in July, and great celebrations for St Andrews Day on 30 November.

In 1987, in common with other places throughout Scotland, St Andrews is honouring Mary, Queen of Scots, 400 years after her execution.

WHAT TO SEE

St Andrew's Cathedral (open standard Ancient Monument times: adults 50p, children 25p) was the largest cathedral in Scotland, seat of the ecclesiastical capital of the country, and even now a truly magnificent ruin. A great twin-towered facade soars towards the sky, surrounded by neat green turf, graves, the foundations of the priory, a few massive walls and a Norman arch.

St Rule's Tower stands next door, like a gaunt chaperone. Here the holy relics were kept until the cathedral was completed. If you feel energetic you can climb the 158 steps inside the tower and see wonderful views of the town and out to sea. It is strange to stand in front of the remains of the high altar and recall that Robert Bruce stood here at the consecration of the cathedral in 1318, 160 years after the building began. Here too stood James V and Mary of Guise at the ceremony of their marriage. In 1559 that zealous reformer, John Knox, preached some stirring sermons on the "cleansing of the temple" and so roused his congregations to hysteria that they stripped the cathedral of its glorious embellishments and riches, leaving it to decay into ruin.

St Andrew's Castle (open standard Ancient Monument times: adults 50p, children 25p) is north-west of the cathedral on a rocky headland overhanging the sea beyond a deep moat. Now a ruin, it was built as the bishop's palace at the end of the 12th century and it witnessed some extremely nasty incidents in the bloodstained history of the Scottish church. George Wishart, the ardent Protestant reformer was burned at the stake in front of the castle in 1545 and tradition tells of the notorious Catholic Cardinal Beaton, lying on velvet cushions inside the castle, watching the death throes. Whether this is true or not, Beaton paid for Wishart's life with his own. A worldly, immoral man, the cardinal did not hesitate to plead for mercy on account of his priestly status, two months later, when he was brutally stabbed to death by a party of avenging reformers. His body was hung over the battlements and then slung into the "bottle dungeon", a fearsome rock pit, where it was preserved in salt until its discovery more than a year later. After the murder, the reformers held the castle against a siege, having been joined by John Knox and others, before they were all captured and sent off to serve time as galley slaves. Knox was a close friend of Wishart: it was to be 14 years before he returned to stir the reforming pot again.

The castle fell into ruin in the 17th century but you can still see the bottle dungeon, its entrance being the neck of the bottle. A large number of the reformers were imprisoned in this hell hole: it is hard to believe that many can have survived. Beaton's apartments are thought to have been in the tower to the south-west.

The Church of St Salvator is among St Andrews many fine university buildings. In North St, it was founded as the university chapel by Bishop Kennedy in 1450, uncle of the beautiful Kate who is feted in the April pageant. You can see the bishop's tomb in the church and a magnificent mace from his time which is still carried on ceremonial occasions. The pulpit was the one John Knox preached from, carried here from the parish church. It is rather uncanny to think of him thumping out his message on that very wood.

Patrick Hamilton, the protomartyr of the Reformation, was burned for his Lutheran heresy in front of **St Salvator's College** in 1528, another of Cardinal Beaton's victims.

The Royal and Ancient Golf Club makes all this history pale into insignificance for golfers. This world-famous establishment determines the rules of the game, although it is by no means Scotland's oldest club. The Autumn Golf Meeting, at the end of September is the main event of the year and when you see the preparations beforehand (the tents and booths and marquees) you would imagine an army was preparing for a major battle. It is at this meeting that the captain for the year plays himself into office, watched by thousands of anxious eyes, in case he should miss that important ball! Of the four courses, "The Old" is the most famous.

St Leonard's College, founded in 1512 and no longer extant, was on the present site of St Leonard's Girls' School, beyond Abbey St. Many ardent reformers, including John Knox it is thought, studied at the college, and the term "to have drunk at St Leonard's Well" was coined from those times, meaning to have listened to the Protestant doctrine. The library of St Leonard's School is in **Queen Mary's House**, in South St, where Mary is believed to have stayed, in 1563, taking a holiday with her ladies from the burdens of state affairs. While she was there she planted a thorn tree that still flourishes in the quadrangle of **St Mary's College**.

The Byre Theatre, which you get to through the attractive South Court, stages an excellent range of productions throughout the year and began its life in a cowshed of the Old Abbey Street Dairy Farm, hence its name. Another place you should visit while you are in St Andrews is the **Crawford Centre for the Arts**, which has a changing programme of art exhibitions, professional theatre and music performances in its drama studio and galleries.

Craigtoun Country Park

Craigtoun Country Park, two miles (3.2 km) south of St Andrews, is 50 acres (20 ha) of parkland surrounding Mount Melville House, now a hospital, and open to the public all year. The park has an Italian garden, a Dutch village, surrounded by an ornamental lake built in 1918, and a picnic area. Craigtoun has a Country Fair in May.

TOURIST INFORMATION
78 South Street, St Andrews, tel 0334-72021. It is open all year.

Leuchars

The railway line to St Andrews was closed some years ago and Leuchars, five and a half miles (8.8 km) north-west is now the station that serves the town. In the village of Leuchars you could easily miss what is perhaps the most beautiful relic of Norman architecture still to be seen in the whole of Britain. Only an apse and chancel remain, incorporated into the parish church, with an arcaded exterior to the apse. If you look carefully you can see the axe-marks of the ancient masons, on the blind arches and pilasters. It is a pity that the modern church is so plain, but perhaps its dullness offsets the triumph of the Norman part.

WHAT TO SEE

Tentsmuir Forest

Going north towards the Tay you come to the Tentsmuir Forest a couple of miles (3.2 km) north-east of Leuchars. This lovely woodland also contains beaches with picnic sites for summer outings. Keep your eyes skinned for deer and families of seals, sunning themselves on the sands, as well as lots of different birds.

Tayport and Newport-on-Tay

Tayport and Newport-on-Tay, five and a half miles (8.8 km) north of Leuchars, are holiday resorts on the southern shores of the Firth of Tay. Both claim to have had the oldest ferry in Scotland and it seems possible that boats might have run from both towns since earliest times. Neolithic remains have been excavated on this north-eastern corner of Fife.

The Tay Rail Bridge

The southern approach to the Tay Rail Bridge is a short distance west of the one that collapsed in a gale on 28 December 1879, sending a train and about 100 passengers into the water, a disaster that shocked the world and still brings a shiver of horror to hearts today. Anyone who has not read the account of the disaster as told by that astonishing poet, William McGonagall, should do so at the first possible opportunity.

So the train mov'd slowly along the Bridge of Tay,
Until it was about midway,
Then the central girders with a crash gave way,
And down went the train and passengers into the Tay!
The storm Fiend did loudly bray,
Because ninety lives had been taken away,
On the last Sabbath day of 1879,
Which will be remember'd for a very long time.

The new rail bridge, built only a few years later is a graceful construction curving across the river like a two mile (3.2 km) memorial to the disaster. The road bridge, two miles (3.2 km) downstream, is a toll bridge.

McGonagall was fascinated by the Tay and wrote several other of his epic verses in its honour. There was one about a monster whale that came to "...devour the small fishes in the silvery Tay..." and one to the railway bridge before it collapsed, and even an address to the New Tay Bridge. In fact, no traveller in Scotland should set out without a copy of the poetic gems of William McGonagall, poet and tragedian!

Balmerino Abbey

Balmerino Abbey (open at any time: admission free) is a ruin three miles (4.8 km) west of the rail bridge, on a hill overlooking the river.

It was founded for Cistercians in the 13th century, by Alexander II, whose mother is buried here. It was mostly destroyed by the English in 1547, during the "Rough Wooing" and a later attempt to restore it was foiled by the Reformation. The last Lord Balmerino was a brave old man, beheaded as a Jacobite in 1746. Seen against a stormy sky, it is a sad, poignant shell, with just the entrance to the chapter house and the roofless sacristy standing among farm buildings.

Lindores Abbey

The scattered remains of Lindores Abbey (open at all times: admission free) are eight miles (13 km) south-west, just before Newburgh, and also overlooking the **Firth of Tay**. This abbey was an important religious community until it was secularised in 1600. The main entrance arch and part of the west tower still stand in jagged isolation, all that remains of a place that witnessed the savage burning of exquisitely illuminated mass books and manuscripts, by John Knox. Lindores was founded in the 12th century for Benedictines and was often visited by Scottish kings.

Newburgh

Newburgh, 13 miles (21 km) south-west of Newport, almost on the border with Tayside, is a royal burgh with a pretty little harbour. In June, it holds a fair, called the Haggis Market, which includes a race for salmon cobbles on the river. On the hill to the south of the town you can see the remains of **Macduff's Cross**, the legendary place of sanctuary for any Macduff who had committed a murder in hot blood. To achieve pardon, the murderer had to touch the cross, wash himself nine times at Ninewells nearby, and forfeit nine cows, each to be tied to the cross.

Falkland

Falkland is nine miles (14.4 km) south of Newburgh, and is one of the jewels of Fife. This ancient, beautiful town clings to the lower slopes of the **Lomond Hills**, looking across the **Howe of Fife**, once a forest full of deer and wild boar, now rich farmland. Many of the 17th to 19th century buildings have been restored, making it a delightful place to wander about in, especially on a fine day when the sun plays tricks with the old stones, dappled with light and shade. In 1987, Falkland is paying tribute to Mary, Queen of Scots, in July and August.

WHAT TO SEE

Falkland Palace (open daily in the summer, and weekends in October: adults £1.40, children 70p; gardens only: adults 80p, children 40p). Built in the 15th and 16th centuries, it was intended as a hunting lodge for the Stuarts and much of it has been carefully restored, giving a wonderful example of early Renaissance architecture—compact and ornate, its massive walls and barred windows reminding us that even hunting lodges had to be fortified. The south wing is the best preserved, with an elaborate façade, mullioned windows and gate house flanked by round towers.

It was in an earlier castle on this site, in 1402, that the heir to the throne, the Duke of Rothesay, was starved to death by the ambitious and greedy Duke of Albany. When James I then eliminated the powerful Albany family by the simple, if somewhat drastic method, of murdering all their menfolk, Falkland was annexed by the crown. The elegance of the architecture was enhanced by French masons employed for James IV and then by his son James V. It was to Falkland that James V came in 1542, after his defeat at Solway Moss, to die a broken man. He had just heard of the birth of his daughter Mary who, he prophesied on his death bed, would be the last of the Stuarts to rule Scotland.

The palace was restored from complete ruin by the Hereditary Keeper, the third Marquess of Bute, in 1887 and he also rescued the gardens and many of the houses in the town. The original **Royal Tennis Court**, 1539 is still in use, as one of Britain's few "royal" or "real" tennis courts. Perhaps Queen Mary had a game here. She certainly played golf and is known to have come often to Falkland on hunting expeditions.

You should take time to wander along the High Street, beyond the palace gates, through the Market Square, and up the Maspie Burn onto East Lomond Law for a splendid panoramic view of the countryside.

From Falkland, back through the hinterland towards St Andrews, the landscape is all rolling hills and rounded hillocks, and attractive little villages with stone cottages and pantiled roofs. This is the Howe of Fife, "how" meaning sheltered place.

Cupar

Cupar, ten miles (16 km) north-east of Falkland, heading back to St Andrews, was once the administrative centre of Fife. It is a cheerful, friendly little town with elegant 18th-century houses built of mellow, honey-coloured stone. In 1276, Alexander III held an Assembly of the Three Estates in Cupar, made up of the Church, the burghers, and the aristocracy. It was this that inspired Sir David Lindsay, who lived in the mount, nearby, to write "Ane Satire of the Thrie Estates", holding them up to ridicule. The play has recently been revived and is aired now and them during the Edinburgh Festival. Cupar has a Gala Week in June.

WHAT TO SEE

Dalgairn House Garden is a must for gardeners (open at weekends in the summer: small fee). On the northern edge of the town, the garden is a delightful, informal collection of old fashioned flowers and edible weeds, all well labelled so that you can see how to use them.

Hill of Tarvit

Hill of Tarvit (open on afternoons in summer, and on April and October weekends: adults £1.40, children 70p; garden only, open all year: adults 60p, children 30p) is a mansion two miles (3.2 km) south of Cupar, dating from 1696 and splendidly remodelled by Robert Lorimer in 1906. The house has a nice lived-in feeling (it is occupied) and sets off the collection of treasures inside: tapestries, porcelain and paintings, and 18th-century English and French furniture. The gardens are laid out in French style, with box hedges and yews.

Scotstarvit Tower

Scotstarvit Tower opposite Hill of Tarvit (open standard Ancient Monument times: admission free) is a five-storey, 16th-century tower house with battlements and turrets. It was the home of John Scott, a 16th and 17th-century scholar and mapmaker.

Pitlessie

Pitlessie, four miles (6.4 km) south-west of Cupar will be familiar to fans of David Wilkie, from his famous painting "Pitlessie Fair". The artist was born at **Cults Manse** nearby in 1785 and many of his wonderful paintings of ordinary everyday life were set locally, so that you find yourself looking round for one of his jovial, bucolic peasants. Very sadly, the manse was destroyed by fire in 1926, together with a wealth of wall paintings done by Wilkie in his youth.

Ceres

Ceres, four miles (6.4 km) east of Pitlessie, is a most attractive village. It has pantiled cottages grouped round a green on which annual games are still held, dating from victory celebrations after Bannockburn in 1314!

The Fife Folk Museum (open daily except Tuesdays in the summer: adults 50p, children 20p) is in a 17th-century **Tolbooth Weigh House** near the medieval hump-backed bridge. The museum is also spread through two cottages and out of doors, with fascinating collections of the domestic and agricultural tools and equipment in daily use before the invention of electricity and the petrol engine. Don't miss the dungeons in the tolbooth. There are also two nature trails from the village, planned by the Scottish Wildlife Trust of Botanical and Geological Interest.

Peat Inn

Peat Inn, three miles (4.8 km) to the south-east, is a hamlet that takes its name from its inn where you can eat as good a meal as you could hope for anywhere in the country.

Magus Muir

Three miles (4.8 km) north of Peat Inn and just south of **Strathkinness**, you pass Magus Muir, a grizzly spot where a party of Covenanters butchered Archbishop Sharp, in 1679, in the presence of his daughter. Sharp's attempts to restore episcopacy to Scotland had not been entirely straightforward and he had won for himself universal detestation. He had gone, as a Presbyterian, to plead the Covenanters cause with Charles II and returned as the consecrated bishop of St Andrews!

Old Dairsie

Old Dairsie, about three miles (4.8 km) west of Magus Muir, has a bridge over the River Eden that was built by Archbishop Beaton in 1522. **Dairsie Castle** (open at all times: admission free) lies above the river, where David II spent part of his youth. **Dura Den** is a wooded gorge south of the bridge, where a large number of fossils has been found. These fossils gave vital clues to the formation of land and life here, over many millions of years. Beside the Ceres Burn that cuts the gorge, you can see the ruins of several linen and jute mills, once an important part of Fife economy.

TOURIST INFORMATION
78 South Street, St Andrews, tel 0334 72021. It is open all year.

WHERE TO STAY
Craws Nest Hotel, Bankwell Road, Anstruther, tel 0333-310691. B&B from £20: 50 bedrooms en suite. A comfortable friendly hotel with good food.

Golf Hotel, 4 High Street, Crail, tel 0333-50500. B&B from £12: categories 3,4,3: 5 bedrooms. A picturesque old building with a nice friendly, old world atmosphere.

Marine Hotel, 54 Nethergate, Crail, tel 0333-50207. B&B from £9: 12 bedrooms, 6 en suite. Comfortable and friendly.

Golf Hotel, Bank Street, Elie, tel 0333-330209. B&B from £18.95: categories 5,4,5: 22 bedrooms en suite. Good food.

Lundin Links Hotel, Leven Road, Lundin Links, tel 0333-320207. B&B from £16.50: categories 3,4,4. 18 bedrooms en suite. Mock Tudor hotel with good service and friendly atmosphere.

The Old Manor Hotel, Leven Road, Lundin Links, tel 0333–320368. B&B from £17: categories 5,5,5: 19 bedrooms, 15 en suite. A comfortable hotel with good food.

Old Course Golf and Country Hotel, St Andrews, tel 0334-74371. B&B from £34: categories 6,6,6: 150 bedrooms en suite. A modern, purpose built hotel with every possible facility and good food.

Rufflets Hotel, Strathkinness Low Road, St Andrews, tel 0334-72594. B&B from £27.50: categories 6,4,5: 21 bedrooms en suite. An attractive house and garden and a country house atmosphere. Very good food.

Russacks Marine Hotel, Pilmour Links, St Andrews, tel 0334-74321. B&B from £25: categories 6,6,6: 50 bedrooms en suite. A large, comfortable hotel with excellent service, friendly atmosphere and good food.

Mayview Hotel, Station Road, St Monans, tel 03337-564. B&B from £10: categories 1,2,4: 5 bedrooms. An attractive house overlooking May Island.

EATING OUT
Craws Nest Hotel, see above. Local fish and shell fish, beef, salmon. Good dinner from £7.50.

The Cellar, Anstruther, tel 0333-310378. Very good food at reasonable prices. Dinner from £7.50.

Caiplie Guest House, 51-3 High Street, Crail, tel 0333-50564. Good Scottish home cooking. Non residents must book. Dinner from £7.50.

Ostlers Close Restaurant, Cupar, tel 0334-55574. Venison, sole, prawns, pigeons, lobsters, duck, game (in season) all local and fresh. Good dinner from £10.

The Peat Inn, Peat Inn, by Cupar, tel 033-484 206. Whatever else you do in Scotland, don't miss out on this restaurant. It is one of the best in Britain, internationally famous, with cooking that will make your mouth water whenever you look back, for years to come. Expensive, but don't think of the bill, even if you have to live rough for the rest of your holiday! Booking essential. Dinner from £14.50.

Rufflets Hotel, see above. Good Scottish cooking. Dinner from £10.

St Andrews Golf Hotel, 40 The Scores, St Andrews, tel 0334-72611. Good Scottish food. Dinner from £10.

Sandford Hill Hotel, Wormit, Newport-on-Tay, tel 0382-541802. Fresh local produce. Dinner from £7.50.

Kind Kyttocks Kitchen, Falkland, tel 033-75 57477. Home baking. Teas. Lunches only, under £5.

CRAFT CENTRES IN FIFE

The following workshops and studios welcome visitors to watch the craftsmen at work. Where a telephone number is given it is best to telephone up first, to check times.

Ceramics

Crail Pottery, Crail, tel 033-35 413. Hand thrown pottery.

Forthside Pottery, Forthside, North Queensferry, tel 0383-418630. All processes connected with hand formed pottery. Throwing demonstrations given on request.

David Heminsley, No 1, Balvirnie Craft Centre, by Markinch, Glenrothes, tel 0592-755975. Throwing and turning on the wheel, finishing, glazing and decorating stoneware.

Largo Pottery, 81A Main Street, Lower Largo. Throwing, glazing, decorating hand made pottery.

Jewellery and Silversmithing

Dust Jewllery, 7 Mill Wynd, Lundin Links, tel 0333-320742. Silver and gold jewellery, specialists in silver and enamel, titanium.

Moray Workshop, High Street, Aberdour, tel 0383-860 248. Hand made silver jewellery, stone setting, engraving, "Repousse", enamelling.

Leatherwork

Eddergoll Studios, Eddergoll House, 29 Bonnygate, Cupar, tel 0334-54757. Leather carving and pressed leatherwork. Specialising in heraldry and Celtic art. Reproduction 17th and 18th-century targes, coasters, tablemats, wall panels, sculptures, boxes, etc.

Part XI

TAYSIDE

Glamis

Somehow Tayside, gateway to the true Highlands, seems to embody more than anywhere else, the ghosts of the Pictish past. Biting into the middle of the eastern sea board, it spreads out around the Tay, offering an enormous variety of scenery. There is the rugged coastline with its red sandstone cliffs and sandy bays; the fertile coastal plain; the gentle Sidlaw Hills; and green moorland giving way to the lovely Strathmore valley backed by the massive Grampians and cut by long, wooded glens. There is everything you could want in Tayside, both in the magnificent scenery and in the range of things to do: golf; fishing (both river and sea), walking; climbing; and endless journeys back into the dawn of history, with more Pictish remains than anywhere else south of Sutherland.

The sun shines kindly on Tayside and the east wind hones its edges. Its people are keen-eyed, resilient, shrewd and industrious: fishermen and farmers mostly, straightforward and down-to-earth, with perhaps a faint mystery about them when one considers that they may have Pictish blood in their veins.

SPECIAL ATTRACTIONS

Among the local events that you should look out for in Tayside, are the Bull Sales in Perth which are a great event in February and October, attracting people from all over the country. In March there is the Perthshire Music Festival and in May the Atholl Highlanders Parade and Games at Blair Atholl. The Dundee Highland Games are in July, as are the Dundee Water Festival, The Arbroath Highland Games and Donkey

Derby. The Scottish Youth Theatre Summer Festival, in Perth, is also in July. In August, both Arbroath and Montrose have Flower Shows, and there are Highland Games in Perth and Birnam. Also in August there is the Aberfeldy, Atholl and Breadalbane Agricultural Shows, and the Crieff Highland Gathering. In Kinross, the International Fly Fishing championships are held in August. Also in Kinross, a traditional Scottish Folk Festival is held for three days every September, drawing groups from all over the country. Pitlochry has Highland Games in September, and Arbroath has a Festival of Highland Dancing. There are Mary, Queen of Scots celebrations, in 1987, in Kinross in May, and during the summer at Glamis.

From the south: on the M90

With several towns to choose from, you have several centres from which to explore Tayside. Coming from the south, you might start at Kinross just off the motorway at a point where you look ahead and suddenly begin to sense the real Highlands, up there beyond the horizon, a tantalising thickening of the skyline.

Kinross

Kinross is a pleasant, sturdy little town, once the county town, its tolbooth dating from the early 17th century, later repaired and decorated by Robert Adam. Kinross is at the heart of the agricultural land; it has a thriving woollen industry and it the only place where cashmere is spun in Britain. The goat hair is imported, but there are plans among Scottish farmers to establish Scottish goat farms which, it is thought, could be an important addition to the economy.

WHAT TO SEE

Loch Leven Castle

Perhaps Kinross is best known for its proximity to **Loch Leven** and, more particularly, to Loch Leven Castle (open daily in the summer: adults £1, children 50p). The castle stands on an island in the loch and is accessible by boat from Kinross. Anyone with a drop of romance in their veins will be compelled to make this pilgrimage, crossing the olive green water in the wake of Mary, Queen of Scots. The solid-looking ruin, dating from the 14th century, with its tower and curtain wall, stands among trees and, as you step ashore, you cannot avoid thinking of Mary, arriving as a prisoner, over 400 years ago.

It was a June day in 1567. Mary was in ragged clothes, her hair shorn, from her days as a fugitive. She was wretched from her defeat at Carberry Hill, already pregnant from her all-too-short marriage with Bothwell; exhausted, sick and utterly despairing. How must she have felt, as she landed at the little jetty, into the custody of unsympathetic Lady Douglas? Not long after her arrival she suffered a devastating haemorrhage and

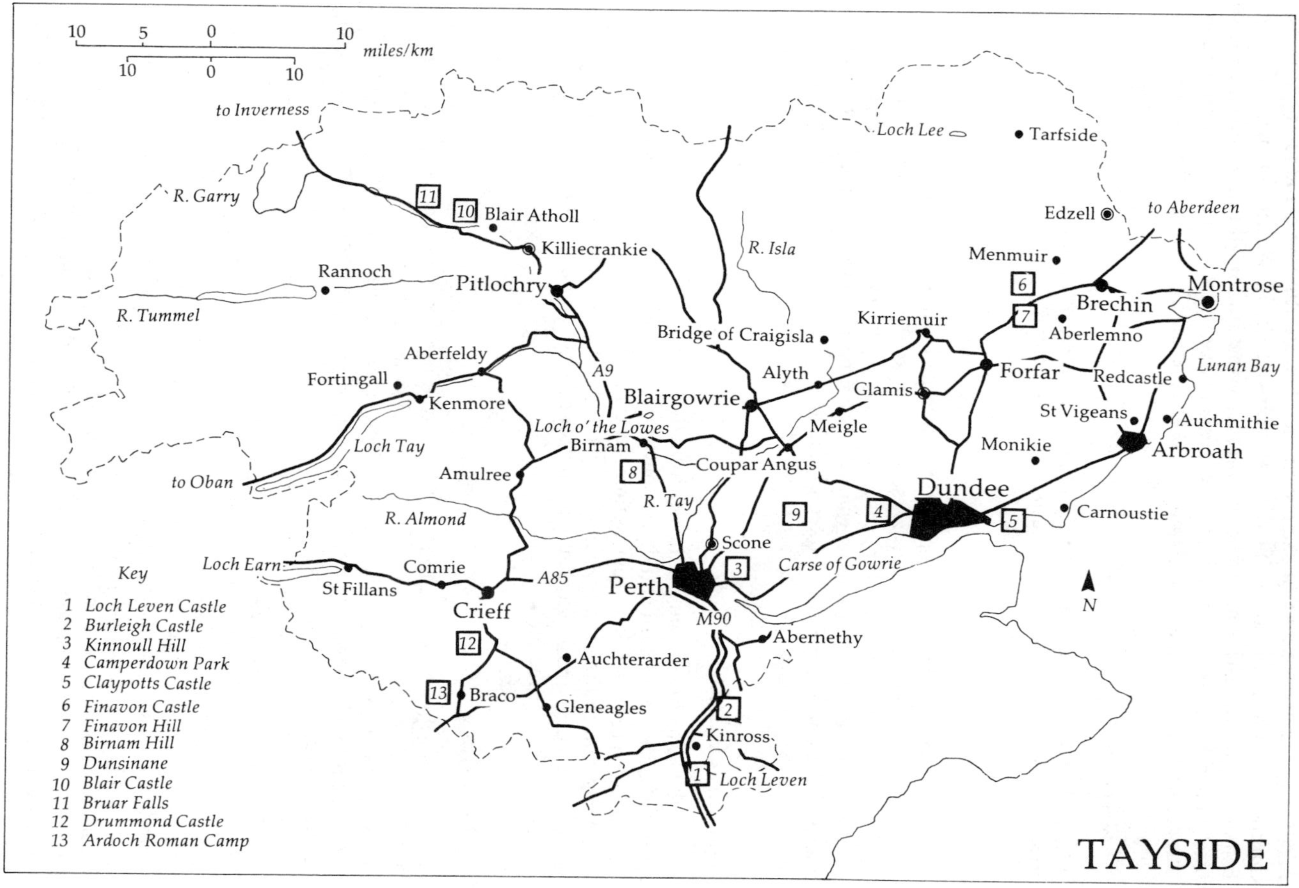

TAYSIDE
10 5 0 10 miles/km
10 0 10
to Inverness
R. Garry
Blair Atholl
Killiecrankie
Rannoch
Pitlochry
R. Tummel
R. Isla
Loch Lee
Tarfside
Edzell
to Aberdeen
Menmuir
Montrose
Brechin
Kirriemuir
Aberlemno
Bridge of Craigisla
Aberfeldy
Fortingall
Kenmore
A9
Alyth
Forfar
Redcastle
Lunan Bay
Glamis
Blairgowrie
Loch o' the Lowes
Meigle
St Vigeans
Auchmithie
Loch Tay
Birnam
Arbroath
Monikie
to Oban
Amulree
Coupar Angus
Dundee
R. Tay
R. Almond
Carnoustie
Scone
Carse of Gowrie
Loch Earn
Comrie
St Fillans
A85
Perth
Crieff
M90
N
Abernethy
Auchterarder
Braco
Gleneagles
Kinross
Loch Leven
Key
1 Loch Leven Castle
2 Burleigh Castle
3 Kinnoull Hill
4 Camperdown Park
5 Claypotts Castle
6 Finavon Castle
7 Finavon Hill
8 Birnam Hill
9 Dunsinane
10 Blair Castle
11 Bruar Falls
12 Drummond Castle
13 Ardoch Roman Camp

miscarriage, and it is said that she lost twins. She stayed in the castle for 11 months, during which time she so charmed an 18 year-old youth, William Douglas, that he helped her to escape. He rowed her ashore, throwing the keys of the locked castle into the loch, from where they were recovered, 300 years later! Mary's elusive spirit haunts this castle more poignantly than almost any other of the places she visited.

St Serfs

The largest island on the loch is St Serfs, with a ruined priory dating from the 9th century, built on the site of an even earlier Celtic settlement.

Loch Leven

Loch Leven is renowned for its pink trout. International fishing competitions are held here annually. The loch is a nature reserve, giving refuge to a large variety of migratory wildfowl; pink-foot and grey-lag geese, and many ducks. If you go there very quietly, in the early morning or late evening, you will hear a marvellous low symphony of chattering birds: little runs and rills of sound; murmurs and mutterings, and an occasional squawk as a fussy mother calls her family to order.

Burleigh Castle

Burleigh Castle (open, you get the key from the farm opposite: admission free) is a mile (1.6 km) north of the loch and dates from 1500. It was the seat of the Balfours of Burleigh who were visited here several times by James VI.

Bishop Hill to the east, the Cleish Hills to the south and the Lomond Hills to the north, combine to create ideal air currents for gliders. There is a gliding centre at Portmoak, just east of the loch.

Abernethy

Going on north, it would be easy to dismiss Abernethy as "just another Perthshire village", but if you take exit 9 off the motorway 11 miles (176 km) north of Kinross, and go 4 miles (6.4 km) to the east, you will find yourself in what was once a Pictish capital. The 74 ft (22 m) high, slender tapering tower, whose lower part dates from the 9th century, is one of only two such in Scotland, discounting the remains of one in Iona, the other being in Brechin. When Abernethy was the centre of the Celtic church, this tower provided the clergy with an almost impregnable refuge, as well as an excellent look-out, in times of threatened Viking or English invasion. The upper part dates from the 11th century and you can see a 7th-century stone, set into the base, carved with mysterious Pictish symbols. Also set into the wall is the "jougs", an iron neck collar by which malefactors were chained for punishment. The design of these elegant towers came over from Ireland with the missionary priests.

It was here in Abernethy, below the Ochil Hills, that Malcolm Canmore was forced to kneel and pay token homage to William the Conqueror in 1071. William had come north, conducting such a brilliant campaign against Scotland that Malcolm's humiliating capitulation seemed the only way to prevent the country being devastated. Perhaps he had his fingers crossed in his pocket. Perhaps he only intended to acknowledge William as his overlord in connection with his English estates. Whatever his motive, he allowed his son by his first marriage, Duncan, to be taken as a hostage to England, and his submission was to create centuries of unrest in both countries.

Perth

Perth is 17 miles (27 km) north of Kinross, and as you come down into it from the motorway, you get a fine view of the town, spread out below you round the Tay. Its two wide green parks, **North and South Inch**, unfold on either side and its spires reach for the sky. This was the first place where it was easy to bridge the river. It was a thriving port in the old days and is now an important livestock market at the centre of a productive agricultural area. A new by-pass has considerably eased the congestion of traffic in the town centre.

Perth's history goes back a long way. Traces of an old city wall indicate that there was a Roman camp here, although the town doesn't appear in the records until the 12th century. A devastating flood destroyed Old Perth in 1210 and William the Lion granted a royal charter to the town that was built in its place the same year. It was the capital of Scotland for a while, until the middle of the 15th century. John Knox preached one of his fire-and-brimstone sermons in St Johns, Perth, in 1559, as a result of which the town's four large monasteries were stripped of their treasures and destroyed.

Among the historical events that touched the city was the Battle of the Clans, a contest between the clans Chattan and Quhele (pronounced Kay), to establish which took precedence in battle. Thirty men from each side were to fight in a tournament, watched by King Robert III, his wife and court, on the North Inch. One of the clan Chattan lost his nerve at the last moment and fled. The rule was that the two sides must be matched man-for-man, so a blacksmith, small and bandy-legged, offered to stand in for the price of half a French crown. All but one of the Quhele clan were slaughtered. Among the survivors of the Chattans was the blacksmith, who had done more than anyone else to secure victory. Walter Scott gives a graphic description of the affair in *The Fair Maid of Perth*. The highly dubious drama of the Gowrie Conspiracy took place in 1600, in the now demolished Gowrie House in Perth. According to James VI, the Earl of Gowrie and his brother, Alexander Ruthven, lured him to an upstairs room in the house and tried to tie him up. He shouted for his lords through an open window, was rescued, and Gowrie and Ruthven were killed in the flurry. The whole affair was shrouded in mystery and speculation, with hints of homosexual motives mingled with hints that the king set the thing up in order to get rid of the brothers, whose political ambitions were notorious.

Apart from its setting, Perth is not a beautiful town, most of its buildings being dourly utilitarian. But if you poke around you will find some traces of the town's past, and, with the river and the Inches, there are several attractive vistas.

WHAT TO SEE

The Tourist Information Centre (open daily, except Sundays in winter) is called The Round House, and is in the Old Waterworks in Marshall Place, on the north-east corner of South Inch. It gives plenty of local information and has an audio visual show that takes you on a complete circle of the town, with slides and a commentary.

Perth Art Gallery and Museum (open daily except Sundays: admission free) in George Street, has local history displays and an exhibition showing the growth of the whisky industry which plays an important part in the economy of the area.

St Johns Church (open daily) was restored in 1923, with a War Memorial Chapel designed by Robert Lorimer. It dates from the 15th century and is on the site of a church built in the 12th century. Edward III is said to have killed his brother, the Earl of Cornwall, in that earliest church in 1335. It was in St John's that John Knox preached one of his iconoclastic sermons in 1559, urging his followers to purge the churches of idolatry. This sermon led to the destruction of a great many of the churches and monasteries in the area. This church alone had at least 40 richly decorated altars, dedicated to saints. A few of the sacred treasures were rescued from the purgers. You can see the 16th-century German Cellini Cup, given to Mary of Guise by the Pope; 17th-century chalices and a 16th-century baptismal basin.

The Fair Maid's House (open on weekdays throughout the year: admission free) is behind Charlotte Street, in North Port. It is the house romanticised by Walter Scott in *The Fair Maid of Perth*. According to Scott's version, it was the suitors of Catherine Glover, who lived in the house, whose rivalry caused the débâcle of the Battle of the Clans. It is one of the oldest buildings in the town, and in it you can see exhibitions of contemporary Scottish crafts and paintings. Perhaps a little over-restored, it is nevertheless an intriguing place.

Blackfriars Street, nearby, was the site of the now long vanished Blackfriars Monastery. This was where James I was murdered in 1437, by Robert Graham and others. Brave Catherine Douglas tried to bar the door to the murderers by thrusting her arm through a staple, in place of a missing iron bar. She survived the mutilation of her arm and went down in history as Catherine Barlass.

Balhousie Castle, a 15th-century castle beyond Rose Terrace on the west side of North Inch, has been restored in imposing Scottish Baronial style. In it is the **Regimental Museum of The Black Watch** (open on weekdays and on Sundays in the summer: admission free). This was the famous regiment that was raised in 1739 to help the government pacify the restless, rebellious Highlanders. There is a comprehensive display of the history of the regiment, with uniforms, weapons, pictures, documents, photographs and trophies, all recording its many honours and triumphs.

Dewars Whisky Distillery, in the western suburbs of Perth, runs free conducted tours during the week, where you can inspect the process of how Scotland's most popular export is made.

Kinnoull Hill rises 729 ft (218 m) above the town to the east, an easy climb giving you a splendid bird's eye view of the "Highland Line", the geological dividing line that runs from the south-west to the north-east.

Scone Palace

Scone Palace (open daily in the summer, or by arrangement, tel Perth 52300: adults £2.20, children £1.80) is two miles (3.2 km) north of Perth on the A93. Pronounced "Scoon", the palace is a 19th-century restoration of 16th-century and earlier buildings, with battlements and a toy fort façade, and the original gateway.

The abbey and palace that stood here in the 16th century were destroyed by John Knox's followers, after he had denounced "idolatry" in his sermon from St John's in 1559.

The palace contains lovely French furniture, including Marie Antoinette's writing desk; 16th-century needlework, including bed hangings embroidered by Mary, Queen of Scots; porcelain, 17th and 18th-century ivories, 18th-century clocks, and walls lined with Lyons silk. There is a coffee shop, with a home baked food, a gift shop and lovely gardens.

In the 9th century, Kenneth Macalpine brought the Stone of Destiny from Dunstaffnage to **The Moot Hill**, at Scone, a solemn meeting place established by the Pictish King Nectan. The stone had been brought over from Ireland, to Dunadd, by the early missionaries, who believed that it carried mystical powers of sovereignty and who used it as a throne during the coronation of Scottish kings. It was moved to Scone when Macalpine united the Scots and Picts, and taken to Westminster Abbey by Edward I, to become part of the Coronation Chair. It has remained there ever since, except for a brief hiatus when Scottish Nationalists removed it and kept it hidden for about three months. The stone is cloaked in mystery. There are many who will tell you that the one you can now see in London is a replica of the Celtic stone, which remains hidden away until such time as its hereditary guardians decide to bring it into the open once more.

TOURIST INFORMATION

Marshall Place, Perth, tel 0738-22900/27108. It is open all year.

Kinross Service Area, Kinross, tel 0577-63680. It is open April to October.

WHERE TO STAY

Windlestrae Hotel, The Muirs, Kinross, tel 0577-63217. B&B from £19.75: categories 6,4,5: 18 bedrooms en suite. Comfortable, with friendly staff.

Green Hotel, The Muirs, Kinross, tel 0577-63467. B&B from £22.50: 40 bedrooms en suite.

Nivingston House, Cleish, near Kinross, tel 05775-216. B&B from £24.25: categories 5,4,5: 76 bedrooms en suite. The hotel lies at the foot of the Cleish Hills in 12 acres (5 ha) of landscaped garden. A 20 minute drive from Perth. It was completely done up recently and is very comfortable. The cook won a gold medal, which says something for the food, if you like sauces.

County Hotel, 26 County Place, Perth, tel 0738-23355. B&B from £13: categories 5,5,6: 23 bedrooms, 12 en suite. Only two minutes walk from the middle of Perth.

Balcraig House, by New Scone, tel 0738-51123-5. B&B from £37.50: categories 5,4,5: 10 bedrooms en suite. A luxury, country house hotel, five minutes drive from Perth. BTA commended and the AA rates it as 3-Star. The restaurant won't disappoint gourmets, nor will the wine list. There is a farm in the grounds and you can go riding and pony trekking. There is also a tennis court, as well as croquet and boules.

Isle of Skye Hotel, 18 Dundee Road, Perth, tel 0738-24471. B&B from £24: categories 6,5,5: 44 bedrooms en suite. The AA and RAC rate is as 3-Star. Dating back nearly 200 years, but recently done up and extended, this is a comfortable hotel with traditional Scottish hospitality.

The Lovat Hotel, 90–92 Glasgow Road, Perth, tel 0738-36555-7. B&B from £19: categories 6,5,5: 35 bedrooms en suite. The AA and RAC rate is as 3-Star. Comfortable with friendly service and good food.

The Queens Hotel, 105 Leonard Street, Perth, tel 0738-25471. B&B from £15: categories 4,5,5: 68 bedrooms, 34 en suite. A modern monstrosity to look at, but comfortable.

The Salutation Hotel, 34 South Street, Perth, tel 0738-22166. B&B from £14.50: categories 5,5,5: 66 bedrooms, 58 en suite. Dating from 1699, this should attract the seekers after history. Prince Charlie made his headquarters here in 1745, in a room you can still see (though there are a few more facilities than in his day). There is a marvellous Adam window in the dining room, complete with a fan light and pillars.

Murrayshall Hotel (and Golf Course), Montague, Scone, tel 0738-51171. B&B from £17.50: categories 6,5,5: 22 bedrooms en suite. Very nice country house hotel in 400 acres (160 ha), with its own 18 hole golf course. The AA and RAC rate it as 3-Star. Fishing and shooting can be arranged.

Ballathie House Hotel, Kinclaven, near Perth, tel 025083-268. B&B from £32: categories 5,4,5: 33 bedrooms en suite. A Baronial style mansion. The AA and RAC rate it as 3-Star. Overlooking the Tay with salmon and trout fishing on the estate. You can sleep in a four poster bed and picture yourself back in the good old days, though there is plenty of modern comfort.

EATING OUT

You could do a lot worse than to eat in some of the hotels listed above, see especially The Ballathie House Hotel, Murrayshall and Balcraig House. All will give you good food. Dinner from about £12.

Croftbank Hotel, 30 Station Road, Kinross, tel 0577-63819. Scottish and international dishes with fresh local ingredients. Dinner from £10.

Rockdale Guest House, Bridge of Earn, tel 0738-812281. Traditional Scottish food. Dinner from £5.

The Coach House Restaurant, North Port, Perth, tel 0738-27950. Has some imaginative dishes: try the breasts of pigeon with mushroom mousse and port and juniper sauce, or noisettes of venison and wild duck, or terrine of scallops. Dinner from £10.

Timothy's, 24 St John's Street, Perth, tel 0738-26641. An informal, relaxed place, half Scottish, half Danish, Recommended by the Good Food Guide, Egon Ronay and Michelin. Dinner from £6.

Patrick's Wine Bar, in Speygate, near the centre of Perth, tel 0738-20539. Consists of the old wine cellars, all stone and wood, very atmospheric with nice, cheap food—burgers, salads, etc, from £5.

North-east from Perth along the Tayside coast

The coastal plain consists of gently rolling farmland in the **Carse of Gowrie**, running back up into the Sidlaw hills where winter can linger into spring, and from whose southern slopes you get magnificent views across the Firth of Tay to northern Fife.

Dundee

Dundee is the fourth largest town in Scotland, 22 miles (35 km) north-east of Perth on the Firth of Tay. Although the history of the town goes way back, there is little to show for it architecturally: what was not destroyed by the English and by the Reformation, the Dundonians have replaced, in the name of modernisation and progress.

Traces of Bronze Age settlements have been found locally, and the many Pictish stones that can still be seen today underline the importance of this area in the Dark Ages. There are the remains of a Roman hillfort on **Dundee Law**, just north of the city centre, and the town was always a busy port. Kenneth Macalpine used it as his headquarters in 834, when he was campaigning for the union of Picts and Scots, and later, in 1190, William the Lion granted it a royal charter.

Fickle in their loyalties, the Dundonians swung between the Jacobite and the Hanoverian causes, conferring the Freedom of the Burgh on Butcher Cumberland after his victory at Culloden. Hereford pounded the town for Henry VIII, during the "Rough Wooing", Montrose stormed it in 1645 during the Civil War and General Monk occupied it in 1651. It was the first town in Scotland to adopt the reformed religion, and it took George Wishart as its paragon, suffering badly as a result, when he was burned at the stake in 1546.

William Wallace went to school in Dundee, which claims, in competition with Lanark, that here was the scene of his tangle with authority that resulted in his being outlawed.

The jute industry, helped by whale oil from a flourishing whaling fleet, flourished in the early 19th century and Dundee became a "boom-town", with factories and tenements shooting up like mushrooms. This prosperity lasted for 100 years until India learnt to develop her raw jute and materials became scarce. Jute still plays a part in the economy but industry has been widely diversified in recent years and includes oil-related enterprises.

The Dundee Highland Games are in July as is the Dundee Water Festival.

WHAT TO SEE

There are three city churches under one roof, just west of City Square, forming a large, cruciform building surrounded on three sides by a pedestrian shopping precinct. The Old Steeple, or St Mary's Tower, is 15th century, the only part that remains of the pre-Reformation church that stood here since the 12th century.

The Howf (meeting-place) is north-west of the square. It was once the orchard of the Greyfriars Monastery, founded in the 13th century. Mary, Queen of Scots gave the land to the city and it became a burial ground. If you wander through it now you can still see a number of quaint old gravestones with curious inscriptions.

The Albert Institute (open daily, except on Sundays: admission free) in Albert St north of City Square, is the **Central Museum and Art Gallery** where you can find local history, archaeology, and a guide to the development of the town. The art gallery contains work by Flemish, Dutch, French and British artists with some lovely Scottish paintings.

The Barrack Street Museum (open daily, except on Sundays: admission free) lies further west, along Meadowside. This museum concentrates on ecology and shipping.

Balgay Hill is one among Dundee's 28 public parks and gardens. It lies north-west of City Square with the **Mills Observatory** on top (open all year, daily except Sundays: admission, a small fee). Here you can look through telescopes and get marvellous close-up views of the surrounding area.

Camperdown Park further north-west, was opened by the Queen in 1946, when she was still Princess Elizabeth. It consists of 600 acres (240 ha) of lovely trees, a golf course, a children's zoo and Camperdown House, and is home of the **Spalding Golf Museum**, where you can trace the history of the game.

Claypotts Castle

Claypotts Castle (open daily in the summer: adults 50p, children 25p) is in the eastern suburbs of Dundee, in a modern housing development just off the busy junction of A92 and B978. It is one of the few castles in Scotland to remain unaltered since it was built in the 16th century. It is a Z-plan tower house, four-storied, with two round towers, crow-stepped gables, tiny windows, massive stonework and parapet walks. Incongruous as the setting now is, the castle somehow manages to retain a splendid dignity, shrugging off the clutter of modern suburbia that sprawls at its feet. It belonged to the Grahams of Claverhouse and was given to the Douglas family after the famous "Bonnie Dundee" Earl of Claverhouse was killed at the Battle of Killiecranke. Keep an eye out for the ghost that haunts its chambers, the vengeful spirit of a hard-working maid servant who was unfairly deposed by a jealous rival.

Broughty Ferry and Castle

Broughty Ferry is on the coast road four miles (6.4 km) to the east, with imposing Broughty Castle (open daily except Fridays and Sundays: admission free) standing on a rocky promontory, towering over a tiny harbour that dries out at low tide. Built in the 15th century on the site of a Pictish fort, it had a commanding position guarding the entrance to the Firth, from which to levy tolls from ships wanting to come up the river. The Gray family who owned the castle also controlled the ferry that linked Broughty with Fife. The fourth Lord Gray sided with the English during the "Rough Wooing", and allowed English troops to occupy this strategic stronghold for three years until the French managed to recapture it for the Scots, in 1550. Extensively restored in 1860, it is now a museum devoted mainly to the whaling industry that once flourished along this coast, and to the ecology of the Tay.

Although the fishing fleet has long vanished from Broughty Ferry, a number of the fisher cottages remain and you can still sense the seafaring history of the community, in the narrow wynds and courtyards off Fisher Street. It is easy to imagine the old fisher-folk mending their nets on the shore, their boats drawn up above the tide on the beach.

Broughty Ferry still mourns the tragic loss of its lifeboat *Mona* in 1959, with her crew of eight brave men, stranded and capsized on nearby Budden Sands in one of the ferocious gales that sweep this coast.

The beach stretches away to the east in a long crescent of sand. You can water-ski here and there is plenty of sailing and windsurfing on the Firth.

Carnoustie

Carnoustie, ten miles (16 km) east of Dundee, is a holiday resort and golf centre, with a championship course. Right on the sea, the town is a popular place in summer with its own musical society, plenty of holiday activities and a conference centre which seats 500 people. Campers will find an attractive caravan site among trees in the grounds of Carnoustie House.

Ardestie and Carlungie

Anyone interested in archaeology should go two miles (3.2 km) inland from Broughty Ferry, to Ardestie, on the A92, and Carlungie, a mile (1.6 km) to the north. Ancient Monument signs will show the way to two very well preserved "souterrains". These underground earthhouses, once covered by stone roofs, have chambers and passages which were the byres and silos of Pictish farmers in the 1st and 2nd centuries. It is thought they did not live in these souterrains, but nothing is certain about the Picts and it is likely that they may have used them as places of refuge. It is strange to stand among these ancient ruins and think of those men, so long ago, busy about their fields and their cattle as their descendants are today, 1,800 years later.

Monikie

At Monikie, five miles (8 km) north of Broughty Ferry, there is a country park round the reservoir, with attractive walks, boating and picnic sites. You get splendid views from up here, down over fertile farmland to the distant coast where the constantly shifting sandbanks have claimed many ships over the centuries. The trees on the ridge above are sculpted into curious wedge shapes by the strong prevailing wind.

TOURIST INFORMATION
Nethergate Centre, Dundee, tel 0382-27723. It is open all year.

WHERE TO STAY
The Angus Thistle Hotel, 101 Marketgait, Dundee, tel 0382-26874. B&B from £19: 58 bedrooms en suite. If you want to indulge yourself you can spend £50 on an "Executive" B&B with four poster bed, whirlpool bath, private suite, etc. The outside of the Angus is extremely modern, but it is comfortable if you like everything ultra convenient and the food is good.

Cambustay Hotel, 2 Dalgleish Road, Dundee, tel 0382-79290. B&B from £18: 7 bedrooms. A family hotel in its own grounds, overlooking the Tay, four miles (6.4 km) from the middle of Dundee.

Taycreggan Hotel, 4 Ellieslea Road, West Ferry, Dundee, tel 0382-78626. B&B from £16: 10 bedrooms, 4 en suite. A Victorian mansion house overlooking the Tay with self-catering cottages in the grounds.

Invercarse Hotel, Perth Road, Ninewells, Dundee, tel 0382-69231. B&B from £17: 41 rooms, 29 en suite. In its own grounds on the outskirts of the city, with views across the Tay, it is comfortable and the food is good.

Tay Hotel, Whitehall Crescent, Dundee, tel 0382-21641. B&B from £27: 87 bedrooms, 30 en suite. Convenient for the middle of Dundee, the hotel has Jaspers Nite Club, open till 2 am at weekends.

EATING OUT

You will get a good dinner in any of the hotels above, from about £10.

Miguel's, 130 Gray Street, Broughty Ferry, tel 0382-730201. A Continental atmosphere and good food. Dinner from £6. Or just next door in 126 Gray Street, is **Boccachos Pizzeria**, under the same management.

Fat Sam's Night Club, Discotheque, Diner, 31 South Ward Road, Dundee, tel 0382-26836. Runs all sorts of special events, such as Fat Sam's Cocktail Night, with cocktails at half price all night. Take your ear-plugs.

Arbroath

Arbroath is 17 miles (27 km) north-east of Dundee. The massive ruin of the red sandstone abbey rises up from the heart of the town, surrounded by lawns and flower-beds, the hub of a thriving holiday resort and fishing centre. The Declaration of Independence was signed in the abbey in 1320 after Robert Bruce's victory at Bannockburn, establishing Scotland's independence from England.

Perhaps Arbroath is best known now as the home of the "smokie", haddock, smoked over wood-chip fires in the backyards of the fishertown between the harbour and the abbey. Many of the cottages display signs, indicating that they sell the freshly smoked fish, and anyone who has not tried an Arbroath smokie should do so. One of the nicest ways to eat them is cold, with brown bread and butter, and plenty of lemon juice and black pepper.

SPECIAL ATTRACTIONS

Arbroath Highland games are in July and there is also a Donkey Derby that month. The Flower Show is a colourful event in August and there is a Festival of Highland Dancing in September.

WHAT TO SEE

Arbroath Abbey (open standard Ancient Monument times: adults 50p, children 25p) was founded by William the Lion in 1178 and dedicated to Thomas à Becket who had recently been murdered in Canterbury Cathedral. You can see William's tomb in the sacristy. The abbey managed to survive the Reformation until 1606, when it was made a temporal lordship. Its final decay was due to neglect rather than vandalism or deliberate destruction. Parts of the ruin date from the 13th century, including the gable of the south transept and the west façade with its tower and entrance. They used to put lamps in the round window that you can see high above the south transept, as a landmark for ships at sea. The abbot's house is now the **Museum** where you get a good idea of the domestic life of the religious community, as well as see a collection of Scottish medieval art.

Signal Tower (open daily except Sundays: admission free) is a museum with exhibitions of local interest. As well, there is an **Art gallery**, in the library, which has works by Breughel as well as a good variety of Scottish paintings.

Whiting Ness, north of the wide promenade, is worth a visit on a fine day. Take the path up on to the cliff. You can walk for miles along the cliff top, with the sea pounding restlessly at the redstone rocks below, honeycombed with caves and deep inlets. Wild flowers cling to the steep slopes and the cries of curlews and oyster catchers can be heard over the booming sea. From the narrow path you get marvellous views out to sea, always dotted with ships and trawlers, oil tankers, coasters and small boats. If the visibility is good you should be able to see the **Bell Rock Lighthouse**, 12 miles (19 km) out to the east and familiar to anyone who learnt Southey's *The Ballad of the Inchcape Rock* at school. The Abbot of Arbroath fixed a warning bell on the hazardous rock, to warn off mariners. Sir Ralph the Rover, a notorious pirate with a grudge against the abbot, cut the bell adrift to spite him. Later, returning home in a fog, the pirate was wrecked on the rock!

Auchmithie

The cliff path takes you to Auchmithie, three miles (4.8 km) to the north. It is referred to as Musselcraig, in Walter Scott's *The Antiquary* and is an ancient, picturesque village believed to have flourished in the 11th century. It is built on a rocky ridge above its tiny harbour, a flat chequerboard of farmland stretching away inland. The caves that you can find up and down this coast were much used by smugglers in the 18th century.

St Vigeans

As you come out of Arbroath going north on the A92, take the road signposted to St Vigeans, on the left. It is less than a mile (1.6 km) and you have to park at the rail bridge and cross the Brothock Burn by footbridge to discover the little gem of a hamlet, nestling out of sight below modern housing developments. A small red sandstone church is perched on top of a steep mound, 40 ft (12 m) high, like an upturned basin, neatly kept and studded with gravestones. Extensive restoration conceals the 12th-century origins of the kirk, but you can find traces inside.

A row of pretty red sandstone cottages with stone-slabbed roofs forms a semi-circle at the foot of the mound, and in one of these is the fascinating **St Vigeans Museum** (open standard Ancient Monument times: admission free). Here you can see a well-displayed and comprehensively explained collection of Pictish and Celtic stones. The Drosten Stone has an inscription in the Pictish language, suggesting that the Picts were more literate than is often supposed. Even if archaeology bores you stiff, you will find that you become more and more intrigued as you examine the intricate carvings on these ancient stones, and read the descriptions: they quickly become more than "just a few more old stones".

Redcastle

Redcastle (open at all times) is seven miles (11 km) up the coast. A 15th-century ruin jutting out on a cliff high above the sea, it dominates the sandy crescent of **Lunan Bay** below. To reach it you have to climb up a short, steepish path through trees and whins. The castle was built on the site of an old fort, to protect the coast from Danish pirates, and William the Lion lived here while he was building Arbroath Abbey. It witnessed several battles and was partly demolished during one that sprang from a feud between its occupant, Lady Invermeith, and her divorced husband, James Gray.

Montrose

Montrose is 14 miles (22.5 km) north of Arbroath, not far from the Grampian border and is almost on an island. It has sea to the east, the **River South Esk** to the south, and a wide tidal basin to the west. There is an airy, spacious feeling about the town, the middle section of its High Street being as wide as a market square. Houses built gable-end-on to the street, lead through to narrow closes and secret courtyards.

Records tell of the Danish invasion of Montrose in 980. The castle that once guarded the town was taken over by Edward I in 1296 and destroyed by William Wallace a year later. It was from here that Sir James Douglas embarked, carrying the heart of Robert the Bruce, on its abortive pilgrimage to the Holy Land (see Dunfermline and Melrose). In 1715, the first of the Jacobite rebellions ended ignominiously in Montrose when the Old Pretender set sail back to France from here. James Graham, the famous, brave, tragic Marquess of Montrose was born in Old Montrose on the south side of the tidal basin.

A tenth of the world's population of pink-footed geese migrate to Montrose's tidal basin every November, from their Arctic breeding grounds. This great wild fowl sanctuary is a marvellous place in winter when you can hear the ceaseless grumble and chatter of the birds as they feed on the mud flats, the sound of their cries haunting the air as they circle in from the sky. It is remarkable to find such a wild haven so close to the bustling town with its docks and shipping, its sturdy buildings and oil-related prosperity.

A profitable slave trade flourished briefly in Montrose, and smuggling was a thriving activity in the 18th century. Because of its out-of-the-way situation, and a shortage of customs officers, the strongly Jacobite population had no conscience about defrauding a Hanoverian government of its income from excise duty. The words "Mare Mitat" (the sea enriches) are aptly inscribed on the Montrose coat of arms. The undulating countryside supports several good golf courses and there is good holiday accommodation around Montrose. In July the town holds its Rose Queen ceremony and in August there is a flower show and a Highland Games.

TOURIST INFORMATION
Market Place, Arbroath, tel 0241-72609/76680. It is open all year.
Montrose, tel 0674-72000. It is open all year.
Carnoustie, tel 0241-52258. It is open all year.

WHERE TO STAY
Hotel Seaforth, Dundee Road, Arbroath, tel 0241-72232. B&B from £17: categories 4,4,5: 20 bedrooms, 11 en suite. Comfortable and friendly.

Lethan Grange Hotel, Colliston, near Arbroath, tel 0241-89 373. B&B from £17: categories 6,5,5: 20 bedrooms en suite. Friendly service in a relaxed atmosphere.

Central Hotel, High Street, Montrose, tel 0674-72152. B&B from £13: categories 3,3,4: 20 bedrooms, 1 en suite.

Links Hotel, Mid Links, Montrose, tel 0674-72288. B&B from £23: 25 bedrooms, 18 en suite.

Park Hotel, John Street, Montrose, tel 0674-73415. B&B from £15: categories 5,6,5: 59 bedrooms, 52 en suite.

EATING OUT
The hotels above will all give you a reasonable meal from about £6. Park Hotel specialises in Scottish food with fresh local ingredients. Dinner from £7.50.

Inland, from Montrose to Perth

Brechin

Nine miles (14 km) west of Montrose is the attractive town of Brechin, sprawled up a steep bank above the River South Esk in the fertile Strathmore farmland.

You can get a good picture of the local history in a small museum in the library.

WHAT TO SEE
The Cathedral and Tower (open at all times: admission free) are the focal points of this ancient town. These red sandstone buildings are perched above the town's twisting wynds, little courtyards and houses built gable-end-on to the road. The tapering tower, restored in 1960, is one of only two such towers in Scotland, the other being in Abernethy. (It is a curious coincidence that Malcolm Canmore was forced to acknowledge the sovereignty of William the Conqueror at Abernethy, in 1072, and the weak John Balliol was forced to renounce his crown to Edward I in 1296, near Brechin, as if the two round towers have survived as monuments to two unhappy events.) Dating from 990, you will see that the tower's door is 6 ft (1.8 m) above the ground, giving the inhabitants greater security. The feet of the crucified Christ, carved on the lintel, are uncrossed, indicating an Irish influence in the design. (There are 76 of these towers in Ireland today.)

Now a parish church, the cathedral dates from the 13th century and was restored in 1900. You can see some Pictish stones inside with interesting carvings on them; a 16th-century font and 17th century pewter and silver.

Maison Dieu, off Market Street, is a single wall with a pointed, arched door, three narrow windows and a piscina—all that remains of an almshouse, hospice and chapel that were founded in 1256.

Edzell

From Brechin, go six miles (9.6 km) north on the B966 to Edzell, in the pretty valley of the **River North Esk**. Here you will see the ruin of 16th-century **Edzell Castle** (open standard Ancient Monument times except Tuesday and Thursday afternoons: adults 50p, children 25p). The castle forms a splendid red backdrop to the **Pleasance**, a walled garden that was designed by David Lindsay, Lord Edzell in 1604. This immaculate formal garden, modelled on the gardens at Nuremburg, has flower filled recesses in the walls, whose intricate heraldic decorations conceal gun loops.

A beautifully kept box hedge, bordering rose beds, has been clipped to spell out the Lindsay family motto: "dum spiro spero" (while I breath, I hope). The foundations of a bath house were excavated in the corner of the garden in 1855, revealing a bath and a dressing and reclining room with a fireplace.

Mary, Queen of Scots held a council in the castle in 1562 and it was garrisoned by Cromwell's troops in 1651. A grisly story is told of a curse, put on the family of the Lindsays of Edzell by a gypsy after they had caused the hanging of her two dumb sons, for poaching. Lady Crawford died the same day and her husband was torn apart by wolves a year later.

Glenesk Folk Museum

Glenesk Folk Museum (open every afternoon in the summer: adults 50p, children 20p) is ten miles (16 km) north-west of Edzell at Tarfside. It contains a collection of exhibits that give you a good picture of what life was like in this area from about 1800 onwards.

Menmuir

The Caterthuns are 6 miles (9.6 km) south-west of Edzell, at Menmuir. These are two Iron Age hill forts on a ridge, the higher one having spilled its masonry down the hill to mix with the lower. The original enclosing wall must have been as much as 40 ft (12 m) thick. If you follow the lovely wooded valley of West Water from here up into the hills towards Loch Lee, you are following in the footsteps of Macbeth, as he fled from his defeat at Dunsinane.

Finavon Castle

Finavon Castle (open at all times: free) is six miles (9.6 km) south-west of Brechin on the A94. This jagged ruin is overgrown by nettles and scrub. It does not look much of a place now, until you look up at the 86 ft (26 m) tower and think of the day when the notorious Earl Beardie Crawford hanged his minstrel from a hook somewhere at the top. This he did because the wretched minstrel had foretold Earl Beardie's defeat at the Battle of Brechin in 1452. The history of the Lindsay family is full of bloodcurdling stories, and it is for these that the ruin is memorable, rather than for its appearance. →

Finavon Hill

Take the little back road that climbs and twists two miles (3.2 km) south-east from Finavon, up over the hills through rugged scenery of dry stone walls and moorland, where black-faced sheep graze the turf between patches of bracken and gorse. As you come down the far side of the ridge, you will see Finavon Hill to your left. It is a short climb to the top where you will find one of the finest vitrified Iron Age hill forts in the land, in a shallow depression. Its shape and turf-covered ramparts are easily seen, and there is a central spring, or well. Excavations in the 1930s revealed evidence of metal working, pot making, and weaving on this lofty summit with its glorious views up Strathmore to the Mearns and west to Blairgowrie. It is strange, to think of those tough Picts busy up here, striving to exist on the hill top, keen-eyed and ever alert for danger.

Aberlemno

If you are interested in the early settlers, go to Aberlemno, just north of the junction, off the back road from Finavon along B 9134 and six miles (9.6 km) south-west of Brechin. Aberlemno is a tiny hamlet that has four Pictish stones. Three stand beside the road, easy to see from your car. The finest, however, is in the kirkyard. The carvings on this stone, 7 ft (2 m) high, are remarkably clear: a Celtic cross on one side, flanked by intertwined creatures, and a stirring battle scene on the other, all with intricate detail. This stone is believed to mark the grave of a Pictish King Feradach. The little kirk is simple and charming. Inside you will find an 18th-century bible which has dates printed at the top of each page, the date of Genesis being set at 4004 BC!

Restenneth Priory

Restenneth Priory (open at all times: admission free) is five miles (8 km) south-west of Aberlemno, just before you get to Forfar on B9134. The priory stands surrounded by gently sloping meadows and scattered trees, rising from a bowl of marshy ground. It was once on a peninsula jutting into a loch which was drained in the 18th century.

In AD 710, Nechan, High King of the Picts was baptised here by St Boniface. Nechan used Northumbrian masons to build a church in Romanesque style, possibly to celebrate his victory over the king of Northumbria at the Battle of Nechtansmere on Dunnichen Hill nearby (a battle which quelled any further Saxon invasion of this part of Pictland). Then, in the 13th century, Augustinian monks built a priory on the same site, incorporating the original tower. It is a lovely, tranquil place, the mellow old stones rising from green sward. You can almost hear the voices of those far off monks, chanting plain-song, as you stand in the ruined choir. An infant son of Robert Bruce is believed to have been buried here.

Forfar

The busy little town of Forfar has little left to see of its history, but plenty of memories.

Once a thriving jute and linen milling centre it now produces man-made textiles, as well as tartans and tweeds.

The Town and County Hall is early 19th century, designed by William Playfair, with a splendid council chamber in which you can see paintings by Raeburn, Romney, Hoppner and Opie. The town centre is attractive, with cobbled streets swirling round an island on which the town hall stands. Just round the corner in West High Street, is the **Meffan Institute** (open daily except Sundays: admission free), which houses, as well as the library, a small museum of local interest, in which you can see the dreadful Forfar Bridle. This is a metal collar, hinged to clip round the neck, with a prong in front to gag the unfortunate women who wore it while being burned at the stake as witches in the 17th century. **Forfar Loch**, west of the town, is a pleasure park, with picnic areas around the small stretch of water.

Kirriemuir

Kirriemuir, is five miles (8 km) north-west of Forfar. It is an attractive little town on a hillside with a straggle of narrow streets lined by picturesque houses. This jute manufacturing town is best known as the birthplace of J. M. Barrie, who renamed it "Thrums' in a series of novels based on small town life in Scotland. The house where Barrie was born, **9 Brechin Road**, is now maintained by the National Trust for Scotland as a **Museum** (open daily in the summer, or by arrangement, tel Kirriemuir 2646: adults 60p, children 30p). You can browse among manuscripts, letters, personal possessions and mementoes of the writer who belonged to a group that was known as "The Kailyard School" at the end of the 19th century. These Kailyard writers exploited a sentimental and romantic image of small town life in Scotland that brought them a certain amount of contempt by their critics. James Barrie was buried in Kirriemuir churchyard in 1937.

A **Camera Obscura** (open in the summer) lies above the town, where you can see, by an ingenious method of reflection, the whole surrounding area.

Glamis

Glamis (pronounced Glarms) is five miles (8 km) due south of Kirriemuir. This tiny hamlet in a wooded hollow lies just off the main road, where you could easily pass a whole summer's day and not be bored.

WHAT TO SEE

Glamis Castle (open during the summer, afternoons daily except on Saturdays or by appointment, tel Glamis 242: adults £2, children £1) is approached down a wide tree-lined avenue. It is so familiar from photographs that the reality is almost an anti-climax. From the top of the avenue it is a splendid spectacle; the pink–grey castle set against the distant hills, with its mass of angles and towers and wings and turrets, its heraldic embellishments and its air of grandeur rather than of beauty. Queen Elizabeth, the Queen Mother, spent much of her childhood here and her daughter Princess Margaret was born here. (It is well worth getting the excellent guide book.)

The land was granted to the Lyon family, Earls of Strathmore, by King Robert II in

1372, and it was their descendants who became Earls of Glamis, Kinghorne and Strathmore. Glamis has the reputation for being the most haunted castle in Scotland and many are the spine-chilling tales that have been born from its stones. No one dares to enter the sealed crypt where huge red-bearded Beardie Crawford played cards with the Devil on the Sabbath; no one can account for the window that looks out from a chamber that does not exist on an upper floor.

The present castle dates mostly from the 17th century, with bits of the older buildings incorporated, including King Malcolm's room, where Malcolm II is said to have died. The oldest part is Duncan's hall, traditionally the setting for Shakespeare's Macbeth.

When you have had your fill of all the treasures that are to be seen in the castle, go to the tea-room and gift shop at the back. You can stroll in the formal 19th-century Italian gardens, and in the extensive parkland.

The Angus Folk Museum (open daily in the summer and on request: adults 90p, children 40p) is in Kirkwynd, the little village beyond the castle. It is to be found past the Strathmore Arms and a thatched cottage (a rare sight among the pantiles and slates in this area). The museum is in a terrace of picturesque cottages, built at the beginning of the 19th century and meticulously restored by the National trust for Scotland in 1957, with stone-slabbed roofs and flagged floors. There are over 1,000 things to be seen, as well as a kitchen from 1807 with all the original fittings and furnishings. The fascinating journey you can make into the past gives you a delightful picture of how country people lived, up to 200 years ago. There is even a Victorian manse parlour.

The Glamis Stone is in the garden of today's Manse, opposite the museum. This 9 ft (3 m) high stone has intricate Pictish carvings. It is also called King Malcolm's stone, from the belief that Malcolm II was buried here in 1034, having died in the castle. In fact, the stone is of an earlier date, possibly 9th century.

If ancient stones are what you enjoy, you will find plenty more nearby: **St Orland's**, or the Crossans Stone, in a field by the railway two miles (3.2 km) to the north. This stone is 7 ft (2 m) high, slender and repaired, with unusual carvings that include men in a boat.

Reekie Linn

Five miles (8 km) or so north-west of Glamis, at **Bridge of Craigisla**, you can take a footpath through the wood to Reekie Linn, a dramatic waterfall haunted by water sprites, and kelpies. The **River Isla**, constricted by narrow rock cliffs, pours down into a deep gorge in a single cascade, the spray rising like smoke, stirring the dark waters of the river into tumult. The path takes you to a spur jutting out level with the top of the falls. If you suffer from vertigo you should go along to the right and see them from further off!

Barry Hill

Barry Hill is beside the road five miles (8 km) to the south from the falls, just short of

Alyth. It is a short, steep climb through whins and bracken, over turf honeycombed by rabbits, to the top where you will find the ruins of a large Pictish fort in a shallow depression. The oblong shape is very clear with round turrets and ramparts. Romance clings to these stones. If you believe the Scottish versions of the Arthurian legends, Queen Guinevere was imprisoned in this fort by King Arthur, because of her love affair with a Pictish prince. If this was true, the captive queen had some glorious views for miles around to comfort her.

Alyth, below the hill, is a pleasant little milling town bisected by the Alyth Burn.

Meigle

Meigle, three miles (1.8 km) to the south-east, is the legendary burial place for poor faithless Guinevere. It also has the most remarkable collection of early Christian Pictish stones in Scotland. You can see them in the old school, now a small **Museum** (open standard Ancient Monument times, except on Sundays: adults 50p, children 25p). There are 25 stones, from the 6th to the 10th centuries, almost all found in or near the old churchyard. There is an excellent booklet in the museum and no one could fail to be fascinated by the amazing carvings that disprove any idea that the Picts were half-naked savages loping around like ape men. These pictures show elaborate clothing, weapons and equipment, and an unquestionable civilised culture.

Coupar Angus

Coupar Angus, six miles (9.6 km) south-west of Meigle is in the Tay valley. It makes a good centre from which to tour this area, lying, as it does, on the edge of lovely Highland scenery. It is a pleasant little market town, very typical of the area and so called to distinguish it from Cupar Fife.

Only the gatehouse remains of a once flourishing Cistercian abbey, beside the Dundee road. It was built about 1164 by Malcolm IV and destroyed in 1559. The parish church stands on the site of the old monks' chapel and you can still see the remains of the original piers from the nave.

The Tolbooth, built in 1769, has recently been renovated, and the **Museum**, at Cumberland Barracks (open weekdays in the summer: admission free) gives you a good picture of the local history.

Blairgowrie

Blairgowrie, four miles (6.4 km) to the north-west, beside the fast-flowing Ericht Water, is a popular tourist centre all the year round. In summer you can explore the Highlands and in winter you can ski at Glenshee. The extremely fertile soil produces abundant raspberry crops.

Ablair Castle (open by appointment only, tel Blairgowrie 2155: small fee). Built in the 16th century on 12th-century foundations, it was the home of the staunchly Jacobite Oliphant family and you can see many of their Jacobite relics. Lady Carolina Oliphant, born in 1766 and named in honour of Prince Charlie, wrote the well-known song *Charlie is My Darling*. You can walk forever round here, once you discover the magic of the surrounding scenery: fast-flowing rivers slicing their ways through steep mountain glens, with sudden glimpses of snow-capped peaks, massing on the horizon.

Glenshee, runs north from Blairgowrie into the Highland region and is one of Scotland's main skiing centres, its challenging *pistes* often icy and demanding. Weather conditions up here can be extreme, the roads sometimes becoming impassable in snow.

Loch of the Lowes

Going west towards Dunkeld, you pass Loch of the Lowes, seven miles (11 km) from Blairgowrie. This is a nature reserve, where you can watch ospreys from a hide. These birds, so common in America, where you find them nesting on every navigation mark in the estuaries, are a rare, protected species in Britain, though their numbers are increasing slightly now.

Dunkeld

Dunkeld, on the banks of the Tay, ten miles (16 km) west of Blairgowrie, is a serene, lovely old cathedral town, small and sheltered by wooded mountains. Its history goes back to early times when it was a refuge for Pictish kings. Being close to the ancient capital of Scone, Dunkeld became a stronghold of Columban monks who founded an abbey here in 729, having been driven from Iona by Norsemen. They enshrined holy relics of St Columba in their abbey. The saint himself is believed to have come to Dunkeld in the 6th century, and to have founded some sort of religious establishment with the help of St Mungo. There is a St Colms Well nearby.

Dunkeld suffered badly during the bitter Covenanting wars and it was here that the Cameronians, extreme Covenanters, held the town against a troop of Highlanders in 1689. Triumphant after Killiecrankie, the Highlanders stormed the town, whereupon the Cameronians set fire to most of its buildings, driving the Highlanders out and securing eventual supremacy for William and Mary.

Dunkeld Cathedral (open standard Ancient Monument times: admission free) is a substantial ruin in a beautiful setting beside the River Tay. The choir has been restored and is the parish church. The nave and great north-west tower date from the 15th century and the original medieval cathedral, which took two centuries to build, was only entire for about 60 years before the reformers reduced it to a roofless ruin. Ironically, it contains the rather splendid tomb and effigy of the Wolf of Badenoch, who was a keen destroyer of churches, Elgin Cathedral included amongst them.

The Little Houses, lining Cathedral Street, were built after the destruction of the town in 1689, and were saved from demolition by the National Trust for Scotland, in 1950. Beautifully restored and privately occupied, they form a delightful approach to the cathedral and give the old part of the town a unique character.

Dunkeld is the sort of town that you want to stroll about in, on a fine day. It seems to exude a feeling of the past. If you are a fisherman, the Tay will give you some of the best salmon fishing in the world. The Scottish Tourist Board have brought out a Perthshire Fishing Guide, for 50p, which will give you all the information you want. It is available at local tourist information offices.

Birnam

Birnam, a mile (1.6 km) south of Dunkeld, is a village that must be familiar to all students of Shakespeare. If you climb **Birnam Hill** you can see **Dunsinane**, 12 miles (19 km) to the south-east. Thus you can picture that day when Macbeth sat in his castle on Dunsinane Hill, confident that he was immortal until "... Birnam Wood shall walk to Dunsinane..." while Malcolm was busy instructing his soldiers to cut down branches from the trees in Birnam Wood, to disguise themselves as they marched on Dunsinane. Some of the trees in Birnam Wood are thought to date from the original forest.

The A9, by-passing Dunkeld, takes you 15 miles (24 km) back to Perth, or northwards.

TOURIST INFORMATION

Montrose, 212 High Street, tel 0674-72000. It is open all year.

Forfar, The Myre, tel 0307-67876. It is open June to September.

Brechin, St Ninian's Square, tel 03562-3050. It is open June to September.

Kirriemuir, Bank Street, tel 0575-74097. It is open June to September.

Blairgowrie, Wellmeadow, tel 0250-2960 (or 2258 when closed). It is open from Easter to mid October.

Dunkeld, The Cross, tel 035-02 688. It is open Easter to October.

SKIING INFORMATION

Glenshee Information Officer, Blairgowrie, tel 0250-5509.

WHERE TO STAY

Apart from the places mentioned here see also the next "Where to stay" section.

The choice in this popular area is enormous and you should look at the tourist brochure for full details and descriptions. The following is just a small, random selection.

Northern Hotel, 2 Clerk Street, Brechin, tel 03562-2156. B&B from £17: categories 4,4,5: 17 bedrooms, 15 en suite.

Royal Hotel, Castle Street, Forfar, tel 0307-62691. B&B from £28: categories 5,4,4: 12 bedrooms, 9 en suite.

Queens Hotel, The Cross, Forfar, tel 0307-62533. B&B from £12: 28 bedrooms, 6 en suite.

Ogilvy Arms Hotel, 6/7 High Street, Kirriemuir, tel 0575-72697. B&B from £10: categories 3,3,5: 10 bedrooms

Kings of Kinloch Hotel, Meigle, tel 08284-273. B&B from £20: categories 3,3,4: 7 bedrooms, 2 en suite.

Altamount House Hotel, Coupar Angus Road, Blairgowrie, tel 0250-3512. B&B from £22.50: categories 5,3,4: 7 bedrooms en suite. A country house hotel. The AA and RAC rate it as 2-Star.

Royal Dunkeld Hotel, Atholl Street, Dunkeld, tel 03502-322. B&B from £6: categories 6,5,6: 33 bedrooms, 12 en suite.

EATING OUT
All the hotels above will give you a reasonable meal, starting at about £6 for dinner. The Altamount House Hotel, in Blairgowrie, has food recommended by the BTA. Dinner from £10.

The Old Mansion House Hotel, Auchterhouse, tel 082626-366/8. Traditional Scottish food using fresh local ingredients. Dinner from about £10.

Glamis Castle Tearoom is open during castle opening times. Well worth a visit. It is in the old castle kitchen, complete with black iron stoves and copper pots. Nice home made soups, sausage rolls, shortbread, etc.

LOCAL SPECIALITY
Mrs MacDonald, Rattray, Blairgowrie. You can't miss the shop, which flies a Swiss flag outside. Switzerland means cheese and chocolate, and Mrs MacDonald can sell you the very best of both.

Tayside: north-west of the A9

Pitlochry

Pitlochry, 13 miles (21 km) north of Dunkeld, is in the middle of Scotland. It has been a popular holiday town since Victorian days. Until General Wade built his network of military roads, after the Jacobite uprisings, linking up the trouble-spots in the Highlands, there was no road north of Dunkeld and Pitlochry was a tiny hamlet. Now, in spite of its popularity, it manages to retain a leisurely, strolling atmosphere, a perfect centre from which to explore the Highlands, in a lovely setting sheltered by hills, where the rivers Tay, Tummel and Garry all converge from their beautiful valleys. The main street is cheerful with its bright façades, hotels and shops, woollen mills, distillery and hydroelectric development.

WHAT TO SEE
The Pitlochry Festival Theatre was founded in 1951. Its lively summer programme includes drama, concerts and variety shows and you can also see exhibitions of Scottish art.

The Hydroelectric development has an observation chamber where you can see its ingenious method of ensuring that the salmon cycle is not broken. Thousands of salmon are "lifted" annually and you can watch them through glass walls. If you look carefully you can often see the water leeches clinging to the fish. There is also a hydroelectric exhibition, giving you an excellent description of all the activities throughout the country and in the Loch Tummel group in particular. Few purists can deny that the hydroelectric schemes often enhance rather than spoil the Highland scenery.

Walking in this area is endlessly rewarding, every path you choose uncovering fresh beauty and unexpected views. There are waterfalls and gorges, festooned with lush ferns; woods and hills; rivers running fast over shallow rocky beds.

Pass of Killiecrankie

The road north from Pitlochry climbs along the upper slope of the Pass of Killiecrankie, a recently opened section of road that cost a great deal of money and took considerable skill to engineer. It clings precariously to the densely wooded gorge where, far below, the River Garry cuts its way through to join up with the Tummel. At the far end of the pass about three miles (4.8 km) from Pitlochry, there is a National Trust for Scotland Visitor Centre (open daily in the summer: admission 10p) where you can see a pictorial description of the history of the Battle of Killiecrankie. Graham of Claverhouse ("Bonnie Dundee") and his brave Jacobite Highlanders, charged the English army under General Mackay, in 1689, in an attempt to depose William of Orange and restore James VII/II to the Scottish throne. The English were almost annihilated by the wild Highlanders, but Claverhouse was mortally wounded and his death, leaving his army without a leader, ensured the subsequent victory of the government troops, three weeks later at Dunkeld.

You can walk down to the river from the visitor centre, past the horrifying **Soldier's Leap**, an 18 ft (5.4 m) jump across the gorge, said to have been made by one of Mackay's soldiers, escaping from the Highlanders. Queen Victoria walked along this path and noted its great beauty in her diary, in 1844.

Blair Atholl

Three miles (4.8 km) north of Killiecrankie, the new road by-passes the village of Blair Atholl and gives you a very good view of **Blair Castle** from across the river. This white, turreted Baronial castle (open daily in the summer: adults £2.20, children £1.20) is the home of the Duke of Atholl, dating from 1269. It has seen many royal visitors: Mary, Queen of Scots stayed here; Prince Charlie accepted hospitality here on his march south in 1745; Cumberland garrisoned his troops here the following year, during which time the Duke of Atholl's brother, Lord George Murray, inflicted severe damage on the castle in his attempts to win it back; Claverhouse stayed here before the Battle of Killiecrankie and it was here that his body lay after the battle.

Queen Victoria visited the castle in 1844 and granted the Duke of Atholl the privilege of being the only British subject allowed to retain a private army, The Atholl Highlanders.

The interior gives you a good idea of what castle life must have been like in the old days, and you can see a vast range of valuable and interesting things that range from arms and armour, to Jacobite relics, china, tapestry, toys, furniture, lace and marvellous paintings (including portraits by Lely, Ramsay and Raeburn). There is even a natural history museum.

North-east of Blair Atholl you will find good walking and climbing country, over moor and scree, with lovely views.

The Bruar Falls

The Bruar Falls are well-signposted, about three miles (4.8 km) west of Blair Atholl and you can park by the road. A short walk takes you up to the falls, where the River

Bruar cascades down through rocky chasms and over great gleaming slabs of granite. Robert Burns came here and was so annoyed by its lack of trees that he wrote "The Humble Petition of Bruar Water", a plea that found its mark and inspired the fourth Duke of Atholl to plant fir trees on the land.

Lochs Tummel and Rannoch

If you take the B8019 west from Pitlochry you find yourself humming Harry Lauder's famous song *The road to the isles*: "... by Loch Tummel and Loch Rannoch and Lochaber I will go..." and you can do a lovely round tour of about 65 miles (104 km): out to **Rannoch Station** on the northern side of the two lochs Tummel and Rannoch to where the road ends, and back along the south side. There is beautiful scenery all the way, with views out between the trees, dominated by the great cone of **Shiehallion** in the south and the lonely wasteland of **Rannoch Moor** stretching away to the west. Loch Tummel is less dramatic than Loch Rannoch, its gentler scenery re-shaped by the hydroelectric development.

Queen's View, two miles (3.2 km) up from the dam, was so called before Queen Victoria visited it in 1866. Perhaps Mary, Queen of Scots also stood on the promontory and looked down to the water, glinting in the sunlight, far below.

The Loch Tummel Forest Centre (open daily in the summer: admission free) at the south-east corner of the loch will tell you anything you want to know about the area, and what places of interest it has to offer. It will tell you, for instance, how to find the **Black Wood**, south of Loch Rannoch, where you can see part of the remains of the old Caledonian Forest.

Harry Lauder must have taken to the moors, when he was "... walking with his crummock to the isles ..." because the road ends at Rannoch Station, appropriately on the border with the Highland region.

TOURIST INFORMATION
Pitlochry, tel 0796–2215/2751. It is open all year.

WHERE TO STAY
Once again the choice is endless and you should look in the tourist brochure for full details and descriptions. The following is just a small random selection.

Acarsaid Hotel, Atholl Road, Pitlochry, tel 0796-2389. B&B from £16: categories 4,4,4: 19 bedrooms, 18 en suite.

Atholl Palace Hotel, Atholl Road, Pitlochry, tel 0796-2400. B&B from £30: categories 5,5,5: 84 bedrooms en suite. The AA and RAC rate it as 3-Star. A chateau style mansion in wooded parkland with swimming pool, tennis courts, pitch and putt, nature trail, snooker, games room, day nursery, cinema, sauna, solarium and gym.

Pitlochry Hydro Hotel, Knockard Road, Pitlochry, tel 0796-2666. B&B from £25: categories 5,4,4: 63 bedrooms, 59 en suite. The AA and RAC rate it as 3-Star. A large hotel in its own grounds with tennis courts, overlooking the town.

Loch Rannoch Hotel, Kinloch, Rannoch, tel 088-22-201. B&B from £15: categories, 6,5,6: 13 bedrooms en suite. In 250 acres (100 ha) of lovely grounds beside the loch, the hotel has pretty well every sort of facility to offer: indoor pool, jacuzzi, sauna, solarium, steam bath, squash, tennis, sailing, windsurfing, canoeing, dry-ski slope, snooker, bicycles, fishing. Live entertainment and Highland evenings.

Dalmunzie House Hotel, Glenshee, tel 025-085 224. B&B from £22: 16 bedrooms, 9 en suite. Known as "The Hotel in the Hills" the house is in 6,000 acres (2,400 ha) of lovely Highland scenery, with a 9 hole golf course, tennis courts, fishing. Shooting and stalking can be arranged. Very comfortable with cosy log fires and good Scottish cooking.

Killiecrankie Hotel, Killiecrankie, tel 0796-3220. B&B from £19.60: categories 4,4,4: 12 bedrooms, 10 en suite. The house used to be a dower house*, in lovely grounds in the Pass of Killiecrankie. Good Scottish food and a friendly welcome.

EATING OUT

The hotels above all give good Scottish meals, in this part of the country, and you can usually eat well from about £8 to £10 and upwards.

Blair Castle has a restaurant, in the castle, where you can have lunch. You can also arrange private lunches and dinners here if you want to impress your friends. Lunches from £5.

Auchnahyle Farm, Tomcroy, Pitlochry, tel 0796-2318. Has its own quail and quails eggs as well as a lot of good local food. It is essential to book. Dinner from £10.

Tayside: south-west of the A9

Five miles (8 km) south of Pitlochry, the A827 takes you 10 miles (16 km) westwards, to Aberfeldy, and then out to Loch Tay through lovely Strath Tay.

Aberfeldy

Aberfeldy is another good centre from which to explore the Highlands. The little town stands on the Urlar Burn at its confluence with the River Tay. Robert Burns poem "The Birks of Aberfeldy" refer to the silver birches which you see beside the burn.

WHAT TO SEE

The bridge over the Tay, at Aberfeldy, was built by General Wade in 1733 and is said to be the best of the many he was responsible for during his arduous task of trying to link up all the remote trouble-spots in the Highlands during the Jacobite uprisings.

The Black Watch Monument is at the south end of the bridge. Here you will see a kilted soldier, erected in 1887 to commemorate the raising of the Black Watch by General Wade in 1739.

The Oatmeal Mill (open Monday to Friday: admission free) in Mill Street, demonstrates the process of milling raw grain into oatmeal. You can buy the finished products.

Castle Menzies

Castle Menzies (pronounced Mingies) (open daily during the summer: adults £1, chil-

* A house set apart for the use of a widow, often on her deceased husband's estate.

dren 30p), a mile (1.6 km) west of Aberfeldy, stands in a field against a wooded backdrop. It is a 16th-century, Z-plan fortified tower house, with carved gables over its dormers. The castle has been well restored after centuries of neglect. It belongs to the Clan Menzies Society and houses their Clan Museum.

Loch Tay

Loch Tay is five miles (8 km) west of Aberfeldy. This long, dark snake of water is bordered by several private estates.

Kenmore, at the head of the loch, was built for estate workers in 1760, by the fourth Earl of Breadalbane. Here you can hire boats for fishing on Loch Tay.

Fortingall, two miles (3.2 km) to the north-west, has the yew tree in the churchyard which is said to be over 3,000 years old. This delightful little village has a single street of cottages, some thatched, and an intriguing tradition that goes back to the lifetime of Christ. Some say that Pontius Pilate was born here, son of a Roman officer who had been sent on a peace mission to the Pictish King Metallanus, who lived in Dun Geal, a fort on the steep, rocky hill behind the village. True or not, it adds romance to an already enchanted spot.

You can see, but not visit, **Glenlyon House**, west of Fortingall. Parts of it date from the days when it was the home of Campbell of Glenlyon, the man who enacted the Massacre of Glencoe. You should park your car if you have time. This is walking and climbing country.

Amulree

Amulree is ten miles (16 km) south of Aberfeldy. This was an important meeting point for the old drover routes from the north, east and west, and you can picture those wild Highland men, meeting up to exchange news and banter, their flocks and herds filling the air with their noise.

The Sma' Glen

The Sma' Glen is the moorland valley, down which the A822 descends from Aberfeldy to Crieff, a famous beauty spot where the hills rise steeply to about 2,000 ft (610 m) on either side. This is another place that is best explored on foot, at a leisurely pace. It follows the River Almond as it thunders down over rapids and falls, with salmon leaping in September and October.

After Newton, look out on the left of the road for **Ossian's Stone**, said to mark the grave of Ossian. The stone was in fact moved to its present position by General Wade's road builders, when it blocked the path of one of their roads. Traces of a pre-historic burial, found when they lifted the stone, were given a re-burial in a secret place by local Highlanders who were convinced that they were indeed the remains of the Gaelic bard and poet. Wordsworth thought so too: "... In this still place, remote from men Sleeps Ossian, in the narrow glen..."

Crieff

Crieff, 23 miles (37 km) south of Aberfeldy, is a delightful Highland holiday town, built on a steep hill, bustling and cheerful. Facing south over the valley of the River Earn, the town is dominated by the Knock of Crieff, 911 ft (277 m) high in the north. This wooded public park has some splendid views from the top.

Nothing much is old in the town today. It was sacked and destroyed by Highlanders during the Jacobite rebellion, later becoming prosperous by bleaching and tanning. It became a spa town in the 19th century and you get a marvellous echo of Victorian splendour as you look at the Crieff Hydro Hotel, above the town, with its glass domes and pavilions. Crieff is an excellent centre from which to explore the Highlands.

WHAT TO SEE

Glenturret Distillery (open on weekdays throughout the year, and also on Saturdays in July and August: admission free) is the oldest in Scotland. You can have conducted tours, to see how the whisky is made. The tour includes a taste, and a visit to the award-winning visitors' heritage centre with an audio visual show, exhibitions, a whisky museum and retail shop.

Stuart Strathearn (open daily throughout the year: admission free) in Muthill Road, is a crystal factory where you can see the whole process of glassmaking, and buy the products.

Comrie

Comrie, six miles (9.6 km) west of Crieff, is a very attractive conservation village in a lovely setting. Here you can see the **Scottish Tartan Museum** (open daily for a small fee) with over 1,300 tartans as well as comprehensive information, a library, weaving demonstrations and a fascinating garden that shows which plants produce what dyes. You can look up your own name and discover which tartan you are entitled to wear.

Anyone interested in social history will find plenty of things to look at in Comrie's **Smiddy Museum** (open Saturdays only, in the summer: admission free). It is full of relics of a past way of life.

St Fillans

St Fillans, on **Loch Earn**, six miles (9.6 km) further west, is a popular holiday resort for anyone who enjoys sailing, water skiing and wind surfing. It is also a good centre for walking and climbing.

Drummond Castle

Two miles (3.2 km) south of Crieff is Drummond Castle, whose Italian gardens are open in the summer (adults 80p, children 40p). The castle is approached down a mile long avenue. The sundial is dated 1630 and there are lovely flowers and shrubs to see against the backdrop of the castle. Founded in 1491, this was the setting for the terrible murder, in 1502. Margaret Drummond and her sisters were poisoned, to prevent James IV from making Margaret his queen (see Dunblane). Cromwell did his best to destroy the castle and it was deliberately damaged in 1745 by its owner the Duchess of Perth, to present Hanoverian troops from taking it over.

There is plenty of good fishing, golf and riding in this area. Flying enthusiasts should visit the **Strathallan Air Museum** (open daily in the summer: adults £2, children £1.50) four miles (6.4 km) south-east of Crieff, where you can see a varied display of civil and military aircraft, mostly from the Second World War but some going back to 1930. The museum sometimes has flying exhibitions.

Tullibardine Chapel

About two miles (3.2 km) south of Strathallan is Tullibardine Chapel, one of the very few of its kind that has not been altered. It was founded as a collegiate church in 1445, by Sir David Murray, whose arms and those of his wife can be seen on the inside west wall. Since the Reformation, this cruciform red sandstone gem has been used as a burial vault for the Drummond Earls of Perth.

Gleneagles

Three miles (4.8 km) south again, and an irresistible magnet for golfers from all over the world, is Gleneagles, Scotland's premier golfing hotel, whose famous courses lie along the edge of the Muir of Ochil, looking towards the Ochil Hills and Glen Devon.

Braco

Not so well-known, but just as much of a magnet for some people, is the **Ardoch Roman Camp** at Braco, always accessible, a couple of miles (3.2 km) west of Gleneagles. This fascinating complex of earthworks is all that remains of a Roman fort, dating from the 2nd century. It was once big enough to house as many as 40,000 men. You can still see the shape of it by its grass-covered foundations—a great rectangle with ditches and ramparts. Here, in wooden dwellings, the Romans tried to subdue the barbaric tribes that swooped down on them from the hills and glens and forests, in an unsuccessful attempt to protect the Antonine Wall, further south. If you go to where the road crosses the **River Knaik**, in Braco, you will see an old overgrown arch, beside the present bridge. This was part of a Roman bridge.

Auchterarder

About eight miles (13 km) south-east of Crieff is Auchterarder, tucked in under the northern slopes of the Ochil Hills. This is another good holiday centre, with a golf course, and good fishing and walks.

TOURIST INFORMATION

Aberfeldy, tel 0887-20276. It is open Easter to mid-September.

Crieff, tel 0764-2578. It is open all year (four hours a day from October to April).

Auchterarder, tel 07646-3450. It is open all year (afternoons only from October to April).

WHERE TO STAY

Once more, the choice is large and you should see the tourist brochure which gives full details and descriptions. The following are just a small, random selection.

The Cruachan House Hotel, Kenmore Street, Aberfeldy, tel 0887-20545. B&B from £12.50: categories 3,3,4: 9 bedrooms, 2 en suite. In three acres (1.2 ha) on the edge of Aberfeldy with lovely views down the Tay valley. Lovely gardens, good food and friendly atmosphere.

The Kenmore Hotel, The Square, Kenmore, tel 08873-205. B&B from £23.10: categories 5,4,4: 38 bedrooms en suite. Scotland's oldest inn, established in 1572 with three miles (4.8 km) of salmon fishing on the doorstep and fishing rights over all Loch Tay. Taymouth Castle golf course is in the grounds and you can get special rates for fishing and for golf if you stay for two nights or more.

Murraypark Hotel, Connaught Terrace, Crieff, tel 0764-3731/3. B&B from £16.50: categories 4,4,5: 15 bedrooms, 10 en suite. BTA commended. The AA and RAC rate it as 2-Star. Relaxed and friendly atmosphere, and good food.

Crieff Hydro Hotel, Crieff, tel 0764-2401. B&B from £14.50: categories 4,4,4: 200 bedrooms, 140 en suite. The hotel beams down on the town from the hill, with its splendid glass pavilion in front. There is an indoor swimming pool, riding, tennis, free golf, sailing, wind surfing and water skiing. In the evenings activities include dancing, films, discos and competitions if you are the sort of person who likes to be organised.

Drummond Arms Hotel, St Fillans, tel 076485-212. B&B from £15: categories 3,3,5: 35 bedrooms, 14 en suite. On the shores of Loch Earn, it is quiet and unspoiled, with a friendly staff and relaxed atmosphere.

Gleneagles, Auchterarder, tel 076-46 2231. Scotland's only 5-Star hotel. Prices and details on application (comfort can come quite expensive). If you get fed up with the sauna, the solarium, the jacuzzi, the gymnasium, the shooting, the fishing, the snooker, the swimming, the squash, the bowling, the croquet and the tennis, you can always fall back on a round of golf.

EATING OUT

Guinach House, Kenmore Road, Aberfeldy, tel 0887-20251. Imaginative Scottish food. Dinner from £7.50.

Murraypark Hotel, see above. Traditional Scottish food. Dinner from £10.

Cultoquhey House Hotel, Gilmerton, tel 0764-3253. A secluded country house in six acres (2.5 ha) with excellent Scottish food, where you can get a four course set dinner for £9.95. (If you are puzzled by the name, "qu" is Gaelic for "w".)

Gleneagles, see above. The hotel's 5-Star rating embraces its kitchen and chef as well as everything else. Don't look at the right hand side of the menu: who wants to toy with an omelette in a place like this!

CRAFT CENTRES IN TAYSIDE

The following studios and workshops welcome visitors. Where a telephone number is given, you should always telephone first to check when you can go.

Ceramics

Bran Clay Pottery, Balquhidder, tel 08774-274. You can watch pots being hand thrown, glazed and fired.

A. W. Buchan and Co Ltd, Muthil Road, Crieff, tel 0764-3515. Thistle pottery is hand made and painted here.

Pitlochry Pottery and Crafts, East Haugh, Pitlochry, tel 0796-2995/2790. Here you can watch stoneware and terracotta being hand thrown and hand modelled. Hand weaving and spinning.

Squire Ceramics, 19 Montrose Street, Brechin, tel 03562-3538. Hand made pottery at all stages, including firing.

Furniture Making

Ben Ghlas Workshops, near Killin, tel 056-72 527. As well as furniture making you can see sheepskin tanning, hand spinning, knitting and weaving and restoration of antiques.

Glass Making

Caithness Glass, Inveralmond Industrial Estate, Perth, tel 0738-37373. You can watch all stages of glassmaking.

Jewellery and Silversmithing

Kor Newhouse, Newcraft, Croft Cottage, Main Street, Balbeggie, tel 0821-4201. Hand made jewellery and tableware in copper and pewter.

Perth Craft Centre, 38 South Street, Perth, tel 0738-38232. All processes of making jewellery in silver, titanium and gold, as well as silversmithing.

Leatherwork

Pibroch Crafts, 86 Burrell Street, Crieff, tel 0764-3197. You can watch hand crafting of soft leather pouch sporrans and handbags.

Perth Craft Centre, 38 South Street, Perth, tel 0738-38232. Here you can see cutting, dying, tooling, finishing and hand stitching of leather such as kilt belts, sporrans, bags, belts and holdalls.

Skins

Jeremy Law (Scotland) Ltd, City Hall, Dunkeld, tel 03502-569. You can watch deerskin manufacture.

Highland Dress

Piob Mhor, 39–43 High Street, Blairgowrie, tel 0250-2131. Here you can watch the making of kilts, bagpipes, sporrans and belts, feather bonnets and other accessories to Highland dress.

Part XII

GRAMPIAN

Craigievar

There is something forbidding about the name Grampian. It sounds angry and stark, but indeed it is neither. On the contrary, it is a rich, fertile region with areas of great natural beauty. Grampian is that shoulder of Scotland that juts out into the North Sea below the neck of Caithness and Sutherland. Like the ribs of an outspread fan, radiating from Aberdeen, the scenery includes the popular beauty spots of Deeside, with its hills and forests, its salmon-filled rivers and sheltered straths. Further north is moorland and undulating farmland, with a wide coastal plain, patchworked with neat fields stretching away to the sea. The coast road links a chain of fishing towns and villages with harbours, giving refuge to boats from the wild North Sea. It is a coastline that is both rugged and gentle, with gaunt rocky cliffs, giving way to vast sweeps of clean sand. It is a land cut by rivers and half-girt by sea, with no notable lochs. To the west lie the mountains and the lure of the ski slopes.

Many pre-historic remains in the lowlands of Grampian tell of early settlements, but the region does not feature much in the history books until Kenneth Macalpine united its Picts with the Dalriada Scots in the 9th century. Its people, like everywhere else in Scotland, are fashioned by their environment. There are the fishermen and oil-men, tough and resilient and full of courage; the farmers and country people, sturdy, intrepid and industrious; the people of Deeside, just a little conscious of their royal connections. The Aberdonian has a reputation for being the epitome of the dour, mean Scotsman: you must get to know him and decide for yourself. Careful, he may be canny and shrewd, but his heart is as soft as butter, his generosity limitless, his kindness unostentatious and sincere.

Grampian offers you such an enormous choice of things to do that there is something for everyone. For sportsmen, some of the best salmon and trout fishing in the world, as well as a large variety of game birds to be slaughtered and deer to be stalked. There is challenging skiing in the west and mountains to be climbed that should satisfy the keenest of 'munro collectors', as well as endless lovely walks, both inland and along the coast. There are sailing, water sports and sea fishing, and there is a large number of golf courses. Grampian has more than its share of castles to be explored, many of which have lovely gardens.

Among the many local events that take place in Grampian, you will find Highland Games play an important part, and of these, the Braemar Royal Highland Gathering is probably the most popular, attended each year by members of the Royal Family, in September. Games are held all over the region, with piping, dancing and all the traditional sports such as putting the weight and tossing the caber. These unique Scottish gatherings, dating from the 11th century when Malcolm Canmore held contests to find the best soldiers for his struggles against the Normans, are usually well supplied with beer tents and side shows.

Aberdeen

Aberdeen is the obvious place from which to begin to explore the Grampian region. It is an ever-changing city, the third largest in Scotland and to learn its true nature, under a brittle, cosmopolitan exterior, you need to live in it for a while. Always a great port, as well as a fish and cattle market, the exporter of granite, textiles and paper, Aberdeen suddenly found itself in the centre of an oil boom, in the 1970s. Country and Western music emanated from dignified old buildings; bars and restaurants changed their characters overnight; American accents were two a penny and the opening ceremony of the American Club was like a visit to Texas. Property prices soared: entrepreneurs flourished.

Somehow, through all this, Aberdeen managed to cling to its own unique character. The Granite City, they call it; and it softens this austere title by decking its streets and parks with what must be some of the most spectacular displays of roses in the British Isles. No oil boom could change the gracious white-granite splendour of the Georgian part of the city, with its lovely terraces and squares and crescents; nor the proud, long sweep of Union Street; nor even, for all the smart new buildings, the waterfront. Expensive oil-rig supply vessels can never spoil the timeless atmosphere of the harbour, with its tang of fish and salt.

Frequently touched by history the city was never a slave to it, as Edinburgh was. Old Aberdeen was granted a royal charter by William the Lion in 1179, now preserved in the Town House in Union Street, endorsing an earlier one granted by David I. Alexander III founded the Blackfriars Monastery in 1222; Edward I passed through in 1296, followed by William Wallace who is said to have burned 100 ships in the harbour. Robert Bruce held a council here in 1308: after the loyal support of the citizens, who forced the English to surrender their hold on the castle, he gave the city its coat of arms and the motto "Bon Accord". Edward III burned down the Old Town in 1336 and it was after that that the southern part of the city was built. The Gordon clan, incomers from Ber-

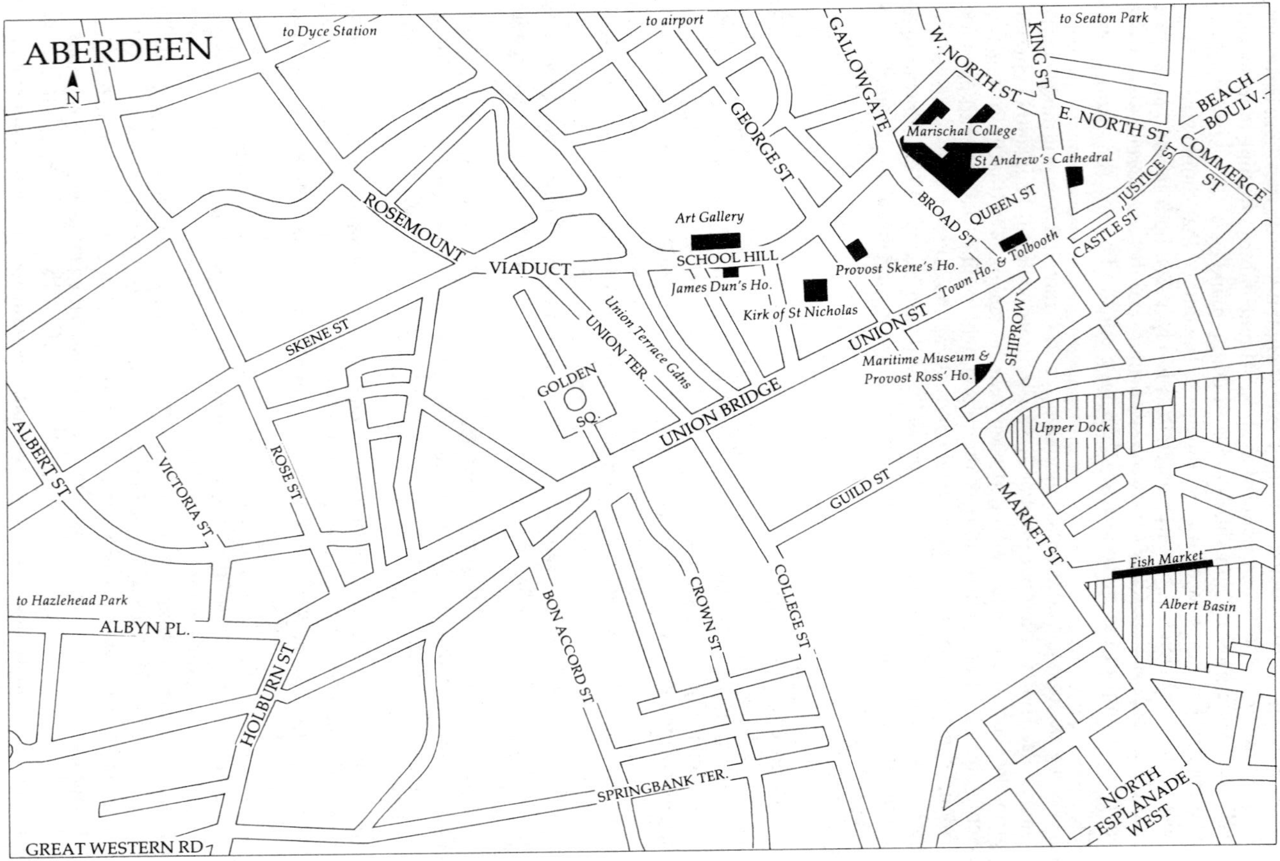

ABERDEEN
N
to Dyce Station
to airport
to Seaton Park
GALLOWGATE
W. NORTH ST
KING ST
E. NORTH ST
BEACH BOULV.
COMMERCE ST
JUSTICE ST
CASTLE ST
Marischal College
St Andrew's Cathedral
QUEEN ST
BROAD ST
GEORGE ST
ROSEMOUNT
Art Gallery
SCHOOL HILL
VIADUCT
James Dun's Ho.
Provost Skene's Ho.
Town Ho. & Tolbooth
Kirk of St Nicholas
UNION ST
SHIPROW
Maritime Museum &
Provost Ross' Ho.
Union Terrace Gdns
UNION TER.
GOLDEN SQ.
UNION BRIDGE
SKENE ST
ALBERT ST
VICTORIA ST
ROSE ST
Upper Dock
GUILD ST
MARKET ST
Fish Market
Albert Basin
COLLEGE ST
CROWN ST
BON ACCORD ST
to Hazlehead Park
ALBYN PL.
HOLBURN ST
SPRINGBANK TER.
GREAT WESTERN RD
NORTH ESPLANADE WEST

wickshire and Lothian, dominated this north-eastern corner for some 250 years, as powerful as kings, and Mary, Queen of Scots was forced by her Protestant half-brother, Moray, to come north in an attempt to quell them, which she achieved by executing Sir John Gordon and by the posthumous trial of the embalmed body of his father, for treason! Montrose sacked the city in 1644; General Monk occupied it for Cromwell. Although nominally Jacobite, the citizens of Aberdeen were not enthusiastic supporters of the cause.

SPECIAL ATTRACTIONS

Among the many events that take place in the city during the year, there is a Marathon Road Race, in May. The Aberdeen Highland Games are in June, as well as a Steam Engine Rally and the Aberdeen Festival. In July there is an Arts Carnival and an international Football Festival. August is the month for the Fish Festival and the Rose Festival and also the International Youth Festival. The Aberdeen Alternative Festival is in October.

WHAT TO SEE

Explore **Old Aberdeen**, north of the city centre, on foot. Walk through it to the **River Don** and stand on the beautiful little **Brig o' Balgownie**, a Gothic gem that spans the river near its mouth and built by Richard-the-mason, on the orders of Robert Bruce. This is the oldest medieval bridge in Scotland. There was a time, some years ago, when the unrestricted discharge of effluent from mills and factories up the river, so polluted the water that you would have had to hold your nose here, looking down into thick green water. Stricter control and conservation have had their effect and the Don flows cleaner now, the salmon once again making their way upstream to spawn. On the north side of the bridge you can see a terrace of charming old stone cottages with pretty, colourful gardens: the one nearest to the bridge was once the ale-house on the old Drove Road.

Walk back through **Seaton Park**, Old Aberdeen, to **St Machar's Cathedral** (open daily: admission free). Founded in 1157, St Machar's stands on a promontory overlooking the Don. It takes its name from the saint who founded a Celtic church here in the 6th century. A 14th-century red sandstone arch is all that remains of an older building, in contrast to the simple dignity of the later granite. Look out for the oak heraldic ceiling, added in 1520, with 48 heraldic shields.

Around this cathedral grew the settlement of Old Aberdeen, an independent burgh with its own council and charter. Today, with its cobbled streets and charming old houses, some of which date back as far as 1500, there is an air of peaceful tranquillity here, unspoiled by the roar of the modern city around it.

King's College (open daily except Sundays: admission free) stands on a green sward, in the High Street of Old Aberdeen with its distinctive "crowned" tower and splendid old buttressed walls. Aberdeen's first university, it was founded in 1495, in the reign of James IV. Its lovely chapel, first Catholic, then Protestant, is now interdenominational and houses the tomb of its founder, Bishop William Elphinstone.

The City

Marischal College, in Broad Street, in "New" Aberdeen, was founded in 1593 as a

Protestant rival to King's, the two colleges being united from Aberdeen University in 1860. This imposing, 19th-century granite building is a great edifice of soaring pinnacles; a neo-Gothic fantasy glittering with mica. The present building, opened in 1906, has some of the older parts incorporated into it. When the university is not using them you can visit the **Hall and Portrait Gallery** (admission free). You can also see the university's **Anthropological Museum** (open on week days: admission free) with local, classical, Egyptian and Chinese antiquities.

Provost Skene's House (open daily except on Sundays: admission free) is opposite the college. Now a museum, this lovely well restored building dates from 1545. It was named after one of its owners, Sir George Skene, provost of Aberdeen in 1676 and responsible for extensive renovation of the house. The Duke of Cumberland lodged here from February until April 1746, on his way to defeat Prince Charlie at Culloden. The house formed two dwellings in those days both of which suffered considerable losses from the misbehaviour of the duke and his officers. They made free with the stocks of provisions: coals, candles, ales and other liquors in the cellars. They milked the cow, spoiled the bed and table linen and robbed their landlady of her hoard of precious sugar!

The house makes a fascinating museum with some of the original decoration. The **Painted Gallery**, known as the chapel, on the second floor of the west wing revealed traces of religious paintings in 17th-century style, showing that medieval ideas and imagery persisted in this north-eastern corner of Scotland far into the Reformation period. On the top floor you can see a range of exhibits illustrating the history and domestic life of Aberdeen over the ages.

From Broad Street, go along Upperkirkgate to Schoolhill, where you will find **St Nicholas**, the old parish church (open daily). It is set among trees in a peaceful churchyard and its 48 bell carillon rings out across the city. Founded in the 12th century and split into two at the Reformation, the present building dates from 1752. In the east part of the church you can see a little stone-vaulted crypt-chapel, St Mary's, dating from the 14th century. Witches were imprisoned down here, in the 17th century and you can see the rings to which they were chained. More prosaically, the chapel has also been used as a plumber's workshop and an early Victorian soup-kitchen.

Aberdeen Art Gallery and Museum (open daily throughout the year: admission free) is also in Schoolhill. Among its vast collection there is a comprehensive display of 20th-century British paintings and sculptures, as well as some excellent Raeburn portraits and many more, including works by Zoffany, Romney, Reynolds, Augustus John and Ben Nicholson. There are regular exhibitions and recitals and a small museum of applied art.

James Dun's House (open daily except Sundays: admission free) is also in Schoolhill. This charming Georgian building has temporary exhibitions of interest to children. In the summer it includes an "Aberdeen Experience" show.

The Regimental Museum of the Gordon Highlanders (open on Sunday and Wednesday afternoons throughout the year and at other times by arrangement: admission free) is in Viewfield Road, south of the city centre. Here you can see comprehensive displays relating to the history of the locally recruited regiment: uniforms, colours and banners, silver and medals and a library with documents and photographs.

His Majesty's Theatre in Rosemount Viaduct, west of the city centre, was built in

1906. Recently refurbished, it is the town's main theatre, seating 1,500 people. Its varied programmes include ballet, opera and concerts.

The Maritime Museum (open daily except Sundays: free admission) is in **Provost Ross's House**, Shiprow, north of Trinity Quay and the Upper Dock. Overlooking the harbour, it is one of the oldest houses in the town and a splendid example of early Scottish domestic architecture. Here are some interesting displays of Aberdeen's maritime heritage of fishing, shipbuilding and trade as well as some fascinating models of offshore oil installations.

Aberdeen Harbour is a wonderful conglomeration of maritime life: fine old buildings line the waterfront where fishing boats are packed tightly into the inner basins, some old and rusty, some so sophisticated that they need an electronics genius to understand them.

Get up early one weekday morning and visit the **Fish Market** (open between 7.30 am–9.30 am). As one of Britain's major fishing ports, Aberdeen exports hundreds of tons of fish daily. Here you can watch the boats unloading box after box of fish, stacking them in the great warehouses, to be auctioned off in a completely unintelligible, esoteric language of grunts, yells, mutterings and gestures that entirely excludes an amateur purchaser. Fat gulls squabble over the fish and the noise, smell and exhilaration of that seething throng is not a thing you easily forget.

Duthie Park Winter Gardens, south of the city on the banks of the Dee, are a riot of exotic plants and shrubs. They include a cactus house, birds, fish, turtles, an amazing display of spring crocuses and a hill of roses that makes you feel exhausted when you contemplate the pruning season!

Two miles (3.2 km) of sand beach stretch northwards from the harbour, with sand dunes laced with marram grass, golf courses and a huge amusement park.

TOURIST INFORMATION

Broad Street, tel 0224-632727. It is open all year.

WHERE TO STAY

There is a very big choice of accommodation in and around Aberdeen, ranging from 4-Star luxury hotels to simple little bed and breakfasts, with an equivalent price range. You should look at the brochure which gives full descriptions and pictures. The following is just a random selection.

The Atholl Hotel, 54 King's Gate, in the west end, tel 0224-323505. B&B from £24: categories 5,5,5: 20 bedrooms, 17 en suite. A comfortable town house hotel with interchange dining facilities at three west end hotels in the city and a private box at Aberdeen FC. Golfing, fishing and shooting can be arranged, and also distillery tours. You can even have secretarial services if you need them.

Caledonian Thistle Hotel, Union Terrace, in the city centre, tel 0224-640233. B&B from £35: categories 6,5,6: 80 bedrooms en suite. Rooms include TV, in-house movies, tea/coffee making facilities, sun-bed and sauna room. Good food, friendly service and special weekend packages available.

Bucksburn Moathouse, Old Meldrum Road, tel 0224-713911. B&B from £30: categories 6,6,6: 99 bedrooms en suite. Comfortable, relaxed atmosphere and good food.

Copthorne Hotel, 122 Huntly Street, tel 0224-630404. B&B from £37.05: categories 6,5,5: 66 bedrooms en suite. Right in the heart of the city, a modern, luxury hotel with a lively night-club called Boodles.

New Marcliffe Hotel, 53 Queen's Road, in the west end, tel 0224-231371. B&B from £28: categories 5,6,5: 27 bedrooms en suite. A new luxury hotel. Rooms with TV and in-house video. Golfing, fishing and shooting arranged and a chauffeur-driven car if you want one, as well as interchange dining facilities with other luxury hotels.

Skean Dhu Hotel, Aberdeen Airport, Argyll Road, tel 0224-725252. B&B from £11.25: (Bargain break on Friday, Saturday and Sunday.) A large luxury hotel. The AA and RAC rate it as 4-Star. Heated swimming pool. Egon Ronay restaurant with very good food.

EATING OUT

As in any city, the choice of eating places is large and always changing and your best way of finding the latest "in" place is to ask around when you get there. The hotels above all have good food, or you could try some of the places listed below.

Mr G's, 74 Chapel Street, tel 0224-64211. A wine bar and restaurant where the food is excellent and the atmosphere friendly. Dinner (in the restaurant) from about £8.

Gerards, 50 Chapel Street, tel 0223-639500. The chef is outstanding, and here you can eat in a garden room with a glass roof and an al fresco atmosphere. Dinner from about £10.

Atlantis Seafood, 145 Crown Street, tel 0224-591403. Good, fresh sea food. Dinner from £6.

Poldinos, 7 Little Belmont Street, tel 0224-647777. Excellent pizzas. Dinner from about £6.

South of Aberdeen

The A92 south from Aberdeen takes you along the coast with extensive views across water that is always busy with shipping.

Stonehaven

Stonehaven is a holiday resort town, as sturdy as its name implies. It is 14 miles (22.4 km) from the city and crouched around a bay below massive red sandstone cliffs. The sheltered harbour is used mainly by pleasure boats now. There is a heated open-air swimming pool, a golf course, boating and wind surfing, fishing and sea angling, pony trekking, a new indoor leisure centre, excellent walks, good accommodation and a cheerful, friendly atmosphere.

WHAT TO SEE

Tolbooth Museum (open daily in the summer, except Tuesdays: admission free) is a

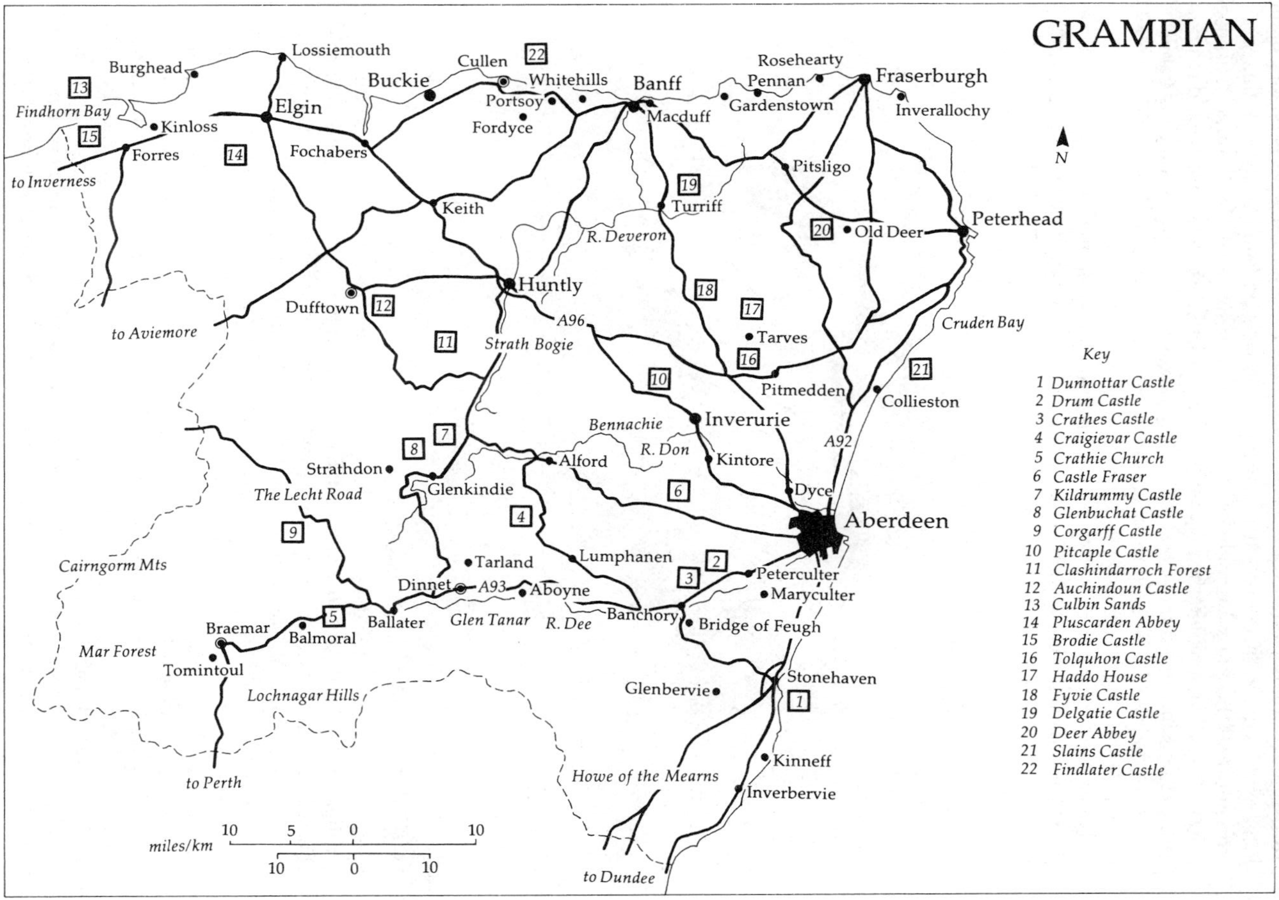
GRAMPIAN
N
Key
1 Dunnottar Castle
2 Drum Castle
3 Crathes Castle
4 Craigievar Castle
5 Crathie Church
6 Castle Fraser
7 Kildrummy Castle
8 Glenbuchat Castle
9 Corgarff Castle
10 Pitcaple Castle
11 Clashindarroch Forest
12 Auchindoun Castle
13 Culbin Sands
14 Pluscarden Abbey
15 Brodie Castle
16 Tolquhon Castle
17 Haddo House
18 Fyvie Castle
19 Delgatie Castle
20 Deer Abbey
21 Slains Castle
22 Findlater Castle
Lossiemouth
Burghead
Findhorn Bay
Kinloss
Forres
to Inverness
Elgin
Fochabers
Buckie
Cullen
Whitehills
Portsoy
Fordyce
Banff
Macduff
Rosehearty
Pennan
Gardenstown
Fraserburgh
Inverallochy
Pitsligo
Turriff
Keith
R. Deveron
Old Deer
Peterhead
Huntly
Dufftown
to Aviemore
A96
Strath Bogie
Tarves
Cruden Bay
Pitmedden
Collieston
Bennachie
Inverurie
R. Don
Kintore
A92
Strathdon
Alford
Glenkindie
The Lecht Road
Dyce
Aberdeen
Cairngorm Mts
Tarland
Lumphanen
Peterculter
Maryculter
Dinnet
A93
Aboyne
Braemar
Balmoral
Ballater
Glen Tanar
R. Dee
Banchory
Bridge of Feugh
Mar Forest
Tomintoul
Lochnagar Hills
Stonehaven
Glenbervie
Kinneff
Howe of the Mearns
Inverbervie
to Perth
miles/km
10
5
0
10
10
0
10
to Dundee

16th-century building on the quay by the north pier. Here you can get a good idea of the local history and archaeology, with a special emphasis on fishing. The building was a storehouse of the Earls Marischal, later used as a prison. In 1748–9, three Episcopal priests were imprisoned in the tolbooth for their insistence in following the old religion. During their incarceration women came from all over the county, smuggling babies in creels on their backs, to hold them up to the barred windows so that the priests could baptise them.

Every New Year's Eve the town celebrates a "Swinging the Fireballs" ceremony, going back to pagan times when fireballs were swung through the streets to ward off evil spirits.

Dunnottar Castle

Dunnottar Castle

Dunnottar Castle (open daily except on Fridays in the winter: adults 55p, children 30p) is about two miles (4 km) south of Stonehaven, just off the A92. This spectacular ruined fortress stands high on a rocky promontory towering 160 ft (48 m) above the boiling sea, protected to landward by a deep natural cleft. It has been written: "... Dunnottar speaks with an audible voice; every cave has a record, every turret a tongue ..." A Pictish fort stood here in the Dark Ages, and one of the earliest Christian chapels. The fort was replaced by a primitive castle in the 13th century. William Wallace stormed the English garrison in 1297, burning down the church where they had taken refuge, but failing to take the castle. Dunnottar was a stronghold of the Earls Marischal of Scotland from the 14th century; the extensive ruins include a great square tower and the chapel, built by Sir William Keith in 1392; and a gatehouse, built in 1575, held to be the strongest in Scotland. In 1645, the seventh Earl Marischal, a stubborn Covenanter, withstood a siege by Montrose, who took his revenge by laying waste to Stonehaven and all the surrounding lands. His actions are recorded by a chronicler as having left the country "... utterlie spoilzeit, plunderit and undone...".

During the Civil War, the Scottish regalia was brought to Dunnottar for safety. The castle was besieged in 1652, but the governor refused to surrender until the regalia had been smuggled out in the apron of the local minister's wife, Mrs Grainger, in a bundle of flax, carried by her servant. It was hidden in the kirk at Kinneff, and kept safe until the Restoration of the Monarchy.

In 1685, 167 Covenanters were imprisoned at Dunnottar in such awful conditions that you can almost sense the horror now, looking at the "Whigs Vault" where many of them were confined "... ankle deep in mire, with one window to the sea ... they had not the least accommodation for sitting, leaning or lying and were perfectly stifled for want of air ... no access to ease nature...". Some tried to escape through the window that overlooks the sea, but were re-captured and cruelly tortured. Many died. It was a chapter in the history of the castle that seems to overshadow it, even now adding a gloomy touch to the very well preserved ruins.

Kinneff

Dunnottar's history is further commemorated at Kinneff, in the 18th-century kirk (usually open). Kinneff is seven miles (11.2 km) to the south, just off the A92. Parts of the old kirk are incorporated into the current building and include those parts in which the Scottish regalia was hidden for nine years by the Rev James Grainger. The hiding place was under the flagstone below the pulpit. You can see memorials to Grainger, his wife, and to Sir George Ogilvy, governor of Dunnottar Castle at the time.

Inverbervie

Two miles (3.2 km) further south you come to the little milling town of Inverbervie, on the banks of Bervie Water. Here, at Craig David on the north shore, David II and his wife, Johanna, were driven ashore by a storm while returning from nine years of exile in France in 1341. King's Step is the rock where David is said to have stepped ashore. He granted the town a royal charter the following year. You can see a memorial to Hercules Linton, the man who designed the famous clipper *Cutty Sark.*

This wild, rugged coastline offers little refuge from the ferocious storms that often rage in from the North Sea. The villagers take what shelter they can from the harbours they have built into the cliffs. You will find several caravan and camp sites, and numerous good picnic spots.

Arbuthnott House and Gardens

Three miles (4.8 km) inland from Inverbervie you come to Arbuthnott House and Gardens (open by arrangement, tel Inverbervie 226: adults 70p, children 35p). The house has a splendid 17th-century Renaissance façade, with 18th-century additions and there is an extensive 17th-century formal garden, attractively terraced with a pretty 18th-century stone bridge. A tower on the site of the house was the home of the Arbuthnott family in 1206. The chancel of the village church, dates from 1242.

The sheltered area to the west of here is called **Howe of The Mearns** and contains several good forest trails and picnic sites.

Glenbervie

Glenbervie, just off the A94, is five miles (8 km) south-west of Stonehaven. It was the home of the ancestors of Robert Burns and you can see the family tombstone and a cairn in memory of the poet, whose father it was that emigrated west to Ayr.

Anyone who has read the trilogy *A Scot's Quair* by Lewis Grassic Gibbon. (James Leslie Mitchell) will recognise in this area much of the setting of the three novels. Mitchell's powerful Scottish, lyrical prose brings to life "the red clay of the Mearns", the land of his childhood, as it was at the beginning of the 20th century.

TOURIST INFORMATION
St Nicholas House, Broad Street, Aberdeen, tel 0224-632727—open all year. Stonehaven, tel 0569-62806—open Easter to September.

WHERE TO STAY
The Commodore Hotel, Cowie Park, Stonehaven, tel 0569-62936, B&B from £22.00. Categories 5,5,5. 40 bedrooms en suite. A modern, purpose built hotel with good food.

Heugh Hotel, Westfield Road, Stonehaven, tel 0569-62379. B&B from £19.00. Categories 5,4,5. 5 bedrooms en suite and warm Scottish hospitality.

Marine Hotel, Shorehead, Stonehaven, tel 0569-62155, B&B from £11.25. Categories 5,2,4. 5 bedrooms. Right on the waterfront in the harbour with a relaxed, friendly staff.

Royal Deeside: from Aberdeen to Braemar

You can enjoy Deeside all through the year: perhaps best of all in autumn when the rich blaze of colour is unforgettable. In winter the landscape becomes a dramatic sweep of snow-covered hills and torrents of ice: a skier's delight, with the Glenshee Ski Centre, to the south. In summer, with a good map and sensible equipment, you could spend a whole holiday exploring the hills and valleys of the Cairngorms and Grampians.

Peterculter and Maryculter

Leaving Aberdeen on the A93, to follow the Dee west, you pass Peterculter and Maryculter (pronounced kooter) seven miles (11.2 km) from the city. Here the Romans once had a camp. William the Lion granted these lands to the powerful Knight's Templar, the soldier-monks of the Crusades, and they built a chapel to St Mary, in the late 12th century. Its ruins can still be seen in Templars' Park on the south bank of the river. The highly coloured statue of Rob Roy that you will see standing above the Leuchar's Burn has no historic significance. It was originally a ship's figurehead and has been replaced twice since it was erected.

WHAT TO SEE

Drum Castle

Drum Castle (open daily in the summer: adults £1.40, children 70p,) is ten miles (16 km) from Aberdeen on the A93 and well worth a visit. A massive granite tower, built towards the end of the 13th century, adjoins a mansion built in 1619. Robert Bruce gave Drum to his standard bearer, William de Irwin, in 1324, and it remained in the possession of the family until they passed it to the National Trust for Scotland in 1975. You can see antique furniture, silver, portraits and family treasures and relics. The grounds are lovely, with rare trees and shrubs, sweeping lawns and woodland nature trails.

Crathes Castle and Gardens

Crathes Castle and Gardens is five miles (8 km) past Drum. (The castle is open daily in the summer: adults £1.40, children 70p. The gardens and grounds are open daily all the year round; adults 50p, children 25p. Combined ticket; adults, £1.80, children 90p.) Crathes will be familiar from the many photographs, both in books and on postcards and calendars, but even so it will give you a delightful nudge of pleasure to see it in reality.

The Burnett family had been granted lands north of the Dee by Robert Bruce early in the 14th century, and it was Alexander Burnett, in 1552, who decided to move from his stronghold on an island in the Loch of Leys nearby, and build a modern house, in keeping with his status as Laird. The castle took many years to complete and the result is one of the best examples of Scottish domestic architecture as it developed from the previously necessary fortified dwellings. It was a style that was to die out within 60 years. When a Victorian extension, overlooking the upper garden, was burnt down in 1966, it was agreed to restore the castle to its original proportions, and that is what you will see today. The interior is beautifully restored, just as it was, with painted decorations on the beams and woodwork, allegorical designs, proverbs and biblical texts. You can see some of the original furnishings, too, among the many treasures that are on show. The little ivory hunting horn, displayed in the main hall, was a symbol of the Burnett's right of tenure of part of the Royal Forest, given them by Robert Bruce.

Crathes has its ghosts, notably The Green Lady, who haunts certain rooms, dressed in green and carrying a baby in her arms. A baby's skeleton was unearthed under the hearthstone in The Green Lady's room, during the 19th century and the story is told of a young girl, under the laird's protection, giving birth to a baby, fathered by one of the servants. Mother and infant died, under mysterious circumstances.

The gardens are a delight in every season of the year and you could happily pass days enjoying them. They consist of a series of small, interlinked gardens, each with its own motif and character, a profusion of glorious colours, scents and blended textures. There are also nature trails laid out in the grounds.

Banchory

Banchory, about three miles (5.6 km) beyond Crathes, is a pleasant, sheltered town on the Dee. It rises in layers of terraced streets, backed by the Hill o' Fare, 1,545 ft (464 m), to the north, and rolling hills to the south. You catch an air of genteel respectability as you stroll among its antique shops and high-class boutiques.

There is a small **Museum** (open on Wednesday, Friday, Saturday and Sunday afternoons in summer: admission free) in the old Council Chambers, in the High Street, where you can learn the history of the area.

In the 5th century St Ternan, a local man and follower of St Ninian, established a monastery where the churchyard now is and you can still see traces of its medieval successor.

Incorporated into the walls of the manse, are delicately carved wheel-crosses that date from this early Christian period. Palaeolithic flints, excavated nearby, suggest a very early settlement. There is a golf course by the river and the salmon fishing is renowned. You can visit the **Ingasetter Lavender Distillery**, on week days, in North Deeside Road. The five-acre (2 ha) field of lavender is a memorable sight and smell, in July and August, before harvest.

Walk to the south of the town, where the Dee is joined by the Feugh, at **Bridge of Feugh**. The footbridge above the rapids gives you a marvellous view of the salmon, leaping up the ledges to get to their spawning grounds. There are lovely forest and riverside walks as well as some more energetic hill climbing.

Aboyne

Aboyne, 13 miles (21 km) to the west, is famous for its annual Games. This splendid Highland Gathering takes place every September on the large green and you can see all the traditional activities such as tossing the caber, putting the weight, piping and dancing. Aboyne is a good base from which to explore this part of Deeside. It has some excellent walks.

Go south, through **Glen Tanar**, in whose woods you can see remnants of the old Caledonian Forest. Tanar oak was much used in the building of ships, being floated down the Dee to Aberdeen, in the 19th century.

The Braeloine Visitor Centre

The Braeloine Visitor Centre (open daily in the summer: admission by donation) is five miles (8 km) south-west of Aboyne. The centre provides all the information you need on this area; its wild life, farming, and forestry, with advice on where to walk. There are several tracks leading south, over the hills, one of which, **Fir Mounth**, is thought to be the route taken by Macbeth as he fled from the castle at Dunsinane to his death at Lumphanan.

Lumphanan

In Lumphanan, five miles (8 km) north-east of Aboyne, you can see the Peel Ring, a medieval motte with wall, earthworks and ditches. This is where Macbeth fought his final battle, against Malcolm Canmore in 1057. **Macbeth's Cairn**, in a circle of trees on the hillside, marks the spot where he actually died.

Craigievar

From Lumphanan it is less than five miles (8 km) north to Craigievar (open every afternoon in the summer: adults £1.40, children 70p). Craigievar is one of the finest 17th-century tower-house castles you will find anywhere. It stands among trees, almost as if it, too, had grown from the ground in a single great trunk, its smooth sides rising to a cluster of turrets, crowstepped gables, balustrades and corbles.

Built between 1600 and 1626, by a rich merchant, William Forbes, Craigievar is a picture book castle with a gorgeously elaborate interior, representing that short period of Renaissance sunshine that preceded the gloom of the Civil War. The painted decorations that were common at that time were being set aside in favour of the moulded plasterwork that was just coming into fashion, and you can see good examples on the ceilings, particularly in the hall. Fortunately, the castle was left unscathed during the vandalism of the civil wars, and in later times the Victorians refrained from adding any of their favourite billiard room wings. Thus, Craigievar is almost exactly as it was when it was built.

Tarland

If you take the B9119, just south of Craigievar, back south-west towards the Dee for six miles (9.6 km), you come to Tarland. This old-world village round a central square, which is the centre of the MacRobert Trust, is a huge and complicated complex of farming and charitable foundations.

Walk a short way to the east, beyond the golf course, to Culsh Earth House, (open at standard Ancient Monument times: admission free), a well preserved souterrain by Culsh Farmhouse. Its roofing slabs are intact over a large chamber.

On a rocky hillock a mile (1.6 km) to the south-east, you can see **Tomnaverie Stone Circle**, unexcavated and recumbent, probably dating from 1800 BC.

Dinnet

At Dinnet, six miles (9.6 km) south, you are back on the A93. You will need special permission to visit the **National Nature Reserve** here. It is a lovely area of heathland, scrub and birchwood, with old oaks, and attractive fenland.

Ballater

Ballater, 11 miles (17.6 km) west of Aboyne on the A93, used to be the end of the line for the Royal Train, before the railway was closed. This is a very popular holiday centre in the summer, in beautiful wooded moorland where you can roam for miles in all directions, discovering more and more enchanted corners.

The town developed in the late 18th century after an old woman discovered the healing powers of the bog, at the foot of Pannanich Hill. Her discovery was exploited by an ex-Jacobite, Francis Farquharson of Monaltrie, 20 years after his exile and near execution, following Culloden. This enterprising entrepreneur built an Inn, at the hamlet of **Cobbletown of Dalmuchie** and developed it into a spa, which quickly became fashionable. After Queen Victoria fell in love with Scotland and came to Balmoral, the whole area developed into the prosperous place that it is today.

Ballater Golf Course must be distracting to play on. The views in all directions, sweeping away to the hills, would kill concentration on the game! You can attend the Ballater Highland Games, every August in Monaltrie Park, with all the traditional events, both athletic and musical, and a Hill Race to Craig Cailleach, south of the bridge.

There are some sizeable hills for you to climb, with panoramic views, and always the sound of rushing water, and the song of skylarks and linnets.

Balmoral

Balmoral (open daily except on Sundays, in the summer when the Royal Family are not at home, gardens only: adults £1.10) is another of those places that is so familiar from photographs that its reality is almost an anti-climax. It is seven miles (11.2 km) west of Ballater. Queen Victoria lost her heart to "this dear Paradise" and she and Prince Albert bought the estate and the old castle in 1852, for £31,000. The old building, however, was too small for the royal household, and Prince Albert commissioned the building of the present white granite mansion in 1853, a Scottish Baronial edifice that was designed by William Smith of Aberdeen. It is still the Royal Family's holiday home, and it holds a place of great affection in most British hearts as being the place where their much-loved "First Family" relax and enjoy the same sort of country pursuits as ordinary people.

Lochnagar, with 11 peaks over 3,000 ft (900 m), towering like massive sentinals over a small loch to the south, inspired Byron to write:

... England! thy beauties are tame and domestic
To one who has roved o'er the mountains afar:
Oh, for the crags that are wild and majestic!
The steep frowning glories of dark Lochnagar...

More recently, Lochnagar inspired another writer, the Prince of Wales, Prince Charles, to write a delightful story, *The Old Man of Lochnagar*, to amuse his brothers during a cruise in the royal yacht.

Crathie Church, just north of the castle, was built in 1895 to replace a series of previous churches whose origins went back to the 9th century. It is now attended by members of the Royal Family when they are on holiday.

Braemar

Braemar, seven miles (11.2 km) to the south-west, is very popular for holiday makers. It lies in the heart of some of Scotland's most beautiful scenery, so spectacular that you almost get indigestion looking at it.

Braemar Castle (open daily in the summer; adults £1.10, children 55p) is a massive great turreted fortress, built by the Earl of Mar in 1628. It was burnt by the Farquharsons in 1689 and was garrisoned by the English after the Jacobite rising in 1715, and again in 1745, to protect the military road from Perth. The castle has great barrel vaulted ceilings, a sinister pit prison, spiral stairways and gun loops. Look out for the carved graffiti on the internal woodwork, left by off-duty soldiers in the 18th century. There is a marvellous "Son et Lumière" (Sound and Light Show) in August and September.

The Invercauld Arms stands on the spot where the Earl of Mar raised the Jacobite standard, in 1715, and you can see a plaque in the hotel, commemorating the occasion.

The Braemar Royal Highland Gathering is held every year on the first Saturday in September, drawing upwards of 50,000 people. It includes all the traditional events both athletic and musical, together with plenty of stalls and sideshows. The Royal Family attend the games, which might be why it is one of the biggest events of its kind in Scotland. The origins of these Highland Games are said to date from the 11th century when Malcolm Canmore held contests to find the best soldiers for his struggles against the Normans.

Linn of Dee

There is a beautiful, though very popular, circular tour of about 12 miles (19.2 km) that takes you west from Braemar through the wooded Dee Valley to the Linn of Dee. Here the river surges through a gorge, in breathtakingly lovely scenery, filling the air with the noise of its tumult and a haze of spray.

TOURIST INFORMATION
Aberdeen, tel 0224-632727. It is open all year.
Banchory, tel 03302-2000. It is open Easter to October.
Stonehaven, tel 0569-62806. It is open Easter to September.
Ballater, tel 0338-55306. It is open Easter to mid October.
Braemar, tel 03383-600. It is open Easter to October.

WHERE TO STAY
This popular area has a wide range of places to stay. Consult the local tourist brochure for full details and descriptions.

Banchory Lodge Hotel, Banchory, tel 03302-2545. B&B from £35: categories 5,4,5: 25 bedrooms, 23 en suite. In a lovely position where the Water of Feugh flows into the Dee, this Georgian hotel has a nice old world hospitality. Popular with the fishing fraternity.

Burnett Arms Hotel, High Street, Banchory, tel 03302-2545. B&B from £16: categories 5,5,4: 17 bedrooms, 10 en suite. A friendly hotel right in the middle of Banchory.

Huntly Arms Hotel, Charlestown Road, Aboyne, tel 0330-2101. B&B from £14:

categories 4,5,6: 44 bedrooms en suite. A family owned and run hotel dating back to 1600, where the Scottish atmosphere is enhanced by the kilted proprietor.

Alexandra Hotel, 12 Bridge Square, Ballater, tel 0338-55376. B&B from £12: categories 4,3,5: 6 bedrooms, 4 en suite. It is very near to the golf course.

The Coach House, Netherley Place, Ballater, tel 0338-55462. B&B from £16.50: categories 4,4,5: 9 bedrooms, 6 en suite. Overlooking the village green in the middle of Ballater, this comfortable hotel will arrange fishing and golf for you.

Craigendarroch Hotel and Country Club, Braemar Road, Ballater, tel 0338-55858. B&B from £37.50: categories 6,6,6: 23 bedrooms en suite. In 29 acres (11.6 ha) of attractive wooded hillside, overlooking the River Dee, and Lochnagar, this hotel has a 55 ft (16.5 m) indoor swimming pool, a whirlpool bath, two saunas, two squash courts, snooker, games room, gymnasium, health and beauty treatment, and a dry ski slope. When you've worked up an appetite there are two restaurants.

Invercauld Arms Hotel, 5 Bridge Square, Ballater, tel 0338-55417. B&B from £16.50: categories 3,4,3: 25 bedrooms en suite. Some rooms with lovely views over the River Dee. A Victorian house with every modern comfort.

Fife Arms Hotel, Mar Road, Braemar, tel 03383-644. B&B from £10.50: categories 4,5,4: 87 bedrooms, 40 en suite. Comfortable and friendly hotel with good food.

Tullich Lodge, Ballater, tel 0338-55406. Dinner, B&B from £55. 10 bedrooms en suite. A Scots Baronial style hotel set on a wooded hill overlooking Ballater. Highly recommended by top food guides. A hotel of real character for those who appreciate individuality.

EATING OUT

All the hotels above will give you a good meal. Dinner from about £7.

The Green Inn, 9 Victoria Road, Ballater, tel 0338-55701. A granite built former Temperance Hotel in the centre of the town, with a patio for summer meals. Good Scottish food. Dinner from £7.50.

Tullich Lodge, Ballater, see above. Delicious meals using fresh local produce in season. Set menu daily from £15. Must book well in advance.

From Aberdeen west to Tomintoul

The A944 from Aberdeen towards the west takes you through farm and moorland towards the hills. Less spectacular than Deeside, it is nevertheless attractive country with an air of prosperity and several large private estates.

Castle Fraser

Castle Fraser (open daily in the summer: adults £1.40, children 70p. Grounds open all year by donation) is about 15 miles (24 km) from Aberdeen, to the north of the road. It is one of the most spectacular of the Castles of Mar, dating from the 16th century and incorporating an earlier castle. If you look closely at the great heraldic panel on the north side, you can see the inscription "I Bel", left by one of the Bel family, master masons who helped in the building. The Bel family was very active in Aberdeenshire and may have had a hand in the building of both Crathes and Craigievar. You can see an exhibition, off the courtyard, showing you the story of the Castles of Mar.

Alford

Montrose fought one of his victorious battles against the Covenanters in 1645 near Alford, ten miles (16 km) further west, on the ground between the village and the bridge over the Don. A sad story hangs over the scant ruin of **Terpersie Castle**, four miles (6.4 km) north-west of Alford, and dating from 1561. The last owner, George Gordon, fought for Prince Charlie at Culloden. He fled to the castle after the battle, to lie low until the worst of the reprisals were over, but his young children, unaware of the threat, revealed that "papa was at home" to his pursuers. He was captured in the castle and later executed.

Kildrummy Castle

Kildrummy Castle (open at standard Ancient Monument times: adults 50p, children 25p) is eight miles (12.8 km) west of Alford, on the A97. Founded in the early 13th century, Kildrummy is one of the most impressive and historic of the castles in this area. Edward I captured it and altered its design. Robert Bruce sent his wife and children here when he went into exile on Rathlin Island, in 1306. The story is told of a treacherous blacksmith who betrayed the fugitives to the English in return for their promise of "as much gold as he could carry". He set fire to the castle, whose inhabitants surrendered, receiving as his reward the molten gold, poured down his throat! The English executed Nigel Bruce, Robert's brother; the garrison was "hangyt and drawyn" but Robert's intrepid wife, Elizabeth, escaped with her children and fled north to Tain. In 1404, Alexander Stewart, son of the Wolf of Badenoch, kidnapped the Countess of Mar, having killed her husband in order to widow her, and forcibly married her in order to gain the title of Mar. Final plans for the 1715 Jacobite rebellion were made at Kildrummy, as a result of which it was forfeited and half destroyed.

It is an extensive ruin, with a broad ditch and curtain wall, round towers, a keep and gatehouse. The gardens are lovely, with a Japanese rock and water garden built in the quarry from which stone was taken for the castle, and a replica of Old Aberdeen's Brig o' Balgownie, spanning the stream among shrubs and alpines.

Glenkindie

If you go two miles (3.2 km) south to Glenkindie, you can see a well preserved earth house in a clump of trees, its short entrance passage leading to two chambers, under massive roof slabs. You need a torch for the inner chamber.

Glenbuchat Castle

From Glenkindie you can follow the course of the Don, through the valley of **Strathdon** and up into the hills to the west. Glenbuchat Castle stands by the road before Strathdon village, and dates from the 16th century. It was the seat of "Old Glenbucket" (sic), a staunch Jacobite who died in exile in France after Culloden.

Corgarff Castle

Corgarff Castle (open at standard Ancient Monument times: adults 50p, children 25p), about seven miles (11.2 km) west of Strathdon, is a 16th-century tower-house. The Hanoverians converted it into a garrison post and barracks, after Culloden, to guard the military road from Perth to Fort George. It is a stark, ugly place with a star-shaped wall with gun loops. As you look up at what was once the tower, think of the terrible day, in 1571, when the family of the Laird, Alexander Forbes, was besieged here by a rival clan, the Gordons. In her husband's absence, Forbes' wife refused to surrender. Edom o' Gordon ordered that the castle be burned, and she died in the flames, with her entire family and household.

This is skiing country, for hardy, experienced skiers who don't need too many sophisticated lifts and resorts.

Tomintoul

The Lecht Road, from Corgarff to Tomintoul, is part of the military road built by the Hanoverians after Culloden. It rises steeply from 1,330 ft (399 m), to 2,100 ft (630 m), within a distance of about three miles (4.8 km). This is an area of wild, bleak moorland that is frequently cut off by snow in winter, with fierce winds causing high drifts. Remote farms and communities can be cut off for days. There is a ski tow half way along, between Tornahaish and Tomintoul.

Tomintoul, on the border with the Highland region, eight miles (12.8 km) north-west of Corgarff, is the highest village in the Highlands, at 1,160 ft (348 m). There is good fishing, skiing, and many lovely walks in the surrounding moorland and hills. It is a place that is easy to drive through in a hurry, so that you miss many of its attractions. Away from your car you will discover remote valleys, hidden in the folds of the hills, with tumbling burns and tiny lochans, rich in bird, animal and plant life.

Tomintoul Museum (open daily in the summer: admission free) gives you a good idea of the social history of the area, including a reconstructed farm kitchen with all the old implements. The Tomintoul and Strathavon Highland Games are held every July.

The **Glenlivet Distillery Visitor Centre** (open weekdays: admission free) is seven miles (11.2 km) to the north. Here you can go on an interesting tour of the distillery, and see the exhibition about whisky.

TOURIST INFORMATION

Broad Street, Aberdeen, tel 0224-632727. It is open all year.

Station Yard, Alford, tel 0336-2052. It is open April to September.

WHERE TO STAY

Forbes Arms, Bridge of Alford, Alford, tel 0336-2108. B&B from £10: categories 3,3,3: 8 bedrooms, 4 en suite. A small, friendly hotel with a cheerful atmosphere.

Colquhonnie Hotel, Strathdon, tel 09752-210. B&B from £9.25: categories 3,3,4: 10 bedrooms. Nice old fashioned hospitality.

Gordon Arms Hotel, The Square, Tomintoul, tel 08074-206. B&B from £13: categories 3,3,4: 32 bedrooms, 6 en suite. A comfortable hotel with good Scottish atmosphere.

Kildrummy Castle Hotel, by Alford, tel 03365-288. B&B from £25: categories 5,4,5: 17 bedrooms en suite. Here you can enjoy the elegance of a real castle with the comforts of a modern first class hotel. There is a good restaurant and you can get very reasonable skiing, fishing and shooting packages.

Blairfindy Lodge Hotel, Glenlivit, tel 08073-376. B&B from £25: categories 4,5,4: 12 bedrooms, 7 en suite. Just another sporting hotel, until you get inside and experience the very friendly atmosphere and the exceptional food, which people come a long way to appreciate.

EATING OUT

Kildrummy Castle Hotel, see above, for good Scottish food with fresh local ingredients. Dinner from £10.

Minmore House Hotel, Glenlivit, tel 08073-378. If you prefer good Aberdeen Angus steak disguised, try it with whisky sauce. Dinner from £7.50.

Blairfindy Lodge Hotel, see above. Very highly recommended. Leave room for the pudding trolley. Dinner from £10.

From Aberdeen: north-west to Forres

The A96 is the main road from Aberdeen to Inverness, flanked by rich farmland and studded with ancient castles. If you take the minor roads you find quiet farming communities in pleasant, rolling scenery.

WHAT TO SEE

Kintore

About ten miles (16 km) from Aberdeen is the little village of Kintore, a royal burgh since 1506. Its quaint town hall, with attractive outside stairs, was built in 1737. The church has a 16th-century tabernacle (sacrament house) decorated with painted angels on a panel. You can see a Pictish stone in the graveyard with carvings on it that are both Christian and pagan; a good example of how confused those early Christians were, and how they were careful not to offend any pagan gods that just might exist in spite of what the missionaries said.

Balbithan House and Garden

Balbithan House and Garden (open by arrangement only, tel Kintore, 32282, in the summer: adults 80p, children 20p) is about two miles (3.2 km) north-east of Kintore. It is a fine 17th-century house with a charming old-world garden, with old-fashioned roses, herbs and yew hedges. In the house you can see a small museum with an interesting collection of antique kitchen equipment and there is usually an exhibition of paintings in the galleried music room.

Inverurie

Inverurie, 16 miles (25.6 km) from Aberdeen, stands in an area rich in Pictish remains. **The Museum** (open daily except Sundays: admission free) has an interesting permanent archaeological exhibition. It also stages three "thematic" exhibitions each year. The Bass is a 60 ft (18 m) high motte, just outside the town, the site of a 12th-century castle. Mary, Queen of Scots visited a castle on this site in 1562. You can see Pictish stones in the cemetery, with some clear carvings on them.

Stones and Monuments

The Brandsbutt Stone is two miles (3.2 km) north of Inverurie. On it are very clear Pictish symbols and Ogham inscriptions, dating from the 8th century. **The Harlaw Monument**, on the B9001 less than five miles (8 km) north of Inverurie, is a red granite obelisk marking the site of a particularly bloody clan battle, in 1411. The Countess of Ross renounced her title to become a nun, leaving two uncles to fight for it: Donald, Lord of the Isles; and Buchan, son of Regent Albany. Donald was beaten and not only lost his claim to the title but was also forced to swear allegiance to the crown at a time when the Lords of the Isles considered themselves to be kings. Not much further along the road you can see the **Loanhead Stone Circle** with a ring of standing stones surrounding a mass of smaller ones that were a burial cairn.

Pitcaple Castle

Pitcaple Castle (open most days in the summer:admission free) is on the A96, south of Loanhead. This 15th- to 16th-century Z-plan tower house has most attractive 19th-century additions, including two round towers. It is still a family home. Mary, Queen of Scots came here in 1562 and danced on the lawn, as did her great, great grand-son, Charles II, in 1650. The tree under which these two monarchs danced was replaced in 1923, by Queen Mary, with the red maple that you can see today. On a tragic day, also in 1650, Montrose was brought here, a prisoner, renounced by the king for whom he had fought, on his way to execution in Edinburgh.

More Stones

A mile (1.6 km) south of Pitcaple, don't miss the **Maiden Stone**, thought to be one of the finest of the early Christian monuments. It is 10 ft (3 m) high and has a Celtic cross and Pictish symbols. It dates from the 9th century.

Bennachie (pronounced Ben-a-hee) is the long, wooded ridge rising to 1,733 ft (520 m), to the south, with a hill fort on **Mither Tap**, one of the peaks. Many claim Bennachie to be the site of the Battle of Mons Graupius, where the Roman Agricola penetrated into the north-east and defeated the tribes in AD 83. The Forestry Commission has made lovely forest walks in this area, well sign-posted. A car park is also provided.

About 13 miles (21 km) north-west of Inverurie on the B9002, you can see the

Picardy Stone, dating to the 7th and 8th century. Its Pictish symbols include a serpent, mirror and the mysterious "spectacles" that are featured so often in those ancient carvings.

Leith Hall

Leith Hall (open every afternoon in the summer; adults £1.40, children 70p; grounds open all year by donation) is four miles (6.4 km) west of the Picardy Stone, down a splendid avenue. The earliest part of the house dates from 1650, a tower house with turrets and gables, with further wings added during the 18th and 19th centuries, around a central court yard. In the exhibition room, you can see a writing case presented to Andrew Hay, the laird, by Prince Charlie on the eve of Culloden, and the official pardon given to Andrew Hay after he had fought for the prince.

The grounds include a splendid zigzag herbaceous border, a rock garden, pond walk with observation hide, picnic area and a flock of Soay sheep.

Huntly

Eight miles (12.8 km) north of Leith Hall, you pass through **Strath Bogie**, with **Clashindarroch Forest** high on the west, its rich valleys running down into the lowland. There are lovely walks up in these wooded hills.

Huntly, 38 miles (61 km) north-west of Aberdeen, is a pleasant 18th-century town on the plain, surrounded by hills, lapped by the Rivers Deveron and Bogie.

WHAT TO SEE

Huntly Castle (open during standard Ancient Monument times: adults 50p, children 25p) is an imposing ruin in a wooded park above Deveron Water. It is a stately 17th-century palace beside a Norman motte, once called Strath Bogie Castle. It was the seat of the Marquesses of Huntly (The Gay Gordons), the most powerful family in this part of Scotland until the middle of the 16th century. The 12th-century fortress on the motte was owned by the Earl of Fife, a Gaelic Norman. Robert Bruce convalesced here in 1307 after an illness, but just before the Battle of Bannockburn, the laird turned against Bruce. After the battle, his lands were forfeited and given to Sir Adam Gordon of Huntly, who had supported Bruce.

In those days the fortress on the motte was made of wood, gradually being replaced by stone and finally destroyed during the Civil War of 1452, in the reign of James II. James IV was a frequent visitor, during an era when the Gordon Earls of Huntly were at the zenith of their power, and it was here that he witnessed the marriage between Catherine Gordon and Perkin Warbeck in 1496. Warbeck was a Flemish impostor, pretender to the English throne, claiming to be Richard, Duke of York, the younger of the two 'princes in the tower'. It suited the Scottish king to encourage his claims, but Warbeck met his cumuppance in the tower of London and was executed in 1499.

The rise and fall of the Gordons was reflected in the rise and fall of Huntly Castle, until the second Marquess of Huntly lost his head for supporting Charles I, having first been imprisoned in the castle. Don't miss the awful dungeons and the basement passage walls marked by the graffiti of the dungeon guards.

Huntly Museum (open Tuesday to Saturday: admission free) in the library in Main Square, gives you a good grounding of local history, with temporary "thematic" exhibitions throughout the year.

Adamson Agricultural Museum (open at all reasonable times, by donation) is two miles (3.2 km) south of the town. It has a large collection of agricultural implements and kitchen equipment, including hand tools and farm machinery, mostly from the north-east of Scotland.

Dufftown

Dufftown, ten miles (16 km) west of Huntly, is known as the capital of Scotland's malt whisky distilling, giving rise to an old couplet:

Rome was built on seven hills,
Dufftown stands on seven stills.

It is the possession of the three essential ingredients that make this area so rich in distilleries: good barley, peat and the right sort of water. The **Glenfiddich** and **Balvenie Distilleries** are open to the public, for free conducted tours on weekdays.

Dufftown Highland Games are held in July.

Dufftown Museum (open daily in the summer: admission free) has a collection of local photographs and shows the process of whisky making.

Auchindoun Castle (open at all times: admission free), 2 miles south-east of Dufftown is a massive ruin on top of an isolated hill, enclosed by pre-historic earthworks. In 1689, a party of Jacobites gathered within these walls to hold a council of war, after the death of their gallant leader, Graham of Claverhouse (Bonnie Dundee) at Killiecrankie.

Balvenie Castle

Some of the stones from Auchindoun were removed and used in the building of Balvenie Castle (open Thursday to Sunday in the summer: adults 50p, children 25p), a mile (1.6 km) north of Dufftown. Now a picturesque ruin, this was a 14th-century stronghold owned by the Comyns. Edward I came here in 1304; Mary, Queen of Scots visited it in 1562, and Cumberland's troops occupied it in 1746.

Keith

Keith is 11 miles (17.6 km) north-west of Huntly, on the Isla. Of interest in an area that is not strongly Catholic, is the Catholic church, with an imposing copper dome. It was built in 1830, helped by a donation from the Emperor Charles X of France, who took refuge in Scotland after he was exiled. The picture over the altar, "The Incredulity of St Thomas", was presented to the church by the emperor. Keith holds a Festival of Traditional Music and Song in June.

The Strathisla Distillery (open on weekdays: admission free) is nearby. It gives you another chance to watch the processes that produce Scotland's most popular export.

Fochabers

Fochabers, eight miles (12.8 km) north-west of Keith, on the Spey, is a good base from which to explore this area with its attractive riverside walks, excellent fishing and chance to take the "whisky trail".

Elgin

Elgin, 17 miles (27.2 km) north-west of Keith, is a popular holiday centre. It is a busy market centre for the rich farmland around and is situated on the banks of the River Lossie. It has one of Scotland's most glorious ruined cathedrals. The town, sturdy and compact, built of granite with a number of old and attractive houses, is drenched in history and is an excellent centre for exploring the north-west corner of Grampian.

James II used Elgin as a royal residence. It is first mentioned in history books in 1190; and was the northern limit of Edward I's progress through the country. The town was partly burned by the Wolf of Badenoch, in 1390 and again in a struggle for power between the Douglases and Huntlys in 1452. Prince Charlie lodged at Thunderton House for 11 days before Culloden.

The town's Highland Games are held in July, and a Fiddlers Rally, in September.

WHAT TO SEE

Elgin Cathedral (open standard Ancient Monument times: adults 50p, children 25p) stands on grass beside the river. It is a lovely soaring symphony of arches, towers and windows, fretted against the sky. It was founded in 1224 and damaged by fire in 1270. In 1390, the Wolf of Badenoch, wild and vicious natural son of Robert II, having been excommunicated by the bishop, burned down both town and cathedral, with his "wyld, wykked Helandmen". After many ups and downs, the cathedral was stripped of its lead in 1567, by order of the Privy Council, in order to raise funds for defence: this act of authorised sacrilege was rewarded by the sinking of the ship that carried the lead. In 1650, Cromwell's troops did their worst to what remained, tearing down a beautiful rood screen and smashing the beautiful tracery of the west window. From then on the lovely building fell into complete ruin. But even now, walking among its mellow stones, looking up at the magnificent relics of its former glory, you get a great feeling of sanctity and peace.

The Bishop's House is just north-west of the cathedral. Here you can see a wing of this old house with the 16th-century coat of arms on the wall.

Elgin Museum (open daily except Sundays, in the summer: adults 25p, children 10p) in the High Street, won an award for its world-famous collection of old red sandstone, Permian and Triassic fossils. Other exhibits include some Bronze Age relics and natural history displays.

Spynie Palace

A couple of miles (3.2 km) north of Elgin, not open to the public but easy to see from

Elgin Abbey

outside, is Spynie Palace. This is the ruined castle of the bishops of Moray in the 13th to 17th centuries. It is strange to think that at one time the sea reached as far as the hillock on which the palace stands, with a good harbour and town. The sea then threw up a bar of sand and shingle across the mouth of the estuary, cutting off Spynie and turning the area into a loch surrounded by marshland. A canal was built in 1808, linking Spynie with Lossiemouth five miles (3.2 km) north on the coast, but great floods in 1829 destroyed all the works and the loch was drained. The old palace saw much history. Mary, Queen of Scots stayed there in 1562 during her tour of the north, and it became a refuge for Covenanters in 1654, during Montrose's campaigns.

Lossiemouth

Lossiemouth, five miles (8 km) north of Elgin, is a popular resort with a pretty harbour and good beach. It is a busy fishing port. Ramsay MacDonald was born here in 1866, the famous British politician whose house is marked with a plaque. This stretch of coast is wild and windswept, with great sweeps of sand, rich in wild fowl.

Burghead

At Burghead, seven miles (11.2 km) to the west, you can find traces of both Iron Age and Norse forts. In the Iron Age fort you can go down steps to what is called the "Roman Well", probably an early Christian baptistry, fed by a natural spring. In common with many communities, Burghead re-enacts ancient ceremonies that were performed to scare away evil spirits: called "burning the clavie", a lighted tar barrel is carried through the streets every January. Burghead Highland Games are held in June.

Findhorn Bay

Findhorn is a small, pretty village seven miles (11.2 km) round Burghead Bay to the west, and on the eastern arm of Findhorn Bay. This bay is a large expanse of tidal flats that dry out at low tide.

In the huge caravan (camper/trailer) park at Findhorn, you will find the **Findhorn Foundation**, an international community of some 200 members, founded in 1962, as a centre for "spiritual and holistic education". The inhabitants stroll about, smiling politely, and you will need determination to get through their apparent unwillingness to communicate with strangers.

In the little village of **Kinloss**, on the southern edge of Findhorn Bay, you will see a small overgrown ruin that was once an important Cistercian centre. It was founded by David I who was led there by a dove after he had lost his way in the forest.

The Culbin Sands that stretch away to the west of Findhorn Bay were formed by a storm in 1694. During this storm mighty rollers, coming in from the sea, brought layer after layer of sand, to create these 3,600 acres (1,440 ha) of dunes and marram grass. Much of this coastline has changed dramatically over the years, as a result of the storms that batter it.

The Kincorth House Gardens (open daily in the summer: adults 40p: children free), south-west of the bay, are worth a visit. Here you can see a wonderful display of specimen trees, rose borders, herbaceous borders, shrubberies and lawns.

Pluscarden Abbey

Pluscarden Abbey (open at all times: admission free) is signposted off the A96, about three miles (4 km) to the south between Elgin and Forres and you should not miss this most priceless gem of the Grampian region. Lying in a sheltered hollow below a ridge of wooded hills in a valley, Pluscarden represents an act of faith that must be an inspiration to believer and non-believer alike. You can hardly fail to come away from this place without feeling spiritually uplifted. The original abbey was founded by Alexander II, in 1230, for an order of white-habited monks, the Valliscaulians, whose mother house was in France. It suffered damage from Edward I, in 1303, and far worse damage from the Wolf of Badenoch, during his revenge on the Bishop of Elgin in 1390. In 1454 it took in Benedictines from Urquhart Priory, probably for economic as well as political reasons. Just before the Reformation took off, a greedy, scheming prior, Alexander Dunbar, anticipating what was to come, managed to 'redistribute' priory funds and lands in favour of his family. He died in 1560 and by the end of that century the priory had passed into the authority of a lay commendator. The estate passed through various hands, gradually falling into disrepair and ruin.

In 1943 the Pluscarden lands were given to the Benedictine community of Prinknash Abbey, near Gloucester, a breakaway community from an Anglican order, whose proposals of doctrinal reform had caused some of its monks to rebel and become Catholic. This order of converted Benedictines started rebuilding Pluscarden in 1948 and today you can see what they have achieved: a truly remarkable feat.

The choir and transepts are entire, as are the domestic buildings. The interior is a haven of calm, timeless tranquillity, lit by a rich glow of colour from the modern stained glass windows and overlaid by a lingering smell of incense. If you are lucky, you may hear, drifting through the stones from the Lady Chapel, the sound of the monks, singing their daily office. You can go into the transept aisles, now a public chapel, and kneel at the south end and look through a wide "squint" into the Lady Chapel.

You can visit Pluscarden at any time, and you will often see the monks busy about their work on the land, dressed in their white habits, investing the place with a medieval atmosphere.

Forres

Forres, 12 miles (19.2 km) west of Elgin, has a long history going back to before the day when Macbeth and Banquo met the witches on the blasted heath, on their way to the town to attend the court of King Duncan. The Forres Highland Games are held in July.

The Crimean Memorial Obelisk, at the west end of the High Street, stands on the site of Forres Castle, where King Duncan held his court.

The Falconer Museum (open daily in the summer: admission free) also in the High Street, gives you an idea of the town's history. It has displays of natural and social history, fossils and archaeology and temporary exhibitions.

The Nelson Tower, high on Cluny Hill and a landmark for miles, was built in memory of Admiral Nelson and you get splendid views from the top.

Sueno's Stone

Less than a mile (1.6 km) out of the town, north-east to Kinloss and Findhorn, look out for one of the most outstanding examples of a Pictish sculptured stone that you will ever see—Sueno's Stone. It stands over 20 ft (6 m) high, a slender sandstone shaft dating from the 9th or 10th century. It is clearly carved with a battle scene on one side, full of bodies and heads and weapons, round a broch, with a cross on the reverse side (probably a cenotaph commemorating a victory). It has a splendid setting, overlooking the Moray Firth, proud and remote.

Brodie Castle

Brodie Castle (open daily except Sundays in the summer: adults £1.25, children 60p) about five miles (7.2 km) west of Forres, stands on land given to the Brodies by Malcolm IV in 1160 and owned by them until the present day. The castle you see now was an 18th- and 19th-century restoration of a predecessor that was destroyed in 1645. It is a fine, pale cream coloured building, with conical turrets and coats of arms on the outer walls and approached down a fine beech avenue. In the castle you can see lovely French furniture, English, Continental and Chinese procelain, and a wonderful collection of paintings. There are woodland walks by a four acre (1.6 ha) loch, a picnic area, adventure playground, car park and shop.

TOURIST INFORMATION
Broad Street, Aberdeen, tel 0224-632727. It is open all year.

The Square, Dufftown, tel 0340-2501. It is open mid-May to September.

17 High Street, Elgin, tel 0343-2666/3388. It is open all year.

Falcolner Museum, Tolbooth Street, Forres, tel 0309-72938. It is open mid May to September.

Church Road, Keith, tel 05422-2634. It is open mid May to September.

The Square, Tomintoul, tel 08074-285. It is open mid May to September.

WHERE TO STAY

Aberlour Hotel, High Street, Aberlour, tel 03405-287. B&B from £12.95: categories 4,4,4: 19 bedrooms, 15 en suite. Comfortable and friendly.

Craigellachie Hotel, Victoria Street, Craigellachie, tel 03404-204. B&B from £21: categories 5,5,6: 31 bedrooms, 26 en suite. Nice rambling old hotel with a warm atmosphere.

Eight Acres Hotel, Sheriffmill, Elgin, tel 0343-3077/3088. B&B from £30: categories 5,5,4: 57 bedrooms, 54 en suite. A modern 3-Star hotel with a sports complex that includes a heated swimming pool, jacuzzi, sauna, solarium, squash and gymnasium.

The Mansion House Hotel, The Haugh, Elgin, tel 0343-48811, B&B from £20: categories 5,5,5: 12 bedrooms en suite, including 2 four-poster suites. A 100 year old mansion house with plenty of modern comforts. They will arrange fishing, shooting golf, etc for you.

Crown and Anchor Inn, Findhorn, tel 03093-30243. B&B from £12: categories 3,2,3: 6 bedrooms en suite. An 18th-century coaching inn on Findhorn Bay with its attractive village. The atmosphere is friendly and lively, and you can get free boats from the hotel.

Gordon Arms, High Street, Fochabers, tel 0343-820508. B&B from £15: categories 4,3,4: 14 bedrooms, 8 en suite. An attractive, old fashioned inn with a good restaurant.

Royal Hotel, Tytler Street, Forres, tel 0309-72617. B&B from £17: categories 3,4,5: 20 rooms, 17 en suite. Comfortable hotel with friendly service.

Castle Hotel, Huntly, tel 0466-2696. B&B from £14: categories 4,4,5: 24 bedrooms, 13 en suite. This imposing building, once the home of the Duke of Gordon, has lovely views from all the rooms. The food and wine are excellent and fishing and golf can be arranged.

Royal Hotel, Church Road, Keith, tel 05422-2528/2313. B&B from £11: categories 4,4,5: 12 bedrooms, 6 en suite. A friendly, comfortable hotel in the middle of the town.

Pittodrie House Hotel, Pitcaple, by Inverurie, tel 046-76 202. B&B from £21: 12 bedrooms en suite. You approach this attractive 15th-century house down a long tree-lined drive, as if you were going to stay in a gracious private house. The illusion is not broken when you go inside to find a warm welcome among lovely paintings, tapestries and antiques, with comfortable bedrooms, Cordon Bleu cooking and a good wine list.

EATING OUT

All the hotels above will give you a good meal from about £7. For a special treat go to the Pittodrie House Hotel, see above. You will get a first class dinner here made with fresh local ingredients. Dinner from about £15.

The Rothes Glen Hotel, Rothes, tel 03403-254. A Scottish Baronial mansion in 40 acres (16 ha) with Scottish Baronial food. Dinner from about £15.

The Park House Restaurant, Elgin, tel 0343-7695. A good dinner of prime beef or local seafood and game. Dinner from about £6.

The north-east corner of Grampian

Taking the A947 from Aberdeen to Banff, you pass **Dyce Old Church**, not far from the airport, seven miles (11.2 km) north-west of the city. Here you can see two more good examples of Pictish symbol stones. Cut across to the B999 that runs parallel four miles (6.4 km) to the east and go seven miles (11.2 km) north to Pitmedden.

WHAT TO SEE

The Pitmedden Garden makes a very good outing, along attractive rural lanes. The garden (open all year, daily: adults £1.10, children 55p) was created by Sir Alexander Seton, who inherited Pitmedden in 1667. It was restored by the National Trust for Scotland in 1952. July and August are the best months to see this re-creation of a formal 17th-century garden, split-level with an upper garden and terraces overlooking the great garden. There are 30,000 bedding plants arranged among symmetrical box hedges, with a centrepiece depicting Sir Alexander Seton's coat of arms, the Scottish saltire and thistle. Pillared gates lead into the great garden, down a graceful twin stairway, with two ogee-roofed pavilions at the corners. There is a fountain in each garden and no less than 27 sun dials, none of which is more than ten minutes off true time. Sir Alexander modelled his floral designs on those used at Holyrood. He did this for Charles I in 1639. Whether you admire formal gardens or not, you cannot fail to appreciate the splendour of this one. You can see Sir Alexander's bath house, in one of the two-storied pavilions, and a key to all the flowers in the garden. In the other pavilion is an exhibition on the evolution of formal gardens.

The Museum of Farming Life (open daily in the summer, garden and museum entrance combined: adults £1, children 50p) has a collection of agricultural and domestic implements. On the 100 acre (40 ha) estate there is a woodland and farmland walk.

Tolquhon Castle

Tolquhon Castle (open at standard Ancient Monument times: adults 50p, children 25p) is a mile north-west of Pitmedden. This attractive ruin was once the seat of the Forbes family; a large quadrangular mansion of the 16th century built onto an early 15th-century rectangular tower. A strong fortress exterior hides a domestic residential inner court. You can still see the kitchen, cellars and stairways, with the hall and Laird's

Room (which has a private stair to the kitchen) on the first floor. An inscription on the gatehouse refers to the laird who did so much to enlarge the original castle: "...Al this wark, excep the auld tour, was begun be William Forbes 15 Aprile 1584, and endit be him 20 October 1589...".

William Forbes' master mason was Thomas Leiper, of a renowned family of masons, and it was he who designed the elaborate Gothic tomb of William and his wife Elizabeth Gordon. This you can see in the church at **Tarves** close by. It is rich in Renaissance detail, with statuettes of the couple standing on either side.

Haddo House

Haddo House (open daily in the summer: adults £1.40, children 70p) is less than four miles (6.4 km) north of Tarves. It is a Georgian house built in 1732 by William Adam on the site of a former house, home of the Gordons of Haddo, earls and marquesses of Aberdeen for over 500 years. The previous house, House of Kellie, was burned down by Covenanters. The present one is charming, standing in a park surrounded by lovely gardens, showing all William Adam's mastery of symmetrical design. It has a wealth of antique furniture, pictures and treasures in its elegant rooms. The stained glass window in the chapel is by Burne-Jones. Haddo has developed its own choral society, with a theatre beside the house. This is now one of Scotland's leading musical bodies with productions of opera and concerts starring international artists. (If you are interested in attending any of its concerts, programme details are available by writing to the Choral Secretary, Haddo House, Grampian. Remember, seating is limited.)

Fyvie Castle

Fyvie Castle (open every afternoon in the summer: adults £1.40, children 70p) is about eight miles (12.8 km) to the north-west. The castle dates from the 13th century and was opened to the public for the first time in 1986. Once described as the "crowning glory of Scottish Baronial architecture", Fyvie stands on a mound above a bend in the River Ythan, approached up a long drive that skirts the lake among trees and rhododendrons. In the days when kings moved from house to house, William the Lion used to visit Fyvie. It passed through many hands over the centuries until the National Trust for Scotland acquired it from the Forbes-Leiths in 1984. The building that you see today is a splendid edifice in which is embodied substantial remains of the medieval Fyvie. Square and round towers soar to a mass of corner turrets, conical roofs and corbels.

Alexander Forbes-Leith bought the estate in 1889. He used the fortune that he had made in the American steel industry to restore the castle, sweeping away much of the ugly additions that had been added over the years, and filling it with the treasures that you will see. Notable are the paintings, which include some of the finest portraits you could ever hope to see, by Gainsborough, Romney, Opie, and Raeburn. The "pièce de résistance", perhaps, is the 18th-century portrait of Colonel William Gordon, by Pompeo Batoni; a deliciously romantic study of a patrician colonel, standing in rich silken tartan, gazing somewhat disdainfully at a statue of Roma. It is a picture you can stand in front of for hours. Fyvie is a stately home you should not miss.

Towie Barclay Castle

Towie Barclay Castle (open by appointment only) lies a mile (1.6 km) to the west. It has a square, 16th-century turreted tower and its upper floors are modernised.

Turriff

Turriff, eight miles (12.8 km) to the north on the A947, stands at the meeting place of the River Deveron and the Water of Idoch. It is a small red sandstone town, dating from at least the 12th century when there was a religious foundation on the site of the present ruined church. The town is still remembered for "The Trot of Turriff", when a party of Royalists defeated the Covenanters in the first skirmish of the Civil War, in 1639. In June there is a pipeband contest in Turriff and the Turriff Show in August.

Delgatie Castle

Delgatie Castle (open by appointment only: c/o Captain Hay of Hayfield, tel 0888-634 79; adults £1, children 50p) is two miles (3.2 km) east of Turriff. This is the tower house home of the Hays of Delgatie, dating back to the 12th century, with later additions. Inside you can see pictures and weapons and fine 16th-century painted ceilings. Mary, Queen of Scots stayed here for three days in 1562 and there is a portrait of her in the room she used. This very striking L-plan house has a turnpike stair of 97 steps, to make you feel giddy.

Eden Castle

Eden Castle (open at all times: admission free) is about six miles (9.6 km) south of Banff. It is a ruin with a legend attached to its 17th-century stones. The wife of a tenant on the estate asked the laird to control her wild son. He did so, by drowning the boy in the river, and the mother's subsequent curse caused the castle to fall down. All that remains now is the tower.

Macduff

Macduff is a plain, unpretentious fishing town three miles (4.8 km) to the north of Eden Castle. It is built around a four-basin harbour, with a thriving fish market and a customs house. If you climb the hill behind the town, to its 70 ft (21 m) high **War Memorial Tower**, you can get splendid views of the rugged coastline.

Tarlair

Just east is Tarlair, a spa in 1770, when a mineral spring was found to have healing properties. Health fanatics used to drink seawater and then the spring water, to ensure good health. The spring was blown up by a mine, during the last war, and there is now a large open-air swimming pool in the rocky bay.

Banff

Banff, less than two miles (3.2 km) to the west, looks across the Deveron Estuary and Banff Bay. It is a splendidly dignified old county town to which the landed gentry retreated in the 16th to 18th centuries. They would do so during the winter months when their castles became too cold and draughty. The elegant town houses that you see today were considerably easier to keep warm. In the Middle Ages, Banff traded with the Low Countries, a thriving exchange of hides, wool, sheepskin and salted salmon. Smuggling was rife along this part of the coast. Banff was an important herring fishing port, until the harbour silted up after a storm and caused the Deveron to change course. The fleet moved across the bay to Macduff.

The town has a Flower Show in August.

WHAT TO SEE

Duff House (open in the summer: adults 50p, children 25p) is beside the golf course. Although incomplete, this house (designed by William Adam for the first Earl of Fife) is among the finest works of Georgian baroque architecture in Britain. Inside there is an exhibition that interprets the motif. Duff House Royal Golf Week is held in September.

Banff Museum (open in the summer: admission free) is a must for ornithologists. It contains collections of stuffed British birds.

If you drive along the coast to the west you will discover a string of charming little fishing villages, each one with its own special character and legend.

Whitehills, is the first village you will come to, two miles (3.2 km) from Banff. Here the women had a reputation for being of a "superior comeliness".

The green and pink serpentine marble of **Portsoy**, six miles (9.6 km) further west, provided two chimney pieces for Louis XIV's Palace of Versailles. Today you can buy small, more portable samples of this lovely stone, in the form of paperweights and knick-knacks.

Three miles (4.8 km) inland at **Fordyce** you will find a picturesque cluster of cottages round a small 16th-century tower and quaint church in a delightful medieval setting.

Three miles (4.8 km) from Portsoy round Sandend Bay mountainous seas crash over the wall into the tiny harbour at **Sandend**. If you walk a mile (1.6 km) or so west along the cliff you will come to the ruin of **Findlater Castle**, a jagged relic of the castle that refused entrance to Mary, Queen of Scots in 1562.

Cullen, six miles (9.6 km) west of Portsoy, tucked in under a steep hill overlooking Cullen Bay, has a wonderful sweep of white sand on which are curious red sandstone rocks called the "Three Kings of Cullen".

Buckie is about eight miles (12.8 km) on round the coast, to the east of Spey Bay. Here, where the River Spey meets the sea, is an important fishing base with all the attendant maritime establishments: chandlers, boat builders, ice works, fish market and the largest scampi processing factory in Scotland. Don't miss **Buckie Maritime Museum** (open all the year except Sundays: admission free) in Cluny Place. There is a comprehensive display of fishing methods, coopering, lifeboats, navigation and all aspects of local maritime history. You should also see the **Peter Anson Gallery**, with water-colours of the east coast villages and the development of the fishing industry in Scotland.

From the mouth of the Spey you can walk eight miles (12.8 km) west to **Lossiemouth** along the beach. This is a perfect place for family holidays.

The coast road east of Macduff, towards Fraserburgh, links up many more of these attractive fishing villages. All have lovely views out to sea and make an extremely pleasant drive on a fine day, especially if you stop off to explore each tiny community.

Gardenstown, a cluster of cliff-hanging houses seven miles (11.2 km) east of Macduff, is believed to have been founded by survivors of the massacre of Glencoe.

Pennan, five miles (8 km) east again, is a picturesque village on a ledge below high red sandstone cliffs with a sandy beach running down to the sea. If it seems familiar to film-goers, it was used as one of the sets in *Local Hero*.

A road runs steeply down to the beach, in **New Aberdour**, three miles (4.8 km) further east, to where St Drostan is said to have landed in the 7th century. He founded a Celtic monastery at **Old Deer**, nine miles (14.4 km) west of **Peterhead**, from which came the *Book of Deer*, the most precious literary relic of the Celtic church. It is a 9th-century Latin manuscript of parts of the New Testament, with Gaelic notes in the margins. This remarkable treasure is now in the University Library at Cambridge.

Rosehearty, five miles (8 km) to the north-east of New Aberdour, was founded in the 14th century by a colony of Danes. It has a small museum giving you the history of this region.

Pitsligo Castle (open at all times: admission free) just south of Rosehearty, is an impressive ruin, dating from 1424. It was last owned by Lord Pitsligo who was remembered for his generosity to the poor and for his highly successful evasion of capture after the final Jacobite rebellion in 1746. The rugged red sandstone cliffs, topped by rolling farmland, give way to low, rocky reefs to the east, running out to sea and providing a severe hazard to ships in bad weather.

Fraserburgh, five miles (8 km) east of Rosehearty, and founded in 1546 by Sir Alexander Fraser, is not a beautiful town, but its large fishing fleet can be seen all round the British Isles. There are several fish curing factories in the town.

Kinnairds Head is a great slate rock that sticks out to the north of the town. On it are the scant remains of **Kinnaird Castle**, built in 1574 by the grandson of the town's founder. The fifth storey was removed in 1787, to make way for a lighthouse. Below the castle you can see a watch tower 25 ft (7.5 m) high and called **Wine Tower**. It was built at the same time as the castle.

Inverallochy is five miles (8 km) to the east of Fraserburgh Bay. It consists of a quaint row of fisher cottages, and the stark tooth of what was **Inverallochy Castle**, to the south.

Four miles (6.4 km) inland, south of Fraserburgh, you can see the **Memsie Burial Cairn**, a large stone cairn that may date from 1500 BC.

On the southern slopes of **Mormond**, 12 miles (19.2 km) south of Fraserburgh and the highest point in this area, at 768 ft (230 m), you can see a white horse and stag, cut out of the hill to expose the quartzite. The horse was said to be a memorial to one killed in battle. The stag was cut in 1870.

You will find no trace today of Cox Haven, or Cockshafen, a tiny hamlet that existed in the 18th century round the Strathbeg Burn, six miles south-east of Fraserburgh on the coast. Thought to have been refugees from religious persecution in Holland, this long-vanished community are believed to have held curious ritualistic ceremonies connected with 'fresh water' dolphins that had been stranded in Loch of Strathbeg by freak waves during a storm.

Peterhead

Peterhead, 18 miles (29 km) down the coast from Fraserburgh, is a town whose houses are built of local pink granite. It was founded in 1593, its harbour growing up round a bay and so ideally placed to cope with the influx of sea traffic during the oil-boom of the 1970s. Surrounded by sandy beaches, golf courses and dunes, it is the largest town in the north-east, after Aberdeen.

The Arbuthnot Museum and Art Gallery (open daily throughout the year except Sundays: admission free) is in Arbuthnot House. Here you can find out about the history of the fishing industry as well as find information about whaling and the Arctic.

Deer Abbey

Nine miles (14.4 km) to the west is Deer Abbey (open at all times). This should not be confused with Old Deer (see above). Here you will see the attractive but insubstantial remains of a Cistercian monastery founded in 1219 by Comyn, Earl of Buchan. It thrived until the late 16th century and you can see the ground plan quite clearly, though most of the masonry was taken away for other uses.

Slains Castle

Walk north a couple of miles (3.2 km) along the cliffs from the sandy sweep of **Cruden Bay**, seven miles (11.2 km) south of Peterhead, till you get to Slains Castle (open at all times: admission free). The castle is situated high above the sea and is an extensive ruin dating from 1598. It was built by the ninth Earl of Errol to replace Old Slains Castle, of which only a fragment remains, four miles (6.4 km) to the south. Slains is a splendid, awe-inspiring ruin and its extremely dangerous situation makes it unsuitable for children to visit unaccompanied. It is amusing to walk among its massive, rather gloomy walls and recall the visit that was paid to it by Johnson and Boswell in 1773. Johnson was most impressed by its position, writing: "... when the winds beat with violence it must enjoy all the terrifick grandeur of the the tempestuous ocean...". Boswell, always fastidious about his comforts, wrote: "...I had a most elegant room: but there was a fire in it which blazed; and the sea, to which my windows looked, roared; and the pillows were made of the feathers of some sea-fowl which had to me a disagreeable smell: so that by all these causes I was kept awake a good while...".

Johnson and Boswell also visited the **Bullers of Buchan**, just north of Slains Castle. Here the sea has eroded a sheer 200 ft (60 m) rock chasm, into which the water pounds through a natural archway. Bullers means "boilers". Johnson wrote of this: "...which no man can see with indifference, who has either sense of danger or delight in rarity...". Much to the horror of Boswell, Johnson insisted on exploring the cavern by boat, writing later: "...If I had any malice against a walking spirit, instead of laying him in the Red Sea, I would condemn him to reside in the Buller of Buchan."

Ythan Estuary

Ten miles (16 km) south the Ythan Estuary cuts deeply inland, with a nature reserve along its shore from **Collieston** to the northern point, and some way inland. This vast area of dunes, heath, pasture and cliff has many species of wild fowl and is a glorious haven for anyone interested in botany. The paths and shore are open for anyone: permits are needed for other parts.

Fourteen miles (22.4 km) of sand stretch south from the estuary to Bridge of Don, above Aberdeen. This area is flanked by golf courses and is ideal for riding.

TOURIST INFORMATION

Broad Street, Aberdeen, tel 0224-632727. It is open all year.

Collie Lodge, Banff, tel 02612-2419. It is open all year.

Saltoun Square, Fraserburgh, tel 0346-28315. It is open mid May to September.

Fyvie, tel 06516-597. It is open mid May to September.

20 Seafield Street, Cullen, tel 0542-40757. Open June to September.

WHERE TO STAY

Banff Springs Hotel, Golden Knowes Road, Banff, tel 02612-2881. B&B from £17: categories 6,5,5: 30 bedrooms en suite. A very modern, comfortable hotel whose staff will arrange golf and fishing for you.

Carmelite House Hotel, Low Street, Banff, tel 02612-2152. B&B from £8: categories 3,3,3: 8 bedrooms, 1 en suite. Friendly, relaxed atmosphere. Not as austere as the name implies.

The County Hotel, High Street, Banff, tel 02612-5353. B&B from £15: categories 5,5,5: 6 bedrooms en suite. An attractive town house with a warm welcome.

Cluny Hotel, 2 High Street, Buckie, tel 0542-32922. B&B from £16: categories 5,3,4: 17 bedrooms, 14 en suite. A solid, old fashioned hotel with a friendly atmosphere.

Cullen Bay Hotel, Cullen, tel 0542-40432. B&B from £15: categories 4,4,4: 18 bedrooms, 10 en suite.

Bayview Hotel, 57 Seafield Street, Cullen, tel 0542-41031. B&B from £15: categories 4,4,5: 6 bedrooms, 2 en suite. A small, friendly hotel overlooking the harbour and the sandy beaches of Cullen Bay. Excellent food.

Ladbroke Hotel, Ellon, tel 0358-20666. B&B from £28: categories 6,5,4: 40 bedrooms en suite. A very modern, purpose-built hotel.

Royal Hotel, 63 Broad Street, Fraserburgh, tel 0346-23352. B&B from £12: categories 4,4,5: 14 bedrooms en suite.

Pennan Inn, Pennan, tel 03466-201. B&B from £12.50: categories 4,4,4: 6 bedrooms en suite. A delightful place, below spectacular cliffs, with great character. If you saw the film *Local Hero*, this was the inn. Excellent local sea food in the Smugglers Restaurant, and water sports available.

EATING OUT

You should get a reasonable dinner in most of the hotels above, from about £7.

The Old Monastery Restaurant, Buckie, tel 0542-32660. An old converted chapel with spectacular cliff-top views, and mouth-watering sea food. The owner-chef has won several awards with justification. Dinner from £10.50.

Hawthorne Restaurant, Church Street, Fordyce, by Portsoy, tel 0261-43003. A beautifully restored 17th-century cottage. Very good Scottish food. Dinner from £10.50.

LOCAL SPECIALITY

A. J. Sutherland in Portsoy are excellent smokers of fish.

CRAFT CENTRES IN THE GRAMPIAN REGION

The following studios and workshops welcome visitors. Where a telephone number is given you should ring up to check times.

Ceramics

Glenbuchat Pottery, Glenbuchat, Strathdon, tel 09753-355. Terracotta garden pottery.

Milton of Crathes Studios, Crathes, Banchory, tel 033-044 601710. Pottery, prints, jewellery and picture framing in all stages of creation.

Portsoy Pottery, Shorehead, Portsoy, tel 026-14 2404. Domestic stoneware and exhibition pieces.

Knitwear

Claire Girdwood, Wester Waterlair, Fordoun, Laurencekirk, tel 056-12 533. Machine knitting.

Margaret Hyne Knitwear, Glenbuchat, Strathdon, tel 09753-355. Machine knitting.

Lapidary

Portsoy Marble, The Marble Workshop, Shorehead, Portsoy, tel 026-14 2404. Jewellery, etc made with local serpentine stone.

Weaving

Pennyfeu Doulies, Oldmeldrum, tel 06513-2419. Handwoven fabrics in pure new wool, silk and mohair. Hand weaving and spinning.

Luther Hand Woven Linens, 15 Main Street, Luthermuir. Handwoven table linen.

Russell Gurney Weavers, Brae Croft, Muiresk, Turriff, tel 08882-3544. Handweaving and handspinning.

Oldcake Studio, Arbuthnott, tel 056-12 474. Weaving and spinning.

Woodwork

The Woodcraft Shop, Invercauld Road, Braemar, tel 03383-657. Wood carving and turning shortbread and butter moulds.

Part XIII

HIGHLANDS

Highland Cow

The Highland region covers two-fifths of Scotland and has more than two million less inhabitants than Strathclyde which is half its size. The main road network is excellent but there are vast tracts of the region that are only accessible by boat or on foot. The landscape is as varied as it is magically beautiful: mountains, deep lochs, rushing rivers and burns of peaty water, sheltered wooded glens and a seaboard that must be the most spectacular in the world. If you want to explore it properly, take the minor roads, many of them single tracks with passing bays, and walk whenever you can. It would be impossible to mention all the beauty spots: you will find them wherever you look, in a million different forms. You can walk for miles over apparently bleak moorland and come suddenly to a secret glen, its steep banks carpeted in lush greenery, with its tumbling river cutting through the rocky bed in a ceaseless torrent. A good bird book, a good wild flower book and an Ordnance Survey map are essential equipment, together with comfortable, sturdy footwear and waterproof clothing, the moment you get out of your car.

Romance and history shroud every inch of the Highlands, as well as tragedy, for it was these lands that suffered the "Clearances" in the 19th century, when the people were turned off their crofts in their thousands to make way for sheep. Some fled to the coast and tried to exist on fishing; many emigrated. Now, as you wander in the hills and glens, you will come upon the stones of ruined crofting townships; bothies and byres, reduced to piles of rubble, where communities once thrived. But it must be said that the Clearances were not as heartless as they have sometimes been painted. For many families they meant the start of a new life in better conditions, with greater hope of prosperity. The old black-houses were not only uncomfortable and damp, they also bred disease, poverty and hardship.

The Highland people, descended from Celtic Scots and from Norse, as well as Pictish settlers, have a natural courtesy, kindness and charm that stem from the old patriarchal clan system which was founded on kindness and justice. Diffidence is blended with an instinctive hospitality that even the influx of tourism has not yet shaken. The Highlander is his own master: this also stems from the clan system when every man bore the name of the chief and considered himself to be part of the clan family, not a servant.

In the remoter parts of the Highlands, you will find that not much has changed in the last hundred years. There may be new hotels, all picture windows and pile carpets and bathrooms-en-suite, but the people who staff them are not very impressed by these modern trappings. Round the back you will find a few dozen derelict vehicles, discarded over the last 20 years; the surrounding countryside will be studded with rusting beer cans and empty whisky bottles, and in the kitchen it would not be unusual to find a live sheep among the inhabitants.

There is no shortage of things to do in the Highlands. Walking, climbing and drinking in the lovely scenery fills up the time too fast. For those who enjoy the slaughter of game there is shooting and stalking. There is excellent fishing in rivers, lochs and the sea. Pony trekking is a nice way to explore the countryside and there are plenty of golf courses. The Highland coastline, particularly in the west, is a sailor's paradise, with potential for all other water sports, including sub-aqua diving. Finally, for skiers, there is challenging skiing in the Cairngorms, from Aviemore, and in Glen Coe.

SPECIAL ATTRACTIONS

Among the many events that take place in the Highland region each year, are Highland Games, where you can see displays of Highland dancing, piping competitions, and all the traditional sports such as putting the weight, tossing the caber and high jump. These gatherings, usually less showy than the smart dress parades of Grampian, are a splendid way of observing the Highlander on holiday. There are side shows and stalls, hot dog stands, fish and chips, and always a beer tent. As you walk round the arena, you find a lone piper, practising a pibroch behind a caravan (trailer) while pacing up and down with precise steps, or a pair of little girls, in full Highland costume, practising the intricate steps of a Highland fling.

The origins of these games were probably as fairs, organised by the chiefs, but some of them had their roots in a more serious purpose, namely, when a king summoned the clans to compete in various contests, so that he could select the strongest men for his armies.

Another popular event to look out for is Sheep Dog trials, where you can watch these most intelligent of the animal kingdom being put through their paces. There can be few things more stirring than to see a first class pair of dogs working a flock of sheep, controlled by a master who appears to communicate by thought rather than word. You can go to the Great Glen Sheepdog trials, in Fort William, in July, for one of the best of these, and you will usually see smaller trials at the many agricultural shows.

TOURIST INFORMATION

Where the local tourist information office is closed in the off season, you can get advice,

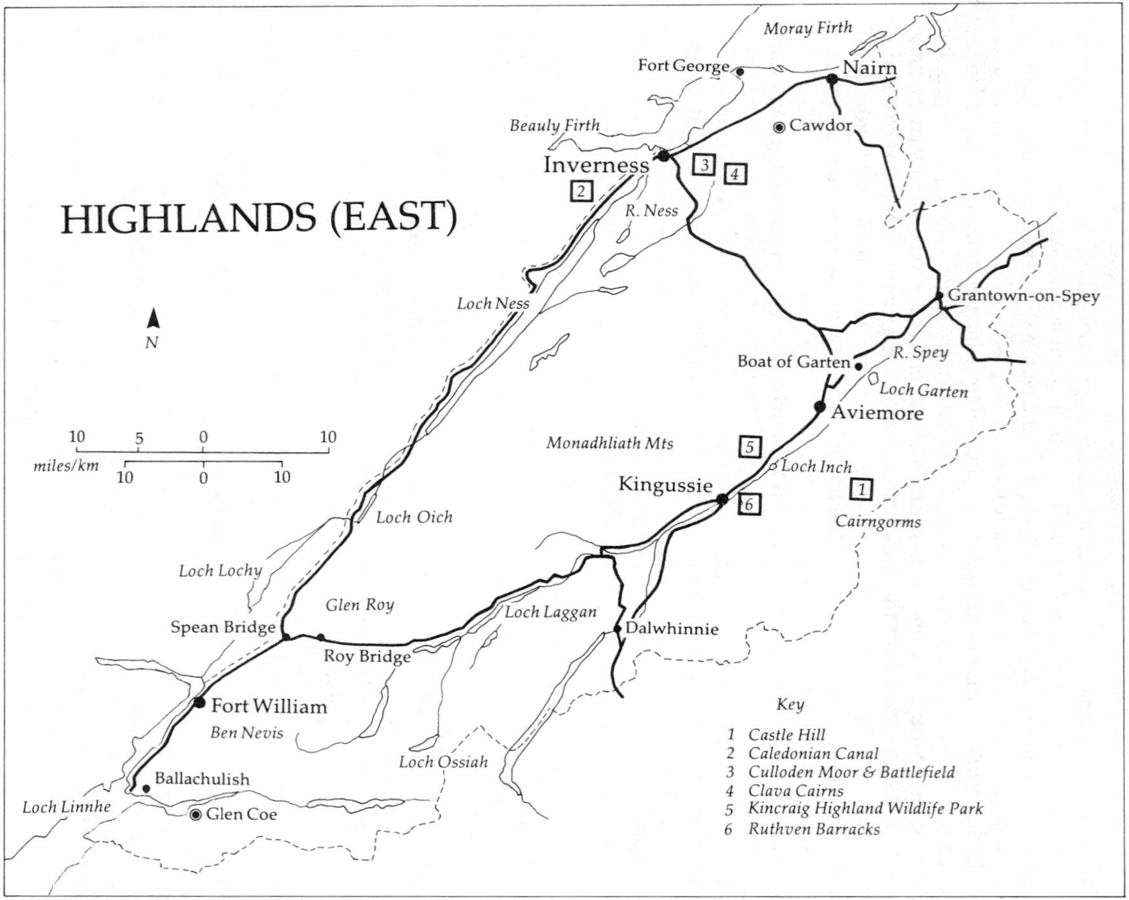
HIGHLANDS (EAST)
N
10 5 0 10
miles/km
10 0 10
Moray Firth
Fort George
Nairn
Cawdor
Beauly Firth
Inverness
R. Ness
Loch Ness
Grantown-on-Spey
R. Spey
Boat of Garten
Loch Garten
Aviemore
Monadhliath Mts
Loch Inch
Kingussie
Cairngorms
Loch Oich
Loch Lochy
Glen Roy
Loch Laggan
Spean Bridge
Roy Bridge
Dalwhinnie
Fort William
Ben Nevis
Loch Ossiah
Ballachulish
Loch Linnhe
Glen Coe
Key
1 Castle Hill
2 Caledonian Canal
3 Culloden Moor & Battlefield
4 Clava Cairns
5 Kincraig Highland Wildlife Park
6 Ruthven Barracks

information and tourist brochures from Inverness, Loch Ness and Nairn Tourist Board, 23 Church Street, Inverness, tel 0463-234353. It is open all year round.

Inverness and Speyside

Inverness

As the capital of the Highlands and the junction of many routes, Inverness is the logical place from which to begin to explore the Highland region. Approaching from the south, on the A9, you come over the final crest and see the town spread out below you, between the **Beauly Firth** and the **Moray Firth**, linked to the misty, blue-grey hills of the **Black Isle** by the graceful span of the new Kessock Bridge. No one could call it a beautiful town, though it has its own charm and some lovely riverside vistas; but its history goes back many centuries.

St Columba is recorded by his biographer, St Adamnan, as having visited the Pictish King Brude in a castle somewhere near the River Ness: this could have been on **Craig Phadrig**, the small hill just west of the town where you can still find the remains of a 4th-century vitrified fort. It is more likely, however, that Brude's stronghold stood on the site of Macbeth's castle on **Auld Castle Hill** east of today's **Castle Hill**.

Historical fact and poetic fiction have become so inextricably interwoven around the story of Macbeth and his bloodstained journey to the throne that you will hear many different claims for the true setting for King Duncan's murder. The most reliable sources will tell you that the deed was done in a house near Elgin, in 1039, and not in Macbeth's castle in Inverness, but it is believed that Malcolm Canmore destroyed the Inverness castle in revenge for Duncan's death. A new castle was built in the 12th century on the site of the present one, and was much abused in subsequent years. The English occupied it in the War of Independence and Robert Bruce destroyed it. Its successor became the hub of conflict between Highlanders and those trying to subdue their wild ways. Jacobites occupied it in 1715 and 1745, after which they blew it up, to keep it from government hands. The present castle was built in the 19th century and still looks brand new, its pinkish walls rising from the small hill exactly like a toy fort. It houses the law courts and local government offices.

The centre of the town is compact, with some excellent shops in a vast new indoor shopping complex, the main streets radiating from the little Station Square, in which stands a statue of a Cameron Highlander, a war memorial to the local regiment, now amalgamated with the Seaforth Highlanders to become The Queen's Own Highlanders.

SPECIAL ATTRACTIONS

The Inverness Highland Games take place in July, during which month there is also a Festival Week, a Cadet Tattoo and a Wool Fair. There is a Folk Festival, in April. The Highland Antiques Fair takes place in the town in August, followed in September by the Northern Meeting Piping Competition, where you will hear the finest pipers of the day competing for the prestigious awards. For the newcomer to the piping scene, remember that a little goes a long way, until you begin to learn the intricacies of the music.

While you are in Inverness, you should go to the Holm Woollen Mills (James Pringle), in the western suburbs, where you can stock up on woollens, tweeds, kilts, rugs, etc, from the Mill Shop.

WHAT TO SEE

Inverness Museum (open from 9 am to 5 pm every weekday: admission free) in Castle Wynd, between the castle and the town hall, has some excellent features of social and natural history, archaeology, and the culture of the Highlands and Jacobite relics. There are often special exhibitions, as well as interesting talks and slide shows.

Perhaps the best view of the town is from the bridge below **Bridge Street**. Fishermen stand, thigh-deep in the fast flowing River Ness, flanked by well-proportioned houses and churches. When the sun shines, it is a curiously continental picture.

St Andrew's Episcopal Cathedral is to the south. An imposing, pinkish building on the banks of the river, it was built less than a 100 years ago, with an octagonal chapter house and a very elaborate interior.

Eden Court is beyond the cathedral. This great glass edifice, built in 1976, incorporates the 19th-century house of Bishop Eden. It is an 800 seat multipurpose theatre, conference centre and art gallery, with an excellent restaurant. Ambitious programmes are laid on throughout the year: concerts, ballet, drama, the latest films and many good exhibitions of art.

The Islands are reached by walking up the river away from Eden Court. These consist of a public park spread over the Ness islands, linked by foot-bridges, with good views back down the river towards the town.

Tomnahurich (The Hill of the Fairies) is the small hillock to the south-west. This is the town's cemetery and it contains many elaborate monuments clinging to the steep, wooded sides and a splendid viewing point from the top. From here you can look down on the environs of Inverness, with its neat, sturdy villas and well-kept gardens, and its air of dependable respectability.

The Caledonian Canal can be seen to the west. This canal links the Moray Firth with Loch Linnhe in the south-west at Fort William. The canal, constructed in the 19th century by Telford, and much used in the old days by boats wishing to avoid the long and often hazardous flog round the north coast, now offers a perfect way for those who enjoy boating to explore the Great Glen. You can hire cabin cruisers in Inverness, or take one of the passenger cruises that operate in the summer.

As you drive out of the town to take the road bridge north, you pass the 19th-century **Cameron Barracks**. These stand high on a ridge to the right, like a wise old guardian looking over the town. This was once the depot of The Cameron Highlanders. From here, many a brave young man walked out, newly trained, to give his life so that his Highland home should remain free.

Culloden

The visitor to Inverness feels an almost magnetic pull to **Culloden Moor**. You should go first to the new visitor centre on the edge of the battlefield. (The visitor centre, cottage and audio visual show are open in the summer, daily: adults £1, children 50p.) The audio visual show gives you the details of the tragic battle, on 16 April, 1746, when Prince Charles Edward Stuart and his 5,000 exhausted, starving and ill-equipped Highlanders were defeated by the Duke of Cumberland, son of George II, and his 9,000 well-trained and equipped army. During that battle 1,200 Highlanders fell; many more were butchered by order of the duke as they lay wounded. The prince watched the battle with tears in his eyes; he was led away and hidden by loyal Highlanders for five months, with a price of £30,000 on his head, until he returned to the Continent in a French frigate, to live out the rest of his life in wretched, debauched exile.

The visitor centre has an exhibition with life-size models and written explanations of history, with good illustrations. There is also a study room for school parties, with a library and Jacobite relics. In addition you will find a coffee shop and restaurant and a first class bookshop with a comprehensive range of Scottish publications.

Outside the visitor centre is the old cottage, the only building that survived the battle and was still inhabited at the beginning of the 20th century but which is now a **Folk Museum**. It still has its old furnishings and domestic equipment. Taped music and Gaelic add an authentic touch to this well-laid-out museum.

On the battlefield, which you can visit at any time of the year, you can see wooden plaques that tell you what clans fought where, and how the battle progressed. There are clan graves: communal burial sites with headstones bearing clan names, and a great memorial cairn, erected in 1881. On the edge of the bleak battle site is the **Well of the Dead** where the wounded Highlanders were slain as they drank water to revive themselves. A single stone bears the inscription "The English were buried here". The flat stone beyond the visitor centre is called the **Cumberland Stone**, thought to have been the vantage point from which the duke viewed the battle.

The Clava Cairns

The Clava Cairns are well signposted, a mile (1.6 km) east of Culloden. These form a remarkable Stone and Bronze Age burial site, possibly dating from 2000 BC. Three large burial cairns in a peaceful glade of beech trees take you back in time to the prehistoric rituals that would have accompanied the interrment of those farmers and herdsmen so many years ago. Two of the cairns have passages leading into them; the third has curious stone strips radiating from it like spokes of a wheel. Each is surrounded by a circle of standing stones, some inscribed with cup and ring symbols. Excavations revealed traces of cremated human bones, pottery and other remains: poignant memorials of men who were alive nearly 4,000 years ago.

The Coastal Strip, south of the Moray Firth

Take the back road from Culloden, signposted to Cawdor, through open farmland with sweeping views over the Moray Firth towards the Black Isle and Easter Ross.

Cawdor

Cawdor, pronounced Cawder, eight miles (12.8 km) north-east of Culloden, is familiar to anyone who has read Shakespeare's *Macbeth*. Within moments of having been told that he was to become Thane of Cawdor by the three witches, Macbeth is told by Ross that the king has indeed bestowed the title on him. The fulfilment of this prophecy encouraged him to bring about the final prophecy, that he should be king, by murdering King Duncan.

WHAT TO SEE

Cawdor Castle (open daily in the summer: adults £1.80, children 90p) dates from 1372, when the central tower was built. Domestic buildings were added in the 16th century and later re-modelled. Protected by a gully on one side and a dry moat on the other, the castle stands in a lovely walled garden which is ablaze with colour in the summer. You go in over the drawbridge and feel that you are in a living home, rather than a museum. There is a cosy, domestic atmosphere that makes it easy to imagine the castle as it must have been in medieval times, with its winding stairways and massive walls. There is plenty to see: Flemish tapestries, paintings, weapons, old domestic equipment and family heirlooms.

Outside there are nature trails, a 9 hole mini-golf course, putting green and picnic spots, as well as a licensed restaurant and souvenir shop.

Cawdor Village, straggling round the castle grounds, is not at all typical of Scottish villages: it has a peaceful cosiness that matches that of the castle. The church is 17th-century, built in thanksgiving, by the twelfth Lord Cawdor after he was saved from a shipwreck.

Cawdor Tavern is in the heart of the village. This delightful inn, has a dark wood and velvet interior and is decorated by ornamental plates and hunting scenes, its atmosphere being almost that of an English pub. A bust of Shakespeare gazes benignly over the saloon and you can get a good lunch here for a reasonable price.

Nairn

Nairn is five miles (8 km) north of Cawdor. This seaside holiday town is sometimes called the Brighton of the North, with its aura of old fashioned respectability. On the mouth of the River Nairn, it has good beaches, several golf courses and a reputation for a high average of sunshine. The Nairn Highland Games are in August. There is a Holiday Week and a Vintage Car Rally in July. The Fairground Fortnight and the Farmers Show are also in August.

Nairn Fishertown Museum (open on summer afternoons: adults 10p, children 5p) is in Laing Hall, King Street. Here you can see photographs and articles relating to the Moray Firth and the herring fisheries during the steam drifter era. There are also good displays of domestic life in a fishing community.

Fort George

Fort George (open during standard Ancient Monument times: adults 50p, children 25p) is ten miles (16 km) west of Nairn, on a windswept promontory jutting out into the Moray Firth. It is the most unspoilt example of an artillery fort in Europe. Built between 1748 and 1769, to replace "Old" Fort George in Inverness, destroyed by Prince Charlie in 1746, it is a classic 18th-century fortress. The defences include the traditional outer works; ravelin, ditch, bastion and rampart, designed by William Skinnor who was in his day the leading expert on artillery fortification. The government contractor who built it was John Adam, oldest son of the architect William Adam whose family has left such a wealth of fine buildings throughout Scotland.

You pass through the stern, forbidding fortifications to be brought to a delighted standstill by the mellow pink sandstone garrison buildings, their impeccable 18th-century proportions mercifully unscarred by Victorian or later "improvement."

The fort was built to house a garrison large enough to overawe Jacobite support in the Highlands, but by the time it was completed the Jacobite threat was finally dead, so it has never had a history of conflict. It became a base where a long series of regiments were mustered and equipped and from whence they embarked for service in America, the West Indies, the Middle East, India and South Africa. In 1881, when each British infantry regiment was allocated its own territorial recruiting area and home base, Fort George became the depot of the Seaforth Highlanders. Generations of Highland soldiers trained there for colonial service, for two World Wars and for modern cold war campaigns.

The regiments of the garrison change over every two years, and they have the privilege to live in barracks that are the oldest in the world still occupied by a battalion of British infantry.

The spirit of permanence is preserved by the **Regimental Museum of the Queens Own Highlanders** (open daily except on Saturdays in the summer and on weekdays in winter: admission free, donations welcome). Formed in 1961 by the amalgamation of the Seaforth Highlanders and the Queen's Own Cameron Highlanders, they are the present day descendants of the two historic regiments of the northern Highlands. In the building formerly used by the Lieutenant Governor, the Queen's Own Highlanders preserve a superb collection of uniforms, pictures, medals, weapons, Colours, artifacts and treasures, representing nearly every major campaign fought by the British army over the past 200 years. The splendour of red coat and tartan, the glitter of gilt plate and dirk, the glint of steel broadsword and bayonet, cannot fail to stir your imagination and make your heart beat a little faster. With its history, its atmosphere and its garrison, Fort George is unique as a 20th-century military base where the 18th century lives on.

TOURIST INFORMATION

Inverness, tel 0463-234353. It is open all year.

Nairn tel 0667-52753. It is open in the summer.

Daviot Wood, by Inverness, tel 046385-203. It is open in the summer.

WHERE TO STAY
The choice is enormous and you should get the tourist brochure which gives full particulars and descriptions. The following is just a small selection.

The Caledonian Hotel, Church Street, Inverness, tel 0463-235181. B&B from £22: categories 5,5,5: 112 bedrooms en suite. A convenient hotel in the middle of town with cabaret most nights.

Bunchrew House Hotel, Bunchrew, tel 0463-234917. B&B from £11.50: categories 4,4,5: 6 bedrooms, 2 en suite. A 17th-century mansion in 20 acres (8 ha) of garden and woodland.

Culloden House Hotel, Inverness, tel 0463-790461. B&B from £42.50: categories 6,4,4: 20 bedrooms en suite. A lovely Georgian mansion with strong Jacobite connections in its colourful history.

Carnach Country House Hotel, Inverness Road, Nairn, tel 0667-52094. B&B from £12.50: categories 5,5,3: 8 bedrooms en suite.

Gold View Hotel, Nairn, tel 0667-52301. B&B from £27: categories 6,6,5: 55 bedrooms en suite. A comfortable, family hotel overlooking the Moray Firth and Black Isle.

Kilravock Castle, Croy, tel 06678-258. B&B from £9: categories 3,3,3: 19 bedrooms, 6 en suite. Pronounced "Kilrawk" this historic old castle, is where Prince Charlie dined before Culloden. It stands in lovely, peaceful grounds near the river.

EATING OUT
Culloden House Hotel, see above. Scottish specialities served in Adam dining-room. Dinner from £10.

Glen Mhor Hotel, Inverness, tel 0463-234308. Good menu of Scottish fare. Dinner from £10.

Golf View Hotel, Nairn, see above. Try the roulade of smoked Findhorn salmon, or collop of fillet steak with scallop souffle. Dinner from £10.

Newton Hotel, Nairn, tel 0667-53144. Good local seafood. Dinner from £10.

The Taste Bud Bar and Restaurant, Nairn, tel 0677-52743. Excellent food in restored listed building in old fisher town. Dinner from £7.50.

Clifton Hotel, Nairn. Good food and classical music. Dinner from £10.

Speyside

The valley of the second longest river in Scotland, the Spey, cuts across the south-east corner of the Highland region, giving mile after mile of astonishing natural beauty. The Spey is born high in the hills above **Loch Laggan**, 40 miles (64 km) south of Inverness. Beginning as a tiny stream it gathers momentum as it flows east and then north to the sea near **Buckie** in Grampian region, fed by many burns that drain from the hills on either side and turn it into a great rushing tumult of water. It is as famous for its salmon as for its surrounding beauty. It runs between the great **Cairngorms** on the east and the **Monadhliath Mountains** to the west and it would take many years to explore completely.

Whatever time of the year you visit Speyside you will be enchanted by its changing scenery: in spring, with the green just coming through the winter browns, snow still capping the mountains; in summer, a glorious patchwork of heather and bracken, water and granite, trees and birdsong; in autumn, with snow already on the hills forming a backdrop to the splendour of the turning leaves; or in winter, a white Alpine world that makes you catch your breath.

The Aviemore Highland Games are in July. There is a Snow Rally in January.

Grantown-on-Spey

Grantown-on-Spey, 6 miles south of the Grampian border, is one of Speyside's tourist centres. A pleasant Georgian town at the junction of several routes, it is well situated as a base for exploring the area. Standing by the river among trees, the town was founded in 1776 by Sir James Grant, one of the Highland's "improving lairds". With the development of skiing in the hills, this area is popular all the year round for holidays that offer a large variety of things to do, for all ages and all incomes. The Grantown-on-Spey Highland Games are held in June. There is a Farmer's Show in August.

The Loch Garten Nature Reserve

The Loch Garten Nature Reserve is eight miles (12.8 km) south of Grantown-on-Spey. It is well known for its breeding ospreys. Americans, accustomed to seeing these "fish-hawks" in countless numbers nesting in their rivers and estuaries, are amused by the tight security that surrounds Scotland's few pairs, but it must be remembered that before the mid 1950s (when one pair set up their nest in a tree at Loch Garten) these birds had not been seen in Britain for almost 50 years. When an over-enthusiastic egg thief robbed this precious nest in 1958 precautions had to be taken. Now, it is not so unusual to look up and see the slow, flapping flight of one of these brown and white birds, or hear its shrill, cheeping cry. The nature reserve has a lot more than ospreys for you to see, if you are lucky and are prepared to stand still and observe. It is rich in other bird life, including blackcock, capercailzie and crossbills and you might see red squirrels and deer. In winter you can stand among the pines and look out over the dark waters of **Loch Garten** and listen to the haunting cry of geese and the eerie honk of whooper swans.

Boat of Garten, west of the loch, is so called after the ferry that operated here until a bridge was built in 1898. It is the home of the **Strathspey Steam Railway Association**, which has its own station and some remnants of the old Highland railway (closed in 1965). It was opened again in 1978 and you can travel to Aviemore behind one of the steam engines of the past. There is a small museum of railway memorabilia, always of interest to steam-engine buffs.

Aviemore

Aviemore, 14 miles (22.4 km) south-west of Grantown-on-Spey, is a thriving tourist centre and ski resort, teeming with holiday makers all the year round. Here you will find every sort of accommodation as well as cafes and restaurants, bistros and bars, gift shops, craft shops, souvenir stalls, amusement arcades and discos. Throughout the year you will see anoraks (parkas) and knapsacks, bright skiing clothes, shorts and tee-shirts, figures plodding along the roads with skis on their shoulders, and figures draped with cameras and binoculars.

From this seething hub of sporting activity you need go only a short distance to discover remote and lovely places. All around are heather-clad moors and craggy mountains, wooded valleys, cool, tumbling burns and deep, mysterious lochs. Beautiful, wild and unspoiled it all lies within easy reach.

The Aviemore Centre (open daily: admission free, with charges for the various attractions) offers a bewildering choice of activity. There is an ice rink and curling rink, swimming pool, theatre, cinema, ballroom, artificial ski slope, games room, sauna, solarium, squash courts, go-kart track, craft village and children's outdoor amusements.

Kincraig Highland Wildlife Park

Kincraig Highland Wildlife Park (open daily from March to November: admission fee) is six miles (9.6 km) south-west of Aviemore. Here you can see animals that used to roam free over the Highlands living in a natural setting: boar, wolves, bears, bison and many more. You drive through the park and must leave any pets in the kennels provided. There are also aviaries where you can see indigenous birds such as capercailzie, eagles and hawks and there is an exhibition on man and fauna in the Highlands.

Loch Inch

Loch Inch is a mile (1.6 km) south-east of Kincraig. It is formed by a widening of the river and is surrounded by blue hills and trees. Here you will find **Loch Inch Watersports Centre** where you can go canoeing, wind surfing, sailing or just swimming. There is a licensed restaurant and instructors are available to give lessons.

On a rocky point at the northern end of the loch you can see a tiny white church, built in the 18th century on a site that is said to have been used by Druids, and which was used continually for Christian worship since the 6th century. Inside there is an 8th-century hand bell that was used to call the faithful to worship, before the days of bells in steeples. **The Rock Wood Ponds**, south-east of the loch are rich in wild life.

Ruthven Barracks

Ruthven Barracks stand on a hillock east of the A9, five miles (8 km) south-west of Kincraig. This great, stark shell of a building, gaunt and substantial is now a ruin. It was the site of a stronghold of the Wolf of Badenoch (notorious son of Robert II) and was built after the 1715 Jacobite uprising to discourage further rebellion. It was extended by General Wade in 1734. Prince Charlie took the barracks from the occupying government troops during his ascendancy, and it was here, after Culloden, that some 1,500 surviving Jacobites assembled, awaiting their prince. They waited in vain, until they received the message that the cause was dead and they must now fend for themselves.

Before disbanding to return to the homes they had so eagerly left, they blew up the barracks.

Kingussie

Kingussie, a mile (1.6 km) to the west and now by-passed by the A9, is another popular holiday resort all the year round. Pronounced Kin-u-sie, it is a pleasant little town with one main street, backed by lovely Highland scenery. The Badenoch and Strathspey Music Festival is held here in March.

The Highland Folk Museum (open daily throughout the summer and on weekdays in the winter: adults £1, children 50p) is a "must" for anyone interested in the old Highland life and folklore. It was founded in Iona, in the 1930s and later moved here under the control of the universities of Glasgow, Edinburgh, St Andrews and Aberdeen. Beautifully arranged, both indoors and outside, you can see an 18th-century shooting lodge, a black-house from Lewis, a clack mill (named from its "clacking" noise) a turf-walled house from the central Highlands and many fascinating exhibits of farming and domestic life. Don't miss the exhibition of Highland tinkers.

Loch Laggan

From Kingussie, south to the Tayside Border, you cross bleak **Dalwhinnie Moor** with its great barren sweeps of upland, inhospitable and windswept: not a place to run out of petrol on a winter's night.

The A86, west from Kingussie, takes you through a valley flanked by steep hills, the road dipping and climbing beside Loch Laggan and alive with the clatter of falling burns. Abandon your car here and you will find glorious walks, up valleys into the hills, past secret lochans and hidden glens.

Glen Roy

Turn right (north) at **Roy Bridge**, 37 miles (59 km) west of Kingussie, and drive nine miles (14.4 km) into Glen Roy. At first it seems to be just another wild glen, the river tumbling down through wooded gorges to flatten out and meander at a more stately pace across the valley floor and the bare hills rising on either side. But stop at the large observation car park some way along and look down the valley. You will see several straight horizontal lines, high up along the hills, each line exactly matched by one on the opposite range. These "parallel roads" are terraces left by the receding water line of the ice lake that once filled the valley. They are geologically famous because of their clarity and they date from a late Ice Age build-up about 11,000 years ago. It is strange to stand there and try to imagine what it must have looked like then.

If you walk from the end of the road, you will discover several secret glens, each with its own character. With the help of a map you will see that is it not far beyond the source of the River Roy to the source of the River Spey, near little Loch Spey, tucked away up in the hills, gathering courage for its long treck to the sea.

TOURIST INFORMATION
Aviemore, tel 0479-810363. It is open all year.

Grantown-on-Spey, tel 0479-2773. It is open all year.
Carrbridge, tel 0479-84 630. It is open in the summer.
Boat of Garten, tel 0479-83 307. It is open in the summer.
Kingussie, 054-02 297. It is open in the summer.
Newtonmore, 054-03 274. It is open in the summer.

WHERE TO STAY

You have a large choice and should consult the tourist brochures which give full particulars and photographs. The following is just a small selection.

Aviemore Centre Chalet Motel, Aviemore Centre, tel 0479-810618. B&B from £9.50: categories 4,2,3: 72 bedrooms en suite. Comfortable, modern and very convenient, with relaxed atmosphere.

Badenoch Hotel, Aviemore Centre, tel 0479-810261. B&B from £12.30: categories 5,5,4: 79 bedrooms, 61 en suite. Large and very modern hotel.

Cairngorm Hotel, Aviemore, tel 0479-810233. B&B from £13.50: categories 4,4,4: 23 bedrooms, 18 en suite. Family house hotel, comfortable and friendly.

The Boat Hotel, Boat of Garten, tel 0479-83 258. B&B from £19: categories 5,4,4: 36 bedrooms, 31 en suite. Old fashioned Highland hospitality.

Craigard Hotel, Kinchurdy Road, Boat of Garten, tel 0479-83 206. B&B from £10: categories 4,4,4: 20 bedrooms, 8 en suite. Friendly welcome and family house atmosphere.

Carrbridge Hotel Carrbridge, tel 0479-84 202/255. B&B from £14: categories 3,5,5: 56 bedrooms, 28 en suite. Comfortable and friendly hotel conveniently situated for touring.

Grant Arms Hotel, The Square, Grantown-on-Spey, tel 0479-2526. B&B from £17: categories 6,5,4: 60 bedrooms en suite. Old fashioned hospitality in the middle of the town.

Spey Valley Hotel, Seafield Avenue, Grantown-on-Spey, tel 0479-2942. B&B from £11: categories 3,4,4: 19 bedrooms. Old family house with friendly welcome.

Duke of Gordon Hotel, Kingussie, tel 054-02 302. B&B from £10.50: categories 5,4,4: 54 bedrooms en suite. Comfortable hotel in nice grounds with lovely surroundings.

Muckrach Lodge Hotel, Dulnain Bridge, tel 047-985 257. B&B from £14: categories 4,4,4: 9 bedrooms, 4 en suite. Nice old family house with good service.

EATING OUT

Inverishie House Hotel, Kincraig, near Aviemore, tel 05404-332. Good local ingredients. Game and fish in season. Dinner from £10.

The Cross, High Street, Kingussie, tel 05402-762. "Dedicated to lovers of food..." Try the Venison Francatelli, or West Coast Prawns. Dinner from about £7.50.

The Osprey Hotel, Kingussie, tel 05402-510. Candlelit dinners. Fresh wholefoods used exclusively. Venison, peat-smoked salmon and trout. Dinner from about £7.50.

Muckrach Lodge Hotel, see above. Good traditional Scottish dishes. Dinner from £10.

The Southern Highland Region

Several routes meet at **Spean Bridge**, three miles (4.8 km) west of Roy Bridge and here you can see the much-photographed **Commando Memorial** by Scott Sutherland, erected in 1952. It is a striking group of Commandos standing on a high promontory looking out over the magnificent view towards Ben Nevis and **Lochaber**, surrounded by the wild, harsh terrain which was their training ground during the last World War.

Fort William

From Spean Bridge it is only seven miles (11.2 km) south to Fort William, at the southern end of the Caledonian Canal, a busy little tourist resort as well as the shopping centre for the whole of this area and the hub of several routes. Fort William is the epitome of a west Highland town, standing under the stern lee of **Ben Nevis**, Britain's highest mountain, 4,406 ft (1,322 m) high, with several ways to the top depending on your skill as a climber and your physical fitness.

The fort from which the town was named was demolished in the 19th century to make way for the railway. It was first built by General Monk in 1655, an earth construction that proved to be of insufficient strength when put to the test by rebellious Highlanders later in the century. It was then re-built in stone and named Maryburgh after the wife of King William III, before being named in honour of the king himself. It withstood Jacobite attacks in 1715 and 1746. The town which grew up around the railway is Victorian and sturdy, with a cheerful holiday atmosphere.

Don't miss the Great Glen Sheepdog Trials if you are here in July. The Highland Games are also in July and the Lochaber Agricultural Show is in August.

WHAT TO SEE

The West Highland Museum (open daily except on Sunday: adults 35p, children 15p) in Cameron Square, is crammed with interesting historical, natural history and folk exhibits. You can see a crofter's kitchen, just as it would have been in the old days with all the original equipment, as well as agricultural implements. Montrose's helmet is also there as are many Jacobite relics, including the bed in which Prince Charlie slept soon after raising his standard at Glenfinnan. There is also a fascinating "secret" portrait of the prince, used in the days when loyal Jacobites toasted "the king across the water", a meaningless blurr of paint until you view it from the right angle through a cylinder, when it is transformed into a recognisable portrait.

It is fun to pass a sunny hour or so leaning over the rails beside the long ladder of locks that bring the Caledonian Canal down to the level of the sea. The locks are only used by pleasure boats now and are worked by hand. You can usually catch them in use, the water boiling through the sluice gates until the level is equal either side.

Eight of the eleven locks that link Loch Linnhe with the canal, are called **Neptune's**

Staircase, a rise of 80 ft (24 m) which presented Telford with an enormous problem when he built the canal.

Ballachulish Bridge

There is a fast road along the east side of Loch Linnhe to the new Ballachulish Bridge, 13 miles (21 km) to the south. (Ballachulish is pronounced Balla-hoolish.) The bridge spans a narrow constriction between Loch Linnhe and Leven, where (not so long ago) a small car ferry used to slither and slide on the fast current. Loch Linnhe is always busy with pleasure boats in the summer.

Glencoe

Glencoe is four miles (6.4 km) to the east. This grim, dramatic pass with its raw peaks reaching up on either side is sliced by white scars of cascading water. There is an unmistakable aura of doom in this glen, enhanced by its well-known history: indeed, Glen Coe means Glen of Weeping, and many tears were shed on 13 February 1692. Macdonald of Glencoe, late with his oath of allegiance to King William III, provided the government with an excuse to get rid of his powerful clan. It was an affair of the greatest possible dishonour. Campbell of Glenlyon billeted himself and 128 soldiers with the Macdonalds for several days, living as guests and accepting the generous hospitality that was such an integral part of Highland life. The Campbells, acting on higher authority, rose one dawn and massacred their hosts as they slept. No one can drive through the glen now, 300 years later, and not glance up into the hills and remember that bitter morning and hear the cries of the women and children, and see the bloodstains in the snow. The **Massacre Memorial** marks the site of the massacre. Here you can see a tall, slender cross, a poignant memorial to a senseless murder.

You can also visit the **Glencoe and North Lorn Folk Museum** (open daily except Sundays in the summer: adults 30p, children 10p) in Glencoe village. It contains many Jacobite and historic exhibits, domestic implements, weapons, costumes, photographs, dolls and dolls' houses, tools, and much else, all housed in a group of thatched houses.

Clachaig

The National Trust for Scotland has a **Visitor Centre** at Clachaig, 2 miles (3.2 km) east of Glencoe village. Here a resident warden will advise you about good walks and climbing in the glen. This is a centre for some of the most challenging mountaineering in the country, much of which is not suitable for amateurs. There is a chair lift and T-bars for skiers at the head of the glen, and good skiing on **Meall a Bhuridh**, when conditions are right.

Loch Ossian

15 miles (9.3 km) north east of Glencoe, tucked into a valley surrounded by hills, is Loch Ossian. Here you will find a youth hostel and **Ossian's Cave**, high on **Aonach Dubh** which is traditionally regarded as the birth place of the great Celtic bard. To get

the best out of this area you must abandon your car, arm yourself with an Ordnance Survey map and keep within your own physical capabilities.

TOURIST INFORMATION

Fort William and Lochaber, Cameron Square, Fort William, tel 0397-3781. It is open all year.

Ballachulish, tel 085-52 206. It is open all year.

WHERE TO STAY

There is a large choice and you should consult the tourist brochures for full details. The following is just a small selection.

Corriegour Lodge Hotel, Loch Lochy, near Spean Bridge, tel 0397-84 285. B&B from £8: categories 2,3,4: 8 bedrooms. Marvellous easy-going atmosphere, very friendly and good food.

Alexandra Hotel, Fort William, tel 0397-2241. B&B from £19.50: categories 5,5,4: 88 bedrooms en suite. Conveniently situated in the middle of lovely holiday country.

Croit Anna Hotel, Fort William, tel 0397-2268. B&B from £19.25: categories 4,5,4: 90 bedrooms, 74 en suite. Comfortable, modern hotel.

The Highland Hotel, Union Road, Fort William, tel 0397-2291. B&B from £15: categories 5,5,5: 82 bedrooms, 39 en suite. Old fashioned welcome and friendly service.

Inverlochy Castle Hotel, Torlundy, Fort William, tel 0397-2177. B&B from £55: categories 6,6,6: 18 bedrooms, 16 en suite. Luxury service in impressive ancestral atmosphere.

Ballachulish Hotel, Ballachulish, tel 08552-239. B&B from £16.50: categories 5,5,4: 36 bedrooms, 27 en suite.

Clachaig Inn, Glencoe, tel 08552-252. B&B from £12.50: categories 3,3,4: 10 bedrooms, 4 en suite. Charming old inn in lovely surroundings.

EATING OUT

The Moorings, Banavie, by Fort William, tel 0397-7550. Traditional Scottish food. Dinner from £5.

Nevisport, Fort William, tel 0397-4921. Traditional Scottish food. Dinner from £5.

Creag Dhu Onich, tel 085-53 283. Local salmon, trout, sea food, game, wholefoods, vegetarian dishes. Dinner from £7.50.

South-western corner

The south-western corner of the Highland region is Jacobite country. It is also yet another enchanted land, full of beauty as well as history. Here, too, you will do best to abandon your car whenever possible and, if it is good weather, take a boat which provides the best way to explore the coast, for those with sailing ability.

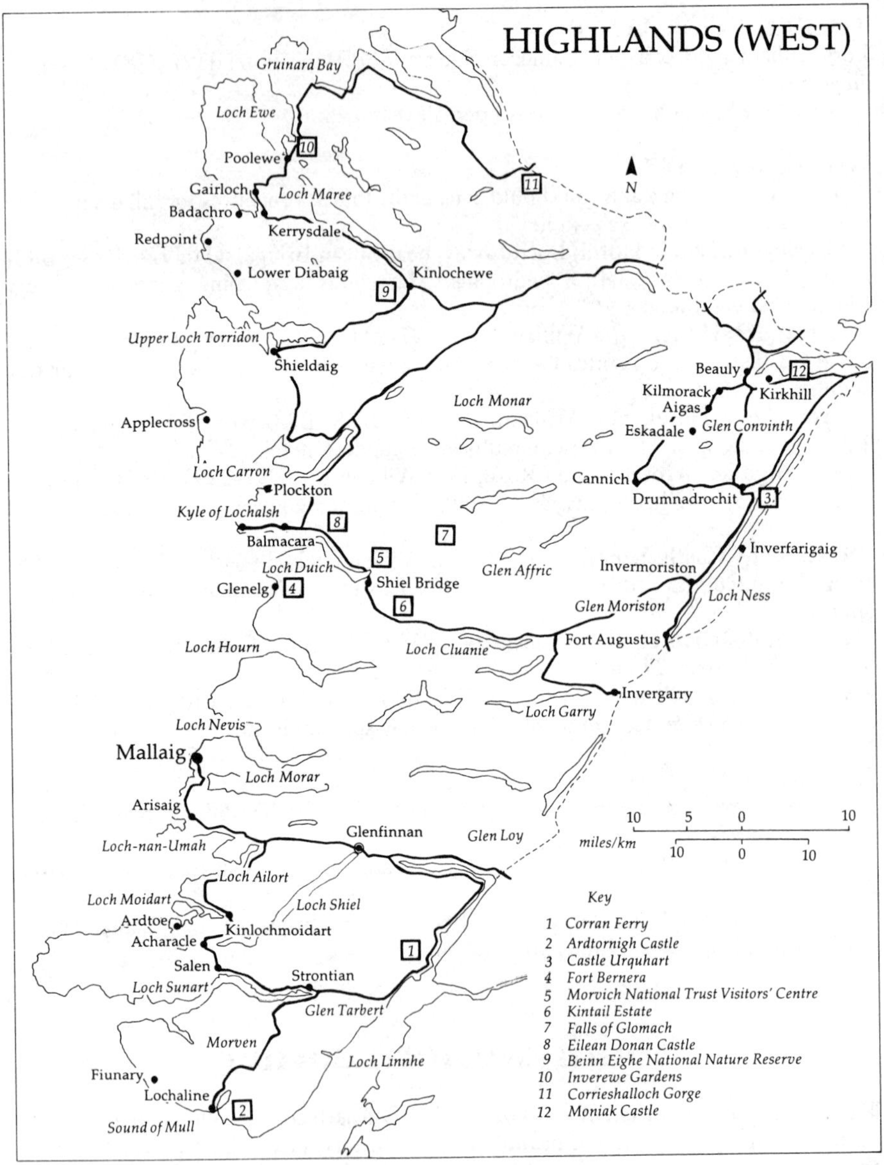
HIGHLANDS (WEST)
N
Gruinard Bay
Loch Ewe
Poolewe
Gairloch
Loch Maree
Badachro
Redpoint
Kerrysdale
Lower Diabaig
Kinlochewe
Upper Loch Torridon
Shieldaig
Applecross
Loch Monar
Beauly
Kilmorack
Aigas
Kirkhill
Eskadale
Glen Convinth
Loch Carron
Plockton
Cannich
Drumnadrochit
Kyle of Lochalsh
Balmacara
Inverfarigaig
Loch Duich
Shiel Bridge
Glen Affric
Invermoriston
Glenelg
Loch Ness
Glen Moriston
Fort Augustus
Loch Hourn
Loch Cluanie
Invergarry
Loch Garry
Loch Nevis
Mallaig
Loch Morar
Arisaig
Glenfinnan
Glen Loy
Loch-nan-Umah
Loch Ailort
Loch Moidart
Loch Shiel
Ardtoe
Kinlochmoidart
Acharacle
Salen
Strontian
Loch Sunart
Glen Tarbert
Morven
Loch Linnhe
Fiunary
Lochaline
Sound of Mull
10 5 0 10
miles/km
10 0 10
Key
1 Corran Ferry
2 Ardtornigh Castle
3 Castle Urquhart
4 Fort Bernera
5 Morvich National Trust Visitors' Centre
6 Kintail Estate
7 Falls of Glomach
8 Eilean Donan Castle
9 Beinn Eighe National Nature Reserve
10 Inverewe Gardens
11 Corrieshalloch Gorge
12 Moniak Castle

The Corran Ferry, nine miles (14.4 km) south-west of Fort William, will take you across Loch Linnhe. It runs frequently and the crossing takes five minutes. There are several districts in this peninsula, each one almost an island, with its own charm and character.

Strontian

The road south from Corran takes you down Loch Linnhe and then through lovely **Glen Tarbert**, 13 miles (21 km) to Strontian, pronounced Stronteen.

WHAT TO SEE
Here there is a **Nature Reserve** and the **Strontian Lead Mines**, opened in 1722. From these mines came the discovery of Strontianite, of which Strontium 90 is an isotope. These mines, manned by French prisoners of war, provided bullets for the Napoleonic wars.

Strontian has a Sheep Shearing Competition in June and an Agricultural Show in August.

Morvern is the area south. It is a district of great beauty, cut by delightful glens, alive with the sound of water and bird song. **Lochaline**, 19 miles (30.5 km) south-west of Strontian, on the southern shore of the peninsula, means "the beautiful loch". From here you can look across the **Sound of Mull** to **Fishnish Point**. There is also a car ferry service to Mull, running fairly frequently, and taking five minutes. (It does not run on Sundays in winter.) Silica sand is mined at Lochaline, for the making of optical glass.

Ardtornish Castle

Walk south-east along the coast from the mouth of Lochaline for a mile (1.6 km) to Ardtornish Castle (open at all times: free). The castle was built in 1340 and was for many years a stronghold of the Lords of the Isles. It stirs the heart to stand looking up at the ruined keep and ramparts, remembering those proud, independent chiefs, ruling over this territory with a total disregard for the authority of the crown.

Fiunary

If you follow the coast road west around Morvern for five miles (8 km), you come to Fiunary, once the home of the Macleods. George Macleod, the left wing, Presbyterian who re-established a community on Iona in 1938, took the name Lord Macleod of Fiunary when he was "elevated" from cleric to life peer in 1967.

Loch Sunart

There are lovely views across the sound, and you can drive round the point as far as Loch Sunart about 12 miles (19 km) to the north. **Salen** is on the northern shore of Loch Sunart, 12 miles (19 km) west of Strontian. It provides a perfect, safe anchorage for boats. There is a well-stocked yacht chandler here and an inn where you may find groups of holiday makers creating their own spontaneous ceilidhs in the summer months.

If you are a sailor, there can be few more memorable occasions than to sail out of Loch Sunart early on a fine morning, the wind on your quarter, the sun on your back, watching the whole of the island-studded Minch open up in front of you.

Ardnamurchan Peninsula

If you are a landsman, there is some rugged terrain as you go west into the Ardnamurchan Peninsula. The ruin of **Mingary Castle**, about 16 miles (25.6 km) along, was once the stronghold of the MacIans of Ardnamurchan. The castle stood on a rock cliff guarding the entrance to Loch Sunart and to the Sound of Mull. James VI came to Mingary to receive the homage of the Lords of the Isles, and was disappointed by their lack of enthusiasm for his sovereignty. The castle was taken by Montrose's men in 1644 and garrisoned in 1745 by government soldiers, who built a barracks within the walls.

Ardnamurchan Point, about 22 miles (35 km) from Salen, is the most westerly tip of the mainland of the British Isles. This wild, heather-clad place has a lighthouse which you may see over at the keeper's discretion. This most dramatic headland takes the full force of westerly gales and can present quite a challenge to small boats, even in lighter winds.

Going north from Salen you come to **Moidart**, where there is a Jacobite legend for every glen and loch.

Acharacle (difficult to pronounce: the "ch" is guttural) is a sheltered little village at the western end of **Loch Sheil**, 3 miles (4.8 km) north of Salen. From here you can go another 3 miles (4.8 km) west to **Ardtoe** on **Kentra Bay**. This sheltered, sandy haven has been turned into a vast seawater reserve for white fish farming. Ardtoe is a delightful little hamlet, very popular with artists.

Castle Tioram

Just north of Acharacle, an unmarked lane to the left twists and turns out to the **South Channel** of **Loch Moidart**, where you can see what must be one of the most stirring, romantic ruins in Scotland, Castle Tioram (always accessible). High on a rocky promontory, it is reached on foot by causeway at low tide. This 13th- to 14th-century castle was the seat of Macdonalds of Clanranald. It was burnt in 1715 by the staunchly Jacobite chief, to prevent it from falling into government hands. The tower dates from 1600; the walls enclose an inner court yard, with several chambers. The castle has witnessed much of Scotland's history. You can explore it any time the tide is low enough.

In 1984 these ancient walls became the fine setting for a gathering of Clanranald Macdonalds from all over the world. They were entertained by their chief, in the roofless banqueting hall, roasting whole lambs in the old hearth, and for a few hours the castle seemed to live again. The darkness was vibrant with the sound of pipe music. The next day an open-air mass was celebrated in the court yard to re-dedicate the Clanranald banner, said to have survived from Culloden. This part of Scotland is predominantly Catholic.

Kinlochmoidart

It was at Kinlochmoidart (kin meaning head), five miles (8 km) north of Acharacle, that Prince Charlie waited while the clans were rallied to his cause, and it was here that his charm won over the chiefs who were reluctant to take part in his ill-fated rebellion.

Loch Ailort

The road north to **Mallaig** takes you through more beautiful scenery with glorious views out to sea. It follows the zigzag of Loch Ailort, 11 miles (17.6 km) to its head, where you turn left (west) for two miles (3.2 km) to **Loch nan Uamh** (Loch of the Caves). Here, on 25 July 1745, Prince Charlie landed from Eriskay, with only seven companions, at the start of his campaign to restore the crown to the Stuarts. You will see the cairn, by the road, commemorating the event. A year later, broken and defeated, the prince embarked from this same place, to return to France, effectively ending what became known as Bliadna Thearlaich (Charlie's Year).

Arisaig

Arisaig, a mile (1.6 km) to the west of the cairn, has a sheltered anchorage and is a peaceful holiday village from which you can take boat cruises out to the islands.

The prominent tower of the Catholic church was erected in memory of Alasdair MacMhaigstir Alasdair, one of the greatest of the Gaelic poets, who took the Jacobite side in 1745. The tower is used as a landmark for boats. Arisaig has its Highland Games in July.

Mallaig

Mallaig is five miles (8 km) north of Arisaig, on the western tip of **North Morar**. This bustling little fishing port is a favourite for holiday makers. The terminus for road and railway is here from which you can take boat cruises out to many of the islands. The quays are a jumble of fish curing sheds and all the clutter of fishing: stacks of creels and fish boxes, piles of netting and gear. The Mallaig and Morar Highland Games are held in August.

Mallaig is a splendid base from which to explore the lovely places in this area. If you want a real treat and you enjoy the sea but do not own a boat, you should try to book on one of the *Hornpipe* cruises. The *Hornpipe* is one of the biggest yachts sailing in the Hebrides. Its dimensions are 62 ft (18.6 m) in length with a 15 ft (4.5 m) beam, a two masted beauty with a working sail area of 1,500 square ft (135 square m). She cruises throughout the Hebrides and the northern isles, in the extremely competent hands of her owners, sailing where the wind blows her. Cruises last for a week, starting and finishing in Mallaig, to coincide with the overnight train from London to Glasgow, the accommodation is comfortable and roomy and the skipper is happy to teach his guests the rudiments of navigation and seamanship. A week on the *Hornpipe* is a week you will never forget. (The weekly rate is £220 per person and you should book early.) Details are available from Hornpipe Cruises, Kingie, Invergarry, Inverness-shire, tel 08092-210 or 031447-6795.

Loch Nevis

Loch Nevis running nine miles (14.4 km) east from Mallaig, is the deepest sea loch in Europe. You can cross by boat from Mallaig and explore **Knoydart** on foot. There are no proper roads on this peninsula, although it is in the process of being developed for holidaymakers, but you can discover many glorious walks. One includes that to **Loch Hourn**, ten miles (16 km) north of Loch Nevis.

Glenfinnan

Glenfinnan is 14 miles (22.4 km) east of Lochailort. It is another milestone in "Bliadna Thearlaich". Here, a column rises from a marshy plain at the head of **Loch Shiel,** where three glens meet, against a splendid backdrop of layers of blue-grey hills. **The Glenfinnan Monument** was erected in 1815 to commemorate the raising of Prince Charlie's standard on 19 August 1745. A Highlander stands on top of the monument, which you can climb if you feel energetic.

It is easier to recall the past if you turn your back on this Victorian folly, and look down the loch and up into the hills. This was where the prince stood on that summer's day, so full of hope, surrounded by those of the clans who had already committed themselves to his cause, waiting to see if Cameron of Lochiel would join them, a man whose great influence would sway the decisions of other clans. This powerful chief had not been enthusiastic about the rebellion, but he was a brave man and a loyal one. "I'll share the fate of my Prince", he had said, and now, in the still afternoon, the waiting clans heard the skirl of pipes. They turned to watch Locheil, at the head of 700 clansmen, marching down from the hills to join Prince Charlie's cause.

The excitement must have mounted to fever-pitch, for Locheil's action quickly brought in the other clans and later in the afternoon the great red and white silken banner was unfurled: the prince's father was proclaimed King James III of Britain, with Prince Charles Edward his regent.

Whatever misguided folly may have influenced this final Jacobite rising, no one with a shred of romance in their veins can stand here, remembering that day, and not feel staunchly Jacobite!

Apart from the monument, there is a **National Trust for Scotland Visitor Centre** (open daily from April to October: adults 55p, children 25p: includes access to the monument) across the road. It provides excellent maps showing the progress of the prince's army, and tracing his wanderings after Culloden out to the islands and finally back to Loch Nan Uamh.

You can see another monument to the prince in the Catholic church nearby. The Glenfinnan Games are held every August on the nearest Saturday to 19th; a Highland event that you should not miss if you get the chance to attend.

TOURIST INFORMATION

Fort William and Lochaber, Cameron Square, Fort William, tel 0397-3781. Open all year

Mallaig, tel 0687-2170. It is open all year.

WHERE TO STAY

Clanranald Hotel, Acharacle, tel 096-785 662. B&B from £9.50: categories 2,4,5: 5 bedrooms. Friendly little hotel with relaxed atmosphere.

Kilchoan House Hotel, Kilchoan, near Ardnamurchan, tel 09723-200. B&B from £12: 7 bedrooms en suite. Comfortable old family house.

Arisaig Hotel, Arisaig, tel 06875-210. B&B from £18.50: categories 3,3,5: 13 bedrooms, 3 en suite. Comfortable and friendly, near the water in lovely setting.

Arisaig House, Beasdale, Arisaig, tel 06875-622. B&B from £28: categories 6,5,3: 16 bedrooms, 3 en suite. Comfortable family hotel with warm welcome.

Glenfinnan House Hotel, Glenfinnan, tel 039783-235. B&B from £14.50: categories 3,4,3: 19 bedrooms, 3 en suite. Splendid old mansion overlooking the site of Prince Charlie's raising of the standard.

Stage House Inn, Glenfinnan, tel 039783-246. B&B from £15.50: categories 4,3,4: 9 bedrooms en suite. Comfortable old inn in lovely surroundings.

West Highland Hotel, Mallaig, tel 0687-2210. B&B from £14: categories 4,4,4: 22 bedrooms, 14 en suite.

Morar Hotel, Morar, tel 0687-2346. B&B from £14: categories 4,4,4: 30 bedrooms, 10 en suite. Seaside hotel with friendly service.

Glenuig Inn, Glenuig, near Lochailort, tel 06877-219. B&B from £13.50: categories 3,3,4: 9 bedrooms. Delightful little inn with friendly welcome.

EATING OUT

Glenuig Inn, see above. Excellent local seafood. Try the salmon and garlic pâte. Dinner from £7.50.

Arisaig Hotel, see above. Traditional Scottish food. Dinner from £7.50.

Glenfinnan House Hotel, see above. Traditional Scottish food, at a reasonable price, in lovely setting. Dinner from £10.

The Great Glen, from Fort William to Inverness

The Caledonian Canal runs about 60 miles (96 km) as the crow flies, from Fort William, north-east to Inverness, through the Great Glen.

The Great Glen

If you are not in a hurry, there are many good walks in this area, and many memories from Scottish history. Of the 60 mile (96 km) length of the canal, only about 22 miles (35 km) have been constructed artificially. The A82 will carry you from one end to the other and give you a good picture of the glen, if you have no time to stop and explore on foot. With more time to spare, take the B8004 from just north of Fort William and go up the western side of the canal to Loch Lochy.

WHAT TO SEE
Two miles (3.2 km) north-east of Fort William at **Lochy Bridge**, you can see **Inverlochy Castle** (always accessible) beside the road. This neglected ruin dates from the 13th century. It has a walled court yard and round corner towers, one of which was the keep, and a water gate. The castle was once a stronghold of the Comyns and scene of several battles, including one, in1645, in which Montrose defeated a Covenanting army under Argyll with a loss of 1,500 men. Legend tells of a Pictish settlement on this site, where King Archaius signed a treaty with Charlemagne in 790.

Glen Loy

Glen Loy, coming in from the west about six miles (8.6 km) is the route taken by Prince Charlie, marching at the head of his army after Glenfinnan and it is worth stopping to walk up the glen and try to picture how these men must have looked—that proud, ill-equipped, untrained column of men, still fired with the heady fuel of loyalty and hope for a better future.

Laggan

You re-join the main road below the Commando Memorial outside Spean Bridge. At Laggan, 16 miles (25.6 km) north-east of Fort William, between Loch Lochy and Loch Oich, there was a ferocious clan battle between the Frasers and the Macdonalds in 1544. It has gone down in history as the Battle of the Shirts, because it was so hot that they all threw off their cumbersome plaids and fought in their shirts.

In the same area, three days before the raising of the standard at Glenfinnan, two companies of government troops surrendered to a handful of Jacobite Macdonalds, having heard a great din of pipes and noise and believing themselves to be in the midst of a mighty army.

Tobar nan Ceann

If you take the minor road east of Loch Oich from Laggan Swing Bridge, you pass a grim monument, less than a mile (1.6 km) on. This depicts the heads of seven men, held together with a dirk through their hair. The monument is called Tobar nan Ceann, the Well of the Heads. It marks the place where Iain Lom MacDonell, poet of his clan, washed the severed heads of the murderers of his chief, Alasdair MacDonell, twelfth Chief of Keppoch, in 1663. He presented the washed heads to MacDonell of Glengarry, who had refused to help him avenge the murder. It was the fifteenth Chief MacDonell of Glengarry who erected the monument in the 19th century. Inscribed in English, Gaelic, French and Latin are the words: "...this ample and summary vengeance...".

Fort Augustus

Fort Augustus is the half-way halt up the Great Glen and a popular tourist centre with an ancient history. The Great Glen Gala is a lively occasion in the town in July.

There is a pre-Christian crannog, **Cherry Island**, just to the north in Loch Ness. The town's original name was Kilcumein (burial place of Cumein) who was one of St Columba's followers.

After the Jacobite rising in 1715, barracks were built in the town to quell further rebellion: you can still see traces of the old buildings behind the Lovat Arms Hotel. General Wade made his headquarters here in 1724, and in 1729 began the building of the fort, beside the loch. It was named Augustus after the Duke of Cumberland, at that time the fat, eight year-old schoolboy, son of George II, who was to go down in history as Butcher Cumberland. Jacobites took the fort in 1745 and held it until after Culloden. Lord Lovat bought the ruins and presented them to a Benedictine community in 1876, for the founding of an abbey. You can see over the abbey, now a school, by appointment with the monks, tel 0320-6232. Much of the old fort was incorporated into the ground floor and you can see a model of what it was like, as well as a Roman stone with pagan carvings, and some very beautiful vestments.

The Great Glen Exhibition (open in the summer: admission free, donations welcome) is in the middle of the town beside the canal. Here, in an open-plan museum, you can see an audio visual show giving the history of the Great Glen. A room has been devoted to Loch Ness and the monster.

Loch Ness

Thanks to Nessie, Loch Ness is world famous: it is also very beautiful. Long and narrow, its steep wooded banks form a wind-funnel, causing surprisingly rough seas at times. Depths of 754 ft (226 m) have been recorded, deeper than much of the North Sea. Four hundred million years ago, Scotland split apart, along what is now called the Great Glen which was later eroded by glaciers in the Ice Age until the final retreat of the ice as recently as ten million years ago.

You have a choice of two roads up Loch Ness: whichever one you take and however logical you may be, you will find yourself anxiously scanning the dark waters of the loch, hoping for one of the rare "sightings" of Nessie.

Balbeg

At Balbeg, 13 miles (21 km) north-east of Fort Augustus, on the main road up the west side of the loch, you can see the memorial cairn to John Cobb. He was killed in 1952, trying to break the world water speed record. The memorial is inscribed in Gaelic: "Honour to the brave and to the humble".

Castle Urquhart

Castle Urquhart (open at standard Ancient Monument times: adults £1, children 50p) is about half way up the west side of the loch, about 17 miles (27 km) from Fort Augustus. It can be clearly seen from the road. You can park at the top and walk down to this extensive ruin, in its lovely setting against the waters of the loch with the dark hills behind. From above you can make out the whole layout of the foundations, with the jagged keep rising proudly from the crumbling walls. This was once one of the largest castles in Scotland, dating from the 14th century. Built on the site of a vitrified fort, it was given to John Grant of Freuchie in 1509, by James IV. In 1692 it was blown up to save it from the hands of Jacobites. The Glen Urquhart Highland Games are held in August

Drumnadrochit

Drumnadrochit is a pleasant tourist centre on a bay beyond Castle Urquhart.

The Loch Ness Monster Exhibition (open daily during peak tourist season, but times should be checked off-season, tel 04562-573: adults £1.35, children 60p) is in Drumnadrochit. Here you can read vivid descriptions of all the attempts that have been made to find and capture Nessie. It is a fascinating study: sceptics may scoff! St Adamnan, not given to telling lies, records a sighting of the monster in his biography of St Columba, in the 6th century. Columba, it seems, had a calming effect on her! Whatever the final truth, there is no doubt that anyone who happens to spend a night at anchor in a boat on the loch, will find themselves starting up a dozen times in the darkness, every time a ripple slaps the hull.

The road up the east side of the loch is prettier and quieter, offering several good walks and some lovely views. Part of the way you are following one of General Wade's military roads, built in preparation for Jacobite uprisings.

Whitebridge

At Whitebridge, ten miles (16 km) from Fort Augustus, the road forks. If you go right for five miles (8 km) you come to **Aberchalder**. Here you can see an alpine garden nestling in a glen in the hills, its ornamental rockeries overlaid by the sweet scent of pines. If you go left, and follow the shore of Loch Ness for a couple of miles (3.2 km) you come to **Foyers**. Here there are lovely signposted woodland walks and a spectacular waterfall.

Inverfarigaig

Anyone interested in pre-historic remains could pass many hours in the stretch of land between Inverfarigaig, about three miles (4.8 km) north-east of Foyers. Here, half way up the loch, is a vitrified Iron Age fort. There are a large number of excavated remains of burial chambers, forts and cairns in this area, some in good condition.

TOURIST INFORMATION

Inverness, tel 0463-234353. It is open all year.

Fort Augustus, tel 0320-6367. It is open in the summer.

Fort William, tel 0397-3781. It is open all year.

WHERE TO STAY

Glengarry Castle Hotel, Invergarry, tel 08093-254. B&B from £14.50: categories 4,4,4: 29 bedrooms, 19 en suite. Gracious living in an imposing mansion with attractive wooded grounds on Loch Oich. Good service.

Glenmoriston Arms Hotel, Invermoriston, tel 0320-51206. B&B from £14: categories 5,4,5: 8 bedrooms, 6 en suite. Traditional Highland inn, good food and wine, and choice of 170 malt whiskies.

Kilmartin Hall, Glenurquhart, tel 04564-269. B&B from £25: categories 3,4,4: 6 bedrooms en suite; elegant, secluded family house with panoramic views.

Foyers Hotel, Foyers, tel 04563-216. B&B from £11: categories 3,4,4: 9 bedrooms, 2 en suite. Traditional Highland hotel with lovely views over Loch Ness.

Drumnadrochit Hotel, Drumnadrochit, tel 04562-218. B&B from £12.75: categories 3,4,4: 25 bedrooms en suite. "The Loch Ness Centre Hotel," complete with monster-hunter bar and monster exhibition.

Lovat Arms Hotel, Fort Augustus, tel 0320-6206. B&B from £15: categories 3,3,4: 25 bedrooms, 3 en suite. A comfortable hotel overlooking Loch Ness and the abbey. Good food.

Knockie Lodge Hotel, Whitebridge, tel 04563-276. B&B from £22: categories 4,3,2: 10 bedrooms en suite. A charming old family house. Surrounded by wild, remote scenery high above Loch Ness, with fishing.

EATING OUT

Knockie Lodge Hotel, see above. Traditional Scottish food, at reasonable prices. Dinner from £10.

Glenmoriston Arms Hotel, see above. Traditional Scottish food. Dinner from £10.

Polmaily House, Drumnadrochit, tel 04562-343. Imaginative cooking, good fish dishes. Try the Highland seafood platter. Dinner from £7.50.

West of the Great Glen

Invergarry is 25 miles (40 km) north-east of Fort William. It is one of the gateways to the west coast. The A87, an excellent new road, takes you out through impressive Highland scenery, along the north side of Loch Garry, over high wild moorland with sweeping views. Five miles (8 km) west of Invergarry, a narrow single-track road takes you out to Kinloch Hourn, Loch of Hell. This, despite its name, is another glorious sea loch, with distant views of Skye to the west. The Glengarry Highland Games are held in July.

Another route west is from **Invermoriston**, 13 miles (21 km) north-east of Invergarry, linking up with the A87 after 17 miles (27 km). On this road, 12 miles (19 km) from Invermoriston, look out for the cairn beside the road beyond **Achlain**. It is in memory of a brave man, Roderick Mackenzie. Mackenzie, an Edinburgh lawyer, had the dubious honour to be a Prince Charlie look-alike. Hoping to deflect government troops from their quest for the Prince's head, after Culloden, he allowed himself to be captured. He lost his life for his gallantry and his head was presented to Butcher Cumberland in triumph, at Fort Augustus.

Five miles (8 km) to the west, the road joins the A87 and runs north of **Loch Cluanie**, through mountain passes that are a patchwork of heather and scree, with rich wooded glens where the many rivers and burns cascade down from the surrounding hills.

If you branch due west off the A87 at **Shiel Bridge**, ten miles (16 km) west of Cluanie Bridge on lovely **Loch Duich**, you find yourself on a narrow, twisting road that takes you up over the **Mam Ratagan Pass**. This was the route taken by the drivers, bringing their cattle and sheep from Skye, down to the tryst at Falkirk, following the course of the military road that ran out to **Fort Bernera**, eight miles (13 km) west of Shiel Bridge. Johnson and Boswell travelled along this road in 1772, when soldiers were still working on it. To the north of **Glenelg**, just before the ferry across to Kylerhea in Sky, you can see the ruin of **Bernera Barracks**, built in 1722 and used until after 1790. These barracks were eyed by Boswell as he shepherded an ill-humoured Dr Johnson towards what proved to be very poor lodgings: "...I looked at them wishfully, as soldiers have always everything in the best order...".

Glen Beg runs east off a narrow road two miles (3.2 km) south of Glenelg. Here you can see two of the most splendid examples of the Iron Age brochs built to provide shelter and refuge for the chiefs and their people: **Dun Telve** and **Dun Troddan**. Their double walls are honeycombed with galleries, and pierced by a single small entrance, easily defended. At the end of the road you will find a track that leads to **Dun Grugaig**, an earlier fort, on the brink of a steep gorge. This whole area is rich in pre-historic remains and the mind is constantly stirred by thoughts of those early pioneers, wondering how they lived and what they looked like. This rough road takes you right on down to **Glen Corran** on Loch Hourn, ten miles (16 km) or so to the south.

If you take the main road round Loch Duich, stop at **Morvich**, two miles (3.2 km) beyond Shiel Bridge at the head of the loch. There is a National Trust for Scotland visitor centre here, with an audio visual exhibition that gives you an excellent picture of the surrounding **Kintail** estate, with its many walks and climbs. Here you can discover the route to the **Falls of Glomach**, three miles (4.8 km) further on by road to the north-east and then about a four mile (6.4 km) walk and climb, that is well worth doing. The 370ft (111 m) falls are among the highest in Britain, falling in two spectacular cascades over a projecting rock, into a breathtakingly deep chasm. The air is full of the sound of water and the sides of the gorge are hung with lush green ferns and foliage.

Eilean Donan Castle

Eilean Donan Castle (open daily in the summer: adults £1) is ten miles (16 km) north-west of Shiel Bridge. It is one of those sights that are familiar from its many published photographs. Standing on a rocky island reached by a causeway, it was built in 1230, on the site of an ancient fort. Eilean Donan was the seat of the MacKenzies, Earls of Seaforth. It was garrisoned by Spanish troops in 1719, supporting one of the Jacobite attempts to regain the throne for the Stuarts: in reprisal it was bombarded by English warships. Now most splendidly restored, it is open to the public and dedicated as a war memorial to the Clan Macrae, who held the castle as constables to the Earls of Seaforth. Among other things you can see some interesting Jacobite relics.

Eilean Donan

Kyle of Lochalsh

Kyle of Lochalsh, is seven miles (11km) further west, and the terminus for the railway from Inverness and the ferry to Skye. This is a busy little holiday resort, with several shops always full of a cheerful crowd of holiday makers, its streets full of cars waiting to catch the ferry to **Kyleakin**, a frequent service that takes only a few minutes. There are plenty of good walks round hcre and you should visit the **Lochalsh Woodland Garden** (open all year: small admission charge) at **Balmacara** just to the east. Here you will see exotic plants, trees and shrubs, and an ecology exhibition, run by the National Trust for Scotland.

Plockton

If you take the coastal route from Kyle five miles (8 km) north to Plockton you get wonderful views across to **Applecross** and **Torridon** to the north. Plockton is an unexpected little tourist community, its neat stone cottages all painted and trim, with velvet lawns and palm trees, lush shrubs, birches and pines, all grouped most attractively round a sheltered bay. Built in the 18th century as a fishing village it is now unashamedly given over to the holiday trade with craft shops and pleasure boats, surrounded by lovely scenery.

Applecross Peninsula

The Applecross Peninsula to the north across **Loch Carron** is another area of striking Highland scenery. Almost every bend of the road opens up fresh vistas. You can drive nearly all the way round its coast from **New Kelso** at the head of Loch Carron, on a minor road that takes you out over the spectacular **Pass of Bealach-nam-Bo**, The Pass of the Cattle, steep and narrow with hair-pin bends that make your scalp prickle. The scenery is almost alpine, fringed by cliffs and rock spurs, dotted with glinting lochans and burns, with the distant hills of Skye ever present to the west. Cattle were driven over this pass from Applecross en route for the lucrative markets on the east coast. Records in 1794 tell of 3,000 cattle leaving the district.

There is a glorious sandy beach at **Applecross**, about 18 miles (29 km) west of New Kelso, in a sheltered bay. An Irish monk, Maelrubha, founded a monastery north of the village, in 673. It became an important centre of Christianity until it was destroyed by Norsemen.

The 26,000 acre (10,400 ha) Torridon Estate, to the north of Applecross, was acquired by the National Trust for Scotland in 1967. It is splendidly preserved by them with a visitor centre (open daily in the summer: small fee) and lies at the road junction at the head of **Upper Loch Torridon**, where you can see an audio visual presentation, telling about the area. There is a deer museum and enclosures, a programme of guided walks and advice on where to go. The 750 million year-old red sandstone mountains dominate the whole of this part of the region with their distinctive white quartzite peaks.

The Beinn Eighe National Nature Reserve

The Beinn Eighe National Nature Reserve, is the area north-east of Torridon, and was the first in Britain established for the preservation and study of the remains of the Caledonian Forest. The wildlife in the area includes deer, wild mountain goat, wild cat and eagles, but you must be prepared to wait, very still and quiet, if you want to see them.

There is another visitor centre (open daily in the summer except Sundays: admission free) at **Aultroy**, a mile north-west of **Kinlochewe**, with a splendid illuminated model of the district and leaflets on the nature trails in the Beinn Eighe Nature Reserve.

Redpoint

You can drive west along the northern shore of Loch Torridon, through scattered crofting townships, with lovely sea views, backed by the massive hills, as far as **Lower Diabaig**, about eight miles (12.8 km). A track takes you further round the coast to a youth hostel. From here it is a lovely walk along the rocky coast to Redpoint where you rejoin the road, about eight miles (12.8 km) in all.

Visitors to Scotland will find their own particular favourite spot; their special corner. For some, this could be Redpoint and the stretch of coast that runs north and east, to join the road to Gairloch. Heather carpeted moorland runs down to rocky cliffs and crescents of red-gold sand, looking across to **South Rona** and **Raasay**, with the island of Skye beyond. Here you can sit on a rock on the cliff watching an otter. Here are wheatears, ringed plovers, linnets, sky larks and many more, filling the air with their song, and colonies of sea birds massed on the rocks: cormorants, shags, gulls, terns, fulmars, gannets. It was of this part of the coast that an old man with piercing blue eyes said: "...You could never be bored, here: if you ran out of things to do you can just sit and watch the weather...".

You can visit the Tweedmakers, on the left of the road just beyond Redpoint. The lovely range of tweeds that you can buy here are woven on the premises during the winter months. Further on, past the attractive bay at **Badachro**, where the community life is centred on a tiny, friendly post office, and past **Shieldaig** with another sheltered anchorage, you come to **Kerrysdale**, about eight miles (12.8 km) north-east of where the River Kerry dashes towards the sea, through mossy glades and silver birches, with a few gnarled oaks and feathery rowans. Here, if you stop and look, you will see a profusion of wild flowers: lousewort, milkwort, primroses, bluebells, wood anemones, orchids, and many, many more.

Gairloch

If you had not taken the detour to Redpoint, you would have driven from Torridon, through Glen Torridon on the A896 ten miles (16 km) north-east to **Kinlochewe** at the head of lovely **Loch Maree**, and turned north-west along the loch, towards Gairloch. Loch Maree is 12 miles (19 km) long, its name derived from St Maelrubha, the monk who founded the monastery at Applecross and who spent some time as a hermit on one of the islands on the loch and is according to tradition, buried there.

About eight miles (12.8 km) along you will see the **Loch Maree Hotel** and it is well worth stopping to drink in an atmosphere that is pure Victorian. Somehow nothing seems to have changed here since Queen Victoria visited in it 1877 and stayed for six days. You can see a rock on a bank in front of the hotel, inscribed in Gaelic, commemorating the queen's visit. The sun lounge may be new: the rest seems entirely as it must have been, and you find yourself whispering, as you ask for the tariff. This is a fishing hotel, with an impressive log of catches on the hall table. Some locals can still remember the day, in the mid 1920s, when a fishing party from the hotel ate sandwiches made from paste that had seen better days. Several of them died from botualism—others were dreadfully ill.

Gairloch is nine miles (14.4 km) north-west of the hotel beyond the road in from Redpoint. It is a well-developed holiday resort with excellent sandy beaches and several hotels. The hub of this community seems to be the Wild Cat Stores, where you can get fresh milk, fresh baps (rolls) and local chat.

Just opposite is the award-winning **Gairloch Heritage Museum** (open daily: adults and children 30p), very easy to miss but well worth a visit. In only a few rooms you can learn a great deal about life in the western Highlands. The exhibits range from Pictish stones and relics to Victoriana. You can see a portable pulpit for outdoor preachers of the Free Church; an old ice-making machine; stuffed birds and wild animals; an illicit still; spinning wheels with the various wools and natural dyes; a wash house; a school room, with Gaelic on the blackboard; a village store; and a fisherman and his gear. The highlight is the replica of the inside of a croft house. This is most beautifully set up so that you press buttons to illuminate it and set the spinning wheel in motion, and animate the old woman in front of the peat fire, who sings a haunting Gaelic lullaby to the baby in the cradle. There is an annex to the museum with interesting history displays and old photographs of the area.

You could spend many days exploring this area and it is impossible to describe it all.

Poolewe

From Gairloch, go five miles (8 km) north-east to Poolewe. Stop on the bridge to watch the mighty force of water from Loch Maree, thrusting its way out into **Loch Ewe**, forming the pool that gave the place its name.

The Inverewe Gardens (open all the year round: adults £1.50, children 75p) at Poolewe, are famous to horticulturists all over the world. They were created by Osgood MacKenzie, a Victorian who had spent much of his early life on the continent. Son of the Laird of Gairloch, he was given the estate at the head of Loch Ewe in 1862: a peninsula of red Torridonian sandstone, pocked by peat-hags and bare of vegetation except for heather, crowberry and dwarf willows. It is hard to believe, now, what this enterprising man achieved from such unpromising beginnings in an era when there were few roads and soil was carried in wicker creels. He planted an outer wind break of Corsican and Scots pine, behind deer and rabbit proof fences. Plants were introduced from all over the world. Now, there are some 2,500 species, in 50 acres (20 ha) of woodland, covering a steep hillside that juts into the loch, sheltered by hills behind. This exotic, sub-tropical paradise lies only a little to the south of the latitude that runs through Cape Farewell, in Greenland! The proximity of the gulf stream is responsible for making this garden what it is. Rock gardens, peat-banks, ornamental ponds, all display a profusion of blooms from Japan, Chile, South Africa, the Pacific, and many other places. They produce a blaze of colour and a blend of scents that leave you gasping with delight.

Gruinard Bay

The road north from Inverewe was called Destitution Road, having been built during the 1851 famine. However, the name is misleading for there is a most attractive route along Loch Ewe and up to Gruinard Bay, about eight miles (12 km) north of Poolewe. Here you will see lovely sandy beaches surrounded by hills, and views out to the **Summer Isles**. It is a magnificent spot, with a camp site right on the beach. Gruinard Island, in the bay, was infected with anthrax during the last war, and has been forbidden territory ever since. It is now being inspected with a view to decontamination.

Sand

Look out for a small sign beside the road as you drive east along the bay. This directs you down a cliff path to the caves, at Sand. The largest of the two caves has been a meeting place for hundreds of years and was used as a church for Presbyterians, as late as 1843. The smaller cave was lived in by an old woman and her girl companion, in 1885. Families evicted from their crofts during the Clearances used to take shelter here.

It is a magic place: you can stand at the entrance to the larger cave, with its protective wall in front, and picture how it was with perhaps several families huddled together inside, with what they had saved of their possessions and livestock. The fire might be burning, children and dogs playing, men coming and going with whatever fish and game they had managed to catch, and women toiling to attend to the needs of their families. Picture it when the wind blew in from the north, rolling the great boulders on the shore. But picture it too, in the summer, with thrift and honeysuckle growing down the rocks, and the sea as calm and clear as a Pacific lagoon.

Rivers Broom, Cuileig and Droma

There is more lovely scenery as you drive south-east on the A832, along Little Loch Broom, and you should stop at the large observation car park just before it joins the

A835 about 25 miles (40 km) from Gruinard Bay. Here there is a staggering view down into a junction of three valleys where the Rivers Broom, Cuileig and Droma meet, their steep, wooded banks ablaze with colour in the autumn. Less than a mile (1.6 km) further on, look out for the sign on your left, to the **Corrieshalloch Gorge** and the **Falls of Measach**. It is only a short walk from the road, or you can approach from round the corner, where there is another car park and signs, on the A835.

Corrieshalloch

Corrieshalloch is surely something you won't easily forget: a mile-long (1.6 km) box canyon, 200 ft (60 m) deep, its sheer sides of metamorphic rock festooned with ferns and mosses, saxifrage, sorrel, tufts of grasses and woodmillet, with miraculously rooted wych elm, birch and hazel, sycamore, Norway maple and beech trees, goat-willows, bird-cherry and guelder-rose. There is an observation platform from which you can look back at the Falls of Measach, a single cascade of 150 ft (45 m) that seems to hang in the air like smoke. If you have a good head for heights, you can get an even better view from the suspension bridge that spans the gorge The deep pools below you are rich in trout, and you should hear, above the roar of the falls, the angry "pruk" of the ravens that nest on a ledge opposite the viewing platform.

Beauly

To complete this section west of the Great Glen, go back towards Inverness on the A835, 27 miles (43 km) to **Contin** on a good road through attractive valleys and moorland. At Contin, go south seven miles (11.2 km) to Beauly. This is Lovat country, the Lovat family having played its part in Scotland's history. The Lovats came to Britain with the Normans and it was their French influence that inspired the name Beauly, Beau Lieu. Beauly has a Gala week, in July.

WHAT TO SEE

The centre of this village is a widening of the main road, to form an attractive rectangular market place with the ruin of **Beauly Priory** (open at standard Ancient Monument times: admission free) at the north end, beyond the old cross. Founded in 1230 for Valliscaulian monks, the priory is now a roofless shell. In the south wall you will see three fine triangular windows embellished with trefoils and which date from the original building. It fell into ruin after the Reformation.

The statue in the Square, in Beauly, is in memory of the sixteenth Lord Lovat, who raised the Lovat Scouts during the South African War. Perhaps the most colourful member of the family was Simon, Lord Lovat, born in about 1667. His many, notorious escapades included the attempted abduction of a nine year-old heiress and his subsequent marriage by force to her mother, a deed that left him convicted of high treason and outlawed. Having come into the title, by devious means, he became a Jacobite agent, involved in conveying false information to the enemy. Outlawed once more, he turned government man and received a full pardon. Swearing loyalty to the crown, he sent his son to fight for Prince Charlie in 1745. He was beheaded, finally, in London, meeting his end with humorous dignity. "You'll get that nasty head of yours chopped off, you ugly old Scotch dog", he was taunted, by a cockney woman in the crowd. "I believe I shall, you ugly old English bitch", he replied. There is a hideous portrait of him by Hogarth that shows him in old age, just before he was helped up the steps to the scaffold; bloated, villainous, with satanic eyebrows and a cruel mouth, wracked by gout. Known as The Old Fox of the '45, he was indisputably a rogue, traitor and hypocrite. He was also intelligent, charming and an elegant courtier, blessed with Celtic wit.

Don't miss out on a visit to the internationally known **Campbells of Beauly**, facing onto the Square. Here you will be tempted by a treasure-trove of tweeds, woollens, tartans and all possible Highland accessories, ready made or custom built. It is a place that visitors return to, year after year, unable to resist the remarkable range and quality of the products, and the unchanging faces of the Campbell family behind the counters.

The Highland Craftpoint (open on weekdays from June to September: admission free) is also well worth a visit. In a pleasant, modern building, approached through a rather forbidding main entrance, there is a large, open-plan showroom displaying all possible crafts: pottery, woodwork, glass, weaving, etc. The object of the place is to promote production and sales of all crafts made in Scotland, with a special emphasis on the creation of jobs. There are workshops in the outbuildings, where crafts can be learnt and instruction is given on marketing, packaging and display. (Wholesale only.)

The Glens of Farrar, Glass and Beauly, Cannich and Affric

From Beauly, take the A831 south-west down **Strathglass** to **Glen Affric**, a beautiful tour through wooded glens following the River Beauly and then the River Glass. You can see the remains of two Iron Age forts, off to the right from **Kilmorack**, two miles (3.2 km) from Beauly. Here, and at **Aigas**, three miles (4.8 km) further on, are hydroelectric dams where you can watch salmon being "lifted" on their way upstream to breed.

There are some lovely walks in this area where the three glens of the Farrar, Glass and Beauly meet; gentler scenery than that of the western Highlands but just as magnificent and not at all spoiled by the hydroelectric developments that have changed the landscape.

Stop off at the chapel of St Mary's, in **Eskadale**, a mile (1.6 km) beyond Aigas. This pretty, early Victorian church was once the main Catholic centre for this area, and in its graveyard you will find a memorial to an almost-forgotten episode in Scotland's history: the graves of the "Sobieska Stuarts". These two brothers, John Sobieski Stolberg Stuart, 1795–1872, and Charles Edward Stuart, 1799–1880, conned Victorian society into accepting them as grandsons of Prince Charles Edward Stuart. They claimed that their father, Lieutenant Thomas Allen, Royal Navy, was Prince Charlie's son. They called themselves Counts d' Albanie and there is a splendid book called *The Sobieski Stuarts*, by H. Beveridge that will tell you all about them. They lived at Eskadale House, further down the valley, and at Eilan Aigas House, where they kept deer hounds and invented several tartans with which further to impress their gullible friends.

More lovely scenery is at **Cannich**, 17 miles (27 km) south-west of Beauly. Here the River Glass meets up with the Rivers Affric and Cannich, and there is also a youth hostel. About three miles (4.8 km) south-east you can see the **Corrimony Cairn**, a Stone and Bronze Age burial cairn, its passage still roofed and surrounded by a stone circle.

Although you should try to walk, it is possible to drive the 12 miles (19 km) up Glen Farrar to **Loch Monar**; or eight miles (12.8 km) up Glen Cannich to **Cozac Lodge**, or ten miles (16 km) up Glen Affric to **Affric Lodge** (one of the most beautiful glens in Scotland). Each glen has its own charm, with tumbling burns, lichen-hung trees, glinting sheets of water, all sheltered by hills. From Affric Lodge there is a good walk, ten miles (16 km) west, to the youth hostel at **Alltbeath**, and then eight miles (12.8 km) to Loch Duich, if you are feeling energetic. It cannot be emphasised too often that anyone walking and climbing here, and anywhere else in the Highlands, should be fit, sensibly equipped, and should carry and know how to use a map and compass.

The Glens of Urquhart and Convinth

From Cannich you can drive 12 miles (19 km) east through lovely Glen Urquhart, back to Drumnadrochit on Loch Ness. Stop off at **Tore**, to visit the restored 18th-century meal mill. You can drive back to Beauly over the moors on an attractive road through Glen Convinth, turning north a mile (1.6 km) short of Drumnadrochit. From Beauly it is 12 miles (19 km) back to Inverness.

Kirkhill

Stop in Kirkhill, three miles (4.8 km) east of Beauly on the back road and visit Drumchardine (open on week days in the summer: admission free). In this converted kirk soap and pot-pourris with lovely Highland fragrances are made.

Moniack Castle Winery and Wine Bar (open on weekdays) a couple of miles (3.2 km) south of Kirkhill serve their own home-produced country wines and meads in converted out buildings in an ancestral setting. You can buy these to take away.

Inverness is about eight miles (12.8 km) to the east, along the south shore of the Beauly Firth.

TOURIST INFORMATION

Inverness, tel 0463-234353. It is open all year.

Fort Augustus, tel 0320-6367. It is open in the summer.

Fort William, tel 0397-3781. It is open all year.

Gairloch, tel 0445-2130. It is open all year.

WHERE TO STAY

The choice is enormous and you should consult the various tourist brochures that cover this area west of the Great Glen. Also see the previous "Where to stay" sections for the Great Glen and for Inverness. The following is just a small selection.

Aigas Field Centre, Beauly, tel 0463-782442. B&B from £10: categories 1,3,2: 12 bedrooms en suite. A Victorian-Gothic castle overlooking the Beauly River, offering wildlife tours and nature trails.

Cozac Lodge, Cannich, by Beauly, tel 04565-263. B&B from £21.50: categories 5,4,4: 7 bedrooms en suite. Comfortable former shooting lodge by the loch in lovely setting. Good food.

Glen Affric Hotel, Cannich, by Beauly, tel 04565-214. B&B from £10.50: categories, 3,3,4: 23 bedrooms, 5 en suite. The hotel is renowned for its salmon and trout fishing, and for its home cooking.

Achnasheen Hotel, Achnasheen, tel 044588-243. B&B from £13: categories 4,4,4: 14 bedrooms en suite. Conveniently situated in the centre of this lovely area.

Dundonnell Hotel, Dundonnell, tel 085483-204. B&B from £16: categories 4,4,4: 24 bedrooms en suite. A comfortable hotel with a friendly atmosphere.

Gairloch Hotel, Gairloch, tel 0445-2001. B&B from £25: categories 5,5,4: 50 bedrooms, 45 en suite. Large, comfortable hotel in lovely surroundings.

Shieldaig Lodge Hotel, Gairloch, tel 04583-250. B&B from £16.50: categories 4,3,4: 14 bedrooms, 6 en suite. Glorious position on the water.

Kinlochewe Hotel, Kinlochewe, tel 044584-253. B&B from £15: categories 3,3,4: 10 bedrooms, 2 en suite. Friendly, relaxed atmosphere.

The Haven Hotel, Plockton, tel 059984-223. B&B from £14: categories 4,4,4: 12 bedrooms, 4 en suite. Friendly hotel in charming holiday village.

Pool House Hotel, Poolewe, tel 044586-272. B&B from £13.50: categories 4,4,4: 13 bedrooms, 6 en suite. Old fashioned hospitality in lovely setting beside the bridge where Loch Maree pours into the sea.

Loch Torridon Hotel, Torridon, tel 044587-242. B&B from £17: categories 4,3,4: 19 bedrooms, 11 en suite. Country mansion in lovely setting.

Cluanie Inn, Invermoriston, tel 0320-40238. B&B from £12.50: categories 1,3,5: 6 bedrooms. The Inn on the Road to the Isles, with a friendly atmosphere, good home cooking and a cosy lounge bar.

Lochalsh Hotel, Kyle of Lochalsh, tel 0599-4202. B&B from £21: categories 5,5,5: Large hotel in lovely setting overlooking the Kyle, to Skye.

EATING OUT

Most of the hotels above will give you a good, reasonable meal.

The Glenmoriston Arms Hotel, Glenmoriston, tel 0320 51206. Traditional Scottish cooking. Dinner from about £10.

Loch Duich Hotel, Ardelve, tel 059985-213. Good seafood. Try the Skye scallops baked in white wine. Dinner from £7.50.

Lochalsh Hotel, see above. Good seafood. Dinner from about £10.

Dundonnell Hotel, see above. Good local produce, beef, lamb and fish. Dinner from about £7.50.

Moniack Castle Wine Bar, Easter Moniack, tel 0463 83283. Excellent inexpensive meals, with home-made country wines and meads. Open 10 am–5 pm, Mondays to Fridays.

The North-east, from Inverness to John o' Groats

The A9 north from Inverness takes you over the elegant Kessock Bridge, where the Beauly Firth meets the Moray Firth, in the lee of the Black Isle. Until 1980 you crossed this narrow neck of water in a small car ferry, side-slipping in the violent currents that run between the two firths.

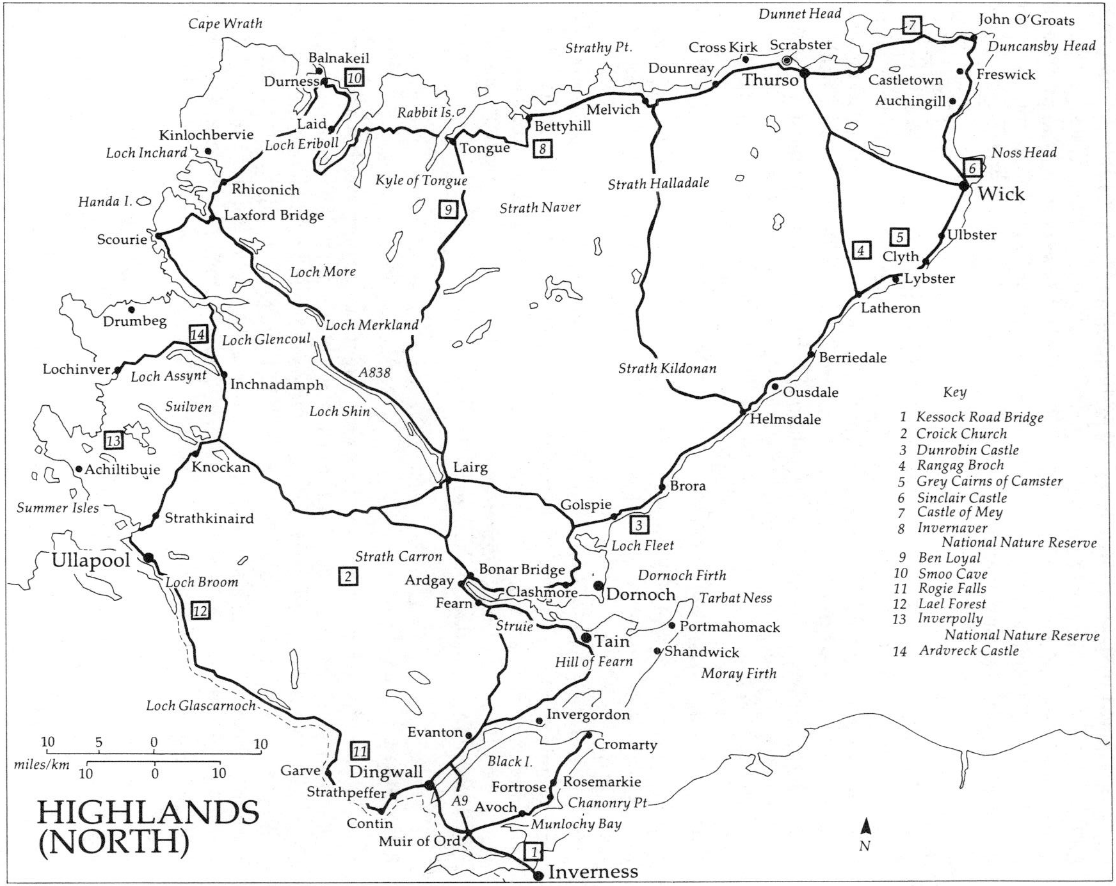
HIGHLANDS (NORTH)
Key
1 Kessock Road Bridge
2 Croick Church
3 Dunrobin Castle
4 Rangag Broch
5 Grey Cairns of Camster
6 Sinclair Castle
7 Castle of Mey
8 Invernaver National Nature Reserve
9 Ben Loyal
10 Smoo Cave
11 Rogie Falls
12 Lael Forest
13 Inverpolly National Nature Reserve
14 Ardvreck Castle
miles/km
10 5 0 10
10 0 10
N
Cape Wrath
Balnakeil
Durness
Laid
Kinlochbervie
Loch Inchard
Loch Eriboll
Rabbit Is.
Handa I.
Rhiconich
Laxford Bridge
Scourie
Loch More
Drumbeg
Loch Glencoul
Loch Merkland
Lochinver
Loch Assynt
Inchnadamph
A838
Suilven
Loch Shin
Achiltibuie
Knockan
Summer Isles
Strathkinaird
Ullapool
Loch Broom
Loch Glascarnoch
Garve
Strathpeffer
Contin
Dingwall
Muir of Ord
Strath Carron
Ardgay
Bonar Bridge
Clashmore
Fearn
Struie
Lairg
Kyle of Tongue
Tongue
Bettyhill
Strath Naver
Melvich
Strathy Pt.
Dounreay
Cross Kirk
Scrabster
Thurso
Dunnet Head
Castletown
Auchingill
John O'Groats
Duncansby Head
Freswick
Noss Head
Wick
Ulbster
Clyth
Lybster
Latheron
Berriedale
Ousdale
Helmsdale
Strath Halladale
Strath Kildonan
Brora
Golspie
Loch Fleet
Dornoch Firth
Dornoch
Tarbat Ness
Portmahomack
Tain
Shandwick
Hill of Fearn
Moray Firth
Invergordon
Evanton
Cromarty
Black I.
Rosemarkie
Fortrose
Chanonry Pt
A9
Avoch
Munlochy Bay
Inverness

The Black Isle

Not quite an island, the Black Isle is joined to the mainland between Beauly and Dingwall and has its own unique character; its people having their own soft, sing-song dialect. It is made up of gentle, rolling farmland, hills, wild-fowl beaches and pretty little fishing villages. The new main road seems to rip through it in a few moments, showing you little of its charms and you should take the coast road up the Moray Firth.

WHAT TO SEE

You will pass **Munlochy Bay**, about seven miles (11.2 km) beyond the Kessock bridge, where the air is vibrant with the cackle of geese in winter, and **Avoch** (pronounced Orch, with a guttural "ch") about five miles (8 km) further. This is a picturesque little fishing village with an attractive harbour. You can walk for miles on the tidal sandflats, with good views across the firth. This is a favourite haunt for those who like to see wild fowl down the sights of a gun barrel.

Fortrose

Fortrose is north of Avoch, ten miles (16 km) north-east of Kessock Bridge, a pleasant, no-nonsense little resort town, sheltered by Chanonry Point and excellent for small boat sailing.

Fortrose Cathedral (open standard Ancient Monument times: admission free) is a mere fragment of the great church founded by King David I in the 12th century. All that remains is the south aisle of the nave and the sacristy. In 1880, a hoard of silver coins was dug up from the green, dating from the reign of Robert III. Cromwell used much of the fabric of the cathedral for building a fort in Inverness.

Chanonry Point

Look out for the memorial stone on Chanonry Point east of Fortrose. It marks the site where the legendary Brahan Seer was burned in a barrel of tar. This enigmatic figure, Coinneach Odhar, went to sleep early in the 17th century on a fairy hillock and awoke to find his head resting on a stone with a hole in it. Looking through this stone gave him the gift of second sight and he made many remarkable prophecies, some of which have yet to be fulfilled but a great many that were accurate. One of his prophecies, forced from his reluctant lips by the Countess of Seaforth, revealed that her faithless husband was dallying in France with a French courtesan. Mad with rage, the countess ordered the savage burning of the seer, but not before he had made some chilling prophecies about the future of her family—prophecies that later came true.

Rosemarkie

Rosemarkie, a mile (1.6 km) beyond the town on the northern side of Chanonry Point, is a popular beach in summer, with golden sand and rock pools. St Mouloag founded a school here in the 6th century and a church, and tradition holds that he is buried below the Pictish stone in the churchyard.

The Groam House Museum (open daily in the summer: adults 30p, children 15p) in Rosemarkie has local and archaeological exhibits.

Golf enthusiasts can enjoy an invigorating game within spitting distance of the sea on the 18 hole Fortrose and Rosemarkie Golf course.

Cromarty

Cromarty is on the north-eastern tip of the Black Isle about 23 miles (37 km) north-east of the Kessock Bridge. It is a delightful old 18th-century fishing town and port and a royal burgh for seven centuries. It is sheltered by the great headland of the South Sutor at the mouth of the Cromarty Firth. You can see rows of terraced cottages, gable-end-on to the street, forming the rope walks where the fisherwomen used to stretch out the new ropes from the rope factory. The town was bought in 1772 by George Ross, some of whose descendants still live there. He built the harbour, founded a cloth factory, a nail and spade factory, a brewery, a lace industry and built the Gaelic chapel for the Highlanders who came flocking to the town for employment. Cromarty has been skilfully and imaginatively restored. The sheltered bay was used as an anchorage for destroyer flotillas, in the First World War.

Hugh Miller's Cottage (open daily in the summer: adults 65p, children 30p) in Church Street, will take you on a nostalgic journey into the past. This long, low, thatched cottage with crowstepped gables, its tiny upper windows half buried in the eaves, was built in 1711 by the great grandfather of Hugh Miller, 1802–56. He rose from simple beginnings to become a famous geologist, stonemason, naturalist, theologian and writer. (Among other things, he wrote about the Brahan Seer, in *Scenes and Legends of the North of Scotland.*) Restored by the National Trust for Scotland, the cottage contains a museum devoted to collections of his writings, personal belongings, geological specimens, and such endearing memorabilia as the wooden chair in which his mother sat to nurse him.

In three restored cottages in the town you can see the work of resident craftsmen and women, who make pottery, silver and knitwear, weaving, textiles, jewellery, etc. There is also a small art gallery with exhibitions of local paintings.

The North and South Sutors

The North and South Sutors guard the entrance to the firth like two massive sentinels: the view north, to the oil installations at **Nigg** is rather marred these days, but if you turn your back, there are lovely foreshore walks and long expanses of sand, lining Cromarty Bay. Charles II landed here on his way to be crowned at Scone in 1650. A passenger ferry runs between **Balblair** a couple of miles (3.2 km) across the Cromarty Firth to **Invergordon**, or you can drive down the coastal plain south of the firth 17 miles (27 km) to **Conan Bridge** and across the neck of land that joins the Black Isle to the mainland, about four miles (6.4 km) to **Muir of Ord**. The Black Isle Show is held just outside Muir of Ord in August.

To complete a circular tour of this attractive peninsula, there is a one-track road that skirts the northern shore of the Beauly Firth, ten miles (16 km) back to the Kessock Bridge immediately beside the water, with its tidal flats rich in wild-fowl, backed by blue-grey hills. The ruined castle that you pass behind a wall at the western end of the Firth is **Redcastle**, originally built by William the Lion in 1178. Its sightless windows were witness to many stirring events. The original castle, Edradour, claimed to be the oldest inhabited house in Scotland and passed through several hands before it was annexed by the Crown after the fall from power of the notorious Douglas family. The Mackenzies held it for 200 years from 1570 and there are spine-chilling stories of sorcery and human sacrifice, in an attempt to save the land from a cattle plague, which brought a curse down on the family of Redcastle.

TOURIST INFORMATION
North Kessock, tel 0463-73 505. It is open all year.

WHERE TO STAY
Conan Hotel, Conan Bridge, tel 0349-61500. B&B from £12: categories 3,3,4: 14 bedrooms. Attractive roadside hotel with comfortable rooms.

Royal Hotel, Marine Terrace, Cromarty, tel 03817-217. B&B from £13: categories 4,4,4: 12 bedrooms, 7 en suite. Wonderful position right on the waterfront.

National Hotel, Dingwall, tel 0349-62166. B&B from £15: categories 3,4,4: 42 bedrooms, 3 en suite. Comfortable hotel well placed for touring the area.

Royal Hotel, Union Street, Fortrose, tel 0381-20236. B&B from £12: categories 3,3,3: 12 bedrooms. Old fashioned hospitality and a warm welcome.

Ord House Hotel, Muir of Ord, tel 0463-870492. B&B from £16: categories 4,4,4: 14 bedrooms, 8 en suite. Charming old family house in lovely grounds.

Munlochy Hotel, Munlochy, tel 046381-217. B&B from £11: categories 3,3,3: 5 bedrooms. Small cosy hotel with warm welcome.

Marine Hotel, Rosemarkie, tel 0381-20253. B&B from £13: categories 3,4,4: 54 bedrooms, 14 en suite. Splendid seaside hotel with family atmosphere.

EATING OUT
Ord House Hotel, see above. Fresh local meat and fish, traditional Scottish cooking, home grown produce. Dinner from £7.50.

Le Chardon, Cromarty, tel 03817-471. Excellent gourmet food in charming bistro-style atmosphere. Very reasonable. Meals from £7.

Dingwall

Dingwall, at the south-western corner of the Cromarty Firth, is at the junction of several main routes. It is a very busy little market town, its curious name being derived from the Norse word "Thing" (parliament or council) and "Volle" (place). Macbeth was born here, presumably in the castle that once stood in Castle Street. It is hard to believe that Dingwall was a thriving port, before the waterway at the mouth of the River Peffery became silted up. You can still see the canal that was built by Telford, at the end of Ferry Road, in an attempt to cut through the encroaching mud-flats.

Dingwall has always been an important cattle and livestock market, and if you hang around the market square any Wednesday you just might catch a few exchanges in Gaelic. The Dingwall Highland Gathering is in July.

WHAT TO SEE

The Town House (open in the summer: admission charge) dating from 1730 is a newly restored museum. Here there is a special exhibition relating to General Sir Hector Macdonald, 1853–1903, a local man who rose from the ranks to become a distinguished soldier, serving in the second Afghan War, the Egyptian Police, the Egyptian Army and given command of troops in Ceylon in 1902. He surpassed himself at the Battle of Omdurman. You can see an impressive monument to him on Mitchell Hill, the local cemetery, a battlemented tower that serves as a landmark for miles around.

A few old stones are all that you will find of the **Castle**. Here, Robert the Bruce's wife was held prisoner during part of his exile.

Black Rock Gorge

From Dingwall, take the back road to **Evanton**, seven miles (11 km) to the north, and follow signs to the Black Rock Gorge, a magnificent two mile (3.2 km) chasm, with sheer sides up to 200 ft (60 m) high and so narrow in places that it would almost be possible to jump across. If you have a good head for heights you can stand on the footbridge that spans the gorge and look down to the River Glass as it tumbles on its way far below. It is not too difficult to catch the quick flash of a water sprite, darting through the fern-hung chasm, in the spray-moist air.

The Indian Temple, on the hill above Evanton, was a folly erected by General Sir Hector Munro, 1726–1805, as a philanthropic gesture, giving work to the unemployed in the area. It is modelled on the gateway of an Indian town that Sir Hector captured in 1781.

Struie

To avoid the ugly industrial sprawl of Invergordon and Nigg, you can take the A836, due north about three miles (4.8 km) beyond Evanton, over the moors and down to the Dornoch Firth. Stop at Struie, at the **Pictish Stone Viewpoint**, ten miles (16 km) up the road, for truly magnificent panoramic views over the **Kyles of Sutherland**.

The Tain Peninsula and the Dornoch Firth

The exploitation of the North Sea oil fields has inevitably transformed the hammer-head peninsula that juts eastwards between Nigg Bay and Tain in the north. There are still a few secluded corners but you must search for them.

Invergordon

Invergordon, 14 miles (22.4 km) north-east of Dingwall, is a busy industrial centre on the western tip of Nigg Bay, and here you can look out on all the surrealistic constructions that are built for the oil industry. The Cromarty Firth is one of the finest deep-water anchorages in the world and is now one of the most important European centres for the repair and maintenance of the exploration rigs. There is something curiously beautiful about some of these giant skeletons whose seemingly fragile girders are built to withstand the full force of a North Sea gale. Inland you will find, here and there, a lane or a wood that is as peaceful as it was before the oil men came.

Fearn

Fearn, 11 miles (17.6 km) north-east of Invergordon, is the hub of the peninsula, with cottages and pretty gardens grouped round a green. Here you can see the restored 13th-century **Fearn Abbey** where the nave and choir are still used as the parish church. Fearn Abbey was the seat of the first martyr of the Scottish Reformation, Abbot Patrick Hamilton, who was burned at St Andrews, for heresy, in 1528 (see St Andrews). The Reformation was responsible for the decay of the original abbey. In 1742, after it had been partly rebuilt to accommodate the parish church, the soaring voices of the parishioners had an unfortunate effect on the stone-vaulted roof, which crashed down and killed 44 of them!

Two miles (3.2 km) north of Fearn there is a **Bird Sanctuary** and **Nature Reserve**.

Tarbat Ness

Tarbat Ness, 10 miles (16 km) beyond Fearn, on the northern tip of the peninsula, has one of the highest lighthouses in Britain, warning ships of the dangerous sandbanks that threaten the entrance to the Dornoch Firth. The Norsemen called them Gizzen Briggs and were no doubt among their earliest victims. You can see over the lighthouse at the discretion of the keeper. The views are stupendous and if you are lucky you may see seals basking on the rocks.

There is a 9 hole Golf Course at **Portmahomack**, a popular resort, a couple of miles (3.2 km) south of the lighthouse, with a small harbour that once supported a fishing fleet.

Shandwick

Shandwick is half way down the east coast, eight miles (12.8 km) south of the ligh-thouse. Fossil hunters may be rewarded if they search below the red sandstone cliffs, and in the caves here. The 9 ft (2.7 m) tall stone cross slab, above the village was erected in memory of one of three Norse princes who were shipwrecked on one of the reefs.

Tain

Tain, derived from the Norse word "thing"—meaning parliament, council or meeting place, is a sturdy little town on the south side of the Dornoch Firth, 11 miles (17.6 km) north of Invergordon. It is a holiday resort and market centre for the surrounding area and has an air of proud antiquity.

St Duthus was born in Tain, in about 1000 and his bones were brought back here after his death in Ireland.

WHAT TO SEE

St Duthus Chapel (always accessible) is an overgrown ruin in the cemetery between the town and the 18 hole golf course. It was built in the 11th century on the saint's birth place and is the repository for his bones. It was built as a "prayer cell" with the resident hermit guarding the sacred relics. Elizabeth de Burgh, wife of Robert Bruce, and her children took refuge here when fleeing to Orkney, relying on its status as a "sanctuary" for fugitives. This was violated by the Earl of Ross, who ignored the safety zone and captured her in 1307—an act that Scotland did not forget. The chapel was burnt down by a smuggler, McNeill of Creich, in 1427, to destroy an enemy he had chased inside.

St Duthus Collegiate Church was built in 1360 on the site of an earlier church, traces of which can be seen in the chapter house. It is now a show place and memorial, no longer used for worship. When the chapel was burnt down, the relics of St Duthus were transferred to this church. They disappeared in 1560. It became a place of pilgrimage. James IV used to come annually, for 20 years, not entirely out of religious fervour: he liked to keep in touch with his subjects all over Scotland and he had established his favourite mistress, Flaming Janet Kennedy in Darnaway Castle, in Moray, giving him an excellent stopping off place on the way. Don't miss the stained glass windows, showing Malcolm Canmore and Queen Margaret, bestowing a royal charter on the town, and an assembly of the Scottish parliament in 1560, adopting John Knox's Confessions of Faith.

The Museum (open daily: admission free) in Castle Street, is well worth a visit. It is full of a large variety of items: relics, manuscripts, photographs, archaeological remains, etc. The museum was founded as an exhibition for the visit of the Queen Mother, in 1966, and became permanent.

The Tolbooth is a lovely example of many others built in the 16th and 17th centuries, with its tall, castellated keep with angle turrets and the original curfew bell of 1616.

The **Highland Fine Cheeses Factory** (open on weekdays all year round: admission free) is worth a visit. Here you can taste the cheeses and watch the processes that go into their making. For an appointment, tel 0862-2034/2734.

North of the town is the famous **Glen Morangie Distillery**, founded in 1843, where Highland Queen whisky is produced, using the waters from the burn.

Croick Church

Driving west along the southern shore of the Dornoch Firth, it is sad to think that this was one of the worst affected areas during the Highland Clearances. Turn left at **Ardgay**, 14 miles (22.4 km) west of Tain, at the head of the Firth and drive ten miles (16 km) up **Strath Carron**, through desolate moorland to little Croick Church. Families who had been evicted from their crofts camped here and you can still see their pathetic, scratched memorials on the windows of the simple kirk, written on the outside because they were not allowed in.

Bonar Bridge

Bonar Bridge, a mile (1.6 km) north of Ardgay, is so called after the bridge that spans the Kyle of Sutherland. It is a good base from which to explore Sutherland and has excellent fishing, walking and boating. **Carbisdale Castle Youth Hotel**, 3 miles north-west, is near the site of the final disastrous battle of Montrose, from which he fled to Assynt.

The wooded road to the east, along the northern shore of the Dornoch Firth takes you past several pre-historic remains: **Dun Creich**, a vitrified fort, on the promontory three miles (4.8 km) out of Bonar Bridge; traces of a chambered cairn at **Clashmore**, west of the school; another cairn at **Everlix**; and a standing stone as you enter Dornoch, ten miles (16 km) east of Bonar Bridge. These remains give an indication of the large number of Pictish and Norse settlers who populated this area.

Dornoch

Dornoch, isolated enough to retain its old world dignity, remains unspoiled by its popularity as a holiday resort. Long famous as a golfing centre, its links have been played on since at least 1616. On the same latitude as Hudson Bay and Alaska, it is the most northerly first class golf course in the world. Excavations have dated settlements here at least as far back as 1000 BC.

WHAT TO SEE

Dornoch Cathedral (open at all times: admission free) dates from 1224 when the town became a bishopric. It was burnt in a clan dispute between Murrays and Mackays in 1570, when only the tower and spire survived. Restored in 1616, it was then further, and tastelessly, restored in Victorian times. Mercifully, in 1924, it was again restored to celebrate its 700th anniversary. Much of the awful Victorian work was stripped away to reveal the original 13th-century stonework. This charming little cathedral is now the parish church.

Dornoch Craft Centre and Town Jail (open all year except winter weekends: admission free) is worth a visit. The restored jail gives you a graphic example of what it would have been like to be imprisoned in the last century and the crafts include the weaving of tartan on power looms, and kilt making.

A stone, near the lower links, marks the spot of the last execution of a witch in Scotland, in 1722. This distinction is claimed by several other places. This witch, Janet Horne, was convicted of having turned her daughter into a pony and ridden her to a witches' meeting place where she arranged for the Devil to shoe her. For this crime she was tarred, feathered, and burnt at the stake. History doesn't relate what happened to her daughter, the pony.

Dornoch is flanked by miles of glorious sand, ideal for holiday makers but not so good for the evicted crofters who, during the Highland Clearances, were expected to settle here and farm the unfertile dune land. Small wonder that so many of them were forced to emigrate.

Embo

If you walk about three miles (4.8 km) north along the sands to Embo you will find the remains of two Stone Age burial chambers dating from 2000 BC, at the entrance to the caravan site. When these were excavated it was discovered that two later cist tombs had been built into the original ones.

Loch Fleet

A couple of miles (3.2 km) further north, on the shore of Loch Fleet, you can see the scant ruin of a 14th-century castle on a grassy mound. It was here, in an earlier, wooden castle, in 1290, that emissaries of Edward I waited to greet the little Princess Margaret, Maid of Norway, whose marriage to Edward's son was to solve the problem of sovereignty in Scotland. Whether it would have done so or not was never to be known for it was here that they heard of the child's death caused by sea sickness on the voyage. This triggered off the Scottish Wars of Independence and Edward's ruthless hammering of the Scots.

TOURIST INFORMATION

Sutherland Tourist Board, Dornoch, tel 0862-810 400. It is open all year.

Bonar Bridge, tel 08632-333. It is open in the summer.

WHERE TO STAY

Fearn Hotel, Fearn, tel 086283-2234. B&B from £14: categories 4,4,5: 7 bedrooms, 6 en suite. A friendly little hotel in the middle of the Tain Peninsula.

Nigg Ferry Hotel, Nigg, tel 086-285 262. B&B from £14.50: categories 1,1,1: 10 bedrooms en suite.

Castle Hotel, Portmahomack, tel 086287-263. B&B from £9: categories 3,3,3: 7 bedrooms. A comfortable, friendly little hotel in a seaside resort.

Royal Hotel, Tain, tel 0862-2013. B&B from £17.50: categories 5,5,5: 25 bedrooms, 22 en suite. Comfortable family hotel in the middle of the town.

Bridge Hotel, Bonar Bridge, tel 08632-204. B&B from £14.50: categories 4,3,5: 16 bedrooms, 10 en suite.

Burghfield House Hotel, Dornoch, tel 0862-810212. B&B from £18: categories 4,4,4: 47 bedrooms, 24 en suite. Comfortable family hotel with warm welcome.

Dornoch Hotel, Dornoch, tel 0862-810351. B&B from £19: categories 4,5,4: 118 bedrooms, 41 en suite. Large, seaside hotel with excellent golf.

Dornoch Castle, tel 0862-810216. B&B from £14.50: categories 4,4,4: 20 bedrooms, 17 en suite. This 400 year old castle was formerly the bishop's palace and retains a splendid atmosphere of history.

Royal Golf Hotel, Dornoch, tel 0862-810283. B&B from £30: categories 5,5,5: 35 bedrooms, 30 en suite. Large comfortable hotel on the golf course.

EATING OUT

Most hotels above will give you a good, reasonable meal.

Dornoch Castle, see above. Specialises in traditional Scottish food. Dinner from £8.

The east coast, from Golspie to John o' Groats

Golspie

The A9 takes you north along the coast through Golspie, nine miles (14.4 km) north of Dornoch. This is the farming centre for the area, with an 18 hole golf course and 17th-century St Andrew's Church where you can see the old, canopied pulpit, some fine panelled walls and carvings. The great statue on Ben Vraggie, behind Golspie, is to the first Duke of Sutherland, a man who was, on the one hand blamed for his harshness to crofters during the Clearances, and on the other praised for sponsoring many social improvements in the area.

WHAT TO SEE

Dunrobin Castle (open daily in the summer: adults £1.80, children 90p) stands on a natural terrace overlooking the sea a mile (1.6 km) north of Golspie. Its situation, on the site of an ancient broch, is magnificent. Dating from the 13th century, this seat of the Dukes of Sutherland was considerably restored in Victorian times, resulting in the huge white extravaganza that you see today. This includes conical towers and turrets and a flamboyant pastiche of French and Scottish architecture in a great park. Formal gardens border a 100 yd (90 m) long terrace, a riot of colour in summer. The castle contains some fine paintings, including two Canalettos, as well as furniture, tapestries, and family heirlooms. There is also a museum, in a summerhouse in the park, with archaeological exhibits, Victoriana, crafts and natural history.

Brora

Brora, five miles (8 km) up the coast from Golspie, is a small tourist resort with good salmon fishing and an 18 hole golf course. The harbour, once used by fishing boats, is now a haven for pleasure craft. In the middle of the 19th century, crofters sailed from here to New Zealand, to start fresh lives away from the threat of eviction during the Clearances. You can visit the **Sutherland Wool Mills** (open on weekdays) famous for their yarn and tweed in many parts of the world. For times, tel 0408-21366/7.

There are two brochs, one either end of Brora, the best being about three miles (4.8 km) north between the road and the sea. This one has domed chambers in the walls and outworkings. Two headless skeletons were excavated from the site in 1880. There is hardly a hill or hummock in this area that is not crowned by some sort of fort or broch and you will notice that there are less Gaelic-derived names as you go north and more with Nordic origins.

Helmsdale

Helmsdale, is ten miles (16 km) north of Brora. At this little fishing and holiday town the road and railway part company.

WHAT TO SEE

The ruin of 15th-century **Helmsdale Castle** (always accessible) overlooks the pretty, natural harbour. It was within these innocent looking walls, in 1567, that Isobel Sinclair poisoned the Earl and Countess of Sutherland, so that her son might inherit the earldom. This somewhat drastic solution failed, however, because her son drank the poison and died with them.

The castle was rebuilt in the early 19th century by the Duke of Sutherland who, having evicted the crofters from his lands, tried to make amends by re-settling them. The streets are laid out in neat geometric parallels, named after the duke's estates.

The River Helmsdale is rich in salmon and trout, and there is a 9 hole golf course.

Suisgill

There is an alternative route north from Helmsdale, inland, up the A897 and 38 miles (61 km) up to **Melvich** on the north coast. This route takes you through wild, windswept, treeless moorland, broken by delightful river valleys, up **Strath of Kildonan**, to Suisgill, ten miles (16 km) from Helmsdale. Here, towards the end of the 19th century, there was a mini goldrush, and a considerable amount of gold was panned from the rivers. Ask in the Helmsdale Tourist Information Centre for details of the Goldrush Heritage Tour. Scattered crofts and roofless ruins are all that remain in this wide valley, flanked by moorland. Kildonan lost four-fifths of its population in the first half of the 19th century, during the Highland Clearances.

Strath Halladale running north from Strath Kildonan on this road, is green and fertile, fed by many rivers and burns: attractive farmland for the invading Vikings so many years ago.

Ord of Caithness

Going on up the A9 from Helmsdale, the scenery becomes more dramatic, with ravines and steep cliffs as the road climbs to a high plateau with spectacular views from the Ord of Caithness about four miles (6.4 km) beyond Helmsdale. No superstitious Sinclair will cross the Ord on a Monday since that Monday in 1513 when the men of the clan passed this way to fight with James IV at Flodden, from which tragic battle not one of them returned. You might easily see red deer up here, specially in the early morning or at dusk.

Ousdale

There is another broch for you to inspect, at Ousdale, a couple of miles (3.2 km) beyond the Ord, where the main road runs inland for a while. If you have time, take the track out to the old hamlet of **Badbea**, two miles (3.2 km) east on the cliffs. Crofters took refuge here during the Clearances and stories are told of the beasts and the children having to be tethered, to prevent them from being blown into the sea!

Berriedale

Langwell House, at Berriedale, three miles (4.8 km) on from Ousdale, is the Caithness estate of the Duke of Portland. It has a garden, opening on certain days of the year, when you can visit the garden centre daily for the sale of plants. White deer are common in this area.

Dunbeath

The 15th-century castle that you can see from the road at Dunbeath, five miles (8 km) north (a private residence), was captured by Montrose in 1650. Six miles (9.6 km) west of here, at **Braemore**, you can see a monument erected after the tragic air crash here that killed the Duke of Kent, in 1942. The Dunbeath Highland Games are held in July.

Two miles (3.2 km) north of Dunbeath, you should visit **Laidhay Croft Museum** (open daily in the summer: small fee) showing a typical Victorian croft house, looking cosier, perhaps, than it may have been in reality. There is also a collection of farm instruments in an outhouse, some of which, like the peat-cutters, are still used today.

Clan Gunn Museum and Heritage Centre

A couple of miles (3.2 km) further north, beyond **Latheron** with its picturesque harbour, you can visit the Clan Gunn Museum and Heritage Centre (open daily except Sundays, in the summer: small admission fee). It is in the old parish church. You can go pony trekking from here; a wonderful way to explore the great tracts of lonely moorland. (For details, tel Latheron 224.)

Lybster

Turn off the broad thoroughfare, flanked by its sturdy, dignified houses, in Lybster, four miles (6.4 km) north of Latheron. Dip down to the delightful harbour, scooped out of rock to provide a perfect haven for the large fishing fleet that once plied from here in the 19th century. The fleet is reduced now to a few lobster boats and a number of pleasure craft, but the atmosphere is still very much that of a fishing community, with its piles of creels and fishing gear, and the salty tang of the sea.

If you go inland from Lybster to join the A895 that runs north 25 miles (40 km) from Latheron to **Thurso**, through barren moorland, you go through the **Shepherdstown Nature Reserve**, two miles (3.2 km) from Lybster. This treasure trove of wildlife is for anyone who is prepared to keep still and observe. Five miles (8 km) up this road from Lybster is the **Ardvanish Standing Stone Circle**, a ritual site in the form of an unusual, truncated oval that may once have contained as many as 60 stones. Less than a mile (1.6 km) west of here, on the main road up from Latheron, you can see **Rangag Broch**, dating from 150 BC, that once stood 40 or 50 ft (about 14 m) high.

Five miles (8 km) to the east, on the minor road north from **Clyth**, beyond Lybster, there are the **Grey Cairns of Camster**, dating from 3000 BC and restored with plaques which give descriptions. The round cairn is one of the best of its kind on the mainland. Its original entrance passage is still intact. Both animal and human remains were excavated from this site.

You must walk a couple of miles (3.2 km) east of here to find the **Hill o' Many**

Stanes, dating from the early Bronze Age. This fascinating fan of stones has ribs, each rib containing about eight or more stones, numbering some 200 in all. This could have been a ritual site for burials, like other henges, or some form of astronomical calculation, lined up with the stars. Whatever the purpose of these stones, it is an eerie feeling to stand here on this lonely, windswept moor, and try to picture how it must have been for those early settlers, so numerous in this northern corner.

Ulbster

Continuing up the coast on the A9, you come to Ulbster seven miles (11.2 km) beyond Lybster where a flight of 365 stone steps twists steeply down the cliff to the old harbour. This is now disused and overgrown but it was once used by fishing fleets to moor and unload their catches, among the cheerful bustle and raucous banter of the fishermen and the teams of women working at the gutting. The steps are only for the sure-footed; they can be extremely slippery.

Wick

Wick so called from the Viking word "vik" meaning bay or creek, is a substantially built sea port, stretching round the sweep of Wick Bay, 15 miles (24 km) north-east of Lybster. This town is a tourist centre, with harbour, airport and railway terminus. The Vikings, those Norse pirates, were drawn to Wick by the shelter of its bay at the mouth of the river, and by the magnet of the rich farmland that beckoned from the west. Created a royal burgh in 1140, it was only properly developed in the 19th century, by the British Fisheries Society, which commissioned Telford to design a model village for them at **Pulteneytown**. It is difficult to believe, now, that 1,122 herring boats once plied from the complex of three harbour basins, before the decline of the herring stock and the development of vast factory ships. White fish trawlers still use the harbour.

WHAT TO SEE

The Heritage Museum (open daily except Mondays, in the summer: adults £1, children 50p) near the harbour, tells the fishing story of Wick. It contains a wonderful collection of displays including a fishing boat, working lighthouse, kippering kilns, blacksmith shop, coopering shop and fishing gear.

The Carnegie Library has a small **Museum** (open during library hours: admission by donation) where you can learn the history of the area, with its domestic and farming life.

The Caithness Glass Factory (open daily except Sundays: free admission) is to the south of the town. You can go into the working area and watch the craftsmen fashioning molten glass, shaping it and engraving it. This factory was established in the slump of the herring industry to offer alternative employment for the fishermen. It is interesting to notice that in this land so full of the echoes of the Norse settlements, the designs of the glass are distinctively Scandinavian.

Also south of the town you can see the shell of **Old Wick Castle** (always accessible) three storeys high on a rock promontory and known to seamen as the Auld Man o'

Wick. Having no water supply, the castle was unable to withstand lengthy sieges and was abandoned in the 16th century.

Look out for the **Brig o' Trams** nearby, a spectacular natural rock arch formed by the erosion of sea and weather.

There are more spectacularly shaped rocks three miles (4.8 km) to the north along the cliffs, at **Noss Head**. You can drive out and park by the lighthouse, but it is a glorious walk, buffetted by the wind. The lighthouse is open to visitors at the discretion of the keeper.

From here you can walk to the **Castle Girnigoe and Sinclair** (always accessible), two dramatic ruins, extending from a keep and lived in as one dwelling by the Sinclairs, Earls of Caithness, for 200 years. The eastern part is 15th century, the western, 17th century. The jagged ruin seems to grow up out of horizontally layered rock on a cliff above a sheltered cove. Ghosts lurk in these history-soaked walls: in 1570 the fourth Earl of Caithness, suspecting his son of plotting to kill him, imprisoned him in the dungeons for seven years till he died of "famine & vermine".

The great sandy sweep of Sinclair's Bay leads you north along coastland that is believed to be among the earliest inhabited in Scotland. Excavations have revealed that Middle Stone Age man existed here in large numbers, on the fertile hinterland.

The tall, slender tower that you can see on top of the cliff at **Keiss** eight miles (12.8 km) north of Wick, is all that remains of Keiss Castle, home of William Sinclair, founder of the first Baptist church in Scotland.

The John Nicolson Museum (open daily except Sundays: small admission charge) in the former schoolhouse at Auchingill, is a must for anyone who wants to find out more about the fascinating archaeology of this area. John Nicolson was a 19th-century antiquarian who lived in the house opposite the museum and spent his life studying the history of the area.

A mile (1.6 km) north is the ruin of the 12th-century **Bucholie Castle**, stronghold of Sweyn Aslefson, a Norse pirate whose name features often in the old Norse sagas. A 10th-century Viking settlement is in the process of excavation, a mile (1.6 km) further north at **Freswick**.

John o' Groats

Although it is neither the most northerly, nor the most easterly tip of Britain, John o' Groats 17 miles (27 km) north of Wick, is loosely accepted as the north-eastern extremity, linked diagonally to Lands End, 876 miles (1,402 km) away in the south-west, which is in fact neither the most southerly, nor the most westerly tip of the country!

Stop as you come over the final curve of the moor and look down on that bleak, scattered village, with the Pentland Firth beyond, its many islands, sometimes so close that you almost feel you can touch them. It is a marvellous vista, making you feel that you are on the edge of the world.

The small settlement, given over to supplying the needs of the dozens of tourists who come here, got its curious name from a Dutchman, Jan de Groot, who established a ferry link with the newly acquired Orkney Islands, in 1496, under the rule of James IV. There are several explanations for the octagonal house he built, with eight doors, no longer standing but represented by the octagonal tower on the hotel which is believed to stand on the site of de Groot's house. One explanation is that he wanted to provide shelter from every point of the fierce wind for his waiting passengers. A nicer theory is that when his eight sons squabbled over who should take precedence at the dinner table, he decided to settle the dispute by having an octagonal table and eight doors, so that each son had his own entrance and no one, or everyone, sat at the head of the table.

Duncansby Head

Boat trips run from the harbour to Duncansby Head, two miles (3.2 km) east, the true "top right hand corner" where you can see many different species of sea birds thronging the dramatic cliffs. You can also drive (or walk) out to the lighthouse and walk on the cliffs from which your view of the Pentland Firth is limited only by the keenness of your eye, and the weather. The 12-knot tide rip here is a notorious hazard to shipping: over 400 wrecks have been recorded there in only the last 150 years. If you go back to the days of the Vikings, the total must be horrifying.

Once you get away from the inoffensive blemishes of tourism, this coastline is perfect for those who like wild places and extremes of weather.

TOURIST INFORMATION

Helmsdale, tel 043-12 540. It is open in the summer.

Wick, tel 0955-2596. It is open all year.

John o' Groats, tel 095-581 373. It is open in the summer.

WHERE TO STAY

You have a good choice of accommodation in this area and you should look in the tourist brochures. These give full particulars of what is available. Here are a few suggestions.

Braes Hotel, Brora, tel 0408-21217. B&B from £9.50: categories 4,3,3: 9 bedrooms. A friendly little hotel in the middle of Brora.

Links Hotel, Brora, tel 0408-21225. B&B from £19: categories 5,5,5: 26 bedrooms, 23 en suite. Comfortable hotel by the golf course.

Forsinard Hotel, Forsinard, tel 06417-221. B&B from £17.50: categories 4,4,4: 10 bedrooms, 8 en suite. Large, comfortable hotel with friendly atmosphere.

Golf Links Hotel, Golspie, tel 04083-3408. B&B from £13.50: categories 5,4,3: 10 bedrooms, 7 en suite. Friendly hotel on the golf course.

Belgrave Arms Hotel, Helmsdale, tel 04312-242. B&B from £9.50: categories 3,3,4: 11 bedrooms. An attractive old inn with a relaxed friendly atmosphere.

John o' Groats House Hotel, tel 0955-81 203. Prices on application. Categories 3,4,4: 18 bedrooms, 10 en suite. Comfortable hotel on the site of Jan de Groot's house, with octagonal tower in memory of de Groot's way of pacifying his family.

Portland Arms Hotel, Lybster, tel 05932-208/255. B&B from £27.60: categories 4,5,4: 19 bedrooms en suite. Very attractive and comfortable hotel with friendly staff.

Ladbroke Hotel, Wick, tel 0955-3344. B&B from £26: categories 6,4,4: 48 bedrooms en suite. Comfortable modern hotel.

EATING OUT
Most of the hotels above will give you a good, reasonable meal.

The North Coast

The road that hugs the north coast, with the choice of several detours into the hinterland, is wild and lonely, with a feeling of end-of-the-worldness to the north, and great tracts of barren, wasteland to the south. Much of the land is very fertile in fact, but the overall impression is of emptiness

The Castle of Mey

The Castle of Mey, seven miles (11.2 km) west of John o'Groats, was built around the middle of the 16th century for the Earl of Caithness and bought by the Queen Mother in 1956. The gardens are open on certain days in the summer in aid of charity

Dunnet Head

Dunnet Head, nine miles (14.4 km) further on, is the most northerly point of Scotland's mainland and you should make time to walk out through a profusion of wild life, both flora and fauna, to the tip. Carpets of pink thrift, laced with tormentil, trefoils, wild thyme and many more, dotted with lochans, make a good setting for the hosts of birds that throng this point. You will see a puffin colony, the endearing birds with their comic tuxedo garb and vivid striped beaks, burrowing in the turf.

The view from Dunnet Head is memorable and if you can coincide your visit with a good sunset, you will never forget it. The village is a scattering of houses near the vast, clean sweep of Dunnet Bay.

The tower of the charming little white church, with its saddle-backed roof, dates from the 14th century, a pre-Reformation survivor that gives a wonderful feeling of continuity in a place where nothing seems to have changed much over the years.

The fishing is good here, both sea and river and loch. A halibut weighing 210 lbs (84 kg) was caught here with rod and line in 1975.

Castlehill Harbour, six miles (9.6 km) south of Dunnet Point is the main centre for the Caithness Flagstone industry.

Thurso

Thurso, 20 miles (32 km) west of John o' Groats, is a large, thriving holiday resort and an important fishing port, built on the River Thurso. Elegant, 18th-century houses built of brown sandstone surround a central square, with a long, narrow harbour. The name stems from the Norse "Thors—a" meaning "river of the God Thor". This important Viking stronghold reached its zenith in the 11th century under Thorfinn, who defeated King Duncan's nephew in 1040 in a mighty battle at Thurso. The town became the chief trading port between Scotland and Scandinavia, in the Middle Ages.

WHAT TO SEE
Thurso Folk Museum (open daily except Sundays in the summer: adults 20p, children 10p) in the High Street, has a good collection of exhibits of local interest, including a reconstruction of a croft house kitchen, with all the homely equipment that was often just as efficient as some of the modern contraptions that have replaced it today. The Pictish "Ulbster Stone" is in the museum, with its intricate carved symbols.

St Peter's Church, near the harbour, dates from the 12th or 13th century. It was restored in the 17th century and used for worship until 1862. Some of the original stone can be seen in the curious choir—a semicircular apse within a square end.

Walk out just over a mile (1.6 km) along the coast to the north-east to **Harold's Tower**, built in the early 19th century as a burial place for the Sinclairs. It stands on the grave of Harold, Earl of Caithness who was killed in battle nearby in 1196, a mighty war lord who ruled over half of Caithness and Orkney.

There are good shops in the town, plenty of places to stay, an 18 hole golf course, and splendid walks all around

Scrabster Harbour

Scrabster Harbour is two miles (3.2 km) round the bay. Here you catch the car passenger ferry, the *St Ola*, to **Stromness** in the Orkneys. It is an invigorating, two hour trip and on Mondays and Thursdays in the summer it links with special bus tours to make a pleasant day excursion, returning to Scrabster in the evening

Crosskirk

St Mary's Chapel, at Crosskirk, six miles (9.6 km) to the west, dates from the 12th century, a simple little kirk with its chancel linked to the nave by a small doorway

Dounreay

You can get tickets from the tourist office in Thurso for a tour of Britain's only prototype **Fast Reactor Power Station** at Dounreay, eight miles (12.8 km) west of Scrabster. There is a **Visitor Exhibition** here which will delight anyone with a scientific turn of mind. In a strange way this vast modern complex is not offensive to the eye in a land of such contrasts

Strathy Point

At Strathy Point, 12 miles (19 km) west of Dounreay, the sea has carved fabulous arches and caverns in the cliffs. The variety of the coastal scenery is amazing; there are many types of rock, sandy beaches, sheltered bays and the restless sea, licking the feet of the cliffs as you walk

Bettyhill

Bettyhill, ten miles (16 km) on, named after Elizabeth, first Duchess of Sutherland, is at the top of **Strath Naver. The Strath Naver Museum** (open daily except Sundays in the summer: admission by donation) is in a converted church. If you are interested in the story of the Clearances, this place will give you a fascinating insight to the Strath Naver chapter of that tragic time. The museum is extremely well laid out, and it is easy to look up what would have been the aisle of the church and picture those terrible Sundays, when the minister read out the eviction notices from his pulpit.

The B873, to the south, takes you through the places depicted in the museum, where many croft houses went up in flames, and where people died of exposure, huddled against the ruins of their homes. It is hardly surprising that feelings ran high, on the subject of the Highland Clearances

Invernaver National Nature Reserve

Invernaver National Nature Reserve, two miles (3.2 km) south of Bettyhill, is a gold mine for nature lovers. It is situated around the mouth of the River Naver, with the finest collection of mountain and coastal plants in the north. Among the rarer birds that breed here you can see greenshank, ring ouzel and twite.

On the edge of the reserve, on a plateau, is **Baile Marghait**, once a Neolithic community, with graves, hut circles and a broch

Tongue

Tongue, 12 miles (19 km) west of Bettyhill, is held by some to be the most attractive place on this northern coast; it has a very special charm. The ruin of **Castle Varrich** dominates the town, once a Norse stronghold in the days when the Vikings occupied these lands.

The Kyle of Tongue is crossed by a causeway, a long, shallow inlet from the wild sea outside, so shallow that at low tide you can walk out to **Rabbit Island**, at its mouth. The lane up the west side takes you among sandy bays, cliffs, weirdly shaped rocks and islands, remote and lovely.

The North Coast Adventure Centre in Tongue, organises watersports and hill walking. This includes climbing **Ben Loyal**, 2,504 ft (751 m) high, its four jagged peaks dominating the skyline five miles (8 km) to the south.

From Tongue, you can take the A836 south, past the lovely stretch of **Loch Loyal** and then through rather dreary moorland, 38 miles (61 km) to **Lairg**

Loch Eriboll

Loch Eriboll, ten miles (16 km) west of Tongue, is a sea loch running ten miles (16 km) inland, very deep and beautiful. This was one of the subjects of a prophecy by the Brahn Seer, early in the 17th century. He named Loch Eriboll as a place where a war would end one day. In 1945, German submarines came into the loch to surrender, at the end of the Second World War. A coincidence ... perhaps?

There are the remains of several ancient settlements around here. About a mile (1.6 km) north of **Laid School** on the west side of the loch, you will find a souterrain, complete and untouched, with curved steps leading down to a round chamber. You will need a torch for this earth house, which can flood after heavy rain.

Durness

Smoo Cave is signposted from the road, three miles (4.8 km) along the coast. This vast limestone cavern has three compartments, two of which are difficult to get to. The main chamber is 200 ft (60 m) long and 120 ft (36 m) high, with holes in the roof. Consult the **Durness Information Centre** for advice on how to reach the inner sections and the 80 ft (24 m) waterfall.

The village of Durness, a mile (1.6 km) west of Smoo Cave, provides a good base for exploring this area and it has plenty of places to stay. The Durness Highland Gathering is in July.

WHAT TO SEE

Durness Old Church, on the bay and dating from 1619, is a roofless shell on the site of an older church. Look for the skull and crossbone carving on the wall; this is thought to mark the site of the grave of a notorious highwayman, Donald MacMurchov, who hoped to buy his way into the afterlife by making substantial contributions to the building of the church! The previous church on this site appears in records in the Vatican as having contributed to one of the Crusades in the 12th century. There was a summer palace for the bishops of Caithness, where the farmhouse now stands, opposite the church

Balnakeil Village

Balnakeil Village, in a former RAF camp, two miles (3.2 km) along the track that runs west from Durness, stands on a lovely white sand bay. Here you can visit craftsmen and women in their workshops and see their creations and watch them at work. Some are open all year round, others in the summer only

Cape Wrath

Boats run from the Kyle of Durness to Cape Wrath, ten miles (16 km) north-west, or you can catch the mini bus that runs from the village every hour in the summer. If you have time, and feel energetic, you should try to walk at least some of the way out to the point. The promontory is an ornithologist's paradise, and you should take binoculars and a good bird book.

Cape Wrath, pronounced Raath, got its name from the Viking word "hvarf" meaning "turning place". It was not named after the furious sea which pounds at the 523 ft (157 m) high cliffs. These cliffs have veins of rich pink pegmatite running through the gneiss. The views from this top left hand corner of Scotland are astonishing. On a clear day you can see the Orkney Islands to the east, some 60 miles (96 km) away, 45 miles (72 km) west to the Butt of Lewis, and 80 miles (128 km) south-west to Harris.

To the north lies the island of North Rona, with Stack Skerry and Skule Skerry further east. Turn your back on the great fort-like lighthouse and look across the bleak moor, **The Parbh**, that stretches away to the south. Wolves once roamed here in great numbers—an eerie thought as the mist comes creeping in across the desolate wasteland and you look around to make sure that the mini bus hasn't left without you.

TOURIST INFORMATION

Wick, tel 0955-2596. It is open all year.

John o' Groats, tel 095-581 373. It is open in the summer.

Thurso, tel 0847-62371. It is open in the summer.

Bettyhill, tel 064-12 342. It is open in the summer.

Durness, tel 097-181 259. It is open in the summer.

WHERE TO STAY

You have a large choice of hotels and should look in the tourist brochures, which give full particulars with photographs. The following is just a small selection. See also the previous "Where to stay" section.

Seaforth Motel, Castletown, tel 084-782 620. B&B from £5.75: categories 1,1,2: 5 bedrooms en suite.

Banniskirk House, near Thurso, tel 0847-83 609. B&B from £8.50: categories 2,2,2: 8 bedrooms. A nice old family house in attractive grounds.

Northern Sands Hotel, Dunnet, tel 0847-85270. B&B from £24: categories 3,4,5: 15 bedrooms, 2 en suite. Comfortable hotel with lovely views.

Ulbster Arms Hotel, Halkirk, tel 084-783 206. B&B from £12: categories 3,4,4: 31 bedrooms, 22 en suite. Large, comfortable hotel with friendly service.

Berriedale Arms Hotel, Mey, tel 0847-85 244. B&B from £8.50: categories 3,5,4: 4 bedrooms. Attractive old inn with a friendly welcome.

Holborn Hotel, 16 Princes Street, Thurso, tel 0847-62771. B&B from £11.50: categories 3,1,3: 12 bedrooms. Covenient hotel in the middle of the town.

Royal Hotel, Traill Street, Thurso, tel 0847-63191. B&B from £15.90: categories 5,5,5: 100 bedrooms, 55 en suite. Large and comfortable, graded 2-Star by the RAC. This hotel offers fishing, both game and sea.

Bettyhill Hotel, Bettyhill, tel 06412-202. B&B from £11: categories 3,3,3: 22 bedrooms, 4 en suite. Comfortable hotel with old fashioned hospitality.

Farr Bay Inn, Bettyhill, tel 06412-230. B&B from £7.50: categories 3,3,5: 6 bedrooms, 2 en suite. Charming old inn with good views.

Parkhill Hotel, Durness, tel 097181-209. B&B from £8: categories 3,3,4: 10 bedrooms.

Smoo Cave Hotel, Durness, tel 097181-227. B&B from £9: categories 3,3,4: 6 bedrooms.

Borgie Lodge Hotel, Skerray, tel 06412-332. Prices on application. Categories 1,3,4: 6 bedrooms. Charming old family house in attractive grounds.

Tongue Hotel, Tongue, tel 084755-206/7. B&B from £11: categories 5,4,5: 21 bedrooms, 17 en suite. Comfortable, friendly hotel with lovely views.

EATING OUT

Most of the hotels above will give you traditional Scottish food, at reasonable prices. Local seafood dishes are usually best.

From Durness to Inverness, via the west coast

The A838 south from Durness runs through a bleak wilderness of rock-strewn glens, forbidding mountains and dark, sombre lochs. **Rhiconich** is 14 miles (22.4 km) south-west and here a narrow lane goes out four miles (6.4 km) west to **Kinlochbervie**, on **Loch Inchard**, another area of great beauty, with a white fish and lobster fishing community. Strong currents around the northern headland makes swimming very dangerous here.

Laxford Bridge

Laxford Bridge is four miles (6.4 km) south of Rhiconich and from here an alternative route south-east takes you through an area of massive rocky mountains that tower threateningly over the road, with sharp turns and blind summits that make your hair stand on end. On a sunny day, with the sparkling waters of **Loch More, Loch Merkland**, and **Loch Shin**, it can be beautiful, but on a grey, sullen day of mist and rain, it is an awe-inspiring route.

Lairg

Lairg, 37 miles (59 km) south-east of Laxford Bridge, at the southern end of Loch Shin, is a fisherman's haven and a good base from which to explore the wild, rugged hinterland of Sutherland. For those who don't want to spend their holiday on the end of a fishing rod, there are good walks around Lairg, particularly one which takes you five miles (8 km) south down the **River Shin**, through beautiful scenery to the **Falls of Shin**, a favourite beauty spot, where you can watch salmon leaping up the falls.

Scourie

From Laxford Bridge, the A894 takes you six miles (9.6 km) west to Scourie, a popular holiday village in a sheltered bay with a sandy beach and rocky pools. Several varieties of orchid thrive in the mild climate here and you can take boat trips to the **Nature Reserve** on **Handa Island** a mile (1.6 km) off the sandy beach north of Scourie. Here you will see a great variety of sea birds, including razorbills, guillemots, puffins, kittiwakes and skua.

Kylestrome

It is a beautiful drive from Scourie, seven miles (11 km) down **Loch a Chairn Bhain**, to Kylestrome, with staggering views across the Minch to Lewis and Harris. There are often long delays here in the summer, to cross the **Kylesku Ferry**, in spite of an almost continuous service during daylight hours, but it is your only way south. You can get boats from **Unapool**, on the south side, down **Loch Glencoul** to the south-east, to see Britain's highest waterfall, **Eas-Coul-Aulin**, a fantastic sight, 658 ft (197 m) high in a wild, melancholy setting that seems appropriate for such a giddy cascade.

Ardvreck Castle

Ardvreck Castle (open at all times: admission free) is a jagged fang of a ruin, three storeys high. It is five miles (8 km) south of Unapool on **Loch Assynt**. Dating from 1490, Ardvreck was one of the few castles to be built in this area where lack of roads in the old days made it difficult to maintain large establishments. It was a Macleod stronghold and carries in its stones an echo of the last days of Montrose. There are several conflicting stories but it is certain that the gallant, tragic hero, Montrose, fighting for Charles II, fled to Assynt in 1650 after his final defeat at Carbisdale, near Bonar Bridge. Some say that he threw himself on the mercy of the Macleod laird of the time, who responded by selling him to the government for £25,000. Others say that Macleod found him and took him prisoner honourably. Whatever the story, Montrose was imprisoned in this grim fortress, on its rocky peninsula jutting into the loch. From here Montrose was taken ignominiously to Edinburgh, tied, back-to-front, on his horse, and abandoned by the king to whom he had given his loyalty.

Inchnadamph Caves, two miles (3.2 km) south of Ardvreck, yielded evidence of occupation by early man and also bones of late Pleistocene animals, going back at least 10,000 years.

Lochinver

Lochinver is ten miles (16 km) west of Ardvreck on the A837l, along the north shore of Loch Assynt, a largish village and the only place of any size between Scourie and Ullapool. It is a delightful place on one of the most beautiful stretches of coastline in Scotland, with heart-stopping views all round.

Two hour wildlife cruises run from Lochinver, in the summer, giving you a chance to see some of the many birds and the colonies of seals that bask on the rocks.

The dramatic sugar-loaf **Suilven**, 2,399 ft (719 m) high, is five miles (8 m) to the south in **Glencanisp Forest**, with **Canisp**, 2,779 ft (833 m), two miles (3.2 km) beyond to the east. Both are well worth climbing, on a clear day.

Ledmore

At Ledmore, five miles (8 km) to the south, an alternative route south-east, runs 30 miles (48 km) through **Strath Oykel** back to Bonar Bridge, leaving the mountains and running through moorland and then attractive wooded valleys. From Ledmore the road runs south through the **Inverpolly National Nature Reserve**, a remote, lonely stretch of moorland dotted with lochs, burns and great jagged red sandstone peaks. These include **Stac Polly**, 2,009 ft (603 m), **Cul Beag**, 2,523 ft (757 m) and **Sul Mor**, 2,786 ft (836 m), all very popular with climbers.

There is a **Nature Conservancy Council Visitor Centre** at **Knockan**, three miles (4.8 km) south of Ledmore, where you can get full information about this area. To enjoy the reserve fully, you should take the "motor trail" which leads west from A835 to **Drumrunie**, eight miles (12.8 km) south of Ledmore, and then winds off to the north between land and sea lochs through some of the loveliest and wildest of Scotland's scenery.

Achiltibuie

Achiltibuie lies to the south of this motor trail, well signposted, about ten miles (16 km) from Drumrunie. Alternatively, it is a lovely ten mile (16 km) walk west from **Strathknaird**, about three miles (4.8 km) south of Drumrunie, along the coast and miles of golden sand. Achiltibuie is a perfect holiday base, and you can take boat trips to the **Summer Isles**, scattered a few miles off the **Coigeach Peninsula**.

Horticulturists should visit the **Hydroponicum**, at the Summer Isles Hotel, in Achiltibuie, which has "Hi-tec soil-less growing houses". One hour lecture tours are given in the summer; these include information on the use of solar energy. For details tel 085-482 282.

The Achiltibuie Smokehouse (open six days a week in summer: admission free). Here you can watch the curing smoking of meat, fish and game. There is a retail shop on the premises. For details tel 085-482 256.

Ullapool

Ullapool, 18 miles (29 km) south-west of Ledmore, is a popular holiday resort as well as an important fishing port and the ferry terminus for boats to Stornoway in Lewis. Freshly painted houses line the sea front, their upper windows sharply gabled, looking down on the jumble of quays and slipways, cluttered with small boats and fishing gear, creels, spars, nets and fish boxes. The town was developed as a fishing port by the British Fishery Society in 1788, Loch Broom providing an excellent deep water anchorage for the boats. Today you can often see the Russian fishing fleet lying at anchor in the bay and you will hear local tales of illegal immigration with people coming and going from the boats with very little interference: splendid material for a spy thriller. The town has a good range of shops, boutiques, restaurants and cafes, bars and every sort of accommodation.

WHAT TO SEE

The Loch Broom Highland Museum (open daily except on Sundays, in the summer: admission free) gives you a good insight into the history of Wester Ross, the life of a fishing village and the story of the Clearances. It also has displays of geology, wild life, military and farming history.

The tourst information office will give you information on sea fishing, boating, pony trekking and cruises. There is a youth hostel and the surrounding countryside is perfect for walking.

From Ullapool, the road goes down the side of **Loch Broom**, with lovely views across the loch, fringed with beaches and good picnic spots. (See the earlier section on the Corrieshalloch Gorge which is 12 miles (19 km) south-east of Ullapool.) **The Lael Forest Garden Trail**, in the area of the falls, has over 150 different species of trees and shrubs to walk among, all labelled. From here you drive through moorland and hydro-electric development to **Garve** 20 miles (32 km) south-east.

The road divides at Garve. You can go south-west along attractive **Strath Bran**, past **Loch Luichart** and out to **Auchnasheen**, a lonely, scattered hamlet where the railway widens to provide a passing place for trains. Here you can go south-west to Loch Carron and Applecross or north-west to Loch Maree.

The Rogie Falls

The Rogie Falls are about four miles (6.4 km) along the south-east route from Garve, well signposted and with a car park. It is only a short walk to the falls where you can see swirling rapids and cascades in attractive mossy woodland, with heather and bracken, birches and rowans, among rocky outcrops. There is a suspension bridge from which you can watch the salmon leaping up the series of falls, often achieving astonishing heights.

Contin

Contin, about three miles (4.8 km) south-east of the falls, has an old coaching inn, on the west side of the **River Blackwater**, from which passengers used to depart on the tortuous journey west to Poolewe and Ullapool, after the roads were built in the 18th century. Telford built the first bridge here, later swept away by flood water. Dealers used to come up from England to the Contin Horse Fair, to buy sturdy Highland ponies for work in the coal mines. Fair days were festive occasions, drawing people in from far afield, to jostle and gossip over the braziers, among the pedlars' stalls and animal pens.

Strathpeffer

Strathpeffer is six miles (9.6 km) east of Contin, a famous spa town until the First World War. It attracted people from overseas, including foreign royalty, to the sulphur and chalybeate springs. The springs were used as early as 1770, but it was not until the first pump room was built in 1820 that Strathpeffer's fame spread over the border. Lying in a sheltered hollow among wooded hills, the little town is a popular holiday centre, with plenty for the visitor to do, including climbing up **Ben Wyvis**, the great bulk of a mountain seven miles (11 km) to the north. Houses and hotels rise in neat terraces from the heart of the town, whose gently refined atmosphere has won it the title "Harrowgate-of-the-North".

SPECIAL ATTRACTIONS

Strathpeffer Highland Games are held in the grounds of Castle Leod on the first Saturday of every August, and here you can see all the traditional events such as tossing the caber, putting the weight, and piping and dancing.

WHAT TO SEE

Strathpeffer Pump Room, restored by the tourist board, is the pump room of the Victorian spa. Here you will see one of the sulphur wells and the chalybeate well, which you can visit in the summer, free. There is a photographic exhibition and you can obtain the "waters"—if you hold your nose.

The Eagle Stone stands 3 ft (0.9 m) high on a hillock to the east of Strathpeffer, reached by a lane near Eaglestone House. It is a Pictish symbol stone with an engraved angel and a horseshoe and was the subject of one of the Brahn Seer's prophecies. If the stone should fall three times, he said, then ships would tie up to it. Setting aside a tidal wave this seems improbable, but the seer had an uncanny eye and it is said that the stone has already fallen twice (hence its having been cemented into place and surrounded by wire) and that on the second occasion the Cromarty Firth flooded up to the old county buildings in Dingwall!

The Strathpeffer Dolls Museum (ring 0997-21549 for details and opening times) in The Square, has a delightful display of antique dolls, toys, costumes, and Victoriana.

The Strathpeffer Craft and Visitor Centre (open in the summer: admission free) has craftsmen and women at work in what was the Victorian Station. There is an audio visual programme called "All change for the Highlands" (shown in the evenings) about the natural history of the Highlands.

To the south, on a ridge called **Druim Chat**, meaning cat's back, there is a well preserved vitrified fort, **Knockfarrel**, one in a line of three great Pictish defence sites, the other two being at Craid Phadrig in Inverness and Ord Hill in Kessock. You can see the foundations clearly; it is a vast place, extending to some 270 yds (243 m). This is believed to have been a stronghold of Fingal and his warriors, and many are the legends told about it.

A terrible clan battle took place to the south-west, at **Kinellan**, between the Macdonalds and the Mackenzies, in the 16th century. The Macdonalds, seeking vengeance after an alleged insult, lost the fight and were later punished by James IV who deposed them as Lord of the Isles.

From Strathpeffer it is about 21 miles (34 km) back to Inverness.

TOURIST INFORMATION

Strathpeffer, tel 0997-21415. It is open in the summer.

Ullapool, tel 0854-2135. It is open in the summer.

Lochinver, tel 057-14 330. It is open in the summer.

Lairg, tel 0549-2160. It is open in the summer.

Durness, tel 097-181 259. It is open in the summer.

WHERE TO STAY

Achnasheen Hotel, Achnasheen, tel 044588-243. B&B from £13: categories 4,4,4: 14 bedrooms, 6 en suite.

Coul House Hotel, Contin, tel 0997-21265. B&B from £17: categories 4,4,4: 20 bedrooms, 15 en suite. Comfortable old family house hotel with a friendly staff.

Garve Hotel, Garve, tel 09974-205. B&B from £12: categories 3,4,4: 34 bedrooms, 15 en suite. Comfortable hotel with relaxed atmosphere in lovely surroundings.

Tir Aluinn Hotel, Leckmelm, Loch Broom, tel 0854-2074. B&B from £12.65: categories 3,3,3: 16 bedrooms, 3 en suite.

Ben Wyvis Hotel, Strathpeffer, tel 0997-21323. B&B from £19: categories 3,5,4: 118 bedrooms, 36 en suite. Large and comfortable in attractive grounds with good views.

Highland Hotel, Strathpeffer, tel 0997-21457. B&B from £22: categories 4,5,5: 138 bedrooms en suite. Old fashioned spar hotel with friendly service, overlooking Strathpeffer.

Altnaharrie, Ullapool, tel 085483-230. B&B from £25: categories 3,3,4: 4 bedrooms, 2 en suite. You have to take Fred Brown's ferry to reach his idylic old drover's inn on the shores of Loch Broom opposite Ullapool. Tiny and intimate with a few simple but prettily furnished bedrooms and the food is out of this world.

The Ceilidh Place, 14 West Argyle Street, Ullapool, tel 0854-2103. B&B from £19: 13 bedrooms, 8 en suite, 11 extra rooms (simpler family accommodation) in clubhouse. A mildly eccentric but fun establishment comprising: hotel, clubhouse, restaurant, coffee shop, bookshop, live shows of jazz, classical and folk music once a week in summer.

Ferry Boat Inn, Shore Street, Ullapool, tel 0854-2366. B&B from £9.50: categories 3,3,4: 12 bedrooms. Overlooking the harbour.

Summer Isles Hotel, Achiltibuie, tel 085482-282/254. B&B from £18: 13 bedrooms, 8 en suite. Set in a relatively remote area, surrounded by spectacular mountain- and seascapes overlooking glorious views of the Summer Isles, Robert Irvine's delightful and sophisticated hotel is almost entirely self-sufficient. The hotel has its own smokehouse; the Hydroponicum (see p. 399) provides fresh fruit and vegetables; it produces its own dairy produce as well as veal, quails, ducks etc.

Inchnadamph Hotel, Loch Assynt, tel 05712-202. B&B from £14.25: 27 bedrooms en suite. Comfortable hotel in lovely surroundings.

Invershin Hotel, Invershin, tel 054982-202. B&B from £14: categories 5,3,5: 24 bedrooms, 12 en suite. Friendly atmosphere with good views.

Kylesku Hotel, Kylesku, tel 097183-231. B&B from £10: categories 3,4,4: 7 bedrooms. On the water overlooking the ferry.

Aultnahar Lodge Hotel, Lairg, tel 054982-245. B&B from £14: categories 4,4,4: 6 bedrooms, 4 en suite. Comfortable family hotel.

EATING OUT

Most hotels above will give you a reasonable meal and many of them specialise in traditional Scottish dishes.

Altnaharrie (see above). Fred's Norwegian partner Gunn Eriksen's imaginative cooking makes the best use of local produce. Culinary delights include elderflower soup, venison paté, langoustines fresh from Loch Broom, breast of pidgeon with juniper sauce, and the lightest of puddings such as cloudberry pavlova. Set dinner £17.50.

Summer Isles Hotel, (see above). At dinner the set menu costs £18. Some excellent wines although you have to rely on the advice and suggestions of the owner as there is no list.

CRAFT CENTRES IN THE HIGHLAND REGION

The following workshops and studios welcome visitors to watch them at work. Where a telephone number is given, you should always ring first to check when they are open

Ceramics

Appin Pottery, Glen Creran, Appin, tel 063-173 319. Hand made and decorated wood fired stoneware.

Cairnbaan Pottery, Lock 6, Crinan Canal, by Lochgilphead, tel 05467-629. Domestic, plant and decorative pottery, sculpture and stoneware. Woodburning kiln; throwing and turning pots.

Caoldair Pottery Company, Laggan Bridge, tel 05284-231. Hand made wood, fired domestic and decorative stoneware and earthenware.

Carron Pottery, Camault, Strathcarron, tel 052-02 321. Hand thrown stoneware pottery.

Culloden Pottery, The Old Smiddy, Gollanfield, Inverness, tel 06676-2340. Throwing, finishing and glazing stoneware and earthenware.

Far North Pottery, Balnakiel, Durness, tel 097-181 353. Hand made domestic stoneware and sculpture.

Highland China (Scotland) Ltd, Kingussie Pottery, Kingussie, tel 05402-576. Highland fine bone china ornaments: shaggy-coated animals and porcelain wild life animals.

Highland Stoneware (Scotland) Ltd, Lochinver, tel 05714-376. All aspects of pottery making including hand decorating.

Mill Street, Ullapool, tel 0854-2980. All aspects of pottery making including hand decorating.

The Potters Shop, George Street, Dingwall. All processes of low-fired stoneware, domestic and decorative.

Nairn Ceramics, Viewfield Street, Nairn, tel 0667-53119. Hand thrown and decorated pottery.

Scarfskerry Pottery, Morrings, Scarfskerry, near Thurso, tel 084-785 324. Hand thrown and decorated pottery.

Riverstone Domestic Stoneware, Insh, near Kingussie tel 05402-287. Handthrown pottery, decorating, glazing and firing

Glass

Caithnes Glass, Harrowhill, Wick, tel 0955-2286. All stages of glass making from raw materials to finished products

Jewellery and Silversmithing

Thomas Buchanan, 12 The Craft Village, Aviemore, tel 0479-810273. All processes of making silver and gold jewellery, including setting of precious and semi-precious stones.

Highland Line, Achnasheen, tel 044-588 227. All aspects of making gold and silver jewellery and small silver ornaments.

Norsaga, Cairnbaan, Lochgilphead, tel 0546-2259. All processes of hand made gold and silver jewellery, with semi-precious stones and enamel. Celtic and modern designs

Lapidary

Orcadian Stone Company Ltd, Main Street, Golspie, tel 040-83 3483. Stone sawing, drilling and polishing, assembly of mineral and geological specimens for jewellery making and ornaments

Weaving

Brough Weavers' Workshop, Ivy Cottage, Brough, Thurso, tel 084-785 695. Hand-weaving of tweed, machine knitting

Other Crafts

Caithness Candles, Old Post Office, Scrabster, tel 0847-5577. More than 100 different styles of candles, handmade.

Garry Crafts, Craigard, Invergarry, tel 080-93 258. The only makers of deer fur flowers.

Knap Studio, North Knapdale, Lochgilphead, tel 054-685 209. Pictures relating to folklore, slate engravings, decorated tiles, plates, small carvings.

Rods and Guns, Fountain Square, Brora, tel 040-82 373. Splitting and planing split-cane fly rods.

Ann R. Thomas Gallery, Harbour Street, Tarbert, tel 08802-390. Printing by offset lithography.

Part XIV

THE ISLANDS

Callanish Standing Stones

(The islands off Strathclyde are dealt with in the Strathclyde section.)

Of the hundreds of islands that lie off the coast of Scotland, only a few are served by public transport. For the rest you need your own boat, a good knowledge of seamanship and many years of leisure. Each one has its own magic, its own character, its own special charm: each one is "...intire of it selfe..." A native of Eriskay can feel homesick, living a mile away across the Sound, in South Uist. Almost untouched by the distractions and bright lights of an increasingly materialistic world, the islanders tend to build their lives around God and the church—a church that varies, depending on the island, from Catholic to extreme Presbyterian, with not a shred of animosity among them.

To understand the people of the islands you need to study their history which here is slow to change; insular communities represent a distillation of the past.

The Western Isles: north of Ardnamurchan Point

From the lone shieling on the misty island
Mountains divide us, and a waste of seas;
Yet still the blood is strong, the heart is Highland,
And we, in dreams, behold the Hebrides.

Canadian beat song

First known to be populated around 3800 BC, the Hebrides are rich in archaeological sites, many of which are yet to be dug. Mesolithic man gave way to Neolithic, who came in boats made of animal hide, bringing skills and culture, and leaving their burial cairns for us to explore. Gaelic immigrants from Europe arrived, with Celtic arts, building their brochs and their mysterious stone circles, practising a Druid religion, worshipping nature gods, until the first Christian missionaries arrived from Ireland early in the 6th century. The Norsemen arrived at the end of the 8th century and remained until the defeat of King Haakon by Alexander III, at Largs in 1263. After this the islands were ceded to the Scottish crown. But stronger than the authority of the crown was the Lordship of the Isles, and the islanders paid no heed to a government that ruled from the east of mainland Scotland.

A succession of Stewart kings tried to whip in the arrogant clans of the Western Isles, but they clung to their own traditions. A patriarchal clan system existed, with every member of the clan family being independent and equal in status, looking to their chief for guidance and justice but not for oppression. This was the foundation of that proud independence that you will find in any Hebridean today, a truly classless pride that endured even the suppression of the clans, after Culloden, and, in the 19th century, the appalling depopulation of the Highland Clearances. This unselfconscious acceptance of freedom from any sort of servility is blended with a gentle courtesy that is more marked here than anywhere on the mainland. Add to this the quick wit, strong imagination and high degree of intelligence that seem to be the natural inheritance of any Celt, and you have a rough sketch of a Hebridean.

The islands to the south of Benbecula never quite caught up with the Reformation and are entirely Catholic: North Uist, Harris and Lewis, and Skye embraced the Reformed church with such enthusiasm that even today visitors must be careful not to offend their strong sabbatarianism.

Most island families have their own croft, or smallholding, their tenancy carefully controlled by the Crofters Commission, brought about in 1886 by public indignation at the Highland Clearances. But crofting is a hard life in the islands. With only a few acres, poor markets and expensive freight, few can exist solely on its returns. Crofting is therefore usually done as an auxiliary occupation, during weekends and days off from more lucrative employment such as building, fishing, and public works.

The old reed-thatched croft houses are being replaced more and more by modern bungalows, but you will still see some of them occupied. These old cottages were preceded by the "black houses" where the byre was part of the dwelling, with the peat fire on a raised platform, its smoke escaping through a hole in the roof. Black houses can only be seen now as museums, dotted over the islands and restored to give a good idea of what life must have been like. The coming of electricity has greatly improved living conditions, but it brought with it the television, which has effectively killed the "ceilidh" tradition.

In the old days, when a crofting township was totally communalistic, the day's work was done on a cooperative basis and in the evenings whole communities gathered together round the fire in one of the black houses, to listen to music and poetry and to tell the old sagas. Attempts are made to capture some of this ancient folklore and imprison it on paper, but it was a living thing, passed verbally from generation to generation, embroidered and altered year by year: its true spirit cannot be appreciated except by ear.

Gaelic is still the first language tor most people in the Outer Hebrides, but an influx of non-Gaelic speakers means that the children of today are growing up speaking English in the playground at school. Those who go to the islands for their holidays are those who enjoy the outdoor life, walking, climbing, boating, fishing. It is a holiday for artists, poets and writers, and for people who enjoy collecting mussels and cockles for supper, and hauling up strings of mackerel and pollack over the side of the unsteady, slippery decked boat, or gathering wild mushrooms from the hillsides. It is a holiday for botanists and bird watchers, and for those who delight in ancient ruins. Look upon good weather as a bonus and you are bound to get some nice days, but in fact you can enjoy things almost as much without the sun. Walk five miles (8 km) out to an isolated beach, collect driftwood and make a fire using dried heather twigs as kindling, cook sausages on the stones and wash them down with peat-coloured water from a burn, have a quick swim, diving into deep water as clear as glass (quick, because whatever people may tell

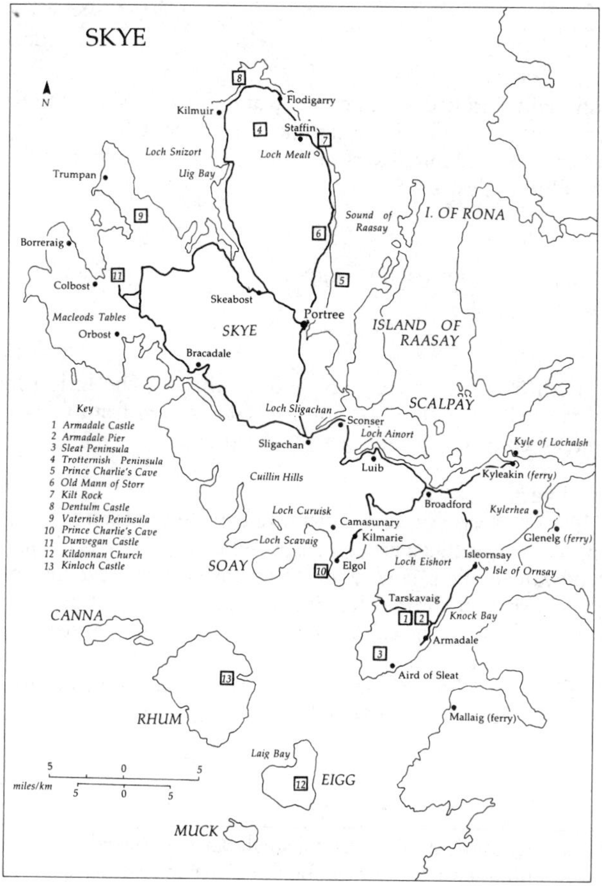

you about the proximity of the gulf stream, the waters of the Minch are icy). This is the sort of day that makes a holiday in the islands memorable.

You won't find smart shops: only general foodstores which stock most things from boots to butter. There are also a few craft shops and weavers, and a post office here and there. Portree and Stornoway have more sophisticated shops, but on the whole, people who enjoy shopping tend to stay on the mainland. For entertainment you may get a local ceilidh or concert in the village halls to mark a particular occasion, and there are Games, in the summer on most of the islands, and touring film shows. Otherwise, your entertainment is what you make for yourself; evenings in front of a peat fire with a good book, or listening to the tales of the local people, who can still tell you much of the old folk lore, and who will often make music for you.

SKYE

GETTING TO SKYE

By sea
Ferrys run continually during daylight hours, from Kyle of Lochalsh to Kyleakin, taking only a few minutes to cross. There is a summer ferry service from Mallaig to Armadale, taking half an hour, and a limited service from Glenelg to Kylerhea. Ferries also run from Uig to the Outer Isles.

By air
There is a daily air service, except on Sundays, between Glasgow and Broadford (Loganair).

By train
You can get a train from Inverness to Kyle of Lochalsh (The Kyle Line), one of the most beautiful you will ever find. Or you can take a train from Glasgow to Mallaig, almost as scenic, to connect with the ferry to Armadale.

Transport in Skye
There is a limited bus service and you can hire cars on the island.

On the map, Skye looks like a great, misshapen claw, its pincers being lumpy peninsulas, separated by deep inlets, surrounded by many islands. Skye, for mountaineers, is the Cuillins, those fearsome, unreal-looking peaks that dominate not only the island but the horizon from the other islands and from the mainland. Romantics dream of a gallant young prince who came "over the sea to Skye" with a price on his head and blood on his conscience. Walkers come to the island for its many beautiful places, sailors return again and again to a coastline that is as lovely and as challenging as anywhere in the world.

Kyleakin

Kyleakin, the ferry terminus, stands round a small bay overlooked by a fragment of a ruin on a knoll, a jagged double tooth that will be familiar from postcards. The 12th-century relic was once a Mackinnon stronghold: Castle Maol or Moil, or Dun-na-Kyne. A story is told of one of its earliest inmates, Saucy Mary, a Norwegian princess, who somehow managed to stretch a barrier across the Kyle in order to levy tolls from passing ships.

Sleat Peninsula

Before you explore the main part of Skye, go down the Sleat peninsula, taking the road to the south a couple of miles (3.2 km) short of Broadford. A single track road goes nine miles (14.4 km) over the moor to **Isleornsay**, on the coast with lovely views across the Sound of Sleat. There is a pleasant hotel and a bar, whose landlord, a recent student of Gaelic himself, encourages his customers to speak Gaelic which is no longer the first language in Skye. The Isle of Ornsay is just off the hotel with a lighthouse and a ruined chapel dedicated to the Columbian monk, Orran.

Knock Bay

Knock Bay, is three miles (4.8 km) further on. **Knock Castle** (always accessible), an overgrown ruin on a rocky peninsula, was once a Macdonald stronghold. It was held on condition that the Macdonalds were always ready to receive the king or one of his representatives. If you stay long enough you may see the "glaistig" who haunts this ruin—a female sprite who will graciously accept libations of milk.

Armadale Castle

Armadale Castle is a further three miles (4.8 km) south. Built by Gillespie Graham in 1815 it was recently restored from a ruined condition, much of it being demolished. It is now the **Clan Donald Centre**, with a good **Museum of the Isles** (open daily in the summer: adults 80p, children 40p). Here you will learn the story of the Clan Donald and the Lords of the Isles in an audio visual theatre. So recently a derelict Victorian eyesore, Armadale has been most imaginatively re-developed, with lovely grounds, a mature arboretum, nature trails and a children's play area. There is a well-stocked book and gift shop, and a restaurant. You do not have to be a Macdonald to find plenty of interest here.

Aird of Sleat

A ferry runs from **Armadale Pier** to Mallaig, in the summer, taking half an hour. The road goes on another five miles (8 km) to the Aird of Sleat with its glorious views across the sound. It is not far to walk out to the southern tip of the peninsula where there is a sandy beach and more good views. Returning on the same road, take the narrow, twisting lane to the west, a mile (1.6 km) north of Armadale, climbing and dipping through woodland and moor, past lonely lochans, and mossy glades among silver birches, and five miles (8 km) out to the west coast of Sleat. Tiny settlements cluster round coves and sandy beaches. The road goes north from **Tarskavaig** about two miles (3.2 km) to **Dunsgiath Castle** (always accessible). This is one of the oldest fortified headlands in the Hebrides, home of the Macdonalds until the late 16th century. Little remains now but stacks of stones on a rock 40 ft (12 m) high, overlooking **Lock Eishort**. Celtic legend tells of Scathac the Wise, Queen of Skye in the Dark Ages, who held court here and preached the arts of peace and war to Cuchullin, an Ossianic hero. Cuchullin went off to practise his newly learnt arts, leaving his beautiful wife Bragela, weeping in vain at Dunsgiath, on "The Isle of Mist". He never returned.

Broadford

From here, it is about 14 miles (22.4 km) to Broadford, rejoining the road you started on. Broadford, though small, is a busy place on a crossroads. It has hotels, shops and, inevitably, groups of people bowed under knapsacks. The Broadford Music Festival is in June.

Take the narrow road south-west signed to **Elgol**, a beautiful drive of 14 miles (22.4 km) and passing several good walks. Elgol is a scattered village with more splendid views and from here you can get a boat across **Loch Scavaig** to **Loch Coruisk**, one of the most beautiful places in the world. For the energetic, a visit to Loch Coruisk is even more memorable if you walk out along the **Camasunary track**, from **Kilmarie**, which you go through about three miles (4.8 km) before Elgol. It is an easy walk over stony ground through bracken and heather, with just one tricky bit called The Bad Step where you must take care. The magic of Loch Coruisk, whether you get there by car and boat or on foot, will draw you back time and time again. It is a long, deep, dark loch, surrounded by high dramatic mountains. If you are lucky enough to catch a good sunset here, the memory of it will stay with you for life. The sun goes down behind the hills sending up great shafts of colour and refracted light, made more splendid by the proximity of the hills.

If you are fortunate enough to be exploring in your own boat, you should put into the perfect natural harbour in the island of **Soay** off the entrance to Loch Scavaig. Here you can see the remains of the shark factory that was established after the Second World War, by the author Gavin Maxwell. His subsequent book, *Harpoon at a Venture* is compelling reading, telling you much about these waters in the days when sharks and whales were plentiful in the Minch. You must return to Broadford on the same road, to rejoin the main road that follows the coast, looping round the long inlets, zigzagging up the hills.

Luib

At Luib, seven miles (11 km) north-west on **Loch Ainort**, you can visit a thatched cottage **Folk Museum** (open in the summer: small fee) furnished in the style of a croft house 100 years ago. For golfers, the main hazard of the 9 hole course at **Sconser** six miles (9.6 km) further on, is that you might hit a sheep.

The Cuillins

There is a delightfully old fashioned hotel at the head of **Loch Sligachan**, five miles (8 km) west of Sconser. It sits on the junction of the east and west routes to the north and is popular with fishermen and anyone planning to climb in the Cuillins. Here, surrounded by the sound of falling water, the Cuillins reign supreme. You can't escape them—they march away from you, in a great fearsome army. They don't look real: they seem to have been pulled upwards from the earth and you can see the runnels left by the fingers of their creator as he shaped them. The Cuillins are the work of a highly imaginative designer of stage-sets. Whether you see them capped with snow, their lower slopes mottled and smeared like camouflage jackets; or in mist, elusive and eerie; or capped by swirling cloud; or in brilliant sunshine against a postcard-blue sky, they seem to present a challenge. Only experienced climbers, with proper equipment, should attempt to conquer these mountains, which have claimed many lives over the years.

Portree

The road up the east side nine miles (14.4 km) north from Sligachan to Portree takes you through attractive valleys, with pine woods and moorland, fast-flowing rivers and burns. Just south of Portree, a minor road takes you out to the east coast that looks over the **Sound of Raasay**, with lovely views and sheltered bays below the cliffs.

Portree is a busy little tourist resort and the only town on Skye. You can take bus and boat excursions from here to many of the island's beauty spots. It is an attractive town, built round a natural harbour with the houses rising steeply from the water, neat and brightly painted. The name Portree is derived from the Gaelic for King's Port, arising from a visit by James V, in 1540, when he came to the islands in an attempt to win the allegiance of the Lords of the Isles. It was in a room in what is now the Royal Hotel, that Prince Charles took his leave of Flora Macdonald. He repaid her half-a-crown that she had lent him, gave her a miniature of himself, and said: "For all that has happened I hope, Madam, we shall meet in St James yet." He bowed and kissed her hand: a fugitive, with a bundle of clean shirts, a chicken, a bottle of whisky and a bottle of brandy tied at his waist, and £30,000 on his head. Such is the romance of Scotland.

Skye Week takes place in Portree in June, with every sort of Scottish entertainment both indoors and out. The Portree Show is in July. The Skye Highland Games also in Portree, are in August, and the Portree Fiddlers Rally sets your feet tapping in September.

Going north-east from Portree up the **Trotternish Peninsula**, you pass **Prince Charles' Cave** about three miles (4.8 km) north and out on the coast, where the prince hid during his escape. The best way to get to the cave is by boat.

The Old Man of Storr

The Old Man of Storr is about seven miles (11 km) north of Portree, to the west of the road. It is another of those landmarks that will be familiar from the many pictures taken of it. The Old Man is the tallest of a group of mighty towers and pinnacles of basaltic rock, the **Storr Ridge**. He is over 150 ft (45 m) high and 40 ft (12 m) in diameter: a great weathered stack, undercut and pointed at the top, like a giant fir cone. As you walk among this silent gathering of wise old sages, look out for the large variety of alpine flowers that grow at their feet.

In 1891, on the shore below the Old Man of Storr, a hoard of treasure was unearthed; a most remarkable collection of silver neck rings, brooches, bracelets and beaten ingots, together with many 10th-century coins, some from Samarkand. You can see these treasures in the National Museum of Antiquities, in Edinburgh. It is believed that they must have been left there by a Norseman, who presumably died before he could claim them.

Loch Mealt

The road twists and turns up the east coast, with lovely view out to sea and to the hills inland. Stop at the car park at Loch Mealt, seven miles (11 km) north of The Old Man of Storr where the road comes to the brink of the cliff. If you have a good head for heights you can watch the waterfall, where the loch drains in a sheer 300 ft (90 m) drop; a white cascade plummeting into the cobalt sea.

On the north side of Loch Mealt you can see the **Kilt Rock**, its vertical columns of basalt over horizontal strips of grey and white oolite looking like the pleats and pattern of a kilt.

The Quiraing

The Quiraing is along a switch-back road, two miles (3.2 km) west of Staffin, which is two miles (3.2 km) north of the Kilt Rock. This is a group of pillars of basaltic rock around an emerald-green grass amphitheatre, where cattle used to be driven for safety during raids in the old days. Walking among these savage-looking columns, you feel you are in some nightmare Gothic cathedral, enhanced by a carpet of alpine flowers.

About three miles (4.8 km) north of Staffin, you pass the house where Flora Macdonald lived after her marriage to Captain Allan Macdonald of Kingsburgh. It stands beside the **Flodigarry Hotel**, whose terrace gives you lovely views across to the Ross-shire coast.

Duntulm Castle

Duntulm Castle (always accessible) is a jagged ruin on the western tip of Trotternish and about four miles (6.4 km) further on. The castle with its water gate stands on a magnificent, easily defended position on a precipitous cliff. Built on the site of an earlier fortress, it was a stronghold of the Macdonalds of Sleat, under the authority of James VI during his attempts to discipline the Hebridean chiefs at the turn of the 16th century. Sir Donald Gorme Macdonald of Sleat was ordered to maintain his fortress in good condition, to restrict his household to six gentlemen, to limit his consumption of wine to four tuns (1,008 gallons, 4,536 l) a year, and to produce three of his kinsmen, annually, as surety for his good behaviour. The family left the castle after a nursemaid dropped the laird's infant son out of a window into the sea. The luckless nursemaid was punished for her carelessness by being cast adrift in an open boat full of holes.

Kilmuir

Going south, down the west side of Trotternish, less than two miles (3.2 km) along, you come to the windswept churchyard at Kilmuir. Below the large white Celtic cross lie the mortal remains of one of Scotland's heroines, Flora Macdonald, her shroud being a sheet on which Prince Charles slept when he was hidden at Kingsburgh House. Flora smuggled the prince, disguised as her maid Betty Bourke, from Loch Uskavagh in Benbecula, to Skye. For this act of courage she was briefly imprisoned. She lived with her family in North Carolina for some years, but returned to Kingsburgh for the last decade of her life, dying at the age of 68.

From the churchyard you can look out across the entrance to **Loch Snizort** to the west, to where Flora and the prince came on their daring voyage. A portrait of Flora by Allan Ramsay shows a woman with a calm, fine-boned face of classic Scottish beauty. Dr Johnson, who was a guest of Flora and her husband at Kingsburgh in 1773, wrote of her: "...Flora Macdonald, a name that will be mentioned in history, and if courage and fidelity be virtues, mentioned with honour. She is a woman of middle stature, soft features, gentle manners and elegant presence..."

The Skye Cottage Museum

The Skye Cottage Museum (open in the summer for a small fee) is close to the churchyard. It consists of a group of old cottages with a "black house", farming and domestic implements and a splendid collection of documents and old photographs, giving you a good idea of what life was like in the old days of crofting. The green plain that stretches away to the south is known as the Granary of Skye, a lush, fertile expanse over which the Macdonalds of Sleat and the Macleods of Vaternish frequently fought for ownership.

Monkstadt House stands to the west of the road, four miles (6.4 km) south of Kilmuir. Flora and the prince landed here, while the house was occupied by Hanoverian troops. The prince hid in the grounds, where he was served by Macdonald of Kingsburgh, who brought him food and wine under the noses of the soldiers.

Uig Bay

Uig Bay, three miles (4.8 km) to the south, lies below a green amphitheatre of hills, its long pier cutting across it like an outflung arm. The tiny hamlet of **Uig** is made busy by ferry traffic, for this is the terminus for the steamer to the Outer Isles. If you are lucky, one of the fishing boats that use the pier may have berthed with a load of scampi, and may agreed to sell you a bagful, scooped up off a great pile on deck. Anyone with a portable camping stove should boil these for just a few moments and eat them while still warm. They taste a hundred times better than when brought to you on a plate, disguised with an exotic sauce and a French name.

Loch Snizort Beag

At **Borve**, 11 miles (17.6 km) south of Uig, take the right turn (west) and stop in **Skeabost**, about three miles (4.8 km) along, a pretty hamlet at the head of Loch Snizort Beag. From the stone bridge you can look down on a rocky island where the river branches. This was the site of an ancient Christian settlement, probably founded by St Columba, whose name it bears, and you can reach it by stepping stones. Among the tumble of weeds there is the ruin of a Celtic chapel and a collection of old gravestones that are carved with effigies of Crusaders, in chain mail.

The scenery is everchanging: hamlets and bleak moorland; lovely views out to sea; great expanses of peat-bog, oozing with riverlets and shallow lochans; everywhere dominated by distant views of the Cuillins and stretches of glinting water.

Vaternish, the peninsula west of Loch Snizort Beag, does not have quite the same outstanding beauty as Trotternish, but it has good views and dramatic cliffs.

Annait

At Annait, a mile (1.6 km) north of **Fairy Bridge**, which is 14 miles (22.4 km) west of Skeabost, you can see the site of what is probably the oldest Christian settlement in these parts. There is the wall and the foundations of a small chapel and the cells of the monks, scattered across a green promontory between two deep gulleys. In this wild and lonely place you can hear only the piping of skylarks, the chatter of running water and the wind.

Trumpan

At the end of this narrow road up the west coast of Vaternish, at Trumpan, ten miles (16 km) north of Fairy Bridge, you will find the scant remains of a church with a murky history. In 1579, the Macleods were attending a service in the church. They were attacked by their bitter enemies, the Macdonalds of South Uist, who massacred them, setting fire to the church and burning the entire congregation except one woman. Cutting off a breast in order to escape through a window, this woman managed to get away and warn the remainder of the Macleod clan. When the Macdonalds returned to their boats they in turn were massacred by the alerted Macleods. This was one of the occasions when the Fairy Flag of Dunvegan was waved (see Dunvegan Castle).

Dunvegan

As you drive south towards Dunvegan you see the outline of **Macleod's Tables** ten miles (16 km) away to the south-west. These two great flat-topped lumps of basalt together with the Cuillins, give Skye its distinctive outline. It is said that when Alasdair Crottach Macleod went to the court of King James V, at Holyrood in Edinburgh in the 16th century, he was asked somewhat patronisingly whether he was impressed by the grandeur of the palace. He replied that he saw nothing to compare for grandeur with his own domain in Skye. When James V then visited Skye, trying to rally support from the Hebridean clans, Macleod gave an open air banquet for him, on the lower of the two "tables", lit by his kilted clansmen, each holding aloft a flaming torch. "My family candlesticks", he told the king, with a sweep of his hand. One can only hope that it was a fine day, and that the monarch was supplied with a good horse or some stout walking shoes!

Dunvegan Castle (open in the summer, daily except Sundays: adults £1.90, children £1) is five miles (8 km) south-west of Fairy Bridge. It has been the seat of the Macleods since at least 1200. It is a massive castle on a rock, displaying a variety of architectural styles, including "country house" windows which soften its otherwise fortress-like stature. From every angle it seems to show you a different face; each one grey, formidable and impressive. Once accessible from the sea only, it is now approached by a bridge over a ravine which formed a perfect moat.

The castle contains a wealth of interesting and beautiful things: There are family heirlooms, pictures, arms, original furnishings, documents and relics. You can trace the history of the Macleods back through 30 generations to their Norse ancestry. The "pièce de résistance" is the Fairy Flag, a frail scrap of faded and worn silk, shot with gold thread and marked with crimson "elf spots". Legend tells of the Macleod who fell in love with a fairy, hundreds of years ago. The lovers were forced to part (at Fairy Bridge, to the north) and the fairy left the flag as a coverlet for their child. This flag had the power to save the Macleod clan from destruction, three times and only if waved in a genuine crises. It has been used twice: once at Trumpan (see above) and once during a famine, caused by cattle plague.

You can take boat cruises from the jetty below the castle to the little islands where seals bask on the rocks. Dunvegan has a Gala Day, in August and the Dunvegan Show, also in August.

Durinish Peninsula

The Durinish Peninsula, topped by the Macleods Tables, stretches away west of Loch Dunvegan. Off the southern tip eight miles (12.8 km) south of Dunvegan, you can see three basalt stacks called **Macleod's Maidens**, called after the wife and daughters of a Macleod, who drowned here in a shipwreck.

The Orbost Art Gallery, three miles (4.8 km) south of Dunvegan on the east side of the peninsula has modern exhibitions in the summer and five miles (8 km) further north you should go to the **Folk Museum at Colbost** (open in the summer for a small fee). Here you can go into a thatched "black house" with its peat fire in the middle of the room and see all the implements and furnishings of the 19th century, as it would have been during the Clearances. There is also an illicit whisky still, once common all over the Highlands. The museum includes a watermill, three miles (4.8 km) to the west at **Glendale**. Also on this road, two miles (3.2 km) north of Colbost, is the **Piping Centre** at **Borreraig**. Here is a cairn marking the site of the piping school where the hereditary pipers to the Macleods, the MacCrimmons of Durinish, lived and taught piping for 300 years.

Dun Beag

Going south on the main road from Dunvegan, after about eight miles (12.8 km) look carefully up to your left as you drop down into **Bracadale**. Dun Beag (always accessible) one of the best brochs in Skye, seems to grow out of the hillside and would be easy to miss. It is only a few minutes climb up over springy turf and stones to this 2,000 year old relic, which once stood 40 or 50 ft (14 m approximately) high. This refuge, once for farmers and herdsmen, has double walls, braced by a honeycomb of chambers and galleries, with cells and passages and stairways, and traces of outbuildings. Axes, hammers, arrowheads, bones and combs were excavated from this site.

As you stand and look down over the hillside to Loch Bracadale in the west, across tufts of reed and rocky outcrops, vivid with heather, and alive with birdsong, it is strange to think that those mysterious ancestors, about whom so little is known, had this same view.

To complete your circular tour of the island, the road south-east takes you along the northern edge of the Cuillins, dappled with brown, tan, grey, blue and ochre; 14 miles (22.4 km) back to Sligachan and the route to the mainland.

Raasay

The island of Raasay can be reached by ferry from **Sconser**. It is a 15 mile (24 km) long strip, sheltered and fertile, once the hiding place of the fugitive Prince Charlie, who spent a couple of nights in a shepherd's hut. Dr Johnson visited the island during his tour of the Hebrides with Boswell and was lavishly entertained at Raasay House, built by the Macleods in 1746. The house and land were badly neglected by an absentee landlord in the 1970s, giving rise to much publicity and local outrage. It now houses the **Raasay Outdoor Centre**.

Castle Brochel (always accessible) is a ruin on a rock on the eastern shore. It has a lovely setting overlooking a bay, with the hills of Torridon massing on the eastern horizon. Boswell, exploring this ruin, discovered that it contained a privy—a convenience that was sadly lacking in Raasay House where they were staying. He pointed this out to their host: '. . . You take very good care of one end of a man, but not of the other . . .".

The island has a ruined chapel dedicated to St Moluag of Lismore, with a carved Celtic cross, and the remains of a ruined broch, **Dun Borodale**.

Having toured Skye by car, you should try to find time to walk, particularly around its glorious west coast.

TOURIST INFORMATION

Meall House, Portree, Isle of Skye, IV51 9VZ, tel 0478-2137. It is open all year.

Broadford, tel 04712-361. It is open during the summer only.

Kyle of Lochalsh, tel 0599-4276. It is open during the summer only.

Shielbridge, tel 0599-81 264. It is open during the summer only.

WHERE TO STAY

There are plenty of hotels, guest houses and bed and breakfast places on Skye and a number of self-catering establishments. You should look at the tourist brochure before you make your choice. Here are a few suggestions.

Broadford Hotel, Broadford, tel 047-12 204/5. B&B from £16.50: categories 3,3,3: 29 bedrooms, 18 en suite. A comfortable, friendly hotel in the middle of Broadford.

The Old Inn, Carbost, tel 047842-205. B&B from £10.50: categories 3,2,3: 4 bedrooms. Small, attractive old inn with a warm, friendly atmosphere.

Duntulm Castle Hotel, Duntulm, tel 047052-213. B&B from £13: categories 4,4,4: 30 bedrooms, 8 en suite. Glorious position, high above Score Bay, looking across to the outer isles.

Atholl House Hotel, Dunvegan, tel 047022-219. B&B from £12.50: categories 4,4,4: 12 bedrooms, 5 en suite. Nice, friendly hotel not far from the castle.

Greshornish House Hotel, Greshornish, near Edinbane, tel 047082-266/255. B&B from £16: categories 4,4,4: 7 bedrooms, 6 en suite. Nice hotel in former family home.

Dunringell Hotel, Kyleakin, tel 0599-4180. B&B from £10.50: categories 3,3,2: 14 bedrooms, 10 en suite. Comfortable hotel in splendid position with attractive grounds.

Caledonian Hotel, Portree, tel 0478-2641. B&B from £13: categories 3,3,4: 12 bedrooms, 5 en suite. Friendly hotel right in the middle of Portree.

Coolin Hills Hotel, Portree, tel 0478 2003. B&B from £18: categories 5,5,4: 27 bedrooms, 20 en suite. A comfortable, hospitable hotel in lovely grounds.

Rosedale Hotel, Portree, tel 0478-2531. B&B from £16: categories 4,4,3: 21 bedrooms, 19 en suite. A comfortable hotel right on the waterfront overlooking the harbour.

Royal Hotel, Portree, tel 0478-2525. B&B from £14: categories 4,5,4: 26 bedrooms, 17 en suite. Full of character, and considerably more comfortable than the days when Prince Charlie took his leave of Flora Macdonald in this hotel.

Viewfield House Hotel, Portree, tel 0478-2217. B&B from £10: categories 3,3,2: 15 bedrooms. On the outskirts of Portree as you come in from the south. Viewfield was until recently a family mansion and stands in lovely grounds.

Sconser Lodge Hotel, Sconser, tel 047852. B&B from £15: categories 3,3,4: 8 bedrooms, 1 en suite. A lovely position at the mouth of Loch Sligachan, looking across to Raasay Island.

Kinloch Lodge Hotel, Isle of Ornsay, Sleat, tel 04713-214/333. B&B from £30: categories 4,4,4: 10 bedrooms, 9 en suite. A converted shooting lodge overlooking the sea, owned and run by Lord and Lady Macdonald. The magic touch of Lady Macdonald, who has written two cookery books, is very evident in the delicious food.

Hotel Eilean Iarmain, Camus Chros, Isle of Ornsay, tel 04713-332. B&B from £13: categories 3,3,4: 13 bedrooms. A comfortable hotel right on the water with an owner/landlord who encourages the speaking of Gaelic in both the hotel and public bar.

Torvaig House Hotel, Knock Bay, Teangue, Sleat, tel 04713 231. B&B from £25: categories 4,4,4: 10 bedrooms, 7 en suite. A comfortable hotel on Knock Bay in lovely grounds.

Sligachan Hotel, Sligachan, tel 047852-204. B&B from £20.50: categories 4,3,4: 23 bedrooms, 9 en suite. A splendid, old world atmosphere, ideally placed for the Cuillins.

Ferry Inn Hotel, Uig, tel 04742-242. B&B from £22: categories 3,3,3: 6 bedrooms, 1 en suite. Charming old inn with a great atmosphere.

Isle of Raasay Hotel, Raasay, tel 047862-222/226. B&B from £17: categories 5,4,4: 12 bedrooms en suite. Very comfortable and friendly, on this lovely island.

It is often more fun, if you have time, to rent a self catering house, giving you more freedom if you want to go off climbing or walking and not be worried about hotel meal times. There are many to choose from. Perhaps the cream of them all is at Braes, high above the Narrows of Raasay south of Portree. This is a charming, cosy, family house, sleeping six to seven people and with everything you could wish for. It costs from £55 to £120 per week. Apply Mrs J. D. Bengough, White Lodge, Church Street, Sidbury, Devon, tel 03957-214.

EATING OUT
Kinloch Lodge Hotel, see above. For a real treat. Food you won't forget in a magnificent setting. Dinner from £10.

Torvaig House Hotel, see above. Good local ingredients. Dinner from £7.50.

The Stables, Clan Donald Centre, Armadale Castle, tel 04714-227. Good variety of fresh, local food, and warm friendly atmosphere. Dinner from £7.50.

The Kings Haven Hotel, Portree, tel 0478-2290. Good local food. Dinner from £7.50.

Skeabost House Hotel, Skeabost, tel 047032-202. Good local food. Dinner from £7.50.

Three Chimneys Restaurant, Colbost, Dunvegan, tel 047081-258. Good local food. Dinner from £7.50.

Harlosh Hotel, tel 047022-367. Specialists in local seafood. Dinner from £5.

CRAFT CENTRES IN SKYE
The following studios and workshops welcome visitors. Where a telephone number is given you should ring up first to check on times.

Candlemaking
Skye Lytes, Three Rowans, Kildonan, Arnisort. Candlemaking and sculpturing.

Ceramics
Edinbane Pottery, tel 047082–234. Manufacture of wood-fired stoneware, tableware and ornaments, some salt glaze.

Knitwear and Crochet
The Gillen Knitwear Workshop, Waternish, tel 047083-267. Machine made wool and cotton garments.

Skye Crotal Knitwear, Camus Chros, tel 04713–271.

Miscellaneous craftwork
Aurora Crafts, 2 Ose, Struan. Lacemaking.

Orbost Gallery, Dunvegan, tel 047022-207. Picture framing, mount cutting, picture and print restoration, calligraphy and illumination.

Skye Original Prints, 1 Wentworth Street, Portree. Printing and sale of colour etchings.

Weaving
Rosalind Burgess, Ardmore, Waternish. Handweaving.

The Small Isles: Rhum, Eigg, Canna, Muck

GETTING TO THE SMALL ISLES
Caledonian Macbrayne run a seasonal service to all four islands on Monday, Wednesday, Thursday and Saturday, from Mallaig. For details write to Caledonian

Macbrayne, The Ferry Terminal, Gourock, Renfrewshire, PA19 1QP, tel 047-042 219.

A local boat also runs cruises from Arisaig to Eigg, in the summer.

RHUM

Rhum is a squashed-diamond shaped island, rising to a massive hump; another unmistakable landmark for sailors, eight miles (12.8 km) west of Sleat in Skye. Inhabited since the Stone Age, its population of over 400 was reduced to one family in 1826, to make way for one sheep farm of 8,000 sheep. Deer were then introduced and it became a private sporting estate until the Nature Conservancy acquired it in 1957. It is now an "outdoor laboratory" trying to discover how the Hebrides can best support wild life and human beings.

The name Rhum is thought to come from the Greek "rhombos", referring to the rhomboid shape. The chief interest of the island is in its geology: special permission must be obtained from the Nature Conservancy warden, to visit most parts of the island.

A herd of half wild golden-brown ponies perserved on Rhum are said to be descended from the survivors of a Spanish galleon which was part of the Armada wrecked off these coasts in 1588. You may also see wild goats, golden eagles and plenty of deer.

The imposing red sandstone castle that looks across the bay as you approach by boat (the only way of reaching the island) is **Kinloch Castle**, built in 1901. It was built by the then owners of the estate, the Bulloughs of Lancashire and is now a hotel. For a very special treat you can spend a few days in the atmosphere of a Baronial seat, with all the original furnishings, and very good food. The hotel is owned by the Nature Conservancy Council and is frequently written up in quality magazines. One of the features is the extremely rare electric 'orchestrarian', a wonderful Heath-Robinson contraption whose parts represent a full orchestra which can play you any piece of music you chose from its vast library of pre-set cylinders. All the working components can be seen in action, in a huge glass chamber in the hall.

For further information about the Kinloch Castle Hotel write to Nature Conservancy Council, Fraser Darling House, 9 Culduthal Road, Inverness, INZ 4AG, tel 0463-239431 or to Kinloch Castle Hotel, Isle of Rhum, tel 0687-2037. The maximum price for full board is £39 a day—one of the biggest bargains in Great Britain. The price descends to cover hostel accommodation and self catering.

TOURIST INFORMATION

Fort William and Lochaber Tourist Board, Cameron Square, Fort William, tel 0397-3781. It is open all year.

WHERE TO STAY

Kinloch Castle Hotel, see above.

EIGG

Eigg is privately owned. It is about four miles (6.4 km) south-east of Rhum. It has chalets and cottages to let and is a perfect holiday island. Shaped like an upturned boat, surrounded by clear, sparkling water, it is a magic place in sunshine, about six miles (9.6 km) by four miles (6.4 km), dominated by the huge black hump of the Sgurr.

Walking up from the little harbour in the south-east and round the bay to the east, you find the ancient burial ground at **Kildonnan Church**, resting place of Macdonalds. It contains a broken Celtic cross and a ruin overgrown with nettles.

Near the harbour there is a cave that you can climb into but you will need a torch. It was here, in the 16th century, that some Macdonalds hid from a party of their deadly enemies, the Macleods of Skye. The Macleods lit a fire at the entrance to the cave and 200 Macdonalds perished. Sir Walter Scott visited the cave in 1814 and found mortal remains from this gruesome event.

It is a pleasant walk up to the north-west corner of the island to the glorious **Bay of Laig**, where you might hear the "Singing Sands" ("the Camas Sgiotaig"). The sands make a curious keening sort of song in certain conditions.

TOURIST INFORMATION

Fort William and Lochaber Tourist Board, Cameron Square, Fort William, tel 0397-3781 . It is open all year.

WHERE TO STAY

Galmisdale House, Isle of Eigg, B&B from £8: 4 bedrooms. With dinner, £18.50.

Mrs M Kirk, Laig Farm, Isle of Eigg, tel 0687-82437. Dinner, B&B from £14: 6 bedrooms.

SELF CATERING

Eigg Holiday Bookings, Maybank, Udny, Ellon, Aberdeenshire, tel 06513-2367. There are five chalets, eight cottages, three houses from £51.75–£293.25 per week.

CANNA

Sometimes called "the Garden of the Hebrides" Canna lies less than five miles (8 km) off the west coast of Rhum. The highest point of this long thin island is only 690 ft (207 m) above sea level. **Compass Hill**, (458 ft, 138.5 m) in the north, is so called because of the magnetic rock in it that can distort the true readings of a ship's compass. Canna is a charming island, serene and lonely, with a good harbour. You can still see the remains of a **Celtic Nunnery** that once flourished, and the ruined tower near the harbour was owned by a Lord of the Isles who is reputed to have imprisoned his beautiful wife in it, suspecting her of infidelity.

WHERE TO STAY
The National Trust for Scotland have a very nice guest house on the island but members get priority. Apply to National Trust for Scotland, 5 Charlotte Square, Edinburgh, EH2 4DU, tel 031-226 5922.

MUCK

Muck, seven miles (11 km) south of Rhum, is the smallest of the group known as the Small Isles, its strange name being derived from the Gaelic "muc", pig. You can visit the island by motor boat from Eigg but there is no accommodation. It is a green, pretty little island with lovely sandy beaches.

The Outer Hebrides

Of all Scotland's islands, the Outer Hebrides seem to inspire the deepest nostalgia, and its exiles to suffer the strongest pangs of homesickness. As you come ashore from the steamer, you are hit by the unforgettable tang of peat-smoke on the clear air. You hear the chatter of Gaelic all around you on the pier, and the magic bewitches you. It is only in these islands that Gaelic is still the first language for many; a living language, though dying and not yet the self-conscious "revival" that it is becoming elsewhere.

The Long Island, as the entire chain is sometimes called, runs about 130 miles (208 km) from the Butt of Lewis, in the north, down to Barra Head in the south, and its main islands include Lewis and Harris, North Uist, Benbecula, South Uist, Eriskay and Barra. Each of these is unique in character, with dialects that differ even between the moorlands of Lewis and mountains of Harris.

North of Benbecula is almost entirely Presbyterian: south is almost entirely Catholic. Although there is no animosity between the two extremes you will notice a far more puritanical attitude towards life in the north, while the south is more easy-going and relaxed.

Scenically, there is everything you could ask for: miles and miles of white sand; acres of machair, rich in wild flowers; rugged mountains; and bleak moorland. The east coast is indented by long sea lochs that provide shelter for boats in bad weather. If you look at an aerial photograph you will see that the land is broken up by a vast number of lochs and lochans which once provided waterways throughout the islands. The climate is unpredictable: you can be lucky and find weather that makes you wonder why anyone ever goes anywhere else for their holiday. On the other hand, it can be very wet and very windy.

It is the people of these islands who are the essence of Gaeldom, with their quiet courtesy, gentle humanity, intelligence, imagination and needle-sharp wit.

Communications are good, but expensive.

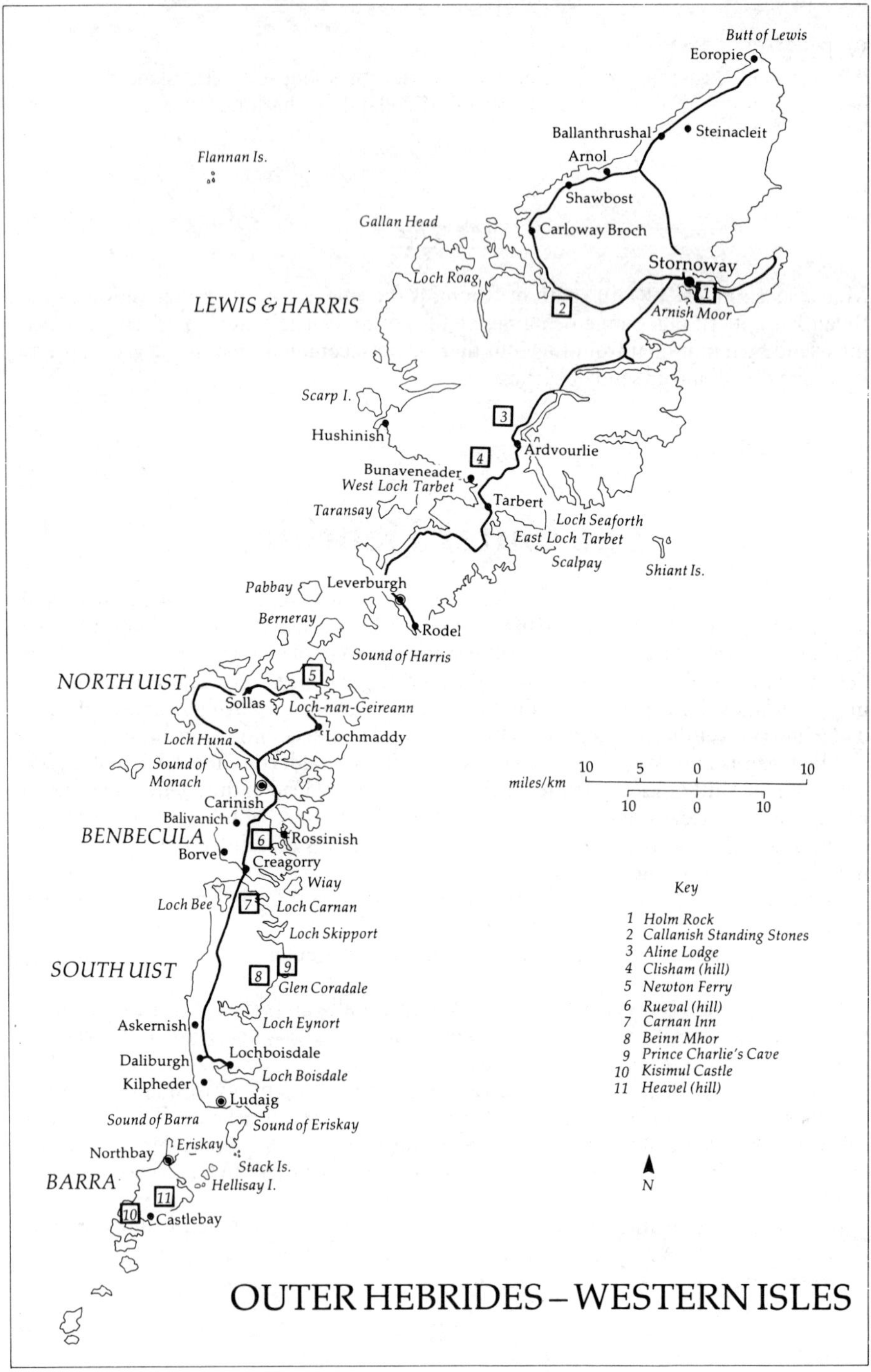
Butt of Lewis
Europie
Ballanthrushal
Steinacleit
Arnol
Flannan Is.
Shawbost
Gallan Head
Carloway Broch
Stornoway
Loch Roag
1
2
LEWIS & HARRIS
Arnish Moor
Scarp I.
3
Hushinish
Ardvourlie
4
Bunaveneader
West Loch Tarbet
Tarbert
Taransay
Loch Seaforth
East Loch Tarbet
Scalpay
Shiant Is.
Pabbay
Leverburgh
Berneray
Rodel
Sound of Harris
NORTH UIST
5
Sollas
Loch-nan-Geireann
Loch Huna
Lochmaddy
Sound of
Monach
Carinish
Balivanich
BENBECULA
6
Rossinish
Borve
Creagorry
Wiay
Loch Bee
7
Loch Carnan
Loch Skipport
SOUTH UIST
8
9
Glen Coradale
Askernish
Loch Eynort
Daliburgh
Lochboisdale
Loch Boisdale
Kilpheder
Ludaig
Sound of Barra
Sound of Eriskay
Northbay
Eriskay
Stack Is.
BARRA
Hellisay I.
11
10
Castlebay
miles/km
10 5 0 10
10 0 10
Key
1 Holm Rock
2 Callanish Standing Stones
3 Aline Lodge
4 Clisham (hill)
5 Newton Ferry
6 Rueval (hill)
7 Carnan Inn
8 Beinn Mhor
9 Prince Charlie's Cave
10 Kisimul Castle
11 Heavel (hill)
N
OUTER HEBRIDES – WESTERN ISLES

GETTING TO THE OUTER HEBRIDES

By sea

Ferrys run from Ullapool to Stornoway in Lewis from Uig in Skye to Tarbert in Harris and Lochmaddy in North Uist, and from Oban to Castlebay in Barra and Lochboisdale in South Uist. The timetable changes for winter and summer and is constantly under review. Write to Caledonian Macbrayne, The Ferry Terminal, Gourock, Renfrewshire, PA19 1QP, tel 047-042 219.

Local boats run between the smaller islands with very flexible sailing times. Anyone will tell you who to consult.

Air

British Airways operate a daily service (except Sundays) from Glasgow/Inverness to Stornoway, Lewis, and from Glasgow to Benbecula. Write to British Airways, Buchanan Street, Glasgow, tel 041-332 9666. Loganair operate a daily service from Glasgow to Barra. They also operate an inter-island service between Stornoway, Lewis, Benbecula and Barra. Charter flights can be arranged. Write to Loganair Ltd, Glasgow Airport, Abbotsinch, Renfrewshire, tel 041-889 1311.

Public transport, once you get there, is almost non existent. You must have your own car or you can hire one locally. Consult the tourist office.

LEWIS AND HARRIS

Lewis and Harris, together, form one island, Lewis being mostly moorland and Harris being mountainous.

LEWIS

Stornoway

Stornoway, the administrative centre for the Western Isles, is an attractive little town on the east coast. It forms a sturdy metropolis with a busy harbour, brightly painted houses, reasonable shops and plenty of amenities. After the First World War, the rich industrialist, Lord Leverhulme bought the island and tried to develop it in order to improve the economy for the benefit of the people. His motives were entirely philanthropic but came to nothing by a mixture of local pride, apathy and governmental bureaucracy. He offered to give the island to the people, having lost a considerable sum of money trying to establish a strong fishing industry, but they refused to accept his gift. Stornoway, however, accepted the castle and grounds.

WHAT TO SEE

The picturesque harbour, with its fishing boat and all the clutter of the waterfront, is the focus of the town. The grounds of **Lewis Castle** are used as a public park and also contain a golf course. The castle, solid and Victorian, has been a technical college since 1953, teaching a range of skills that includes navigation (using a minesweeper as a classroom), textile making and building. All are useful subjects for an island student. The present castle was built on the site of the stronghold of the original lairds, the Seaforth Mackenzies. It was destroyed by Cromwell.

The Stornoway Museum (open in the summer: admission free) is in the Old Town Hall. Here you can discover some of the island's history.

If you walk out past the castle, about four miles (6.4 km), to the edge of **Arnish Moor**, you can see the cairn that commemorates the night Prince Charlie spent in a house here, while trying to negotiate for a boat. He came to Stornoway during his fugitive days after Culloden.

The local minister, Aulay Macaulay, was the only man, during the five months of the prince's escape, who contemplated with avarice the £30,000 reward offered for his capture.

On New Year's Day, 1919, a troop ship, the *Iolaire*, hit **Holm Rock,** across the harbour, and sank, drowning 200 men returning from the war.

The Butt of Lewis

The Butt of Lewis is a bleak headland on the northern tip of the island, 27 miles (43 km) from Stornoway by road, and topped by a lighthouse. Here you can see many different species of sea birds, filling the air with their sound.

At **Eoropie**, the little hamlet here, you can see the restored 12th century **St Moluag's Chapel**, known as Teamphull Mhor and built on the site of an early Christian chapel. You can get the key for this charming little place from the shop. Episcopal services are held occasionally and there is a strong feeling of the simple, uncomplicated faith that keeps such a remote church alive.

Going down the west coast from the Butt, about 11 miles (17.6 km), you come to **Steinacleit**. Here, surrounded by bleak moorland, is a ruined burial cairn within a stone circle.

Next to it is the 20 ft (6 m) high monolith called **The Thrushel Stone**, in **Ballantrushal**. It is the largest single stone in Scotland, another relic from the pre-historic settlers in these islands.

Five miles (8 km) further on at **Arnol**, you can visit a **Black House Museum** (open in the summer: small fee). It is a good example of the way the crofting families lived with their implements and simple furnishings in the time of the Highland Clearances.

The Shawbost Folk Museum (open in the summer: small fee) is at Shawbost, five miles (8 km) to the south. This museum has a splendid exhibition covering the old way of life in Lewis. It includes a restored Norse watermill about a mile (1.6 km) to the west. The entire museum was set up by pupils of the school.

You can also visit the craft centre and tea room at nearby **Rabhat**.

Carloway Broch

Carloway Broch (always accessible) is on the northern shore of East Loch Roag, six miles (9.6 km) south-west of Shawbost. It is the best preserved broch in the Hebrides, on a wonderful site overlooking the sea. Part of it rises to about 30 ft (9 m), and you can picture those families, 2,000 years ago, crowding inside the massive walls to take refuge from invaders.

The Callanish Standing Stones

The Callanish Standing Stones (always accessible) are five miles (8 km) south-east of Carloway along the northern shore of East Loch Roag. They rank in importance with Stonehenge, being one of the most complete pre-historic sites in Britain. The stones are laid out to depict, more or less, a Celtic cross, with a burial cairn at the centre, approached from north and south by avenues of pillars. Traces of cremated bones were found in the cairn. The central pillar casts its shadow exactly along the entrance passage into the grave at sunset on the days of the equinox. It is a most dramatic place, set in moorland overlooking the loch and surrounded by hills. It stirs the imagination as you try to picture the burial of some priest-king, all those years ago, with all the ritual that was practised in the centuries before Christianity.

There is a craft centre nearby and a tea room, and a **Mini Museum** (open in the summer). Here you will find information about the stones.

On a clear day you can see the **Flannan Islands**, 15 miles (24 km) to the west. In 1900, a gale raged at Christmas and all three of the lighthouse keepers vanished without trace.

It was at **Gallan Head**, on the western tip of **West Loch Roag**, 11 miles (17.6 km) across the water from Callanish, that the famous Lewis Chessmen were discovered in 1831, made of walrus-ivory. Replicas can now be bought all over the islands. The originals, in the British Museum in London, are thought to have been hidden by nuns to save them from plunder. These nuns lived in a Benedictine convent nearby. There are lovely walks along the west coast, all the way down into Harris.

Although scenically Lewis is not remarkable, apart from some lovely coastal views, it has plenty of things to see including craft centres, pottery centres and weavers, all with their own shops, and all well signposted as you drive round the island.

HARRIS

Aline Lodge, at the head of **Loch Seaforth**, marks the boundary between Harris and Lewis, and it was at **Ardvourlie**, on the west side of the loch, that Prince Charlie landed before walking to Arnish, near Stornoway, to look for a boat.

WHAT TO SEE

From the moors of Lewis you come to a lumpy mass of hills in Harris, dominated by **Clisham**, 2,600 ft (780 m). This is the highest mountain in the Western Isles and towers to the south of Ardvourlie.

Tarbert

Tarbert, at the head of **East Loch Tarbert** on the east coast, is the main village. It is a thriving centre with good shops and the ferry terminus for Uig in Skye and Lochmaddy in North Uist. It is a good centre for fishermen, both for salmon, sea trout and trout, and for sea fishing. You can also visit local tweed suppliers and watch Harris Tweed being woven.

When weather permits you can take a boat cruise from Tarbert to the **Shiant Islands**, 12 miles (19 km) to the east, a wonderful wild cliff land with masses of birds.

Harris is divided into north and south by a narrow isthmus at Tarbert, between East and West Loch Tarbert. It was on **Scalpay Island**, at the mouth of East Loch Tarbert, that Prince Charlie stayed for a time, as a guest of Donald Campbell. Campbell was not a Jacobite, but he had all the Gaelic sense of hospitality and he protected the prince from a boat-load of armed men, led by the Reverend Macaulay, who had come from the north to try to claim the £30,000 reward for the capture of the prince. Donald Campbell's house is now the Free Church Manse.

Bunaveneader

The road to the west from Tarbert takes you through 14 miles (22 km) of lovely scenery with views out to sea, among hills sliced by cascading burns and carpeted in heather. There was a whaling station along this road, at Bunaveneader, built by Norwegians in 1912, when whales were plentiful in these waters.

Near **Amhuinnsuid Castle** (a private residence) about seven miles (11 km) west of Tarbert, you can see salmon trying to jump the falls where **Loch Leosaidh** pours down the cliff into the sea.

Scarp, the island off the tip at **Husinish**, 14 miles (22 km) north-west of Tarbert, was to be the recipient of a very advanced method of postal delivery in 1934. The mail was to be fired off in a specially designed rocket. A special stamp was issued, coveted by philatelists, and the first rocket was fired. Unfortunately it exploded, as rockets tend to do on impact, doing no good to the mail and effectively killing the project.

At the southern end of Harris, **Rodel Church of St Clements** dates from the 12th century and has some intriguing carved kilted figures on its tower. Among the tombs there is one of Alastair Crotach, 1528, the Macleod chief from Dunvegan, who entertained James V at Macleod's tables.

Leverburgh

Leverburgh, on the south coast, a couple of miles (3.2 km) north-west of Rodel, was developed by Lord Leverhulme after his plans for Stornoway had collapsed. He put a great deal of money into developing the harbour. He built a large pier, houses, kippering sheds, roads and lighthouses, and blasted rocks to improve the harbour. But he died a year after the fishing began to flourish, and with him died the drive and energy to keep things going as he had planned.

A passenger ferry runs from Leverburgh to North Uist.

TOURIST INFORMATION

4 South Beach Street, Stornoway, Isle of Lewis, tel 0851-3088. It is open all year.

Tarbert, Isle of Harris, tel 0859-2011. It is open in the summer.

WHERE TO STAY

Lewis

Baile-Na-Cille, Timsgarry, Uig, Isle of Lewis, tel 08505-242. B&B from £14, 5 bedrooms, 1 en suite. A converted 18th-century manse on the sea shore. Simple but very comfortable with good country cooking. Set dinner £10.

Cross Inn, Ness, Isle of Lewis, tel 085181 378. B&B from £12: categories 1,3,4: 5 bedrooms. Attractive old inn with lovely views.

Claitair Hotel, Shieldinish, South Lochs, Isle of Lewis, tel 085183 345. B&B from £10: categories 3,5,5: 8 bedrooms. Comfortable hotel with warm, Highland hospitality.

Caberfeidh Hotel, Manor Park, Stornoway, Isle of Lewis, tel 0851-2604. B&B from £23: categories 5,5,5: 38 bedrooms en suite. Modern purpose-built hotel with all comforts.

Seaforth Hotel, Stornoway, Isle of Lewis, tel 0851-2740. B&B from £21: categories 5,5,5: 58 bedrooms, 56 en suite.

Harris

Scarista House, Scarista, Isle of Harris, tel 0859-85 238. B&B from £23: categories 4,4,2: 7 bedrooms en suite. Georgian manse in lovely surroundings overlooking spectacular stretch of beach. Friendly and very civilised. Peat fires, good library. Delicious food and interesting, quite extensive wine list. Set dinner £14.

Harris Hotel, Tarbert, Isle of Harris, tel 0859-2154. B&B from £13.95: categories 3,3,4: 26 bedrooms, 14 en suite. Comfortable and friendly with relaxed atmosphere.

MacLeods Motel, Tarbert, Isle of Harris, tel 0859-2364. B&B from £10.95: categories 3,4,5: 16 bedrooms. Comfortable hotel with traditional Scottish hospitality.

EATING OUT

You will get a reasonable meal in any of the hotels above. Go for the local seafood wherever possible.

NORTH UIST

The island of North Uist is about 17 miles (27 km) long and 13 miles (21 km) wide, and a great deal of it is water. Wild peat moors cover the eastern side, with gentler green farmland to the west and glorious sandy beaches.

WHAT TO SEE

Lochmaddy is the port; a sprawling village with a sheltered harbour. It has several shops, a bank, hotel, and guest houses. The name comes from the Gaelic for dog ("madadh") and you can understand this when you look at the three rocks at the harbour entrance, shaped like crouching dogs.

Black House

each croft having its own place to cut; most people cook on it and use it to heat their houses, supplemented by calor gas, and, in recent years, electricity. The peat is cut in spring and stacked on the site until it is dry enough to cart. It is then built into great piles beside the houses, and used for the rest of the year.

There are several pre-historic remains to look at as you go round the island. Going about three miles (4.8 km) west from Lochmaddy you pass three standing stones on the slope of **Blashaval**. These are known as the **Three False Men**, said to be three men from Skye who were turned to stone by a witch as punishment for deserting their wives.

Five miles (8 km) west of Lochmaddy you can take the small road four miles (6.4 km) north to **Newton Ferry**. In a loch on the right of this road, just before the end, you will see a very well preserved fortress, **Dun-an-Sticir**, reached by a causeway. It was occupied as late as 1601.

Eilean-an-Tighe

Eilean-an-Tighe is a rocky islet in **Loch-nan-Geireann**, back on the circular road, two miles (3.2 km) west. It was the site of a Neolithic potters' workshop, the oldest to be excavated in western Europe. The pottery that was found here was a very high quality, better than that of later times, and there was so much of it that the factory must have supplied a large area.

In **Sollas**, three miles (4.8 km) west, a medieval settlement is being excavated, revealing valuable information about life here all those years ago.

Vallay

Vallay is an island at the entrance to a wide, shallow bay that runs north and west from

Sollas. Here stands a Victorian house that is sadly dying of neglect, inhabited only by birds and the occasional carcase of a sheep. You can walk out to Valley at low tide, but watch out for the flood tide which comes in like bath water and it is very easy to get cut off.

Huna

Follow the road about four miles (6.4 km) round the coast westwards to Huna. Here, if you take the footpath two miles (3.2 km) east across the moor, you come to a chambered cairn on **Clettraval**. This was built before peat covered the land, in the days when birchwood copses grew here. Birch wood was found inside the cairn. A fort was built over it, later, in the Iron Age, from which pottery was excavated and found to be the same as that made in the factory at Eilean-an-Tighe.

Unival

Unival is a hill north of the road, six miles (9.6 km) south-east of Huna. If you walk across the moor, up its eastern flank, on the west side of **Loch Huna**, you will find another chambered burial cairn with a small cist.

A couple of miles (3.2 km) further down, the road forks, south to the right, and north-east to the left. If you take the left hand road you complete the circle of the island and take in two of its greatest treasures.

Pobull Fhinn

Two miles (3.2 km) along this road back to Lochmaddy, a track to the right is signposted to **Langlass Lodge Hotel**, less than a mile (1.6 km) away. Park at the hotel and take the footpath up behind it, a ten minute climb through heather, bracken and bog-myrtle. On the hillside you come to an oval of standing stones, called Pobull Fhinn (Finn's People) a pre-historic site that is so overlaid with mysticism that you want to make some small gesture of recognition to those ancient gods.

It is believed that this may have been one of the sites where an annual ritual included the ceremonial sacrifice of the king, hundreds of years before Christ. Whatever its origins, you come away from this magic mystery deeply moved.

Barpa Langass

Go back to the road and continue less than a mile (1.6 km) north-east. On the right, on the shoulder of **Ben Langass**, you see a grey lump, obviously man-made, shaped like a squashed beehive. Take a torch, and walk up over the peat-bog for five minutes, to Barpa Langass (always accessible). This is a truly magnificent burial cairn, thought to date from about 1000 BC, the tomb of a chieftain. You have to crawl along a short entrance tunnel over rough stones into the chamber. Inside, when your eyes get used to the dimness, you can see great stone slabs lining the interior, and traces of where other cells may have led off the main chamber. Amazingly well preserved, this cairn takes you back 3,000 years into a past that you can only guess at, and, like Pobull Fhinn, you come away strangely moved.

From here it is about six miles (9.6 km) on to Lochmaddy, to complete the circle of the island.

Going back south-west, to the fork, go left.

Carinish

Carinish is two miles (3.2 km) down the road, with one of the most interesting, though by no means the oldest, remains in North Uist.

Teampulla-na-Trionaid (Trinity Temple) is a ruin on the top of a knoll on the Carinish promontory at the southern end of the island. Dating from the early 13th century, it is thought to have been founded by Bethog, the first Prioress of Iona. It is a large building with a detached side chapel which is reached by a vaulted passage. This church was regarded as an important seat of learning for the training of priests.

The last battle to be fought in Scotland using just swords and bows and arrows, was the Battle of Carinish, in 1601, between the Macdonalds of Uist and Macleods of Harris. The cause of the battle appears to have stemmed from an insult dealt by one of the Macdonalds, who divorced his Macleod wife and sent her home. The Macleods descended on Carinish in a wild frenzy but in the furious battle that ensued all but two of them were killed. **Feith-na-Fala** (The Field of Blood) marks the site of the battle, just north of the **Carinish Inn**.

Ben Lee

You should find time to climb Ben Lee, 896 ft (269 m) high, south-east of Lochmaddy. It provides a marvellous view of the island, with its mass of lochs and great expanses of moorland and hill.

Like all the Outer Isles, North Uist is a place to be enjoyed on foot, or from a boat, with plenty of time and keen eyes. On a clear day you can see St Kilda from the hills, 45 miles (72 km) to the west.

ST KILDA

St Kilda consists of four islands and five great rock stacks and is the most westerly of the British Isles apart from Rockall. You can only visit these lonely islands by special arrangement with the National Trust for Scotland, who own them. The history of St Kilda is one of decline due to isolation, in a world obsessed by centralisation and conformity. A small, patriarchal, strongly Presbyterian, society subsisted here, paying its rent with meat, feathers and oil from the sea birds caught and often cut off by storms. In 1930, the younger members of the community, brainwashed by the lure of the outside world, persuaded the older ones that they should move to the mainland. Some of the houses, at **Village Bay** on **Hirta**, have been preserved, and you can see the cleits, beehive-shaped cells of rough stone that were the islanders' larders and storerooms. The careful design of these cleits allowed the air and wind to circulate inside and preserve the meat of the sea birds. It also kept clothes and gear dry.

TOURIST INFORMATION-

4 South Beach Street, Stornoway, Isle of Lewis, tel 0851-3088. It is open all year. Lochmaddy, tel 08763-321. May–September.

WHERE TO STAY

Langlass Lodge Hotel, Locheport, North Uist, tel 08764-285. B&B from £12.50: categories 3,3,5: 4 bedrooms. Remote and friendly converted shooting lodge overlooking Loch Langlass. Good traditional Scottish cooking.

Lochmaddy Hotel, Lochmaddy, North Uist, tel 08763-331. B&B from £12: categories 3,3,4: 15 bedrooms, 2 en suite. Close to the ferry terminus, comfortable hotel with old fashioned hospitality.

EATING OUT

Both hotels above will give you an excellent dinner, from about £10.

BENBECULA

Benbecula, over three miles (4.8 km) of causeway, is south of North Uist. The low tide route across North Ford by foot, once the only way, is extremely dangerous for those who don't know the path. Locals will tell you hair-raising stories of lost travellers and quicksands. From the causeway you look out across rocky inlets washed by the ever-changing tides.

The name Benbecula is derived from Beinn a'bh-faodhla, "the mountain of the fords". The only mountain on the island is **Rueval** in the east, a small, round hillock only 409 ft (123 m) high, but with good views from the top. The island is flat and waterlogged, with a fertile strip on the west side. The main road cuts through the middle of the island with minor roads off to the east and a circular road round the west coast.

WHAT TO SEE

Benbecula is the home of the British army who run the rocket range to the south. In the north-west corner there is a large army base with all the accompanying rash of utility buildings, not always designed to please the eye. The airport is just beside the army camp, at **Balivanich**.

Near the airfield you can see the remains of **St Columba's Chapel**, dating from early Christian times. Nearby is a well, now marked by a cairn, where people came to drink the holy water.

Benbecula was part of the patrimony of the Macdonalds of Clanranald, from the 13th to 19th centuries, when the lands were sold off. Most of the ruins are of Clanranald origins.

Nunton

Nunton, two miles (3.2 km) south of Balivanich, has a ruined chapel that belonged to a nunnery. The nunnery was destroyed during the Reformation and the nuns were brutally massacred. The stones of the farm that you can still see by the road came from the nunnery.

Borve Castle

Borve Castle is a gaunt ruin of a keep near the road, four miles (6.4 km) south of Balivanich, and scene of many a bloody skirmish. A Clanranald stronghold, it was finally burnt down by clansmen who opposed their chief and supported Hanoverian George II. You can still see the scant remains of the castle chapel nearby.

Wiay, an island off the south-east tip of Benbecula, is a bird sanctuary supporting snipe, duck, geese and swans.

It was from **Rossinish**, on the north-east corner, that Prince Charlie sailed "over the sea to Skye" disguised as Betty Bourke, the servant of Flora Macdonald.

TOURIST INFORMATION
4 South Beach Street, Stornoway, Isle of Lewis, tel 0851-3088. It is open all year.

WHERE TO STAY
Creagorry Hotel, Creagorry, Benbecula, tel 0870-2024. B&B from £12.50: categories 3,4,4: 14 bedrooms.

Dark Island Hotel, Liniclate, Benbecula, tel 0870-2414/2283. B&B from £15: categories 6,5,5: 29 bedrooms, 26 en suite. Modern hotel with good food.

EATING OUT
Both hotels above will give you a good meal, from about £8.

SOUTH UIST

A straight causeway links Benbecula with South Uist, less than half a mile (0.8 km) across **South Ford**, a white strand that yields an abundant harvest of cockles at low tide. When the tide is out you can usually see at least one stooped figure, scooping up the white-shelled molluscs into a bucket. A roadside shrine to the Virgin Mary, just south of the causeway, reminds you that you have left the Presbyterian north and are on the threshold of the Catholic south.

South Uist is about 20 miles (32 km) long and about 7 miles (11 km) wide at the widest point, with mountains and long sea lochs to the east; sand and machair to the west; peat bog and moorland in between. **Ben Mhor**, less than half way down in the east, is the highest peak, 2,033 ft (610 m), and well worth the effort of climbing, with a terrifying sharp serrated-edge summit, and views to take your breath away.

WHAT TO SEE
Eochdar Cottage Museum (open in summer: for a small fee) is clearly signposted, just down the road to the west, immediately after you come off the causeway. It is in an old black house, with lots of interesting relics from the old days of crofting.

The main road runs straight from north to south, mostly single track with passing bays, but, here and there, with a sudden stretch of new highway, wide and fast and somewhat unnerving. Lateral roads branch off like the veins of a leaf, leading out to the many crofting townships that scatter the island.

The first road to the east, a mile (1.6 km) south of the causeway, takes you two miles (3.2 km) out to **Loch Carnan**, a beautiful fiord-type sea loch with a pier for large boats.

Loch Bee

The main road crosses Loch Bee on a causeway, three miles (4.8 km) south, one of the largest swan reserves in Britain. The area of marshland to the east is a nature reserve, with an observation tower. It is the breeding ground of many wild fowl including greylag geese.

The hill on your left, just south of Loch Bee, is **Rueval**, and the "outer-space" contraption that you can see on top is the Army Range Head. You can often see rocket targets out to sea, and hear the muffled bang of firing.

Look up to your left as you come round the shoulder of Rueval: you will see the classically beautiful statue, by Hew Lorimer, of Our Lady of the Isles. Carved from white granite, it stands high on the hillside, the child held up on his mother's shoulder. The clean-cut simplicity of the statue seems to embody the deep faith that exists in these islands.

The next road east, a mile (1.6 km) south, runs four miles (6.4 km) out to **Loch Skipport**, where there is a deep water anchorage, a salmon farm and a skeleton pier: another lovely fiord-like sea loch.

Drimisdale

Less than two miles (3.2 km) further south on the main road, beyond the road west to Drimisdale, you will see a small loch with a ruined castle on an island in the middle. To reach the island you must make your way along a submerged causeway whose uneven surface, below the dark peaty water, can cause the unwary to take an involuntary swim. The castle, **Caisteal Bheagram**, is a 15th or 16th-century keep, once a Clanranald stronghold, all that is left of what must once have been an extensive building. The present Captain of Clanranald recently led a large team of experts in an attempt to map out the original layout of the castle, revealing that its foundations cover almost all the island.

A mile (1.6 km) south, the side road runs west a mile (1.6 km) to **Howmore**, with an ancient burial ground and early Christian stones.

Ormaclete Castle

Ormaclete Castle (always accessible) is three miles (4.8 km) to the south on the western machair, in a farm steading between the main road and the sea. This massive keep was built in seven years, between 1701 and 1708, as a home for the Clanranald chief. Only seven years after its completion, it was accidentally burnt down on the day of the Battle of Sherrifmuir, in which the chief was killed.

On the main road east of Ormaclete, a road runs east to **Loch Eynort**, another lovely sea loch, cutting deep into the east coast.

Glen Corodale

From here you can walk north to Glen Corodale, about four miles (6.4 km) north-east of the end of the road, and you will need a map. This wild country east of the high mountains of **Ben Mhor** and **Hecla**, was where Prince Charlie took refuge for a while, hiding in a cave in a shieling. The cave is marked on the map but is very difficult to find. It is glorious walking and climbing terrain from Loch Eynort right up to Loch Skipport and you can explore places that are only otherwise accessible by boat.

Milton

Three miles (4.8 km) south of the turning to Loch Eynort, a road runs west, signposted to Milton, where you can see a cairn marking the birth place of Flora Macdonald who was born in 1722. Flora's father was a tacksman. She had come to attend her brother's cattle in the shieling about three miles (4.8 km) from here, when the prince was brought to her, needing help, and her part in the well-known story of his escape began.

Askernish

Askernish, a mile (1.6 km) south, has a 9 hole golf course on the machair, where players must dodge sheep and plovers' nests among the dunes. Here, in July, you can attend the South Uist Games, usually followed by a dance or a concert in the church hall. Everyone on the island turns out for the games, where you can see piping, dancing and all the traditional sports.

Daliburgh

Daliburgh is a village on the crossroads west of Lochboisdale. Here there is the hospital run by nuns, attached to the convent; the old people's home with a charming garden sheltered from the wind by a glass partition; a hotel; shops and a post office. The road to the west leads to the parish church of **St Peters**, a large, simple building, weathered and unadorned. This is the living heart of the island, filled to capacity at every Sunday mass, and well attended throughout the week, as indeed are the other churches that support it to the north and south.

North-west of St Peters is what must be one of the most beautiful, lonely burial grounds in the country, on the edge of the machair, overlooking the wild Atlantic; a place where any restless spirit must feel at peace.

Loch Boisdale

The road east from Daliburgh goes three miles (4.8 km) east to Loch Boisdale. Half way along on the right, look in at the Knitwear Factory, where a team of women work out intricate patterns and create a huge range of Hebridean knitwear. You can watch them at work and buy the products from the shop at very reasonable prices.

Lochboisdale is the port, with a hotel, bank, shop, police station and harbour. It is at its busiest early in the morning and late at night, for those are the times when the Caledonian Macbrayne steamer comes and goes, turning the quay into a bustling crowd of people, with a wonderful atmosphere and a babble of Gaelic voices. A few visiting yachts anchor in the small bay in the summer and the hotel, overlooking the harbour with its excellent reputation for fishing and for food, attracts many visitors.

Towering over the northern side of Loch Boisdale is **Beinn Choinnich**. This provides a challenging race every year for the young men of the area, who may take whatever route they chose to the top.

Kilpheder

Going on a mile (1.6 km) south from Daliburgh you can take a small road about two miles (3.2 km) west to Kilpheder. Then take a track out onto the machair, over a ditch, to an Iron Age Pictish wheel house. These communal dwellings had a central hearth with cells radiating from it like the spokes of a wheel, elaborate drainage systems and storage places sunk into the floor.

South Lochboisdale

To find one of the most enchanted secret places in Scotland, you need a map and a ten mile (16 km) walk (round trip). Two miles (3.2 km) south of Daliburgh, go east for two miles (3.2 km), through South Lochboisdale to the parking bay at the end. From here you must use your map and follow the not always obvious track over the hills and moor, along **Lochs Kerrsinish, Marulaig** and **Moreef**, five miles (8 km) south west to the coast. **The Bun Struth** is a loch joined to the sea by a narrow passage of sheer rock, surrounded by hills. It is a forgotten corner, inaccessible except by boat or on foot, peopled only by sheep and birds and the ghosts of the people who once lived in the now ruined croft houses that lie scattered over the valley. When the tide is out the loch is higher that the sea, draining over a shelf of rock in the entrance passage and marooning boats until the next tide, which comes in through the passage with all the force of the ocean behind it.

As you walk back, look up into the hills north of Loch Marulaig: you will probably see golden eagles, gliding in the wind.

All this south-eastern foot of the island is good walking country, and the views from the summits of the hills are spectacular. On a clear day you can see Ardnamurchan Point, on the mainland. The road out to the west, opposite that to South Lochboisdale, takes you to a white beach where you can see the remains of a once flourishing seaweed factory. A few years ago any islander could cut seaweed—a very laborious job—and sell it to this factory where it was processed into alginates, for use in a large number of products ranging from soap to cosmetics.

The white beach runs for miles in a great sweep of sand where you can find tiny pink cowrie shells. Its surface is so hard that cars can drive on it and the machair borders it, with its glorious carpet of wild flowers in the summer.

Garrynamonie

The road south climbs to the wedge-shaped church at Garrynamonie which was built in 1963. It has an enamelled mosaic behind the side altar and some beautiful Stations of the Cross, designed by a priest from Barra, Father Calum McNeil. Here, as in the other churches, you can hear mass in Gaelic, with a haunting, almost Moorish, chant from the choir.

At the end of the road, five miles (8 km) south of Daliburgh is the **Pollachar Inn**, overlooking the most beautiful view in Scotland, across the **Sound of Barra** to **Barra** and east to **Eriskay**. You can pick up a lot of local atmosphere and stories of the past, in the Pollachar.

Ludaig

The road runs east for a couple of miles (3.2 km) along the south coast as far as Ludaig, where you can get a ferry to Eriskay and to Barra. A lovely sandy bay beyond, at **South Glendale**, dries out at low tide and makes an excellent picnic spot, sheltered all round by turf-covered rocks.

East of South Glendale, along the rocky shore and below the water, lies part of the wreck of the *Politician*, immortalised as the *Cabinet Minister*, by Compton Mackenzie in his book *Whisky Galore*. The true story was only slightly embroidered in the novel. The ship was carrying 20,000 cases of whisky to America in 1941, at a time when whisky was scarce in the islands. Magnetic minerals in the rocks distorted the *Politician*'s compass readings and she went off course, riding over **Hartamul**, the rock at the entrance to the **Sound of Eriskay**, and finishing up against the cliff. The islanders made a valiant attempt to "rescue" the whisky, thwarted by the bureaucracy of the customs and excise department, and not a few families can still show you a much-valued "Polly bottle" today. Stories are still told, with a twinkle and a knowing shake of the head, of animals reeling down the road, and of bottles dug up on the machair that have been buried for years, forgotten in the mist of those halcyon days.

South Uist is littered with places where Prince Charlie is said to have sheltered during his wanderings. He certainly hid for a time on **Calvay Island**, the island you see as you enter Loch Boisdale in the steamer from Oban. The prince hid there in the ruined castle that still stands jagged against the sky.

ERISKAY

For some, the tiny island of Eriskay is the jewel of them all. You can take your car on the ferry from Ludaig in South Uist, but it is not necessary as the road is barely two miles (3.2 km) in length. The boat takes you a mile (1.6 km) across the sound, to **Haun**, a smiling village of freshly painted white cottages with roofs of bright blue, pink, green and red, sheltered by hills with its church perched up on a shoulder above the harbour.

This church, with its altar shaped like the prow of a ship, is the pulsing heart of the island, built by Father Allan MacDonald in 1903, the man who wrote down much of the songs and folklore of the Hebrides. The ship's bell that stands outside, beyond the church, was rescued from the *Derflinger*, one of the German ships that sank in Scapa Flow.

Just beyond the village on the western shore there is a delightful crescent of sand called **Prince Charlie's Bay**. This was where the prince landed from France on 23 July 1745 and where he spent his first night on Scottish soil. The black house he stayed in was only pulled down in 1902. Its smokey interior drove him out into the fresh air several times during the night, drawing reproof from his host. It was a simple place, like all the others of its kind, with cupboard beds, hens running over the earth floor, and wooden trunks holding the family possessions. If you look in the machair round Prince Charlie's Bay, you should find the pretty pink convolvulous, called Prince Charlie's Rose, said to have been introduced here from a seed dropped from his shoe.

You will have to ask a local man to take you by boat to the **Stack Islands**, off the south of Eriskay. There is a rock creek on the main island where you can get ashore and climb the precipitous cliff to the **Weaver's Castle** at the top. Here lived a notorious Macneil, who was a much-feared wrecker and pirate along the coast. He built the castle as a hideout and stole a girl from a shieling in South Uist, to be his wife, and the mother of a large number of sure-footed children.

TOURIST INFORMATION

Outer Hebrides Tourist Board, 4 South Beach Street, Stornoway, Isle of Lewis, tel 0851-3088. It is open all year.

Lochboisdale, Pier Road, South Uist, tel 08784-286. Seasonal.

WHERE TO STAY

Borrodale Hotel, Daliburgh, South Uist, tel 08784-444. B&B from £12: categories 4,4,6: 13 bedrooms en suite.

Lochboisdale Hotel, Lochboisdale, South Uist, tel 08784-332. B&B from £16: categories 4,4,5: 20 bedrooms, 16 en suite. Lovely views overlooking Loch Boisdale, by the ferry terminus.

Polochar Inn, Kilbride, South Uist, tel 08784-215. B&B from £12: categories 1,1,2: 5 bedrooms. Charming old inn overlooking the Sound of Eriskay towards Barra. One of the most beautiful views in Scotland.

SELF-CATERING

Boisdale House, South Lochboisdale, tel 08784-314. A perfect holiday house by the water, sleeps twelve. From £140 per week.

EATING OUT

Both the Borrodale Hotel and the Lochboisdale Hotel, see above, will give you a good meal. Dinner from about £8.

BARRA

Ringed by a number of smaller islands, Barra, four miles (6.4 km) south of South Uist at the nearest point, has its own unique charm and atmosphere. One road circles the main part of the island, with an arm running north to the airport and **Scurrival Point**.

The name Barra stems from St Barr of Cork, the patron saint of the island, who converted its people to Christianity.

WHAT TO SEE

No one arriving in the steamer from Oban forgets their first sight of **Castlebay. Kisimul Castle** (open Wednesday and Saturday afternoons in the summer, accessible by boat from the pier: for a fee) stands on a rock in the middle of the harbour. It is one of Scotland's oldest castles, built in 1060, a splendid sight in any weather but most romantic when silhouetted against a half-dark sky on a summer night. The Macneils, famous for their lawlessness and piracy, acquired the castle as a reward for fighting for Robert Bruce at Bannockburn. It was virtually destroyed by fire at the end of the 18th century and remained in ruins until the forty-fifth chief of the Macneil clan, returning from his adopted homeland in America, restored it to its present, excellent condition.

Neat little shops and houses line the road that climbs from the harbour, overlooked by the lovely statue of the Blessed Virgin and Child, which stands on the southern shoulder of **Heavel**, 1,260 ft (378 m) high, a mile (1.6 m) to the north, Barra's highest peak. The statue was erected in 1954 during the Marian Year, carved from Carrara marble; a symbol of the deep faith that governs the lives of these islands.

Like all the islands, Barra has its ancient remains. Going clockwise, two miles (3.2 km) west from Castlebay, you see standing stones beside the road past the Isle of Barra Hotel, said to mark the grave of a Norse pirate.

A mile (1.6 km) inland from the chapel at **Gariemore**, a mile (1.6 km) further north, is **Dun Bharpa**, a large chambered cairn beyond the hamlet, surrounded by standing stones.

Wherever you look in Barra you get magnificent views; seascapes and landscapes that have inspired a vast number of artists.

On the eastern side of the peninsula that runs north four miles (6.4 km) on from Gariemore, past **Northbay** the great sweep of white sand is the landing strip for the daily Loganair air service. Two square miles (5 sq m) of dazzling cockle shell strand, the **Traigh Mhor** is washed twice a day by the tide and provides a firm touchdown for the little plane that comes droning in like a bumble bee, its timetable as flexible as the tide!

The house at the end of this great strand was the home of Compton Mackenzie, the writer who caught the spirit of the Highlands more perceptively than anyone. He is buried in the graveyard at **Eoligarry**, just to the north. Here you can see the ruins of a chapel and burial slabs that are said to have arrived from Iona, being used as ballast in an ancient galley.

Another famous name can be seen in the cemetery: that of John Macpherson, better known to lovers of Gaeldom as "The Coddy" who died here in his native island in 1955. "Tales from Barra," recorded in both Gaelic and English, are a large collection of folk tales told by the Coddy in his inimitable voice, delighting exiled Scots all over the world and well worth getting hold of if you haven't heard them.

A grassy mound is all that remains of **Eoligarry House**, a three storied house built by the Macneils after Kisimul Castle burned down in 1795. It was a substantial ruin until very recently.

The islands that lie off Barra are each a delight to visit if you have your own boat, or if you can persuade a local man to take you. Golden eagles and a number of black rabbits will greet you in **Hellisay**. The sea birds are magnificent; the wild flowers a constant delight; the sea so clear that 20 ft (6 m) of water seems no more than a few inches.

TOURIST INFORMATION

Outer Hebrides Tourist Board, 4 South Beach Street, Stornoway, Isle of Lewis, tel 0851-3088. It is open all year.

Main Street Castlebay, Barra, tel 08714-336. May to September.

WHERE TO STAY

Castlebay Hotel, Castlebay, tel 08714-223. B&B from £10: categories 4,4,4: 13 bedrooms, 3 en suite.

Clachan Beag Hotel, Castlebay, tel 08714-279. B&B from £12: categories 3,3,5: 5 bedrooms.

Craigard Hotel, Castlebay, tel 08714-200. B&B from £22: categories 4,4,4: 7 bedrooms.

Isle of Barra Hotel, Tangusdale, tel 08714-383. B&B from £18.50: categories 5,4,4: 30 bedrooms en suite. Extremely comfortable, modern purpose built hotel overlooking glorious crescent of white beach. There are also self-contained apartments.

EATING OUT

You will get a reasonable meal in all the hotels above. Go for the local seafood wherever possible.

CRAFT CENTRES IN THE OUTER HEBRIDES

The following workshops and studios welcome visitors. Where a telephone number is given, you should ring first to check times.

Ceramics

Breanish Pottery, Breanish, Uig, Isle of Lewis, tel 185175-349. Hand throwing of earthenware pottery.

Fear an eich, Coll Pottery, 22a Coll, Back, Isle of Lewis, tel 085182-219. All aspects of pottery making.

Borve pottery, Borve, Isle of Lewis, tel 085185-345. All aspects of pottery making.

Dolls and Toys

Glendale Crafts, Glendale, High Borve, Isle of Lewis, tel 085185-409. Making of chess sets, wooden toys, soft toys, hand puppets and knitwear.

Raebhat Originals Ltd, Raebhat House, Shawbost, Isle of Lewis, tel 085171-205. Teddy bear and rag doll making.

Farming and Processing

Margaret Ponting, Olcote, New Park, Callanish, Isle of Lewis, tel 085172-277. All stages of wool preparation from sheep to finished garment, shearing, carding wool from fleece, spinning, knitting. Archaeological display and sale of books on Lewis.

Jewellery and Silversmithing
Hebridean Jewellery, Iochdar, South Uist. Hand made jewellery.

Knitwear and Crotchet
Co Chomunn Eirisgeidh Ltd, Community Hall, Eriskay, tel 08786-236. Hand knitted sweaters.

Creag-an-Sgairbh Crafts, Cnoc Sitheal, 11 Malaglate, Sollas, Lochmaddy, North Uist, tel 08766-214. Hand knitting using Harris, Shetland, and Icelandic wools.

Heather Graham Crafts, Borve Cottage, Isle of Harris, tel 085985-202. Knitwear and sporran making.

Hebridean Croft Originals, 4a West Kilbride, Lochboisdale, South Uist, tel 08784-483. Hand framed and hand made knitwear.

Hebridean Knitters, Unit 2, 7 James Street, Stornoway, Isle of Lewis, tel 0851-3773. Knitwear finishings.

Macramé, etc
Lochside Crafts, Leverburgh, Harris, tel 085982-343. Photography, pyrography, macramé work.

Weaving
Breanish Tweed, Breanish, Uig, Isle of Lewis, tel 085175-349. Hand weaving of pure new woollen tweed.

Clansman Tweed Company, 28–30 Bells Road, Stornoway, Lewis, tel 0851-3065. Harris tweed carding, spinning, finishing and baling. Yarn and cloth.

Croft Crafts (Harris), 4 Plocropool, Drinishader, Harris, tel 085981-217. Harris tweed weaving, warping, etc.

Lindsay Gray Textiles for Interiors, 4 Leurbost, Lochs, Isle of Lewis, tel 085186-379. Hand weaving of rugs, hangings, cushions, throws, shawls, also some handspinning.

John MacGregor, 27 Garenin, Carloway, Isle of Lewis, tel 085173-257. Hand weaving and warping of Harris tweed.

Flora Ann Macleod, Harmony Villa, Scadabay, Harris, tel 085981-221. Hand weaving of Harris tweed.

Annie Morrison, Post Office, Drinnishadder, Isle of Harris, tel 085981-200. Hand spinning, hand weaving, warping Harris tweed, twisting Harris wool.

Woodwork
Gisla Woodcraft, Uig, Isle of Lewis, tel 085175-371. Wood turning.

The Northern Isles

These were called the "Nordereys" by the Norsemen. Although separated by 60 miles (96 km) or so of ocean, the Orkney Islands and the Shetland Islands have a common history and tend to be bracketed together.

Both groups, about 70 Orkney Islands and 100 Shetland Islands, were inhabited in the Stone Age. The Picts colonised them in the 1st century AD and were subjected to continual harassment from the Vikings for centuries until the Norse King, Harold Harfagri annexed them in 875. The story behind this conquest is rather interesting. When King Harold succeeded to the throne of Norway in about 860, large parts of his kingdom didn't recognise the authority of the crown—like the Lords of the Scottish Isles. Harold was in love with a Princess Gyda, daughter of one of the rebel "kings" and she refused to marry him until he had conquered all Norway. He vowed that he would not cut his hair, or his beard, until he'd done this, and it must have been a very hairy bridegroom who claimed his bride, ten years later. All the dispossessed "jarls" or minor kings, took refuge in the Orkney and Shetland Islands and from here proceeded to raid Norway in wild Viking raids. King Harold, exasperated, collected up a fleet and sailed down to put an end to their tactics. He landed at what is now Haraldswick, in Unst, in the Shetlands and declared all the islands to be a "Jarldom".

The centuries of Norse occupation of these islands are recorded in the romantic and stirring sagas that have been handed down over the years, "The Orkneyinga Saga" being one of the best known.

By the 13th century, although still under Norse rule, the islands were presided over by Scots' earls. When Princess Margaret of Norway and Denmark became betrothed to James III of Scotland, her father, King Christian I, pledged the islands to Scotland, as part of her dowry in 1468. Scotland formally annexed them in 1472 and from then on they have been part of Scotland.

Norse place names are still predominant and the people of these northern islands are a blend of Norse and Scots, very different in character to the dreamy Celts of the Hebrides. They are extrovert and stolid, industrious and mainly Presbyterian. Their accent is sing-song: the old "Norn" language disappeared during the 18th century, although you may still hear curious phrases that have remained.

The coming of the oil boom obviously struck hard at the old roots bringing many innovations that are not always popular, but on the whole the islanders have managed to retain their old way of life.

ORKNEY

GETTING THERE

By sea

P&O operate a daily roll-on, roll-off car ferry service (except on Sundays) from Scrabster near Thurso to Stromness on Mainland Orkney. There is also a passenger ferry, daily in the summer, from John o' Groats to Burwick.

By air

British Airways operate a daily service from Glasgow, Inverness and Aberdeen to Kirkwall.

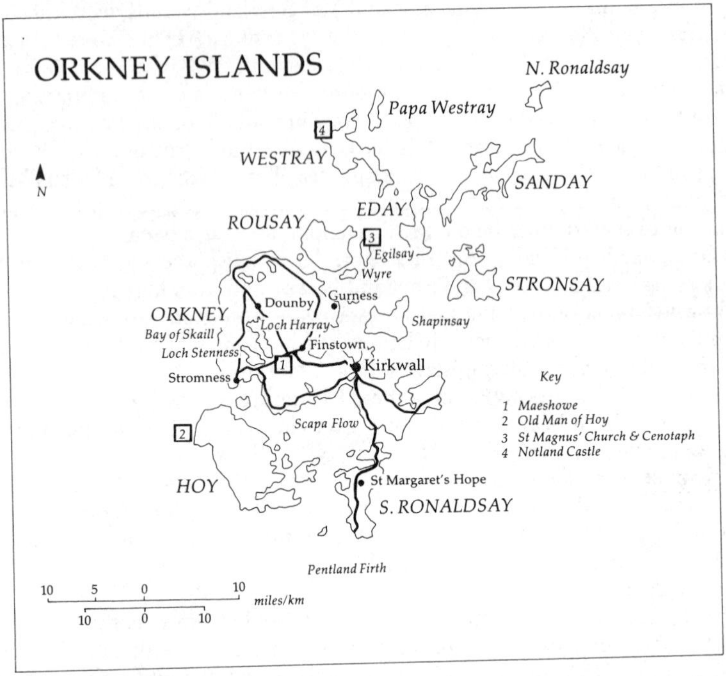

Loganair operate a daily service from Glasgow, Edinburgh, Inverness and Wick.

Once you are there, there is a very good inter-island air service, as well as ferries. It is easy to hire cars and there are causeways to some of the islands.

WHAT TO SEE

Of the 67 islands of Orkney 21 are inhabited, and when an Orkadian talks of the Mainland, he means Mainland Orkney—the big island. Although there is plenty of accommodation, you should book well in advance.

An unforgettable bonus to a holiday in the northern isles is the Midsummer Twilight, "Grimlins", from the Norse word "Grimla", to glimmer or twinkle. It is possible to read a book outside at midnight during this midsummer period. The long winter nights are easier to put up with when you look ahead to summer evenings. Apart from the extremely hospitable friendliness of Orkadians, your first impressions are of emerald-green plateaux of turf above sheer rock cliffs, under a great dome of clean, pure skies that seem to cast a wonderful greenish light. Ornithologists will find every possible species of sea bird; botanists will find a wealth of rare wild flowers; fishermen will leave Orkney with enough fishing stories to keep them talking till they return—the brown trout are the best in Britain and fishing is free, thanks to ancient Udal tradition and Norse law. Sub-aqua divers will find excellent facilities and wonderful clear water, especially for wreck-diving in **Scapa Flow**.

For archaeologists, there are more pre-historic remains than anywhere else in Scotland, some in a remarkable state of preservation: brochs, standing stones, burial cairns—an average of three sites per square mile (2.5 sq m).

It is beyond the scope of this book to describe each of the many hundreds of historic sites and antiquities that pepper the Orkneys. The Scottish Tourist Board's Information Office, in Broad Street, Kirkwall, has brought out a first class free booklet on what to see and you are strongly advised to get hold of it. Careful planning is needed if you are to make the best use of the transport available for visiting as much as possible within the time you have to spare. The tourist office will advise you of the best tours to take, by sea and air, and will give you up-to-date opening times.

Among the events that take place in Orkney throughout the year, the St Magnus Festival in Kirkwall in June is a week of music, drama and art that is rapidly growing in popularity. For two weeks in July there is a Craftsmen's Guild in Kirkwall, where you can see demonstrations of local craftwork. Stromness has a Folk Festival in May and a Shopping Week in July.

TOURIST INFORMATION
Orkney Tourist Board Information Centre, Broad Street, Kirkwall, tel 0856-2856. It is open all year.

MAINLAND: ORKNEY

Kirkwall

Kirkwall is the capital of Orkney and one of the earliest established Norse trading towns, referred to in *The Orkneyinga Saga* as Kirkjuvagr, Church-bay-of-the-Vikings, indicating that the Norsemen found an early Christian church here when they arrived.

Sir Walter Scott wrote of the town:

'Tis a base little borough,
Both dirty and mean;
There's nothing to hear
And there's nought to be seen.

But he must have come on a bad day. It is a cheerful, bustling, sturdy town; an ideal centre from which to explore these fascinating islands.

The St Magnus Festival, in June, attracts companies from many countries and the standard is high. July is the month for the Craftsmen's Guild and August for the St Magnus Fair. Kirkwall has its own, unique "Ba Game", loosely described as football. It is played on Christmas and New Year's Day, between the "uppies" and "doonies" and often involves as many as 150 men from either end of the town. If the ball finishes up in the harbour it is victory for the "uppies": if it reaches the goal at the old castle, then the "doonies" win. The game can last all day and dates from Norse times.

WHAT TO SEE
St Magnus Cathedral (open daily except on Sundays when it is only open for services: admission free) dominates the town. It is a massive red sandstone cruciform building, founded in 1137. St Magnus, who was murdered in 1116, and whose canonisation may

have been more political than spiritual, was the uncle of Jarl Rognvald Kilson, the founder of the cathedral. The bones of both these men now lie below the columns of the central bay of the choir. They were discovered, hidden in chests, during repair work in this century, one with a pierced skull. The cathedral has been carefully restored: the rose window is modern but the east window dates from 1511. Although still called a cathedral the services are Church of Scotland.

The old part of the town clusters round the cathedral, with the ruin of the 12th-century **Bishops Palace** (open at standard Ancient Monument times, closed Friday afternoons and Saturdays in winter: adults 50p, children 25p) next door to it. It was here that poor old King Haakon of Norway died, having struggled back this far from his defeat by Alexander III at Largs in 1263.

Across the road from the Bishop's Palace you can see the still beautiful ruin of the **Earl's Palace** (open at standard Ancient Monument times, closed Friday afternoons and Saturdays in winter: adults 50p, children 25p) built by forced labour for a much loathed tyrant, Earl Patrick Stewart at the beginning of the 17th century. The palace is L-shaped, with attractive angle-turrets, once described as "... the most mature and accomplished piece of Renaissance architecture in Scotland". Earl Patrick was steward of Orkney and Shetland and entirely corrupt. He was finally executed for his awful crimes against humanity, having been granted a week's reprieve so that he could learn the Lord's Prayer!

The Tankerness House Museum (open daily except on Sundays: admission free) is in a well-restored 16th-century merchant's town house, with an attractive court yard and garden. Here you can see the history of Orkney, going back over 4,000 years.

The Library (open daily except Sundays: admission free) founded in 1683, is the oldest public library in Scotland and it has an excellent Orkney Room, if you want to go more deeply into the history of the island.

Among the other things you can visit in the town are the **Silver Works** and the two malt whisky distilleries, **The Highlands Park Distillery** and **Scapa Distillery**, all of which welcome visitors, free, on weekdays.

Stromness

Stromness, about 17 miles (27 km) west of Kirkwall, is the only other proper town in Orkney. This pretty place with a sheltered harbour has houses dating from 1716. It was once a principal port on the sailing route round the north of Scotland and base for the Hudson Bay Company ships. Many local men went to do contract work in Canada. The houses, many of them with their own jetties, seem to jostle each other aside, to get the best position along the mile of waterfront. Stromness is the terminus for the car ferry from Scrabster. Stromness has a Traditional Folk Festival, in May and a "Shopping Week" in July when all the shops compete for your business and so offer many a good bargain!

WHAT TO SEE

Pier Arts Centre (open daily except Sundays: admission free) is in well-restored 18th-century buildings, with exhibitions of modern paintings.

Stromness Natural History Museum (open daily except Thursday afternoons and

Sundays: small fee) has collections of birds, fossils, shells and butterflies. There are also exhibitions covering whaling, fishing, the Hudson Bay Company, Scapa Flow and the German fleet.

Scapa Flow

Scapa Flow is a great inlet to the south of Mainland, surrounded by protective islands; a perfect deep-water anchorage up to ten miles (16 km) wide, adapted as the main base of the Grand Fleet, in 1912. At the end of the First World War, the German navy sailed their fleet into Scapa, having surrendered. Then, on the order of Rear-Admiral Ludwig von Reuter, the whole fleet of 74 warships was scuttled, on 21 June 1919. At the beginning of the Second World War a German U-boat crept through the defences and sank the *Royal Oak*, after which the Churchill Barriers were erected, making the anchorage almost impregnable.

Scapa is very popular with sub-aqua divers and its clear water offer a great scope for wreck diving. There are good supplies of air obtainable locally.

The following is a small selection of some of the very many historic, and pre-historic antiquities that there are to be seen in the Orkneys. Do consult the tourist office in Broad Street, Kirkwall for more detailed information and advice as how best to fit in as much as possible.

Maes Howe

Maes Howe (open at standard Ancient Monument times: adults £1, children 50p) is ten miles (16 km) west of Kirkwall, just off the main road to Stromness. It is a huge Stone Age burial cairn, unquestionably the most outstanding in Britain. The passage into the cairn, made of huge single slabs of stone, is so aligned that a shaft of sunlight pierces its 36 ft (11 m) length into the chamber on only one day a year, that of the winter solstice. Burial cells lead off the main chamber which has massive stone buttresses in each corner.

When Maes Howe was first excavated, in 1861, the cells were found to be empty and this fact, together with runic Viking inscriptions on the walls, misled archaeologists into thinking the tomb was Norse. It then became obvious that the structure dates back many centuries before that time and probably to around 2700 BC. The Vikings then came, much later, sacking the tombs and leaving their graffiti on the walls.

In fact the graffiti is just as fascinating as the much older cairn. There are references to treasure, and to the Crusades and a collection of sex slogans that are as modern as any you might see today: "Thorny was bedded, Helgi says so" reads one; "Ingigerd is the best of them all" says another! There is an excellent guide book that you can buy at the site.

Beside the car park is **Tormiston Mill**, a restored 19th-century water mill with a restaurant and a craft centre.

The Ring of Brodgar

The Ring of Brodgar (always accessible) is on the narrow neck of land between Harray

Stromness

and Stenness Lochs, four miles (6.4 km) north-west of Maes Howe. From the original 60 stones, 36 remain. They are precisely set, being 6° apart, with a surrounding ditch cut from bedrock, as much as 9 ft (2.7 m) deep and 27 ft (8 m) wide, crossed by two causeways. These stones date from about 1560 BC and are believed to be some sort of lunar observatory, a splendid reminder that those Stone Age men may have been primitive but they certainly weren't stupid.

The Stones of Stenness

The Stones of Stenness (always accessible) nearby, date from around the third millennium BC and only four stones remain of the original circle. Excavations uncovered an almost square setting of horizontal stones, scattered with fragments of cremated bones, charcoal and shards of pottery, indicating that this must have been some sort of cremation and burial site. The two outlying stones, **The Barnhouse** and **The Watch Stone**, were probably associated with this circle, as must have been the many cists and cairns that have been unearthed in this area.

Skara Brae

Skara Brae (open at standard Ancient Monument times: adults £1, children 50p) is five miles (8 km) north-west of the Stones of Stenness, on the west coast and on the southern arm of the sandy sweep of **Bay of Skaill**. This was a Stone Age settlement that became engulfed in a massive storm that buried it in sand for about 4,000 years. Another storm then blew away some of the sand to reveal the village to archaeologists. It is unique, giving an insight into the whole way of life of those pre-historic tribes, rather than just revealing a burial cairn which only tells a fraction of their story. Careful excavation has un-sanded about six of the original ten one-roomed houses, and a workshop, with covered passages from one to another and a communal paved court yard.

Lack of wood meant that they used stone for their furniture and you can see the old bed platforms, cupboards, hearths, fish tanks and tables, as well as a fascinating collection of tools and implements. Recent progress in carbon-dating means that more and more information is coming to light about those mysterious settlers and you can get an excellent guide book with up-to-date findings. There is a small museum and you can visit the site daily. Midden (dunghill) excavations have revealed that the inhabitants of this earliest fishing village in Scotland were also farmers.

Click Mill

Beyond **Dounby**, about eight miles (12.8 km) north-east of Skara Brae, is the only surviving Click Mill (always accessible). It is a horizontal water wheel, built in about 1800 from an earlier design, and so called from the noise it makes as it turns. It is preserved in working order, although the pond has been drained.

Gurness

Gurness, five miles (8 km) north-west of the Click Mill, on the coast opposite Rousay Island, has a magnificent **Broch** (open at standard Ancient Monument times: small fee). It is the best broch in Orkney, on a wild, windswept headland, and you should get the booklet from the custodian, to try to sort out the very complicated layout of the site. Built as a broch it was added to over the centuries by the Norsemen, and includes many domestic buildings, Norse longhouses, partitioned chambers and a well.

The islands off Mainland: to the south

Lamb Holm

Lamb Holm, linked by a mile (1.6 km) of causeway, south of Mainland, has a heart-stirring little chapel, created out of Nissen huts by Italian prisoners-of-war during the Second World War. They were building the Churchill Barrier, after the sinking of the *Royal Oak* and they made the chapel in their spare time, using scrap metal. It is a miracle of faith, with delicate wrought-iron tracery, and frescoes, whose artist, Dominico Chiocchetti returned, in 1960, to restore the original work. You don't have to be either Catholic or even Christian to feel extremely humble and moved by this exquisite work of love that transcends the hatred and bitterness of war.

South Ronaldsay

South Ronaldsay, joined to Lamb Holm by four miles (6.4 km) of causeway, across Burray, has a picturesque village with a poignant memory—**St Margaret's Hope**. In 1290, the seven year old Princess Margaret, Maid of Norway, died of sea sickness in the ship that was bringing her from Norway, to marry Prince Edward of England. (The marriage had been planned as a way of uniting Britain.) The ship, bearing the wasted body of the little princess, put in to St Margaret's Hope.

Hoy

Hoy, the largest island apart from Mainland, about three miles (4.8 km) south of Stromness, is the only one that is not flat. Here **Ward Hill** rises to 1,500 ft (450 m).

The Old Man of Hoy is an incredible rock stack that rises 450 ft (135 m) from a promontory above the sea. This is a favourite challenge to serious rock climbers, a towering pinnacle of horizontally layered rock.

St John's Head, on north-west Hoy, is part of a 1,140 (342 m) high vertical cliff, teeming with sea birds and many rare plants.

The islands off Mainland: to the north

Birdsay and Brough of Birdsay

Birdsay and Brough of Birdsay are less than a mile (1.6 km) off north-west Mainland and you can walk out at low tide. Here you can see the remains of early Christian and Norse settlements.

Rousay

Midhowe is a burial cairn, on Rousay, a couple of miles (3.2 km) north-east of Mainland. This cairn has a long chamber, 76 ft (23 m) by 7 ft (2 m), has 24 burial cells leading off it, in which the remains of 25 human bodies were found.

Of the other tombs on Rousay, **Taversoe Tuick** is unusual in being two-storied, one over the other, each with its own entrance passage. Rousay has also a very well-preserved broch, with a complex of cells, cubicles, passages, stairs and doorways, and outbuildings.

Wyre

On Wyre, a mile (1.6 km) south-east of Rousay, you can see the ruin of a 12th-century stone castle, one of the oldest in Scotland, known as **Cubbie Roo's Castle** and probably the stronghold of a Norse robber baron. There is also a ruined 12th-century chapel, **St Mary's**.

Egilsay

On Egilsay, two miles (3.2 km) east of Rousay, you can see **St Magnus' Cenotaph**, marking the site of the murder of Jarl Magnus in 1116, after whom the cathedral in Kirkwall is named. The ruin of St Magnus' Church dominates this small, low-lying island, with a tall, tapering round tower at the west end. This design is of Irish origin, indicating close contact between Ireland and Orkney during Viking times. It was probably built in the 12th century, and its walls still stand to their full height. The tower, nearly 50 ft (15 m) high was once taller still and it seems to beckon you from all round. Magnus was killed on the order of his rival, Earl Haakon, who wanted sole power over Orkney.

Eday

On Eday, four miles (6.4 km) to the east of Egilsay, there are chambered tombs and an Iron Age dwelling that was once a roundhouse with radial divisions inside, dating from several centuries BC.

Westray

Westray, seven miles (11 km) north of Rousay, has the formidable ruin of **Noltland Castle**, built in 1560 by Gilbert Balfour, Master of the Household to Mary, Queen of Scots. Its design is Z-plan, with all round visibility and an almost extravagant provision of gun loops. It was burned by Covenanters in 1650.

Papa Westray

Papa Westray, two miles (3.2 km) off the north-east tip of Westray, is so called from the hermits who lived in the cells that you can see. This island was part of an important Norse family estate in the 11th and 12th centuries and archaeologists discovered the remains of Neolithic settlements which have provided valuable clues to the lifestyle of those ancient inhabitants.

North Ronaldsay

The most northern of the Orkneys is North Ronaldsay, 15 miles (24 km) east of Papa Westray and 32 miles (51 km) north-east of Kirkwall. It is surrounded by a sea dyke that is designed to keep the unique breed of sheep off the grass, so that they feed from the rich seaweed on the shore. The meat of these small, sturdy animals has a distinctive flavour.

TOURIST INFORMATION

Orkney Tourist Board, Broad Street, Kirkwall, Orkney, tel 0856-2856. It is open all year.

Ferry Terminus, Stromness, tel 0856-850716. Open daily May to September and 2 hours daily October to April.

WHERE TO STAY

There is a large choice of accommodation in Orkney and you should consult the tourist office brochure which gives descriptions and details. The following is just a small selection.

Barony Hotel, Birsay, tel 0856-72 327. B&B from £10: categories 3,3,4: 8 bedrooms.

St Lawrence Motel, Burray, tel 0856-73 298. B&B from £10.20: categories 3,2,3: 12 bedrooms.

Smithfield Hotel, Dounby, tel 0856-77 215. B&B from £10: categories 3,3,4: 6 bedrooms, 1 en suite.

Woodwick House, Evie, tel 0856-75 330. B&B from £10: categories 3,3,4: 4 bedrooms.

Merkister Hotel, Loch Harray, tel 0856-77 366. B&B from £15: categories 3,4,5: 19 bedrooms.

Burnmouth Hotel, Hoy, tel 0856-79 297. B&B from £7: categories 3,3,3: 3 bedrooms, 1 en suite.

Ayre Hotel, Kirkwall, tel 0856-2197. B&B from £10: categories 3,4,5: 31 bedrooms, 3 en suite.

Kirkwall Hotel, Kirkwall, tel 0856-2232. B&B from £17: categories 4,5,4: 41 bedrooms, 12 en suite, 2 suites.

Queens Hotel, Kirkwall, tel 0856-2200. B&B from £13.80: categories 1,1,3: 7 bedrooms, 5 en suite.

Royal Hotel, Kirkwall, tel 0856-3477. B&B from £14.95: categories 3,4,5: 33 bedrooms, 17 en suite.

Trumland House, Rousay, tel 0856-82 263. B&B from £14: categories 4,4,3: 5 bedrooms, 3 en suite.

Ferry Inn, Stromness, tel 0856-850280. B&B from £14: categories 4,4,5: 15 bedrooms, 6 en suite.

Royal Hotel, Stromness, tel 0856-850342. B&B from £10.85: categories 3,4,4: 4 bedrooms.

Stromness Hotel, Stromness, tel 0856-850298. B&B from £8.50: categories 4,4,5: 40 bedrooms, 34 en suite.

EATING OUT

Most of the hotels above will give you a very reasonable meal. You should go for the fresh local seafood where it is offered, or the local lamb.

CRAFT CENTRES IN ORKNEY

The following studios and workshops welcome visitors. Where a telephone number is given, you should ring up first to check times.

Ceramics

Fursbreck Pottery, Harray, Orkney, tel 085677-419. Highly finished glazed terracotta pottery.

Knowtoo Pottery, Sandwick, Orkney. All aspects of pottery making.

Dairy work

Claymore Creamery, Deerness Road, Kirkwall, tel 0856-2824. Cheese making, butter making.

Swannay Farms, Swannay, Birsay, Orkney, tel 085672-365. Making of farmhouse cheese.

Fish processing
Rousay Processors, Trumland Pier, Rousay, Orkney, tel 085682-216. Shell fish processing and lobster ponds, fish smoking.

Furniture making
Robert Towers, Rosegarth, St Ola, Kirkwall, tel 0856-3521. The making of the straw-backed traditional Orkney chair.

Brian Winter, Hall of Heddle, Firth, Orkney, tel 085676-437. Furniture making and wood turning.

Glass
Orkney Glass, Skaebreck, Northdyke, Orkney, tel 085684-593. Production of kiln-fired stained glass, historical plaques in glass for museum, handmade paper.

Jewellery and Silversmithing
Ola Gorie, 11 Broad Street, Kirkwall, Orkney, tel 0856-3251. Jewellery making.

Ortak Jewellery, Hatston Industrial Estate, Kirkwall, Orkney, tel 0856-2224. Making of sterling silver and 9 ct. gold jewellery.

Knitwear and Crochet
Judith Glue, 25 Broad Street, Kirkwall, Orkney. Knitting workshop.

Orcadian Crafts, 8 Bridge Street, Kirkwall, Orkney, tel 0856-2846. Knitting

Graphics and Painting
Geoffrey Popplewell, Blett, Island of Eday, Orkney, tel 08572-248. Painting, drawing, cartoons, spinning.

Skin craft
Lindor Sheepskins, Braevilla, Rendall, Orkney, tel 085676-356. Tanning of sheepskin rugs.

Whisky Distilling
James Grant, Highland Park Distillery, Holm Road, Kirkwall, Orkney, tel 0856-3107. Whisky distilling, including traditional floor maltings, mashing, fermentation, distillation and maturation of whisky.

Taylor and Ferguson, Scapa Distillery, Orkney, tel 0856-2071. All aspects of distilling.

SHETLAND

GETTING THERE

By air
British Airways operate four flights a day from Aberdeen. Loganair operate a daily service from Edinburgh. Inverness runs a daily service, via Orkney.

By sea

P&O ferries operate a passenger and car ferry service, three times a week from Aberdeen. Departure is at 6 pm from Aberdeen on Monday, Wednesday and Friday, to arrive at 8 am next day. For information and booking write or phone P&O Ferries, PO Box 5, Jamieson's Quay, Aberdeen, tel 0224-572615.

Transport on the islands

There are good bus and taxi services from the airport, as well as plenty of rental cars. There are inter-island ferries and planes.

WHAT TO SEE

Sixty miles (96 km) north of Orkney and half way to Norway, the Shetland Islands have their own character, and scenery that is very different from that of Orkney. Though almost on the same latitude as Greenland, the winter climate is startlingly mild because of the Gulf Stream, with plenty of sunshine in early summer and less rain than the Western Isles.

Of the 100 islands in the archipelago, only 17 are inhabited. According to Tacitus, when the Romans sailed round the north coast of Scotland and found out that Britain was an island, they "discovered and subdued" Orkney but they left Shetland alone because of the wild seas that lay between them. He called Shetland "Thule", that mythical island which the ancients believed to lie on the edge of the world. As in Orkney, Shetland has the long summer nights, the "simmer dim" twilight of midsummer, adding a touch of timelessness to your holiday. The name Shetland is derived from the Norse word "hjaltland", meaning Highland. The terrain is mostly peat bog and rough highland hillside, carpeted with heather and turf and dotted with many small lochs.

Ronas Hill (in the middle of Mainland, the principal island) is the highest point, at 1,475 ft (446 m), and nowhere is more than three miles (4.8 km) from the sea.

You will find wonderful cliff scenery with long winding inlets, called voes, battered into amazing arches, fissures and jagged stacks. Few trees survive the gale-force winds that lash the islands and there isn't much agriculture: sheep-farming is important, including the black and brown Shetland sheep. Shetland knitwear is world famous: the wool is plucked, or "roo'ed" from the sheep's neck by hand, being too fine for shears. A true Shetland shawl should be so fine that you can draw it through a wedding ring.

You can still see wild Shetland ponies roaming over the hills, once bred for work in coalmines and with "... as much strength as possible and as near the ground as can be got...".

The old life of crofting and fishing was greatly changed when the oil boom hit Shetland, but the oil depots are well confined to the Sullom Voe area, on Mainland, and have not spoiled the rest of the islands, while at the same time bringing a new prosperity that must make life a lot easier for many.

It is said that, while Orkadians are crofters who also fish, Shetlanders are fishermen who own crofts.

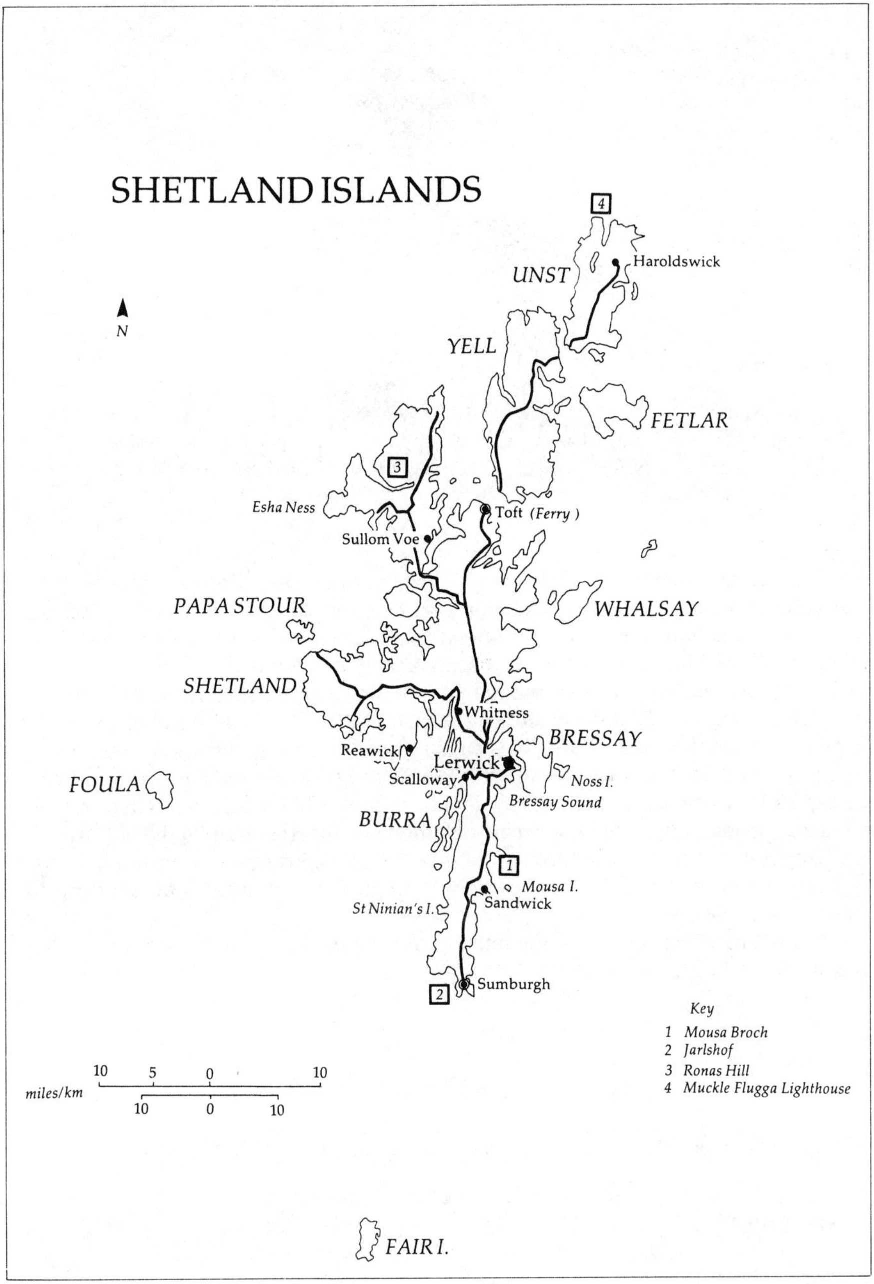

SHETLAND ISLANDS
N
UNST
Haroldswick
YELL
FETLAR
Esha Ness
Toft (Ferry)
Sullom Voe
PAPA STOUR
WHALSAY
SHETLAND
Whitness
BRESSAY
Reawick
Lerwick
FOULA
Scalloway
Noss I.
Bressay Sound
BURRA
Mousa I.
Sandwick
St Ninian's I.
Sumburgh
1
2
3
4
Key
1 Mousa Broch
2 Jarlshof
3 Ronas Hill
4 Muckle Flugga Lighthouse
miles/km
10 5 0 10
10 0 10
FAIR I.

Ewe and Lamb

The bird life on Shetland will delight any ornithologist, with vast colonies of sea birds, both northern and migrant. Fair Isle, half way to Orkney, has an observation station and is famous for the migrants who come to rest on its shores. The wild flowers are marvellous. The history of the occupation of Shetland is the same as that for Orkney. Norse names are still predominant, though Norn is no longer spoken.

Up-Helly-Aa is held in Lerwick, on the last Tuesday in January and is a wonderful hang-over from the Viking days. This pagan fire festival used to mark the end of Yule-tide and symbolise the desire for the sun to appear again after the long winter nights. A Viking galley is carried to the harbour amidst a forest of blazing torches, and set alight while the people sing "The Norseman's Home" as a funeral dirge. In the old days blazing barrels of tar were rolled through the streets. The midsummer Carnival in Lerwick is a marvellous celebration that goes right through the light night. The Shetland Folk Festival is at the end of April.

Shetland roads are good and the inter-island ferries are excellent. Many are roll-on, roll-off.

MAINLAND: SHETLAND

Mainland is by far the biggest of the islands, its chief town being Lerwick.

Lerwick

Lerwick, from the Norse 'leir-vik' meaning clay creek, is Britain's most northerly town.

Even so, in spite of its geographical isolation it is a lot more up-to-date and cosmopolitan than many of the towns in the Highland region of Scotland. It was a stopping-off port for Norsemen. King Haakon re-provisioned his fleet here on the way to Largs in 1263.

Lerwick was always important for fishing: not only are the home waters productive but it lies on the edge of the valuable northern fishing fields. Dutch fishing fleets were based here in the 17th century and by the 18th century the export of salt fish was thriving. In the 17th century the town became important as a base for the British Navy. Fort Charlotte was built in 1665 to protect the Sound of Bressay from the Dutch.

The buildings that grew up round the port were sturdy and compact, designed to withstand the violent storms, many of them the town houses of Scottish lairds who had taken over from the Norsemen and who found winter conditions rather bleak in the outlying countryside.

Looking over sheltered **Bressay Sound**, Lerwick has always been a refuge for seafarers.

Up-Helly-Aa, is in January, there is a Folk Festival at the end of April and a midsummer Carnival in June.

The *Dim Riv* is a replica Norse longship, over 40 ft (12 m) long, and you can take trips round the harbour in her on summer evenings.

WHAT TO SEE

The harbour is a lively, bustling place with a picturesque waterfront, and a charmingly haphazard, flagstoned Commercial Street, straggling up behind. Commercial Street, the main shopping centre of the town, and the steep, narrow lanes around it, are said to cover a network of secret tunnels and passages, used by smugglers in the olden days.

Fort Charlotte (open at standard Ancient Monument times: admission free) built by Cromwellian troops, was partly burned by the Dutch in 1673. It was repaired and restored in 1781 and garrisoned during the Napoleonic wars. It is the only Cromwellian military building still intact in Scotland.

Above Commercial Street, in **Hillhead**, you will find the **Town Hall**, a great Victorian-Gothic building, partly resembling a church, with tower and rose window. It doesn't look very different from countless other such Victorian buildings, until you notice that the upper floor, with its four corner turrets and central oriel window, has stained glass windows. These tempt you to go inside and climb the main staircase to the main hall. Here you will discover a fascinating parade of the history of Shetland, beginning with the Scandinavian conquest in 870, and represented by full length figures of Norway's King Harald Harfagri, the conqueror of the islands, and Rognvald, Jarl of More, to whom Harald offered the first earldom. The windows take you on through the main events that make the islands what they are today, and include one of the Maid of Norway, who died at sea nearby.

The **Shetland Museum** (open daily except on Sundays: admission free) is opposite the town hall. It has four galleries devoted to the history of man in Shetland, from prehistoric times to the present. Look out for the fascinating Papil Stone, dating from the 7th century, showing a procession of papas, or priests, one of whom is on a horse. Other exhibits include the history of Shetland knitting, and the history of the island's marine and fishing past. You can also see replicas of the treasure found on St Ninian's Isle.

These beautiful islands are a great inspiration to artists and you can see exciting exhibitions of local art and crafts in the **Shetland Workshop Gallery** (open all the year: admission free) in Burns Lane.

On the western outskirts of the town you can see **Clickhimin Broch** (always accessible) standing on its own island in a loch and reached by a causeway. It is 65 ft (20 m) in diameter, its walls 18 ft (5.4 m) thick and 15 ft (4.5 m) high, on a massive stone platform. Excavations on this site suggest that it may have been a late Bronze Age settlement.

A frequent car ferry crosses to the island of **Bressay** just east of Lerwick, and from here you can get a boat across to **Noss** (only 200 yds (180 m)). Here is a bird sanctuary whose population includes a colony of gannets, those great yellow-headed Solen Geese who dive from great heights to fish, plummeting into the water like arrows.

From Victoria Pier in Lerwick, two and a half hour boat excursions are run giving you a good look at the surrounding coast.

Scalloway

Scalloway is Mainland's other town, seven miles (11 km) west of Lerwick, and the capital until 200 years ago. Now it is a centre for fish processing. Visitors are welcome in some of the factories.

Lunna House, near the town and now a guest house, was the headquarters of the Norwegian resistance movement, during the last war. Small Norwegian fishing boats crossed to Nazi-occupied Norway to carry out sabotage or to land secret agents and bring back refugees. "To take the Shetland Bus" meant to escape from Norway to Shetland. (See *The Shetland Bus* by David Howarth.)

Scalloway is in an attractive bay at the southern end of the agricultural valley of **Tingwall**, so called after the site of the old Norse parliament, or "ting", at the north end of Tingwall Loch, reached by stepping stones.

Overlooking Scalloway is the forbidding ruin of the castle (always accessible) built by Earl Patrick Stewart, in 1600. Stewart was the notorious despot who tyrannised Orkney and Shetland until he was executed. Built in medieval style, the roofless shell, with corner turrets and gables, stands on a narrow promontory by the water. It was left to rot after the earl's death. It is said that he used to hang his victims from an iron ring in one of the chimneys. It is difficult to imagine the terror with which local people must have viewed this now harmless stronghold.

Scalloway is much older than Lerwick and retains a quiet, old fashioned atmosphere. You can cross by bridge to the islands of **Tronda** and **Burra** just to the south.

Whitness

Whitness, 7 miles (11 km) north of Scalloway, has the Hjaltasteyn Workshop (open on weekdays: admission free) where local semi-precious stones are polished and mounted in silver and enamel. Not far north, at **Weisdale**, Shetland Silvercraft also make high quality Celtic and Viking design jewellery.

Reawick

Reawick, or Red Bay, seven miles (11 km) west of Scalloway across Weisdale Voe, is a dangerous place to visit with a cheque book. The sheepskins that you can buy from the Reawick Lamb Marketing Co are very tempting indeed.

South of Lerwick

Mousa Island

Mousa Broch (open at standard Ancient Monument times: admission free) is one of Shetland's main archaeological treasures. You get to it, weather permitting, by boat from Sandwick, 11 miles (17.6 km) south of Lerwick. Mousa Island, a mile (1.6 km) offshore, is inhabited only by sheep and ponies, and its broch is the best preserved in existence. It is a thrilling experience to climb its steps, and know that you are walking in the footsteps of its Pictish builders, left 2,000 years ago. Over 50 ft (15 m) in diameter, 45 ft (13.5 m) high, with walls that taper from 12 ft (3.6 m) to 7 ft (2 m) in thickness, this is in fact one of the smallest of the brochs and probably one of the latest. You can follow the galleries in its walls and walk its stairways and parapet round the top. You can see how they tapered the walls inwards to within about 10 ft (3 m) of the top, and then sloped them outwards, making it impossible for invaders to climb up.

Mousa appears romantically in two of the old sagas. In 1150, a Norwegian Prince Erland abducted a famous beauty and held her in the broch until her son, a Jarl, unable to storm the impregnable fortress, had to consent to their marriage. Another saga tells of a young man called Bjorn, who brought Thora, a girl he had seduced, to Mousa in 900 and here they set up home together.

St Ninian's Isle

St Ninian's Isle is four miles (6.4 km) south-west of Sandwick, off the west coast of Mainland. You can walk to it along a glorious white crescent of sand, called a tombolo, creating a causeway. Here you can see the foundations of a 12th-century chapel (always accessible) that was buried by sand for many hundreds of years. In 1958, Aberdeen University began excavating the site and discovered not only the foundations of the chapel, but also a Bronze Age burial ground and the remains of a pre-Norse church.

Under a stone slab in the chapel nave they found a hoard of 8th-century Celtic silver, now in the Museum of Antiquities, in Edinburgh, with a replica collection in the museum in Lerwick. It is believed that this wonderful hoard was buried by the monks who lived here, probably during an invasion threat from Vikings. The treasure includes silver bowls, delicate brooches and a communion spoon. Lengthy litigation followed the finding, it being disputed whether the crown could claim treasure in a land where Udal law still applies.

The Shetland Croft Museum

The Shetland Croft Museum (open daily except Mondays in the summer: adults 50p, children 20p) is at **Southvoe**, in the south of Mainland, seven miles (11 km) south of

Sandwick. The museum is a restored croft house, typical of the mid-19th century. Inside the cottage you can see original driftwood furniture as well as get a very good idea of how crofters lived in the last century. You can also see the old watermill, down the hill by the burn.

Sumburgh

Sumburgh, with the airport, is at the southern tip of Mainland, 27 miles (43 km) south of Lerwick. The modern, clean cut buildings that you see as you arrive by air present a remarkable contrast to the antiquity of **Jarlshof**, just next door. **Jarlshof** (open at Standard Ancient Monument times, except shut Tuesday and Wednesday afternoons: adults 50p, children 25p) was a name invented by Sir Walter Scott in *The Pirate*, when he visited the island in 1814 and was impressed by the laird's hall. He was not to know how misleading this name was to prove, because it was not until 1905 that a violent storm revealed that this was a site that had been occupied for over 3,000 years, by seven distinct civilisations of which the Norse Jarls were by far the most recent.

The remains of these village settlements, from Bronze Age to Viking, are sprawled over a low green promontory by the sea. The first house dates from the early or middle part of the second millennium BC. It would be impossible to sort out the various ages and purposes of the conglomeration of stones without the excellent explanation that are displayed, and the very helpful guide book. The Bronze Age huts include cattle stalls and a metal workshop; the Iron Age settlement has two earth houses and a broch. The three 8th-century wheel houses are fascinating: thought to be family dwellings, they consist of a number of individual recesses separated as if by the spokes of a wheel, all around a central hearth. A confusion of longhouses is all that is left of the Norse occupation, and then there is a medieval farmhouse and the remains of the 16th-century house owned by the Stewarts. There is a little museum where you can see some of the things that have been dug from the site as well as good ground plan.

Fair Isle

Fair Isle is 24 miles (38 km) south-west of Sumburgh. You can get boats to it from **Grutness Pier**, also on Sumburgh Head. Fair Isle, the 'Far Isle' of the Vikings, half way between Orkney and Shetland, a buffer between the Atlantic and the North Sea, must be the most gale-battered territory in Britain. It presents a tough challenge to the 60-odd people who live there. The bird population is enormous, preserved by the warden of the Observatory. Among the varieties of species included here are puffins and kittiwakes. Paying guests can stay at the Observatory in the summer and you could be lucky and spot one of the rare birds that occasionally appear, such as a rubythroat, from Siberia, or a sandhill crane from North America.

There is only one woman left who hand knits the traditional Fair Isle jumpers (sweaters), but there is a thriving island cooperative, men and women, working machines and hand finishing only 200 orders of Fair Isle jumpers, scarves, hats and gloves a year. These are sold only on the island. Each jumper costs around £55 and takes seven hours to finish by hand. The designs date back to Viking times, possibly influenced by the Moorish patterns learnt from the survivors of a Spanish Armada shipwreck, in 1588, who were given shelter by the islanders.

North of Lerwick

Papa Stour

Sandness is about 25 miles (40 km) north-west of Lerwick and from here you can get a boat to Papa Stour, a couple of miles (3.2 km) off the coast, three times a week. The sea caves are believed to be the finest in Britain, and you will need to hire a boat locally to see them properly. The scent from the wild flowers on Papa Stour, was said to be so strong that fishermen could fix their position from it if caught in fog out at sea!

Brae

At Brae, about 23 miles (37 km) north of Lerwick, a very narrow neck of land prevents the north-west corner of Mainland from being an island. You can stand on this "anchor cable" of land and throw a stone one way into the Atlantic, and the other way into the North Sea.

The Sullom (pronounced Soolem) Voe Oil Terminal, with its complex of buildings and jetties, is on the peninsula of **Calback Ness**, seven miles (11 km) north-east of Brae, joined to Mainland by reclaimed land. The terminal is tucked away so discreetly that you are hardly aware of it. **Firth**, nearby, is the village that was built to house the oil men. **Toft** is four miles (6.4 km) east of Sullom Voe. Here you catch the car ferry for Yell, three miles (4.8 km) north-east, for Unst, two miles (3.2 km) north-east of Yell, and for Fetlar, three miles (4.8 km) east of Yell.

This northern part of Mainland is dominated by **Ronas Hill**, Shetland's highest point, 1,475 ft (443 m) high, ten miles (16 km) north of Brae. You should climb Ronas if you get the chance, for lovely views over the islands.

Esha Ness

Esha Ness, on the coast of Mainland, 15 miles (24 km) north-west of Brae, has precipitous cliffs and breathtaking views of the **Drongs**, a collection of weird stacks carved by the force of the ocean. These stacks include a huge natural arch called **Dore Holm**.

Yell

The island of Yell, 17 miles (27 km) by 6 miles (9.6 km) to the north, is mostly peat moor. It was described by Eric Linklater, as "...dull and dark and one large peat bog". Although the second largest of the Shetlands it has suffered from depopulation and is rather depressing.

Fetlar

Fetlar, east of Yell and much smaller, derives its name from the Norn name for "fat land" and is the most fertile of the islands, with a large number of birds.

Unst

Unst is Britain's most northern island, not counting the rock off its north tip with the **Muckle Flugga** lighthouse on it. The lighthouse was built by Robert Louis Stevenson's father, and while he was designing and building it, his son stayed on Unst, dreaming up the story of *Treasure Island.* Unst supports a number of Shetland ponies and it has wonderful cliff scenery.

Philatelists can get a special frank on their letters, at Britain's most northerly post office, in **Haroldswick**, in north-east Unst, the place where Harald Harfagri landed from Norway to subdue the troublesome Vikings

Whalsay

Whalsay, a couple of miles (3.2 km) off north-east Mainland, is important for fishing and fish processing. On the pier you can see a 17th-century Hanseatic trading booth. The Hanseatic League merchants, pioneers of today's Common Market, came to Shetland to trade, buying fish and salting it for export, until salt tax was introduced in 1712. The Baltic traders set up booths like this one, from which they offered fine cloth, fishing tackle, exotic foods, tobacco, fruit and gin at a farthing a pint, in exchange for fish, butter, wool and fish oil. It is strange to look at this quiet, peaceful place and picture how it must have been when the merchants set up their booths and bartering was in full swing.

Whalsay has two pre-historic sites: the **Standing Stones**, at **Yoxie**, and the **Benie Hoose**, thought to have been the dwelling for the Druid priests who were responsible for the ceremonies performed around the standing stones.

Foula

The island of Foula, 27 miles (43 km) west of Mainland, has more dramatic cliff scenery and a colony of skuas. Still inhabited, it is often cut off in bad weather. This was the last place where Norn was spoken, in the 19th century.

Everywhere you go among these wonderful islands, you find views that you will remember forever, sudden glimpses of sea, dramatic rocks and cliffs, all suffused by an extraordinary clarity of light. The colours must have influenced the natural shades used in the knitwear, particularly those in the Fair Isle designs. Somehow it does not seem surprising that so much of Shetland's talent is in the creative arts.

TOURIST INFORMATION

Tourist Information Centre, Lerwick, Shetland, ZE1 0LU, tel 0595-3434. It is open all year.

WHERE TO STAY

There is a large choice and you should consult the tourist brochure that you can get from the tourist information office. The following is a small selection.

Grand Hotel, Commercial Street, Lerwick, tel 0595-2826. B&B from £16: categories 3,3,4: 25 bedrooms, 9 en suite.

Lerwick Thistle Hotel, South Road, Lerwick, tel 0595-2166. B&B from £25: categories 5,5,5: 60 bedrooms en suite.

Queens Hotel, Commercial Street, Lerwick, tel 0595-2826. B&B from £16: categories 4,4,4: 34 bedrooms, 22 en suite.

Shetland Hotel, Holmsgarth Road, Lerwick, tel 0595-5515. B&B from £26: categories 6,5,5: 64 bedrooms en suite.

Scalloway Hotel, Main Street, Scalloway, tel 0595-88 444. B&B from £13: categories 5,4,5: 12 bedrooms, 8 en suite.

Sumburgh Hotel, Sumburgh, tel 0950-60201. B&B from £13.50: categories 3,3,4: 23 bedrooms en suite.

Burrastow House, Walls, tel 0595-71 307. B&B from £24.75: categories 5,4,4: 3 bedrooms en suite. Charming, listed 18th-century Haa with a private beach. A warm welcome from owners, Harry and Stella Tuckey. Delicious home cooking.

Sullom Voe Hotel, Graven, tel 0860-242283. B&B from £13: categories 1,1,1: 12 bedrooms, 5 en suite.

Busta House, Busta, tel 080-622 506. B&B from £15: categories 5,5,5: 21 bedrooms en suite.

St Magnus Bay Hotel, Hillswick, tel 080623-372/3. B&B from £17: categories 5,4,6: 26 bedrooms, 12 en suite.

Fair Isle Lodge and Bird Observatory, tel 03512-258. Dinner, B&B from £12: inclusive categories 3,3,3: 12 bedrooms.

EATING OUT

Most of the hotels above will do you very well. The local food is memorable. Nowhere else will you find better lamb, shell fish and seafood. Reestit Mutton is a local speciality, with a strong, distinctive flavour.

CRAFT CENTRES IN SHETLAND

The following studios and workshops welcome visitors. Where a telephone number is given you should ring up first to check times.

Jewellery and Silversmithing

Hjaltasteyn, Whiteness, Shetland, tel 059584-351. Jewellery making, including lapidary work, silver and goldsmithing, enamelling.

Shetland Silverware, Soundside, Weisdale, Shetland. Jewellery making.

E. W. J. Wishart, Stapness, Walls, Shetland. Making and repairing of jewellery.

Knitwear and crochet

Barbara Fraser, Heatherbraes, Gulberwick, Shetland, tel 0595-3308. Knitting workshop.

Veronica Sheehan, Westhouse, Cunningsburgh, Shetland, tel 09503-346. Knitting workshop.

Scottish Monarchs

Kenneth Macalpine: 843–860
Constantine I: 863–879
Donald I: 892–900
Constantine I and II:
Donald II: 900–943
Malcolm I: 943–954
Kenneth II: 954–994
Malcolm II: 1005–1034
Duncan I: 1034–1040
Macbeth: 1040–1057
Malcolm III, Canmore: 1057–1093
Donald Bane: 1093 (six months)
Duncan II: 1094 (six months)
Edmund: 1094 (six months)
Donald Bane: (again) 1094–1097
Edgar: 1097–1107
Alexander I: 1107–1124
David I: 1124–1153
Malcolm IV, the Maiden: 1153–1165
William I, the Lion: 1165–1214
Alexander II: 1214–1249
Alexander III: 1249–1286
Margaret: 1286–1290
Interregnum
John Balliol: 1292–1296
Interregnum
Bruces
Robert I: 1306–1329
David II: 1329–1371
Stewarts
Robert II: 1371–1390
Robert II: 1390–1406
Regent Albany: 1406–1419
Regent Murdoch: 1419–1424
James I: 1424–1437
James II: 1437–1460
James III: 1460–1488
James IV: 1488–1513
James V: 1513–1542
Mary: 1542–1567
James VI/I: 1567–1625
Charles I: 1625–1649
The Commonwealth: 1649–1660
Charles II: 1660–1685
James VII/II: 1685–1688
William and Mary: 1689–1694
William (alone): 1694–1702
Anne: 1702–1714
Hanoverians
George I: 1714–1727
George II: 1727–1760
George III: 1760–1820
George IV: 1820–1830
William II/IV: 1830–1837
Victoria: 1837–1901
Edward I/VII: 1901–1910
George V: 1910–1935
Edward II/VIII: 1935–1936
George VI: 1936–1952
Elizabeth I/II: 1952–

Some milestones in Scottish History

82	Defeat of Picts at battle of Mons Graupius by Roman Agricola.
141	Building of Antonine Wall.
397	Founding of Christian church at Whithorn by St Ninian.
410	Departure of Romans from Britain.

500	Invasion of Scotland by Irish Scots, settlement of Dalriada.
563	Landing of St Columba in Iona, conversion of Picts to Christianity.
794	Invasion of Hebrides by Norsemen.
844–60	Kenneth Macalpine unites Picts and Scots.
1034	Whole of Scotland united into one kingdom under Duncan I.
1040	Duncan I murdered by Macbeth who is in turn murdered by Malcolm Canmore.
1057–93	Anglicising of Scotland under Queen Margaret.
1102	Western Isles granted to Magnus of Orkney.
1124–53	David I founds many abbeys and burghs, grants land to Normans.
1174	William Lion forced to acknowledge supremacy of Henry II.
1200	Beginning of Auld Alliance of Scotland and France against England.
1214	Alexander II, Golden Age of Scottish history.
1263	Battle of Largs, defeat by Alexander III of King Haakon of Norway. Annexation of the Hebrides.
1286	Death of Alexander III, succeeded by Maid of Norway.
1290	Death of Maid of Norway at sea on her way to Scotland.
1291	Edward I arbitrates between Robert Bruce and John Balliol. Balliol gets crown.
1296	Balliol renounces his crown in favour of Edward I.
1297–8	William Wallace stirs up resistance, defeats Edward at Stirling Bridge, and is defeated at Falkland. Goes into hiding.
1305	Capture and execution of William Wallace.
1306	Robert Bruce slays John Comyn and is crowned at Scone.
1307	Edward I dies.
1314	Battle of Bannockburn, Bruce defeats English.
1326	First Scottish parliament at Cambuskenneth.
1346	Battle of Neville's Cross. David II taken prisoner by English.
1371	Robert Stewart crowned, Robert II, first Stewart king.
1406	James I captured, regency of Duke of Albany.
1414	Foundation of St Andrews, Scotland's first university.
1450–55	Struggle for supremacy between Stewarts and Douglases. Douglases crushed by James II.
1469	Orkney and Shetland pledged to James III as part of dowry of his wife, Margaret of Denmark.
1476	Overthrow of Lords of the Isles.
1495	Perkin Warbeck claims English throne, encouraged by James IV.
1513	Battle of Flodden, death of James IV.
1528	Burning of Patrick Hamilton, proto-martyr of Reformation.
1538	Marriage of James V to Marie de Guise.
1542	Defeat of Scots at Solway Moss, death of James V, accession of his infant daughter Mary.
1544	Rough Wooing, devastation of Lowland Scotland by Henry VIII.
1546	Burning of George Wishart, murder of Cardinal Beaton.
1554	Regency of Marie de Guise.
1557	Signing of first Protestant Covenant.

1558	Marriage of Mary to Dauphin of France, Francis II.
1559	John Knox preaches Reform.
1565	Marriage of Mary to Darnley.
1566	Birth of James VI.
1567	Murder of Darnley, marriage of Mary to Bothwell, defeat, imprisonment and abdication.
1568	Mary, finally defeated leaves Scotland.
1587	Mary executed.
1600	The Gowrie conspiracy, a squalid attempt to abduct James VI in dubious circumstances.
1603	Accession of James VI to English throne making him James VI/I (VI of Scotland, I of England). Establishment of Episcopacy in Scotland.
1637	Riots of Edinburgh against Charles I's Episcopacy.
1638	Signing of National Covenant to uphold Presbyterian worship.
1643	Signing of Solomn League and Covenant recognised by English parliament.
1645	Battle of Philiphaugh. Defeat of royalist Montrose by Covenanters under Leslie.
1649	Execution of Charles I, Charles II proclaimed king in Scotland.
1650	Signing of covenants by Charles II. Invasion of Scotland by Cromwell.
1653	United Parliament at Westminster.
1660	Restoration of Monarchy.
1662	Renunciation of Covenants by king and re-establishment of Episcopacy.
1666	Start of the Killing Times, persecution of Covenanters.
1688	James VII/II tries to restore Catholicism. He is deposed in favour of William and Mary.
1689	Highlanders, under Claverhouse, Bonny Dundee, defeat King's army at Killiecrankie.
1692	Massacre of Glencoe.
1698	Failure of Darien Scheme.
1707	Union of Parliaments.
1715	Rebellion in favour of the Old Pretender.
1736	The Porteous Riot, Scots rebel against English domination.
1745/6	Final Jacobite rebellion. Defeat of Prince Charles Edward Stuart at Battle of Culloden. Repression of Highlands. Soon followed by the beginning of the Highland Clearances which lasted for over 100 years and depopulated the Highlands.
1845/6	Extensive Irish immigration after severe potato famine in Ireland.
1947	Founding of Edinburgh International Festival, putting Scotland back on the cultural map.

Biographical notes

The following names are mentioned in the text but are not necessarily explained.

Adam, William and his four sons, John, Robert, James and William. Renowned Scottish-born architects, Robert, 1728–92 being the best known.

Adamnan, Saint. c. 624–704. Ninth Abbot of Iona and biographer of St Columba.

Bean, Sawney. Apocryphal 17th-century cannibal who lived with his incestuously bred family in a cave in Ayrshire, existing on the flesh and gold of unwary travellers.

Beaton, David. Cardinal and Archbishop of St Andrews, 1494–546. Notorious for persecution of Reformers. Burned George Wishart for heresy and was murdered in revenge in St Andrews Castle.

Boswell, James. 1740–95. Scottish lawyer, writer and admirer of great names. Met Dr Johnson in 1763 and toured Hebrides with him in 1773. Wrote *Life of Samuel Johnson*. A volatile, promiscuous man given to fits of depression. Of great value to anyone visiting Scotland is to read his *Journal of a Tour of the Hebrides*, in conjunction with Dr Johnson's account.

Bothwell, James Hepburn. Earl of, 1537–78. Powerful and ambitious. Closely involved in murder of Mary, Queen of Scots' husband, Darnley. Abducted Mary, raped her and married her after quick divorce from his wife. Escaped when Mary was deposed. Imprisoned in Denmark where he died insane.

Brahn, Seer. Coinneach Odhar. 17th century. Given gift of second sight after falling asleep on a fairy hill. Made astonishing prophecies, many of which have been fulfilled; some of which may yet be. Murdered by Countess of Seaforth having told her of her husband's infidelity.

Burns, Robert. 1754–96. Born at Alloway in Ayrshire of humble parents and rose to become lionised as Scotland's greatest vernacular poet. Renowned almost as much for his enthusiastic love life and "joi de vie" as for his marvellous verse. Among the many classics he wrote were *Tam o' Shanter, My Love is like a Red, Red Rose, A Man's a Man, for a' that* and *Auld Lang Syne*.

Columba, Saint. c. 521–597. Of royal Irish blood, he was exiled from Ireland, settled in Iona in 563 and founded a religious community, launching-pad for missionaries who then converted Scotland to Christianity.

Cromwell, Oliver. 1599–1658. Led parliamentarians in England's civil war and was responsible for execution of Charles I.

Cumberland, William Augustus. Duke of, 1721–65. Fat son of George II, defeated Prince Charles at Culloden 1746, winning nickname of Butcher Cumberland for his brutality.

Douglas. Ancient Scottish family, often so powerful that they were a threat to the crown. Divided into the Black Douglases and the Red Douglases, they appear for better or worse throughout Scottish history. The Black Douglases were finally subdued by James II. The Red Douglases, who "...rose upon the ruins of the Black..." held considerable power until deposed by James V.

Dundee, Graham of Claverhouse. Viscount "Bonnie Dundee". 1649–89. Royalist and notorious persecutor of Covenanters. Led early Jacobite rebellion after James VII/II was deposed, and was killed defeating William's army at Killiecrankie.

Hamilton, Patrick. 1502–28. Proto-martyr of Scottish Reformation, influenced by Erasmus and Luther. He returned to his native Scotland and was burned for heresy by Beaton at St Andrews. In spite of his youth, he was titular Abbot of Ferne.

Hertford, Edward Seymour. Earl of, 1506–52. Leading aggressor in Henry VIII's "Rough Wooing" of Scotland, to punish them for cancelling marriage between Mary, Queen of Scots and Henry's son, Edward. He was responsible for appalling destruction to many of Scotland's finest Lowland buildings, including the Border abbeys.

Hogg, James. 1770–1835. Protégé of Sir Walter Scott, known as the Ettrick shepherd. Prolific poet and novelist.

Johnson, Samuel. 1709–84. English lexicographer, critic and poet, whose reputation as a man and a conversationist is as great as his literary fame. Dogmatic, unreasonable, humble, pious and loveable, his account of his tour of the Hebrides with James Boswell, in 1773, makes marvellous reading and is full of acute observations on life in the Highlands after Culloden and the Act of Proscription.

Jones, John Paul. 1747–92. Born in Kircudbrightshire, son of a gardener. He received commission in American navy and returned to harass the English, but always with honour. Stories told of his chivalrous treatment of his victims.

Knox, John. c. 1505–72. Leading Scottish Reformer. Spent 19 months as French galley-slave, returning to preach fiery iconoclastic sermons in Perth and St Andrews in 1559 which led to destruction of monasteries. Minister of St Giles, in Edinburgh during which time he tangled with Mary, Queen of Scots. The phrase "monstrous regiment of women" was coined from his pamphlet called: "The First Blast of the Trumpet Against the Monstrous Regiment of Women". Although dogmatic, he had a keen sense of humour.

Lauder, Sir Harry. 1870–1950. Mill boy and miner who became a much-loved writer and interpreter of Scottish songs, including *The Road to the Isles*.

Leslie, David. 1601–82. Scottish Covenanter and general. Defeated Montrose at Battle of Philiphaugh. Supported Charles II in 1650 and was defeated by Cromwell at Dunbar. Imprisoned in Tower of London till Restoration of Monarchy, and then made Lord Newark.

Macdonald, Flora. 1722–90. Born in South Uist. Tacksman father died when she was two. Adopted at 13 by Lady Clanranald wife of chief of clan, and brought up in Skye. She smuggled Prince Charlie from Benbecula to Skye, disguised as her maid, Betty Burke, thus helping to save his life. Was imprisoned for a year on a troopship. Married son of Macdonald of Kingsburgh and entertained Dr Johnson during his tour of Hebrides in 1773. Emigrated with family to North Carolina where her husband became a brigadier-general in American War of Independence. Returned to Scotland in 1779 and died at Kingsburgh.

Macpherson, James. 1736–96. Scottish poet who "translated" the Ossianic poems.

Many believed that these works were genuine and they were certainly of great value, but others, including Dr Johnson, doubted their authenticity and it is now believed that he collected a quantity of Gaelic material and composed his own poems from them. In their own right, whatever the source, they are a valuable and beautiful contribution to Gaelic past.

Monk, George. 1608–69. Parliamentary general in Scotland, fighting for Cromwell at Dunbar and then governor of Scotland in 1653–58. When Cromwell died he saw that the only way to heal the turmoil in Britain was to restore the monarchy and he was instrumental in bringing Charles II back to the throne.

Monmouth, Duke of, 1649–85. Bastard son of Charles II by Lucy Waters, he claimed that his parents had been married and raised a revolt against James VII/II, for which he was executed.

Moray, James Stuart. Regent, 1531–70. Bastard son of James V, half-brother to Mary, Queen of Scots. Sided with Lords of the Congregation and became regent on Mary's abdication. Shot while riding through Linlithgow.

Ossian. 3rd-century Gaelic bard, possibly son of Fingal, chief of the Fenians, semi-mythical military body said to have been raised for defence of Ireland against Norse. Countless tales told. (See Macpherson.)

Queensberry, "Old Q." fourth Duke, 1724–1810. Notorious gambler, despoiled many tree plantations in Scotland, to pay his debts.

Ramsay, Allan. 1686–1758. Scottish poet, best known for *The Gentle Shepherd*.

Ramsay, Allan. 1713–84. Son of above. Famous portrait painter.

Rob Roy, Robert MacGregor. 1671–1734. Known as Rob Roy (red Robert) from colour of his hair. Romanticised by Walter Scott as philanthropic Robin Hood, he was in fact a cattle-raider and smuggler. Died peacefully, having been imprisoned in London and pardoned.

Scott, Sir Walter. 1771–1832. Prolific poet and novelist. Remarkable for his efforts to pay off debts of £130,000 after collapse of his publisher hence the amazing volume of his work. He also did much for Scotland after the despair that followed Culloden. It was he who organised the search for the Scottish regalia, and he who organised the State Visit of George IV.

Stevenson, Robert. 1772–1850. Scottish engineer responsible for many important lighthouses, including Bell Rock.

Stevenson, Robert Louis. 1850–94. Grandson of above and son of another engineer. Prolific writer, best known for *Treasure Island, Kidnapped, Master of Ballantrae*, and *Dr Jekyll and Mr Hyde*.

Telford, Thomas. 1757–1834. Scottish engineer famous for his bridges, of which many still exist, his roads and his canals including the Caledonian Canal.

Thomas the Rhymer. c. 1220–97. Thomas Learmont of Erceldoune (Earlston) Scottish seer and poet, many of whose prophecies were fulfilled. Said to have lived with the Fairy Queen for three years in the Eildon Hills. He foretold the death of Alexander III at his wedding feast.

Wade, George. 1673–1748. English general, sent to Scotland in 1724 to try to bring the Highlands into control. Built a system of metalled roads and bridges that opened up the north.

Warbeck, Perkin. 1474–c.99. Claimed to be one of the princes murdered in the Tower.

Put forward by English Yorkists as rightful king. Made three futile "invasions", was caught and executed. He was in fact the son of a Flemish boatman.

Wishart, George. c. 1513–46. Scottish reformer, burned by Cardinal Beaton in St Andrews, for which the cardinal was later murdered.

Wolf of Badenoch. died 1394. Bastard son of Robert II, Alexander Stewart, Earl of Buchan. Also known as "Big Alastair, son of the King". Brutal and merciless, terrorising countryside from his castles of Ruthven and Lochindorb. Excommunicated by Bishop of Elgin in 1390 for which he destroyed Elgin Cathedral and much else.

Suggested reading

For those rainy days here are some recommended books which will prove valuable companions to anyone visiting Scotland. They are all thoroughly "readable" for pleasure as well as for information

History

A Concise History of Scotland, Fitzroy Maclean
The Lion in the North, John Prebble
These two histories of Scotland are beautifully written, easy to read, and tell you all the interesting bits!

Also by John Prebble:
Culloden
The Highland Clearances
Glencoe
The Darien Disaster
Mutiny, Highland Regiments in Revolt

Mary, Queen of Scots, Antonia Fraser
The Prince in the Heather, Eric Linklater. The story of Prince Charlie's escape after Culloden.
In Search of Scotland, H. V. Morton
In Scotland Again, H. V. Morton
These two were written in 1929 and 1933 and are as fresh and readable today as then.
The Highland Clans, Sir Iain Moncreiffe of that Ilk. Not quite so "readable" but an erudite book of great value.
A Journey to the Western Islands, Samuel Johnson
Journal of a Tour to the Hebrides, James Boswell
These two can be got in one volume and should be read together.
The Drove Roads of Scotland, A. R. B. Haldane
The Fringe of Gold, Charles MacLean. Wonderful collection of anecdotes about the fishing villages of the east coast.
The Islands of Western Scotland, W. H. Murray
The Prophecies of the Brahn Seer, Alexander Mackenzie
A Macdonald for the Prince, Alasdair Maclean. The story of Neil MacEachen, native of Uist and father of Napoleon's Marshal MacDonald.
Tales of a Grandfather, Walter Scott. The history of Scotland as told by Walter Scott to his young grandson. Delightful!
Edinburgh: A Travellers' Companion, (ed) David Daiches. Excellent new anthology of

historical accounts of the city, its life and customs.
Scotland: An Anthology, Paul Harris. Delightful, idiosyncratic literary collection covering all aspects of Scotland.

Novels
Whisky Galore, Compton Mackenzie. Any of Compton Mackenzie's books make amusing reading.
The Waverley Novels, Walter Scott
The Song of the Forest, Colin Mackay. A beautiful piece of contemporary writing, giving a picture of life in the Dark Ages.

Poetry
Robert Burns
William McGonagall (Scotland's worst poet—compulsive reading)
Hugh MacDiarmid

Light Relief
The Old Man of Lochnagar, HRH The Prince of Wales

INDEX

Page references in *italics* refer to maps

Abbotsford House 113
Aberdeen 307–312
  events 309
  history 307, 309
  map *308*
Aberdour 258
Aberfeldy 300
Aberlemlo 291
Abernethy 278, 279
Aboyne 318
accommodation 20, 23–25
Achiltibuie 399
Ailsa Craig 184
Aird of Sleat 409
air travel 8, 10–14
Alford 323
angling 35, 36
Annait 414
Annan 125–127
Anstruther 264, 265
Antonine Wall 235
Applecross Peninsula 369
Arbigland 132
Arbroath 286–289
Arbuthnot House and Gardens 315
Ardeslie 285
Ardnamurchan Peninsula 360
Ardrossan 190
Ardtornish Castle 359
Ardwell House Gardens 148
Arisaig 361
Armadale Castle 409
Arran 197–202
Askernish 434
Athelstaneford 176
Auchindrain Museum 212
Auchmithie 287
Auchterarder 303
Auld Alliance 42
Aviemore 351, 352
Ayr 187–193
Ayton 97, 98

Balbeg 365
Balbithan House and Garden 325
Ballachulish Bridge 356
Ballantrae 184
Ballater 319, 320
Balloch 205, 206
Balmerino Abbey 269, 270
Balmoral 320
Balnakeil Village 395
Balquhidder 246
Balvenie Castle 328
Banchory 318
Banff 337, 338
banks 28
Bannockburn 241, 242
Barholm Castle 140
Barns Ness 154
Barpa Langass 429
Barra 438–440
Barry Hill 293, 294
Beauly 373, 374
Beecraigs Country Park 168
Beinn Eighe National Nature Reserve
Benbecula 431, 432
Ben Lee 430
Bennane Head Cave 184
Biggar 196, 197
Berriedale 387, 388
Bettyhill 393, 394
Birdsay 448
birdwatching 37
Birham 296
Black Isle 378
Blackness Castle 165
Black Rock Gorge 381
Blair Atholl 298
Blair Drummond Safari Park 243
Blairgowrie 294, 295
Blairlogie 238
Bonar Bridge 383
Bo'ness 165
Bonnington Nature Reserve 195
Borders 93–119
  Common Riding Festivals 94
  craftwork 117
  map *95*
  tourist information 94
Borthwick Castle 172, 173
Borve Castle 432
Bowhill 111
Braco 303
Brae 459
Braeloine 318
Braemar 321
Breacachadh Castle 230
Brechin 289, 290
Broadford 410
Broch of Dun Mor 230
Brodick 198, 199
Brodie Castle 332
Brora 386
Broughton 116, 117
Broughty Ferry 284
Bruar Falls 298
Bruce, Robert 44, 187, 189
Bunaveneader 426
Burghead 330
Burleigh Castle 278
Burns, Robert 187–189
Burntisland 259
bus travel 12, 14
Bute 202–204
Butt of Lewis 424

Cairnpapple 168
Caithness glass 389
Caledonian Canal 363
Callander 245, 246
Callanish Standing Stones 425
Campbeltown 214, 215
Campsie Fells 240
canoeing 33
Canna 420, 421
Cape Wrath 395
Cardoness Castle 139
Carinish 430
Carleton Castle 184
Carloway Broch 424
Carlungie 285
Carnasserie Castle 218
Carnoustie 285
Carrick Forest 185
Carron Valley 239, 240
Castle Campbell 237
Castle Douglas 135–137
Castle Duart 228
Castle Fraser 322
Castle Menzies 300, 301
Castle Stalker 220
Castle Sween 214
Castle Tioram 360
Castle Urquhart 365
Cawdor 348
Ceilidh 5, 6
celebrations 6
Central Scotland 233–249
  craftwork 249
  festivals 234
  map *236*
  tourist information 234
Ceres 272
Chanory Point 378
Charles I 48, 49
Charles II 49
Charles Edward Stuart 50, 51
Charleston 254
Chirnside 98
Christianity 41
churches 30, 31
Clachaig 356
Clan Gunn Museum and Heritage Centre 388
clans 4, 45, 46
Clatteringshaws Loch 141
Clava Cairns 347
Claypotts Castle 284
Click Mill 447
climate 2
climbing 33–35
clothes 19
Clyde 204
Cockleroy Hill 167, 168
Coldingham 96, 97
Coldstream 101–103
Colinsburgh 262
Coll 229, 230
Colonsay 224, 225
Comrie 302
Consulates 31
Contin 400
Corgarff Castle 324
Corrie 199
Corrieshalloch 373
Corsewall point 147
Coupar Angus 294
Cowal Peninsula 207, 208
craftwork 77, 117–119, 149, 150
Craigcleuch Scottish Explorers Museum 124, 125
Craighouse 224
Craigievar 319
Craignethan Castle 195, 196
Craigtown Country Park 268
Crail 265
Cramond 164
Crarae Woodland Garden 213
Crathes Castle 317
Crianlarich 247, 248
Crichton Castle 173
crofting 6
Croich Church 383
Cromarty 379
Crosskirk 393
Crossraguel Abbey 240
Cuillins, the 410, 411
Culcreach Castle 240
Culloden 346, 347
Culross 251–254
Culzean Castle 185
Culzean Country Park 185, 186
Cupar 271
curling 35
currency 28
customs allowances 19

Dalbeattie 136
Dalgety Bay 258
Daliburgh 434
Dalkeith 172–174
Dalmeny 163, 164
Dalyell, General Tam 165
Davaar Island 215

David I 42
David II 44, 45
Dawyck House Gardens 116
Deer Abbey 339
Deeside 316–322
Delgatie Castle 336
Dervaig 226
Devils Beef Tub 129
Dingwall 380, 381
Dinnet 319
disabled travellers 17, 18
diving 35
Dollar 238
Dornoch 384
Douglases, the 45, 46
Doune 243, 244
Dounreay 393
Drimisdale 433
drinking 27, 32
driving 9, 12, 14, 18
Drum Castle 317
Drumcoltran Tower 132
Drumelzier 116
Drumlanrig Castle 134
Drummond Castle 302
Drumnadrochit 366
Dryburgh Abbey 113
Dufftown 328
Dumbarton 205
Dumfries 130–133
Dumfries and Galloway 120–150
  craftwork 149
  map *123*
  tourist information 121
Dunbar 152–155
Dun Beag 415
Dunbeath 388
Dunblane 242–245
  Cathedral 243
Duncansby Head 391
Dundee 283–286
Dundrennan Abbey 138, 139
Dunfermline 254–257
  Abbey 255
Dunkeld 295, 296
Dunnet Head 392
Dunnotar Castle 314
Dunoon 208–210
Dunrobin Castle 386
Duns 99–101
Dunskey Castle 147
Dunstaffnage Castle 219
Duntulm Castle 412
Dunure 186
Dunvegan 414, 415
Durisdeer 134
Durness 395

East Neuk 263–266
eating out 25, 26
Ecclefechan 128
Eday 449
Eden Castle 336
Edinburgh 52–78
  accommodation 72, 73
  art galleries 66–68
  Arthur's Seat 62
  Botanic gardens 68, 69
  Butterfly Farm 71
  Castle 54–58
  Cathedrals 68
  craftwork 77
  Craigmillar Castle 71
  Dean Village 70
  eating out 73–75
  entertainment 75, 76
  Esplanade, The 56
  events 77, 78
  Festival 71
  Grassmarket 63, 64
  Greyfriars Bobby 64
  history 52, 53
  Holyrood 61–63
  Lauriston Castle 70
  Leith 69
  map *55*
  New Town 65–68
  Old Town 54–65
  Princes Street 65, 66
  Royal Mile 58–61
  St Giles Cathedral 59, 60
  shopping 75–76
  tourist information 72, 73
  Warriston Cemetery 69
  Zoo 70
Edinshall Broch 100
Edward I 43, 44
Edzell 290
Egilsay 448, 449
Eglinton Castle 190
Eigg 420
Eilean-an-Tighe 428
Eilean Donan Castle 368
electricity 19
Elgin 329
Embo 384, 385
Eriskay 436, 437
Eyemouth 96–99

Fair Isle 458
Falkirk 234, 235, 239
Falkland 270, 271
Fast Castle 97
Fearn 382
ferries 14–17
Fetlar 459
Fidra Island 158
Fife 250–274
  craftwork 274
  East Neuk 263–266
  festivals 251
  map *252*
  tourist information 251
Finavon Castle 290, 291
Findhorn 331
Finlarig Castle 24
Finlaystone Estate 192, 193
fishing 35, 36
Fiunary 359
Flodden 46, 47
Floors Castle 104
Fochabers 329
food 24–27, 32
Forfar 291, 292
Forres 332
Fort Augustus 365
Fort George 349
Fortrose 378
Fort William 355–357
Foula 460
Foulden 98
Furnace 212, 213
Fyvie Castle 335

gaelic 5
Gairloch 371
Galashiels 112–114
Garrynamonie 436
Garvald 178
Gatehouse of Fleet 139
geography of Scotland 1
Gifford 178
Gigha Island 216
Gilnockie Tower 124
Girvan 182–187
Glamis 292, 293
Glasgow 79–92
  accommodation 89, 90
  "Barras, The" 88
  Botanic Gardens 88
  Burrell Collection 87
  Cathedral 81
  eating out 90, 91
  entertainment 91, 92
  events 92
  festivals 88, 89
  Fossil Grove 88
  George Square 83, 84
  history 81
  map *81*
  museums and galleries 84–87
  Provand's Lordship 83
  shopping 91, 92
  tourist information 88
  Zoo 87
glass 32, 389
Glenapp Castle 185
Glenbuchat Castle 323
Glencoe 356
  massacre 49
Glen Corodale 434
Gleneagles 303
Glenesk Folk Museum 290
Glenfinnan 362
Glen Kindie 323
Glen Loy 364
Glen Roy 353
Glenshee 295
Glentress Forest 116
gliding 36
golf 36, 37, 185, 285, 303
Golspie 386
Gosford Sands 159
Gourock 191, 192
Grampian 306–341
  craftwork 341
  maps *313*
Grantown-on-Spey 351
Grass Point 228
Great Cumbrae 191
Great Glen 363–367
Greenlaw 100
Greenock 192
Gretna Green 121–124
Greyfriars Bobby 64
Grey Mare's Tail 129
Gruinard Bay 372
guides 31
Gullane 158
Gurness 447

Haddington 174–177
Haddo House 335
Hailes Castle 175
Hallowe'en 6
Harris 425–427
Hawick 107–109
  Hermitage Castle 108, 109
health 18
Hebrides, Outer 421–440
  craftwork 439, 440
  getting there 423
  map *422*
Hebrides: Strathclyde 222–231
Helensburgh 206, 207
Helmsdale 386, 387
Hermitage Castle 108, 109
Highlands 342–404
  craftwork 402–404
  events 343
  maps *344, 358, 377*
  tourist information 343, 345

Hillend Dry Ski Slope 171
Hill of Tarvit 271
hill-walking 33–35
history 40–51, 462–464
Auld Alliance 42
biographies 465–468
Flodden 46, 47
Jacobites 49
Mary Queen of Scots 47, 48
Massacre of Glencoe 49
monarchs 462
Normans 42
Norse invasion 41, 43
prehistory 40
Romans 40, 41
Union with England 48, 50
Wars of Independence 43, 44
hitch-hiking 14
Hogmanay 6
Holy Loch 208
Hopetoun House 164
horn-work 32
hotels 23–25
House of the Binns 164, 165
Hoy 448
Huna 429
Huntly 327, 328

Inchcolm 258
Inchkeith 260
Inchmahome Priory 246
insurance 18
Inverbervie 315
Invererary 212
Inverfarigaig 366
Invergary 367, 368
Invergordon 381, 382
Inverkeithing 257, 258
Invernaver National Nature Reserve 394
Inverness 345, 346
Inverurie 326
Iona 228, 229
Irvine 190
Isle of Whithorn 144
Islay 222–224

James I 45
James IV 46, 47, 102
James Edward Stuart (the Old Pretender) 50, 103
James Stewart 48
Jedburgh 105–107
jewellery 32
John O'Groats 390, 391
Jura 224

Keith 328
Kellie Castle 264
Kelso 103–105
Kenneth McAlpine 41
Kilberry 213–214
Kildonan 200
Kildrummy Castle 323
Killiecrankie, Pass of 298
Killin 247
Kilmarnock 189, 190
Kilmory Knap Chapel 214
Kilpheder 435
Kincardine 235, 237
Kincraig Highland Wildlife Park 352
Kinghorn 259, 260
Kingsbarns 266
Kingussie 353
Kinlochmoidart 361
Kinmount Gardens 126
Kinneff 315
Kinross 276
Kintore 325
Kintyre Peninsula 214–217
Kircaldy 260, 261
Kirkcudbright 137–140
Kirkhill 375
Kirkpatrick Fleming 122
Kirkwall 443, 444
Kirkwynd 293
Kirriemuir 292
Kirtlebridge 122
Knapdale 213, 214
Knock Bay 409
Knox, John 47
Kyleakin 408
Kyle of Lochalsh 369
Kyles of Bute 203
Kylestrom 397

Ladykirk 102
Laggan 364
Lairg 397
Lamb Holm 447
Lamlash 201
Lammermuir Hills 177–179
Lanark 194–197
Langholm 124, 125
Largo 262
Largs 191–193
Laxford Bridge 397
Leadhills 196
Ledmore 398
Leith 69
Leith Hall, Grampian 327
Lennoxlove House 175
Lerwick 454–456
Leuchars 268, 269
Leven 262
Lewis 423–425
Limekilns 254
Lindores Abbey 270
Linlithgow 166–169
Linn of Dee 321
Lismore Island 219
Loch Airlort 361
Loch Awe 220
Loch Bee 433
Loch Boisdale 434, 435
Loch Doon Castle 185
Loch Earn 247
Loch Eriboll 394
Loch Fleet 385
Loch Fyne 210, 212
Loch Garten Nature Reserve 351
Lochgilphead 213, 217, 218
Loch Inch 352
Lochinvar Castle 140, 142
Lochinver 398
Loch Katrine 246
Loch Laggan 353
Loch Leven 276, 278
Loch Lomond 205–207
Lochmaben 127
Lochmaddy 427
Loch Mealt 412
Lochnaw Castle 147
Loch Ness 365
Monster Exhibition 366
Loch of the Lowes 295
Loch Ossian 356
Loch Rannoch 299
Lochranza 199
Loch Snizort Beag 413
Loch Sunart 359, 360
Loch Tay 301
Loch Tummel 299
Lockerbie 127, 128
Logan Botanic Gardens 148
Lossiemouth 330
Lothian 151–180
coast 162–166
craftwork 179, 180
map *153*
tourist information 152
Ludaig 436
Luib 410
Lumphanan 319
Lybster 388

Macbeth 42
Macduff 336
Machrihanish 215
MacLellans's Castle 138
Maes Howe 445
Magus Muir 272
Mallaig 361, 362
Malleny House Gardens 171
Manderston 100
map of Scotland *7*
Maryculter 316
Mary Queen of Scots 47, 48, 276
Maxwelton House 135
May Island 266
McGonagall, William 269
Meigle 294
Melrose Abbey 114
Menmuir 290
Mey, Castle of 392
midges 6
Milton, South Uist 434
Moffat 128–130
money 28
Monikie 285
Montrose 288, 289
Mote of Mark 136
Mote of Urr 136
Mousa Island 457
Muck 421
Mull 225–228
Mull of Galloway 148
Mull of Kintyre 215
Musselburgh 160, 161

Nairn 348
national dishes 26, 27
national symbols 5
National Trust for Scotland 38
Newark Castle 110, 111
Newburgh 270
New Galloway 140, 141
New Lanark 195
Newton Stewart 141–143
Norman influence 42
North Berwick 155–159
Northern Isles 440–461
North Queensferry 257
North Ronaldsay 449
North Uist 427–430
Nunton 431, 432

Oakley 254
Oban 218–222
Old Dairsie 272, 273
Oldham Stocks 178, 179
Ord of Caithness 381
Orkney 441–451
accommodation 449, 450
craftwork 450, 451
eating out 450
getting there 441
Kirkwall 443, 444
map *442*
tourist information 443, 449
Ormaclete Castle 433
ornithology 37

Oronsay 225, 226
Ousdale 387
Outer Hebrides *see* Hebrides

Paisley 194
Papa Stour 459
Papa Westray 449
Pass of Killiecrankie 298
Peat Inn 272
Peebles 115–117
Pentland Hills 169–171
Perth 279–282
Peterculter 316
Peterhead 339
Picts 41, 42
Pinkie House 161
Pirnmill 200
Pitcaple Castle 326
Pitlessie 272
Pitlochry 297
Pittenweem 264
Plockton 369
Pluscarden Abbey 331
Pobull Fhinn 429
pony trekking 37
Poolewe 371
Port Ellen 222, 223
Port na Croise 227
Portpatrick 147
Portree 411
post offices 28, 29
Pressmennan Glen 177
Preston Mill 176
Prestonpans 161, 162
Prestwick 8, 189
public holidays 30

Queen Elizabeth Forest Park 246
Queensferry 162, 163, 257
Quiraing, the 412

Raasay 416
Rammerscales 128
Redcastle 288
Redpoint 370
Reekie Linn 293
religion 2, 3, 41
Restenneth Priory 291
Rhinns of Galloway 146–150
Rhu 207
Rhum 419
Ring of Brodgar 445, 446
Rogie Falls 400
Rosemarkie 378
Roslin 170, 171
Rosyth 257
Rothesay 203
Rousay 448
Roxburghe 104
Rumbling Bridge 237
Ruthven Barracks 352, 353
Ruthwell 126

St Abbs 97
St Andrews 266–268
St Andrew's Day 6
St Columba's Cave 214
St Fillans 302
St Kilda 430, 431
St Mary's Loch 111
St Monance 264
St Ninian 41
St Ninian's Isle 457
St Vigeans 287
Saltcoats 190
Sand 372
Sanda Island 216
Sanquhar 133–135
Scalloway 456
Scapa Flow 442, 445
Scone Palace 280, 281
Scottish Museum of Woollen Textiles 114
Scourie 397
Scrabster 393
Seil 218
Selkirk 110–112
Shandwick 382
Shetland 451–461
  accommodation 460, 461
  craftwork 461
  Croft Museum 457, 458
  getting there 451, 452
  Lerwick 454–456
  map *453*
  tourist information 460
shooting 38
shopping 31, 76, 77, 91, 92, 112
skiing 37, 38, 295, 296, 352
Skye 408–418
  accommodation 416, 417
  Cottage Museum 413
  getting there 408
  Portree 411
  tourist information 416
Slains Castle 339
Sleat Peninsula 409
Sma' Glen, the 301
Southend 215, 216
South Lochboisdale 435
South Queensferry 162, 163
South Ronaldsay 447, 448
South Uist 432–436
Spedlins Tower 128
Speyside 350–354
Spynie Palace 329
Stenton 176, 177
Stewarts, the 45
Stirling 240–242
  Castle 240, 241
Stonehaven 312, 314
Stornoway 423, 424
Stranraer 146–149
Strathclyde 181–232
  craftwork 231
  maps *183, 211*
  tourist information 182
Strathpeffer 400, 401
Strathy Point 393
Stromness 393, 444, 445
Strontian 359
Struie 381
sub-aqua 35
Sueno's Stone 332
Suisgill 387
Sumburgh 458
Sutors 379
Sweetheart Abbey 132

Tain 382, 383
Tarbat Ness 382
Tarbert 426
Tarlair 336
tartan 4, 5, 302
tax 33
Tay Bridge 269
Tayside 275–305
  craftwork 305
  events 275, 276
  map 277
telephones 29
Temple, Lothian 173
Tentsmuir Forest 269
Teviothead 108
thistle, origin of emblem 5
Threave Castle 135
thundergay 200
Thurso 392, 393
time zone 27
Tinto Hill 197
tipping 29, 30
Tiree 230, 231
tobar nan Ceann 364
Tobermory 225, 226
toilets 30
Tolquhon Castle 334
Tomintoul 324
Tongue 394
Torhouse Stone Circle 142
Torland 319
Torosay Castle 228
tourist offices
  abroad 9, 10
  in Scotland 20–23
tours to Scotland 8, 9
Towie Barclay Castle 336
tracing ancestors 33
Traprain Law 175
Traquair House 116
travel in Scotland 12–17
  air 12, 13
  bus 14
  car 14
  ferry 14–17
  hitch-hiking 14
  train 13
Travelpass 12
travel to Scotland 8–12
Treaty of Union 50
Troon 189
Trossachs, The 245, 246
Trumpan 414
Tullibardine Chapel 303
Turnberry 185
Turriff 336
tweed 31, 32
  origin of name 112
Tyndrum 248
Tyninghame House gardens 154

Uig Bay 413
Ulbster 389
Ullapool 399, 400
Unival 429
Unst 460

Vallay 428, 429

Wallace, William 44
Wanlockhead 134
watersports 38
Wemyss 262
Westerkirk 125
Western Isles 405–418
  map *407*
Westray 449
Whalsay 460
whisky 302, 324, 328
Whitebridge 366
White Corries Chairlift 219
Whithorn 143–145
Whitness 456
Whiting Bay 200
Wick 389, 390
Wigtown 142
wool 31, 32
Wyre 448

Yell 459
youth hostels 23
Ythan Estuary 340